THE COVENANTS OF THE PROPHET MUHAMMAD WITH THE CHRISTIANS OF THE WORLD

الله
رسول
محمد

THE COVENANTS
of the
Prophet Muhammad
with the
Christians of the World

By
John Andrew Morrow

Angelico Press
Sophia Perennis

First published in the USA
by Angelico Press / Sophia Perennis, 2013

For information, address:
Angelico Press / Sophia Perennis
info@angelicopress.com
See also www.covenantsoftheprophet.com

Library of Congress Cataloging-in-Publication Data

Morrow, John A. (John Andrew), 1971–
The covenants of the Prophet Muhammad with the
Christians of the world / Dr. John Andrew Morrow.

p. cm.

Includes bibliographical references and index.
ISBN 978-1-59731-465-7 (pbk: alk. paper)
ISBN 978-1-59731-466-4 (hardback: alk. paper)
1. Muhammad, Prophet, –632—Relations with Christians.
2. Islam—Relations—Christianity. Christianity and
other religions—Islam. I. Title.
BP172.M647 2013
297.2'83—dc23 2013035953

Cover Design: Cristy Deming
Cover image: Turkish language copy of the *Achtiname* or
Covenant of the Prophet Muhammad with the Monks of Mount Sinai,
from 1638 (by permission of St. Catherine's Monastery, Egypt)

CONTENTS

PART I: CONTEXT

PART II: TEXTS

PART III: CHALLENGES

PART IV: BACKMATTER

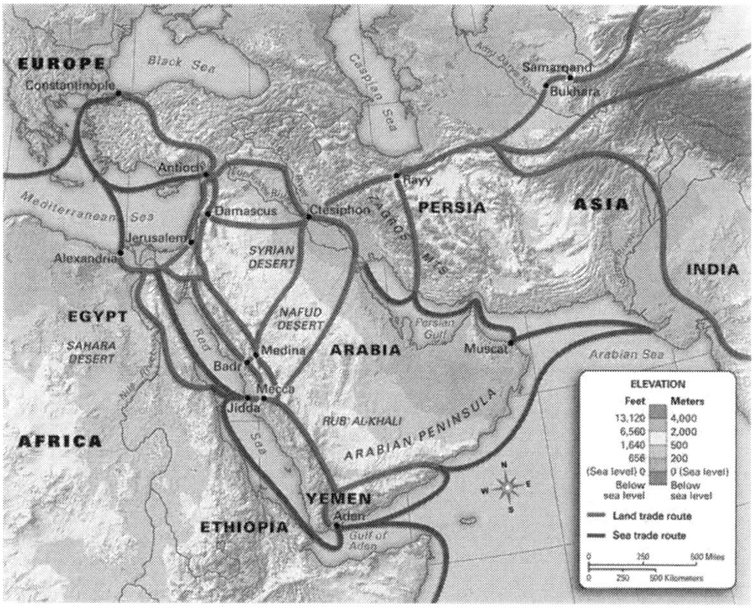

1. Ancient Arab Trade Routes

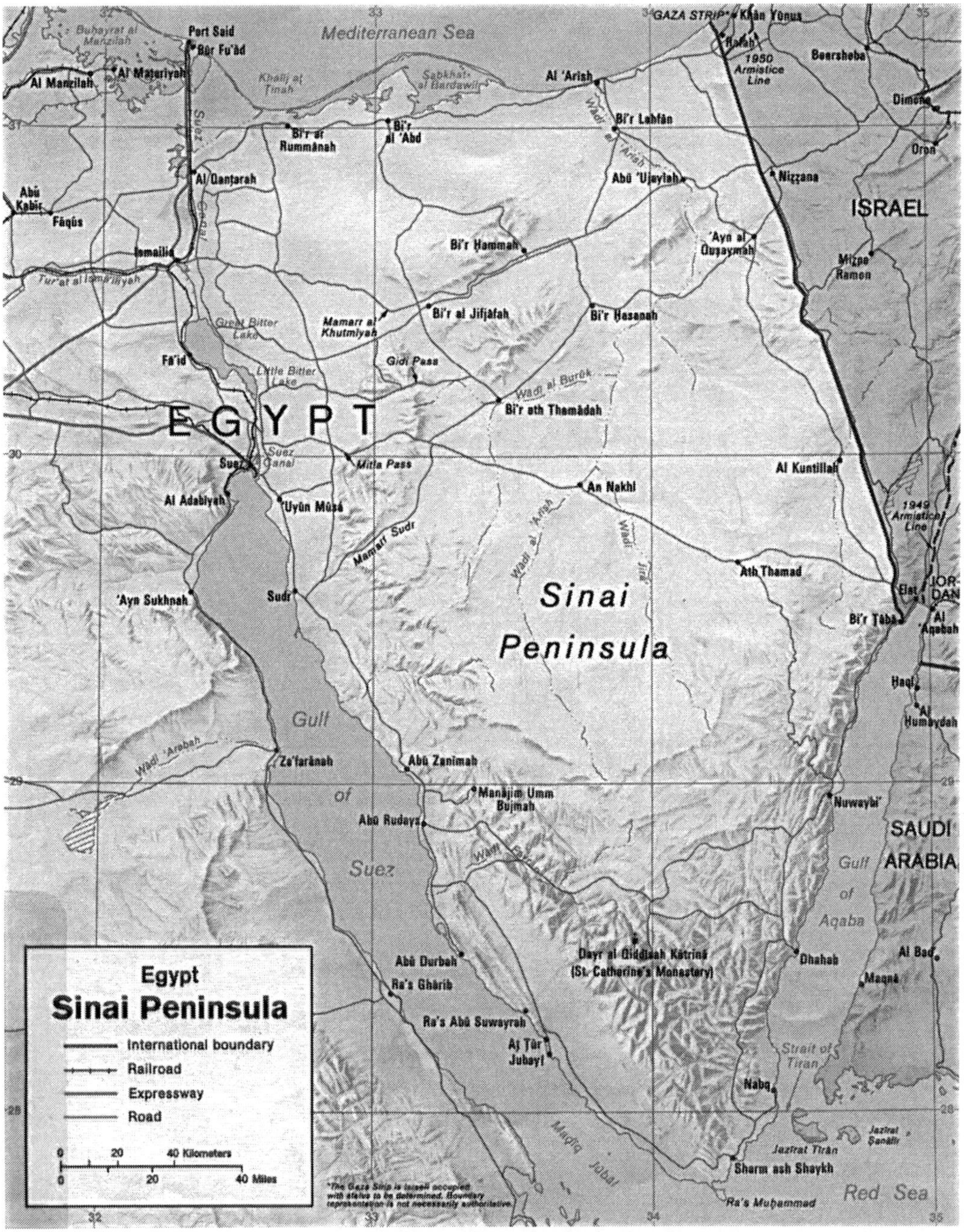

2. Map of the Sinai

Foreword

By Charles Upton

The two foundational sources of the Islamic tradition have always been the Holy Qur'an—the direct Word of Allah as revealed to his Prophet Muhammad, peace and blessing be upon him—and the prophetic *hadith* literature, the record of the sayings of Muhammad as remembered by his wives, his close companions, and others who had been in his presence and heard his words. (The tradition of *sirah* or prophetic biography is also important, but it has never held the same pre-eminent position as these two.) When, after the Prophet's death, his wife 'A'ishah was asked what his character was like, she answered: "It was exactly like the Qur'an."

With the publication of *The Covenants of the Prophet Muhammad with the Christians of the World* we may in fact be witnessing—unexpectedly, miraculously, at this extremely late date—the emergence of a third foundational source for Islam, one that is entirely consonant with the first two: the application of western methods of textual and historical research to the documents composed by the Prophet himself during his lifetime. These documents—letters, covenants, treaties etc.—while they have been known to a few scholars for many centuries, have been largely neglected by both traditional Muslim and modern western scholarship, and are virtually unknown to the mass of believers. One of the most valuable contributions of this work is that it represents a comprehensive treasury of rare, ancient, Islamic sources, many of which have been quite difficult to obtain. Rather than spend their time scouring European and Middle Eastern archives, scholars will now have all the sources they need to conduct further studies on the Covenants and advance our knowledge in this fascinating field. Not only has Dr. Morrow included the original primary sources in Arabic and Persian, he has provided corrected versions of most of these in modern Arabic typescript, along with a wide variety of translations for the purpose of comparative analysis. Consequently, the *Covenant of the Prophet Muhammad with the Christians of the World* represents a necessary and foundational resource and source of reference for all subsequent studies.

In many cases, textual criticism by modern secular scholars has had a negative effect on our understanding of the scriptures and traditions of the Abrahamic religions, at least from the standpoint of the believer. Differences in style and genre in texts traditionally attributed to a single writer are often parceled out to several writers—writers *invented* by the critics themselves—with little justification outside the unwarranted belief that no writer of ancient times could have commanded a spectrum of styles, used them for distinct purposes, or directed them to different audiences. And one effect of this prejudice has been the tendency to view a given sacred tradition as a kind of pastiche, accidentally, arbitrarily, or cunningly sewn together from God-knows-what mass of heterogeneous influences, usually for the purpose of pulling the wool over the eyes of the "ignorant masses." Needless to say, the notion that the Holy Qur'an could have been dictated, word for word, to the Prophet Muhammad, on specific known occasions, sometimes through the intermediary of the Angel Jibra'il, sometimes directly by Allah, is disallowed from the outset.

Dr. John Andrew Morrow has done us all the great service of applying the strict standards of western scholarship to the written documents of the Prophet Muhammad in the context of faith, not doubt. In these post-modern if not post-human times, we are used to thinking of "faith" as synonymous with prejudice, in the belief that only doubt can lead us to the truth, taking doubt as synonymous with "objectivity." Dr. Morrow, on the contrary, has brilliantly demonstrated how doubt is more often synonymous with scholarly dishonesty and prejudice, while faith is a light that—God willing—can show us things as they really are. Certainly faith can degenerate into the kind of compulsive belief that violates objective truth, but *true* faith—defined by St. Paul as "the presence of things hoped for, the evidence of things not seen"—can reveal to us realities that the narrow, tunnel-vision of doubt can never imagine, and therefore will never see. The scholar who has no faith in some order of truth beyond him or herself, or beyond the habitual notions of colleagues whose acceptance he covets and whose opposition he fears, is left with nothing but his own pre-conceived or self-interested concepts. On the other hand, the scholar who sees with the eyes of faith, and who is willing to let that faith challenge his own unconscious assumptions and received ideas, will have the humility—and also the courage—to accept, and let himself be informed by, new paradigms, new discoveries, and will never be scandalized by ancient truths. And in the field of religion particularly, the attempt of scholars who do not believe in the existence of God to present religion in a true light may be compared to the self-defeating struggle of some mythical physician to treat his patients when he does not believe in the existence of health. Those who would successfully study a particular object must first believe that it exists.

The author of this book has opened up the world of the Prophet and his contemporaries as few before him. Who knew that, before the Crusades, Muslims on the *hajj* visited Christian and Jewish sacred sites on their way to Mecca? Who knew that Christians as well as Muslims, in the time of the Prophet, were called by the title *al-mu'minin*, "the faithful"? Who knew that Christian knights and warriors sometimes fought side-by-side with the armies of Islam? Who knew that even Crusaders were given safe-conduct by Muslim authorities to make pilgrimages to the Christian holy sites controlled by Islam? Dr. Morrow makes a compelling case that the original intent of Muhammad was not to create a strictly Muslim state, but rather a confederation of the People of the Book. Muslims, as the founders of this confederation, would retain their pre-eminence, but all the peoples of the Islamic *ummah* were to enjoy the rights accorded to citizens of that confederacy—rights that were extended, under certain circumstances, even to pagan polytheists. In recent times we have heard protestations that "Islam is a religion of peace," and that "Islam was never spread by the sword"—claims that, in the absence of the kind of exhaustive scholarship provided by Dr. Morrow, have tended to ring hollow. Certainly the Islamic *ummah* was forged in battle; nonetheless, the principle that no-one was to be converted to Islam by force—as the Qur'an declares, *there is to be no compulsion in religion* (2:256)—was established by the Prophet, repeated by Caliphs, and became enshrined in the holy *shari'ah*. Violations of this principle, which certainly did take place, were nothing less than crimes, deserving, in the Prophet's words, the severest punishment in this world and the next.

It is nothing short of providential that *The Covenants of the Prophet Muhammad with the Christians of the World* has seen the light of day at this precise historical moment. The covenants of the Prophet with various Christian communities of his time, which Dr. Morrow has rediscovered in obscure monasteries and collections, providing cogent arguments for their validity, uniformly state that Muslims are not to attack peaceful Christian communities, rob them, stop churches from being repaired, tear down churches to build mosques, prevent their Christian wives from going to church and taking spiritual direction from Christian priests and elders, etc. On the contrary, the Prophet commands Muslims to actively protect these communities "until the End of the World." In view of the contemporary, massively-destabilizing attacks by the Western powers on many Muslim nations, and the continued spread of the Wahhabi/Salafi version of Islam—a form of willful and militant ignorance which has been the social and ideological seed-bed for so much "Islamic" terrorism, and which is opposed in so many particulars both to the rulings of the Prophet Muhammad, peace and blessings be upon him, and the clear teachings of the Holy Qur'an—even making itself vulnerable, in certain instances, to manipulation by the very Western powers who are apparently dedicated to the total destruction of traditional *dar al-islam*—the revelation of newly rediscovered documents recording the Prophet's very words, which command Muslims to *protect and defend* peaceful Christian communities, not attack them, could not be more timely, more crucial, and in greater need of wide and rapid dissemination. *The Covenants of the Prophet Muhammad with the Christians of the World* represents a type of "ecumenism" which does not arise, as so much interfaith activity apparently does today, from a weakening of religious faith and a desire to accommodate to the secular "liberal" values of an increasingly anti-liberal world, but rather one which is intrinsic to the Islamic revelation itself. In the words of the Holy Qur'an:

> He has revealed unto you (Muhammad) the Scripture with truth, confirming that which was (revealed) before it, even as He revealed the Torah and the Gospel. (3:3)

> Say (O Muhammad): 'O people of the Scripture: Come to a word that is just between us and you, that we worship none but God, and that we associate no partners with Him, and that none of us shall take others as lords besides God.' (3:64)

> And do not dispute with the followers of the Book except by what is best, except those of them who act unjustly, and say: We believe in that which has been revealed to us and revealed to you, and our God and your God is One, and to Him do we submit. (29:46)

> Verily! Those who believe and those who are Jews and Christians, and Sabians, whoever believes in God and the Last Day and do righteous good deeds shall have their reward with their Lord, on them shall be no fear, nor shall they grieve. (2:62)

As the author himself puts it:

> Although there is unity in religious diversity, there is no place for syncretism. Equality does not mean that all are identical. Each religious system is coherent within itself. Each religion is an ecosystem. Combining two ecosystems would ruin the fragile ecological balance. There are barriers in nature and the universe. There are also certain boundaries within religions that need to be respected....While Muslims may not agree with Christians on all matters doctrinal, they must respect Christianity as a crystallization of the divine message. Although, from a Muslim perspective, certain Christian beliefs and practices are incorrect, many Christian beliefs are correct from an Islamic standpoint. The same can be said of Judaism. The similarities between Islam, Christianity, and Judaism far outweigh any differences. To disrespect Christianity is to disrespect Christ in the same fashion that disrespecting Judaism is to disrespect Moses. Muslims do not have *carte blanche* to denigrate divinely revealed religions and then cry bloody murder when Islam is attacked. Jews, Christians, and Muslims must defend each other from the onslaught of the secular New World Order which is deeply committed to destroying them all.

May the publication of *The Covenants of the Prophet Muhammad with the Christians of the World* be an occasion for a new alliance between those of the Abrahamic faiths who are dedicated to preserving the divine revelations entrusted to them both from traitors within their midst, and from the unrelenting attacks of the modern world.

Acknowledgments

First and foremost, I would like to thank my wife and children for providing me with a peaceful, loving, and supportive home environment in which I can cultivate my scholarship. Secondly, I express my gratitude to Carol Gibbs, Interlibrary Loan Clerk at Ivy Tech Community College in Fort Wayne, Indiana, for happily helping me obtain all the books and articles I required in order to complete my research. Thirdly, I wish to recognize my friends and associates, Héctor Manzolillo and Barbara Castleton, for investing so much of their free time to the careful review of this work. The dedication and devotion of these fine human beings is simply unparalleled. Fourthly, I am grateful to Fatima Ezzahra Kaanoune and Fatiha Bejja for typing the covenants of the Prophet in Arabic. Fifthly, I am deeply grateful to Dr. Said Mentak and 'Abdullah Shahin for reviewing, editing, and correcting my English translations of the covenants and including the short vowels and case endings on the Arabic. These two colleagues were especially helpful in helping to properly decipher obscure aspects in the primary sources and to correct the shortcomings of the ancient scribes. Sixthly, I would like to express my sincere appreciation to Charles Upton, James Wetmore, and John Riess for copyediting the final manuscript, and the first for providing the Foreword to this work. I would also like to commend them for their profound faith in the value of this project and their efforts to advance the cause of the covenants. Last, but not least, I express my profound appreciation to Angelico Press/Sophia Perennis for supporting scholarship that encourages socio-spiritual solidarity between members of the Abrahamic faiths. I cannot imagine a more proper place to publish a work on the covenants of the Prophet with the Christians of the World.

Permissions

The author and publisher gratefully acknowledges the University of Texas Press, Joseph J. Hobbs, Abomajid Ahmed Qassim Sultan, the Armenian Missionary Association of America, Inc., Erik Smith, and Oxford University Press for allowing us to reproduce photos and/or long citations which are under their copyright.

Conventions

Unlike most academic monographs, which are written by scholars solely for scholars, this work is aimed at two audiences, academics and educated readers. While I have endeavored to adhere to the established norms of Arabic transliteration, I have intentionally avoided the use of diacritical marks. For the sake of consistency, and to avoid annoying the eyes unnecessarily, I have attempted to standardize certain terms, preferring "Allah" to "God," for example, and "Messenger" to "Apostle." When translations were particularly poor, and grammar, spelling, and syntax were incorrect, I have been either benevolent enough or audacious enough to improve the works of others rather than repeatedly splatter them with *sic errat scriptum*, thus it was written, to indicate that the spelling is incorrect. I have also mildly modernized the archaic spelling of many of my old English and French sources. Finally, in keeping with the conventions of the English language, I have suppressed the honorific titles and formulaic benedictions which traditionally accompany the names of certain religious personalities. The absence of these reverential titles and invocations should not be interpreted as an indication of disrespect as readers are free to include them wherever and whenever they are called for. It goes without saying that any shortcomings in this study are mine and mine alone.

Concerning the Covenants

The *Testamentum et pactiones initae inter Mohammedem et Christianae fidei cultores*, known in Arabic as *al-'Ahd wa al-shurut allati sharataha Muhammad rasul Allah li ahl al-millah al-nasraniyyah*, which literally means *The Treaty and Covenant which Muhammad, the Messenger of Allah, Concluded with the Christian Community*, was first published by Antoine Vitré, whose last name was also spelled Vitray, in 1630 in an edition prepared by Gabriel Sionita (1577–1648 CE). Born Jibra'il al-Sahyuni at Ehden in Lebanon in 1577, Gabriel Sionita was a learned Maronite famous for publishing the 1646 Parisian polyglot of the Bible. Sionita's edition includes the original Arabic of the *Covenant* along with a Latin translation. It also features the *Pact of 'Umar*. To all appearances, only three copies of this first edition remain in existence, housed in the rare books collections of the Hesburg Library at the University of Notre Dame, as well as the University of Chicago Library and Bizzell Memorial Library at the University of Oklahoma.

A second edition of *al-'Ahd wa al-shurut allati sharataha Muhammad Rasul Allah li ahl al-millah al-Nasraniyyah* was also printed in Paris in 1630 which, if the catalog entry is correct, apparently did not mention the name of the publisher, translator, and editor. A single copy of this edition is stored in the Harvard College Library. A third edition of the *'Ahd wa al-shurut*, edited by François Hotman, and featuring the Latin translation of Gabriel Sionita was newly published in Paris in 1630 by Antoine Vitré, a copy of which exists in the Universitätsbibliothek Marburg in Germany. A fourth edition of the *Testamentum et pactiones* was published by J. Fabricius in 1638. The edition of this Protestant scholar apparently only included the Latin translation.

A fifth edition of *al-'Ahd wa al-shurut allati sharataha Muhammad Rasul Allah li ahl al-millah al-Nasraniyyah* was published in Lugduni Batavorum, namely, Leiden, in the Netherlands, in 1655 with a Latin translation by Johann Georg Nissel (1621–1662 CE). A German born in Palatinate, but who lived most of his life in Leiden, he self-financed the publication of a Hebrew Bible, circa 1659, which is reported to be accurate. He also published many other religious works in Arabic and Latin. Nissel's work also includes the Arabic versions of two Qur'anic chapters, *Surah Ibrahim* (14) and *Surah al-Hijr* (15), along with their literal Latin translation. The Columbia University Library in New York City and the Vrije Universiteit Amsterdam in the Netherlands each have a copy of the *'Ahd wa al-shurut*. According to their catalogues, the work was translated by Johann Georg Nissel (1621–1662 CE), along with Robert of Chester (active from 1140–1150 CE), Hermann of Carinthia (c. 1100–c. 1160 CE), and André du Ryer (c. 1580–1660 CE), the former vice-consul of France in Egypt and ambassador of France in Constantinople. Obviously, this appears silly as Chester and Carinthia were not the contemporaries of Nissel and Ryer. The editor, evidently, was pointing to the fact that some of their translations of the Qur'an had been included in the work and not that they had co-authored it.

It seems that Nissel's translation was published in several runs. Some libraries speak of three editions. However, it is not always clear whether one is dealing with different editions or the same single edition which was catalogued differently. In any event, copies of Nissel's translation can be found in the following British, German, Swiss, and French libraries: the British National Library, the British Library, St. Pancras, Bibliotheek Universiteit Leiden, Herzog August Bibliothek Wolfenbüttel, Niedersächsische Staats-und Universitätsbibliothek Göttingen, Universitätsbibliothek Rostock, Herzogin Anna Amalia Bibliothek/Klassik Stiftung Weimar, Staatsbibliothek zu Berlin-Preussischer Kulturbesitz, Thür-inger Universitäts-und Landesbibliothek, Universitäts und Forschungsbibliothek Erfurt/Gotha, Universitäts- und Landesbibliothek Sachsen-Anhalt/Zentrale, Universitätsbibliothek Greifswald, Bibliothèque Cantonale et Universitaire-Lausanne, Koninklijke Bibliotheek, Bibliothèque nationale de France,

Zentralbibliothek Zürich, Bayerische Staatsbibliothek, and Niedersächsische Staats-und Universitätsbibliothek Göttingen.

In his edition of *al-'Ahd wa al-shurut allati sharataha Muhammad Rasul Allah li ahl al-millah al-Nasraniyyah*, Johann Georg Nissel (1621–1662 CE) denounced the translation and edition of Gabriel Sionita (1577–1648 CE) as being corrupt, full of major mistakes, lacking diacritical marks, and being unclear and unfaithful to the text. There is no doubt that the Arabic type employed in Gabriel Sionita's edition differed from the norm. For example, it uses the letter *fa* with no dot above and three dots below to represent the letter "p." The *alif maqsurah* or isolated *alif* is written as a *ya* and the final *hamzas* at the end of words are not represented. Since this final feature was a trait of the Prophet's Arabic, which was not accepted when Classical Arabic grammar was standardized, this makes us wonder what source was employed by Sionita. His unusual spelling conventions may have been a faithful transcription of the original text. It should be stressed, however, that as much as Sionita's edition appears to be handwritten, it is the product of the printing press. It was printed by Vitré using Brève's Arabic types (Hamilton and Richard 47). These fonts had actually been molded in Istanbul (Bernard 45, note 1).

As for the Arabic transcription of Johann Georg Nisell, it is, without a doubt, far superior, according to modern standards: the text is printed in a fully-vocalized 'Uthmani script as found in contemporary Qur'ans. One wonders whether Sionita and Nissel were both working from the same original Arabic source. The origin of the *Covenant of the Prophet Muhammad with the Christians of the World* is especially obscure. Since Sionita was an Arab, he may have obtained a copy of the *Covenant* from a community in the Levant. As a cleric, he may also have obtained it through ecclesiastic sources or Church channels. The connections of Nissel to the *Covenant* are even less clear. Since the French were close allies of the Turks at the time, it seems that the Ottomans had encouraged the dissemination of the *Covenant of the Prophet*. Who, one must ask, was the intended audience? Were the Ottomans attempting to prove to the French that they were protecting the Christians who lived in their lands? Were they trying to gain popular support from the educated French? Or did the Ottomans intend to distribute copies of the *Covenant* to Muslim scholars around their empire in order to promote positive relations with the People of the Book? And why would Johann Georg Nissel (1621–1662 CE) be so concerned about using a clear, fully-vocalized, Arabic script, if the intended readers were educated Europeans? Such a text would only have been of value to Arab readers. While the Arabic fonts he employed seem superior, in a certain sense, Nissel's Latin translation is far from being an entirely accurate rendition of the *Covenant*. To be blunt, both Latin translations are poor.

In 1672, Jacobo Nagy de Harsany (b. 1615 CE), the Hungarian scholar and professor, also included a Latin translation of the *Testamentum et pactiones* in his *Colloquia familiar turco-latina*. This would be the sixth edition of the *'Ahd wa al-shurut*. Since it did not include the original Arabic text, it was certainly aimed at educated Europeans. There was also a seventh edition published in 1690 which featured a German translation by Abraham Hinckelmann (1652–1695 CE), a German Protestant theologian and Islamologist who was the first to print a complete copy of the Qur'an in Hamburg, which seems to have been lost. This would have been the first translation of the *'Ahd wa al-shurut* into a modern European language. His motivation in publishing the work is unclear. If his goal in publishing the Qur'an was to attack it, what benefit would the publication of the *Covenant of the Prophet Muhammad with the Christians of the World* bring to his controversial cause? Besides their ties with the French Catholics, it is known that the Ottomans also flirted with Protestant princes, seeking to draw them to the side of the Turks. Could Hinckelmann, like Nissel and Sionita, have received a copy of the *'Ahd wa al-shurut* through Turkish diplomatic channels? If anything is clear it is that Hinckelmann had an important collection of Arabic and Islamic manuscripts. While most were auctioned by his family after his death, never to be seen again, many have survived. Unfortunately, the *'Ahd wa al-shurut* does not appear to be among them.

Gabriel Sionita (1577–1648 CE) is single-handedly responsible for spreading the word of the *Covenant of the Prophet Muhammad with the Christians of the World* to the Western world. Considering the magnitude of its importance, it is stunning that the Prophet's *'Ahd wa al-shurut* has never been published in the Muslim world. While it is not clear how many copies of the *Covenant* were printed in Europe in the 1600s, it appears that fewer than thirty of them have survived into the 21st century. Once again, the Arabic version of the Prophet's *'Ahd wa al-shurut* came dangerously close to oblivion.

The first scholar to translate the *Testamentum et pactiones* into English appears to have been Sir Paul Rycaut in his *History of the Ottoman Empire.* This work was translated into French by Monsieur Briot. This French translation, which appeared in 1670, reappeared in several works during the 19th century. In 1826, M. Grassi (Alfio) included Briot's French translation of the *Traité de Mahomet avec les Chrétiens* in his *Charte Turque ou Organisation religieuse, civile et militaire de l'empire ottoman.* This was followed by Alexandre de Miltitz, the former minister of the Prussian king to the Ottoman Porte, who included the *Privilège accordé par Mahomet aux Chrétiens* in his *Manuel des Consuls*, which was published in 1838. In 1881, Edward A. Van Dyke, a consular clerk of the United States at Cairo, published an English translation of the *'Ahd wa al-shurut* in his *Capitulations of the Ottoman Empire.* This was not a direct translation from the original Arabic. This was actually an English translation of Briot's French translation which was based on Ricaut's English translation. It is unclear to me whether Ricaut's translation was based on the Arabic, Turkish, Latin or German versions of the *'Ahd wa al-shurut.* Hence, many editions of the covenant underwent a process of double, triple, and even quadruple translations.

The present edition of the *Covenants of the Prophet Muhammad with the Christians of the World* includes six of the covenants concluded by the Messenger of Allah with distinct communities all of which were translated directly from the original Arabic. It features modern typed versions of the *Covenant of the Prophet Muhammad with the Monks of Mount Sinai*, the *Covenant of the Prophet Muhammad with the Christians of Najran*, the *Covenant of the Prophet Muhammad with the Christians of the World*, the *Covenant of the Prophet Muhammad with the Christians of Persia*, and the *Covenant of the Prophet Muhammad with the Assyrian Christians.* It also includes scanned copies of the *'Ahd wa al-shurut* published by Gabriel Sionita in 1630 and Johann Georg Nissel in 1655 as well as a copy of what appears to be the original covenant brought from Palestine to Paris by Father Pacifique Scaliger in 1629. This possible source covenant, which dates to 1538, has never been previously published. Likewise, besides being cited over the centuries in various sources, the *Covenant of the Prophet Muhammad with the Monks of Mount Sinai* has never been fully published in book format in both Arabic and English. There was a 1902 translation into English by Anton F. Haddad; however, this was completed on the basis of Naufal Effendi Naufal's Arabic translation of a Turkish copy of the *Achtiname.* Considering that both Haddad and Naufal were Arabs, the former a Baha'i and the latter a Christian, it is academically inexcusable that they did not rely on the original Arabic. The only complete Arabic versions I have come across was published by Shuqayr in 1916 and by Bernhard Moritz in 1918. The subsequent versions which I have seen, in Arabic or English, were either incomplete or inaccurate. This is not to say that these earlier translations are of no benefit. On the contrary, they all have value as they capture different shades of meaning from the original Arabic. It is for this reason that I have included several translations of the *Covenant of the Prophet Muhammad with the Monks of Mount Sinai*, not to be tedious and torment readers, but rather, to provide scholars with all translations in a single source.

As for the *'Ahd wa al-shurut* or *Covenant of the Prophet Muhammad with Christians of the World,* it has not appeared in Arabic in three and a half centuries and, to my knowledge, was last published in English by Van Dyke in 1881. The *Covenant of the Prophet Muhammad with the Assyrian Christians*, a work widely unknown, was first published in Persian and English by George David Malech in 1910. With regard to the *Covenant of the Prophet Muhammad with the Christians of Najran*, it was published in Arabic and French in 1919. Although the French translation by Archbishop Addai Scher is quite good, there are some omissions and additions. As for the Arabic version of this covenant, it reappeared in print in 1956 in Muhammad Hamidullah's *Majmu'ah al-watha'iq al-siyasiyyah li al-'ahd al-nabawi wa al-khilafah al-rashidah* and in 2002 in Muhammad 'Amarah's *al-Islam wa al-akhar.* Unfortunately, this critically important covenant remains virtually unknown outside of a small circle of religious clerics, professors, and educated readers. The same applies to the *Covenant of the Prophet Muhammad with the Christians of Persia,* which was published in English by Leon Arpee in 1948. And while the *Covenant of the Propet Muhammad with the Armenian Christians of Jerusalem* has circulated, to a limited extent, among clerics and educated members of this denomination, it remains virtually unknown to outsiders. Certainly, the rediscovery and reappearance of these covenants in the current volume is of the greatest historical significance.

The Covenants Initiative

In response to the clash of barbarisms that is presently laying the world in ruins, interested Muslims have elected to take the rare opportunity presented by the publication of *The Covenants of the Prophet Muhammad with the Christians of the World* to launch "The Covenants Initiative," which asks Muslims to append their names to the following declaration:

> *We the undersigned hold ourselves bound by the spirit and the letter of the covenants of the Prophet Muhammad (peace and blessings be upon him) with the Christians of the world, in the understanding that these covenants, if accepted as genuine, have the force of law in the* shari'ah *today and that nothing in the* shari'ah, *as traditionally and correctly interpreted, has ever contradicted them. As fellow victims of the terror and godlessness, the spirit of militant secularism and false religiosity now abroad in the world, we understand your suffering as Christians through our suffering as Muslims, and gain greater insight into our own suffering through the contemplation of your suffering. May the Most Merciful of the Merciful regard the sufferings of the righteous and the innocent; may He strengthen us, in full submission to His will, to follow the spirit and the letter of the covenants of the Prophet Muhammad with the Christians of the world in all our dealings with them.* In the name of Allah, Most Gracious, Most Merciful. Praise be to Allah, the Cherisher and Sustainer of the worlds:
>
> *Luqman Ali, Founding Director, Khayaal Theatre Company; Rachida Bejja, Clinical Director, Quality Counseling & Psychological Services; Dr. Bridget Blomfield, Asst. Prof. of Religious Studies, Univ. of Nebraska; Charles Daines; Marina (Nouria) Bouteillier, Shadhili Sufi Order; Alicia Carrara; Yousef Casewit; Adam Deen, The Deen Institute; Saimma Dyer; Daniel Dyer; Dr. Mohamed Elkouche, Prof. of English at Mohamed I University in Oujda, Morocco; Dr. Muhammad-Reza Fakhr-Rohani, Scholar of 'Ashura' Literature in English, University of Qom, Iran; Dr. Aida Shahlar Gasimova, Prof. of Arabic, Baku State University, Azerbaijan; Prof. Alan Godlas, University of Georgia; Shaikh Kabir Helminski, Mevlevi Sufi Order; Jeremy Henzell-Thomas; John Herlihy, author; Nigel Jackson, author;*

Matthew Johnson; Irving Karchmar, Nimatullahi Sufi Order; Qaisra Ehsan Khan; Farah Kimball, The International Peace Project; Amnah Malik; Sadat Malik; Hector Manzolillo, translator; Zachary Markwith, Graduate Theological Union; Dr. Said Mentak, Senior Lecturer of English at Mohamed I University; Dr. John Andrew Morrow, Professor, Author, and Research Scholar; Dr. John Parks, M.D.; Dr. Hisham M. Ramadan, Muslim jurist and professor of Criminology, Kwantlen Polytechnic University; Imam Feisal Abdul Rauf, Founder and Chairman, Cordoba Initiative; Saqib Safdar, Teacher of Mathematics; Dr. Omid Safi, Professor of Religious Studies, Univ. of North Carolina; Yusuf A.H. Salaam; Kathryn Qahira Santana; Dr. Amar Sellam, Professor of Linguistics at Mohamed I University; Dr. Reza Shah-Kazemi, The Institute of Ismaili Studies; Kamal Southall; Dr. Mahdi Tourage, Assoc. Prof. of Religious Studies, Univ. of Western Ontario; Charles Upton, author; Dr. Cyrus Ali Zargar, Asst. Prof. of Religion at Augustana College.

We will forward this declaration and the endorsements we receive, along with copies of *The Covenants of the Prophet Muhammad with the Christians of the World*, to Christian leaders in the Middle East, Africa, and elsewhere in the world, many of whose communities are now under serious attack by Muslim "extremists." In view of the bombings and brutal massacres committed in the name of Islam in the past, as well as others that—God forbid!—may take place in the future, it is safe to say that if there was ever a time when Muslims need to do something to break the growing identification of Islamicist terrorism with all Islam in the minds of the non-Muslim populations of the western nations, it is now. Islam has been on tthe losing end of virtually every interaction with the western wworld during the past two centuries, and is presently under relentless attack both from without and from within. Why, then, should Muslims make a point of drawing public attention to the sufferings of contemporary Christians? One reason is that compassion extended to fellow sufferers by those who themselves are in great need of compassion is a powerful and chivalrous act. Those who come with demands drive people away from them; those who come with offers of help draw them closer. It is time for Muslims to move beyond simply protesting, once again, "but we're not all terrorists!"—a phrase which, for all its obvious sincerity, has rather a self-serving ring to it for many non-Muslims, whether it is believed or disbelieved—and take a vigorous, proactive, and public stance in support of peaceful Christians presently being attacked by some seriously misguided "Muslims," doing so in the name of the Prophet Muhammad himself, peace and blessings be upon him, based on newly rediscovered documents that record his very words. This project, *insha' Allah*, will have three good effects, which we will list in ascending order of importance: 1) Like nothing else we can imagine, it will present Muslims in a positive light to those who are still capable of human feeling; 2) It might save a few lives; and 3) It is a worthy thing to do in the sight of Allah, according to His clear Command as transmitted by His Prophet Muhammad, peace and blessings be upon him.

Peace is not made by generating peaceful feelings and/or attending exclusively peaceful gatherings. It is made by facing and enduring conflict, while never departing from the remembrance of God. It is a rare occurrence when strategic advantage, moral rectitude, and Divine Command apparently converge so as to point out a particular course of action; we believe that the Covenants Initiative represents just such a convergence. If you are a Muslim, and feel moved by your own conscience, after reading *The Covenants of the Prophet Muhammad with the Christians of the World*—remembering, always, that no-one can decide for you or compel you in any way, seeing that *there is to be no compulsion in religion*—to add your name to this Initiative, space is provided at the following link: http://covenantsoftheprophet.com.

Chasing History: Appendix to the Covenants Initiative

Books are slow, but events happen swiftly. Muslims, including traditional authorities, in both Egypt and Syria—the Egyptian Grand Mufti among them—have made strong statements condemning so-called "Islamicist" violence against Christians, and we have seen ordinary Muslims coming to the aid of their Christian brothers and sisters who have been the victims of such violence. In a book like this we can only note the fact that such things have happened; any exhaustive treatment of traditional Islam's response to Wahhabi/Salafi violations of the teachings of the Qur'an and the sunnah of the Prophet (whether such violators are acting on their own initiative or as the agents of other players) will have to wait until the dust settles—if it ever does. At this point we can only briefly quote from two news stories which, however, will retain their historical value, whatever course events may take in ensuing months and years. The first item, from November 14, 2011, is already ancient history:

> Patriarch Kirill Gundyaev of Moscow and all the Russias and Chief Mufti Sheikh Ahmad Badreddin Hassoun (Ahmad Badr Al-Din Hassoun), the top Sunni cleric in Syria, agreed at a meeting on Sunday in Damascus, that they'll work together to combat extremism through religious education.... Mufti Hassoun... noted that Christianity spread throughout the world out of Syria (through the missionary work of Apostle St. Paul). He said, "The Orthodox Church continues to keep true to its roots. The Church of Jerusalem won't give up one metre of its patrimony, even though they'd been tempted to sell off part of it to the Zionists. It's a timely message to Israel.... Christianity is in the region to stay. We must rethink our teaching in our mosques and churches so that we can give our young people a basic defence against extremism, Islamic, Christian, and Jewish...." http://o2varvara.wordpress.com/.

The second item, from Intifada, Voice of Palestine website, August 19, 2013, speaks to the moment when this book first saw the light:

> [B]oth the Coptic Pope Tawadros II and the Grand Imam of al-Azhar Mosque stood side by side declaring that Muslims and Christians of Egypt are brothers and will work together on protecting Christian properties and rebuilding churches. Many local Muslims rushed to protect churches against Muslim Brotherhood terrorists. http://www.intifada-palestine.com/2013/08/egypts-painful-birth-pangs/

Many more statements could certainly have been found from all over the Muslim world, enough to make a whole book in themselves, but there was neither the time to collect them nor the space to include them; we invite the reader to do his or her own investigation of this vast trove of information.

Part I

CONTEXT

"By the Fig and the Olive, and the Mount of Sinai" (95:1–2)

"By the Mount (of Revelation)" (52:1)

Chapter 1

The Prophet Muhammad and the People of the Book

Introduction

The covenants concluded by the Prophet Muhammad (570–632 CE) with the Christians of Mount Sinai, Najran, Assyria, Persia, Palestine, Egypt, Armenia, and the World are some of the most important, yet notably neglected, literary monuments in the history of Islam. Considering that the continued conflict between Christians and Muslims across the world has been artificially ignited by the forces of imperialism, especially in Africa, the Middle East, and Asia, the content of these priceless historical documents can shed light on the early history of Islam. Via this information, we are witness to the primordial relationship between Muslims and People of the Book. Thus, these covenants can serve as a source of inspiration for the establishment of insuperable harmony between the three Abrahamic religions: Judaism, Christianity, and Islam.

The Prophet's Early Life and Encounters with Christians

Muhammad, the son of ʿAbd Allah and Aminah, was born in Mecca in 570 CE, in what was henceforth known as the Year of the Elephant, owing to the fact that his birth coincided with the attempted destruction of the Kaʿbah at the hands of Abraha, the Christian ruler of Yemen. His father having died while his mother was pregnant, Muhammad was cared for by his mother and his grandfather ʿAbd al-Muttalib. As was customary, Muhammad's mother sent him to live with the Bedouins of the desert for the first five years of his life. Throughout his life, Muhammad would harbor fond memories of his nurse-mother of the desert tribe, Halimah, who cared for him during his early years. Shortly after the young boy, Muhammad, returned to live with his mother Aminah, she passed away, leaving her son in the sole care of his grandfather at the age of six. Alas, the grandfather had died as well by the time the boy reached the age of eight, at which time an uncle, Abu Talib, became Muhammad's guardian or foster-father. Thus, several times an orphan, Muhammad had to rely on his own intellect and determination to pull from the future the threads of his later success. Historians and mystics have reviewed his life minutely, looking for signs and symptoms of what was to come.

According to the traditional biography of the Prophet, Muhammad first worked as a shepherd, during which time his boundless curiosity led him to study the marvels of nature and creation. Later, he was taken on as a helper in his uncle Abu Talib's shop in Mecca. According to traditions found in Majlisi's *Bihar al-anwar*, Muhammad was recognized by the Jews as a future prophet when he was seven years old (Dar Rahe Haqq 20). Since prophets do not consume forbidden food, the Jews gave a stolen hen to Abu Talib, Muhammad's uncle, without his knowing. After it was cooked and served, all but Muhammad consumed the impure chicken. When asked why he refrained from eating, he replied: "This food is forbidden by God and God protects me against anything that He has forbidden" (20). Later, the Jews took a hen from a neighbor's house, intending to pay for it later, and sent it to Abu Talib's home where it was cooked. Again, Muhammad refrained from eating on the grounds that the food was doubtful. Having tested the young Muhammad, the Jews concluded that "This child has an extraordinary character and a supreme position" (21). In his *Aʿlam al-nubuwwah*, al-Mawardi mentions that a group of Christians from Syria met the seven-year old Muhammad in Mecca, marveled at his belief in the One God, and proclaimed his prophethood (Roggema 41–42). Ibn Saʿd al-Baghdadi (d. 845 CE) also stresses that the People of the Book had recognized Muhammad as a prophet before he had turned nine years of age (Roggema 41).

When Muhammad was but a child, his uncle Abu Talib took him on a trade journey to Syria. This decision, to give the boy a rare exposure to the world and its diversity, demonstrated both caring and trust. In some Sunni accounts, Muhammad is said to have been nine years old; in others, twelve. If we believe Muhammad Baqir al-Majlisi (1616–1689 CE), and I believe in this case we should, it appears that there was not one but two trips (Chapter 5). In any event, it was during this first trip that Muhammad had an unusual encounter with a monk named Bahira who lived in Busrah, Syria, a city located 145 kilometers to the south of Damascus which is also spelled Busrah, Bosra, Bosrah, Bostra, Bustra, and Bustrah. 'Abdullah Yusuf 'Ali (1872–1953 CE) also mentions "another Busra in Edom, north of Petra in Transjordania" (7) which is certainly not the correct site as it has no religious or historical sites related to Bahira. Regarding the term *sawma'ah* or cell used in the tradition, Barbara Roggema writes that "[t]his term should not be understood as a cell that is part of a larger monastic complex, but rather as the dwelling place of a solitary monk and probably a vertical, tower-like structure" (38, note 4). While she does not seem to have seen the traditional hermitage attributed to Bahira in Busrah (45, note 33), her definition of the term coincides perfectly with the site located on the south-west side of the city. Curiously, Aminah, the mother of Muhammad, had dreamed of the castles of Busrah in Syria while she was pregnant with the Prophet (Ibn Ishaq 69). These castles may have in fact been the monastic towers in which mystics and ascetics such as Bahira resided. This dream or divinely-inspired vision may have foretold that her future son, Muhammad, would be recognized as the Messenger of Allah. As Reza Shah-Kazemi asks: "Can we see here a luminous anticipation of the mutual recognition between the Prophet and the monks—each recognizing the light of God in each other?"

Well-versed in the knowledge of the Christians, the monk Bahira is said to have possessed unadulterated ancient scriptures which had been passed down from generation to generation. *Bahira*, it appears, was probably a title of respect such as "Reverend," as opposed to a proper name; this explains the existence of apparently disparate accounts. In some sources he is referred to as "Rabbi," leading to suggestions he was Jewish or a Messianic Jew (Sprenger 578). However, this is also the term that Nestorian Christians use to address their clerics. Although Bahira typically paid no mind to the many Arab caravans that passed by, a manifestation he saw in his cell, and which is nowhere defined, inspired him to prepare Abu Talib's group a great feast. Apparently, the monk was moved by the fact that a cloud was hovering over Muhammad as the caravan approached, a curious and unlikely event in those desert regions. However, since he was not yet a grown man, the men of Quraysh left Muhammad behind under the shade of a tree. Thus, it came to pass that Bahira insisted the boy be brought to join them in the meal.

When Muhammad was fetched and arrived to partake of the meal with the rest of the men, Bahira examined him closely, seeking confirmation of the signs of his description which were found in his ancient Christian scriptures. After the meal was finished, and the guests had left, Bahira got up and asked Muhammad: "Boy, I ask you by al-Lat and al-'Uzza to answer my question," to which he responded, "Do not ask me by al-Lat and al-'Uzza, for by Allah, nothing is more hateful to me than these two." Seeing the boy in person, Bahira determined that he matched the physical description of the awaited prophet, and confirmed the belief in monotheism in his heart. Next, Bahira proceeded to ask him questions about his affairs. The responses provided by Muhammad coincided with what the monk knew from the texts. Emboldened, Bahira looked at the young boy's back and found there the seal of prophethood between his shoulders, precisely at the place described in his scroll.

When Bahira had finished interviewing Muhammad, he approached his uncle, Abu Talib, seeking further information about the identity of the young boy. When Abu Talib described Muhammad as his son, Bahira told him that he was not since the boy's father could not possibly be alive. Abu Talib admitted that "He is my nephew," and he recounted for the monk Muhammad's history and the fact that his father had died before the child was born. "You have told the truth," said Bahira. "Take your nephew back to his country and guard him carefully against the Jews," he warned, "for, by Allah, if they see him and know about him what I know, they will do him evil; a great future lies before this nephew of yours, so take him home quickly" (Ibn Ishaq 81). This, of course, is a simplified account of the event. The version found in Muhammad Baqir al-Majlisi's *Hayat al-qulub* is far more detailed and elaborate as it integrates elements from a larger body of sources. According to the Shi'ite version, monks from far and wide were drawn to Muhammad when he journeyed to Syria and many more miraculous events took place in his presence (Chapter 4).

While many who read the story of Bahira imagine a Christian hermit living in an isolated cave in some mountainous region in the desert, correct contextualization provides an entirely different image. As Barnaby Rogerson elucidates,

> By the time Muhammad visited Bostra it had been the capital of eastern Syria for five hundred years. It bustled with officialdom; it was the sea of the Byzantine governor and the commander of a legion and the Archbishop of Bostra lorded over some thirty-three junior bishops. At the time Muhammad would have known it Bostra was a great walled city whose skyline was dominated by the newly completed domed cathedral. . . . Bostra was surrounded by the Hauran, a productive hinterland of agricultural villages. Roads led across this busy landscape to Antioch, Damascus, Palmyra and the Red Sea. It was appropriate that the caravan from Mecca should stop there; indeed it may well have been an administrative necessity. The tradition of scholar hermits also ties in with the Christian sects known to be active in this period, such as the Jacobites and Nestorians. Even now Bostra is impressive. . . . The mosque of Mabrak is traditionally considered the site where the young Muhammad dismounted from his camel, while an old Roman basilica has long been considered to be Bahira's church. (63–64)

Both the hermitage of Bahira the Monk, and the church, monastery or cathedral where he officiated, remain places of religious and historical importance in southern Syria, drawing travelers and pilgrims alike. As the ruins of the ancient city testify, Busrah was a bustling metropolitan center during the time of Muhammad. While the Sunni version stops short at Busrah, the Shi'ite version states that the caravan continued on to Damascus where a monk by the name of 'Abd al-Muwayhab also recognized Muhammad as the future Messenger of God (Majlisi, Section 4).

The event of Bahira, which is cited by Ibn Ishaq (704–761/770 CE), al-Baladhuri (d. c. 892 CE), al-Tabari (838–923 CE), and al-Tirmidhi (824–892 CE), among several other authors (Roggema 39, note 7), has prompted a great deal of discussion among scholars. For skeptical scholars like Richard Bell (1876–1952 CE), "[n]o credence can be given to the stories of his contact with Christian monks at this stage" (21). He fails, however, to provide any proof to support his claim. Even for scholars sympathetic to Islam, such as Karen Armstrong (b. 1944 CE), the stories surrounding the birth, childhood, and youth of Muhammad are merely "pious legends" with a symbolic purpose (1993: 48). Since the story of Bahira does not possess a complete chain of transmission, and is cautiously introduced by "it is supposed," many Muslim scholars have simply treated it as a legend. Consequently, some biographers of the Prophet, such as al-Ya'qubi (d. 897/898 CE), Ibn Hazm (994–1064 CE), and Muhammad Zafrulla Khan (1893–1985 CE), make no mention of the event in their works (Roggema 46). While al-Dhahabi (1274–1348 CE) reviews several versions of the episode in *Tarikh al-Islam*, he dismisses them as *munkar jiddan* or very weak (Roggema 46). However, simply because the event was not passed down by a complete chain of narrators does not imply that it is untrue. After all, the episode predates the *hadith* period, most of which took place during the ten years the Prophet spent in Medina.

The story of Bahira, however, has been related in the works of early Muslim historians such as Muhammad ibn Jarir al-Tabari (838–923 CE) and Ibn Sa'd al-Baghdadi (c. 784–845 CE).

After deconstructing the various conflicting accounts of *The Legend of Sergius Bahira*, even Barbara Roggema admits that a historical kernel may remain at its root (51). While Richard A. Gabriel seems to accept the fact that Muhammad encountered monks along the caravan route, he disregards the account of miraculous happenings and prophecies (56). As a historian, he may be entitled to ignore the supernatural; however, he cannot, in good faith, ignore centuries and centuries of sources which stress that something spiritually and politically significant took place during Muhammad's encounters with the monks. As a historian, he is required to rely on sources and the sources are unanimous on this subject. In fact, based on evidence contained in the Qur'an, Francis Edward Peters (b. 1927 CE) concludes that Muhammad was well acquainted with the customs of Christian monks (166). While Goddard admits that the status and reliability of traditional Muslim biographies of Muhammad are the focus of scholarly dispute, he admits that "there seems to be no good reason to discount the accounts" of his encounters with Christians (19). Sir John Glubb (1897–1986 CE) also attests that "[t]he story may well record some meeting between the boy Muhammad and a Christian hermit, of whom there were many at this time on the borders of the Syrian desert" (70–71). And Robert Brenton Betts entertains the possibility that "Rahib al-Buhayra may have been a wandering Syrian monk" (5). "Why do the Muslim sources include such narratives?" asks Omid Safi; "A simple answer might be because they happened, and indeed, there is no reason to suspect that they did not" (80). In fact, after perusing all of the Bahira stories, Aloys Sprenger (1813–1893 CE) came to the conclusion that Bahira was a historical figure. He insists that the tradition of Bahira found in Tirmidhi (824–892 CE) is the oldest and most authentic (588, 592) and that the account cited by al-Waqidi "bears equally the stamp of high antiquity" (592).

Since secular scholars refuse to accept that Muhammad was a prophet, their default setting is to reject any evidence that would support this claim. Their first approach, then, is denial. When denial fails, opponents of Islam will often delve into distortion. Consequently, Bahira, a Syriac Christian, was accused by Christian polemicists of having been a Bahrani Nestorian, an Arian, or even a Jacobite. As for Arianism, it refers to the doctrine of Arius (256–336 CE), an Alexandrian priest, and later Libyan bishop, who, from the year 318 CE onwards, propagated the idea that God consists of a single person, the Father, as opposed to three. In other words, Jesus was not God but had been created by God out of nothing as part of His Greater Plan. Jacobism, of course, refers to a form of Monophysite Christianity which holds that Jesus has but a single, divine, nature. Identified as Sergius, Georgius or Nestorius by opponents of Islam, and later as Baeira or Pakhyras, Bahira was accused of inspiring Muhammad to create his own heresy. As Robert Irwin recognizes, however, "Christian polemicists . . . invented tales about how a monk (in some versions actually a renegade cardinal) instructed Muhammad in the elements of a pernicious Christian heresy" (20).

While many have claimed that Bahira was the actual author of the Qur'an (Vernet, 1991: 233), there is simply no way that he could have given a book to an illiterate boy of nine or fifteen years only to see it resurface twenty-five to thirty-one years later when Muhammad was forty years of age.

While it is difficult to determine the precise denomination to which Bahira belonged, he may have considered himself one of the relatively few remaining Unitarian Christians who, according to some Muslim scholars—though orthodox Christians will disagree—had preserved the original teachings of Jesus (for more on the subject, see Thomson and 'Ata'ur-Rahim). John of Damascus (c. 645 or 676–749), who is an earlier source than Ibn Ishaq, wrote that Bahira was an Arian (Rhodes 150, note 265). For Rhodes, "Arian influence on Islam would be more believable than Nestorian influence" (150, note 265). The issue, however, is not one of influence but one of recognition. From a theological point of view, it seems far more likely that Arian or Nazorean Christians would have been awaiting a final prophet to revive what they saw as the monotheistic faith of Jesus as opposed to Trinitarian Christians such as the Nestorians or Jacobites. As Donner (b. 1945 CE) admits, "Arabia may also have been home to some communities of Jewish Christians called Nazoreans, who recognized Jesus as messiah but adhered to bans on consuming pork and wine" (30–31). The monks that Muhammad met may very well have been monotheistic followers of Jesus who abided by the laws of Moses. As Hans-Joachim Schoeps observes, "the Arabian Christianity which Mohammed found at the beginning of his public activity was not the state religion of Byzantium but a schismatic Christianity characterized by Ebionite and Monophysite views. From this religion many beliefs flowed in an unbroken stream of tradition into the proclamation of Mohammed" (136–137). According to Schoeps, the "extensive similarity in structure between Jewish Christianity and Islam explains why the population of the countries bordering Arabia, areas permeated with Monophysitism and Nestorianism, could so quickly become Mohammedan" (139).

Another example of how the encounter of Muhammad and Bahira has been misinterpreted comes from a text which completely confuses Muhammad's encounters with Christians in Syria and the Egypt. Richard Pococke (1704–1765 CE), an English Orientalist and Protestant bishop, went so far as to allege that a Greek monk named Sergius helped Muhammad write the Qur'an during his visit to Saint Catherine's Monastery in the Sinai (151; Stanley 326, note 111). This fanciful fabrication was spread widely centuries before the author of *Relation d'un voyage fait au Levant*, Jean de Thévenot (1633–1667 CE), related details of his travels through the holy land between 1655 and 1663 (72). He claimed that the Qur'an was patchworked by Sergius on the basis of the Old and New Testaments. He also asserted that the Qur'an abounded with ridiculous tales related by various rabbis (72). Closer reading of this volume demonstrates that, though it was alleged that the French Orientalist was a polyglot who was proficient in Arabic, he was abysmally ignorant of all matters Arabic and Islamic. As the content of his works make clear, his knowledge of the Qur'an and Islam was null as he merely repeated the various legends that had circulated among the illiterate masses in Europe.

When Antoninus Martyr visited the Sinai around 570 CE, the year in which Muhammad was born, he reported that "In the monastery are three fathers expert in languages, who speak Latin, Greek, Syriac, Coptic, and Persian, and also many interpreters for particular languages" (Skrobucha 35). Were there actually those proficient in Arabic in the Monastery of Saint Catherine, no doubt they would have been referred to by Antoninus more specifically. Thus, during the time of the Prophet's peregrinations, no one was likely available to offer substantive Arabic instruction or influence. Of course, this argument has less weight if one subscribes to the absurd notion that the Qur'an is actually Aramaic. As Ratliff relates, "It was [only] during the first century of 'Abbasid rule that the Christian community, particularly Palestinian monastic communities, began translating Christian texts into Arabic" (16). While there was a Saint Sergius, he died in the fourth century CE. There was also a hermit called Sargarius who supposedly lived in a grotto on Mount Sinai. However, there is no evidence that any person of this name resided in the region of the Holy Mountain during the period of the Prophet's visits. As for the claims concerning a late origin for the composition of the Qur'an, they are easily dismissed. In the words of Maurice Bucaille (1920–1998 CE), "There is absolutely no doubt about it: the text of the Qur'an we have today is most definitely a text of the period" (120).

If we have expounded upon the story of Bahira in a scholarly capacity it is to illustrate the distinct historical possibilities of the event. But the tree should not prevent us from seeing the forest. The certainty or uncertainty of a single event or series of events does not change one iota the essence of the message brought by Muhammad. As to what took place between the encounter with Bahira in 582 CE and Muhammad's marriage to Khadijah (d. 619 CE) in 595 CE, the sources are silent with the exception of spurious allegations that he participated in the Sacrilegious War or *Harb al-fijar* when he was twenty years of age. It can only be assumed that Muhammad, from the age of twelve to the age of twenty-five, continued to acquire experience leading caravans in his uncle's family business. Due to the qualities he exhibited, both personally and professionally, Muhammad was eventually granted the honorific titles of *al-Sadiq* [the Truthful] and *al-Amin* [the Trustworthy].

In 595, after having proven himself a worthy caravaneer with a reputation for honesty, integrity, and honor, Muhammad was hired by Khadijah bint Khuwaylid, a wealthy merchant woman from Mecca, to lead one of her trade missions to Syria, as she herself did not travel with her caravans. He was, however, to take a young servant of hers with him. Known by the name of Maysarah, the boy would witness the next miraculous encounter between Muhammad and members of the Christian faith in Syria. As Ibn Ishaq (704–761/770 CE) relates,

> The Messenger stopped in the shade of a tree near a monk's cell, when the monk came up to Maysara[h] and asked who the man was who was resting beneath the tree. He told him that he was of Quraysh, the people who held the sanctuary; and the monk explained: 'None but a prophet ever sat beneath this tree.' (82)

Identified in Sunni sources as Nastur or Nasturah [Nestor], the person in question may simply have been a Nestorian monk. He was not, Shi'ite historians stress, the same monk whom the Prophet had met as a child (Dar Rah Haqq 175, note 32). Although Ibn Ishaq's (704–761/770 CE) version is truncated, Majlisi's (1616–1689 CE) version describes in meticulous details the events that occurred (Section 4):

> When the caravan neared Syria they camped near a monastery. The Holy Prophet sat down under a tree and all the members of the caravan dispersed.
>
> The said tree had dried up since long but it became green instantaneously. Branches and leaves sprouted and fruits also hung down from it. Greenery spread all around. Seeing this, the monk rushed out and went to the Holy Prophet. He had a book from which he was reading and then looking at the elegance of the Holy Prophet said: 'By the One who sent the *Injil* [Gospel], this is him.' When Khuzaymah heard this, he feared that perhaps he would harm the Prophet, so he drew his sword and cried: 'O people of Ghalib! Beware. Take care!'
>
> All the members of the caravan rushed there and the monk fled and hid himself in his house, went up the roof and said there from: 'Why do you want to harm me? By the one Who has raised the sky without pillars, you are the dearest of all the caravans who have ever passed by me. This Book says that this youth who is sitting under the tree is the Messenger of the Lord of the heavens and the earth and who will be appointed to wage armed *jihad* and kill innumerable unbelievers. He is the last prophet. One who obeys him will get salvation and one that disobeys him will lose the way.'
>
> Then he asked Khuzaymah: 'Do you belong to his community?' He said: 'No. But I am his servant.' Then he narrated to the monk all the miraculous things observed by him on the way. The monk reiterated that he was the prophet of the last age. 'I tell you a fact which you must keep confidential. I have read in books that he will conquer the whole world and control all communities. He will never return from any war but as a conqueror. His enemies are many and most of them are Jews. So protect him from them.' Then that caravan left that place and reached Syria and earned a lot of profit.
>
> On the return journey when they approached Mecca, Maysarah said to the Holy Prophet: 'O virtuous and selected one! We have seen many miracles from you in this journey. Every rock and tree by which we passed, saluted you saying: 'Peace be upon you, O Messenger of Allah.' The valleys on the way which could be earlier crossed in many days were crossed this time, because of your auspiciousness, within a night. The profit made by us in this journey is the best we earned in the last forty years. So it is better if you yourself go to Khadijah and give the good news of this easy journey and profitable trade so that she is pleased.' Thus the Prophet went ahead of the caravan and turned to Khadijah's house who was at that time sitting with some other ladies in the upper apartment with an eye on the road.

> Suddenly she saw a mounted man arriving and she also observed a cloud shading him and that two angels, one on his right and the other on his left, were accompanying him with naked swords. A lamp of emerald hung over his head from that cloud. All around that cloud was a tent of topaz spread in the space over him. Seeing this, Khadijah prayed in her heart with astonishment: 'My Lord! Be it so that this youth who is beloved to You may come to my humble home.' (Section 5)

While the version found in Ibn Ishaq (704–761/770 CE) is more sober, it still shares the same common elements as the account narrated by Majlisi (1616–1689 CE). It should be noted, however, that Ibn Ishaq alludes to the fact that he has condensed the story, perhaps suppressing elements that sounded too mythological for his taste. In any event, after selling his goods in Syria, the Prophet commenced his return journey to Mecca. According to Ibn Ishaq,

> The story goes that at the height of noon when the heat was intense as he rode his beast Maysarah saw two angels shading the Messenger from the sun's rays. When he brought Khadijah her property she sold it and it amounted to double or thereabouts. Maysarah for his part told her about the two angels who shaded him and of the monk's words. (Ibn Ishaq 82)

Ibn Ishaq relates what happened thereafter in the following terms,

> Now Khadijah was a determined, noble, and intelligent woman possessing the properties which God willed to honor her. So when Maysarah told her these things she went to the Messenger of God and —so the story goes—said: 'O son of my uncle I like you because of our relationship and your high reputation among your people, your trustworthiness and good character and truthfulness.' Then she proposed marriage. Now Khadijah at that time was the best born woman in Quraysh, of the greatest dignity and, too, the richest. (82)

Impressed by Muhammad's remarkable character, Khadijah had developed a fondness for him. Muhammad, in turn, had developed feelings for the honorable, independent, and industrious woman that was Khadijah. At a time when marriages were arranged in one's infancy, when men only asked women in marriage, and when people married merely for the purpose of political ties and prosperity, Khadijah proposed marriage to Muhammad, and both married out of love despite their difference in age and social status. According to Ibn Ishaq (704–761/770 CE),

> Khadijah had told Waraqah b. Nawfal . . . who was her cousin and a Christian who had studied the scriptures and was a scholar, what her slave Maysarah had told her that the monk had said and how he had see the two angels shading him. He said, 'If this is true, Khadijah, verily Muhammad is the prophet of this people. I knew that a prophet of this people was to be expected. His time has come' or words to that effect. Waraqah was finding the time of waiting wearisome and used to say 'How long?' (83)

While little to nothing is known about Muhammad's life during the decade prior to his prophetic mission, we have the evidence of his industry to support the likelihood that he would have traveled to Syria during the summer and to Yemen during the winter. In addition to the southern route to Yemen; the northern routes to the Levant and Syria; the eastern routes to Basrah, in what is modern day Iraq; and the route to Gerrha, in what is now Bahrayn; there was also a trade route that passed through Medina on the way to ʿAqabah from where it continued on to Nakhl, in the central Sinai, to its final destination of Alexandria, in Egypt. At that location, the Arabian trade routes connected with the trans-Saharan ones (see Porter 93). According to Muhammad Hamidullah (1908–2002 CE), the Prophet traveled extensively along the coast of the Persian Gulf and perhaps even made it as far as Abyssinia (*Muslim Conduct* xi). Theophanes (early 9th century), George Hamartolus (late 9th century), and Thomas Arcruni (early 10th century) all reported that Muhammad made mercantile journeys to Egypt (qtd. Thomson, "Muhammad" 833, 836, 837). According to Pierre Belon (1517–1564 CE), Muhammad had made many voyages to Persia, Egypt, and Syria in the company of Khadijah (380). As Hamidullah reports,

> Later, we see him sometimes in the fair of Hubashah (Yemen), and at least once in the country of the 'Abd al-Qais (Bahrain-Oman), as mentioned by Ibn Hanbal. There is every reason to believe that this refers to the great fair at Daba (Oman), where, according to Ibn al-Kalbi (cf. Ibn Habib, *Muhabbar*), the traders of China, of Hind and Sind (India, Pakistan), of Persia, of the East and the West assembled every year, travelling both by land and sea. There is also mention of a commercial partner of Muhammad at Mecca. This person, Sa'ib by name, reports: 'We relayed each other; if Muhammad led the caravan, he did not enter his house on his return to Mecca without clearing accounts with me; and if I led the caravan, he would on my return enquire about my welfare and speak nothing about his own capital entrusted to me.' (*Introduction* 5)

This business partner of Muhammad, whose full name was al-Sa'ib ibn Abu al-Sa'ib ibn 'Abid ibn 'Abd Allah ibn 'Umar ibn Makhzum, was probably the person with the most detailed knowledge of his early travels. Ibn Hisham reports that "there is a tradition that the Prophet said that he was an excellent partner who was never ill tempered or obstinate" (Ibn Ishaq 747, note 520). According to the information available to Ibn Hisham, Sa'ib "became an excellent Muslim" (Ibn Ishaq 747, note 520). Ibn 'Abbas reported that Sa'ib ibn Abu al-Sa'ib was one of the Quraysh who swore fealty to the Messenger of Allah and that the later gave the former a share of the booty of Hunayn (Ibn Ishaq 747, note 520). Ibn Ishaq, however, alleges that Sa'ib was among the polytheists killed at Badr (338).

If anything is clear, it is that the Prophet was well-traveled. Consequently, the claim of Sayed Mujdtaba Moussaoui-Lari (1925–2013 CE) that Muhammad only left "Saudi" Arabia on two occasions prior to the declaration of his prophetic mission (12) is patently false. Considering that Muhammad had been "a trader and caravan leader on the Incense Road between Arabia and Syria" (Franck and Brownstone 190) for more than two decades, fifteen at the service of his wife Khadijah, it is a logical impossibility that he made merely two trips. If this had been the case, Khadijah would hardly have been the wealthy and successful business woman that she is made out to be. Such notions are often based on a habit of seeing Muhammad as an illiterate who had little or no contact with Christians. This habit stems from the fear, likely based on an over-reaction to certain ideas of the Orientalists, that Muhammad might have been overly influenced by the Judeo-Christian tradition. As the Qur'an and Sunnah evidence, the Prophet was fully familiar with the environment in which he operated. He could identify all the political and religious leaders in Arabia, Byzantium, Egypt, and Persia. He was well aware of the theological disputes which divided the Christian community.

Outside of intriguing elements found in the Qur'an and the Sunnah, the historical record is a virtual void when it comes to the period between Muhammad's marriage and the descent of revelation on the Mountain of Light. It was precisely during this obscure decade that Muhammad is said to have come into contact with another Christian community, that of the monks of Mount Sinai. As Aziz Suryal Atiya (1898–1988 CE) acknowledges, "Muhammad . . . is said to have visited the Monastery during his early peregrinations" (xviii). According to both the monks and Bedouins of Mount Sinai, "Muhammad had already visited the monastery before his revelations began, on one of his journeys as a merchant" (Hobbs 159). They describe the auspicious arrival of a man who would eventually be appointed as the Final Messenger of Allah in the following terms:

> As he rested with camels on Jebel Munayja at the head of Wadi ad-Dayr, an eagle was seen to spread its wings over his head, and the monks, struck by the augury of his future greatness, received him into their convent, and he in return, unable to write, stamped with ink on his hand the signature to a contract of protection, drawn up on the skin of a gazelle, and deposited in the archives of the convent. (344)

As a monk explained to Joseph J. Hobbs, "Muhammad and his companions were taken in by the monastery and treated very well by the monastery, as well as was possible in those days. For that reason he guaranteed the safety and protection of this place. That is one of the reasons for its longevity" (159). Apparently, Muhammad was so moved by the hospitality of the monks, who assisted him during difficult times, that he "later rewarded them by issuing a covenant whereby their lives and property became secure under Moslem rule" (Atiya xviii).

At first thought, the presence of an Arab trade caravan in the vicinity of Mount Sinai seems strange indeed since caravans from Mecca passed through Medina, Mada'in Salih, and Tabuk, crossing over into the Sinai from 'Aqabah on their way to Alexandria. Since the southern Sinai is very mountainous, caravans would cross the interior in the middle part of the peninsula. Why, then, was Muhammad attempting to follow a coastal route? There was, indeed, a route that went from Aylah or 'Aqabah down eastern coast of the Sinai and all the way up the western coast. Close to Nuwaybah, a route crossed inland toward St. Catherine's Monastery, passed by Fayran [Pharan], and reached the Gulf of Suez. If caravans crossed the Sinai, stopping at Nakhl, it was because it was the shortest distance between two points. If the destination was Alexandria, heading south into the Sinai more than doubled the distance—unless, of course, that the intended goal was Mount Sinai.

Despite the fact that the monks of Mount Sinai were a numerically small community, could commerce have been the major motivator? After all, according to Greffin Affagart (d. c. 1557 CE), the distance between Mecca and Mount Sinai was fourteen days by camel caravan (203). This estimate, however, is inaccurate, and the voyage would have been substantially longer. While the population of Saint Catherine's Monastery may have been small compared to that of cities such as Alexandria and Damascus, it was actually much greater than imagined. According to John Lewis Burckhardt (1784–1817 CE), there were six to seven thousand monks spread throughout the Sinai at the time of the Muslim conquest (546). The monk market was thus of substantial size. What, one wonders, could the monks have possibly traded to the Arabs for needed supplies? If the monks were relatively self-subsistent, they might only have been in need of spices, incense or articles of clothing. It is possible, however unlikely, that Muhammad had strayed from the major trading routes for reasons unexplained. It is far more likely that he combined both religion and commerce. However, the most likely answer to all of these questions may be found in one of the earliest accounts of Muhammad's encounter with the monks.

The current version of Muhammad's encounter with the Monastery of Saint Catherine, namely the one shared by the monks in the 20th and 21st centuries, differs in some details from one of its earliest recorded accounts. Balthasar de Monconys (1611–1665 CE), who traveled to Mount Sinai in 1646–47, returned with the following account of Muhammad's contact with the monastery:

> Muhammad, being a friend of one of their monks, gave him a charter containing a number of privileges and all kinds of tax exemptions. He also subjected all the Arabs who serve them. In return, however, the monks were obliged to feed all the Arabs that came. . . . Muhammad signed the charter with the figure of his hand which he dipped in ink and applied to the paper. This charter, in turn, was taken from them by Selim, the Emperor of the Turks, who brought it to his Treasury after leaving behind a copy for them along with a confirmation and amplification of said privileges. . . . (228–229)[1]

During his travels through the holy land between 1655–1663, which were recorded in his *Relation d'un voyage fait au Levant*, Jean de Thévenot (1633–1667 CE) relates the following version from the Greek monks of the time:

> One day, Muhammad, who, according to the Greek monks, was their camel driver, had brought them some provisions on his camels. As he was tired, he fell asleep in front of the door of the monastery. While he was sleeping, an eagle appeared which circled around his head for a long time. When the doorman saw this, he ran to the Abbot, who came

1. For the convenience of the reader all passages from French texts have been translated into English.

right away and saw the same thing, causing him to reflect upon the matter. When Muhammad awoke, he asked him whether he would be willing to do some good, seeing that he was a great and powerful lord. Muhammad responded that he was no such person and, as such, was in no position to help. Seeing that the other continued to insist on his supposition, Muhammad assured him that, were he able, he would not hesitate to help them greatly considering the fact that they were the ones that fed him. The Abbot, however, wanted to obtain his promise in writing. However, since Muhammad was unable to write, the Abbot asked that an inkwell be brought and Muhammad, having soaked his hand in the ink, applied his palm on a sheet of white paper, where his palm-print remained marked, and gave this to them as an assurance of his promise. A short time after having reached the heights that were foretold by the Eagle, he remembered the promise he had made and protected and conserved their Monastery with all of their land on the condition that they fed the neighboring Arabs.... (*Relation* 322–323; *Voyages* 536–537)

While St. Catherine's Monastery did not lie on any major trade route, it was in close proximity to Aylah, the point of intersection of the Silk Road, the Spice Route, and the Incense Road (Franck and Brownstone: front and back endpapers) during Roman times. If Aylah, on the eastern side of the Sinai lost its importance during Muslim times, the western side of the peninsula continued to form a major part of the Spice Route. Evidently, there were many minor trade routes which delivered supplies to communities which were off of the major routes and roads. As a young man, Muhammad may very well have been contracted by the monks to act as their caravaneer. In fact, this is exactly the account we find in *Relation historique d'un voyage nouvellement fait au mont de Sinaï et à Jerusalem*, published in 1704, by Sieur Antoine Morison Chanoine de Bar le Duc who was a Knight of the Holy Sepulchre. Speaking of the Monastery of Saint Catherine, he wrote that

Muhammad, the imposter and false prophet, who was an Arab by nationality and of very low birth, stayed there for a few years, as if he were seeking refuge from the miseries of his low condition, taking care of the camels and other animals destined for the use and service of the monks. Having later removed himself from servitude, as all do, he showed his change of fortune to the entire monastery by means of the considerable gifts that he gave in consideration for a monk he was particularly fond of and in recognition of the bounties they had bestowed upon him during his stay in that place. Besides the presents, he granted it great privileges for perpetuity and, among other things, an exemption from all types of taxation, and absolute power over the Arabs who wished to work for them. However, he required some charity of the monastery which is still not denied to this day to the poor Arabs who (as I have seen myself) come in rather large numbers to the convent and who are never denied bread. These conditions were confirmed by letters of patents which were not signed by Muhammad (as he never knew how to read) but marked with his hand which had been soaked in ink and which was his normal signature in important affairs. Selim the first, known as the emperor of the Turks, confirmed these privileges, removed this patent, a signed copy of which he gave the monks of Mount Sinai, and placed the original in the Treasury of the Serrail in Constantinople, where it is conserved as a very precious trust. (105–106)

In his *History of the Growth and Decay of the Othman Empire*, which was originally written in Latin, Demetrius Cantemir (1673–1723 CE), the Prince of Moldavia, shared a similar account which, he says, was found solely "in a fabulous treatise by a Sinaitic monk" (168). This version, which appears to be the oldest of all, and on which most of the oral accounts seem to be based, is as follows:

They say, though fabulously, that Mahomet being of mean birth, us'd to drive in his youth hir'd camels from place to place. In these journies, as he one day approach'd Mount Sinai, the Abbot saw a cloud hovering over Mahomet's head as he lay asleep in the open field, and defending it as it were from the sun-beams. The Abbot thence conjecturing there was something more in the youth than was promis'd by his outward appearance, because so singular an omen, in his opinion, could only happen to the future Lord of those Regions, and therefore he went and saluted him very civilly, inviting him into his room and bidding him take his rest quietly.

When he thought he had gain'd his good-will by all kind of civilities, he ask'd him, if ever he should become Sovereign of those parts what his pleasure would be concerning the monks? Mahomet answer'd, 'He would free them as *Rubban*, (Keepers of the Life or Course), dispers'd through the world from all tribute, and hold them in great honour.' He gave him this promise in an Arabic writing, and confirm'd it, for want of a Seal, with the Palm of his hand dipt in ink and impress'd on the paper. Long after, when Sultan Selim was in Egypt, the Abbot of Mount Sinai humbly came to him with Mahomet's true or forged instrument, which the Emperor purchased of the monks for four thousand gold crowns, with a declaration of their being free from all tribute, and a confirmation by his *Chatisherif* of this and their other privileges. (168)

If this is indeed the oldest account of Muhammad's contact with the monks of Mount Sinai, and if it is really drawn from an ancient treatise by a Sinaitic monk, as opposed to the oral tradition, it provides some critically important details. To commence, it states that it was a cloud, and not an eagle, that followed Muhammad overhead. This is the same phenomenon that was observed when Muhammad traveled to and from Syria during his youth. It also explains that Muhammad used his hand-print to sign the document, not because he could not write, but because he did not have a seal. The allegation that the Prophet could not write, and for which he was mocked by many European travel writers, appears to be a later development. While it may have been the result of ill-will on the part of certain Christians, it may have also been in keeping with a belief in the Prophet's illiteracy, a doctrine that only became entrenched among the Sunnis centuries after his passing. This account also clarifies the details surrounding the transfer of the covenant from the Sinai to Istanbul. Rather than being seized, it was purchased by Selim I at the exorbitant amount of four thousand gold crowns. The Ottoman Caliph, guided by his Grand Vizier, and counseled by the greatest scholar of Islam, would not have spent such a spectacular sum on a spurious document.

When J.N. Fazakerley visited the Monastery of Saint Catherine in 1811, the monks also proudly showed him the famous *achtiname* of Muhammad. As he relates in his "Journey from Cairo to Mount Sinai:"

We were shown what professes to be the celebrated *firman* of Mahomet, granting many privileges, particularly to the priests of this Convent, and generally to Christians; there is, however, reason to suppose that the original document was taken away by Sultan Selim, the conqueror of Egypt, who thought it too precious and sacred a monument to be left in Christian hands. The original was signed by 'Ali, and Abu Bekr, and many of Mahomet's chieftains, the Prophet having consecrated it with his own seal. Selim, at all events, left a *firman* confirming the same privileges. (375–378)

Sir Frederick Henniker (1793–1825 CE), who traveled to the Sinai in 1820–21, also spoke of the *Covenant of the Prophet Muhammad with the Monks of Mount Sinai*, with one caveat: he was not allowed to see it:

Among the talked-of curiosities of Mount Sinai, is said to be an impression of the hand of Mohammed, under which the convent enjoys many immunities; I requested to see it, but the superior tells me that it is now at Constantinople, for the Gran Seignor having desired to look at it, retained it. The history of it he gave as follows: It happened that Mohammed, when an unknown youth, was encamped in this neighborhood, an eagle was observed to hover over him, and one of the monks predicted his future greatness. Mohammed, well pleased with the gipsy tale, made liberal promises to the convent; a piece of paper was produced, but Mohammed, being unable to write, smeared his hand all over with ink, and made his mark. In about fifteen years afterwards the augury was fulfilled; the soothsayer hastened to Mecca, and claimed performance of the note of hand. Mohammed kept his promise, and swore by the token that the convent should remain forever sacred; that the country, as far as eye can scan, should belong to it; and all the inhabitants thereon its slaves. (233–234)

When Francis Arundale, the British architect, visited the Monastery of Saint Catherine in 1831, the *Covenant of the Prophet* was still not on display. Rather, it was stored in the archives. As he explains:

> Amongst the most curious manuscripts preserved at the Library, is one to which the Fathers attach great importance; it is the copy of an edict from the Prophet, addressed to all Christians. The original, written in Cufic characters upon the skin of a gazelle, and upon which still remain marks of the Prophet's fingers, is at present in the possession of the Sultan; though formerly preserved in this Convent. In 1517, after the conquest of Egypt, Selim demanded it, and placed a copy, in parchment, certified by himself, among the archives of this monastery. (28)

The two details that stand out are 1) that the covenant was written on the skin of a gazelle and 2) that it was written in Kufic script. The material is consistent with the period of the Prophet and the script is consistent with Imam 'Ali personal artistic preference.

If the events related by the monks of Mount Sinai, which were recorded by a large number of pilgrims over the past millennium, are true, then this would enrich our understanding of an obscure period during the life of Muhammad. Many Muslims, of course, would reject these accounts, perhaps rightfully so, on the basis that they are related by Christians who had an unfavorable view of the Prophet of Islam. Still, this might amount to a short-sighted or even rash assessment. It should be recalled that little to nothing is known about the life of Muhammad from his voyage to Syria with his uncle Abu Talib in 582 CE to his marriage to Khadijah in 582 CE. Sayyed Safdar Husayn (1932–1989 CE) erroneously claims that Muhammad spent the following years in the luxury of Abu Talib's house where he observed the pious offerings and prayers conducted by the guardians of the holy sanctuary (32–33). In other words, this author alleges that Muhammad was immersed in pagan piety during his teenage years. He also wrongly alleges that Muhammad participated in the Sacriligious War in 585 CE, another offense to the personality of Muhammad who had been protected from sin. The bibliography of Muhammad goes blank for another ten years during which he supposedly participated in the *Hilf al-fudhul* in 595 CE, a league devoted to defending the oppressed (33–34).

There is thus a period of ten years in the life of Muhammad, from the time he was fifteen to the time he was twenty-five, that is unaccounted for. There is also a second period of fifteen years, from the time he was married, at the age of twenty-five, until he declared his prophethood, at the age of forty, that is equally unaccounted for. These two blocks of time represent twenty-five years of silence. Where, then, was Muhammad, and what on earth was he doing? If the sources with Arab roots are silent on the subject, it may be because he simply was not in Arabia. Tellingly, when news of Muhammad disappears in the Hijaz, news of him reappears in the Sinai. It therefore seems highly improbable that the monks of Mount Sinai invented the account of Muhammad's residence at the Monastery of Saint Catherine in the Sinai. Since the biography of Muhammad is the most meticulously detailed of any historical figure, either past or present, the odds of being able—dishonestly but convincingly—to place him at a specific place at a precise time are slim. Any account which conflicted with the biography of Muhammad would have been exposed as a fraud. Either the monks of Mount Sinai were experts in *sirah* literature, extremely lucky, or honest and truthful. The evidence points to the latter. As all Muslims authorities on the biography of the Prophet will agree, a piece in the puzzle is missing. There is a gaping void which spans twenty-five years. Astonishingly, the monks of Mount Sinai appear, to all evidence, to have the missing piece. Admittedly, anyone can make up a piece of a story, but not everyone can make it fit. The piece of the puzzle provided by the monks of Saint Catherine's Monastery fits: it completes the picture of Muhammad's early life.

Muslim critics may commend this creative reconstruction of Muhammad's youth; however, they will object that it is uncorroborated by Islamic sources. But is it really? There may be no surviving signs of this period in the extant *sirah* literature. Or are there? The Prophet Muhammad used to say,

"There is no prophet but has shepherded a flock" (Ibn Ishaq 72). His Companions asked him if this included him. He responded in the affirmative (72). But when and where was the young Muhammad a shepherd? Was it in Mecca? If so, for whom did he work? Was it while he lived with the Bani Sa'd ibn Bakr when he was a boy? Could this tribe's range have extended into the Sinai? Or was it in the Sinai where Muhammad tended the flocks that belonged to the Monastery of Saint Catherine? In "The Shepherds, the Baptist and the Essenes: A Response to *The Life of Christ and Biblical Revelations* by Anne Catherine Emmerich," Charles Upton sheds light on the symbolism of the shepherd. As this author explains,

> Those "shepherds keeping watch over their flocks by night" mentioned in Luke 2:8 were undoubtedly the leaders of secret or esoteric spiritual schools, 'night' being a symbol of both outer secrecy and hidden matters of the Spirit. Such esoteric groups could also have actually made their living as shepherds, which would have allowed them to carry messages, gather intelligence and spread their teaching over a wide area, shepherds being relatively mobile as compared to town dwellers, and thus able to travel without arousing suspicion. (199)

According to Upton, Jesus, the "Good Shepherd" and "Lamb of God," along with John the Baptist, may have belonged to, or been a "graduate" of, the Nazirite Order, which seems to have been associated with sheepherding. The Talmud mentions a "Nazirite shepherd," and the Prophet Amos, himself a shepherd, lamented the degeneration of the Order. For some, this might suggest the possibility that Muhammad may have come across Judeo-Christian mystics during his wanderings as a young shepherd.

If the Prophet stayed in the Cave of Moses at the top of Mount Sinai, it may have been in the course of his shepherding. Intentionally or not, he was reenacting the movements of Moses. Muhammad's connection to Moses must have been profound. While he recognized that Jesus was the Messiah, but not the son of God, Muhammad also insisted that the Law of Moses remained binding with some minor modifications which resulted from the final revelation. After all, Muhammad proclaimed the need to follow the laws that God had imposed on the Children of Israel in his Covenant with the Christians of Najran. A further fascinating fact involves the image of the Virgin Mary and the infant Jesus, surrounded by angels, which the Prophet Muhammad found in the Ka'bah, and which he protected from destruction with his hand during the Conquest of Mecca (Flood 245). This very same image, which was found in the Ka'bah, in the middle of the 7th century, is also found in the Holy Monastery of Saint Catherine at Sinai. This icon, known as the Virgin and Child with Saints and Angels, also features the Hand of God and dates from the 6th to 7th century CE (Thomas 127, fig. 55). It is as if the Prophet had seen the icon, made of encaustic paint on wood, with the Hand of God granting protection to the Holy Family, at the Monastery of Mount Sinai and re-enacted the same scene in the Ka'bah by protecting the image with his own hand. In this sense, it was not truly the Hand of Muhammad, but rather, the Hand of Allah that protected the sacred symbol. Muhammad, as Prophet and Messenger, also had a profound impact on the Christian faith. While most Muslims and Christians are ignorant of the possibility, it appears that the first person to formulate the doctrine of the Immaculate Conception was Muhammad himself, a fact conceded by both Catholic and Protestant theologians (Grassi 74). Some assert that the Prophet learned such doctrines from the Eastern Christians, but ignore the strong evidence that the Christians might in fact have learned it from him.

The Messenger of Allah did not create an amalgam of Judeo-Christian beliefs and practices together with pagan Arab elements. As far as Muslims are concerned, Muhammad purified, perfected, and completed the primordial mono-theistic tradition of Adam, Abraham, Moses, and Jesus. The issue, then, is not of borrowing, but rather of belonging, reviving, revitalizing, and renewing.

But what does the Qur'an say on the subject of Muhammad's sojourning in the Sinai? Stunningly, it seems to support it. According to the thousand year old accounts of the monks of Mount Sinai, which were documented by pilgrims from many parts of the world over the centuries, Muhammad was an orphan. He had lost his father; he had lost his mother; and he had lost his grandfather. He had lost it all. He was destitute and all alone in the world. As the monks of Mount Sinai explained, they came across this young man, and were convinced of his great potential. They saw in him the seeds of a great leader. Perhaps—just perhaps—they believed he might be the awaited prophet foretold in the Old and New Testaments. They took him in. They cared for him. They sheltered him. As Almighty Allah asked the Prophet in the Holy Qur'an: "Did we not find thee an orphan and give thee shelter (and care)? And He found thee wandering, and He gave you guidance" (93:6–7). These Christians, who were cut off from the more established Church, appear to have been expecting the arrival of a Final Prophet, the *parakletos* (comforter, helper) whom Jesus predicted would come after him (cf. John 16:7–11), and may have interpreted this word as *periklytos* (praiseworthy one), identifying the expected figure with Muhammad, one of whose epithets, *Ahmad*, means "praiseworthy." They may have also interpreted the New Heaven and the New Earth, which is described in the Book of Apocalypse as being of equal length, breadth, and height, as being the Ka'bah or Cube, a veiled prediction of Islam. They may also have been relying on ancient scriptures which have been lost or destroyed.

There are numerous reports in both Sunni and Shi'ite sources that Muhammad's life has been in peril since the moment of his birth. The Jews, it is reported, would have killed him given the opportunity. The Christians, however, had recognized his future greatness and had offered him protection. As Ibn Ishaq reports, a group of Abyssinian Christians had seen Muhammad with his foster-mother, asked questions about him, and studied him carefully. They then said to Halimah, Muhammad's wet-nurse: "Let us take this boy, and bring him to our kind and our country; for he will have a great future. We know all about him" (73). Is it possible that Abu Talib placed Muhammad in the care of a remote Christian community for the sake of his own safety? The sources record that many such offers were made by Christians who came across Muhammad while in the custody of Abu Talib. Were the Christians or *nasara* [i.e., Abrahamic Arab monotheists, Jews, and Christians], from the root *nsr* or "to help," destined by the vocabulary of the Qur'an to protect the future prophet? The evidence appears to indicate that it was so.

According to the monks of Mount Saint Catherine, Muhammad eventually returned from the Sinai to Mecca where he came into wealth. Was this as a result of his marriage to Khadijah? Almighty Allah appears to allude to this event, when He says: "And he found thee in need, and made thee independent" (93:8). These are not the only Qur'anic verses which appear to echo these early events in the life of Muhammad. Take, for example, *Surah al-Tin* or The Fig, which reads:

> By the Fig and the Olive,
> And the Mount of Sinai,
> And this City of Security.
> We have indeed created man in the best of moulds.
> Then do we abase him to the lowest of the low,
> Except such as believe and do righteous deeds: for they shall have a reward unfailing. (95: 1–6)

These verses connect Sinai, the Mount of Revelation, with Mecca, the City of Security, which also features the Mountain of Light, another Mount of Revelation. The man created in the best of moulds is none other than the Prophet: *al-insan al-kamil*, the Perfect Human Being, the man of sublime character. Tried and tested, the young Muhammad wandered the wastelands of Arabia working as a shepherd and caravaneer. Like Job, who was tested to the extreme, the young Muhammad never lost his faith. Since the slayers of prophets were awaiting the arrival of a final prophet from Arabia, Muhammad's life had been in imminent danger from the day he was born. He found protection with Halimah, his nurse-maid, among the Bedouin Arabs. He would later be protected by an isolated community of monks who lived at Mount Sinai. Having helped him get on his feet until he reached manhood, they sent him back to Mecca where he married Khadijah al-Kubra and where his fortune changed. The unfailing reward was nothing less than the sublime rank of prophethood.

The Qur'an also refers to *Jabal Sinai* by the ancient name of *Jabal Tur* suggesting intimate familiarity with the region. Chapter 52 of the Qur'an is actually named *al-Tur* which is a synonym for *al-Sina'* or Sinai. Almighty Allah even invokes the Holy Mountain, saying: "By the Mount [of Tur]" (52:1). As such, the Prophet's knowledge of the Sinai would have derived, not only from divine inspiration, but from personal experience as well. Some may claim revisionism; however, what is more improbable: that Muhammad was a prototypical pagan until he received revelation or that he was a seeker of truth who sought out the *hanafiyyah*, the *yahud* and the *nasara* [i.e., Abrahamic Arab monotheists, Jews, and Christians]? I would prefer a Muhammad who was mentored by monotheistic holy men than a Muhammad who cared for the idols in the Ka'bah. Jesus may have been a Jew who was taught by rabbis; however, that did not prevent him from founding a new faith. The value of Christianity is not weakened by its Jewish origins nor is Islam weakened by the fact that it is a continuation and completion of the Judeo-Christian tradition.

If the versions of Thévenot (1633–1667 CE) and Morison (17th–18th centuries CE) are correct, they clear up some of the confusion surrounding the origin of the covenant that the Prophet entered into with the monks of Mount Sinai. The origin of this *achtiname* would be prior to the declaration of prophecy, consisting of an oral promise sealed with a palm-print or, according to another version, a document redacted by the monks and sealed by Muhammad (Mouton 177). Thus, the actual charter of rights and privileges would date back to the early days of Islam. This certainly makes a lot of sense. It is equally plausible that Muhammad, as the head of a small caravan, had intentionally set off for the Sinai for religious reasons. He may even have provided caravan services for religious pilgrims. The current structure of the Monastery of Saint Catherine was built under Emperor Justinian (r. 527–565 CE), namely, in the years immediately before the birth of Muhammad in 570 CE. Word of this new construction, and its spiritual significance, must certainly have been known throughout Arabia, particularly among caravaneers. As Ratliff reports, "[t]ravel to visit holy places and holy figures flourished in the century before the Arab occupation of the region" ("To Travel to the Holy" 87). During Muhammad's life, the "See of Jerusalem and the monasteries of Mar Saba in the Judean desert and Saint Catherine in the Sinai were important intellectual centers" (Ratliff, "Christian..." 38). As a spiritual seeker and contemplative, he may have yearned to visit one of the most sacred sites on earth. After all, few places in the world have such religious and historical significance as the Sinai:

> The Monastery itself was built over the traditional site of the bush from which God spoke to Moses in the fire, and nearby grows the sacred tree which, according to tradition, sprang from Aaron's rod. At the summit of Mt. Sinai or Jebel Musa, one can feel the very presence of the great lawgiver himself, for this seems to be the top of the Biblical world. To the south lies the tip of Sinai and the Red Sea; to the east across the mountains is the Gulf of Aqaba from which Solomon once sent his trading ships; to the north is the wilderness of Zin, and on the west is the land of the Pharaohs. Here at the top, Moses is commemorated by a chapel and Moslem mosque. The cave in which he is said to have lived alone for forty days and nights lies near the mosque, which is still a place of pilgrimage for Moslems. Nearby, tradition claims, the Lord gave Moses, the 'tablets of stone, and a law and commandments which I have written; that thou mayest teach them' (Exodus 24:12). (Atiya x-xi)

According to the Jabaliyyah, the Arab inhabitants of Mount Sinai, Muhammad spent a night in the cave in question when he visited the area as a caravaneer (Hobbs 169). It is an accepted fact that Muhammad was fond of solitude. In Mecca, in the years immediately prior to receiving his first revelations, he used to spend extended periods of time meditating, fasting, and praying in a cave on what is now known as the Mountain of Light. This period of religious seclusion, known as *tahannuth*, would last a month (Ibn Ishaq 105). Since his travels to the Sinai took place before he declared his prophecy, his practice of praying in caves may have commenced in the very cave in which the Prophet Moses retired on a spiritual retreat that lasted forty days and forty nights. At the very least, the cave of Moses on Mount Sinai may have been the immediate precursor to the cave of Hirah on the Mountain of Light. In this sense, Muhammad was very much in communion, not only with the Divine, but with the spirit of Moses in the same way that the encounter with Bahira placed him in contact with the tradition of Christ.

The cave on Mount Sinai, in which the Prophet Muhammad spent the night, has long been revered as a sacred site. Located ten meters south of the church on the top of Jebel Musa is a small mosque known as *Jami' Fatimah* [The Mosque of Fatimah], which dates from Fatimid times (Hobbs 169). In fact, it was built by Emir Anushtakin, during the reign of Abu 'Ali al-Mansur (r. 996–1021 CE), the tenth of the Fatimid Caliphs. Its purpose was to allow the Bedouins to have their own place of prayer (Mouton 181). The Jabaliyyah, however, "believe it dates from the rule of Caliph 'Umar" (Hobbs 634–644). It may be that the Fatimid mosque was built on the foundations of an earlier commemorative mosque, although Mouton is certain that it was built on the foundations of an ancient Christian chapel (181). Since Bernstein reports that "[t]he Moslems . . . constructed a small fort on the peak of Mount Sinai, in order to defend the southern route to Egypt from the Crusaders" (12) in the 12th century, it seems more logical to assume that the mosque was built on the foundation of an earlier fort or perhaps a small mosque which served the detachment of Muslim soldiers. What is clear is that the mosque and the fort that preceded it were built using the vestiges of an ancient church or convent (Dahari 153). In fact, the remains of four earlier churches can be discerned in all the debris, all of them predating the current church, and mosque, which stand at the top of Jabal Musa (153). Regarding the mosque itself, Hobbs has the following to say:

> The mosque is situated above a site sacred to the Jabaliyyah, a cave in which they say Moses lived and fasted during his forty days and nights on the mountain—a tradition shared by fifteenth-century monks—and where the Prophet Muhammad spent a night when he visited the area as a caravaneer. Ten steps lead down into the cave, where there is a small altar and a *mihrab* niche indicating the direction of Mecca. (Hobbs 169)

With regard to the prayer niche in the cave of Moses, Mouton believes that is was carved out of stone at the same time the mosque was built (181). Despite the fact that this is a sacred site to the Bedouins, they never prevented Christians from praying at the spot (181).

In reference to the mosque, which is located inside the monastery proper, there are a number of different traditions. The most unusual of these allege that the mosque dates back to the time of the Prophet Muhammad himself. In *A Journal from Grand Cairo to Mount Sinai*, which relates the voyage of the Franciscan prefect to Egypt to the sacred site in 1722, it is mentioned that "there is a mosque with a turret for the Turks, which stands near the western door of the great church, for the preservation of which . . . they have several immunities granted them under the hand of the Prophet Mahomet" (16). The same story was shared with Arthur Penrhyn Stanley (1815–1881 CE), the English churchman, professor of ecclesiastic history, and Dean of Westminster, when he visited Saint Catherine's in 1858. He wrote that:

> There still remains, though no longer used, the mosque on top of the mountain, and that within the walls of the convent, in which the monks allowed the Mahometan devotees to pray side by side with Christian pilgrims; founded, according to the belief of the illiterate Musulmans, in whose mind chronology and history has no existence, in the time of the Prophet, when Christians and Musulmans were all one, and loved one another as brothers. (120)

Although it would be foolhardy to assert that the mosque was built during the rule of the Prophet, the entire account cannot be dismissed as it contains elements of truth. The mosque, all agree, was built on the spot where Muhammad once stood. It was thus built on holy ground. So, while it was not literally constructed during the time of the Prophet, it was founded by his footstep. What is most interesting about this Arab Bedouin account is the nostalgia it conveys. It speaks fondly of a time when Muslims and Christians were united as one and filled with brotherly love. Something, it seems, had gone wrong at some point in early Islamic history.

Another tradition, this time more rooted in history, asserts that the mosque at the heart of the Monastery of Saint Catherine dates back to the time of ʿAmr ibn al-ʿAs (592–664 CE), the general who conquered the Sinai. Although this view is generally rejected by scholars (ʿAbd al-Malik 171), it remains remotely possible. After all, the construction of mosques accompanied all of the early Muslim conquests. In fact, the Mosque of ʿAmr ibn al-ʿAs, which was constructed in the newly-founded capital of Fustat, Egypt, in 642 CE, was the first mosque built, not only in Egypt, but on the continent of Africa. The Muslims who conquered the southern Sinai must also have established early prayer-halls or mosques. They may have adapted existing structures or may have built entirely new ones. So, whatever purpose the original structure served, it may have been used for congregational prayers by the Muslim conquerors.

Sir Frederick Henniker, who visited Mount Sinai in 1820–21, came to his own conclusions regarding the *raison d'être* of a mosque in the center of a Christian monastery. "The mosque," writes Henniker, "strange as it appears adjoining to a church, is necessary to the existence of this Christian foundation—it sanctifies the place in the eyes of the Musulman, and professes to acknowledge his superiority" (224). During the early days of Islamic expansion, Muslims would build their mosques next to existing Christian churches or holy sites. When building mosques, the Muslims would sometimes attach small churches to the Islamic prayer hall. It is possible, as Henniker suggests, that this was done to demonstrate the power of Islam. It is equally possible that it was done to sanctify, and thus protect, Christian holy sites. If Christian churches, holy sites, and monasteries, formed part of the same Islamic complex featuring mosques and prayer halls, the odds of any misguided Muslim attacking any one of them was remote. It would seem that the early generations of Muslims embodied the teachings of the covenants of the Prophet which commanded Muslims to protect and maintain Christian churches and monasteries. What better way to do so than to grant them the protection of Islam?

One of the most common claims is that the mosque at Saint Catherine's Monastery was built by the monks to appease al-Hakim (r. 996–1021 CE) (Galey 13), the unpredictable Fatimid Caliph, around the year 1000 CE. Impressed at the monks' courage, Muslim troops supposedly spared the monastery on the condition that a mosque be erected on the place where the Prophet Muhammad had once set foot (Bernstein 124). A similar legend was related to Lord Alexander William Branford Crawford Lindsay (1812–1880 CE) during his visit in 1837. He wrote that:

> Close to the church rises a minaret of a mosque! Built, for the nonce, three centuries ago, when the convent was threatened by the Paynim Soldan of Egypt; he spared the convent for its sake. It is plain and unornamented . . . and is seldom used unless some Turkish pilgrim of rank visits Mount Sinai. (290)

For any scholar with a sense of history and chronology, this account makes little sense. If the mosque was built in 1537, it was built during Ottoman times. It would thus be much more recent than believed. The title of *Paynim Soldan* is garbled. There was, of course, no Sultan in Egypt; he ruled from Istanbul. The allusion to the ruler of Egypt may imply the Fatimids; however, they did not employ the title of *Sultan* and they were certainly not in power in 1537. Even if we assume that the monks were mixed up, and not just making this stuff up, the claim that the mosque was built to protect them from al-Hakim is not supported by existing evidence.

In reality, the existing structure was built during the reign of his fourth successor, Abu ʿAli al-Mansur, al-Amir bi-Ahkam Allah, who ruled from 1102 to 1131 CE. Its purpose, according to Bernstein, was to serve the religious needs of Muslim soldiers sent to the Sinai to fight the Crusaders (124). While this theory, like many others, is perfectly plausible, it is contradicted by some of the ancient Arabic manuscripts housed at the Monastery of Saint Catherine which John Lewis Burckhardt came across in 1816. As this young explorer explains:

> I read a circumstantial account how, in the year of the Hedjra 783, some straggling Turkish Hadjis, who had been cut off from the caravan, were brought by the Bedouins to the convent; and being found to be well educated, and originally from Upper Egypt, were retained there, and a salary settled on them and their descendants, on condition of their becoming the servants of the mosque. (qtd. Manley and 'Abdel-Hakim 144)

While Burckhardt interprets this as proof that the mosque dates to 1381 CE, to me it implies that the mosque already existed and that the monks merely hired some stranded Muslims to act as its guardians and custodians. Alexandre Dumas (1802–1870 CE) favored a later date. He alleged that "the Greek convent in token of servitude has been compelled to erect a Turkish edifice within its sacred compound" (246). For this ignorant tourist, the purpose of the mosque was to grieve and humiliate the poor monks beyond all expression (246).

If anything, the origin of the mosque appears to be lost in time. The construction dates proposed by many writers merely seem to mark other events including periods of repair, reconstruction, and renovation. For the time being, the mystery of the Jami' mosque remains to be resolved. It is time, then, to turn to its design itself. According to an article on "St. Catherine Monastery Mosque," published in *Arabic News* in 2004,

> The mosque is divided into six rooms by two pillars with irregular sides.... The minaret ... was the only high tower in the vicinity of the monastery until the Russian Tsar gave the monastery bells to the tower in the 17th century as gift. The floor of the minaret is made of wood and carried by wooden rams that extend inside the wall. The upper part of the 12 meter high minaret is square in shape and covered by a round dome.... [T]he minaret is very much like that of al-Gioshi Mosque in Cairo.

The pulpit of the mosque, which is only one of three *mimbars* that have survived from the Fatimid era, was built in the year 1106 CE, and was donated by Shahan Shah al-Afdal, a powerful chancellor of the Fatimid Empire (Skrobucha 61). The only other two come from Kous, in Upper Egypt, and Hebron, in Palestine (Champdor 48). The *kursi*, or Qur'an stand, which is also sculpted out of wood, dates from the same year (Champdor 48). An inscription on the *minbar* reads as follows:

> In the Name of Allah, the Compassionate, the Merciful. There is no God but Allah; He has no fellow; to Him belongs dominion and to Him honor is due. From His gracious hand come life and likewise death, and He is mighty over all things. From God comes victory, and mastery is near for the bondservant of Allah and his representative. Abu 'Ali al-Mansur, the Imam al-Amir bi-Ahkam Allah, Commander of the Faithful, Allah's blessings be upon him and his honored fathers and his expected sons. This preaching-desk was ordered to be made by the right honorable lord, Prince of the Army, Sword of Islam, Helper of Islam, Protector and Judge of Humankind, Guide and Protector of the Faithful, Abu al-Qasim Shahan Shah, through him may Allah uphold religion and give joy to the Commander of the Faithful through his long life and uphold his power and exalt his sword. Done in the month of Rabi I, of the year 500 [AH], to the glory of Allah. (qtd. Skrobucha 61)

There are other scholars, like Bernhard Moritz (19th to 20th century CE), who allege that the mosque was built during the Crusades, around 1090 CE, in order to accommodate a detachment of Muslim troops (Skrobucha 62; Mouton 179). The markings on the *mimbar*, however, take precedence since physical evidence must always prevail over speculation. There can be little doubt that the mosque was built at the beginning of the 12th century. As Albert Champdor has explained, the Caliph, al-Amir (r. 1101–1130 CE), went so far as to ensure that he had the blessing of the Patriarch of Jerusalem prior to commencing the construction (47). The mosque was built to allow the

Muslim vassals of the Monastery, as well as those living in the Sinai Peninsula, to perform their religious obligations (47). For Champdor, "the church bell and the minaret, side by side, are a moving symbol" (47). Others, however, feel that the mosque seems out of place in the Monastery. According to J. Daumas, however, it was simply built upon the site of an ancient chapel dedicated to Saint Basil, the founder of the Order of Greek Monks (qtd. Champdor 47–48). This view traces back to Basile Posniakov who visited Saint Catherine around 1560 CE (de Khitrowo 303; and repeated by Rabino 39). Champdor, though, seems to believe that the only new thing that was built was the minaret, and that the chapel in question was simply converted into a mosque (34). In contrast, for Freeman-Grenville, the mosque was "originally built as a hospice for pilgrims in the sixth century" (217). This hypothesis was first asserted by George H. Forsyth (7). In recent decades, however, this historic symbol of Islamo-Christian co-existence has been shattered by the closing of the mosque by the monks and the planting of a cross on its dome.

All of the aforementioned theories regarding the origin of the mosque located in the Monastery of Saint Catherine are of modern origin. What do ancient sources actually say about the mosque? Jean Thenaud, who performed a pilgrimage to Mount Sinai in 1512 CE, had the following to say about its origin: "In front of that church is a Muslim mosque which was built by prior [a *prieur de leans*] who became a Muslim when asked to assume its administration" (72). The expression "to become a Mameluke" has both the sense of "to embrace Islam" and "to become an apostate [from Christianity]." In Europe, it could have been used for Catholics who became Protestants; however, in the context in question, the meaning is absolutely clear: the current mosque at the Monastery of Saint Catherine was built or re-built by a head monk who converted to Islam. While he certainly could not continue to act as a Greek Orthodox Abbot, the Fatimids, who were the rulers at the time, granted him the administration of the mosque on their behalf. Thenaud also relates that the privileges that Muhammad granted the monks of the Church of the East were also stored in the mosque. This would mean that the *Covenant of the Prophet Muhammad with the Monks of Mount Sinai* was in Muslims hands from the moment the mosque was built in the 12th century CE until it fell into disuse in the 14th century CE. By appointing a two man team, consisting of an imam and a muezzin, the Fatimids, it appears, wanted to ensure that Muslims, and not Christians, acted as the custodians of the *Covenant of the Prophet*. This may also explain why the earliest copies of the covenant have been lost. They may very well have been taken to Cairo by the Fatimids. Considering that Salah al-Din al-Ayyubi (1138–1193 CE) would soon subject the Fatimid domains to a scorched earth policy which included the deliberate destruction of one of the greatest Islamic libraries in the world, said to have contained over a million and a half volumes (Bolman 282, note 17), there is little hope that these early copies of the *Covenant of the Prophet* could have survived.

Although there are only two ancient mosques that remain at Mount Sinai, one in the Monastery of Saint Catherine, and the other at its summit, many more mosques were built in the vicinity during the 11th and 12th centuries (Mouton 178; 182, note 10). Sami Salah 'Abd al-Malik writes that twenty-one buildings, including mosques and prayer halls, all built between 900–1517 CE, have been listed to date (171). It was the Shi'ite Fatimids, more than the Sunni Ayyubids, Mamluks and Ottomans, who showed the most interest in the famous Mount of Moses, perhaps as a result of this strain of Islam's greater appreciation for sacred sites and spiritual pilgrimages. In fact, "six mosques were erected upon the order of a Fatimid emir between Feiran and Mount Moses, one of which was located in the very heart of the Monastery of Saint Catherine" (171.) As 'Abd al-Malik explains, "they were built for Muslims passing through the Sinai: pilgrims on the way to Mecca or to Mount Moses." It appears that the flow of pilgrims to Mount Sinai was far greater during Shi'ite times than under Sunni rule. With the fall of the Fatimid Caliphate, the importance for Muslims of the Monastery of Mount Sinai seems to have diminished significantly. As *Arabic News* reports, "During the Ayyubid and Mamluk ages, only little was known about the mosque [of Saint Catherine] through travelers who had visited the monastery."

The mosques in question, including the one at the heart of Saint Catherine's Monastery, were not merely physical signs of Islamic rule: they were fully functioning mosques during medieval times and beyond (Mouton 179). The personnel in charge of the mosque were directly appointed by the chief *qadi* [judge] in Cairo and typically consisted of one or two people who served as imam, muezzin, and superintendent of the building (Mouton 179). Frequented by Muslim pilgrims returning from the *hajj*, as well as Muslim soldiers stationed in the Sinai, the mosque at Saint Catherine's Monastery was always closed to the troublesome local Bedouins with full support from Islamic authorities in Cairo (Mouton 179). For centuries, the sound of ringing church bells came from the monastery's tower while the Muslim call to prayer was emitted from the minaret. This aural manifestation of monotheistic unity would have made the Messenger of Allah proud. According to *Arabic News*,

> The mosque . . . remained in use up till the 14th century AD, although it was neglected for a long time during the Ottoman age when it became a store-house for grains and fruits. According to the manuscript preserved at the library of St. Catherine, monks of the monastery used to confer in the mosque round AD 1508.

When Sir Frederick Henniker (1793–1825 CE) visited the Monastery of Saint Catherine in 1820–21, he remarked that the monks allowed for one person to enter the mosque on the Turkish Sabbath, namely, on Friday (224). When Alexandre Dumas (1802–1870 CE) visited the *masjid*, it was moldering and deserted (246). Little attention was paid to the mosque by Muslim authorities until the early 20th century when King Fu'ad (1868–1936 CE) of Egypt "provided the mosque with carpets and decorated the pulpits with green flags" (Arabic News). As for the *jami'* mosque located inside the Monastery, it was only officially closed in 1986 (Mouton 179; 'Abd al-Malik 171). According to *Arabic News*, "The SCA carried out a restoration process of the mosque in 1986 by means of grant from Sultan Qaboos of Oman" and "[a] budget has been allocated for the mosque for periodical maintenance." Considering that Saint Catherine's is the only monastery in the world to embrace both a church and a mosque, it is encouraging to see that efforts are underway to preserve and protect this unique site and what it symbolizes.

In addition to the cave in which the Prophet spent the night, the Sinai contains many other sites sacred to Muslims, including the tomb of the Prophet Salih in Wadi al-Shaykh (Skrobucha 55). The Arabs of the region celebrate Nabi Salih with a festival of several days which concludes with a sacrifice on Jabal Musa (55). They also revere a print they believe was made by Salih's camel or, according to some, by Buraq, the mystical beast that the Prophet mounted during his Night Journey (Freeman-Grenville 210; Skrobucha 56; Clayton 20; Van Egmont and Heyman 166–167; Stanley 246; Henniker 233). As Hobbs explains,

> Approximately 200 meters northwest of the summit is a hollow in the rock which in size and shape is remarkably like the hoofprint of a camel. The Jabaliyyah claim it is the Print of the She-Camel (*Matabb an-Naaga*) of Nabi Saalih Rashiid, a man they believe was either an early Muslim prophet or the progenitor of the Bani Saalih tribe. Earlier Bedouins told travelers that the hoofprint belonged to the Prophet Muhammad's she-camel, an animal of such stature that its other legs rested in Mecca, Jerusalem, and Damascus or in Mecca, Cairo, and Damascus. (169–170)

The earliest accounts that stipulate that the mark was made by Buraq are to be preferred due to their antiquity and the fact that they concur with ancient Islamic tradition. After all, authenticated *ahadith* or prophetic traditions assert that Muhammad, while on his Night-Journey or *Isra wa Mi'raj*, was physically transported from Mecca to the precinct of the Temple of Solomon in Jerusalem on the back of Buraq. While some sources suggest this voyage was simply spiritual, the Family of the Prophet always insisted that it was physical. During the journey, and in the company of the archangel Gabriel, Muhammad was made to stop and perform ritual prayers in Medina, Mount Sinai, Bethlehem, and Jerusalem. So, whether or not one believes that Muhammad visited Saint Catherine's Monastery at the age of twenty-five, it is an article of faith among Muslims that the Prophet was physically present on Mount Sinai around the year 621 CE.

In the account of his pilgrimage to Mount Sinai, Sieur Antoine Morison (17th to 18th centuries CE), mocks the "the extravagant object which is venerated by the Turks" (95). He relates that, according to the Turks,

> Muhammad climbed to the top of that mountain, mounted on his camel, and, in order to leave a permanent testament and a precious monument of the devout pilgrimage that he undertook, he wanted his animal to leave the miraculous print that is seen today and which they revere. I know full well that that great legislator of the Muslims had the honor of being a valet and camel-handler for the Monastery of Mount Sinai; however, I am certain that he would never have risked such a stunt, which would have risked his life, which he held so dear, and which has since being fatal to an infinite number of souls who were deceived by its enchantments. (95)

As Albert Champdor reports, the Bedouins of the Sinai visit the site every year to sacrifice a goat or, on particularly favorable years, a camel, on the rock in question (50). The blood of the sacrificial animal was then used to soak the lintel and the side-posts of the sanctuary in an act reminiscent of the sacrifice which God commanded of the Hebrews during the last of plague to fall upon ancient Egypt (50). In 1598, Christophe Harant (1564–1621 CE), the Czech nobleman, traveler, soldier, and writer, reported that the Jabaliyyah Bedouins would perform a certain number of rites each time they passed the spot of the camel-print, kissing it, and touching their foreheads against it (119). Unfortunately, many a monk has mocked the Muslims for honoring this mark over the past millennium (see Stephens 221 for one such example). However, as the author of *A Journal from Grand Cairo to Mount Sinai* remarks, if the knees and hands of Moses are said to be engraved in stone in the Sinai, why not the hoof-print of the Muhammad's camel? (Clayton 20). Other monks, mentions Francis Arundale (1807–1853), are "careful not to efface the impression, since the veneration for the spot serves to check the constant inclination of the Arabs to plunder the Convent" (32). Besides the Print of the She-Camel, the list of holy sites in and around Mount Sinai is exceptional. It includes,

> the cave on the summit, where Moses sojourned; Horeb . . . whither Elijah fled from Ahab; Elijah's cave and altar sacrifice; the open space where Aaron and the seventy stood; while Moses was receiving the Law; the Burning Bush. . . ; the spot where Moses received the command to put off his shoes; the two sites where the Israelites encamped; when Moses went up the Mount; the place where the golden calf was made; the open space from which Moses caught sight of his people dancing around the golden calf; the stone on which Moses broke the tablets of the Law; the site where the golden calf was destroyed; the rock from which Moses gave the people water to drink; and the places where the manna and quails provided food for the Israelites. . . . (Skrobucha 27–28)

There are other sites as well, including the Monastery of the Forty Saints, the place where Saint Catherine's body was carried by angels and where it rested for three centuries; a monastery which had no bells but from which bells miraculously sounded; and the bushes from which Moses made walking-sticks (Freeman-Grenville 212). The area also comprises the valley where the Israelites defeated the Amalekites (Affagart 197), the twelve fountains for the Twelve tribes (198), the place where the women of Israel melted their jewels in order to forge the golden calf (199), the mountain where the golden calf was adored and where the Jews celebrated (199), as well as the creek in which Moses cast the dust of the golden calf which he had destroyed (199). In addition, there is the footprint of the Prophet Harun [Aaron] as well as a shrine in his honor (Hobbs 173). The Fountains of Moses, an oasis located twelve kilometers from El-

Shatt, also holds great significance (Champdor 58).

The importance of Saint Catherine of Alexandria (c. 282–c. 305 CE) cannot be ignored. While martyred nearly 500 miles away, Christian tradition asserts that angels carried her body to the top of Mount Catherine, a peak next to Mount Sinai, where it remained for three hundred years, until it was moved to the monastery established by Emperor Justinian in the middle of the 6th century CE. According to Jabali Arab tradition, however, Catherine had lived on Mount Sinai for a long time during the early days of Islam. After becoming a Muslim, she returned home. Her Christian father was so infuriated by her conversion that he beheaded her on the spot. It was then that the angels took her body to what is now known as Jabal Katerina, the Mountain of Catherine.

While Skrobucha views Arab beliefs as "naïve" (62), and further claims that the Prophet created the Qur'an on the basis of Jewish and Christian traditions passed down through oral tradition (53), he, rather inconsistently, treats Jewish and Christian traditions as if they were fact. The Arabs also assert that the foundation of the monastery traces back to Moses himself who wished to memorialize the deliverance of the monotheists from the oppressive hands of Pharaoh (57; Bernstein 123). Again, for Skrobucha, of course, this is simply an "incongruous legend" (57). Such double standards have no place in the true academic tradition. Since the three major monotheistic religions, Judaism, Christianity and Islam, all hold the majestic Mount Sinai in high honor, a degree of respect is due to all of their traditions.

Furthermore, it should be acknowledged that without the good offices of the mountain-dwelling Arabs of the Sinai Peninsula, neither Jew nor Christian or even Muslim would be familiar with any of the holy sites in the region - since the Sinai Arabs were the ones who had preserved the memory of such places for thousands of years. The Marquis of Labode, for one, expressed his admiration at the accuracy of Arab traditions (204). Jewish people eventually lost the geographic details of their wanderings in the Sinai, leaving scarcely any documentation. As for the Christians, their earliest traditions identified Mount Sinai as Mount Serbal where a monastery was founded in the 4th century CE. It was only in the 6th century CE that it was relocated to the base of Mount Catherine based on the belief that Mount Sinai must have been the tallest mountain in the region. Finally, it was only in the 15th century that Mount Horeb, which is adjacent to Mount Catherine, was identified as Mount Sinai. This recognition was based on the Bedouin tradition that had long taught that the mountain in question was the Jabal Horeb, also known as Jabal Musa, the site where the Israelites received the Ten Commandments. Other sites have been proposed for Mount Sinai, including Jabal Lawz in Arabia, and Jabal Shara in Jordan. Curiously, Jabal Lawz is identified with Mount Sinai in some contemporary Islamic sources. One such map, which charts the course of Muhammad's early caravan routes, indicates that he passed by the [Saudi] Arabian site of Mount Sinai. It is quite possible that the source misidentified the route followed by Muhammad. Nonetheless, the Prophet was certainly familiar with the site. He may also have visited the area in 631 CE when he signed the *Treaty of Maqnah* with the Jewish inhabitants of the oasis, which is accessible by foot from Jabal Lawz. Despite claims to the contrary, "Jebel Musa is generally acknowledged as the true peak, and is accepted by all three of the religions in which it plays a role, partly because there is little religious desire to prove what is essentially unprovable" (Hazleton 5).

Currently, despite the fact that it contains sacred sites which are of importance to Muslims, it is mainly Christian or secular visitors who tend to visit Mount Sinai in Egypt. Shi'ites, it would seem, appear to be an exception to this rule. As Hobbs relates,

> Gordon Brubacher, a leader of Biblical tour groups, told me that he had seen hundreds of Shi'ite pilgrims 'from all over the world, judging by their dress,' camped on Jebel Musa on the last night of Ramadan of several years of the 1980s. Jebel Musa was the third most sacred pilgrimage destination

for Shi'ite pilgrims after Mecca and Karbala, he said. (219)

Up to the 14th century, Muslims from all schools of law and thought regularly made pilgrimage to Mount Sinai and prayed in the mosque located in the monastery (Hobbs 161). When Greffin Affagart (d. c. 1557 CE) visited Mount Sinai between the years 1533–1534 CE, he observed that

> The Turks and the Moors have a singular devotion to this place, not only for the mysteries of the Old Testament that took place there, but also for the holy virgin Catherine, whom they reverence, for which reason they have built a mosque in the monastery, namely, a church with a priest who is charged with maintaining it and officiating in their fashion, and in which are found the privileges which Muhammad granted to the monastery. (190–191)

As was the custom with many European writers of the time, Affagart applies Christian terminology to Islamic concepts. Hence, when he speaks of a "church with a priest," he actually means a *masjid* or mosque under the direction of an *imam* or Muslim prayer leader.

If it is now customary for Muslims who go to Mecca for the *hajj* to also pay a visit to the Prophet's tomb in Medina, prior to the establishment of Israel in 1948 Muslims typically included a visit to the Mosque of al-Aqsa in Jerusalem as well. It seems that, in past centuries, some Muslims also used a route past Mount Sinai for their journey. However, since it was somewhat out of the way, and entailed an additional expense, the pilgrimage route that passed Mount Sinai was never a major one. As David W. Tschanz explains, some outlying *hajj* routes did "not follow the shortest distance between two points, but were intended to allow the pilgrim to visit mosques and holy places along the way to Makkah." Furthermore, the route via Mount Sinai was the only one that was feasible for pilgrims from North Africa and Egypt as it was out of the way for pilgrims coming from other parts of the Muslim world.

Since many pilgrim routes were also trade routes, the flow of visitors to Mount Sinai reflects, to a certain extent, economic prosperity, and appears to be partially related to issues of infrastructure. When al-Tur, the port city in proximity to the Monastery of Saint Catherine, replaced Clysma as the main Red Sea Port in 1058 CE, large numbers of traders, goods, and pilgrims started to travel overland to and from Cairo. Within a century and a half, however, the flow of Muslim pilgrims seems to have slowed to a trickle undoubtedly due to the presence of hostile Christian forces in the region. As F. E. Peters (b. 1927 CE) explains, the Gulf of Aqaba and the fortress of Aylah fell into the hands of the Crusaders at the beginning of the 12th century (Peters 90). Since Frankish Crusaders controlled the land routes in the region, caravans were forced to take long detours in an attempt to slip into the Hijaz (90, 93). As Ibn Jubayr (1145–1217 CE) related, the most direct way to Mecca from Cairo "was . . . by way of the Aqaba or Ayla to the Holy City of Medina, a short trip during which the sea is on his right and the Jabal Tur [the traditional Mount Sinai] is on his left" (qtd. Peters 93). Unfortunately, since the Franks had a strongly guarded fortress in the area, pilgrims were prevented from using this route" (qtd. Peters 93).

In 1378 CE, after a brief decline, al-Tur resumed its role as a major Red Sea port. In 1384 CE, Lionardo di Nicolo Frescobaldi (14th century to post 1405 CE), found two hundred monks living at Mount Sinai (357). By 1479 CE, however, the Monastery of Saint Catherine was temporarily abandoned as a result of the fall of the Byzantine Empire. In 1517 CE, with the advent of the Ottoman Empire in the Sinai, a period of intense fortress building took place at al-Tur, Nakhl, Nuwaybah, al-Arish, and Kusayr, bringing increased security to the region. Don Aquilante Rochetta, a knight of the Saint Sepulcher, who visited the Sinai in 1598–1599 CE, reports that Sultan Selim had built a double wall around the Monastery of Saint Catherine to protect it from any attackers, be they Muslim or non-Muslim (159). While the prosperity of the Monastery of Saint Catherine fluctuated during the 16th and 17th centuries, al-Tur declined as a major port and settlement as a result of increased Western domination of trade and maritime routes. Interest in Saint Catherine increased as a result of the Napoleonic expedition to Egypt in 1797–1804. When the JL Stephens reached Saint Catherine in 1836, he found it inhabited by fifty monks. When he visited Mount Sinai in 1837, Lord Lindsay only found twenty-two monks living there (291). It was not until the 1869 construction of the Suez Canal, however, that prosperity and strategic importance returned to the Red Sea region and the Sinai. As a result of the efforts of the Egyptian regime to develop the southern Sinai, the Monastery of Saint Catherine has become, for better or worse, a major attraction drawing thousands of tourists per day along with a small number of true pilgrims.

It is equally possible that the pilgrimage route to Mecca, via Mount Sinai, declined due to the gradual suppression of inter-religious ties from earlier years. In fact, most of the Muslims in the Middle East, North Africa, and Europe, that is, those who were of Christian ancestry, continued to celebrate major Christian holidays for centuries after embracing Islam. In some communities, relations between Muslims and Christians were so cordial that they celebrated Christmas, Easter and Eid together as well as slaughtering a sheep in honor of the Virgin Mary (Berkey 160). Some Muslim sects, like the Alavis, celebrate Christmas, Easter, and Epiphany to this day, along with Persian holy days. It almost makes one wonder whether the Alawis of Syria and the Alevis of Turkey practice a primitive form of Islam which has remained frozen in time and which only appears heterodox in comparison with Islam's fully developed form. Often accused of suffering from partial Islamization and engaging in religious syncretism, the devotional practices of the Alawis and Alevis share many similarities with early Islamic expressions in Mecca and part of the Medinan period. It was only with the concerted effort of Muslim clerics that such holidays were suppressed and Christmas was replaced by *mawlid al-nabi*, the Celebration of the Birth of the Prophet.

Although rare, such egalitarian convergence of monotheistic believers occurred from time to time during Islamic history. In 1311 CE, for example, when a plague broke out, the Jews, Christians, and Muslims of Damascus all marched together in procession, praying, holding their sacred scriptures, and reciting supplications (Limor 221). In 1317 CE, in the face of a serious famine caused by drought, the Muslims, Christians, and Jews of Jerusalem all assembled and prayed for rain together (Limor 220). Their prayers were actually answered on the third day (220). In 1384 CE, Frescobaldi reported to his Christian readers that Muslims revered the Virgin Mary, John the Baptist, and, *nota bene*, Saint Catherine (101). The Christian-Muslim cult of Saint Catherine remained alive and well in the 14th century. Alas, such examples of spiritual solidarity have rarely been seen since.

Although there appears to have been a significant decline in Muslim pilgrims to Mount Sinai by Mamluk times, some continued to make the journey. As Brandie Ratliff writes, "[a]ll of the preserved documents mention the monastery receiving, at Mount Sinai and at its properties, pilgrims, who in the Mamluk period are identified as Muslims traveling to and from Mecca" (15). In their *Travels through Parts of Europe, Asia Minor, the Islands of the Archipelago, Syria, Palestine, Egypt, Mount Sinai, etc.*, Van Egmont and John Heyman, who traveled in the East between 1700 and 1723, reported that "All the Turks that visit Mount Sinai, from religious principles, are lodged and entertained in the convent, the very women not excepted" (167). Considering that women are prohibited from entering the monastery, as is true of any Eastern Orthodox monastery where even female animals are not admitted, this concession made to Muslim women was quite exceptional. By the late 18th century the flow of pilgrims from Cairo to Saint Catherine was down to a trickle. As Constantin-François de Chasseboeuf de Volney (1757–1820 CE), the French historian, Orientalist, and politician, reported in his *Voyages en Égypte*, which took placed in the years 1783, 1784, and 1785, "these trips only take place once a year" (204). By 1836, when J.L. Stephens visited Saint Catherine's, he reported that both the church and mosque at the summit of Mount Sinai were in ruins (219). He seemed to have been saddened by the sight for "on this sacred spot the followers of Christ and Mohammed have united in worshipping the true living God" (219). Since Mount Sinai formed part of one of the pilgrim routes to Mecca, we find Muhammad 'Ali of Egypt (r. 1805–1848 CE) making reparations to the monastery during this rule. There are also reports, as late as the mid-19th century regarding occasional Muslim visitors (161). The period of significant decline seems to be the 18th to early 19th centuries CE. While the issue deserved in-depth examination, as many events occurred during this period, the one major development that comes to mind is the rise of Muhammad ibn 'Abd al-Wahhab (1703–1792 CE). There are also reports from the Sinai Bedouins of the time regarding pressures placed upon them by the Wahhabis who did not view them as *bona fide* believers. It may very well be that the rise of Salafism rendered the region unsafe for both Christians and traditional Muslims.

By 1885/1886, when Mirza Mohammad Hosayn Farahani (19th century CE) performed the pilgrimage, the later Ottomans were using the *wadi* of Mount Sinai as a post-*hajj* quarantine station in response to the outbreak of cholera (qtd. Wolfe 290–291). The pilgrims, it appears, were oblivious to the fact that they were at the foot of one of the most significant religious sites in the monotheistic tradition. By the 1930s, the mosque in the monastery was less accessible, with the monks only allowing Muslims to enter it during the month of Ramadan (161). While Muslim guests and Jabaliyyah employees of the monastery continued to use the mosque until modern times, "a chill in relations between the monks and Egyptian authorities forced its closure" (161) in the mid-1980s. Concurrent with the rise in influence of the Muslim Brotherhood in the second decade of the second millennium, monastic authorities are concerned that extremists, such as the Salafi group, might usurp and potentially desecrate and destroy the sacred sites. As Patrick Kingsley and Marwa Awad reported on September 5, 2013, the Monastery of St. Catherine was forced to close its doors due to the deteriorating security situation in the Sinai; in other words, the spread of the Takfiri Jihadists in the region.

As a result of the spread of Salafism, which holds that pilgrimage to other than Mecca is a prohibited form of polytheism, pseudo-Sunnis rarely show their respect for sacred sites and relics. Shi'ite Muslims, however, who follow the example of the Prophet and His Household, show a great deal of respect for the signs of Allah (Qur'an 22:32; 40:81; 5:29; 31:32). As such, they consider pilgrimages to sacred sites as meritorious acts of piety. They visit the graves of the Fourteen Infallibles, the Prophet, Fatimah, and the Twelve Imams from their family, the graves of famous figures, including martyrs, saints, and scholars. They also visit sites associated with Biblical prophets in Iran, Iraq, Syria, Jordan, Palestine, and Egypt. In so doing, Shi'ites feel connected to their religious past and relive important moments in Islamic history in their minds. Evidently, true, traditional Sunnis, in whose hands a multitude of sacred sites remain, continue to respect the signs of Allah, and revere holy places throughout the Islamic world. In the Holy Land, this includes the Tomb of David on Mount Zion (Limor 223), the Tomb of Saint Pelagia, Rabi'ah al-'Adawiyyah, and prophetess Huldah on the Mount of Olives (227), the Tomb of the Virgin Mary in the Vale of Jehoshaphat, the Church of the Ascension (220), as well as the Temple Mount among many other such sites. In the 8th century, a *mihrab* was added in the Church of the Kathisma on the Jerusalem-Bethlehem road, "where the Virgin was believed to have rested" (Ratliff, "Christian communities..." 34). Caliph Hisham (r. 724–743 CE) even relocated his royal residence to Rusafa or Sergiopolis, "the seat of the popular cult of Saint Sergios," where he built a mosque next to the famous church (Ratliff, "Christian communities..." 34; Flood 248). Muslims built the Great Mosque of Damascus "on the site of the basilica of Saint John the Baptist" (Ratliff, "Christian communities..." 34). During Ottoman times, Muslims even visited the Church of the Holy Sepulchre (Faroqhi 170–171). Like Mecca, Medina, Kufah and Karbala, as well as other holy sites, Mount Sinai is believed to be not of this world and, indeed, the peak acts as a spiritual vortex between our world and the spiritual world. As Hobbs has clearly comprehended, "Through the Angel Gabriel, God revealed the Mount Sinai tradition to the Prophet Muhammad, so that in the Qur'an it forms part of the bedrock on which Islam is founded" (33).

Despite claims that the Prophet prohibited pilgrimages to all but Mecca, Medina, and Jerusalem, Muhammad himself made pilgrimages to holy sites both before and after his proclamation of prophecy. He visited holy sites in the Sinai and the Levant as a young man and visited the graves of the martyrs of Islam. The Prophet Muhammad, it is reported, performed his prayers on a clay tablet. While this practice is simply considered a tradition among *ahl al-sunnah* [the Followers of the *Sunnah*; i.e., the Sunnis], it is treated as obligatory by the followers of *ahl al-bayt* [the Household of the Prophet; i.e., the Shi'ites]. Interestingly, the tradition of carrying away clay tokens from sacred pilgrimage sites pre-dates Islam. In fact, it was a common Christian custom. These tablets, which combined sacred matter and images, were said to possess spiritual and medicinal power (Flood 250). Believers used to seek blessings from such relics, touching them with their eyes, mouth, and forehead (Ratliff, "To Travel to the Holy" 86). If Shi'ite Muslims pray on the sacred soil of Karbala', Najaf, Mashhad, and other sacred sites, did the Prophet himself prostrate on the sacred soil he brought back from Mount Sinai? If not, he certainly continued with a custom of prophets past. According to the teachings of traditional Islam, the Prophet had rendered the earth clean for prostration by his sacred steps and had rendered the soil of Medina curative by means of his saliva.

Revelation Received: The Proclamation of Prophecy

Muhammad's contact with Christians in Syria, Arabia, and the Sinai seems to have had a profound impact on his personality. Such incidents did not inspire Muhammad to proclaim his prophecy and they certainly do not suggest that he was taught by Jews or Christians as his detractors, both past and present, have alleged without any evidential support whatsoever. These early encounters with hermits, monks, and priests, did, however, confirm his status as the prophet long-awaited by both the Jews and Christians, and seem to have inspired a confidence in his ability to count on the spiritual solidarity of the People of the Book. This view, however, is not shared by all biographers. "Whatever the truth about this story [of Bahira] and the other reports," writes M.A. Salahi,

> it is certain that they did not influence Muhammad in any way. . . . Moreover, it seems that the men who heard Baheera's conversation with Abu Talib did not bother to relate it to other people. The only value of these reports is that they confirm the fact that learned men of other religions were aware of the imminent appearance of a Prophet in Arabia. (31)

Salahi, however, evidently operates on the basis of the belief that Muhammad merely became the Messenger of Allah upon the receipt of revelation at the age of forty. According to traditional Islam, Muhammad was always a prophet. In fact, he was a prophet prior to Creation. Protected by God and assisted by angels, Muhammad's life, from birth to death, was surrounded by profound spiritual significance, the signs of which manifested themselves on numerous occasions. Hence, as a result of his repeated interaction with Christians of all kinds from his childhood into adulthood (Haya 1–3), Muhammad realized that he had much more in common with the followers of Christ than with the idol-worshippers who surrounded him.

When, in the year 610 CE, at the age of forty, Muhammad received his first revelation, Khadijah, who had been Muhammad's wife and confidant for fifteen years, was the first human being to embrace his prophetic message. Although she did not belong to the designated People of the Book, she was, like Muhammad, a member of the Hanafiyyah, a small sect of Arabs who had maintained the primitive monotheistic religion of Abraham. She was also closely connected to Christianity via her cousin, Waraqah ibn Nawfal. In fact, after the Angel Gabriel appeared to Muhammad, 'A'ishah reports that:

> The Prophet returned to Khadijah while his heart was beating rapidly. She took him to Waraqah ibn Nawfal who was a Christian convert and used to read the Gospel in Arabic. Waraqah asked [the Prophet], "What did you see?" When he told him, Waraqah said, "That is the same angel whom Allah sent to the Prophet Moses. Should I live till you receive the Divine Message, I will support you strongly."(Bukhari)

In a more detailed version of the events, 'A'ishah related that:

> Khadijah then accompanied him to her cousin Waraqah ibn Nawfal ibn Asad ibn 'Abd al-'Uzza, who, during the pre-Islamic period became a Christian and used to write the writing with Hebrew letters. He would write from the Gospel in Hebrew as much as Allah wished him to write. He was an old man and had lost his eyesight. Khadijah said to Waraqah, "Listen to the story of your nephew, O my cousin!" Waraqah asked, "O my nephew! What have you seen?" Allah's Apostle described whatever he had seen. Waraqah said, "This is the same one who keeps the secrets [Angel Gabriel] whom Allah had sent to Moses. I wish I were young and could live up to the time when your people would turn you out." Allah's Apostle asked, "Will they drive me out?" Waraqah replied in the affirmative and said, "Anyone who came with something similar to what you have brought was treated with hostility; and if I should remain alive till the day when you will be turned out I would support you strongly." But after a few days Waraqah died. (Bukhari)

Just as Waraqah predicted, the Prophet was persecuted by the polytheists. His confidence in the Christian community, however, remained strong. If Cansino Assens (1882–1964 CE) and Aloys Sprenger (1813–1893 CE) are correct, and Bahira actually relocated to Mecca to be in close proximity to the Prophet (Sprenger 591; Assens 148), Muhammad's confidence in his mission could only have increased. The Messenger of Allah, however, was, by all standards, severely tested. By the year 615 CE, when conditions had become truly unbearable for his followers in Mecca, the Prophet suggested that they resettle in Abyssinia as religious refugees under the protection of al-Najashi, a wise Christian king. According to Mawardi and Abu Musa, a man by the name of Bahira returned with Ja'far ibn Abi Talib from exile in Abyssinia (Sprenger 591). Ibn Hajar believed him to be a different person; however, Ibn al-Athir identified him as the Bahira from Busrah (Sprenger 591).

Not long after, in the year 619 CE, both Khadijah, Muhammad's beloved wife, and his admirable uncle, Abu Talib, passed away, leaving him with even less support than before. In the year 620/621 CE; however, the Prophet received great solace as a result of his *Isra* and *Mi'raj* or Night-Journey in which, within the span of a single night, he traveled from Mecca to Syria, the land of Ibrahim [Abraham]; then to Palestine, the land of 'Isa [Jesus]; and then to Mount Sinai, the land of Musa [Moses]. The route of his miraculous journey was succinctly summarized in the Qur'an. The following oath came from Almighty Allah: "By the Fig and the Olive, and the Mount of Sinai, and this City of Security" (95: 1–3). Since Abraham, Moses, and Jesus were all prophets who had received a *shari'ah* or a legal code, in the form of a sacred scripture, the *Sahifah* [Scroll] for the first; the *Tawrah* [Torah] for the second; and the *Injil* [Gospel] for the third, Almighty Allah was thus confirming that indeed Muhammad was the Final Messenger of Allah. He was the custodian of the last revelation, the *Qur'an* or Recital. After a decade of extreme difficulties, the Prophet finally saw the light at the end of the tunnel.

The Constitution of Medina

Having heard about the mission of Muhammad, and after meeting with him on two occasions, the Arabs of the rich but self-destructive city of Yathrib invited the Prophet to settle in their midst as their religious and political leader. In the estimation of Michael Lecker, some unusual reports suggest that a treaty might have been concluded between the Quraysh and the Ansar, the early Muslims of Medina, which aimed at preventing bloodshed (2000: 157–167). With his presence, the inhabitants of the troubled city, divided between warring Arab tribes and their Jewish allies, came to believe that the Prophet could act as an efficient arbitrator. The Jews were not clients, as so many have claimed, but powerful and influential allies of the Arabs (Lecker 2000: 67). After arriving in Yathrib in 622 CE, the Prophet presented a pact known as the *Constitution of Medina* or the *Charter of Medina*. The document explicitly contained the rights and obligations of all members of the community.

Although the *sirah*, the orthodox biography of the Prophet, claims that this took place immediately upon his arrival, Francis E. Peters (b. 1927 CE) believes that "the provisions likely date from within a few months after Muhammad's arrival in Medina" (200). This makes sense as Muhammad would need time to assess the socio-political situation in the oasis. Hence, scholars like John L. Esposito (b. 1940 CE) believe it dates from between 622–624 CE (80). The document may even date from a later period since it fails to include the names of the Banu Qurayzah, the Banu Nadir, and the Banu Qaynuqa'. Either it was written after the expulsion of these aggressively hostile Jewish tribes or their names were removed from the original document since it seemed redundant to include tribes that were no longer covered by the terms of the covenant. There also exists the possibility that these three Jewish tribes were not from Medina, but rather from Khaybar, as stipulated in early Islamic sources (Scholler 30, note 44).

Michael Lecker (b. 1951 CE), however, has shown that greater Medina was actually a combination of Yathrib and a cluster of nearby towns. While the Banu Nadir and Banu Qaynuqa' lived in the towns of al-Quff and Zuhra in what is now eastern Medina (2010: 66, 70), the Banu Qurayza lived in the southeast (65). Not only did they prevent the spread of Islam into parts of Medina, they engaged in actions that were detrimental to the Muslim community's social and economic interests. As Michael Lecker has made clear, "The main Jewish tribes [of] Nadir, Qurayza, and Qaynuqa' are not listed among the participants [in the *Constitution of Medina*] for the simple reason that they were not part of it" (68). While they may not have been included in the *Charter of Medina*, perhaps because they lived in communities in the outskirts of the city, al-Waqidi (748–822 CE) insists that

> [w]hen the Messenger of God arrived in Medina, the Jews, all of them, were reconciled with him, and he wrote an agreement between him and them. The Prophet attached every tribe with its confederates and established a protection between himself and them. He stipulated conditions to them, among which it was stipulated that they would not help any enemy against him. (87)

If this is indeed the case, then this treaty or series of treaties must have been distinct from the *Charter* or *Constitution of Medina*. In any event, the *Sahifat al-Madinah* stipulates the following:

The Constitution of Medina

In the Name of Allah, the Most Compassionate, the Most Merciful

[Preamble]

This is a document from Muhammad, the Prophet [governing the relations] between the believers and Muslims of Quraysh and Yathrib, and those who followed them and joined them and labored with them. They are one community [*ummah*] to the exclusion of all men. The Quraysh emigrants according to their present custom shall pay the blood wit within their just number and shall redeem their prisoners with the kindness and justice common among believers.

[1: The Blood-Wit]

1.1 The Banu 'Awf according to their present custom shall pay the blood wit they paid in heathenism; every section shall redeem its prisoners with the kindness and justice common among believers. The Banu Sa'ida, the Banu al-Harith, the Banu Jusham, and the Banu al-Najjar likewise.

1.2 The Banu 'Amr b. 'Awf, the Banu al-Nabit, and the Banu al-'Aws likewise.

1.3 Believers shall not leave anyone destitute among them by not paying his redemption money or blood wit in kindness.

[2: Loyalty and Unity of the *Ummah*]

2.1 A believer shall not take as an ally the freedman of another Muslim against him. The God-fearing believers shall be against the rebellious or him who seeks to spread injustice or sin or enmity or corruption between believers; the hand of every man shall be against him even if he be a son of one of them.

2.2 A believer shall not slay a believer for the sake of an unbeliever, nor shall he aid an unbeliever against a believer.

2.3 Allah's protection is one: the least of them may give protection to a stranger on their behalf.

2.4 Believers are friends one to the other to the exclusion of outsiders.

2.5 To the Jew who follows us belong help and equality. He shall not be wronged nor shall his enemies be aided.

[3: Rules of Engagement]

3.1 The peace of the believers is not divisible. No separate peace shall be made when believers are fighting in the way of Allah. Conditions must be fair and equitable to all.

3.2 In every foray a rider must take another behind him.

3.3 The believers must avenge the blood of one another shed in the way of Allah.

[4: Code of Conduct]

4.1 The God-fearing believers enjoy the best and most upright guidance.

4.2 No polytheist shall take the property or person of [any of the] Quraysh under his protection nor shall he intervene against a believer.

4.3 Whosoever is convicted of killing a believer without good reason shall be subject to retaliation unless the next of kin is satisfied [with blood-money], and the believers shall be against him as one man, and they are bound to take action against him.

4.4 It shall not be lawful to a believer who holds by what is in this document and believes in Allah and the Last Day to help an evil-doer or to shelter him. The curse of Allah and His Anger on the Day of Resurrection will be upon him if he does, and neither repentance nor ransom will be received from him.

[5: The Guardianship of the Prophet]

5.1 Whenever you differ about a matter it must be referred to Allah and to Muhammad.

[6: The War Effort, Military Matters, and Support]

6:1 The Jews shall contribute to the cost of war so long as they are fighting alongside the believers.

6.2 The Jews of Banu 'Awf are one community with the believers, the Jews have their religion and the Muslims have theirs, their freedmen and their persons except those who behave unjustly and sinfully, for they hurt but themselves and their families. The same applies to the Jews of the Banu al-Najjar, Banur al-Harith, Banu Sa'ida, Banu Jusham, Banu al-'Aws, Banu Tha'laba, and the Jafna, a clan of the Tha'laba and the Banu al-Shutayba. Loyalty is a protection against treachery.

6.3 The freedmen of Tha'laba are as themselves. The close friends of the Jews are as themselves. None of them shall go out to war save with the permission of Muhammad, but he shall not be prevented from taking revenge for a wound.

6.4 He who slays a man without warning slays himself and his household, unless it be one who has wronged him, for Allah will accept that.

6.5 The Jews must bear their expenses and the Muslims their expenses. Each must help the other against anyone who attacks the people of this document. They must seek mutual advice and consultation, and loyalty is a protection against treachery.

6.6 A man is not liable for his ally's misdeeds.

6.7 The wronged must be helped.

6.8 The Jews must pay with the believers so long as war lasts.

6.9 Yathrib shall be a sanctuary for the people of this document.

6.10 A stranger under protection shall be as his host doing no harm and committing no crime.

[7: Rights of Women]

7.1 A woman shall only be given protection with the consent of her family.

[8. Binding Nature of the Covenant]

8.1 If any dispute or controversy likely to cause trouble should arise it must be referred to Allah and to Muhammad the Messenger of Allah.

8.2 Allah accepts what is nearest to piety and goodness in this document.

8.3 Quraysh and their helpers shall be given no protection.

8.4 If the contracting parties are bound to make peace and maintain it they must do so; and if they make a similar demand on the Muslims it must be carried out except in the case of holy war.

8.5 Every one shall have his portion from the side to which he belongs; the Jews of al-'Aws, their freedmen and themselves have the same standing with the people of this document in pure loyalty from the people of this document.

8.6 Loyalty is a protection against treachery: He who acquires aught acquires it for himself.

8.7 Allah approves of this document.

8.8 This deed will not protect the unjust and the sinner.

8.9 The man who goes forth to fight and the man who stays at home in the city is safe unless he has been unjust and sinned.

[Epilogue]

Allah is the Protector of the good and God-fearing man and Muhammad is the Messenger of Allah. (Ibn Ishaq 233)

The Constitution Critically Contextualized

As can be appreciated, the *Sahifat al-Madinah* or *Constitution of Medina* is one of the most important relics of early Islam and one that sheds an enormous amount of light on the foundations of the Muslim faith. As Robert G. Hoyland (b. 1965 CE) recognizes, "[i]ts authenticity has been accepted by most scholars" (2000: 290, note 58). He even points out that Patricia Crone (b. 1945 CE), a person with little love towards Islam and Muslims, admitted to its authenticity in *Slaves on Horses* (7). While his theories on the origins of Islam can and should be criticized as utterly unfounded, Donner (b. 1945 CE) can be credited with one thing, admitting the antiquity of the *Constitution of Medina*. As he explains in *Muhammad and the Believers*,

> [T]he *ummah* document . . . seems to be of virtually documentary quality. Although preserved only in collections of later date, its text is so different in content and style from everything else in those collections, and so evidently archaic in character, that all students of early Islam, even the most skeptical, accept it as authentic and of virtually documentary value. (72)

The historical value of the *Sahifah al-Madinah* or *Constitution of Medina* having been established, an analysis of its content is in order. For this purpose, a phenomenological approach is appropriate, presenting the document in cultural context while comparing its contents to practices current in the period. The political elements of the *Constitution* must also be duly addressed considering their implications for Islam in the world today.

Determined to bring an end to the bitter infighting between the Arab war-lords of the tribe of Khazraj and their Jewish rivals, the Prophet prepared the *Constitution of Medina* and, in so doing, established the first Islamic State. Identity and loyalty were no longer to be based on family, tribe, kinship, or even religion: the overriding identity was membership in the *ummah* of Muhammad. The *Constitution of Medina* decreed that the citizens of the Islamic State were one and indivisible regardless of religion. Be they heathen, People of the Book, or Muslims, all those who were subject to the *Constitution* belonged to the same *ummah*. In so doing, he created a tolerant, pluralistic government which protected religious freedom. The importance of this is so extraordinary that it is often misunderstood.

When confronted with the clause that "The Jews of Banu 'Awf are one community with the believers," Orientalists like Peters (b. 1927 CE) are simply startled: "If the Jews were permitted from the outset to practice their religion *within* the newly constituted *ummah*, then Muhammad's original Medina 'community' was a purely secular one, and the word *ummah* was being used in a sense different from its Qur'anic occurrences" (201). For most people, including the majority of Muslims, the nature of the original Islamic State is outside their frame of political reference. As such, it has been referred to as a kingdom, a theocracy, or even a secular state, all of which definitions are incorrect. The Prophet Muhammad's Community was a unique system which had never existed before and which has never been seen since despite honest efforts to emulate it. As Karen Armstrong (b. 1944 CE) clearly comprehends,

> In the Qur'anic vision there is no dichotomy between the sacred and the profane, the religious and the political, sexuality or worship. The whole of life was potentially holy and had to be brought into the ambit of the divine. The aim was *tawhid* (making one), the integration of the whole of life in a unified community, which would give Muslims intimations of the Unity which is God. (2000: 14–15)

In Greek or Athenian democracy (5th century BCE), for example, the only individuals considered to be citizens were free adult males who were natives of Athens or Sparta. Slaves, women, children, and foreigners, as well as the majority of peasants, who represented more than 50% of the population, were all excluded. In other words, more than half of the population was composed of human "objects" as opposed to human beings. What was called "democracy" or "rule of the people" was, in effect, "pro-slavery democracy" or "slave-master democracy." And while it is true that Islam did not abolish slavery in a single stage, it established a system that would gradually eradicate it. For in Islam, slavery is not a permanent state. Not only can all slaves earn their freedom by work or conversion, all children born of slaves are free in Islam. Islam also decreed that slaves should be treated humanely and considered the freeing of slaves as a pious act. In fact, in many cases, freeing slaves was a required act of expiation for certain sins.

It could be argued in passing that the resemblance of Greek democracy to the current "liberal" democracies of the Western world is no coincidence. The *Constitution of Medina* can also be compared with that of the Roman Republic (509 BCE–27 BCE). The Republican Romans also spoke of the "government of the people;" however, this was more fictitious than real. The consuls—those who ruled the people—acted like kings, presided over the Senate and the People's Assembly, which was composed of representatives of military units, and simply represented the economic elite. As for the Senate, made up of the dominant players in matters of politics, it represented the aristocracy. Common people were simply numbers to be counted. (Ironically, in some present-day democracies, the roll of the populace in the political process is similarly nullified.) As for the plebeians (from *plebs* or masses), which comprised the vast majority of Romans, they could not rule, elect rulers or make use of land, all of which was reserved for the patricians or nobles. These same landowners controlled the Senate. However, in the community created by means of the *Constitution of Medina*, every single member of society enjoyed equality before the law as all privileges of class were abolished. The rich and the poor; the noble and the laymen; the Arabs and the non-Arabs; the blacks and the whites; the men and the women; and the children and the adults all had the same rights. Even Muhammad, as the Messenger of Allah, was not above the law. As he himself said in a rhetorical question, even if his daughter Fatimah were to steal which, as a saintly soul is inconceivable, he would have given her the punishment for theft. Given the *Constitution of Medina*'s genuinely progressive mandate, one might question why this document is ignored in favor of the less democratic offerings from the "Greek democracy" and the "Roman Republic."

In contrast to post-prophetic interpretations of Islam, in which the People of the Book are considered as *kuffar* or infidels, and only the best of Muslims are considered *mu'minin* or Believers, the Prophet created an inclusive Community of Believers which included members of all the Abrahamic faiths. In the time of the Prophet, the *ahl al-dhimmah*, both Jewish and Christian, belonged to the community of believers. The term *kuffar* was reserved for those who actively attacked and plotted to destroy Islam. This is not to say that Islam was not a distinct faith as Fred M. Donner (b. 1945) has argued (58), or that it was a Jewish or Christian heresy, as some Orientalists have asserted. It simply shows that Islam, as the culmination of divinely-revealed religions, viewed Judaism and Christianity as the foundational stepping stones of God's final revelation. While Donner is right that the Community of Believers was ecumenical and included Jews and Christians, this simply serves to show the unifying nature of early Islam. Although the early Muslims were tolerant of the People of the Book, and embraced them as fellow monotheists, they did indeed have a distinct identity. This can clearly be seen in the brotherhood that the Prophet established between Muslim Emigrants and Muslim Helpers. These bonds of brotherhood were based not on kith or kin or color or class but on the collective belief in Islam.

Donner's claim that the words *islam* and *muslim* "did not yet have the sense of confessional distinctness we now associate with 'Islam' and 'Muslim'" (71) demonstrates a misunderstanding of basic Arabic. When the Qur'an speaks of *islam* as "submission," and *muslim* as "one who submits," the words are indefinite. However, when the Qur'an speaks of *Islam*, as a religion, and *Muslim*, as a follower of that religion, they are definite. When the Qur'an says that *Inna al-dina 'inda Allahi al-Islam*, it means, very much, "Verily, the religion with Allah is Islam" (3:19) and not "Verily, the religion with God is submission." The same applies when Allah says: "This day have I perfected your religion for you, completed My favor upon you, and chosen for you Islam as your religion" (5:3). The word is *al-Islam*, not *islam*; thus, it refers specifically to Islam as a religion and not some vague state of submission. The religion revealed to Muhammad was not intolerant and exclusivist. It was a revival and rectification of the religion of Abraham, Moses, and Jesus, under its final Messenger, Muhammad. As Stephen O'Shea has understood, "The message given to Muhammad, the last in a long line of prophecy, improved and supplanted all that had come before" (15). While Islam confirmed the Abrahamic religions that came before it, it came to correct them and complete them. Had they not gone astray in matters of orthodoxy and orthopraxy, there would have been no need for a final prophet and messenger. Islam was revealed in order to update, supplement, and correct pre-existing spiritual knowledge rather than depart from it. As far as Muslims are concerned, Judaism and Christianity are steps on the path to spiritual salvation. The final step, in the words of Allah, is Islam. Since it is the completion of the monotheistic message, it has essentially encompassed and fulfilled all previous revelations.

There is also no basis for Donner's belief that the fifth Umayyad Caliph, 'Abd al-Malik ibn Marwan (r. 685–705 CE), helped convert the Believer's movement into "Islam" (194–224). Muhammad clearly identified himself as the Prophet and Messenger of Allah, his religion as Islam, and his followers as Muslims in the many letters he sent which still exist in museums to this date. Of the sixty-two letters said to have been sent by the Prophet Muhammad in Hebrew, Syriac, and Arabic (Zeitlin 131), the texts of twenty-nine of them are available (Dar Rah Haqq 133–134). This, of course, does not include the *Covenant of the Prophet Muhammad with the Monks of Mount Sinai*, the *Covenant of the Prophet Muhammad with the Christians of Najran*, the *Covenant of the Prophet Muhammad with the Assyrian Christians*, the *Covenant of the Prophet Muhammad with the Christians of Persia*, the *Covenant of the Prophet Muhammad with the Armenian Christians of Jerusalem*, and the two versions of the *Covenant of the Prophet Muhammad with the Christians of the World*, among possible others. Hence, over thirty-five letters of the Prophet appear to have survived over the course of the centuries. Donner, of course, devotes his time casting doubt on sources produced in the centuries immediately after the Prophet while completely ignoring the sources produced by the Messenger of Allah himself. If the claim that Islam, as a distinct religion, developed under the rule of 'Abd al-Malik, is false, it is nonetheless true that "[t]he relationship of mutual trust and even conviviality that characterized Christian and Muslim during the early Umayyad days began to change, however, during the reign of Caliph 'Abd al-Malik (685–705 CE) and his four sons who succeeded him in turn" (Betts 9). As Ingrid Mattson (b. 1963 CE) argues, "Muslims seem to have been articulating a more distinct identity with respect to the People of the Book, while at the same time trying to reach out across a doctrinal divide that possibly could be bridged" (149).

This hardening of position, which was started under 'Abd al-Malik, manifested itself in many ways. As part of his broader program of Islamization, the Caliph constructed the Dome of the Rock as a symbol of Muslim superiority and imposed Arabic as the official language of the administration (Foss 136). Not only did he remove the cross from coinage, in favor of religious slogans exclusively in Arabic, he also printed a couple of controversial coins (136). The first coin, numbered 89A, features the image of a man on the obverse believed by some to be the Standing Caliph but said by Foss and Hoyland to be the Prophet Muhammad himself. On the reverse is another intriguing image. For some, it is a *qutb* or pole which symbolizes the Caliph as the center of the community (Foss 137, 142, 287 note 8). For others, however, it resembles a broken cross symbolizing the triumph of Islam over Christianity. Since the object is the mirror image that appeared in previous coins (140, fig. 65, 86A), with only the horizontal bars of the cross missing, I can only conclude that it represents a broken cross (142, 89A). Actually, it may also be an allusion to the *hadith* of the Prophet Muhammad which asserts that Jesus Christ would break the crosses during his second coming. Whatever it means, it marks a monumental change in the relationship between Islam and Christianity. Whether the bearded Arab with a sword is 'Abd al-Malik or the Prophet Muhammad (142, 89 A), he clearly represents the power of Islam. Even more intriguing is the image of the man who appears on the back of coin 89c and the front of 89e. As Foss writes, "[t]he figure they portray is different from the caliph in the main series. Their inscription names Muhammad messenger of God. The conclusion seems obvious and very surprising: Could this be the image of the Prophet himself?" (137). These Standing Caliph coins, issued between 694/95 and 692/697 CE, were the last to depict a human image. But let us return to the Prophet's early period in Medina.

As the Arabs of Medina were known to be violent and bellicose warlords with a deeply-ingrained culture of revenge, the Prophet Muhammad sought to settle all past grievances with kindness and mercy. Since perceived past wrongs and demands for blood posed a grave danger to the fledgling Islamic State, and threatened to ignite ancient feuds at any time, the *Constitution of Medina* devoted great detail to the peace process and fostering stable tribal relations. If an eye for an eye was the law of nomadic Bedouins, it was not a philosophy that sedentary populations could ever follow if they wished to prosper. As such, the payment of blood money between families or tribes for the unjust slaying of individuals replaces the *lex talionis*. In his effort to create safety and security, the Prophet proclaimed Medina a *haram* or sacred place, thus barring all violence and weapons. The Prophet's attempt at peace and reconciliation was embraced by the majority of the inhabitants of Medina. The hypocrites, however, among both the Arabs and the Jews, made every attempt to undermine the Prophet's peace commission, hoping for a return to the time-honored ways of settling accounts through slaughter. (The term "hypocrites" or *munafiqin* denotes those who outwardly professed Islam but secretly held different beliefs.)

Departing from the lawless tradition of tribal anarchy, in which the strong oppressed the weak and the rich exploited the poor, the Prophet Muhammad granted protection to the most vulnerable members of society including women and the destitute. Importantly, all believers were equal before the law. At a time when the wronged had no recourse before the law, as there was no law, the Prophet established a judicial system based on the teachings of Allah. The Qur'an and the Sunnah were enshrined as the sole basis for legislation. All affairs were to be referred back to Allah and the Prophet Muhammad.

Although non-Muslims shared the same rights as Muslims, and were granted autonomy in religious matters, they were not obliged to participate in the religious wars of the Muslims. In this sense, they were granted rights without obligations. Both Muslims and Jews, however, were committed to protecting one another if they were attacked by enemies. In such cases, Muslims were bound to protect the Jews from their enemies. Likewise, Jews were bound to protect Muslims. In such cases, in which both communities fought alongside each other, the cost of war was to be equally shared. Once again manifesting a merciful nature, the Prophet Muhammad extended protection to both combatants and non-combatants so long as they had not engaged in any crimes or atrocities.

In the newly-formed *ummah* of Muhammad, loyalty was no longer to tribe or kin. Loyalty was to the law. All believers were brothers to one another. By way of putting theory into practice, the Prophet instituted brotherhood between the Emigrants [*muhajirun*], those Muslims who followed the Prophet on his *hijrah* from Mecca to Medina, and the Helpers [*ansar*], pairing the rich with the poor, the black with the white, and the noble with the commoner. This was the dawn of a new day and the birth of a new culture and civilization. What the Prophet had created was unprecedented: a Free State, "the first of its kind in the intellectual and political history of human civilization" founded "more than thirteen hundred years before the Universal Declaration of Human Rights (1948)" (Khan 1). Considering the unprecedented level of rights, freedoms, and protections that the Prophet was prepared to provide, integrating into the Islamic *ummah* was particularly appealing to the pagan Arabs, a few Jews, and an important number of Christians. Pluralistic in nature, the *Consitution of Medina* was, very much, a call for peaceful co-existence. It provided rights to non-Muslims and encouraged their participation in the broader Muslim community.

The Judeo-Christian Response to the Advent of Islam

After arriving in Medina, the Prophet had the great pleasure of meeting Salman the Persian (d. 654 CE), a spiritual wayfarer who had travelled far and wide in the search of truth. Originally a Zoroastrian, he had converted to Christianity and had served two bishops and three priests, the last of whom informed him of the imminent arrival of the predestined prophet. A pious priest told him that the awaited one would rise from Mecca, would migrate to a city full of date trees, would have the seal of prophecy between his shoulder blades, and would eat food only if it were a gift and not charity. In his zeal to find the personification of prophecy, Salman asked some Arabs from the tribe of Kalb to take him to Arabia in exchange for money. Breaking their promise, the Arabs sold Salman to a Jewish man. After working for him for a while, the slave master sold Salman to his nephew who belonged to the Banu Qurayzah of Yathrib. So occupied was Salman with his slave duties that he was unaware that Muhammad had proclaimed his prophecy in Mecca and was calling people to Islam. As the years passed by, the Prophet eventually migrated to Yathrib. It was then that Salman learned of his arrival. Overwhelmed with excitement, Salman eventually made his way to the Prophet. As Salman explained,

> When it was evening, I took some food with me and went to the Prophet. The Prophet was in Quba at the time. I said, 'Word has reached me that you are a very pious man, and that you have some travelers in your company. I had some charity and thought that you would be most deserving of it. This is it; you may have some to eat.' The Prophet withdrew his own hand, not eating from it, but told his Companions to eat. At the time, I thought, 'This is one of the characteristics my mentor told me of.'
>
> On my way back, I saw that the Prophet was heading to Medina. Thus, I took the food to him, saying, 'I saw that you were not eating from this charity. As a matter of fact, I presented it as a gift and not charity.' This time, the Prophet also ate with his Companions. 'That makes two signs,' I thought.
>
> Later on, I approached the Prophet as he was walking behind the corpse in a funeral. I remember that at the time, he was covered in two sheets, and that his Companions were with him. I was trying to steal a look at the Seal on his back, when the Prophet saw me glancing. Realizing that I wanted to verify what someone had told me, he let his cloak drop a little, and I managed to see that the Seal between his shoulder blades was exactly the way my Mentor had described it. I threw myself down before the Prophet kissing (his blessed hands/feet) and started to cry. The Holy Prophet said, 'O Salman! Reveal your story.'
>
> So I sat in front of him, relating my story to him and hoping that his Companions could also hear it. When I had finished, the Prophet said, 'O Salman! Make a deal with your owner to free you.' Consequently, my master did agree to free me, but in exchange for the following: 'Three hundred date trees, as well as one thousand six hundred silver coins.' Hence, the Sahabah helped by providing around twenty to thirty date plants each, and a tenth of every man's land in accordance to how much he owned. The Prophet said to me, 'Dig a hole for each date-plant. When you are finished, let me know so that I can personally fix all the date-plants into place with my own hands.' Thus, with the help of my friends, I dug holes wherever the date-plants were to be put. Later on, the Prophet came. We stood by his side holding the plants as he fixed them into the ground. I swear by the Being Who sent the Prophet with the Truth, not a single plant died out.
>
> Nevertheless, I still had the silver to pay. A man came to the Prophet bringing from the mines some gold which was roughly the size of a pigeon's egg. The Prophet said, 'O Salman! Take this and pay off whatever you have to.' I replied, 'O Messenger of Allah! How will this be enough for my debt?' He said, 'Allah will surely make it sufficient for your debt.' As a result to this statement, I swear By Allah, it outweighed the one thousand six hundred coins. I not only paid off my dues, but what I had left with me was equivalent to what I had given them. (Inter-Islam)

As a result of Muhammad's personal virtues and foretold physical characteristics, Salman embraced Islam and was released from slavery by the Prophet who paid his Jewish master the stipulated price. Considering that Salman, a learned Christian, recognized him as the final Messenger of God, Muhammad held high hopes that the Jewish tribes of Yathrib would also embrace Islam. Besides extensive Christian-oriented content, the Qur'an also directed much of its wisdom towards the Children of Israel. In matters of monotheism, ritual purity, dietary laws, and prayers in the direction of Jerusalem, Islam was very much a revival of the true teachings of Judaism. The story of al-Husayn ibn Sallam ibn al-Harith (d. 630 CE), the most learned Jewish rabbi from Yathrib, shows the appeal of Islam to the Hebrew people:

> When I heard of the appearance of the Messenger of Allah, peace be on him, I began to make enquiries about his name, his genealogy, his characteristics, his time and place and I began to compare this information with what is contained in our books. From these enquiries, I became convinced about the authenticity of his prophethood and I affirmed the truth of his mission. However, I concealed my conclusions from the Jews. I held my tongue. . . .
>
> Then came the day when the Prophet, peace be on him, left Mecca and headed for Yathrib. When he

reached Yathrib and stopped at Quba, a man came rushing into the city, calling out to people and announcing the arrival of the Prophet. At that moment, I was at the top of a palm tree doing some work. My aunt, Khalidah bint al-Harith, was sitting under the tree. On hearing the news, I shouted: *Allahu Akbar! Allahu Akbar!* [(God is Great! God is Great!]. When my aunt heard my *takbir*, she remonstrated with me: 'May God frustrate you.... By God, if you had heard that Moses was coming you would not have been more enthusiastic.' 'Auntie, he is really, by God, the brother of Moses and follows his religion. He was sent with the same mission as Moses.' She was silent for a while and then said: 'Is he the Prophet about whom you spoke to us who would be sent to confirm the truth preached by previous prophets and complete the message of his Lord?' 'Yes,' I replied.

Without any delay or hesitation, I went out to meet the Prophet. I saw crowds of people at his door. I moved about in the crowds until I reached close to him. The first words I heard him say were: 'O people! Spread peace.... Share food.... Pray during the night while people (normally) sleep ... and you will enter Paradise in peace....' I looked at him closely. I scrutinized him and was convinced that his face was not that of an imposter. I went closer to him and made the declaration of faith that there is no god but Allah and that Muhammad is the Messenger of Allah. The Prophet turned to me and asked: 'What is your name?' 'Al-Husayn ibn Sallam,' I replied. 'Instead, it is (now) 'Abd Allah ibn Sallam,' he said (giving me a new name). 'Yes,' I agreed. 'Abd Allah ibn Sallam (it shall be). By Him who has sent you with the Truth, I do not wish to have another name after this day.' (Islamic Web)

Besides Salman the Persian, other Christians embraced Islam, including Addas, a young Christian boy from Nineveh who was enslaved in Ta'if. The most significant conversions from Christianity to Islam occurred during the early days of Islam. As Ibn Ishaq (704–761/770 CE) reports,

While the Messenger was in Mecca some twenty Christians came to him from Abyssinia when they heard news of him. They found him in the mosque and sat and talked with him, asking him questions, while some Qurayshites were in their meeting round the Ka'bah. When they had asked all the questions they wished the Messenger invited them to come to God and read the Qur'an to them. When they heard the Qur'an their eyes flowed with tears, and they accepted God's call, believed in him, and declared his truth. They recognized in him the things which had been said of him in their scriptures. When they got up to go away Abu Jahl with a number of the Quraysh intercepted them, saying, 'God, what a wretched band you are! Your people at home sent you to bring them information about the fellow, and as soon as you sat with him you renounced your religion and believed what he said. We don't know a more asinine band than you,' or words to that effect. They answered: 'Peace be upon you. We will not engage in foolish controversy with you. We have our religion and you have yours. We have not been remiss in seeking what is best.'

It is said that these Christians came from Najran, but God knows whether that was so. It is also said, and again God knows best, that it was in reference to them that the verses 'Those to whom we brought the book aforetime, they believe in it. And when it is read to them they say We believe in it. Verily, it is the truth from our Lord. Verily aforetime we were Muslims' as far as the words, 'We have our works and you have your works. Peace be upon you; we desire not the ignorant.' (28:52–55) (179)

The Christians of Najran, explains Goddard, were followers of Monophysite Christianity (16). According to Betts, however, this was not the case at the time of the Prophet: "[t]he Christians of Najran north of al-Yaman, at first Monophysites under the influence of the Ethiopian occupation, turned to Nestorianism when they came within the Persian sphere in 575" (5). If the Nestorians were 'olive oil and water' Christians, who believed that the human and divine natures of Jesus cannot mix, the Monophysites were 'wine and water' Christians who believed that, although both natures mixed, the mix was impenetrable to theological analysis (Rogerson 82). In matters of belief and practice, they shared much in common with the Muslims, a fact that may have helped precipitate their proselytization.

Other famous figures are said to have embraced Islam at the hands of the Prophet, including Qays 'Abd al-Rashid (575–661 CE), the semi-legendary ancestor of the Pashtun people. Although the pre-Islamic Afghans were said to practice Buddhism, Zoroastrianism, Hinduism, and Judaism, they identified themselves as the Children of Israel. Qays 'Abd al-Rashid, for example, is alleged to have been a 37th descendant of King Saul through Malak Afghanah, a grandson of King Saul. After hearing of the advent of Islam in Arabia, Qays was supposedly sent to Medina to meet the Prophet. Convinced of the truth brought by Muhammad, Qays returned to Afghanistan and converted his tribe to Islam.

Not only did the chief rabbi of the Jews of Yathrib embrace Islam, so did his immediate family. As 'Abd Allah explained,

> I concealed the matter from the Jews, and then went to the Messenger and said, 'The Jews are a nation of liars and I wish you would take me into one of your houses and hide me from them. Then ask them about me so that they may tell you the position I hold among them before they know that I have become a Muslim. For if they know it beforehand they will utter slanderous lies against me.' The Prophet housed me; the Jews came; and the Messenger asked them about my standing among them. They said: 'He is our chief, and the son of our chief; our rabbi, and our most learned man.' When they said this, I emerged and said: 'O Jews, fear God and accept what He has sent you. For by God you know that he is the Messenger of Allah. You will find him described in your Torah and even named. I testify that he is the Messenger of Allah, I believe in him, I hold him to be true, and I acknowledge him.' They accused me of lying and reviled me. Then I reminded the Messenger that I had said that they would do this, for they were a treacherous, lying, and evil people. I publicly proclaimed my conversion and my household and my aunt Khalidah followed suit. (Ibn Ishaq 241)

Though detractors attempted to discredit 'Abd Allah ibn Sallam, his integrity is even attested to in the Qur'an, which presents him as a Jewish witness to the truth:

> Say: See ye? If (this teaching) be from Allah, and ye reject it, and a witness from among the Children of Israel testifies to its similarity (with earlier scripture), and has believed while ye are arrogant, (how unjust ye are!) truly, Allah guides not a people unjust. (46:10)

While many other Jewish people acknowledged that Muhammad was the Messenger of Allah, most of them opted to oppose him due to the fact that he descended from Isma'il [Ishmael] as opposed to Ishaq [Isaac]. As Safiyyah bint Huyyay ibn Akhtab, the Jewish wife of the Prophet reported,

> I was the favorite child of my father and my uncle Abu Yasir. When I was present they took no notice of their other children. When the Messenger was staying in Quba' with the Banu 'Amr b. 'Awf, the two went to see him before daybreak and did not return until after nightfall, weary, warn out, drooping and feeble. I went up to them in childish pleasure as I always did, and they were so sunk in gloom that they took no notice of me. I heard my uncle say to my father, 'Is he, he? Do you recognize him, and can you be sure?' 'Yes!' 'And what do you feel about him?' 'By God I shall be his enemy as long as I live!' (Ibn Ishaq 242)

Besides 'Abd Allah ibn Sallam, the only other prominent Jew to embrace Islam was another rabbi by the name of Mukhayriq, described by Ibn Ishaq (704–761/770 CE) in the following terms:

> He was a learned rabbi owning much property in date palms. He recognized the Messenger by his description and his own learning, and he felt a predilection for his religion until on the day of Uhud, which fell on the Sabbath, he reminded the Jews that they were bound to help Muhammad. They objected that it was the Sabbath. 'May you have no Sabbath,' he answered, and took his weapons and joined the Messenger in Uhud. His parting testimony to his people was: 'If I am killed today my property is to go to Muhammad to use as God shows him.' He was killed in the battle that followed. I am told that the Messenger used to say 'Mukhayriq is the best of the Jews.' The Messenger took over his property and all the alms he distributed in Medina came from it. (241)

As for the rest of the Jews in Medina, they allied themselves with the hypocrites in an attempt to extinguish the growing flame of Islam. These adversaries of the Prophet did their best to annoy him and stir up confusion. Some rabbis went so far as to falsely convert to Islam in an attempt to undermine Islam from within. As Ibn Ishaq (704–761/770 CE) relates,

> These hypocrites used to assemble in the mosque and listen to the stories of the Muslims and laugh and scoff at their religion. When some of them were there one day the Messenger saw them talking with lowered voice among themselves huddled together. He ordered that they should be ejected and they were put out with some violence. (246)

Finding vehement opposition to the Prophet, both internal and external, to be insufficient, the Jews of Medina actually plotted against him with the polytheists in the hope he would killed and that the Muslim movement would be wiped off the face of the earth with his demise.

The Jewish Opposition: The Case of the Banu Qaynuqa', Banu Nadir, and Banu Qurayzah

After the devastating defeat of the Meccans in the Battle of Badr in 624 CE, the Prophet reportedly assembled the Jews of the Banu Qaynuqa' and invited them to Islam with the following words: "O Jews! Beware lest God bring upon you the vengeance that He brought upon Quraysh and become Muslims. You know that I am a prophet who has been sent—you will find that in your scriptures and God's covenant with you" (Ibn Ishaq 363).

Far from being tactful, the response from the Jews was a declaration of war. "O Muhammad," they replied, "You seem to think that we are your people. Do not deceive yourself because you encountered a people with no knowledge of war and got the better of them; for by God if we fight you, you will find that we are real men!" (Ibn Ishaq 363). As Ibn Ishaq (704–761/770 CE) reports, the following verses were revealed in response:

> Say to those who reject Faith: 'Soon will ye be vanquished and gathered together to Hell, an evil bed indeed (to lie on). There has already been for you a Sign in the two armies that met (in combat): One was fighting in the cause of Allah, the other resisting Allah. These saw with their own eyes twice their number. But Allah doth support with His aid whom He pleaseth. In this is a warning for such as have eyes to see.' (3:12–13)

Since they had broken their treaty obligations and threatened the Prophet, Muhammad is reported to have moved against the Banu Qaynuqa', besieging them for fourteen to fifteen days. After engaging in negotiations, the tribe is said to have surrendered unconditionally. Since they had betrayed the trust of the Muslims, and might act as fifth column allies of the polytheists, Muhammad would have been within his military rights to put them to the sword. As a man of mercy, however, Muhammad decided to show leniency towards the tribe and simply requested their exile. He even allowed them to collect the debts that were owed to them by other Medinans (Waqidi 89). Allowed to take all of their belongings, the Banu Qaynuqa' relocated to the Jewish colonies in Wadi al-Qura, north of Medina. Eventually, they settled permanently in Der'a in Syria, to the west of Salkhad, where they assimilated into the existing Jewish communities of the region.

If the Jews of Banu Qaynuqa' opposed Muhammad verbally, the Jews of Banu Nadir initiated a treacherous plot against the Prophet's life. After at least two attempts on the life of the Prophet, including an incident in which Muhammad was as close as a poisoned mouthful away from death, the Commander-in-Chief of the Muslim Community opted to exile the Banu Nadir from Medina in the year 625 CE. Having opted originally to comply, the Jews of Banu Nadir were convinced by 'Abd Allah ibn Ubayy, the chief of the hypocrites, to hunker down in their fortresses where their supposed ally falsely promised two thousand reinforcements. The Jews of Banu Nadir were roundly defeated by the Muslims. Rather than put them to the sword, the Prophet granted them free passage. Most of the Jews of Banu Nadir settled in Khaybar while others migrated to Syria. The remaining Jews, however, continued to harbor animosity against Islam. If the plots of the Banu Nadir had initially failed, the Jews of Banu Qurayzah moved from targeted assassination to military conspiracy with the enemy.

In 627 CE, when the Muslims were besieged by the idolatrous Quraysh, the Jews of Banu Qurayzah, in defiance of their treaty obligations, entered into negotiation with the besiegers. The plot was to combine an external attack by the polytheists with an internal attack by the Banu Qurayzah. In the words of Qureshi,

> During the *ghazwah* [raid] of Ahzab, the Banu Qurayzah joined hands with the enemy and did not regard the stipulations of the *Charter of Medina.* The Muslims had signed two treaties with them, one was *Charter of Medina* and the other signed at the time of the battle with the Banu Nadir. (261)

As soon as the conspiracy was revealed, the Jewish tribe was charged with treason. Seeking refuge in their fortress, the Banu Qurayzah was besieged for twenty-five days, ending in the tribe's surrender. Some members of the Banu Qurayzah embraced Islam during the siege. They recognized that Muhammad was indeed the prophet that their elders had testified about. In so doing, they saved their lives, their property, and their families (Waqidi 247). Despite having broken their treaty obligations, the Prophet's emissary urged the Banu Qurayzah to enter, once again, into an agreement with the Messenger of Allah (247). Otherwise, they were offered the opportunity to profess Judaism and pay the *jizyah* (247). The Banu Qurayzah, however, remained defiant, and stated that they preferred to die than to pay taxes (247). As such, the siege intensified until the Jews could no longer withstand it. Surrendering unconditionally, they asked only to be judged by a member of the Arab tribe to which they were adherents (Nafziger and Walton 9–10). "This was granted them," writes George F. Nafziger (b. 1949 CE) and Mark W. Walton, "but the judgment rendered was brutal" (10). Condemned for treachery, the obstinate male members of the tribe are alleged to have been beheaded while their women and children were reduced to slavery. One such captive, Rayhannah bint Zayd ibn 'Amr, married the Messenger of Allah and eventually embraced Islam. She died in 631 CE, shortly after the Prophet's Farewell Pilgrimage, a mere one year before his death.

It should be stressed, however, that the historicity of this mass execution, which had been decided by a judge appointed by the Jewish people, and who had ruled on the basis of the Torah, has been called into question (Donner 73). The clashes between the Prophet and the Jews of Medina may have been greatly exaggerated and some of the details may have been completely fabricated (73). While the sequence of events presented by Ibn Ishaq (704–761/770 CE) has become the "orthodox" version, others sources, such as Muhammad al-Kalbi (737–819 CE), make no mention of the Banu Qaynuqa' incident (Schöller 26–27). If Ibn Ishaq places the Banu Qaynuqa' episode after Badr, the Banu Nadir episode after Uhud, and the Banu Qurayzah episode after the Battle of the Trench, al-Kalbi's account explains that no conflict with the Jews occurred prior to Uhud (26–27). For Schöller, the evidence "does seem to imply that there was neither a B. Qaynuqa' nor a B. al-Nadir episode as we know it from the 'orthodox' *sira* version" but rather a single larger episode of conflict (28–29). According to Schöller, this confrontation between the Prophet and the Jews may have taken place in Medina or, maybe, even in Khaybar (30). As for what happened in Khaybar, the versions are many.

Rather than execute the Jews of Banu Nadir, the Prophet had allowed them to relocate to the oasis of Khaybar located 150 kilometers from Medina where other Jewish tribes resided. Instead of making amends with the Muslims, the Banu Nadir started to incite the Arab tribes of the region against the Islamic community. Preferring polytheists over monotheists, the Jews of Khaybar posed a major political, military, and economic threat to the Muslims of Medina who were, in effect, surrounded by enemies on all sides: the Jews of Khaybar and their Arab polytheistic allies to the north and the Arab pagans of Quraysh in Mecca to the south. The Muslims marched on Khaybar, surrounded the city, and compelled the Jews to surrender. One of the captives of the battle, a seventeen year old Safiyyah, soon embraced Islam and became wife to the Prophet Muhammad. The

Messenger of Allah had proposed Islam to her and said: "If you will be in your religion, we will not compel you; but if you choose God and His Messenger I will take you for myself" (Waqidi 348). She replied, "Rather, I will choose God and His Messenger." In return, he manumitted her and married her, with her freedom being her dowry (348).

If anything seems clear, it is that the Jews of Khaybar surrendered without any significant fighting and that a treaty was concluded by means of emissaries (39). As for what followed, the claims are three: 1) the Prophet left the land to the Jews on the condition of crop-sharing, 2) he took some land for himself and distributed the rest among his combatants, or 3) Fadak fell to Muhammad alone, but he left the land to the Jews on condition of share-cropping (Schöller 38–39). This final version is the most sound and supported by the impeccable testimony of Fatimah, the daughter of Muhammad. While not entirely convincing, Syed Barakat Ahmad's (d. 1988 CE) *Muhammad and the Jews: A Re-Examination* also cast doubts on the credibility of Ibn Ishaq's account of early relations between the Prophet and the Jews which may have been colored by 'Abbasid ideas. More likely, it was Ibn Hisham (d. 833 CE), the editor who "abbreviated, annotated, and sometimes altered" (Guillaume xvii) the work of Ibn Ishaq, who was responsible for this more polemical perspective. As far as Ahmad is concerned, no Jews were executed or expelled from Medina during Muhammad's life. In fact, many traditions state that the Jews were only expelled from Khaybar by the Second Caliph, 'Umar ibn al-Khattab (579–644 CE) (Schöller 39, note 78). After all, "there were more than twenty Jewish tribes living in Medina when the Messenger of Islam began his mission" (Levy 158) and the historical record only indicates that he had problems with a number of them.

If, indeed, we believe that the seven hundred men of Qurayzah were killed, and their women and children sold as slaves, and, increasingly, the evidence suggests that we cannot, such a horrible incident must not be judged according to the standards of our times. As Karen Armstrong points out,

> This was a very primitive society: the Muslims themselves had just narrowly escaped extermination, and had Muhammad simply exiled the Qurayzah they would have swelled the Jewish opposition in Khaybar and brought another war upon the *ummah*. In seventh-century Arabia an Arab chief was not expected to show mercy to traitors like the Qurayzah. The executions sent a grim message to Khaybar and helped to quell the pagan opposition in Medina, since the pagan leaders had been the allies of the rebellious Jews. This was a fight to the death, and everybody had always known that the stakes were high. The struggle did not indicate any hostility towards Jews in general, but only towards the three rebel tribes. The Qur'an continued to revere Jewish prophets and to urge Muslims to respect the People of the Book. Smaller Jewish groups continued to live in Medina, and later Jews, like Christians, enjoyed full religious liberty in the Islamic empire. (2000: 21)

While he won a small segment of the Jewish community to Islam, the majority of the Hebrew people rejected Muhammad's message for what they admitted were racist reasons: the fact that he descended from Isma'il [Ishmael] as opposed to Ishaq [Isaac]. If they submitted, paid the tribute, and lived in peace with the Muslims, Jews would still remain in Arabia. Opting for hypocrisy, treason, and treachery, they allied themselves with the infidels, claiming that polytheists were preferable to Muslims. By so doing, they effectively sealed their own fate. Acting swiftly and decisively, the Prophet inflicted important military and economic injuries upon the Jews and forced them into exile. If the Prophet's treatment of the Jews differed from his way of dealing with the Christians, the reason cannot be ignored. As Qureshi has expressed, "The real danger to Islam was from the polytheists and the Jews because the Christians were not active in Arabia" (274). Although "[t]he polytheists and Jews among the people of Medina hurt the Prophet and his companions grievously," wrote al-Waqidi (748–822 CE), "God, Most High, commanded His Prophet and the Muslims to be patient and forgiving" (91). The Prophet's approach was always centered on peace. He urged the Jews to enter into treaties and covenants with the Muslims. When they broke them, he urged them to repent and renew their allegiance. When they refused, he called upon them to submit and pay taxes. It was only after the Messenger of Allah had exhausted all avenues, and that the Jews themselves had chosen war, that he resorted to military action. As for the Jewish tribes and clans that had remained neutral, writes the *Encyclopedia Judaica*, they "were allowed to remain in Medina unmolested" (qtd. Levy 162).

Consolidating the Monotheistic Movement

Besides small groups of Jewish, Christian, and *Hanafiyyun* converts or reverts to Islam, the main body of the Prophet's followers had previously been polytheists. With his Jewish opponents sent into exile, the Messenger of Allah could concentrate on disseminating Islam among the remaining tribes of Arabia and consolidating his hold on the Peninsula. Both the picture given by the Orientalists, who allege that the Prophet spread Islam by the sword in the sense of forcibly converting conquered peoples, and the arguments of those misguided Muslim apologists who claim that the Prophet practiced some sort of "peace jihad," are incorrect. The Messenger of Allah employed a time honored political and military strategy: he presented all of the benefits that could be obtained by those who agreed upon an accord or, in the event the offer was rejected, the conditions to which they would have to adapt.

The benefits, of course, were not theoretical or declarative. They were a real and constant practice developed by the Prophet and his Companions. Furthermore, the beauty of the Qur'an, the wisdom of the Prophet's sayings, and his sublime ethics were so alluring that, for many, Islamic rule became simply irresistible. The benefits expounded by the Messenger of Allah came in the form of generous and benevolent treaties, accords, and covenants which he offered to those communities which willingly submitted to the Islamic State. In many instances, the terms of alliance were so utterly altruistic that allies were granted rights and privileges without reciprocal obligations of any kind. The Prophet truly had one mission in mind: to open the hearts of the unbelievers to the message of Islam.

If, however, the mutually beneficial covenant offered by the Prophet was not only rejected, but violently opposed, its opponents knew full well that they would have to face brave and battle-hardened Muslim warriors. It is said that while they were like lambs among the believers, they were like lions among unbelievers in the battlefield. News of the Prophet's miraculous victory at Badr (624 CE), in which a force of just over 300 Muslims overwhelmed 900 enemy combatants, spread like wildfire along the caravan routes of Arabia, reaching every far corner of the Peninsula. After a minor set-back at Uhud, which left the Muslims bewildered, the Prophet Muhammad inflicted important blows upon his enemies both militarily and materially leading to a loss of morale.

A formidable military commander, the Prophet Muhammad engaged in a large number of caravan raids and expeditions, including those of Waddan, Buwat, Safwan, Dhul Ashir, the First Badr, Kudr, Sawiq, Qaynuqa', Ghatafan, Bahran, Uhud, al-Asad, Najd, the Second Badr, the First Jandal, the Trench, Qurayzah, the Second Lahyan, Mustaliq, Hudaybiyyah, Khaybar, Fadak, the Third Qurah, Dhat al-Riqa, Baqra, Mecca, Hunayn, Awtas, Ta'if, and Tabuk. He also sent his troops to participate in a long series of forays in which he himself did not participate directly, including those of Nakhlah, Najd, the First Asad, the First Lahyan, al-Raji, Umayyyah, Bir Ma'una, the Assassination of Abu Rafi, Maslamah, the Second Asad, the First Thalabah, the Second Thalabah, Dhu Qarad, Jumum, al-Is, the Third Thalabah, Hismah, the First Qurah, the Second Jandal, the First 'Ali, the Second Qurah, Uraynah, Rawaha, 'Umar, Abu Bakr, Murrah, Uwwal, the Third Fadak, Yemen, Sulaym, Kadid, Banu Layth, Amir, Dhat Atlah, Mu'tah, Amr, Abu 'Ubaydah, Abi Hadrad, Edam, Khadirah, the First Khalid ibn Walid, the Demotion of Sumwa, the Demolition of Manat, the Second Khalid ibn Walid, the Demolition of Yaghuth, the First Awtas, the Second Awtas, Banu Tamim, Banu Khatham, Banu Kilab, Jiddah, the Third 'Ali,

Adhruh, the Third Khalid ibn Walid, the Fourth Khalid ibn Walid, Abu Sufyan, Jurash, the Second 'Ali, the Third 'Ali, Dhul Khalasa, and the Army of Usamah, which was the final expedition ordered by the Messenger of Allah.

By raiding enemy caravans, the Prophet placed the business interests of the polytheistic Arabs in peril. Then, by targeting pagan tribes, the Prophet placed pressure upon them to turn towards the emerging Islamic power-base. The more fortified cities that the Prophet conquered and the more arable land he acquired, the more powerful he became. Since people respect power and wealth as opposed to weakness and poverty, the Prophet's increased military and economic strength earned him greater authority. Despite a staggering number of raids, excursions, and expeditions in which the Prophet and his Companions engaged, most of them took place with little to no bloodshed. The bulk of these were short actions, not long campaigns. It is estimated that during his entire life Muhammad spent no more than 89 days in battle. Clearly, the Prophet did not use violence *per se* to bring people into his fold. He did, however, use the threat of violence as a stratagem in order to convince particular tribes that it was in their best interest to join the brotherhood of believers. By sending his troops throughout Arabia, leaving no major settlement untouched, the Prophet made a significant show of strength. His brilliant strategy worked wonders. He single-handedly brought the entire Arabian Peninsula under Islamic rule at the cost of approximately one thousand casualties. His conquests were so remarkable that "[e]ven Western skeptics may wonder about the divine nature of the Islamic conquest" (Nafziger and Walton 24). Following in the footsteps of the Prophet, the Companions soon showed the super-powers of that age, the Byzantine Romans and the Persians, that Islam was a force to be reckoned with. As fierce as they were in battle, the early Muslims administered their territories gently and justly, granting rights and protections to minorities, and creating the first cosmopolitan culture. How was this accomplished? As far as Nafziger (b. 1949 CE) and Walton are concerned, "only one possible explanation remains for the Arab success—and that was the spirit of Islam" (34). For Fowden, it was "Muhammad's proclamation of a fresh revelation from the one God, together with his political theory and practice, that created such a powerful expansionist impulse" (qtd. Zeitlin 164).

The Prophet's Domestic and Foreign Policy

Ultimately, the Prophet Muhammad was a man of peace. As such, he promoted peace everywhere. Now, it may seem paradoxical and disingenuous to present the Prophet as a person of peace knowing full well that he declared battle and waged war. Yet, in reality, there is no contradiction at all. Rather, there is complete and total coherence. It is not the same to operate on the basis of social interests as it is to act on the basis of individual interests. The interest of the group takes precedence over the interest of the individual. If an individual wishes to turn the right cheek after he/she has received a blow to the left cheek, such a person is free to do so. It is an individual decision. However, when the safety and security of an entire nation is at stake, the common good is always the determining factor. The issue changes completely when one is dealing with social as opposed to individual interests. In this case, a person who represents a movement that seeks peace, that loves peace, and that wants to ensure cordial relations between human beings throughout the world, will never achieve any such aims by accepting or tolerating injustice in any form. And it was precisely this role that the Prophet played. He was a leader and the standard-bearer of a movement that sought world-wide social harmony. It is in this capacity that he set in motion a movement that would uniformly neutralize sordid egotistical interests and it is for this reason that he was opposed. The Prophet was a man of kind words; however, he was also a man of action as encapsulated in his saying, "Both I smile and I fight" (Ibn Taymiyyah qtd. Hamidullah, *Muslim Conduct* 157).

If the Prophet Muhammad was resisted by certain sectors, it was because Islam, as a complete and total life transaction, was a threat to their vested economic interests. Since he prohibited oppression and exploitation, the source of the oppositions' wealth and power was placed in peril. As such, they determined to rise up against the Prophet's peace movement. The statement of Flavius Renatus Vegeitus, which was made towards the end of the 4th century CE, "If you want peace, prepare yourself for war," was never applied better. It should be made clear, as many commentators have done, that such a saying does not encourage aggression or imperialistic expansionism. Rather, it promotes the very opposite: a strong military acts as a deterrent to outside aggression and can neutralize the forces of any aggressors. The Prophet, basing himself on the doctrine revealed by God, was acting upon this principle. Whosoever wants world peace the most must struggle all the more against injustice in all forms and attempt to eradicate it from the face of the earth.

More than anyone, the Prophet Muhammad comprehended that the essential and irreplaceable ingredient for peace was justice. He understood that peace was necessarily based on the existence of a divinely-ordained socio-economic and political system which was, in its most elevated expression, integral to the revelation he received. After a decade of persecution in Mecca, the Messenger of Allah finally found an abode of relative peace in Medina. After neutralizing his internal enemies who were allied with his external enemies, the Prophet adopted a proactive peace-building policy. Whoever was at peace with Muslims, Muslims were at peace with them. Consequently, the Prophet offered generous covenants to any tribes or nations, be they pagan, Jewish or Christian, who were willing to forge alliances with the Muslims.

If any tribes or nations expressed hostility towards Islam, the Prophet warned them of dire consequences: submit to Islam or suffer conquest. This is not to say that such peoples had to convert. A visionary long-term planner, the Prophet understood that the spread of Islam could take centuries. What he sought to create were the conditions under which the seeds of Islam could be planted and watered, thus enabling Muslim seeds to sprout, grow, and spread. If a population preferred to remain heathen, Christian or Jewish, they were entitled to do so as long as they entered into a covenant with the Islamic State as protected people. If they refused the Prophet's peaceful advances, and expressed hostility or engaged in aggression, they would be duly conquered. Although they would be subjected to taxation, they would still not be compelled to convert. As the Qur'an clearly commands, "There shall be no compulsion in religion" (2:256). And as Allah explained, "Had your Lord willed, those on earth would have believed, all of them entirely. Then, [O Muhammad], would you compel the people in order that they become believers?" (10:99). As Islam has clearly established, Allah loves and appreciates diversity. In the words of Almighty Allah,

> O humankind! We created you from a single (pair) of a male and a female, and made you into nations and tribes, that ye may know each other (not that ye may despise (each other). Verily the most honored of you in the sight of Allah is (he who is) the most righteous of you. And Allah has full knowledge and is well acquainted (with all things). (49:13)

In the year 2 AH, the Prophet put in place a treaty with the Chief of the Banu Damrah. The treaty stipulated that "He [the Prophet] will not attack the Banu Damrah, nor will they attack him, nor swell the troops of his enemies, nor help his enemies in any way" (Ibn Sa'd and al-Qari, qtd. Bahnasawy 78). After more families rallied together in support of the treaty, its content was expanded from non-aggression to include a pact of mutual aid and neutrality in certain circumstances. The terms of the expanded agreement were as follows:

> In the Name of Allah, the Most Compassionate, the Most Merciful. This is the writ of Muhammad, the Messenger of Allah, in favor of the Banu Damrah, assuring them of the security of their persons and their properties: that they may count on his help if anybody takes aggressive action against them, except in the case of fighting in the name of religion.

> This assurance is valid so long as the sea wets the shells. Similarly, when the Prophet requires it of them, they will help him; and they pledge that for God and His Messenger. To help them will depend on their loyalty and piety. (qtd. Hamidullah, *Muslim Conduct* 629–30)

As a result of the Prophet's military and diplomatic efforts, many Arab populations submitted to Islamic rule without fighting.

Despite their long-standing hostility towards the Prophet, and their participation in numerous wars against the Muslims of Medina, the Messenger of Allah eventually concluded a treaty with a branch of the Banu Ghatafan. In the *Treaty of Ashjah*, which was dictated to Imam 'Ali (d. 661 CE), the Prophet confirmed the commitment of help between both parties:

> In the Name of Allah, the Most Compassionate, the Most Merciful. This treaty is a pledge concluded by Na'ym ibn Mas'ud al-Ashja'i. He has concluded it on the condition of help. This assurance is valid so long as the Mountain of Uhud remains standing and the sea wets the shells. (qtd. Qureshi 153)

In return for this pledge of mutual support and solidarity, the entire clan in question embraced Islam in the year 5 AH.

According to the *Chronicle of Séert*, the Arabs commenced their conquests in the year 5 AH and Islam became a powerful force with which to be reckoned (627/28 CE) (Scher 280–281 / 600–601). In response to the rise of Islam, the chronicles of the Nestorian monks assert that the inhabitants of Najran, headed by Sayyid Ghassani, went to meet the Prophet, sharing presents and praise with him (281 / 601). While they did not embrace Islam, they offered to support him and to fight under his banner if the Messenger of Allah ordered them to do so (281 / 601). The Prophet accepted their presents and bestowed on them a covenant (281 / 601). This covenant is reported to have been recognized by 'Umar ibn al-Khattab (579–644 CE), who provided the Christians with a second pact of protection during his rule, which essentially summarized and reiterated the privileges provided by the Prophet (281 / 601). The *Covenant of the Prophet Muhammad with the Christians of Najran* would represent the first major treaty of protection with the Christian community and apparently predates the *Covenant of the Prophet Muhammad with the Monks of Mount Sinai.*

Fulfilling a promise he had made to the monks many years ago, the Prophet was especially eager to engage in a treaty with the Monastery of Saint Catherine in the Sinai. As with the treaty he concluded with the Christians of Najran, the Messenger of Allah did not expect the Christians of the Sinai to embrace Islam. He simply sought their solidarity. The *Treaty of Saint Catherine*, which was dictated by the Prophet to Mughirah, and signed in the year 6 AH (628 CE), stipulated the following:

> Whatever goods that the neighbors of Allah and His Messenger have in their churches, monasteries and bishoprics, however small or great they may be, will remain in the possession. No bishop is to be driven out of his bishopric. No monk is to be expelled from his monastery. No changes will be made with regards to their rights and sovereignty or anything in their possession provided that they remain friendly [towards Islam and Muslims]. They will reform the rights incumbent on them. They will not be oppressed nor will they oppress. (qtd. Qureshi 155)

In his "Letter to the Ruler of Yamamah," which was delivered by Sulayt ibn 'Amr al-'Amiri, the Prophet dictated:

> In the Name of Allah, the Most Compassionate, the Most Merciful. From Muhammad, the Messenger of Allah, to Hawdah ibn 'Ali. Peace be upon the follower of the straight path. Know that my religion will prevail everywhere. You should thus embrace Islam. If you do so, whatever you possess will remain under your control. (qtd. Qureshi 40)

Hawda ibn 'Ali sent the following response to the Prophet:

> The faith, to which you invite me, is very good. I am a famous orator and poet. The Arabs highly respect me and I am well-known among them. If you include me in your government, I am prepared to follow you.

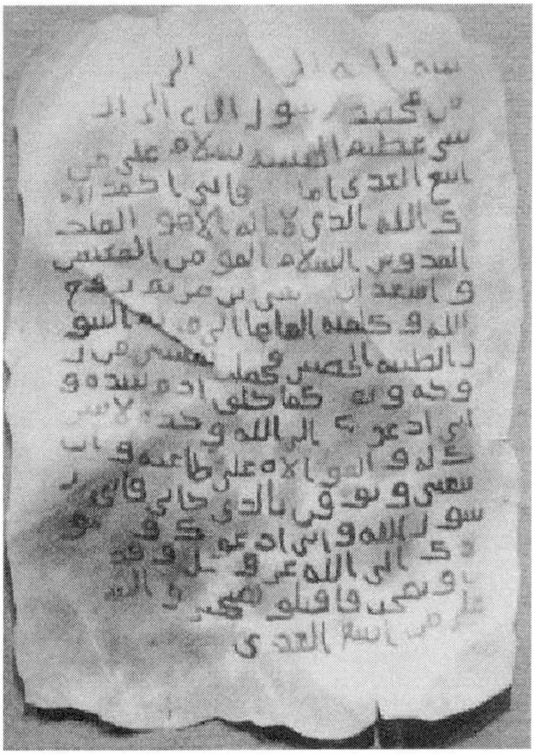

Letter of the Prophet to the Emperor of Abyssinia

Although the Prophet did not accept Hawdah's demands, saying that such matters were in the hands of Allah, he did make an ally, but one who unfortunately died shortly after.

It was the custom of the Prophet to contact world leaders, invite them to Islam or, in the event they opted to maintain their current creed, ask them to enter into an alliance. Having had diplomatic communications with the King of Abyssinia in the past via the Companions he had sent there as refugees, the Prophet established official contact with the Negus after he secured for himself a position of authority in Medina. In his "Letter to the Negus," the Prophet dictated:

> In the Name of the Most Merciful and Beneficent God! From Muhammad, the Messenger of Allah, to Negus al-Asham, the King of Abyssinia: Peace! First of all, I praise Allah, the King, the Holy, the Peace, the Faithful, and the Watcher. I bear witness that Jesus, son of Mary, is the Spirit of Allah and His Word which He cast to Mary, the Virgin, the good, the pure, so that she conceived Jesus. God created Christ from His Spirit and His Breath as He created Adam by His Hand and His Breath. Now I call you to God, the Unique, without partner, and to His Obedience. Always submit to Him and follow me and believe in that which came to me, for I am the Messenger of Allah. Before this I have already sent to you my cousin Ja'far with a number of Muslims. Take care of them. Negus! Leave pride because I invite you and your court to Allah. Mind it that I have accomplished (my duty) and my admonitions. Now it is better for you to receive my advice. Peace upon those that follow true guidance. (qtd. Qureshi 34–35; see also Ibn Ishaq 657)

The Negus responded:

> From the Negus al-Asham ibn Abjar. Peace be upon you, O Prophet of Allah, and mercy and blessing from Allah beside Whom there is no god, who has guided me to Islam. I have received your letter in which you mention the matter of Jesus and by the Lord of heaven and earth there is not one scrap more than what you say. We know that with which you were sent to us and we have entertained your nephew and his companions. I testify that you are

Letter of the Prophet to al-Najashi,
Ruler of Abyssinia

> Allah's Messenger, true and confirming (those before you). I have given my fealty to you and to your nephew and I have surrendered myself through him to the Lord of the worlds. I have sent you my son Arha. I have control only over myself and if you wish me to come to you, O Messenger of Allah, I will do so. I bear witness that what you say is true. (Ibn Ishaq 657–658)

Since the Negus had honored his obligations, hosted Muslim refugees, and made peace with the Prophet, the Messenger of Allah viewed the Abyssinians as friends and allies. Understanding that the political and religious climate could change in the future, the Prophet gave his Companions the following command: "Leave the Abyssinians in peace, so long as they do not take the offensive" (Abu Dawud and Nisa'i). In other words, the Prophet was at peace with those who were at peace with him. However, anyone who expressed hostility towards him or who exhibited belligerent or combative behaviors would be subject to conquest.

In his "Letter to Heraclius," which was probably sent in 627 CE, the Prophet invited the Roman ruler to embrace Islam:

> In the Name of Allah, the Most Compassionate, the Most Merciful. From Muhammad, the Messenger of Allah, to Heraclius, the Emperor of the Romans. Peace be upon him who follows the straight path! I invite you to embrace Islam. If you embrace Islam, you will be secure. If you embrace Islam, Allah will give you a double reward. However, if you refuse to do so, the responsibility for misguiding an entire nation will be yours. 'O People of the Book! Come to common terms as between us and you: That we worship none but Allah; that we associate no partners with him; that we erect not, from among ourselves, Lords and patrons other than Allah.' If then they turn back, say ye: 'Bear witness that we (at least) are Muslims (bowing to Allah's Will)' (3:64). (qtd. Qureshi 37–38)

While initially inclined to embrace Islam, Heraclius was pressured by his ecclesiastic advisors to reject Muhammad's invitation. Rather than opt for peace, he prepared his troops, mobilizing them near Damascus. After conquering the cities of Lakhm and Judham, he intended to invade Medina. When the Prophet reached Tabuk, he sent the following message to Heraclius (r. 610–641 CE):

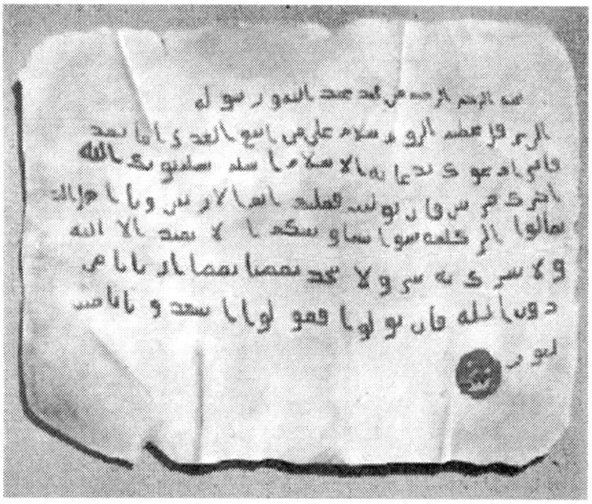

Letter of the Prophet to Heraclius

> From Muhammad, the Messenger of Allah, to the Byzantine Emperor. I invite you to embrace Islam. If you do, you will enjoy the same rights as Muslims and will have the same obligations as them, but if you refuse, you will have to pay *jizyah*. Allah, glorified and exalted be He, says: 'Fight those who believe not in Allah nor the Last Day, nor hold that forbidden which hath been forbidden by Allah and His Messenger, nor acknowledge the religion of Truth, (even if they are) of the People of the Book, until they pay the *jizyah* with willing submission, and feel themselves subdued.' (qtd. Bahnasawy 13–14)

The *jizyah*, it should be stressed from the onset, is a "collective military tax paid by tribes who did not have to share in the Muslims' military engagements, but in exchange for which the Muslim authority was to ensure their defense, their protection, and their survival, if necessary" (Ramadan 189). While for some modern thinkers this treatment amounted to second-class citizenship, "it was very advanced" (Esposito 71). As John L. Esposito (b. 1940 CE) stresses, "No such tolerance existed in Christendom, where Jews, Muslims, and other Christians . . . were subjected to forced conversion, persecution, or expulsion" (71). In fact, "[o]ver the centuries it was generally better to be a Christian or a Jew in an Islamic society than a Jew or Muslim in a Christian society" (Armour 29). While the Prophet's demand of conversion or taxation may seem startling to modern minds, it was, in reality, quite revolutionary. Rather than make peace with the Prophet and conclude a treaty, Heraclius assumed an aggressive attitude towards the Prophet. While the Messenger of Allah had promised to protect the People of the Book, Heraclius took the opposite attitude a couple of years later. In fact, "[i]n AD 632, on the very eve of the Arab invasion, the emperor Heraclius had ordered the baptism of all Jews within the Byzantine Empire" (Armour 27). As a result, "Jewish sympathies would hardly have been with the Byzantines" (27). By rejecting the Prophet's offer, and attempting to impose Christianity by force, Heraclius sealed his fate as Jews and persecuted Christian groups sided with the Muslim armies who had promised to protect their rights. As Steven Fine opines, "[m]any Jews saw the Islamic invaders as nothing less than harbingers of the Messiah, rescuing them from 'the Evil Empire' made up of Bible-reading, deeply supersessionist Christian 'pagans'" (103).

In his "Letter to the Ruler of Alexandria and Egypt," which was delivered by Hatib ibn Abu Balta'a al-Khami, and which is preserved in a library in Egypt, the Messenger of Allah sent a similar message:

> In the Name of Allah, the Most Compassionate, the Most Merciful. From Muhammad, the Servant and Messenger of Allah, to Muqawqis, the Coptic King. Peace be upon the follower of righteous guidance! I invite you to embrace Islam. If you embrace Islam, you will be at peace with Allah, and He will grant you a double reward. If, however, you do not embrace Islam, you will be held responsible for the suffering of the Coptic Christians. 'O People of the Book! Come to common terms as between us and you: That we worship none but Allah; that we associate no partners with him; that we erect not, from among ourselves, Lords and patrons other than Allah.' If then they turn back, say ye: 'Bear witness that we (at least) are Muslims (bowing to Allah's Will)' (3:64). (qtd. Qureshi 39)

Muqawqis had the Prophet's letter placed in an ivory casket and asked his scribe the send the following response to Muhammad:

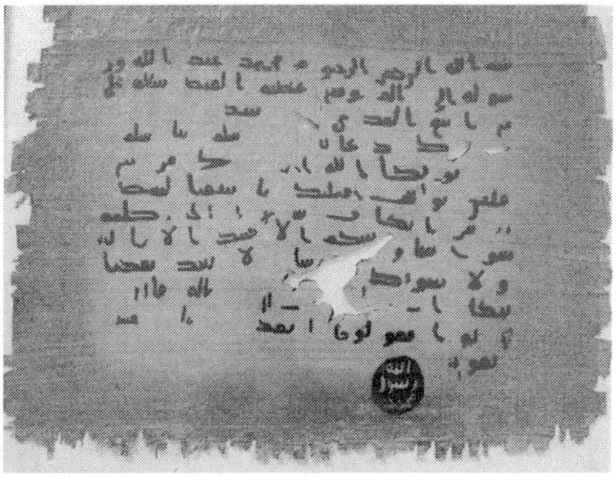

Letter of the Prophet to Muqawqis, Ruler of Egypt

> In the Name of Allah, the Most Compassionate, the Most Merciful. From Muqawqis to Muhammad ibn 'Abd Allah. Peace be upon you! I have read your letter and understood its contents and what you are calling for. I already know that the coming of a Prophet is still due, but I used to believe that he would be born in Syria. I am sending you as presents two maids, who come from noble Coptic families; clothing and a steed for riding upon. Peace be upon you. (qtd. Qureishi 40)

Not all leaders had the tact of Muqawqis, as can be seen with the case of Chosroes. In his "Letter to Chosroes," the Prophet dictated,

> In the Name of Allah, the Most Compassionate, the Most Merciful. From Muhammad, the Messenger of Allah, to Chosroes, the King of Persia. Peace be upon him who follows true guidance! Believe in Allah and His Messenger and testify that there is no god but Allah, the One, without associate, and that Muhammad is his Servant and His Messenger. I invite you to accept the religion of Allah. I am the Messenger of Allah sent to all people in order that I may place the fear of Allah in every living person, and that the charge may be proved against those who reject the Truth. Accept Islam for your salvation. Otherwise, you will be held responsible for the sins of the Magians. (Dar Rah Haqq 134)

The Prophet's letter, which was directed to Chosroes, so infuriated the new Persian Emperor that he tore it to pieces. He was incensed that the Prophet addressed him on equal terms: "From

Muhammad ibn 'Abd Allah to Chosroes, the Emperor of Persia." When word reached him of the Emperor's reaction, the Prophet said, "Even so, O Lord, tear from him his kingdom." As historians will acknowledge, it came to pass that the Muslims conquered Persia within ten short years. Since both the Egyptian, Roman, and Persian leaders expressed anger and hostility towards the Prophet, they were considered enemy powers that would be dealt with at some future point in time after the Muslims had grown and greatly expanded their forces. In the meantime, the Prophet focused on expanding his sphere of influence in the Arabian Peninsula.

In his "Letter to the King of Bahrayn," the Messenger of Allah invited the Persian inhabitants of the island nation to embrace Islam. If they did so sincerely, and performed their religious obligations, they would maintain all the property rights they had upon converting to the Muslim faith. In order to support the Islamic State, they would be required to provide a portion of their date and grain crops to the government. The only additional claim the Prophet made was with regard to the Temple of Fire. He determined that when the people embraced Islam, the edifice would be turned over to the Islamic State for demolition or conversion into a place of prayers for the Muslims. If the people of Bahrayn opted to remain Magians, they were perfectly entitled to do so, on the condition that they paid the *jizyah* or *per capita* tax as a sign of submission to Islamic rule. The conditions put forth by the Prophet were as follows:

> Salutations! If you keep up prayer and give *zakat*, and show sincerity towards Allah and His Apostle, and give *ushr* on dates and half *ushr* on grain, and will not convert your progeny into Magians, then you will remain owner of all those things which were in your possession at the time of embracing Islam. But Allah and His Messenger will have their right to the Temple of Fire. If you refuse, then you will have to pay *jizyah*. (qtd. Qureshi 35)

In response, Mundhir ibn Sawa, the ruler of Bahrayn, sent the following message to Prophet:

> Messenger of Allah! I received your injunctions. Prior to this, I read your letter, which you wrote to the People of Bahrayn extending them an invitation to Islam. Islam appealed to some of them and they entered into the fold of Islam while others did not find it appealing. In my country, there are Magians and Jews. Please inform me as to how they should be treated. (qtd. Qureshi 35)

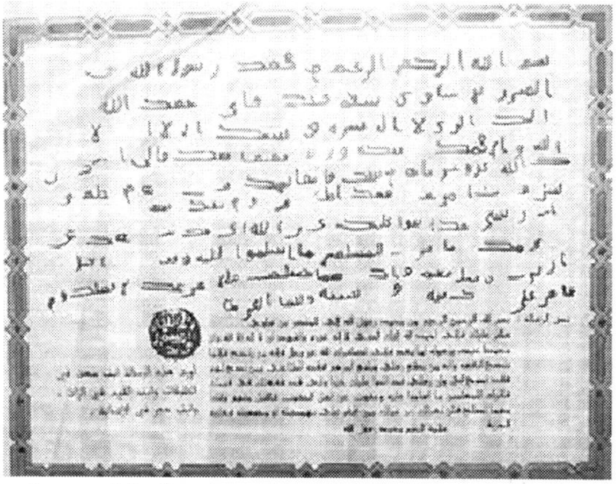

Letter of the Prophet to Mundhir ibn Sawa al-Tamimi

The Messenger of Allah forwarded the following response to the leader of Bahrayn:

> In the Name of Allah, the Most Compassionate, the Most Merciful. From Muhammad, the Messenger of Allah, to Mundhir ibn Sawa. Peace be upon you! I praise Allah, who has no partner, and bear witness that Muhammad is His Servant and Messenger. Thereafter, I remind you of Allah, the Mighty and Glorious. Whoever follows my messengers and acts in accordance with their guidance, he, in fact, accepts my advice. My messengers have highly praised your behavior. You shall continue in your present office. Give the new Muslims the full opportunity to preach their religion. I accept your recommendation regarding the people of Bahrayn, and I pardon the offenses of the offenders. Therefore, you should also forgive them. If any of the people of Bahrayn wish to maintain their Jewish or Magian faith, they should be made to pay the *jizyah* [poll-tax]. (qtd. Qureshi 35)

In his follow-up letter, the Prophet informed the leader of Bahrayn that so long as he continued to act with integrity, he would not be deposed. In other words, those who embrace Islam have nothing to fear and nothing to lose. He also provided assurances to the People of the Book, saying that

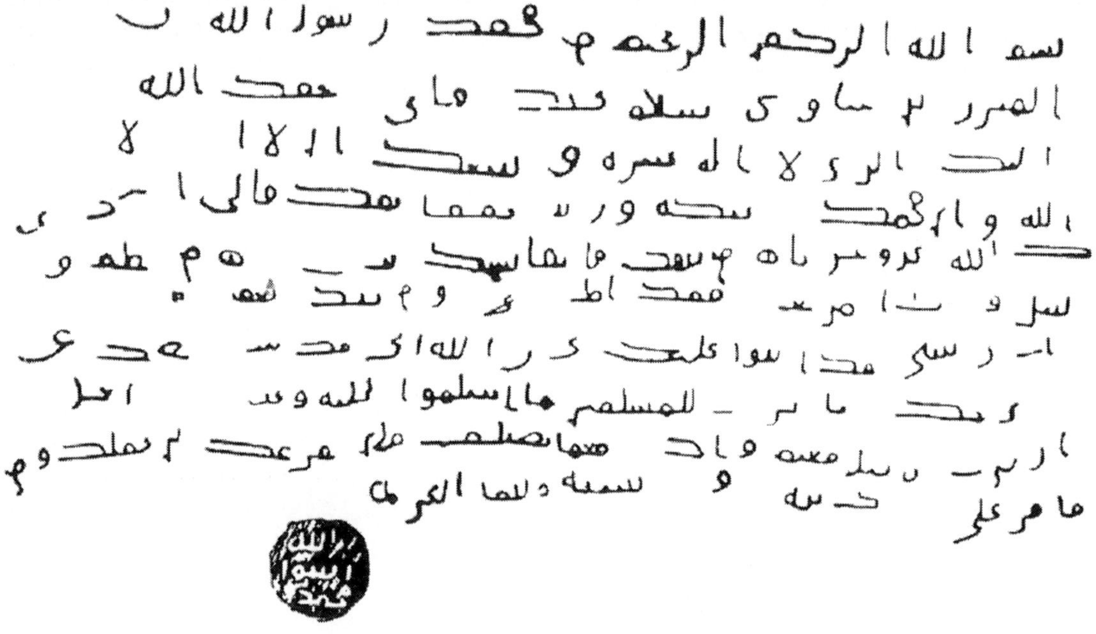

Letter of the Prophet to Mundhir ibn Sawa, Governor of Bahrayn

those who did not leave the Magian religion or Judaism would be levied the *jizyah* [*per capita* tax]. In other words, those who embraced Islam would be subjected to the obligatory religious contributions known as *zakat* [2.5% tax on livestock and agriculture] and *khums* [20% of one's yearly profit after expenses] while the non-Muslims would be required to pay the *per capita* tax in exchange for not participating in Muslim military service. The people of Bahrayn submitted, some embracing Islam, and other maintaining their ancestral religions. Abu Hurayrah (603–681 CE), the Companion of the Prophet, was sent to the island to collect the taxes in question (36).

In his "Letter to the Kings of Oman," which was written by Ubbay b. Ka'b, and delivered by 'Amr ibn al-'As (d. 664 CE), the Prophet Muhammad made the following offer to the rulers of this kingdom in the southeastern Arabian Peninsula:

> In the Name of Allah, the Most Compassionate, the Most Merciful. From Muhammad, the Messenger of Allah, to both the sons of Julunda: Junayfir and 'Abd. Peace be upon the follower of the straight path. I invite both of you to embrace Islam. If you both embrace Islam you will live in peace. I have been sent as the Messenger of Allah to all of humankind so that I may frighten them from opposing Allah and impose the Rule of Allah upon the infidels. If you both embrace Islam, you will remain the rulers of your country. Otherwise, you will lose your kingship. My horsemen will enter your lands and my prophethood will dominate over your kingdom. (36)

After much debate and discussion, the two ruling brothers embraced Islam, supported the Prophet, and played an important role in the spread of the Muslim faith.

If individual nation-states entered into treaties and covenants with the Islamic State, they were embraced as brothers and sisters in a mutually-beneficial union which provided for economic prosperity, socio-religious solidarity, and military protection. If tribes, nations or empires eschewed the Prophet's advances, reacting with anger or hostility in response to his friendly advances, Muhammad adjusted his foreign policy. Such enemy forces would be tolerated so long as they did not infringe upon Islamic lands or persecute Muslim populations. If they engaged in bellicose action against Islamic interests, the Prophet would declare a *jihad* against them. Such was the case with the Ghassanids.

According to Goddard, "the Banu Ghassan . . . was among several tribes that possibly accepted Christianity in the fourth century, and in the 6th century the Ghassanids acquired a position of political dominance in the region as a result of the designation of their leader Harith ibn Jabala by the Byzantines as 'phylarch' or tribal leader" (15). Vassals of the Byzantines, the Bani Ghassan chief, Mundhir ibn Harith, had been granted the title of

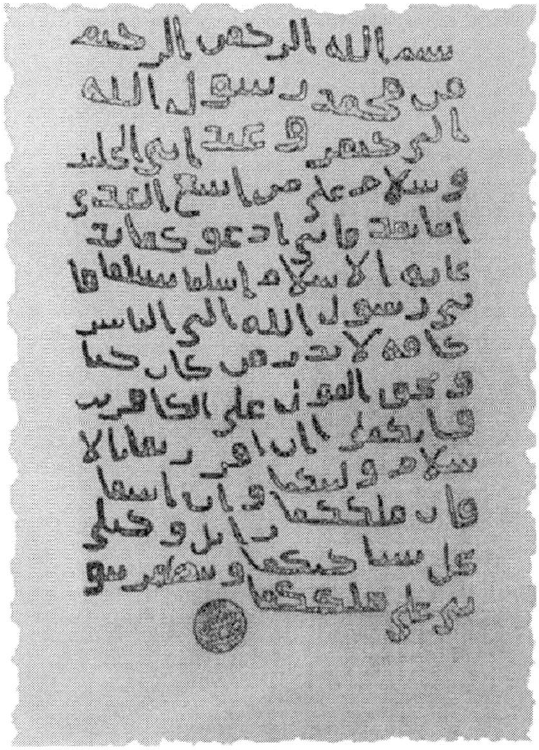

Letter of the Prophet to the Rulers of Oman

"King of the Arabs" by Emperor Heraclius (Shoup 12). As Christians, "[t]he Ghassanid kings were great supporters of the Monophysite Jacobite Church" (Rogerson 82). In fact,

> They had established a whole chain of monasteries and hermitages the length for the Red Sea coast and were well established in the Yemen. Najran, Dhufar, Aden, San'a, Socotra and Marib are all confirmed Christian sites within pre-Islamic Arabia. The story about the Christian hermits of Bostra—Bahira and Nestor—recognizing Muhammad as a prophet almost certainly involved the Jacobite Church in Arabia. They also had a useful patron in the Abyssinian Negus who supported their activities. (Rogerson 82–83)

Around the year 628 CE, the Prophet Muhammad reached out to al-Harith, the ruler of Ghassanids, asking him to reconsider his alliance with the Byzantines and to side with the Islamic State. The "Letter to the Ruler of Ghassan," which was carried by Mubarak Shuja' ibn Wahab al-Asadi, reads as follows:

> In the Name of Allah, the Most Compassionate, the Most Merciful. From Muhammad, the Messenger of Allah, to Harith ibn Abi Shimr. Peace be upon the one who follows the straight path, believes in Allah, and testifies to it. I invite you to believe in Allah, who is Unique and without partners. If you do so, your country will remain yours. (qtd. Qureshi 41) [see illustration next page]

After the letter was read to al-Harith ibn Abi Shimr, the ruler of Damascus became so infuriated that he asked: "Who dares dispossess me of my country? I will fight him." Since Harith opted to oppose Islam, the Prophet sent his forces to conquer the region of Ghassan. Over time, there were other political entities that switched sides when they realized the military might of the Prophet. Such was the case with the Prince of Dumat al-Jandal.

The city of Dumat al-Jandal, modern al-Jawf, which is located five hundred miles from Medina, and some seven days by caravan south of Damascus, had initially antagonized the Muslims by stopping traffic to Medina and threatening to invade the City of the Prophet. Located at the southern end of the Wadi Sirhan, Duma was "an important route connecting northern Arabia and southern Syria" (Hoyland, 2001: 68). Inasmuch as the city was a major intersection of trade routes from Mesopotamia, Syria, and the Arabian Peninsula, the Prophet was compelled to protect the economic interests of the Islamic community.

The Messenger of Allah reacted swiftly, sending seven hundred men under the command of 'Abd

Letter of the Prophet to the Ruler of the Ghassanids

al-Rahman ibn 'Awf to confront the marauders. The Prophet exhorted his commander to "Fight everyone in the way of Allah [who attacked you or betrayed you] and kill those who disbelieve in Allah" (672). "Do not be deceitful with the spoils; do not be treacherous; nor mutilate, nor kill children," he warned, "This is Allah's ordinance and the practice of his Prophet among you" (Ibn Ishaq 672).

Following Islamic practice, 'Abd al-Rahman called the people to Islam, granting them three days to submit in peace as Muslims or face a military assault. Al-Asbagh, the Christian leader of the Banu Kalb, embraced Islam, as did many of his followers. Those who opted to remain Christian where granted the right to do so on agreement to pay the *jizyah* on a regular basis. In order to consolidate the ties between both communities, al-Asbagh offered his daughter, Tamadhir, in marriage to 'Abd al-Rahman ibn 'Awf (d. 652 CE). Thus, the daughter of the Christian king returned with the Prophet's deputee to Medina.

Several years later, the successor of al-Asbagh instigated problems for the Prophet by harassing the caravans that came from the north. On that occasion, the Messenger of Allah sent Khalid ibn al-Walid (592–642 CE) to confront Ukaydir 'Abd al-Malik al-Kindi, the Christian prince of Dumat al-Jandal. During the course of fighting, Ukaydir's brother was killed, yet the prince himself was taken captive and brought back to the Prophet. Rather than kill him for breaching the treaty al-Asbagh had entered into, the Prophet spared his life on the following conditions. First, the prince was required to embrace Islam. Next, he was to make peace with the Muslims. And, third, he was to collect the tribute from Dumat, Tabuk, Aylah, and Tayma'. After doing so, the Prophet ransomed Ukaydir for two thousand camels, eight hundred sheep, four hundred coats of armor, and four hundred lances. Most importantly, the Prophet granted him a treaty. Known as the *Treaty of Dumat al-Jandal* or the *Treaty of Ukaydir*, the document reads:

> In the Name of Allah, the Most Compassionate, the Most Merciful. This is a treaty between Muhammad, the Messenger of Allah, and Ukaydir, who has embraced Islam, forsaking false gods and idols as well as the Pole of Duma. That portion of the ponds situated outside the population, barren lands and forests, uninhabited lands, coats of arms, armors, weapons, horses, camels, and small forts are for us. To you shall belong the walled palm groves as well as the running water in the cultivated lands. Your grazing animals will not be driven away from the pastures. The beasts which are more than the prescribed number will not be counted at the time of *zakat*. Your plants will not be prevented from growing. You will have you pay your *zakat* accordingly. In return, you will be assured of our good faith and scrupulous observance. You deserve our sincerity and the fulfillment of our promises. Allah and the present Muslims stand witness to it. (qtd. Qureshi 179)

This document, which appears in a slightly different version in the Faizer's English translation, is said to have been sealed with the thumb-print of the Messenger of Allah as he did not have his seal with him at the time (Waqidi 505). Obviously, the translation provided by Qureshi is poor. However, questions of content are more compelling than shortcomings in style and syntax. Why, for example, would the Prophet speak of forsaking false gods and idols when corresponding with a Christian leader? The false god in question may refer to Jesus, who is worshiped as God by most Christians, but whose divinity is denied in the Qur'an. The false idols may refer to statues of Jesus, Mary, and the Saints which, again, were superstitiously adored rather than venerated by some Christians, contradicting Church doctrine. How Christianized the Ghassanids were is also subject to question.

Many Christianized populations in Africa, the Americas, and elsewhere, practice hybrid religions, combining animism, paganism, and polytheism with Christianity; in its first centuries the Christian religion had to struggle against this very sort of paganization in the Greco-Roman world. Was Jesus just another deity added to the pantheon of the pagan Arabs? After all, images of Jesus and Mary were included among the idols of the Ka'bah. It is equally possible that the Ghassanids were Christians who ruled a population consisting predominantly of pagans. Hence, by introducing Islam, the Prophet was not only commanding the polytheists among his people to forsake their false gods, but helping purify Christianity from invasive pagan influences.

In any event, after the Prophet freed Ukaydir, "several treaties were concluded with other Christian governments" (Qureshi 288). Soon, though, and despite the generous terms of the treaty, Ukaydir broke his word and the covenant offered by Muhammad. Still, the Prophet continued his campaign of creating alliances with Christians throughout the Middle East. In the year 8 AH (630 CE), for example, the Prophet received a deputation from the Tribe of 'Abd al-Qays. The tribe, which was a branch of the Banu Rabi'ah, had settled in Bahrayn and included some Christians. A fourteen member delegation, headed by Jarud ibn 'Amr, who professed the Christian faith, visited the Prophet in that year specifically to submit to his sovereignty.

In approximately the same period, "the Prophet Muhammad established treaties with the Christian and Jewish leaders of al-'Aqabah, Maqnah, Adhruh, and al-Jarbah in southern Jordan" (12). In his "Letter to the Jews," the Prophet wrote:

> In the Name of Allah, the Most Compassionate, the Most Merciful. This is a letter from Muhammad, the Messenger of Allah, the brother of Musa ibn 'Imran [Moses the son of Amran], and his co-missionary. Allah has assigned to Muhammad the same mission He had assigned to Musa. I swear to you by Allah and by the sacred commands descended upon Moses on Mount Sinai: Have you found in your Holy Book predictions of my prophetic mission to the Jewish community as well as to all other peoples? If you have found this, then fear Allah and convert to Islam. If you have not found such a divine prediction, then you will be excused. (qtd. Dar Rah Haqq 137–138)

In the *Treaty of Maqnah*, which was made between Muhammad and the Jews of the Banu Janbah, Banu Habibah or Banu Haninah, in the year 9 AH, the Prophet made the following agreement with the Jewish inhabitants of the port city on the Gulf of 'Aqabah:

> In the Name of Allah, the Most Compassionate, the Most Merciful. From Muhammad, the Messenger of Allah, to Bani Habibah and the people of Maqnah. You may be in peace. I have come to know that you people are going back to your village. When this letter of mine comes to you, you are in security. You have the protection of God and the protection of His Messenger. The Messenger of Allah pardons you for your evil deeds and all your faults. Towards you is no wrong and no enmity. After today you will not be subjected to oppression or violence. And the Messenger of Allah will save you from all things from which he saves himself. Besides the things exempted by the Messenger of Allah or his representatives, your woven clothes, slaves, horses, and the coats of armor are for the Messenger of Allah as is one fourth of the products from your oases, the fish caught by your boats, and whatever is spun by your wives. The rest is yours. Furthermore, the Messenger of Allah has exempted you from *jizyah* and compulsory labor. If you hear and you obey it will be incumbent upon the Messenger of Allah to honor the honorable men among you and to pardon the wrong-doer. Whoever the Banu Habibah and the People of Maqnah elect as a ruler, he will be respected as such. Whoever harms a Muslim will have to face the same. Nobody will rule over you but a person from among yourselves or a member of the Household of the Prophet. (qtd. Qureshi 182)

A superior, slightly divergent, version of the treaty in question has been provided by Moshe Gil in his *History of Palestine*. It reads:

To the sons of Haninah, who are Jews of Maqnah, and the people of Maqnah, near Aylah. Your request has reached me [which was sent] when you returned to your village. With the arrival of this letter your security is ensured and you are granted Allah's protection and that of His Messenger; Allah's Messenger forgives you the wickedness you have done and for all the sins you have committed. Therefore you are granted Allah's protection and that of His Messenger; no one will do you injustice or harm, for it is the Messenger of Allah himself who gives you protection from what he himself will not do to you. Your arms belong to the Messenger of Allah; as well as all the slaves that are with you, and the rings, apart from what the Messenger of Allah, or the envoy o the Messenger of Allah, will allow you to keep. And from onwards you will owe a quarter of your date harvest and a quarter of your fishing yield, and a quarter of the yarn spun by your women. Except for these you will be free of any levy or impressments. If you will listen and obey, the Messenger of Allah will respect the honorable amongst you and forgive the sinners amongst you. And for the information of the believers and the Muslims: anyone coming to the people of Maqnah who is concerned with their well-being will benefit; and anyone who intends doing them harm will suffer. There will be no chief over you other than one of you or one of the Messenger of Allah's people. And peace. (29)

In his "Letter to the People of Adhruh," the Prophet made the following assurances:

In the Name of Allah, the Most Compassionate, the Most Merciful. From Muhammad the Prophet and [Messenger of Allah] to the people of Adhruh. They [will live] securely by virtue of the letter of security from God and from Muhammad. They are due to pay 100 dinars, good and weighed, on every Rajab. And if one [of them] flees from the Muslims, out of fear and awe—for they feared the Muslims—they shall live securely until Muhammad will visit them before he leaves. (qtd. Moshe 30; see also Waqidi 505)

In his "Letter to Yuhanna ibn Ru'bah," who ruled over the region of 'Aqabah on the Red Sea, the Prophet dictated:

To Yuhanna bin Ru'bah and the worthies of Aylah. Peace be with you! Praise be Allah, there is no God save Him. I have no intention of fighting you before writing to you. Thou hast to accept Islam, or pay the tax, and obey God and his Messenger and the messengers of His Messenger, and do them honor and dress them in fine clothing, not in the raiment of raiders; therefore clothe Zayd in fine robes, for if you satisfy my envoys, you will satisfy me. Surely the tax is known to you. Therefore if you wish to be secure on land and on sea, obey God and his Messenger and you will be free of all payments that you owed the Arab [tribes] or non-Arabs, apart from the payment to God [which is] the payment of his Messenger. But be careful lest thou do not satisfy them, for then I shall not accept anything from you, but I shall fight you and take the young as captives and slay the elderly. For I am the true Messenger of Allah; put ye your trust in Allah and His Books and His Messengers and in the Messiah, son of Maryam, for this is Allah's Word and I too, put my trust in him, for he is the Messenger of Allah. Come then, before a calamity befalls you. As for me, I have already given my envoys instructions with regard to you: give Harmal three *wasqs* of barley, for Harmal is your well-wisher, for if it were not for Allah and if it were not for this, I would not be sending you messengers, but rather you would be seeing the army. [A *wasq* equals sixty *saa'*, a *saa'* is four *mudds*, and a *mudd* is what an averabge m an can scoop up iwth two hands.] Therefore if you honor my messengers, you will have the protection of Allah and of Muhammad and all that stand at his side. My messengers are Shurahbil and Ubayy and Harmala and Hurayth b. Zayd who is one of the sons of the Banu Tayy'. All that they decide with regard to you shall be according to my wishes, and you will have the protection of Allah and of Muhammad the Messenger of Allah. And peace will be with you if you obey me. And the people of Maqnah thou shall lead back to their land. (Moshe 28–30)

Not only did Yuhannah b. Ru'bah respond, he came in person to Medina to meet with the Prophet. The Messenger of Allah treated him as a guest, engaged in deliberations, provided him with a cloak, and concluded the following accord known as the *Treaty of Aylah.*

In the Name of Allah, the Most Compassionate, the Most Merciful. This is a writ of protection from Allah and Muhammad, the Prophet and the Messenger of Allah, in favor of Yuhannah b. Ru'bah and the people of Aylah for their ships and their caravans by land and sea. They and all that are with them, men of Syria and Yemen, all seamen, all have the protection of Allah and the protection of Muhammad, the Prophet, Should any one of them break the treaty by introducing some new factor then his wealth shall not save him; it is the fair prize of him who takes it. It is not permitted that they shall be restrained from going down to their wells or using their roads by land or sea. (qtd. Qureshi 180; qtd. Peters 241)

As the inhabitants of the region were a Christian people, they were taxed one dinar per adult as *jizyah*. They also committed to providing room and board to any Muslim forces that were passing through the region (Qureshi 117–18). The people of Tabalah also opted for the same approach. In exchange for embracing Islam, the Prophet agreed to maintain their status quo. In return, they were required to collect one dinar per person from community members who remained People of the Book and provide Muslim forces with supplies when required (184).

In the tenth year of the *hijrah*, the Christian kings of Himyar notified the Prophet Muhammad that they had rejected polytheism, opposed its adherents, and accepted Islam. The Messenger of Allah sent them the following letter:

Letter to the Kings of Himyar

In the Name of Allah, the Most Compassionate, the Most Merciful.

I praise Allah, the only God, unto you. Your messenger reached me on my return from the land of the Byzantines and he met us in Medina and conveyed your message and your news and informed us of your Islam and of your killing the polytheists [who waged war against Allah and His Messenger]. Allah has guided you with His guidance. If you do well and obey Allah and His Messenger and perform prayer, and pay alms, and Allah's fifth and the Messenger's share and selected part, and the poor tax which is incumbent on believers from land, namely a tithe of that watered by fountains and rain; of that watered by the bucket, a twentieth; for every forty camels, a milch camel; for every thirty camels, a young male camel; for every five camels, a sheep; for every ten camels, two sheep; for every forty cows, one cow; for every thirty cows, a bull calf or a cow calf; for every forty sheep at pasture, one sheep. This is what God has laid upon the believers. Anyone who does more it is to his merit. He who fulfills this and bears witness to his Islam and helps the believers against the polytheists he is a believer with a believer's rights and obligations and he has the guarantees of Allah and His Messenger. If a Jew or a Christian becomes a Muslim he is a believer with his rights and obligations. He who holds fast to his religion, Jew or Christian, is not to be turned [seduced] from it. He must pay the poll tax—for every adult, male or female, free or slave, one full dinar calculated on the evaluation of its values or its equivalent in clothes. He who pays that to Allah's Messenger has the guarantee of Allah and His Messenger, and he who withholds it is the enemy of Allah and His Messenger.

The Messenger of Allah, Muhammad the Prophet, has sent to Zur'a Dhu Yazan: When my messenger Mu'adh ibn Jabal and 'Abd Allah ibn Zayd, and Malik ibn Ubadah, and 'Uqbah ibn Nimr, and Malik ibn Murra and their companions come to you I commend them to your good offices. Collect the alms and the poll-tax from your provinces and hand them over to my messengers. Their leader is Mu'adh ibn Jabal, and

let him not return unless satisfied. Muhammad witnesses that there is no God but Allah and that he is His Servant and Messenger.

Malik ibn Murra al-Rahawi has told me that you were the first of Himyar to accept Islam and have killed the polytheists, and I congratulate you and order you to treat Himyar well and not to be false and treacherous, for the Messenger of Allah is the friend both of your poor and your rich. The alms tax is not lawful to Muhammad or his Household; it is alms to be given to the poor Muslims and the wayfarer. Malik has brought the news and kept secret what is confidential, and I order you to treat him well. I have sent you some of the best of my people, religious and learned men, and I order you to treat them well, for they must be respected. Peace upon you and the mercy and blessings of Allah. (Ibn Ishaq 643–644)

As he bid farewell to Mu'adh ibn Jabal, who was known for his excessive fervor, the Messenger of Allah instructed him to "[m]ake things easy for them and do not put them into difficulty. Be lenient, not harsh; encourage, rather than repress. Talk to them pleasantly, and not in a manner that might repel them. Reconcile, and do not alienate" (Bukhari). "You are going to People of the Book," the Prophet continued:

> First of all invite them to worship Allah [alone] and [acknowledge] that I am His Messenger. When they come to know Allah, then teach them that Allah has enjoined on them five prayers every day and night, and if they start offering these prayers, then tell them that Allah has made it an obligation for them to pay the *zakat* from their property. It is to be taken from the wealthy among them and given to the poor among them. And if they obey you in that, then be cautious! Do not take their best properties [as *zakat*] and be afraid of the curse of an oppressed person as there is no veil between his prayer and Allah. (Bukhari)

Concluding his description of the best manner in which to disseminate Islam, the Prophet added: "Make your character good for the people, Mu'adh ibn Jabal" (Malik). Clearly, Islam should be introduced in stages and taught by example.

In the year 10 AH, a delegation from the Yemen presented itself to the Prophet Muhammad in order to submit to Islam. The delegation of fifteen to twenty men was led by Surad ibn 'Abd Allah, whom the Prophet recognized as the ruler of the clan. As an ally of the Prophet, Surad was vulnerable to attacks from the enemies of Islam and, in consequence, would have to defend the territorial integrity of the Islamic State. Surad ibn 'Abd Allah set forth towards the fortified city of Jurash where members of the Khatham tribe had also sought refuge from the advancing Muslim forces. Despite a month-long siege, the inhabitants refused to open the gates to the city. Surad decided to change his strategy and feigned a withdrawal. In truth, Surad simply retreated to the surrounding hills to lay ambush to the people of Jurash. The non-Muslims fell into the trap and suffered heavy casualties. Although the belligerents had attacked Muslims without provocation, and despite the fact that they had refused the peace settlement, the Companions of the Prophet only killed those combatants who took up arms against them. As for the rest of the population, they were levied one dinar per person per year as *jizyah* along with a commitment to care for Muslim travelers crossing the region (Qureshi 175). This sum, which is repeated in numerous letters, treaties, and covenants, is also confirmed in another document attributed to the Prophet which was in the possession of Imam Muhammad al-Baqir (676–733 CE). Containing instructions on *sadaqah* or charity, the document concludes with the words: "Whoever is Jewish or Christian and refuses to convert from it, one dinar from every adult male or the equivalent in clothes" (Waqidi 531).

The year 10 AH also saw the complete submission of the Christians of Najran in southern Arabia. As a result of the submission of the Banu al-Harith, the Messenger of Allah made the following covenant with them:

Letter to 'Amr ibn Hazm of the Banu al-Harith

In the Name of Allah, the Most Compassionate, the Most Merciful.

This is a clear announcement from Allah and His Messenger. O you who believe, be faithful to your agreements [5:1].

The instructions of Muhammad, the Prophet, the Messenger of Allah to 'Amr ibn Hazm, when he sent him to the Yemen. He orders him to observe piety to Allah in all of his doings for Allah is with those who are pious and who do well; and he commanded him to behave with truth as Allah commanded him; and that he should give people the good news and command them to follow it and to teach men the Qur'an and instruct them in it and to forbid men to do wrong so that none but the pure should touch the Qur'an and should instruct men in their privileges and obligations and be lenient on them when they behave aright and severe on injustice, for Allah hates injustice and has forbidden it. 'The curse of Allah is on the evil-doers' [7:44]. Give men the good news of paradise and the way to earn it, and warn them of hell and the way to earn it, and make friends with men so that they may be instructed in religion, and teach men the times of the *hajj*, its customs and its obligations and what Allah has ordered about it: the greater *hajj* is the greater *hajj* and the lesser *hajj* is the *'umra*; and prohibit men from praying in one small garment unless it be a garment whose ends are double over their shoulders, and forbid men from squatting in one garment which exposes their person to the air, and forbid them to twist the hair of the head [if it is long] on the back of the neck; and if there is a quarrel between men forbid them to appeal to tribes and families, and let their appeal be to Allah; they who do not appeal to Allah but to tribes and families let them be smitten with the sword until their appeal is made to Allah; and command men to perform the ablutions, their faces, and their hands to the elbows and their feet to the ankles, and let them wipe their heads as Allah has ordered; and command prayer at the proper time with bowing, prostration, and humble reverence; prayer at daybreak, at noon when the sun declines, in the afternoon when the sun is descending, at even when the night approaches not delaying it until stars appear in the sky; later at the beginning of the night; order them to run to the mosque when they are summoned, and to wash when they go to them, and order them to take from the booty Allah's fifth and what alms are enjoined on the Muslims from land—a tithe of what the fountains water and the sky waters, and twentieth of what the bucket waters; and for every one camel, two sheep; and for every twenty camels, four sheep; for every forty cows, one cow; for every thirty cows, a bull or cow calf; for every forty sheep at grass, one sheep; this is that Allah has enjoined on the believers in the matter of alms. He who adds thereto is a merit to him. A Jew or a Christian who becomes a sincere Muslim of his own accord and obeys the religion of Islam is a believer with the same rights and obligations. If one of them hold fast to his religion must pay a golden dinar or its equivalent in clothes. He who performs this had the

guarantee of Allah and His Messenger; he who withholds it is the enemy of Allah and His Messenger and all believers. (Ibn Ishaq 647–648)

Despite the preponderance of passive, apolitical clerics, who oppose efforts to create Islamic states, who object to the establishment of Muslim rule, and who rail against the desire to implement Islamic law, "the Prophet, it needs emphasizing, had established the Islamic State in Madinah" (Bangash, "Following the Lead"). As Zafar Bangash (b. 1950 CE) observed, there are some scholars, like Shah Waliullah Dehlvi, from 18th-century India who suggested that the Prophet had created a state in Mecca, albeit with limited power. This obviously refers to the time before the *hijrah*, which is cause for controversy. "There is, however, no disagreement," affirms Bangash, "about the fact that the Prophet had established the Islamic State in Madinah which, less than ten years after its creation, dominated the entire Arabia Peninsula." As Bangash clearly comprehends, "in following the Sunnah, Muslims are obliged to live in the Islamic State or, if one does not exist, to strive to establish one." Muslims who do not accept the sovereignty of the *shari'ah*, preferring monarchy, despotic dictatorship or "democracy" in the lands of Islam, act in clear contradiction to the Qur'an and the Sunnah. Any Muslim scholar who opposes Islamic rule in Muslim lands calls his own orthodoxy into question. As the Nestorian monks who authored the *Chronicle of Séert* acknowledged, "Muhammad ibn 'Abd Allah was strong and powerful" (280 / 600). The strength of the Prophet was not simply spiritual; it was also political and military.

By embracing Islam or simply becoming allies with the Islamic State, leaders of tribes and nations were assured of their continued sovereignty. The Prophet was clearly no imperialist. He was more concerned with the spread of Islam than the colonization of neighboring kingdoms and empires. If anything, the conversion of numerous kingdoms to Islam was aimed at creating a "United States of Islam" or an "Islamic Union." The Prophet was divinely inspired to lay down the foundation of the Muslim *ummah*, the World Community of Muslims, in which regional rule was not only allowed but encouraged so long as solidarity towards Islam came first and foremost. Although many polytheists, Jews, and Christians did not honor their treaties, as was the case with the Banu Kuza'ah, Banu Mudlij, Banu Bakr, Banu Damrah, and Banu Sulaym, the rightly-guided Companions continued to follow the Prophet's precedent in their treatment with non-Muslims, be they the Christians and Jews of the Middle East, North Africa and Europe, or the Hindus and Buddhists of South-East Asia.

When, in 634 CE, the forces of 'Umar ibn al-Khattab (579–644 CE) spread into the Sinai, under the command of 'Amr ibn al-'As (d. 664 CE) "the conquerors displayed not the slightest interest in the conversion of the Christian monks" (Crone and Cook 120). In *Hagarism*, "a book written by infidels for infidels" (viii), authors Patricia Crone (b. 1945 CE) and Michael Cook (b. 1940 CE) argue that such behavior suggests that the Arabs were not "Muslims" in the sense we understand the term today (8). "Why, then, were the Muslim conquerors relatively benign?" asks Zachary Karabell (28). The answer is simple: "the Qur'an instructed Muslims to respect the People of the Book, and that is precisely what they did" (28). As Karabell explains, 'Amr ibn al-'As took advantage of the fact that the Coptic Christians were Monophysites, namely, that they believed that Christ was a single person with a single nature, in order to stress their similarity with Islam, which objected to the concept of Trinity (28). This would explain why Egypt fell quickly to an army of less than five thousand soldiers (28). According to Karabell,

> Later Arab chroniclers even claimed that the Coptic Church actively aided the Arabs and helped them defeat the Byzantine garrisons in the Delta, having been promised by 'Amr that their churches would be undisturbed and their tax burden manageable. For the Copts and their bishops, it was a tolerable trade-off. They knew they had to pay taxes to someone, and at least the Muslims would allow them to

practice their faith the way they wishes, free from the repressive, arrogant authority of Constantinople. (28)

This argument, however, is not completely convincing since the overwhelming majority of the Catholic population of the Iberian Peninsula eventually embraced Islam. While traditional Muslims view Trinitarianists as somehow falling short of strict monotheism, they do not consider them polytheists. Nowadays, it would be absurd to obstinately place Unitarianism and Trinitarianism at the center of discussion and argue that the acceptance of one and the rejection of the other were a question of "life or death." More specifically, it would be absurd, in our days, to debate whether Christians are monotheists beyond the fact that they theoretically accept that there are "three in one" and "one in three." God is, and has always been, one for Christians. In fact, Catholic theologians have always insisted that God is one and that His Nature is a mystery that we will never comprehend.

If, in our day and age, Muslims insisted that Christians must reject Trinitarianism in order to be able to sit down with them to talk about ways of creating a more just society than the one imposed by blood and fire by capitalism and communism, the followers of Muhammad would find themselves in an illogical position. As a Muslim leader said to a Catholic leader at the end of the 1970s: "Let us work together to create a more just society and let us leave discussions such as Unitarianism and Trinitarianism to our scholars to talk about in private." This is exactly one of the characteristics of the covenants of the Prophet of Islam with the Christian community. And it is precisely for this reason that Christians accepted these covenants. Consequently, when one speaks about or debates such topics, one must always position oneself correctly. One must always keep the most important things in view, in order to counter those who do not seek to establish a logical and natural understanding between Christians and Muslims, but instead stir up discord and bloody conflict under the Machiavellian slogan of "divide and you will rule," a strategy that has been applied in the most atrocious ways. So, setting aside the mystery of the Trinity, the main sticking point between Muslims and Catholics is the belief in the divinity of Christ; in this regard, the differences between Christian denominations dissipate. And while the Qur'an strictly forbids Muslims to attribute divinity to Jesus, this being the worst of sins, the sin of *shirk*, it is clear that Muhammad, since he must have known that the vast majority of Christians considered Jesus "the only-begotten Son of God," was much more tolerant of the divinization of Jesus by the Christians themselves, in line with the Qur'anic verses: "And do not dispute with the followers of the Book . . . and say: 'We believe in that which has been revealed to us and revealed to you, and our God and your God is One'" (29:46); and "So vie with one another in good works. Unto Allah ye will all return, and He will then inform you of that wherein ye differ" (5:48). If the Prophet Muhammad had attacked Christians on every point where Christianity differed from Islam, or involved himself in Christian sectarian disputes, no matter how significant these were in terms of Christianity itself, he could never have built a unified empire. Such toleration was not just based on political expediency, however, though it definitely included that. It was also undoubtedly founded on the recognition that theological matters that went beyond the most fundamental tenets of monotheism—the existence of One God, the impossibility of identifying this God with any object in creation since any such identification would constitute idolatry, and so forth—were best discussed among scholars, theologians and esoterics, in line with the wise and balanced Islamic separation between the Outer and the Inner, between that which must be accepted by all Muslims and that which will necessarily be understood only by the few.

Jonathan Swift in *Gulliver's Travels* wrote about the dispute between the Big-Endians and the Little-Endians, who went to war over whether a soft-boiled egg was to be cracked at the big or little end; it was his way of satirizing theological disputes. But such theological questions as whether the Jinn can act as intermediaries between human beings and Allah, or whether Allah has "daughters," or whether the Qur'an could have come to anyone but just "happened" to descend upon Muhammad, were crucial issues that had to be settled if Islam was to take hold, though most of such issues were settled by the Qur'an itself. They were not just questions of style or personal preference falsely inflated to the theological level; they had everything to do with whether one would inherit the Garden or the Fire. Likewise many (though not all) of the disputes between Christian sects were and are of real spiritual import. However, as I have pointed out, Muhammad's practice of allowing great latitude among the Peoples of the Book as long as they agreed on the most basic principles of monotheism: the existence of One God, the impossibility of identifying this God with any object in creation since any such identification would constitute idolatry, and so forth. If he had become embroiled in Christian sectarianism, his work to build a unified *ummah* would have been compromised. But when it came to the Muslims themselves, he and the Qur'an were much stricter.

The question as to why the Christians of Egypt and surrounding regions sided with the Muslims has not been satisfactorily answered. What is clear, however, is that "[t]he Muslims, with their mild tax, were generally welcomed as liberators, not conquerors" (Nafziger and Walton 33). "The God of vengeance," wrote Michael the Syrian, a Patriarch of the non-Chalcedonian Syrian Church, "seeing the evilness of the Romans [= Byzantines] led the sons of Ishmael from the region of the south to deliver us from Roman hands" (Binns, qtd. 172). According to William Ainser Wigram, "the coming of the Arabs must have been a relief" for the Assyrian Christians (Wigram, *The Assyrians* 33). As for the Christians of Persia, "the advent of the Islamic army was universally regarded as the hope of salvation from the tyrannical rule of Paganism" (Emhardt and Lamsa 75). Many scholars have attempted to explain the reasons why the Monophysite and Judeo-Christians sided with the Muslims. For some, it was a natural socio-political and economic response to the oppression of the Byzantines. For others, it was due to their religious opposition to the Catholic Church. For Claude Cahen (1909–1991), there may have been a different reason altogether. As he explains:

> Islam, it is well known, recognizes the message of God to the Jews and Christians as authentic despite the fact that it was incomplete and subsequently corrupted. In the East, there probably existed a reciprocal mentality that led many minds to admit the existence of an inferior, but authentic, revelation destined to those who had not been reached by Christianity. More explicitly, it is known that certain sects professed the continued coming of prophets, even after Jesus. (57)

Rather than proving that they did not really identify themselves as "Muslims," the actions of the early Arabs conquerors undeniably confirm that they were Qur'anically-conscious, *bona fide*, believing, Muslims. As Richard Fletcher writes,

> In the written traditions of Islam . . . there is an embedded cordiality towards Christianity. In practice, of course, this was not always observed. Patriarch Sophronius lamented the destruction of churches and monasteries which occurred during the Muslim invasion of Palestine. Such things happen in wartime. But the record of such capitulation treaties as survive shows that the leadership sought to observe Koranic precept. (20–21)

As John F. Esposito (b. 1940 CE) expounds,

> When Muslims conquered Byzantium, they were welcomed by some Christian sects and groups, who were persecuted as 'heretics' by 'official' Christianity, that is, Catholicism. Many Christians welcomed Muslim rule that gave them more freedom to practice their faith and imposed lighter taxes. Despite initial fears, the Muslim conquerors proved to be far more tolerant than imperial Christianity had been, granting religious freedom to indigenous Christian churches and Jews. (82)

"To the persecuted Monophysite Christians of Syria and Egypt," writes Richard Fletcher, "the Muslims could be presented as deliverers. The same could be said of the persecuted Jews of Spain" (16). When the Muslims entered Spain in 711 CE, at the request of the oppressed Jews who had come to them requesting liberation, "the

Arabs promised the local inhabitants that their homes and land would not be seized and that their religious customs would not be curtailed" (Karabell 66). As John L. Esposito explains, Muslim rule also "offered the Christian and Jewish populations seeking refuge from the class system of Europe the opportunity to become prosperous small landholders" (83).

When Salah al-Din al-Ayyubi (1138–1193 CE) took Jerusalem in 1187 CE, he mirrored the magnanimity of the Messenger of Allah: "He granted its people clemency and allowed freedom of movement to Christian pilgrims throughout his domain" (Hobbs 226). The historical literature is simply replete with evidence of Muslim military mercy. The *Decree of Jerusalem*, issued by Sultan Selim I (r. 1512–1520 CE) after his conquest of the Holy Land, provides an outstanding example of such tolerance (Qaturi). "In general," writes John Galey, "Muslims have a better record of religious tolerance than Christians, as is best proven by the fact that the monastery, a Christian enclave within Islamic territory, has an unbroken tradition" (13). The Monastery of Saint Catherine was protected by the Prophet as well as by the Caliphs and Sultans that followed him. In 1517 CE, when the Sinai fell under Ottoman control, Selim I issued a *firman* to Joachim, the Patriarch of Alexandria (c. 1448–1567 CE), safeguarding all patriarchal privileges, freedom of religion, and protection from persecution. According to al-Safsafi Ahmad al-Qaturi, "the decree of Selim I to the monks of Saint Catherine Monastery was preserved there until the Israeli occupation of Sinai." Apparently, its whereabouts are now unknown. Fortunately, I was able to locate a translation of Selim's Charter in the *History of the Growth and Decay of the Othman Empire* by Demetrius Cantemir (1673–1723 CE). While in Adrianapole, he was fortunate enough to read a Turkish translation of the original Arabic. I provide below the English version of Cantemir's Latin translation which was completed by N. Tindal (1687–1774), the Vicar of Great Waltham in Essex:

> Since the monks of Mount Sinai are come to our sublime Divan, and have humbly represented, that Muhammad el Mustapha (one whom be peace and health) being heretofore by their Monastery hospitably receiv'd in his travails, and according to their slender abilities ador'd with all kind of honour and reverence, graciously exempted this community of Nazaraean Monks from their annual tribute, and in confirmation of it was pleas'd to give an holy writing signed with his own hand, after his example we also out of our great clemency do ordain that the aforemention'd monks be free from the yearly tribute paid by the rest, and to suffer'd without molestation to enjoy their churches and rites according to their obsolete law. To this end, we have graciously order'd them an authentic copy of the Instrument of God's Holy Prophet, confirm'd by our Inscription. We therefore enjoin every person exercising dominion or jurisdiction throughout our whole kingdom, not to burthen the said monks of the tribe of Jesus with tribute or other political contributions. And whoever shall act contrary to our *Chatifsherif* and mandate, know that he shall be certainly punish'd and chastis'd. Given at Cairi, &c. (168–169)

From the time of Selim I to the end of the Ottoman Empire, it was protocol for each new sultan to instruct the pasha of Egypt to protect the monastery at Mount Sinai (Hobbs 160). As Brandie Ratliff writes, "Documents issued by the Islamic government in Cairo . . . reference the tradition of Islamic beneficence towards the monastery, and during the Ottoman period, the Pasha of Egypt renewed these protections yearly" (15). "Generally speaking," admits Tomadakis, "the Moslems respected the Monastery [of Mount Sinai]" (14). "This tolerance," he continues, "is attributed to the famous *Achtiname*, the 'Testament' of the Prophet Mohammed who protected the monks from many dangers and exempted them from heavy taxation" (14).

While it is true that the Arab Bedouins of the Sinai attacked the monastery on numerous occasions, Islam can hardly be held to blame. As Greffin Affagart (d. c. 1557 CE), the French pilgrim, observed in his *Relation de Terre Sainte* (1533–1534), the Bedouins claim to be Muslims; however, they do not observe Islamic law (186). He describes them as a detestable and tyrannical band of brigands that do not hesitate to raid caravans consisting of five or six thousand merchants, regardless of whether they were Turks, Moors, Jews or Christians (186). Although the Prophet and the Islamic rulers that followed him granted protection to the Monastery, the lawless Bedouins repeatedly attacked and robbed the monks, often forcing them to flee to Pharan or elsewhere (Champdor 33). The behavior of the Bedouin Arabs at the time was consistent with their description in the Qur'an:

> The desert Arabs say, 'We believe.' Say, 'Ye have no faith'; but ye (only) say, 'We have submitted our wills to Allah,' For not yet has Faith entered your hearts. But if ye obey Allah and His Messenger, He will not belittle aught of your deeds: for Allah is Oft-Forgiving, Most Merciful.' (49:14)

As for the sedentary Muslims of Egypt, Affagart, the French knight, is surprisingly indulgent. He describes them as truthful, trustworthy (186), and honest gentlemen (Affagart 188). As Mouton writes, the Bedouins of the Sinai "represent, more often as not, a category of Muslims who escape the control of both the monks and that of the Muslim authorities" (180). The Bedouins in question had a long history of pestering the monks in a multitude of ways (Mouton 181). Time and again, however, the various Islamic authorities of the day ruled in favor of the monks as opposed to the conflict-causing Bedouins (Mouton 179–181). Still, despite some discord, "the monks of St. Catherine's" have lived "in symbiosis with the Bedouins for more than 1,300 years" (Soskice 116).

Conclusions

With unfortunate exceptions, Muslim rule, in its multifarious forms, has almost always assured protection for members of minorities, a policy that did not always extend to all Islamic schools and sects. There were, of course, exceptions, such as the case of Yazid II (r. 720–724 CE) who persecuted Christians and destroyed their icons throughout the Caliphate (Irwin 23). However, these were despots who oppressed all of their subjects, Muslim or non-Muslim, regardless of their religion. Still, even when injustices were committed against Christians, they rarely lasted long and were soon rectified. For example, Walid ibn al-Malik (r. 705–715 CE), the Umayyad Caliph, confiscated a church from the Christians in order to expand a mosque. When his successor came to power, the Christians complained at the injustice committed by his predecessor. The new Caliph ordered that the church be returned to the Christians even if it entailed the destruction of the mosque (Haya 5). If this is how the Umayyads, the most wretched rulers of Islam behaved, one can only imagine the exalted treatment the Prophet (570–632 CE) and Imam 'Ali (r. 656–661 CE) reserved for their subjects.

When he appointed Muhammad ibn Abi Bakr (631–658 CE) as the Governor of Egypt, the First Imam and Fourth Caliph instructed him thus: "I recommend to you to be equitable to the [Christian] subjects, to do justice to an oppressed person, to be severe upon the oppressor, and to be indulgent towards the people as far as possible and to be kind to them" (qtd. Jordac 186). "Do not be unjust to the Muslims," Imam 'Ali instructed Ma'qal ibn Qays, "and do not oppress the [Christian] subjects" (qtd. Jordac 185). He also taught that "If you follow the path of truth, and the tenets of Islam become clear to you, neither Muslim nor [Christian] subject will be oppressed" (qtd. Jordac 185). In his testament to Malik al-Ashtar (d. 658 CE), the Governor of Egypt, Imam 'Ali wrote that "There are two kinds of persons among the subjects, out of whom some are your brethren-in-faith [i.e., Muslims] and others are creatures of God like you [i.e., Christians], and you should be forgiving towards them just as you wish God to be forgiving towards you" (qtd. Jordac 183). As George Jordac or Jurji Zaydan (1861–1914 CE) has eloquently expressed, "A Muslim is the brother of a Christian whether he likes it or not, because a man is the brother of a man whether he admits it or not" (184). As a result of his lofty qualities, "'Ali was loved very much for his justice by the knowledgeable Christians during his own time as well as afterward. All of them lauded and praised him. 'Allamah ibn Abu al-

Hadid writes thus in *Sharh Nahj al-balaghah*: 'What should I say about that man ['Ali] whom the [Christian] subjects loved ardently although they did not acknowledge the prophethood [of Muhammad]'" (186).

Still, despite their well-documented defects, the Umayyads were an example of "the inherent Islamic tolerance toward Christians" (Shboul 127). In fact, "[i]t had always been a point of honor among Arabs to treat their clients well, to come to their aid, or to avenge an injury done to them" (Armstrong, 2000: 31). Although the Imams after 'Ali were politically powerless, they still insisted on the implementation of true Islamic teachings. When detailing rights, obligations, and duties in Islam, Imam 'Ali Zayn al-'Abidin (d. 712 CE), wrote that "The right of the people under the protection [of Islam] (*dhimmah*) is that you accept from them what God has accepted from them and you do not wrong them as long as they fulfill God's covenant" (18).

Muslim political theorists like Ayatullah al-Uzma Muhammad Baqir al-Sadr (1935–1980 CE) (al-Rikabi 258) and Imam Ruhullah Khomeini (1902–1989 CE) (42) have all insisted on the fact that any Islamic system must guarantee the rights and liberties of all citizens, regardless of religion. Imam Khomeini even promised protection to Israeli Jews: "Jews are different from Zionists; if the Muslims overcome the Zionists, they will leave the Jews alone. They are a nation like other nations; their life continues on and they cannot be rejected by Muslims" (42). Inspired by the teachings of the Prophet, the Hizbullah in Lebanon called for constant dialogue between Muslims and Christians and called for the establishment of a non-confessional political system (Mamdani 172). It is both policy and practice to back Sunni and Christian candidates in order to broaden their appeal (172). Such an attitude requires an enormous amount of forbearance considering the atrocities that Lebanese Christians committed against Lebanese Muslims during the Civil War (1975–1990). The Phalange, a fascist movement composed of Maronite Christians, slit the throats of three hundred Muslims at road-blocks on Black Friday in 1975 and massacred Palestinians in the camp of Tel el-Za'tar a year later (Dalrymple 226). Acts of terrorism carried out by Muslims—or sometimes, if we are to believe various accounts of *agent provocateur* action, by persons posing as Muslims—as well as all sorts of planned attacks, usually thwarted at the last moment, are liberally reported by the Western media. What is not reported is the long history of European colonialism, and European and American neo-colonialism, both military and economic, under the relentless blows of which the Muslim world has been the loser, almost every time. Islam is ideologically violated and its holiest figure slandered on a daily basis, sometimes by the very people who pretend to value "diversity," "multiculturalism," and "religious pluralism." Yet it was under the rule of Islam, not Western liberal democracy—whether or not this form of government was imposed upon a particular unwilling population by force of arms—that the Muslims of the world enjoyed the fullest rights, protections, and liberties. Conversely, the periods of greatest intolerance have coincided with Western imperialist occupation both past and present.

Not all of them are alike; of the People of the Book are a portion that stand (for the right); they rehearse the Signs of Allah all night long, and they prostrate themselves in adoration.

They believe in Allah and the Last Day; they enjoin what is right, and forbid what is wrong; and they hasten (in emulation) in (all) good works; and they are in the ranks of the righteous.

Of the good they do, nothing will be rejected of them; for Allah knoweth well those that do right. (3:113–115)

Chapter 2

The Prophet Muhammad and the Monks of Mount Sinai

Introduction

The *Covenant of the Prophet Muhammad with the Monks of Mount Sinai* is a controversial and highly disputed document. While many Orientalists summarily dismiss it as spurious, the venerable Greek Orthodox Church and generations of Muslim scholars from all schools of law have insisted upon its authenticity. Despite its importance as a major milestone in Muslim-Christian relations, the *Covenant of the Prophet* is virtually unknown to most Muslims and has historically received greater circulation and recognition among Arabic, Latin, and English-speaking Christians. Is it true or false? Is it an invaluable authentic artifact or an infamous forgery? Such are the the issues that confront any scholar who studies the *Covenant of the Prophet Muhammad with the Monks of Mount Sinai.*

Arabic Copies of the Covenant of the Prophet in Scroll Format

Roll No.	*Dimensions* (cm)	*Material*	*Date*
1	78 x 27	Paper	1150 AH / 1737–38 CE
2	50 x 27	Paper	1192 AH / 1778 CE
3	61 x 22	Paper	1215 AH / 1800–01 CE
4	44.5 x 24.5	Paper	Undated
5	49 x 38	Paper	Undated (Atiya 26)
961	53 x 49	Paper	Undated (74)

Arabic/Turkish Copies of the Covenant of the Prophet in Codices

Codex No.	*Dimensions* (cm)	*Material*	*Date*
695	14.5 x 10	Paper	1683-1684 CE
696	19 x 14	Paper	1561 CE (same as 695)

Issues of Authenticity

The *Covenant of the Prophet Muhammad with the Monks of Mount Sinai* was concluded in the second year of the *hijrah.* This date is consistent with the chronicles kept by the monks since the early days of Islam. Considering that the *Covenant* was a writ of protection provided by the Prophet himself, the document was guarded preciously by the monks at Mount Sinai for nearly nine centuries. According to Marie-Joseph de Géramb (1772–1848 CE), a French General and Trappist monk, the *Covenant of the Prophet with the Monks of Mount Sinai* had been kept in the Convent of the Holy Transfiguration of God at the Monastery of Saint Catherine (Géramb, *Pélerinage* 294; *Pilgrimage* 245). "When Ottoman troops occupied Sinai in 1517," however, "they sent the original *firman* to the palace of Sultan Selim I in Istanbul" (Hobbs 160). According to Griffith, "the monks of Mount Sinai presented him with the original *Achtiname*, bearing it into his presence on a tray, covered with green brocade, a color traditionally associated with Muhammad" (64). Prior to sending the original covenant to Turkey for safe-keeping, it was replaced "with a copy the monks display in one of the most heavily traveled corridors in the monastery, where all visitors may see it" (160). As Hobbs rightfully acknowledged, "This may be the most important document in the monastery's vast collection" (160). Other scholars, such as Albert Champdor, certainly count the *Akd Nâmé* or *Achtiname* of Muhammad as one of the most famous works found at the Monastery.

In his *Arabic Manuscripts of Mount Sinai*, Atiya (1898–1988 CE) mentions that the Monastery of Mount Sinai contains six Arabic copies of the *Covenant of the Prophet* dating from unknown periods to 1800/01 CE.

There are also a large number of Turkish translations of the *Covenant of the Prophet*, numbering 1 to 43, listed in Appendix I (Atiya 80). These dates, however, give the false impression that the oldest copies of the covenant are only four-and-a-half centuries old, dating from the reign of Sulayman the Magnificent (r. 1520–1566) (Mouton 182, note 7; Moritz, 190: 91 & 96; Clark 38 & 52; Fatal 30). Despite his valuable contribution to scholarship, Atiya's list of Arabic manuscripts is incomplete. In addition, as he himself admitted, "[t]he dating of many documents bristles with difficulties" (xxx). Since many of the manuscripts have not been dated, one cannot state with certainty that the earliest copy dates to 1561 CE. Some of the undated covenants may actually be older.

As previous copies became old and brittle and started to disintegrate, new copies of the *Covenant* were created for the sake of posterity. Evidently, the fact that some of the existing copies of the *Covenant* are only centuries old has caused some scholars to call its authenticity into question. However, considering that several of the covenants are not dated, it is quite possible that one of the undated copies represents the initial copy that was made from the original document.

Scholars who stress the spurious status of the *Covenant of the Prophet Muhammad with the Monks of Mount Sinai* rely primarily on specious arguments. They argue, for example, that the oldest extant copies of the *Covenant* date to the 16th century. The oldest version of the *Iliad* dates to the 10th century yet Homer lived in the 8th century BCE. The oldest known version of the *Tanakh* or Hebrew Bible was written between 150 to 70 BCE. The oldest complete copy of the New Testament is contained in the *Codex Sinaiticus*, a work which dates back only 1,600 years. The oldest complete copy of the Qur'an dates from the year 651 CE, nineteen years after the death of Muhammad. There are, of course, segments of the Qur'an which were written by the scribes of the revelation during the Prophet's lifetime (Aydin 87–90). The oldest existing anthologies of *hadith* were compiled one hundred and fifty years after the Prophet's passing. Consequently, the argument goes, one cannot claim an earlier date of composition. This sort of "logic" is intellectually inadmissible, and one might reasonably suspect that an attitude of rejection has preceded any investigation or analysis.

When certain *a priori* assumptions exist, the assertion of which promises to provide compelling benefits, whether substantial material rewards or powerful support for cherished ideologies, a common strategy is to invent or propose arguments which appear, on a stylistic level, to be logical and reasonable, all in an attempt to convince people that the rejection of a particular thesis (decided beforehand) is the final result of a broad, serious, scientific, well-organized, meticulous, and, above all, objective investigation. In other words, the verdict may have been given even before the case commenced. In order to better understand this tendency, an example might be in order, taken, in this case, from the contentious case of creationism versus evolutionism. Richard C. Lewontin (b. 1929), of Harvard University, openly admits that the starting-point of his research is an *a priori* judgment, namely, that anything subjected to study must always lead to results which support materialism and the non-existence of God. As this evolutionary biologist and geneticist admits,

> It is not that the methods and institutions of science somehow compel us accept a material explanation of the phenomenal world, but, on the contrary, that we are forced by our *a priori* adherence to material causes to create an apparatus of investigation and a set of concepts that produce material explanations,

no matter how counter-intuitive, no matter how mystifying to the uninitiated. Moreover, that materialism is absolute, so we cannot allow a Divine Foot in the door. (28)

In the same way that some scientists consider an *a priori* rejection of creationism more important than impartial analysis, there are certain historians for whom it is more important to reject the true and original positions of Islam with respect to Christianity and Christians than accept logical, well-grounded analysis of true Islamo-Christian relations. Some of those so inclined are motivated by political and ideological considerations, while others are simply seduced by the prospect of worldly benefits.

But let us return to the matter at hand. Though carvings in stone and the bones of animals can last thousands of years, and wooden tablets for centuries, most manuscripts have been produced on more malleable and manageable material such as papyrus, parchment, or paper. Papyrus, which was first manufactured in Egypt over three thousand years BCE, is remarkably durable in dry conditions. The material, however, is vulnerable to moisture, which leads to mold, and also to excessive dryness, which results in the fragile material becoming extremely brittle. Outside of Egypt, in regions such as Europe, it was a singular occurrence for papyrus to last more than one or two centuries. The climate worked against its preservation. Parchment, which is made from a thin layer of sheep, goat or cow hide, was developed during the first few centuries BCE. Considerably stronger and more durable than papyrus, parchment could last for centuries so long as it was kept dry. Moisture, however, is its undoing, encouraging rot and decomposition. Excessive dryness was equally a problem. Although strong and initially durable, parchment would lose its natural oils over time becomes very brittle and powdery dry. The high cost of production was an additional limitation.

The earliest precursor to paper appeared in China during approximately two centuries BCE. It was only in the 10th century that paper-making technology spread to the Middle East and eventually into Europe and the rest of the world. If paper came to prevail, it was because it could be mass-produced rather inexpensively. It was not the most durable material, however, as some paper becomes brittle after twenty-five to thirty years and only the highest quality paper promises to last a century in prime condition. Again, the durability of paper and its deterioration depend on many factors including its chemical composition and storage conditions. This is why some one hundred and fifty year old books are in better condition than some 50-year-old books. The point here is that five hundred, one thousand, and fifteen hundred year old parchment would be in particularly poor condition. If the *Covenant of the Prophet Muhammad with the Monks of Mount Sinai* was taken from the monastery by Sultan Selim I after the Ottoman invasion in 1517, as reported by Balthasar de Monconys (1611–1665 CE) (*Le voyage* 92), Pococke (1704–1765 CE) (148), Oumanetz, who is cited in Volkoff (128), along with Skrobucha (57) and Hobbs (160), it was already almost 900 years old. Had the original charter remained at Saint Catherine's, it may have turned to dust by now. If the existing copies of the *Covenant* have survived until the present it is due to geographic factors and questions of climate. In fact, out of over one hundred official letters sent by the Prophet Muhammad as part of his diplomatic campaign, the texts of only sixty or so have survived in ancient historical sources and less than ten original copies have endured the vicissitudes of time.

Although some authors, like Dean Arthur Stanley (1815–1881 CE), believe that the *Covenant of the Prophet*, "if ever it existed, has long since disappeared," having been "taken by Sultan Selim to Constantinople, and exchanged for a copy, which, however, no traveler has ever seen" (344–344), Tomadakis, in vehement contrast, is confident that the original *Covenant of the Prophet* still exists today:

With the conquest of Sinai by the Turks, a worthy Greek named Tsernotabey assisted in the renewal of the Monastery's privileges. Tsernotabey had some influence with the Sultan Selim and in 1517, while the latter was in Cairo, he arranged a meeting of Sinai monks with the Sultan in order that they should show him the Achtiname and thus secure more privileges. Selim, however, took possession of the original document and took it to Constantinople where it must still exist in the archives. (16)

The *Covenant* in question, given the proper conditions, could have survived in storage in Turkey, just as numerous copies of the Prophet's letters have survived the test of time. The oldest Arabic document housed in the library at Mount Sinai belongs to the Fatimid period and was perhaps written in 1106 CE (Digbassanis 361). According to Digbassanis, "Documents of the Fatimids, the Ayyubids and the Mamluk Caliphs from the 12th century CE and thereafter have been preserved in their original form or as copies" (361). This demonstrates that the copies made over the centuries were authentic reproductions of original documents which had been held on to until they virtually turned to dust.

Thus, while the oldest existing copies of the *Covenant* stored in the Monastery of Mount Sinai date from the rule of Sulayman the Magnificent (r. 1520–1566 CE), the existence and presence of the original copy was certified to by Greffin Affagart (c. 1490 or 1495–c. 1557 CE) who performed a pilgrimage to Saint Catherine between 1533–1534 CE. Then, when John Lewis Burckhardt visited the monastery in 1816, he had the opportunity to examine the copy of the *Covenant* on display and which, in all probability, was the one dated from 1800/01 CE. He observed, and this is of absolute importance, "in a note it is expressly stated that the original, written by 'Ali, was lost, and that the present was copied from a fourth successive copy taken from the original" (Chapter 7). Since a paper manuscript is supposed to last one hundred years in the best of conditions, it would make perfect sense that a new copy was made approximately every century. Paper scrolls, which are rolled and unrolled, suffer more wear and tear than single flat sheets of paper. Considering their size, some copies of the covenants appear to have been rolled as scrolls. This strongly supports the argument that the original *firman* was housed at Saint Catherine until the 16th century. The original would have been kept in safe storage with display copies reprinted every hundred years or so. After all, the monks of Mount Sinai were prolific and prodigious scribes. Copying and recopying documents was their *raison d'être*. If the copy made in the 1800s is identical to the copy made in the 1700s and the copy made in the 1700s is identical to the copy made in the 1600s, it is only logical to extrapolate on that data and conclude that the chain of faithful transcriptions traces all the way back to the original *Covenant* concluded by the Prophet Muhammad himself and which was scribed by the hand of Imam 'Ali ibn Abi Talib (d. 661 CE). There are centuries and centuries of copies of the *Covenant* at the Monastery of Saint Catherine all of which are identical in content, the only differences being the official seals, notes, and observations of scribes, scholars, and jurists who certified them.

While every authority has accepted 1517 as the year in which the *Covenant* was taken to the capital of the Ottoman Empire and replaced with a copy (Ratfliff 14–15), Affagart wrote that the original was still at the mosque of the monastery seventeen years after the supposed transfer took place. As he explains in his *Relation de Terre Sainte*, which I have translated from Middle French,

> The monks told us that he [Muhammad] had visited this place during his lifetime and that they asked him for some privileges to prevent his people from hindering them. He granted them that which they asked, and requested that he place his signature. However, since the dummy did not know how to write, he dipped his hand in ink, and pressed it against a piece of paper since he could not sign any other way. The Turks offered to give them a great deal of money in exchange for that sign, which is in the form of his hand, in order to make it a relic, but they never accepted to get rid of it since, by means of it, they are free from [paying] any tribute. (191)

If Greffin Affagart (d. c. 1557 CE) is correct, two points are particularly critical: one, that the *Covenant of the Prophet* was stored, not in the monastery, but in the mosque; and two, that the Turks had not yet convinced the monks to sell the original and content themselves with a copy. Did Affagart actually see the *Covenant* in the mosque? Was he told that it was located there or did he assume that it was displayed there? If the French knight and Lord of Courteilles du Bois is correct, the chronology of the *Covenant* must be modified. The Sultan, Selim I, may have purchased or simply seized the *Covenant* at a later date. If the original was indeed at Saint Catherine's between 1533–1534, then it may have been taken by Sultan Sulayman the Magnificent, who ruled from 1520 to his death in 1566 (Mouton 178). This is perfectly plausible as this particular ruler encouraged and enjoyed positive relations with the Catholic French and even reached out to Protestant princes (Karabell 178–179).

Since Sultan Selim I (r. 1512–1520 CE) sent his emissaries far and wide throughout the Islamic world in search of sacred relics, it seems logical that he would have taken the *Covenant of the Prophet* to the Treasury at Topkapi Palace. In fact, an entire section of that palace, the Chamber of the Relics, is devoted to the holy artifacts that Selim I brought back from his conquest of Egypt in 1517. The Chamber of Relics contains the Prophet's mantle, his swords, and the letter he wrote to Muqawqis, the ruler of Egypt. Also kept safe are the hairs from his beard, soil from his tomb, one of his teeth, as well as imprints of the Prophet's footstep. These are only some examples of the sacred relics that Selim I brought to Istanbul from the treasuries of the Mamluk State, the 'Abbasid Caliphate, and the Hijaz Emirate. For a full appreciation of these treasures, and the account of their acquisition, readers are referred to *The Sacred Trusts* by Hilmi Aydin, a truly sublime work. "With the title and the emblems of Islam," explains Andrew Wheatcroft, "the Ottoman sultans assumed the unquestioned leadership of the Islamic world" (52). As guardian of the holy places, and guarantor of the pilgrimage routes, "[p]ossession of the sites sacred to Islamic orthodoxy could only imbue the Ottoman dynasty with greater legitimacy" (Finkel 110). After all, it was as a result of the conquest of Egypt, and the symbols he secured, that "Selim was also able to induce the titular Caliph" (Eversley 112).

The possibility that the original *Achtiname* remains stored in some forgotten archive, perhaps in the Palace of Topkapi in Istanbul, Turkey, is tantalizing to say the least. Its rediscovery would mark a monumental event in Islamic history, reconfirming not only the historicity of the Prophet but also his benevolent dealings with the People of the Book. This is especially important since, as Pococke (1704–1765 CE) has pointed out, the *Patent of Muhammad* was granted, not only to the Monks of Mount Sinai, but to Christians in general (289). While most sources simply say that Sultan Selim took the covenant back to Istanbul, several of them specify that it was stored in the Serrail (Morison 105–106) or Seraglio (Van Egmont and Heyman 161). Although the terms *Serrail* or *Seraglio* apply primarily to the Topkapi Palace, they are also applied more generally to other traditional Turkish palaces. Hence, while the search must start at the Topkapi Museum, it should be extended to other ancient palaces as well.

As demonstrated by the records in Chapter 1, a copy of a treaty with the Monastery of Saint Catherine does indeed exist in Islamic sources. Although there are some similarities in content when it comes to the protection granted by the Prophet Muhammad to the monks, the version cited by Ibn Sa'd (d. 845 CE) is far shorter than the *Covenant* on display at the Monastery of Mount Sinai. Still, this does not constitute proof that the *Covenant of the Prophet Muhammad with the Monks of Mount Sinai* is a forgery. Ibn Sa'd is a secondary source. He essentially presented a citation from a treaty, while not necessarily being in possession of the full document. The information he cited may have been passed down through the oral tradition; however, it was probably based on a partial written version. The current monks of Mount Sinai possess a primary source, albeit, a copy of a copy of a copy passed down from generation to generation and guarded as the most prized possession of the monastery. Since the Prophet made and remade numerous treaties with the same parties, often renewing them and expanding upon them, it is quite possible that more than one treaty was signed with the monks of Mount Sinai. As Hobbs summarizes,

> Some monastery records say that a delegation of monks traveled to Medina in 625 CE. and met with the Prophet in an effort to obtain his patronage and protection. Both the monks and Bedouins say Muhammad had already visited the monastery before his revelations began, on one of his journeys as a merchant. By some accounts the Prophet granted his protection of the monastery on that visit. (159)

Clearly, the Prophet and the monks of Mount Sinai had a continued contractual relationship. As I have already pointed out, he appears to have visited the Monastery prior to receiving his first revelation, during the days when he directed caravans for his wife Khadijah, or even earlier. According to some monastery records, a delegation of monks traveled to Medina in 625 CE, namely, in the second to third year of the *hijrah*, shortly after Muhammad assumed a position of political power. As he did in similar instances, it seems virtually certain that the Prophet provided the monks with a treaty of protection. The monastery chronicles are in agreement with the content of the *Covenant* itself which says that it was written by the hand of 'Ali ibn Abi Talib (d. 661 CE) on the second year of the *hijrah*. It would seem, then, that the *Treaty of Saint Catherine*, which was signed in the year 6 AH, was a reiteration and confirmation of the content found in the initial long-form covenant.

As custodians of the *Covenant of the Prophet*, the monks of Mount Sinai have always unanimously and unequivocally endorsed its authenticity, their assertions spanning centuries. If the monks of Mount Sinai perpetrated a fraud, it would be one of the best held secrets in history. Since the region was invaded by the French from 1798 to 1801 and subjected to British rule from 1882 to 1952, the monks of the Sinai had over a century and a half of European Christian domination to come clean with regards to the *Covenant of the Prophet*. Rather than reject the *Covenant*, Napoleon (1769–1821 CE), who claimed not only to be a Muslim but the manifestation of the Mahdi, endorsed its authenticity. As Tomadakis relates,

> During Napoleon I's campaign in Egypt, Sinai benefitted greatly. Napoleon not only assisted in the rebuilding of the Monastery's north wall which had collapsed after long and heavy rain in December, 1798, but he also issued a special decree on 8 December, 1798 by which the privileges of Sinai were confirmed and, furthermore, he allowed the monks free communication and exempted them from various financial obligations. (16)

In fact, the decree issued by Napoleon on 19 December 1798, in which he placed the monastery under his protection, actually confirms the privileges that were granted by the Prophet. As Albert Champdor confirms, "this order of protection and privilege . . . matches, corresponds to, and acts as a counterpart to the *Akd Nâmé* of Muhammad" (35). In fact, an article published in 1986, in *Le Figaro* (vols. 351–354) affirmed that Napoleon consciously imitated and revindicated the Prophet's *achtiname* (114). The decree, which was seen by Fazakerley during his 1811 visit to the Monastery of Saint Catherine (378), stresses the French Republic's respect for the Law of Moses, the Jewish Nation, and the educated inhabitants of the monastery. Its articles prevent warring Bedouins from seeking asylum in the monastery; guarantees their freedom of religious practice; and even releases them from the obligation of paying tribute, taxes, or duty on any goods (99–100). If Moritz rejects the authenticity of the *Covenant of the Prophet Muhammad with the Monks of Mount Sinai* because he finds it unbelievable that the monks would be exempted from taxation, he should certainly question the authenticity of Napoleon's decree on the same grounds. After all, how often does any politician abolish taxes?

The authenticity of the *Covenant of the Prophet Muhammad with the Monks of Mount Sinai* was confirmed by the Fatimids (r. 901–1171 CE), the Ayyubids (r. 1174–1249 CE), the Mamluks (1250–1517 CE), and the Ottomans (1517–1805 CE) through a long series of decrees (Atiya 32–35; 80).

These decrees were issued by the Fatimids as early as 975, 1109, 1110, 1135, 1154, and 1156 CE (26), by the Ayyubids in 1195, 1199, 1201/02, and 1210/11 CE, by the Mamluks in 1259, 1260, 1272, 1268/69, 1280 and 1516 CE, and by the Ottomans from 1519 to 1818/19 CE. As Atiya (1898–1988 CE) explains,

> The decrees are the charters of liberties granted by the caliphs and sultans of mediaeval Egypt to the Monastery. In this manner, they are supposed to be following in the steps of the Prophet in his famous covenant. The oldest decrees date from the Fatimid period. During the reign of the Mamluk Dynasties, they increase considerably in numbers, and some sultans issued several of them to the Monastery in one and the same reign. Signatures and signs of the sultans appear at the head of numerous decrees, often coupled with other signs of the various vizirs and their diwans at the royal court of Cairo. These documents are of singular importance.... (xxix)

Not only did these various Muslim dynasties recognize the authenticity of the *Covenant of the Prophet Muhammad with the Monks of Mount Sinai*, they insisted on regularly reaffirming it by means of political proclamations. A total of 1,742 Arabic and Turkish *firmans* are housed in the library at Saint Catherine's Monastery, including 210 royal mandates or decrees from twenty-one Ottoman sultans in succession (Atiya xxxi). As Atiya (1898–1988 CE) explains,

> A survey of the monumental Firman collection in the Monastery Library proves that the covenant of the Prophet, whether forged or authentic, was renewed by the successive Moslem potentates in Egypt, and the privileges of protection and safe-conduct to the monks of St. Catherine were freely upheld throughout the Islamic period. (xviii)

Since worldly authority is subject to change, and recognition of temporal power is time-bound, the Christians of the Sinai also obtained edicts, rulings, or *fatwas* from the four Sunni schools of jurisprudence as well as the Fatimid school in support of the *Covenant of the Prophet Muhammad with the Monks of Mount Sinai*. In the words of Atiya (1898–1988 CE),

> The importance of the *fatwas* or legal opinions chiefly lies in the fact that the privileges accorded to the monks were upheld by the imams of the four Islamic rites: Maliki, Shafi'i, Hanbali, and Hanafi. The subject of each *fatwa* is presented at the top, and this is succeeded by a signed opinion of each of the imams. (xxx)

While the earliest of these edicts were passed by Fatimid Shi'ite jurists in 975, the latest was issued by Ottoman Sunni scholars in 1888. If the original charter was conveyed by Sultan Selim I to Istanbul after the Ottoman invasion of Egypt in 1517, Muslims scholars had already had access to it for 542 years. If they issued edicts, they did so because they were convinced of the authenticity of the document in form and content. As for the scholars who issued decrees for the 371 subsequent years, they have been equally convinced that the covenant they reviewed was a true and accurate transcription from the original document. The same applies to the Ottoman viceroys of Egypt who issued "166 decrees safeguarding the Monastery and the monks" (Atiya xxxi). As a result, the *Covenant of the Prophet Muhammad with the Monks of Mount Sinai* was recognized by the political and religious leaders of Islam for more than a millennium. As the Greek historian, Amantos, writes,

> The monastery of Sinai could not possibly have survived without the protection afforded by Mohammed and his successors.... Moreover, the great number of decrees which the Mohammedan rulers of Egypt issued confirming the protected status of the monastery must have resulted from the fact that Mohammed himself had granted protection to Sinai. (qtd. Shah-Kazemi)

To summarily dismiss one thousand years of scholarly consensus without advancing any evidence-based arguments falls short of the accepted standards for scholarship and may, at the very least, be the product of some political and ideological prejudice. Take, for example, the case of J. Muehleisen Arnold, who wrote: "Were the celebrated *Testamentum et pactiones initae inter Mohammedem et Christianae fidei cultores* (Paris 1630 and Hamb. 1690) a *genuine* document, which it is not, it would only be a 'snare and delusion.'" In other words, if a document presents a positive image of Islam, it must be false. However, even if it were true, it most certainly represents a ruse. Such contradictory reasoning, of course, is not surprising coming from a reverend and missionary like Arnold who announced, on the front cover of his book, that "the entire proceeds of this work will be given towards founding a 'society for propagating the gospel among the Mohammedans.'"

"While some doubt that the *Achtiname* is genuine," writes Tomadakis, "the fact that it was always respected by Moslem leaders, the Arabs to begin with, and later the Turks, indicates that the Moslems did consider it the will of the Prophet" (14). As Demetrius Cantemir (1673–1723 CE) has explained,

> 'Tis certain the exemption of these monks from tribute remain'd in force through all the Turkish dominions till the time of Soliman II, Great-Uncle of the present Emperor, when the Turks began to collect the *Haraj* upon them, and that by means of... Mustafa Pasha, who made no scruple to charge the whole Diploma with forgery. To prevent this, some of the monks of Mount Sinai were sent to Adrianople with the instrument of Exemption, in whose hands I both read and transcrib'd it. They indeed preserv'd by their petitions to themselves and society, a freedom from tribute, but could not prevail for the rest of the monasteries. (169)

As Cantemir makes manifest, the Grand Vizier Merzifonlu Kara Mustapha Pasha, who served Sulayman II from 1663–1666, denounced the *Covenant of the Prophet with the Monks of Mount Sinai* as a forgery as a pretext to subject Greek Christians to the *kharaj* or land tribute. When faced with the facts, he himself conceded that the monks of Mount Sinai were granted immunity by the Messenger of Allah. However, this did not stop him from restricting the Muhammad's Charter to the monks of Mount Sinai (Cantemir, *Histoire* 357). Jurisprudentially, he believed that the conditions contained in the *Covenant of the Prophet* were not applicable to all Christians at all times and places. However, convinced that the document represented the will of the Prophet, he continued to exempt the Monastery of Saint Catherine from taxation.

What is remarkable, and what must be remembered, is that the *Covenant of the Prophet Muhammad with the Monks of Mount Sinai* was accepted by both Shi'ites and Sunnis. The Sunnis, in general, are quite suspicious of Shi'ites, and tend to summarily reject their sources. The Ottomans, who were Sunnis, received the *Covenant of the Prophet* from the Mamlukes, whom, despite being Sunnis, were viewed by the Turks as heretics and apostates for supporting the Safavid Shi'ites. The Mamluks, who were Sunnis, received the *Covenant of the Prophet* from the Fatimids, who were Shi'ites. The Fatimids, who were Shi'ites, received the *Covenant of the Prophet* from their enemies, the Sunni 'Abbasids. The 'Abbasids, who were Sunnis, received the *Covenant of the Prophet* from the Umayyads, who were considered evil-doers if not infidels by the 'Abbasids who rose to power by exploiting Shi'ite sentiments. The Umayyads, who were headed by Mu'awiyyah (d. 680 CE), and who were infamous for their hatred of the Household of the Prophet, received the *Covenant of the Prophet* from Imam 'Ali (d. 661 CE), from whom they usurped a large segment of the Islamic *ummah*. Despite all of their differences, and the deep divide between Sunnism and Shi'ism, Muslims have always regarded the *Covenant of the Prophet Muhammad with the Monks of Mount Sinai* as a constant. There is no evidence at all that Sunnis rejected the *Covenant* on the grounds that it was a *rafidi* Shi'ite imposture. (This is a pejorative term which means "extremist," "critic," "heretic," "innovator," "misguided," "renegade," "deserter," etc., all of which are characteristic of traitors, liars, and disloyal individuals.) Likewise, there is no evidence at all that Shi'ites rejected the *Covenant* on the grounds that it was a *nasibi* Sunni fabrication. (This is a term that Shi'ites apply to those who hate them, namely, those who hate the Household of the Prophet of Islam. Muqtada al-Sadr uses it to refer to the Salafis.) The *Covenant*, it almost seems, brought Sunnis and Shi'ites together. While they may not have agreed with one another on other issues, they all seem to have agreed on the manner in which all Muslims should treat peaceful, law-abiding, Christian minorities.

Despite this unparalleled consensus among Muslim authorities over the ages, some scholars still suggest that the *Covenant of the Prophet Muhammad with the Monks of Mount Sinai* dates to 1517 CE. Such claims can be dismissed with assurance, as the famous *Pact of Muhammad* had been confirmed by Muslims leaders and religious authorities as early as 975 CE. Consequently, the suggestion that the *Covenant* was a "ploy" perpetrated by the Greek monks in 1010 CE lacks the barest substance. In a rare moment of objectivity in the history of Western Orientalism, Albert Champdor asserts that the *Covenant of the Prophet with the Monks of Mount Sinai* was indeed in existence during the rule of the Caliph ʿUmar (r. 634–644 CE). As this expert explains,

> the monks of the Sinai were barely tolerated by the Arabs of the Caliph ʿUmar who settled in the oasis of Pharan in 634 after having expelled its Christian communities. The knights of Allah, however, never dared to occupy the monastery of Saint Catherine, something they would have done without incurring any risks, because that holy site was protected by an *Akd Nâmé* redacted by [ʿAli ibn] Abu Talib and signed by Muhammad, yes, by Muhammad himself! It goes without saying that a simple ʿUmar, as powerful as he may have been as a Caliph, would never have allowed himself to ignore this diplomatic decree which accorded to the monks of Saint Catherine, in return for the hospitality they had one day offered the Prophet, the right to worship God as they deemed fit and to serve him freely. In addition, this Decree freed them from any and all servitude to Muslim authorities. (32)

Helen C. Evans also argues that the *Achtiname* of the Prophet was given to the Monastery of Saint Catherine at Sinai "in the first years of the Muslim advance across the Sinai Peninsula" (10). The implication is that it dates from the time of ʿUmar when, in reality, it was simply renewed. Establishing a tradition that would last until Ottoman times, ʿUmar ibn al-Khattab (579–644 CE) not only recognized the *Patent of Muhammad* with the Monks of Mount Sinai, he issued an edict endorsing its content. The treaty in question is the antithesis of the discriminatory demands of the so-called *Pact of ʿUmar.* Not only does Champdor acknowledge that the *Covenant of the Prophet* existed during the rule of the Second Caliph, establishing a clear and unbroken chain of transmission from the time of the Prophet to the present, he equally admits that the *Patent* of the Prophet was generally respected by Muslim rulers. "In general," writes Champdor, "the Caliphs of Baghdad, Cairo or Damascus respected the clauses of this Gentleman's agreement and confirmed them on numerous occasions" (32). However, this adherence to the Prophet's words and wishes was not accepted across the region. The Arabs of the Sinai Peninsula, in fact, questioned its authenticity or ignored its existence as a pretext to assault and pillage the powerless monks (32–33).

Despite suffering, from time to time, from the reprehensible actions of some superficially Islamized Muslims who did not follow the example of Muhammad, the monks of Mount Sinai have always defended the authentic status of the *Covenant of the Prophet Muhammad* throughout recorded history. As Father Makarios, a monk at Mount Sinai, has said: "Where would the monastery be today if it had turned Muhammad away when he came?" (qtd. Hobbs 280–281). According to Konstantinos A. Manafis,

> The preservation of the Monastery's Greekness was due to its own resources, and especially to the position taken by the monks who managed to gain the respect and protection of the Arabs, the Turks and the Egyptians by means of the famous *Charter* or *Achtiname* given by the founder of the Islamic Faith, the Prophet Mohammed himself in order to preserve the Monastery's rights. (22)

While some may say that it was in the vested interests of the monk to defend the authenticity of the *Covenant*, this was certainly not the case under European occupation. Pulling off such a forgery would have been a formidable feat. Had it been exposed, it would have meant certain death for the monks involved and the probable destruction of the monastery. Furthermore, it seems highly unlikely that anyone at the monastery would have had a sufficiently sophisticated knowledge of Arabic to imitate the substance of the Prophet Muhammad's speech and the handwriting style of Imam 'Ali (d. 661 CE), not to mention the intimate knowledge of early Islamic history required for such a risky endeavor. Even Atiya (1898–1988 CE), who was Christian, admitted that

> Copies of the covenant of the Prophet Muhammad are identical in their purport and terms. These are presumably reproductions of an original written by the Caliph 'Ali and sealed by the hand of the Prophet, whereby all the faithful Muslims are enjoined to protect the monastery and safeguard the monks. Some of the copies are certified in court by judges of Islam and are sealed by them as official testimony to the authenticity of the covenant. The story is circulated that the original covenant of the Prophet was taken to Istanbul by Sultan Selim I at the time of his conquest of Egypt in 1517. It is also said that he gave the monks a certified copy in its place to ensure their security under the banner of Islam. It is noteworthy at this juncture to say that the *firman* of Selim I has actually been located in the Turkish collection; and, although it does not contain the text of the covenant at all, it is nevertheless a clear guarantee of safe conduct for the monks of Mt. Sinai. (xxix)

The only difference between the various copies involves decorative elements. "Some of the later copies," writes Digbassanis, "apart from the depiction of the Monastery and Mt. Sinai," include "the imprint of a palm and five fingers, namely the symbol of the Prophet Mohammed and his blood relatives Fatima, Ali, Hasan, and Hussein" (361). If the original *Covenant of the Prophet* actually contained the palm-print of the Prophet, the symbol of *ahl al-bayt*, the Holy Household of the Prophet, it would certainly support the Shi'ite claim regarding Imam 'Ali's right to succession and the fact that the Messenger of Allah had appointed his direct descendants as Imams and Caliphs over the Muslim Community. By signing with his hand, the five fingers of which stand for Muhammad, Fatimah, 'Ali, Hasan and Husayn, and the fourteen bones representing the fourteen infallibles, namely, the Prophet, his daughter, and the Twelve Imams, the Messenger of Allah would have been granting protection to the Christians of Sinai in his name and the names of his entire Holy Household. This is not as far-fetched as is sounds and may explain the suppressed history of Shi'ism in Egypt. The region, after all, was under the rule of 'Ali ibn Abi Talib, and governed by Muhammad ibn Abi Bakr, the Imam's adopted son, who was a staunch partisan of 'Ali. It was only as a result of the insurrection of Mu'awiyyah ibn Abi Sufyan that the region fell into Umayyad hands in 658 CE. When Francis Arundale (1807–1853 CE) completed a voyage to the Sinai in 1831, he noted that most of the Bedouins were Shi'ites. As he explained:

> The Bedouins, or wandering Arabs . . . are amongst the largest of the tribes, and governed by their own Emir and Sheikhs. They have a contempt for the Turks, whom they consider as usurpers in their country. Their religion is a reformation of the Mahomedan, and though they practise the same forms in their prayers, and observe the same fasts, yet there is a great difference in their religious sentiments, being for the most part followers of 'Ali.

Obviously, being followers of 'Ali, as the Bedouins apparently were, does not mean that 'their religion' was 'a reformation of the Mahomedan' (6–7). This may, in fact, be the real reason why the Umayyads, 'Abbasids, Mamluks, and Ottomans have portrayed the Bedouins of the Sinai in such a poor light. It may not be that they were "bad Muslims," but merely because they were the "wrong kind of Muslims." Since they refused to submit to central authority, they were deemed a threat. This may also explain why the *Covenant of the Prophet Muhammad with the Monks of Mount Sinai* eventually went missing from the Treasury in Istanbul. It is possible that the enemies of *ahl al-bayt* destroyed it on grounds that it was too favorable to the Shi'ite cause.

Digbassanis, of course, is wrong to suggest that the hand-print was a latter addition to the covenant as it is attested in many ancient sources. In the *Jeux d'esprit et de mémoire*, published in 1697, the author, M.L.M.D.C., reports that the Prophet Muhammad provided great gifts to the Monastery of Saint Catherine motivated by the friendship he had with one of the monks, granting it beautiful privileges, among others, an exemption from taxation (85–86). The author also mentions that these rights were bestowed by means of a Patent signed with his hand (86). The Prophet, the writer continues, used to soak his hand in a big basin full of ink and would press his hand against the parchment (86). The author also explains that Muhammad never used any feather or writing instrument apart from his hand (86). The text proceeds to paraphrase the opinion of a Maréchal on the subject:

> The general officer continued to speak, saying that he had once read the History of the Turks and that he remembered perfectly well that it was Selim, the Emperor of the Turks, who officially removed this precious Relic and Patent which was in the Monastery of those monks of the Church of the East. It was a double and true Patent since it was covered with all of its forms and, furthermore, it was the exact figure of the Hand of Muhammad which is the greatest Relic of the Ottomans. (87)

Rather than a later addition, the presence of the Hand of Muhammad or *khamsah* on the *Covenant* has been attested to in all of the ancient sources. The sole exception appears to be the account of Van Egmont and John Heyman which claims that the Prophet simply dipped one of his fingers in the ink and signed the covenant with a fingerprint (161). Since neither of these men seems to have actually seen the *Covenant*, their version can be discounted as a mere misunderstanding.

Considering that some copies of the *Covenant of the Prophet Muhammad with the Monks of Mount Sinai* date from the 16th century CE, some scholars, who cast doubt on its content, claim that the treaty was a fraud perpetrated by the monks in a desperate attempt to save themselves from the blood-thirsty Muslim military. As Hobbs observes, some scholars suggest that the *Covenant of the Prophet* may have merely been a ruse (160). The idea of "monkish impostures" has a long history among Protestant scholars due to their hatred of Catholics. Although he fails to mention who they are or the evidence they presented to support their allegations, Hobbs states that "several observers believe that monks rather than the Prophet Muhammad drafted the original *firman* of protection when a Muslim army threatened the monastery in about 1010 CE" (160–161). In the opinion of the author,

> A real threat may have caused the monks to take such an extraordinary step to protect themselves, and they have certainly taken others. In 1009 in an assault on Christianity the allegedly psychotic Caliph al-Hakim of the Tunisian Fatimid dynasty destroyed the Church of the Holy Sepulchre in Jerusalem. His forces then reportedly set out to raze the Monastery of St. Catherine. There are several versions of what followed. One is that the Prophet's *firman*—perhaps freshly written—repelled the army. Another account is that the caliph decided not to attack the monastery and even repented when he learned the mountain was once again in flame. In another version a party of monks met the caliph as he was on his way to destroy the monastery, imploring him to save it as a holy place for Muslims. As they met, another party of monks worked feverishly to erect a mosque within the monastery walls atop a spot where they would say the Prophet Muhammad had stood. This is the account today's monks relate. Yet another version is that al-Hakim, initially bent on the monastery's destruction, was talked out of his plan by the monks, and then ordered the monks to build a mosque where Muhammad had stood in order to 'pacify his soldiers' thirst for Christian blood.' In fact, the mosque was apparently constructed around 1106 during the reign of al-Hakim's successor, the Fatimid Caliph al-Afdal. The Crusaders had taken Jerusalem in 1099; the mosque may have been built to service a Muslim detachment sent to defend the site against the Crusader army, or perhaps as a device to ward off an attack by Ottoman troops. (Hobbs 161)

As Hobbs admits, however, "There are conflicting accounts of the Prophet Muhammad's contact with the monastery" (159). This is a sound historical assessment. It is the second part of the sentence, "and there are questions about whether contact took place at all" (159) which poses the problem. If there are many versions of an event, it suggests that an event took place. It does not suggest that an event did not take place. In the absence of definitive proof that a renowned historical document is spurious, historians should refrain from questioning its validity by mere hypothesis. As Shi'ite jurists acknowledge, there is no *ijtihad* or interpretation against the text. As Digbassanis explains,

> the Arabic section of the Archive contains documents which inform us about the relations of the Monastery with the Arab chiefs and with the centers of the Islamic world from a very early date. For example, copies of the 'Achtiname' (the Holy Testament) are preserved, that is, the first guarantee given by Mohammed which, according to tradition, the Prophet himself sanctified by stamping his palm over it. The copies date to the 16th century when the original was given to the Sultan Selim I after he conquered Egypt in 1517. (361)

If the records of the monastery date back to the early days of Islam and if these documents clearly chronicle the contacts between the monks of Mount Sinai and the Prophet Muhammad, they serve to confirm the authenticity of the *Covenant.* Those who would argue otherwise would need to demonstrate, not only the falsehood of the *Covenant*, but the fact that large portions of the monastery archives have themselves been forged. The onus of proof is on the accuser and, so far, no serious repudiation of the *Covenant* has ever been formulated. As Stanley (1815–1881 CE) wrote over a century ago,

> No one can now prove or disprove the tradition that Mahomet, whilst yet a camel-driver in Arabia, wandered to the great Convent, then not a century old. It is at least not impossible, and the repeated allusions in the Koran to the stone of Moses, evidently that now exhibited; to the holy valley of Tuwa, a name now lost, but by which he seems to designate the present valley of the convent; and to the special addresses made to Moses on the western, and on the southern slopes of the mountain, almost bring it within the range of possibility. His name certainly has been long preserved, either by the policy or the friendliness of the monks. Nowhere else probably in the Christian world is to be found such a cordial, it might also be said such a tender feeling towards the Arabian prophet and his followers, as in the precincts and the memorials of the Convent of Mount Sinai. 'As he rested,' so the story has with slight variations been told from age to age, 'as he rested with his camels on Mount Menejia, an eagle was seen to spread its wings over his head, and the monks, struck by the augury of his future greatness, received him into their convent, and he in return, unable to write, stamped with ink on his hand the signature to a contract of protection, drawn up on the skin of a gazelle, and deposited in the archives of the convent.' (344–345)

As Stanley recognizes, the differences between the various accounts are slight and are the natural result of an event having been related over the ages. As Hobbs points out, the local Jabaliyyah Arabs who live in the Sinai mistakenly believe that the *Covenant* was written by Caliph 'Umar ibn al-Khattab (579–644 CE). Apparently, they simply confused the *Covenant of the Prophet* with the *Pact of 'Umar* and Imam 'Ali (d. 661 CE) with Caliph 'Umar. "The document itself," however, "claims to have been dictated by the Prophet and written by his cousin and son-in-law 'Ali in 623 CE" (Hobbs 159). The text must take precedence over oral tradition. According to Hobbs, the Jabaliyyah relate that Caliph 'Umar (r. 634–644 CE) "imposed a decree ordering all of Sinai's inhabitants except the monks to convert to Islam, and that copies of this decree survive in the monastery" (158). As historical record indicates, this was simply not the case. Furthermore, there is no record of any such decree in the archives of the Monastery at Mount Sinai. Rather than prove that the story is fake, the various "conflicting" versions concerning the relations of the Prophet with the Monastery seem to confirm repeated contact between both parties. It seems that the various visits back and forth have been merged into a single narrative over time. Although they differ in details and dates, the various accounts all confirm the good relations between the Prophet Muhammad and the Christians of Mount Sinai and the fact that a series of treaties and covenants were concluded. Still, this does not suffice for a handful of Salafi opponents.

Although most traditional Muslim *'ulama'* accept the *Covenant of the Prophet Muhammad with the Monks of Mount Sinai* as authentic, its content is roundly rejected by certain groups of Islamist extremists. These Wahhabis, habitually essentialists and fundamentalists, namely, people who insist in a single literal interpretation of sources, appear completely disconnected from the Islamic scholarly tradition as they declare that the only legitimate sayings of the Prophet Muhammad are those that are confirmed in books of tradition by his Companions and the Followers of the Companions. Since the *Covenant of the Prophet* does not contain an *isnad* or chain of narration, they choose to view it as a fabrication. The utter absurdity of such an argument is startling. Chains of narration were not needed in the lifetime of the Prophet, his Companions, or their Followers. People quoted the Prophet directly because they had heard him directly. It was only after a century, when memory had started to fade, that the need for chains of narration arose and an entire, widely accepted, science of prophetic traditions or *hadith* was developed. Since most of the traditions of the Prophet were only compiled six generations after his passing, a process of authentication was required. No such standard, however, is required when dealing with a primary document, a covenant which was dictated by the Prophet, written by 'Ali, witnessed by other Companions, and sealed with the hand-print of the Messenger of Allah. Furthermore, there are numerous examples of prophetic sayings which are considered authentic or at least acceptable despite the fact that their chains of narration are weak, incomplete, or even completely absent. Ideally, both the content and the chain of the tradition should be sound. However, the chain is not the only criterion of *hadith* sciences. It would be foolish to accept an illogical or absurd tradition simply because its chain of narrators is sound. Any *'alim* or Muslim scholar worth the turban on his head can easily forge an *isnad*. Likewise, it would be foolish to reject a tradition which agrees with the Qur'an and Sunnah simply because its chain of authorities is absent or incomplete.

The few Salafis who have even heard about the *Covenant* argue that it is not authentic since it is not found in the surviving *hadith* collections. It is, however, found in partial form in classical Islamic historical literature. However, since the books of history like Tabari (d. 923 CE), Ibn Sa'd (d. 845 CE), and others do not include chains of narrations, the anti-intellectual Wahhabis duly dismiss them. If the covenants are authentic, why are they not found in the canonical books of traditions? Well, for starters, *hadith* scholars were interested in compiling sayings of the Prophet, as opposed to historical accounts, treaties, and covenants, which they left to historians. This is certainly a shame since the covenants of the Prophet are of important jurisprudential value. In fact, a large number of *shari'ah* rulings can be derived from them. While they may have traveled much of the Middle East in search of such sayings, few *hadith* scholars went to North Africa, and even fewer reached al-Andalus. Furthermore, they tended to limit their search for prophetic traditions to large urban centers where Muslims were concentrated. They rarely, if ever, reached isolated outposts such as the Monastery of Saint Catherine at Mount Sinai. In the mind of any *muhaddith*, there were no traditions of the Prophet to be found in Christian monasteries in the Sinai, Arabia or Iraq.

Many such Muslims would even discard the covenants because they were preserved and passed down by Christians. The original copy of the *Covenant of the Prophet Muhammad with the Monks of Mount Sinai* was lost. Hence, all we have are the copies produced by generations of monks over the centuries. The original copy of the *Covenant of the Prophet Muhammad with the Christians of Najran*, which was found by the monk Habib in 878/879 CE, is only preserved in a Christian chronicle. As for the *Covenant of the Prophet Muhammad with the Christians of the World*, it has only reached us thanks to Arab and European Christians from the 1500s and 1600s. As the result of their deep-seated distrust of Christians, not to mention many cases of overt hostility and hatred, some Muslims would reject the covenants categorically. For scholars and historians free from the limitations of fundamentalism and fanaticism, the arguments of these theoreticians of terror hold no sway. For, surely, one should not shoot the messenger, especially when he may be delivering priceless jewels and gems. After all, the *Treaty of Maqnah* was purchased by al-Saffah, the first of the 'Abbasid caliphs, from the people of Aylah, for three hundred dinars (Gil 29, note 25). Besides the letter of protection, they had also preserved the Prophet's cloak, which he had given them as a gift (29, note 25). The same applies with the Prophet Muhammad's "Letter to Muqawqis, Leader of the Copts" which was "discovered inside a Coptic Bible cover in the monastery at Ahmin, near Saide, Egypt, in 1850 by a Frenchman named Barthlmy" (Aydin 96). If many Muslims, including the Sultans of the OttomDar al-islaman Empire and scores of Muslim scholars, have accepted this letter, discovered in 1850 CE, as authentic, the covenant of the Prophet published in Paris in 1630 CE, the covenant of the Prophet uncovered in 878/879 CE, the covenant of the Prophet from 1538 CE, which I recently rediscovered, and the *Treaty of Maqnah*, which was purchased between 750–754 CE, should be received with the same, if not greater, acclaim since they are so much older.

There are those, of course, who will insist that Muslims cannot rely on Jewish or Christian sources when constructing or reconstructing their religious history. They will argue that Islam can only be based on Islamic sources, specifically the Qur'an and the Sunnah. However, this ignores the fact that the Islamic tradition is simply saturated with Jewish and Christian material. Again, I am not saying that early Muslims copied the Jews and Christians. Rather, they accepted anything and everything from these Abrahamic faiths which did not contradict the Qur'an and the Sunnah. After all, the Prophet is reported to have encouraged his Companions to "Narrate [traditions] from the Children of Israel for there is nothing objectionable in that" (Shafi'i). While the integrity of Ka'b al-Ahbar (d. 652 CE) was called into question by Imam 'Ali, it is difficult to discount the Jewish and Christian traditions transmitted by Wahb ibn Munabbih (655–732 CE), and particularly those related by Ibn 'Abbas (619–687 CE). Since Muslims have a long tradition of relying on Jewish and Christian religious sources in order to confirm the content of the Qur'an and Sunnah, there is no reason they cannot do the same with the various covenants of the Prophet. Muslims also have a long history of relying on Greek, Persian, Indian, and even Chinese sources in order to increase their knowledge in all fields. As for the argument that Jewish and Christian sources are oceans of falsehood, the same argument can be applied to the Islamic *hadith* literature. As all Muslim *hadith* scholars are aware, out of the millions of sayings attributed to the Prophet, only a small number are genuine. Hence, simply because there is some falsehood in non-Muslim sources does not mean that we have to dismiss them entirely. By applying a critical scholarly methodology, it is possible to distinguish between what is sound and what is spurious. In the quest for knowledge, Muslims should avail themselves of all sources. For verily, the Prophet asked his followers to "Seek knowledge, even in China" (Bayhaqi). We are thus entirely justified to seek knowledge in the Sinai.

The Salafis set aside, the most detailed criticism of the *Covenant of the Prophet Muhammad with the Monks of Mount Sinai* belongs to Bernard Moritz. However, since this scholar wrote in German, and this book is intended for an English audience, I shall spare my readers and provide the summary provided by Skrobucha who happens to share the views of Moritz. In the opinion of Skrobucha:

> That this copy should be based on an authentic writing of the Prophet, signed by him with two fingers of his hand, has been disproved by Moritz on grounds of date, style, and content. The chief argument which he adduces against the genuineness of the document is that, in contrast to the Prophet's surviving genuine letters of protection, there is no demand for the fulfillment of any single duty, but in spite of this, very far-reaching promises are granted. That, for example, the Christians themselves are empowered to fix the amount of their taxes, is con-

trary to Muslim government practice and is unparalleled in our sources.

It is also noticeable that the monastery of Sinai is not expressly mentioned, and that parts of the contents, for example the passage about women, military service, and commerce, have no relevance to the monastery and its special conditions. Nevertheless, this presumed letter of protection of Muhammad's may be identical with the document named in the *firman* of 1134. . . . Persecution of Christians, destruction of their churches and monasteries, and oppression of the subject population reached a peak in Egypt under Caliph Hakim (AD 996–1020); hence this document from Sinai may well have originated in Egypt at that period. In this connection, the fact that it was not a very skilful forgery is explained by 'the Mohammedans' lack of critical sense in religious matters and their reverence' for the Prophet. It must be borne in mind that there had been undoubtedly genuine letters of protection of the Prophet's, for example to the Jewish community at Maqnah on the Gulf of Aqaba.

It has been shown that when faced with the existence of both genuine and forged letters of protection from the Prophet, the Muslim rulers made it their principle in doubtful cases to favor the presumption of authenticity, even to the extent of renewing the right of protection in the absence of documentary evidence, original or secondary. It is related of the Mameluke Sultan Jakmak (1438–53) that in the year 1442, stirred up by the fanatical clergy, he inquired of the Coptic and Greek patriarchs, and also of the heads of the Orthodox, Karaite, and Samaritan Jewish communities, concerning the 'letter of protection, which had been issued to their forefathers.' As they knew nothing about them, the council of state decided 'to renew their protected status according to the precedent set by the Caliph 'Umar ibn al-Khattab.'

For the fate of the Christian monastery on Mount Sinai the Muslims' belief in the Prophet's promise of protection was of extraordinary importance. Improbable as the existence of a letter of protection from the Prophet is, the effect in history in this case, as so often, did not depend on any questions about the reality, the authenticity of the document. (Skrobucha 58–59)

Although Skrobucha agrees with the arguments made by Moritz, and does not believe that the existing copy of the *Covenant of the Prophet Muhammad with the Monks of Mount Sinai* is genuine, he thinks that it may have been based on earlier sources:

> Undoubtedly certain ancient documents—whether genuine or otherwise may be left an open question—must have existed, for a Caliph as early as al-Hafiz (1132–49), in a *firman*, advises the governor of 'Aqabah to honor the ancient agreements with the monks, and other *firmans* also contain explicit references to a holy letter of protection of the Prophet's. (57–58)

The claim that the *Covenant of the Prophet Muhammad with the Monks of Mont Sinai* was forged during the despotic reign of Caliph Hakim (r. 996–1021 CE) is without foundation. In 1134 CE, when al-Hafiz, the eleventh Fatimid caliph, commanded his governor to observe the ancient agreements with the monks of Mount Sinai, these documents were already ancient. As Hieromonk Justin of Sinai writes, "[t]hese documents, considered old at the time, must have already existed for some centuries" (51). Clearly, if they were three to four hundred years old at the time, they could not have been a century-old forgery.

The arguments advanced by Bernhard Moritz in *Beiträge zur Geschichte des Sinai-Klosters Im Mittelalter Nach Arabischen Quellen* (1918) and espoused by Skrobucha are neither compelling nor convincing for several reasons mentioned previously. Mr. Moritz, who had served as the director of the Khedivial Library in Cairo, was not an objective, impartial, man. He was a German imperial field agent and propagandist (McMeekin 88, 92, 96, 147, 372, note 12). In the opinion of Leo Frobenius (1873–1973 CE), another zealous spy and political agent, Moritz was "in his innermost heart a despiser of Oriental peoples" (qtd. McMeekin 147). Moritz belonged to a small clique of German operatives who thrust the Islamic world into conflict in order to suit their own political, economic, and military ends. In the same fashion that the British spear-headed the spread of Wahhabism and "Islamic" extremism during the Arab Revolt in order to destroy what remained of the Ottoman

Empire, the Germans also appealed to Arab nationalism and Muslim religious sentiment to support their cause. Agents like Moritz were charged with convincing the Arabs that German interests and Islamic interests were one. By paying off Sunni and Shi'ite religious authorities as some sort of *jizyah*, they were able to obtain *fatwas* in support of the German jihad against the Allies (McMeekin 200, 201–209, 214–15, 233). While these corrupt clerics described such pay-offs in religious terms, all parties knew what they were: bribes in exchange for collaborating with the colonial powers. If the Germans were garnering the support of the Turks, the Berbers, the Persians and some Arabs, the British were spreading Salafism in what is now Saudi Arabia in an attempt to oust the Ottomans from the Middle East. As the United States rose to imperial status in the 20th century, it inherited the Salafi movement from the British and used it to advance its own agenda in the Muslim world. For more on the subject, readers are referred to *The Two Faces of Islam* by Stephen Schwartz (b. 1948 CE) and *God's Terrorists: The Wahhabi Cult and the Hidden Roots of Modern Jihad* by Charles Allen.

As Sean McMeekin makes manifest in his *Berlin-Baghdad Express: The Ottoman Empire and Germany's Bid for World Power*, these Orientalists/covert operatives gathered armies of Islamists and, through the use of selected citations of the Qur'an taken totally out of context, insisted that it was an Islamic obligation for the pro-German jihadists to kill Jewish and Christian infidels, excluding, of course, the Deutschen *dhimmis* who spurred them on (86–93, 96–99, 118, 124–37, 160–161, 172–179, 181, 202–209, 216, 258, 263–265, 267–268, 271, 273–274, 333, 338). Since Moritz worked on behalf of the German Propaganda Ministry, his scholarship can be dismissed precisely as that: propaganda. Moritz was a man who wanted Muslims to kill and persecute Christians. Of course he dismissed the *Covenant of the Prophet Muhammad with the Monks of Mount Sinai* as a forgery. It was against German imperial interests for Muslims to treat the People of the Book with tolerance. While one may have expected Moritz to have learned his lesson after Germany's defeat in World War I, he allied himself with the Nazis in the years to come and even reviewed the Arabic translation of Hitler's *Mein Kampf* (Herf 24–25). As Jeffrey Herf details in *Nazi Propaganda for the Arab World*, "'Jihad made in Germany' and the appeal to Arabs to revolt against British and French colonialism had been a component of German policy during World War I" (6) and continued with great intensity both before and during the Second World War. All of these facts need to be borne in mind when considering the claims made by Moritz about the *Covenant*.

Despite claims by Moritz to the contrary, the *Covenant*'s date is confirmed by Islamic sources as well as the chronicles from the Monastery of Saint Catherine. As for the style and content of the *Covenant*, they are consistent with other authenticated accords concluded by the Prophet. The main argument made by Moritz against the authenticity of the *Covenant* revolves around the fact that no demands were made of the Christians. For Moritz, this stands in clear contrast to the Prophet's surviving genuine letters of protection. This claim is as clear as clouds. Muhammad's logic in this regard is evident. If the Messenger of Allah made no demands, it was because he was dealing with monks, with a religious order, with an isolated brotherhood of believers who had devoted their lives to adoration and contemplation. If the Prophet made demands in his other covenants, it was because he was dealing with monarchs, states, communities, and even municipalities, groups who were engaged broadly in agriculture and commerce. Moritz also argues that empowering the Christians of Mount Sinai to determine their level of taxation was contrary to Muslim government practice and is unparalleled in other sources. Again, were the Prophet dealing with an actual city-state, such an argument would be acceptable. However, what is remarkable and telling in this instance was that the Prophet made a treaty with a specific monastery out of gratitude for their kindness. Nowhere else is this the case. If the details of the document were distinctive by the omission of expected elements, it is because the case was exceptional. The Messenger of Allah catered to the specific conditions of particular communities. Finally, since there were existing peace treaties concluded with the Prophet, for instance, the *Constitution of Medina*, the treaties with the Meccans at al-Hudaybiyyah, with the Jews of Khaybar, and with the Christians of Najran and other communities, the monks of Mount Sinai had no reason to forge a treaty. And if they decided to forge one, they would have had the common sense to include direct references to themselves. Rather than run the risk of being charged with blasphemy for authoring falsehoods and attributing them to God and His Prophet, the monks of Mount Sinai could simply have asked the Muslims to respect the precedents set down previously by the Prophet and of which they had specific knowledge. In fact, when the Muslims came across new communities of Jews and Christians, none of the parties thought to perpetrate such a fraud. As Jacques Waardenburg writes, the peace treaties previously concluded by the Prophet "served as models for treaties during and after the Arab conquest" (17, note 22). Even Brandie Ratliff admits that

> The document bears close resemblance to a number of other documents found in religious communities in the Near East. These documents are remarkably similar to the letter of Muhammad addressed to the Christians of Najran and discovered in 878 in a monastery in Iraq; the letter is preserved in the *Chronicle of Séert*. The letter grants Christian communities in Islamic lands protection against acts of violence, protection for Christian cult sites, and exemption from taxes. (15)

Although the evidence confirms a common origin, the fact that the Prophet could have produced such documents is apparently unpalatable to Ratliff. Failing to follow the scientific method, which demands that one focus first on the most likely cause as opposed to far-fetched theories, she relates that a Christian convert from Islam, who had become a monk at Mar Saba, made his way to Mount Sinai, and eventually became its Abbot (16). Born Rabi ibn Qays ibn Yazid al-Ghassani in the city of Najran, this person is said to have changed his name to ʻAbd al-Masih. As mundane as this may be, Ratliff is fascinated by the fact that an Arab Christian convert rose to preeminence at the Monastery of Saint Catherine. The manuscript on which this information is based originates from Mount Sinai and dates from the 9th or 10th century. According to Sidney H. Griffith, ʻAbd al-Masih was martyred in the 860s (Ratliff 17, note 23). While she is not bold enough to come out and say it directly, the implication is clear: Ratliff alleges that ʻAbd al-Masih, an Arab and former Muslim, had both the linguistic skills and religious knowledge to forge the famous *Patent of Muhammad*.

Although Ratliff shies away from saying so herself, she gives credence to the claims of the incredulous. Regarding the *Letter of Protection* of the Prophet, Ratliff writes that "[s]ince the nineteenth century, scholars have questioned aspects of the document" (17, note 9; see also Mouton 177). One of the first to do so, of course, was Johann Ludwig Burckhardt (1784–1817 CE), the Swiss traveler and Orientalist, who summarized his arguments as follows:

> It is a favorite belief of the monks of Mount Sinai, that Mohammed himself, in one of his journeys, alighted under the walls of the convent, and that impressed with due veneration for the mountain of Moses, he presented to the convent a Firmahn, to secure to it the respect of all his followers. Ali is said to have written it, and Mohammed, who could not write, to have confirmed it by impressing his extended hand, blackened with ink, upon the parchment. This Firmahn, it is added, remained in the convent until Selim the First conquered Egypt, when hearing of the precious relic, he sent for it, and added it to the other relics of Mohammed in the imperial treasury at Constantinople; giving to the convent, in return, a copy of the original certified with his own cipher. I have seen the latter, which is kept in the Sinai convent at Cairo, but I do not believe it to be an authentic document. None of the historians of Mohammed, who have recorded the transactions of almost every day of his life, mention his having been at Mount Sinai, neither in his earlier youth, nor after he set up as a prophet, and it is totally contrary to history that he should have granted to any Christians such privileges as are

mentioned in this Firmahn, one of which is that the Moslems are bound to aid the Christian monks in rebuilding their ruined churches. It is to be observed also that this document states itself to have been written by Ali, not at the convent, but in the mosque of the Prophet at Medina, in the second year of the Hedjra, and is addressed, not to the convent of Mount Sinai in particular, but to all the Christians and their priests. The names of twenty-two witnesses, followers of Mohammed, are subscribed to it; and in a note it is expressly stated that the original, written by 'Ali, was lost, and that the present was copied from a fourth successive copy taken from the original. Hence it appears that the relation of the priests is at variance with the document to which they refer, and I have little doubt therefore that the former is a fable and the latter a forgery. (Chapter 7, 546–47)

Known also as John Lewis or Jean Louis, Burckhardt had converted to Islam, sincerely or otherwise, dressed as an Arab, and went by the name of Shaykh Ibrahim ibn 'Abd Allah. If his conversion was genuine, as Paul Lunde believes, his *Travels in Syria and the Holy Land* would represent the first Islamic critique of the *Covenant of the Prophet Muhammad with the Monks of Mount Sinai.* Although his family members always rejected claims that John Lewis Burckhardt converted to Islam, he was indeed buried as a Muslim in Cairo, at the age of 32, under the name of Shaykh Ibrahim. In all likelihood, Lewis simply pretended to be a Muslim, as others had done, to facilitate his travels throughout the Holy Land, including the sacred city of Mecca.

Regardless of his religious convictions, Burckhardt made some interesting observations. He points out that "None of the historians of Mohammed, who have recorded the transactions of almost every day of his life, mention his having been at Mount Sinai, neither in his earlier youth, nor after he set up as a prophet" (Chapter 7). The Swiss Orientalist seems to forget that virtually nothing is known about Muhammad's life prior to the proclamation of prophecy. By the time he was in his forties, most of the adults who accompanied him as a child were dead. Besides the Prophet himself, and the monks of Mount Sinai, few, if any, witnesses to those early events still existed. Still, it is possible that the story of Bahira the Monk was an echo of the Prophet's encounter with the monks of Mount Sinai. Burckhardt's claim that "it is totally contrary to history" that the Prophet "should have granted to any Christians such privileges as are mentioned in this *Firmahn*, one of which is that the Moslems are bound to aid the Christian monks in rebuilding their ruined churches" (Chapter 7) is manifestly untrue. As this study makes abundantly clear, the Prophet issued numerous edicts providing protection to the People of the Book and signed many memorandums of understanding.

The Swiss Orientalist also argues that the *Covenant* "states itself to have been written by 'Ali, not at the convent, but in the mosque of the Prophet at Medina, in the second year of the Hedjra, and is addressed, not to the convent of Mount Sinai in particular, but to all the Christians and their priests" (Chapter 7). Had Burckhardt been familiar with the letters and treaties of the Prophet, he would have known that many of the declarations of the Messenger of Allah did not refer directly to their intended recipients. When confronted with a question, he would provide a direct, but distant, ruling, a tradition followed to this day by Shi'ite jurists. The response is supposed to be applicable to all. The principles the Prophet set forth applied not only to the monks of Mount Sinai, but to Christians around the world. This universal approach is seen in the other covenants concluded by the Messenger of Allah. On the basis of his cumulative arguments, Burckhardt concludes that the relation of the priests is a fable and that the covenant is a forgery (Chapter 7).

Rather than weigh the arguments of their predecessors for significance and veracity, Orientalists like Ratliff and Mouton merely ingest them, digest them, and redeliver them; in this case, the issue of the twenty-two witnesses. In the words of Mouton, "The lists of witnesses attesting to the authenticity of the document is also suspect: some of them, such as Abu Hurayrah and Abu al-Darda' had not yet converted to Islam at this date and even fought against it" (177).

Since the *Covenant of the Prophet Muhammad with the Monks of Mount Sinai* is dated on the third of Muharram of the second year of the *hijrah*, which corresponds to July 7th, 623 of the Gregorian calendar, and Abu Hurayrah (603–681 CE) reportedly joined the Prophet in Medina in the year 7 AH (628/629 CE), Mouton concludes that the covenant is a fake (182, note 5). What he fails to mention, however, is that Abu Hurayrah is also reported to have visited the Prophet in Mecca during the early years of Islam. Consequently, as an acquaintance, even before he was a Companion, Abu Hurayrah may very well have visited the Messenger of Allah on other occasions.

As for Abu al-Darda', Mouton writes that he only converted to Islam after Battle of Badr in 624 and was the last of his family to do so (182, note 5). Since the battle took place on March 13, 624 CE, and the covenant was concluded on July 7, 623 CE, Mouton concludes that the patent is a forgery. Mouton gives the impression that Abu al-Darda' fought on the side of the Meccans against the Muslims from Medina. What he fails to realize, however, is that Abu al-Darda' was not a Meccan but a Medinan. Thus, the claim that Abu al-Darda' fought Islam is based on a false premise. A member of the Ansar of Medina, Abu al-Darda' was a cautious person who did not act precipitously. While Abu al-Darda' may have converted in 624 CE; it is also reported that he converted one year after the *hijrah*, which would have been 623 CE, the very year in which the covenant was concluded with the monks of Mount Sinai. Whether he converted in the first or second year of the *hijrah* is immaterial. The fact that he lived in Medina, was a respected merchant and member of the community, had good relations with the Prophet, and was friendly towards Islam are weighty justifications for his appearance as a witness to the covenant concluded with the Christians from the Sinai.

It should be recalled that *isnads* or chains of narration only came to prevail as a means of authentication over a century after the passing of the Prophet. While the events were proximate to memory, and witnesses to the facts were alive and available, there was no need to substantiate all accounts. This is a distinction that is often ignored by historians and Islamic scholars. It was only later, after the passing of the Companions and the Followers of the Companions that scholars felt obliged to develop a system of authenticating narrations. As such, they started to attach chains of narrations to the sayings of the Prophet and even included them in historical texts. In many instances, these chains of narration were produced centuries after the fact. This does not necessarily mean that the saying or account is spurious, though a scholar could have certainly made an honest mistake in trying to trace back a tradition. Furthermore, since many of the surviving documents produced by the Prophet do not include witnesses, it is possible that the witnesses cited on some of the covenants were added after the fact to meet the scholarly demands of the day and to silence doubters. A mistake in a chain of narration is simply that: an error due to neglect, oversight, forgetfulness or lack of information. It should also be recalled that only Muslims have used these chains of narration to trace back a saying to its origin. According to the scholarly standards of the rest of the world, a single reference is sufficient to establish authority. Muslim scholars, on the other hand, demanded a complete history of citation by demonstrably trustworthy authorities, a much higher standard of scholarship. It is ironic, then, that the works of non-Muslims, which lack chains of narration, have not aroused legions of critics in the Muslim world alleging that they are not authentic, seeing that the Muslim methodology of documentation is unsurpassed even by modern researchers (Azami 75).

Based on the proliferation of "sic" throughout his Arabic rendition of the *Covenant of the Prophet Muhammad with the Monks of Mount Sinai*, it would seem that Moritz was suggesting that such shortcomings were somehow suspicious (6–8). Since the Qur'an was the first book committed to writing in the Arabic alphabet, grammar and orthography had yet to be formalized, a process that would take centuries. Hence, it is not at all unexpected to find so-called "spelling mistakes" in early Arabic manuscripts. In most cases, these are simply variants, similar to those found in other sources from the period. Earlier written English also exhibits a lack of standardized spelling. The last will and testament of William Shakespeare was signed both "Shakspere" and "Shakspeare" in his own hand; the name of Sir Walter Raleigh was written by his contemporaries either as Raleigh, Raliegh, Ralegh, Raghley, Rawley, Rawly, Rawlie, Rawleigh, Raulighe, Raughlie, or Rayly. And while these variants may have existed in earlier manuscripts, they could also be of later origin, having been caused by the slips of some scribe or copyist. In terms of spelling, style, and usage, the covenant in question contains many archaic traits.

In what he hoped would be the death-blow to the *Covenant of the Prophet Muhammad with the Monks of Mount Sinai*, Jean-Michel Mouton points out that it was dated on 3 Muharram in the year 2 of the Hegira while "the hijri calendar did not yet exist; it was only established in 637 by the Caliph ʿUmar who, in retrospect, made it start in 622" (177). What Mouton chooses to ignore, however, is that it was Imam ʿAli ibn Abi Talib (d. 661) who proposed the *hijri* calendar to ʿUmar ibn al-Khattab (579–644 CE). Since he had conceived of the *hijri* calendar, it is conceivable that Imam ʿAli had long been employing this method of dating. Furthermore, he was the scribe who wrote down the covenant in question, and it is reasonable to suppose that he would date it according to the *hijri* system. It is also widely accepted in Shiʿite scholarly circles that Imam ʿAli, and the eleven Imams who followed him, had inherited the knowledge of the Prophet. In other words, much of the knowledge that Imam ʿAli possessed came directly from the Messenger of Allah and this might well include the Islamic calendar.

While it is possible that ʿUmar ibn al-Khattab was the first to actually mandate the official use of the Islamic calendar at a time when various calendars were in use, this does not negate the distinct possibility that the *hijri* calendar had been employed at an earlier date. It is a phenomenon well-known throughout the world that populations often adopt civil measures informally long before they become part of a body of law. During the time of the Prophet and the covenant in question, many conflicting dating systems were being used. Hence, for the sake of simplicity and uniformity, the Second Caliph officially imposed the Islamic calendar. As Mouton admits, dates were then adjusted retrospectively. Hence, when an old document which contained a superseded dating method was copied anew, the new dating system was employed. This entire line of argument, however, is contingent upon the claim that Imam ʿAli conceived of the Islamic calendar and convinced Caliph ʿUmar to introduce it universally.

What Mouton conveniently ignores is the fact that some Muslim scholars believe that the hegira dating system was developed by the Prophet himself. As Kasim Sulum explains, the Islamic calendar was developed in the 2nd year of the *hijrah*. Without a functioning Islamic calendar, the practices of fasting and sacrifice could not have been established. As a result, "the calendar must also be regarded as a part of the developments in calendar practices of the period of Holy Prophet." Although minor modifications were made by ʿUmar in his "official Islamic calendar," these were all based on the "original Islamic calendar" which had been used by the Prophet since the second year of the *hijrah*.

As for the disparity in dates on ancient Islamic documents, they are easily explained. To begin with, documents were rarely, if ever, dated in earlier times. "[T]he ancient Arabs," writes Lammens, "were not familiar with calculation in years" (195). It was only later generations of scribes who attempted to date documents to establish the proper sequence of events. According to Ibn Qutaybah (828–885 CE), Hudayfah ibn al-Yaman (d. 656 CE), a Companion of the Prophet admitted that: "We are Arab people; when we report, we predate and postdate, we add and we subtract at will, but we do not mean to lie" (qtd. Berkey 58). As a result of this retrospective tracking, some historical events and documents may be off by a few years. Issues with early Islamic dating have been addressed by numerous scholars. As F.E. Peters (b. 1927 CE) explains,

Later Muslim authorities seem to give tacit recognition to the uncertainty of any of the chronological indications passed on about the Prophet's life at Mecca. They, like us, must have felt that the historical ground grew firm only at Muhammad's migration to Medina. (103)

As Hashim Amir 'Ali (1903–1987 CE) admits, "there is more calendrical confusion connected with these ten years of Muhammad's mission in Medina than with any other decade of human history either before or after this period" (qtd. Peters 253). The lunisolar calendar used during the early days of Islam involved intercalation, namely, the inclusion of a leap month. It is not known exactly when the Prophet suppressed this intercalary month (Lammers 204). When the Caliph 'Umar (579–644 CE) introduced a purely lunar calendar it "ousted to some extent the older chronology involving intercalation and . . . naturally found its way into the chronicles of many historians of the period" (Peters 309, note 11). Although the Muslim era began with Muhammad's migration to Medina, an event that took place in September 622, "[t]he initial date of the new era was, however, pushed back for calendrical purposes to the first day of the first month of that year, 1 Muharram or July 16, 622 CE" (Peters 252–253). While this move introduced order and a new degree of self-identity into the affairs of the new Muslim Commonwealth, "one perhaps unanticipated side-effect was to introduce a degree of anarchy into the Muslims' recollection of the date of events during the intercalation era at Medina" (Peters 253). Many dates were also adjusted to match auspicious astrological dates or sacred days. Mnemonic devices were used to provide a proper narrative pattern (Faizer xv). Even the ages of certain personalities were altered for various, often symbolic, ideological or symmetrical reasons, including the date of birth of Muhammad, the age of Khadijah upon marriage, and the birth of Fatimah al-Zahra. As speculation abounded, honest mistakes were also made. For Prince Leoni Caetani (1869–1935 CE), there exists a possibility of error of three years in the Prophet's chronology (Lammens 188). For Henri Lammens (1862–1937 CE), a scholar who viewed the Qur'an with "pious contempt," and who was known for skewing sources to support his contentious claims, a full ten years may have been added to Muhammad's existence (197). According to a rock inscription, "Abraha conducted large-scale raids against defiant Arab tribes near Mecca in 552 CE" (Schulz). As a result, "[a] few Western historians consider this to be the true year of Muhammad's birth."

With regard to the *Covenant of the Prophet Muhammad with the Monks of Mount Sinai*, Davenport made the following important observation: "It not being customary in those days to date documents, it is very probable that the original patent had no date, and that the one given in the text was assigned to it at a subsequent period by the writer" (151). It is equally possible that the Monastery at Mount Sinai had more than one version of the *Patent*, as it was the practice of the Prophet, and his successors, to renew such covenants on an almost yearly basis. In all probability, however, both the dates, the name of the scribe, and those of the witnesses were added at a later time when such information was viewed as imperative by scholars specializing in prophetic sayings. As far as Josée Balagna is concerned, the manuscripts witnessed by Mu'awiyyah (602–680 CE) in the fourth year of the *hijrah* are anomalous; however, the manuscripts attributed to 'Ali, which were written in the second year of said calendar, are "plausible or likely" (66–67).

The order of the witnesses is especially suspicious, listing Abu Bakr first, 'Umar second, 'Uthman third, 'Ali, fourth, and Mu'awiyyah, fifth, as this is the traditional order of the Caliphs for the Sunnis. Although most Sunnis ignore the fact, 'Ali was only added to the list of "rightly-guided" Caliphs during the time of Imam Ahmad ibn al-Hanbal (780–855 CE) two centuries after his rule. Not only was 'Ali not considered a Caliph by the Umayyads, those who coined the term *ahl al-sunnah wa al-jama'ah* as an act of opposition against the *ahl al-bayt* of the Prophet, he was the subject of ritualized cursing throughout the empire. If anything, the order of the witnesses suggests that it was attached at a later period, no earlier than the rule of ʿUmar ibn ʿAbd al-ʿAziz (r. 717 to 720 CE), the Umayyad Caliph who halted the long-standing custom of cursing Imam ʿAli (d. 661 CE) at the end of Friday sermons. ʿUmar II, as he was known, is also credited with ordering the first official compilation of *hadith* which, he feared, were in danger of being lost forever. Evidently, the list of witnesses may have been attached at a later period; however, it could not conceivably have been attached any earlier according to this hypothesis.

In order to support his allegations that the Prophet's visit to Mount Sinai is a legend, and that the *firman* attributed to him is a forgery, Jean-Michel Mouton insists that the document conserved at Saint Catherine contains nothing really original and that it belongs to a body of similar documents preserved by several institutions from the medieval Near East (177). For Mouton, all of these documents come from the same source, a so-called letter of Muhammad addressed to Christians which was "discovered" in 878 CE in an Iraqi monastery (177). In peremptory fashion, Mouton alleges that "This original letter was also false and was, without a doubt, forged on the order of the Banu Makhlad, a family of viziers of Nestorian origin. They forged such documents out of concern to protect their community of origin" (177).

While it is true that the document conserved at Saint Catherine repeats the same points made in the *Covenant of the Prophet Muhammad with the Christians of Najran* which was found in Iraq, it is not true that "There was no visible effort of adaptation on the part of the monks who forged the *firman* of Saint Catherine" (177). Mouton, as usual, operates in a world of groundless assumptions and conjectures. He has not provided a shred of proof that the monks of Mount Sinai forged their covenant on the basis of another supposedly forged covenant found in Iraq. While most of the points are similar—which makes sense if they were written by the same person—they are not identical in content. Having carefully compared both documents, I can confirm that no "cut and paste" job ever took place. Despite the fact that both covenants are written in the Classical Arabic of the period, there are differences in style. The covenant from the Sinai is more direct while the covenant from Iraq is much more elaborate, at least in the long introductory section which precedes the actual list of privileges. Furthermore, there is no evidence whatsoever that proves that the Banu Makhlad was engaged in forging prophetic treaties for the purpose of protecting the Christian community. Certainly there were senior officials of the ʿAbbasid Caliphate, such as Saʿid ibn Makhlad (d. 889 CE), who were Nestorian Christian converts to Islam and who rose to prominence as viziers; in this instance, during the regency of al-Muwaffaq over his brother, al-Mu'tamid, who was the nominal Caliph 878–885 CE. However, there is no evidence whatever that they ordered anyone to falsely attribute traditions to the Prophet Muhammad. In fact, Saʿid ibn Makhlad's career came to an abrupt end as a result of his Christian brother's attempt to obtain special concessions for the Christian subjects of the Caliphate. Another famous vizier was al-Hasan ibn Makhlad ibn al-Jarrah (d. c. 882 CE), a senior official of the ʿAbassid Caliphate, who served as secretary under Caliph al-Mutawakkil (r. 847–861 CE), and vizier under al-Mu'tamid (r. 877; 878–879 CE). Another Nestorian Christian who converted to Islam late in life, al-Hasan ibn Makhlad, was also dismissed, this time by al-Muwaffaq, the Caliph's brother, and sent into exile in Egypt and then Antioch. It is highly unlikely that peddling a previously unknown patent from the Prophet would have gone unnoticed and little chance that it would have gone unpunished. A record of any such scandal should have reached us as the *hadith* science literature provides plenty of examples of famous forgeries of prophetic traditions. Finally, although the ʿAbbasids employed many non-Muslims in their administration, they were careful not "to give the People of the Book too much influence over the court and the empire" (Karabell 46).

While most of the focus has been directed towards the credibility of the *Covenant of the Prophet Muhammad with the Monks of Mount Sinai* itself, no attention has been paid to the actual story surrounding it; in particular, the presence of an eagle. According to all of the various versions which narrate the pilgrimage of Muhammad to Mount Sinai, an auspicious eagle appeared, circling above the future prophet, and spreading its wings over his head. The eagle, of course, is considered the messenger of the Creator in many cultural traditions. In the Jewish context, the eagle symbolizes the divine powers of deliverance and watchful protection. In the Christian context, the eagle is one of the Four Living Creatures surrounding the Throne of the Lamb in the Apocalypse and the symbol of Saint John the Evangelist while in the Islamic context it was associated with the Angel Gabriel. The fact that the eagle circled Muhammad symbolized that he was divinely-protected. Since Saint John the Evangelist predicted the coming of the Comforter or Paraclete (14:16; 15:26; 16:7), the eagle may have been pointing out that Muhammad was the long-awaited one. As the symbol of Gabriel, the eagle was the embodiment of the angel of revelation. Buraq, the mystical animal that the Prophet mounted on his Night-Journey, is also described as having the wings of a giant eagle. While the eagle is not a major symbol in Islam, it is curious to note that the Black Standard of Muhammad was known as *rayat al-ʻuqab*, namely, "the Banner of the Eagle," even though it was solid black. Could the Prophet's flag have been an allusion to his divine appointment at Mount Sinai? It seems that only God and the Prophet could say.

The image of the eagle is particularly rare in Sunni sources; it does not appear in any other accounts of Muhammad's contacts with Christians. In the story of Bahira, it was a cloud, and not an eagle, that followed Muhammad overhead. The story of the eagle seems to be uniquely associated with Muhammad and the monks of Mount Sinai. Shiʻite sources, however, seem to contain echoes of the event. In Majlisi's *Hayat al-qulub*, for example, one finds that Muhammad has extensive contact with Christian monks from the time he was a small child until adulthood. As an infant, Muhammad was taken by ʻAbd al-Muttalib to a monastery in Johfa where he was attended by a Christian physician who recognized him as a future prophet (Section 4). While under the care of his foster-mother, Halimah, the Muhammad was identified as a future messenger of God by forty Christian monks (Section 4). On another occasion, when Muhammad was but a little boy, a white bird is said to have carried him to a spot where he ate fruit and drank water from a stream. That angelic bird was described by Muhammad as being the Angel Gabriel (Section 4). So, Shiʻite sources, at least, speak of Muhammad's meetings with monks during his early age and the providential presence of a heavenly bird. While many may dismiss these accounts from Majlisi as late mythological developments, similar stories are also found in early Christian sources.

One of the earliest existing biographies of Muhammad completed by a Christian is the *Istoria de Mahomet* or *Life of Muhammad*, a scurrilous Latin work which dates to circa 850 CE. While slanderous and salacious and produced with propagandist intent, its anonymous author appears to have had a "significant degree of familiarity with Islam" (Gervers 95). He relates, for example, that the devil sent a golden-faced vulture to Muhammad who convinced him that he was the Angel Gabriel (Tolan 42; Christys 62; Constable 48–49; Gervers 97–99). Since the author deliberately corrupted details of Muhammad's life, he appears to have turned the eagle into a vulture and Gabriel into a demon. This, however, is not the most interesting thing. The real question is where did this Latin author derive this information? The story of Muhammad at Mount Sinai does not exist in any of the surviving Arabic and Islamic sources. Unless the author had access to Muslim sources that did not survive the test of time, he must have obtained this information from Christians.

The *Tultusceptru del libro domni Metobii*, included in the *Liber apologeticus martyrum* of Eulogius of Córdoba also makes mention of Muhammad and a bird-type creature. In this bizarre account, an abbot named Osius experienced a vision from an angel who instructed him go preach the truth to the pagans of Erribon or Yathrib in Arabia (Gervers 94). Realizing that his failing health would prevent him from fulfilling his duties, he sent one of his monks, Ozim, in his place. On his way to his destination, the boy encountered an *angelus malignus*, namely, a fallen angel or demon, perched on an oak tree (94–95). The evil angel, who claimed to be the same angel as had appeared to his master Osius, asked him to change his name to "Mohomad," and ordered him to preach a terribly transliterated formula which sounds like: "Allah is Great, Allah is Great, there is no god but Allah and Muhammad is his Messenger" (95). According to the author, the naïve young boy, Ozim-Muhammad, was unaware that he was invoking demons (95). As a result of the intervention of the evil angel, Muhammad corrupted the true message of Osius and misguided the Arabs that he had planned to save (94–95).

Since both of these early Latin accounts of the life of Muhammad speak of flying creatures and monks, it may be that they were drawing upon early accounts of the Prophet's interactions with the monks of Mount Sinai. This would prove that stories of miraculous events surrounding Muhammad's pilgrimage to the Sinai were in circulation in the mid-9th century rather than having been spontaneously generated in Fatimid times centuries later by Christians for the purpose of self-preservation. As abominable as they may be, these early accounts share a series of core elements with the accounts passed down by the monks of Mount Sinai. As such, they may actually serve to corroborate the true, traditional, account of events. When scholars like Arthur Jeffery (1892–1959 CE) argue that legendary development found in sources like *Hayat al-qulub* is of Christian origin (352), they do so in order to disprove Islamic tradition. However, in the case of the Prophet's encounters with Christian monks, such an argument can be used to confirm it. While the *Legend of Sergius Bahira* was invented in the 9th century to undermine Islam, it makes mention of a revelation that Bahira received on Mount Sinai. This is certainly strange since no Islamic account of Bahira associates him with the Sinai. And although this Aramaic and Arabic legend is little more than a litany of lies fabricated by Christians, it draws, in part, on elements found in the Islamic versions of the event. The fact that Mount Sinai does not appear in the Muslim traditions about the mysterious monk makes one wonder whether the Christian forgers of the *Legend of Sergius Bahira* were familiar with the story of Muhammad's early peregrination to the Monastery of Saint Catherine. While their intent was polemical, the Christians who composed the legend may have inadvertently helped preserve proof of some sort of connection between Muhammad and that monastery.

Returning to more modern times, the allegation that the Ottomans rejected the *Covenant of the Prophet Muhammad with the Christians of the World* must be addressed. While it is possible that some Turks refused to accept the covenants, it was not necessarily on the grounds that they were fakes. It may simply have been because they prevented them from taxing, forcibly converting, and even killing Christians. Such motivations are socio-political and economic; not religious. The fact that some Turks objected to the covenants is not proof that they are false for just as many, if not more, insisted that they were authentic. For Father Golubovich, these Turkish administrators were "accomplices" of the Orthodox Christians (L'École Pratique d'Études Bibliques 637). But what could possibly have motivated Muslims to forge something in the name of the Prophet Muhammad? What did they have to gain? Why would any Ottoman diplomat risk the ire of Allah, the Prophet, the Imams, the Sultans, the Grand Viziers, the *'ulama'*, the janissaries, and the Muslim masses?

If the *Covenant of the Prophet Muhammad with the Monks of Mount Sinai* dates to the 16th century why are there allusions to it in the 15th century? In a treaty concluded between the order of St. John of Jerusalem and the Sultan of Egypt in 1403 CE "mention is made . . . of the pilgrims who repaired to St. Catherine of Mount Sinai, and permission is given to that convent to repair its buildings and to construct new ones" (Laborde 332–333). This decision was in keeping with the Prophet's command to protect, build, and repair the churches and monasteries of the Christians. Simon Joseph Léon Emmanuel Marquis de Laborde (1807–1869 CE), the French archeologist and politician, pointed out that this treaty was made in the middle of the Crusades. As Laborde concedes, "[i]t is surprising to observe the indulgence with which the Saracens treated those Christians who thus traversed their country" (333). Although European Christians had been at war with the Muslims for two centuries, the custodians of the sacred sites—and by this, I mean, all holy places, whether Jewish, Christian or Muslim—continued to host Christian pilgrims from the Western world. If, even under siege by Crusaders, the Muslims persisted in protecting sacred Christian spaces, and those that visited them, they must have been abiding by commands of a higher order. To be quite blunt, this example of Muslim tolerance made little military sense as many of the pilgrims were Christian knights.

Simply because a covenant was copied in 1630, 1561, 1538 or at some point in the 10th century CE does not mean it was created on that date. It is unreasonably cynical to assume that all of the covenants were forgeries. If all of the covenants of the Prophet are fakes, fabricated, say, in the 9th century, by Christian priests or monks, why is it that all of the injunctions they contain had been applied by Muslims since the first days of the conquest in the 7th century? If one looks at the laws implemented by the early Caliphs (Fortescue 226), they are virtually identical to those contained in the covenants. This suggests that the covenants were known and observed from the earliest days of Islamic rule. Hence, the fact that the oldest extant copies date from the 9th, 16th, and 17th centuries is immaterial.

Commentary on the Content of the Covenant

The *Covenant of the Prophet Muhammad with the Monks of Mount Sinai* commences with the invocation of God's greatness and quickly moves into specifics: "As God is great and governs, from whom all the prophets are come, for there remains no record of injustice against God." Not only is God great, dictates the Prophet, but He also governs. The point is important both theologically and politically. Theologically, the Jews and Christians were engaged in a series of polemics concerning the role of the Creator. Some Jewish scholars argued that God has retired from active participation in the world after Creation, a view shared by the Deists of the Enlightenment and also by some contemporary Christian thinkers, such as Ernesto Cardenal. The Islamic position, espoused by the Prophet, is in agreement with the Catholic tradition which holds that God is actively engaged in a continuous process of Creation and Re-Creation. Hence, He is very much the Creator and Sustainer of the Universe.

If God rules, then, it follows that the rule of God should be established upon the earth; as the Lord's Prayer beseeches, "Thy will be done on earth as it is in heaven." This raises the critical questions of who is invested with the authority to implement the Law of Allah upon the land. Islam answers: none other than the prophets of God; among whom Muhammad, the Messenger of Allah, represents the completion of the prophetic mission. Hence, the importance of Muhammad as *khatim al-anbiya* or the Seal of the Prophets, he who is the "careful guardian of the whole world." As such, the covenant he bequeathed to the monks of Mount Sinai is directed, not only to the entire Muslim *ummah*, but to the Christian Nation as well. As the Prophet proclaimed: he "has written the present instrument to all those who are in his national people, and of his own religion, as a secure and positive promise to be accomplished to the Christian nation." During a period in which class was everything and strictly defined one's role in society, the Prophet did not direct his covenant to the rich, the powerful, and the noble. He did not give his word simply to the ecclesiastic establishment. His covenant was concluded with each and every Christian: "whosoever they may be, whether they be the noble or the vulgar, the honorable or otherwise." The *Covenant*, then, conveyed a clear rejection of classism, elitism, and racism. It is thus in complete agreement with the contents of the *Constitution of Medina*: all are equal before God for whom the most important thing is not language, skin color, social status or class position which exclude others, but rather the degree of piety, humanity, love for others (which includes not only human beings but the entire natural order), sincerity of faith, the acceptance of His Commandments, and complete certainty as to the special place occupied by His Prophets, Messengers, and Imams.

As the covenant was made in the Name of Allah and His Most Noble Messenger, it was binding upon all Muslims at all times. The first item of the covenant is a stern warning directed to those who violate the Prophet's promise:

> I. Whosoever of my nation shall presume to break my promise and oath, which is contained in this present agreement, destroys the promise of God, acts contrary to the oath, and will be a resister of the faith, (which God forbid) for he becomes worthy of the curse. . . .

Once again, the Prophet reiterates his rejection of racism, elitism, and classism, warning that the curse of Almighty Allah will befall on any of those who betray his oath "whether he be the King himself, or a poor man." If a man's word is gold, the Prophet's word was made of platinum and the most precious and priceless jewels. The Prophet personally promised to grant protection and safety to all Christians covered by the covenant:

> whenever any of the monks in his travels shall happen to settle upon any mountain, hill, village, or other habitable place, on the sea, or in deserts, or in any convent, church, or house of prayer, I shall be in the midst of them, as the preserver and protector of them, their goods and effects, with my soul, aid, and protection. . . .

Since all Muslims must submit to the will of Allah and His Messenger, the *Covenant of the Prophet* is binding on all believers. The promise of protection is made, not only in the name of God and His Prophet, but in the name of all of his followers. As the Prophet makes explicitly clear, the covenant is concluded "jointly with all my national people." Rather than view Christians as Others and Outsiders, the Messenger of Allah insists that "they are a part of my own people, and an honor to me," clearly comprehending that those who possess power are judged on the basis of how they treat the minorities in their midst. As categorically demonstrated by this covenant, there is truly nothing honorable in exterminating members of minorities or engaging in religious, ethnic or racial "cleansing." The honor of the law resides in embracing diversity and multiculturalism, as the Qur'an affirms (49:13). The French, the English, and the Spanish, on the other hand (to cite only a few examples), spent over a millennium attempting to impose a single language and a single religion upon their nations to the detriment of religious and linguistic minorities. Australia—which, like Canada, earlier promoted multiculturalism—now advocates assimilation. By defending diversity, the Prophet Muhammad established a norm of social justice rare in any time. The Prophet never imposed *shari'ah* law on non-Muslims. Jewish people were judged on the basis of Jewish law and Christians were judged on the basis of Christian law. The example of the Prophet was emulated by Imam 'Ali (d. 661 CE). After receiving the pledge of allegiance from the people, Imam 'Ali made the following famous statement:

> Question me before you lose me. Question me, for I have the knowledge of those who came earlier and those who will come after. If the cushion (on which a judge sits) was folded for me (to sit on), I could give judgments to the people of the Torah by their Torah, to the people of the Gospels by their Gospels, to the people of Psalms by their Psalms, and to the people of the *Furqan* (i.e. Qur'an) by their *Furqan*, so that each one of these books will be fulfilled and will declare, 'O Lord, indeed 'Ali has given judgment according to Your Decree.' (Mufid 21)

Because the monks comprised a religious community, as opposed to a commercial enterprise, the Prophet granted them tax-free status. "I command all officers," he wrote, "not to require any poll-tax of them, or any other tribute, because they shall not be forced or compelled to anything of this kind." Unlike despots and dictators, from both past and present, who have often raided the coffers of religious authorities, the Prophet viewed them as non-profit entities engaged in charitable, social service, and spiritual activities. Not only did he grant them ecclesiastic autonomy, he even granted them politically autonomy, like a free associated state or an autonomous region. However, unlike free associated states such as Puerto Rico, whose people are deprived of the right to vote, the Christian communities were free to elect their own political representatives and members of their judiciary: "None shall presume to change their judges or governors," declares the Prophet, "but they shall remain in their office, without being deported." Again, in contrast to other rulers who would eliminate the previous administration after assuming power, removing—by exile, imprisonment or execution—the remnants of any earlier regime and replacing them with loyalists, the Prophet would keep the same administrative and judiciary structures in place, seeking only love and loyalty in return. Most leaders of the time, and many leaders of the present, act according to the animal order. Like dominant lions and bears, who go to the extreme of killing cubs of previous or potential competitors, many victorious political and/or military leaders still physically purge the leaders of the preceding administration. Based on his actions, it is clear that the Messenger of Allah was not a centrist but rather a federalist. Centrism is the concentration of political power in a single center. Federalism is a political organization based on the voluntary integration of provinces or states which delegate some of their powers to the central power while maintaining their autonomy. Federalism is thus the most pragmatic and convenient method of constructing a government that recognizes diversity of its constituents and allows them to maintain their principles. So, what the Prophet was creating were provinces or states that had a wide range of rights and freedoms within the larger framework of the Islamic *ummah*. This is federalism. It may be Islamic Federalism but it is federalism nonetheless.

The fifth item promised by the Prophet was freedom of movement, a right taken for granted by many people in the world today. Yet, even in recent times, freedom of movement was not granted in most Communist countries. Even non-Communist countries, like Saudi Arabia, require its citizens to obtain permits to travel within their own homeland. In the kingdom in question, women cannot even drive much less travel without the permission of their father, husband, or senior male relatives. In Morocco, a *grand taxi* needs a special authorization simply to leave the outskirts of a city. Papers are routinely checked at check-points throughout the country. All entrances and exits to towns in certain regions are blocked by military check-points and barracks. One has to permanently carry identification at the risk of immediate imprisonment. The movement of people in many nations is controlled at all times. However, before the dawn of Islam, and in its early years, there was no freedom of travel or, more specifically, little assumption of safety with regard to travel. The lands were overrun with highwaymen, robbers, thieves, rapists, pillagers, murderers, and human traffickers. Consequently, the Arabs always had to be armed and travel in large groups for the purpose of protection. In lands under the rule of Islam, the Muslim State promised, and provided, protection for travelers along the vast trade and travel routes. Whether they were Jews, Christians, Muslims, or members of other faiths, the Prophet promised that "No one shall molest them when they are travelling on the road."

In item six, the Prophet provided protection to all religious establishments. "Whatever churches they are possessed of, no one is to deprive them of them." In most Communist countries, religious communities had few or no rights. In the Soviet Union and China, for example, tens of thousands of mosques were destroyed. Muslims in France are denied places of worship through deliberate governmental policies. Even in the 21st century United States, Muslims in certain areas face almost insurmountable obstacles when they apply to build mosques. In many Western countries, even those which purport to uphold "human rights" and "religious liberty," mosques have been vandalized and set ablaze while authorities turn a blind eye. The Prophet, however, personally promised to protect all places of worship. Consequently, the building of synagogues and churches actually flourished during the Golden Age of Islam. This is not to say that an Islamic State can allow prosyletization within its midst. While non-Muslims are allowed freedom of religious practice; they are not allowed to engage in missionary activity among Muslims. Nothing prevents them, however, to spread the Gospel among pagans and polytheists.

In the manner of a great teacher, the Prophet regularly repeated his most important points. Item seven is not a right: it is the repetition of his initial warning: "Whosoever shall annul any of one of these my decrees, let him know positively that he annuls the ordinance of God." As for those who pretend to be *ahl al-Qur'an* and yet reject the Sunnah, they should know that they stand in opposition to both. As we read in the Holy Qur'an, Muslims are obliged to obey both Allah and His Messenger (2:285; 3:32; 4:13; 4:14; 8:1; 8:20; 8:24; 8:46; 9:71; 24:51; 24:52; 33:33; 33:66; 33:71; 48:17; 49:14; 58:13; 64:12; 72:23). While the Qur'an takes precedence, and though the Sunnah must be subjected to the highest degree of scientific scrutiny, it is an obligation to follow the true traditions of the Messenger of Allah. While a majority of Muslims meticulously follow the teachings of the Prophet on a myriad of issues, many, if not most of them, have neglected his instructions concerning tolerance towards religious minorities living in their midst. If mosques were historically open to anyone interested in Islam, they are now closed to non-Muslims in many countries. If "Allah" is merely the name of the One God in Arabic, the Malaysians seek to prohibit Christians from employing it when they should be encouraging it. Rather than honor their Jewish and Christian minorities, many Muslim countries have oppressed them and expelled them. While "Islam has traditionally been tolerant of religious minorities," writes William Dalrymple, "that Islamic tradition of tolerance is today wearing distinctly thin" (19). "After centuries of generally peaceful co-existence with their Muslim neighbors," he laments, "things are suddenly becoming difficult for the last Christians of the Middle East" (19).

Muslims, of course, are not entirely to blame for failing to live up to the ideals of early Islam. Often, they are responding to centuries of Crusades, colonialism, imperialism, and neo-imperialism. If Muslims were generally tolerant of the People of the Book, their attitude gradually changed in response to changing circumstances. By the 14th and 15th century, Muslim jurists adopted a more restrictive approach towards non-Muslims. As Humphreys observes, "Many of these texts are quite late . . . and represent a period when the status of non-Muslims had sharply degenerated from earlier times; here as elsewhere no one text should be made the basis for sweeping generalizations" (259). In other words, for every action, there comes a reaction. If Jews and Muslims once lived in harmony in many Arab countries, sharing the same common language, culture, and traditions, the establishment of the State of Israel ruined a millennium and a half of conviviality. Centuries of colonial aggression, which continues to the present through Western intervention, invasion, and occupation, has done nothing but increase animosity towards Christians as a whole. Campaigns to convert Muslims to the Christian faith, and continued attacks against everything Muslims hold to be sacred, such as the Qur'an and the Prophet Muhammad, have led many Muslims to view all Christians with suspicion and their churches as Trojan horses.

Expanding upon the fifth item, the Prophet addresses the issue of taxation, for a second time, in item eight: "Neither their judges, governors, monks, servants, disciples, or any others depending on them, shall pay any poll-tax, or be molested on that account." Fearing, rightfully so, that those who would succeed him might attempt to "read between the lines" of item five and argue that only the monks were granted tax-free status, and that such status did not apply to their judiciary, servants, students or dependants, the Prophet stresses that the freedom from the poll-tax applies to the entire Christian community at Mount Sinai. Once again, he reiterates his warning. In the words of the Most Noble Messenger, "I am their protector, wherever they shall be, either by land or sea, east or west, north or south; because both they and all that belong to them are included in this my promissory oath and patent." The Prophet is not merely their ruler. He is their protector. The Messenger of Allah was not merely the local warlord who reigned over Medina. He was not simply the leader of the Muslim community. He was, as he says so himself, the Rightful Ruler of the World, by the grace of God, and the guardian, not only of Islam, but of all Abrahamic religions. As such, he was the Patron of the People of the Book.

Because pan-Arabia contained a relatively large number of hermits, monks and wandering ascetics, including the likes of Bahira and other famous figures, the Prophet provided protection for all of them:

> And of those that live quietly and solitary upon the mountains, they shall exact neither poll-tax nor tithes from their incomes, neither shall any Muslim partake of what they have; for they labor only to maintain themselves.

Not only did he extend protection to the pious contemplatives among the People of the Book, he required that they be provided for: "Whenever the crop of the earth shall be plentiful in its due time, the inhabitants shall be obliged out of every bushel to give them a certain measure." In so doing, the Prophet demonstrated that he cared, not only for their spiritual vocation, but for their physical well-being. By supporting the People of the Book, the Prophet aimed to encourage good-will and cordial relations between the Christian and Muslim communities. When a government cares for its people, those people, save for the treacherous, will always be loyal and loving. The Prophet's policy was to win the hearts of the non-Muslims through selfless acts of kindness and consideration.

Since the monks of the Monastery of Saint Catherine were a peaceful people who had devoted their lives to prayer, the Prophet could never conceive of an occasion which would warrant sending them off to war. Consequently, he excluded them from military service. As item eleven establishes, "Neither in time of war shall they take them out of their habitations, nor compel them to go to the wars, nor even then shall they require of them any poll-tax." When dealing with Jewish and Christian tribes and communities, the Prophet typically accepted the poll-tax in lieu of military service. These communities in question could independently decide whether they wanted to pay the tax or whether they wanted to join the military when required. However, that distinction was for general populations, not the monastery. From them, the Messenger of Allah required neither taxes nor military service. In short, they were provided with rights and protections without any obligations save loyalty to the Prophet Muhammad. With regard to this "loyalty," it was not a dog-like loyalty to one's master or the servile attitude of lackeys such as was shown by some Hindus towards the British occupiers. Instead, loyalty meant a sincere respect for the covenants that had been concluded.

As the document explains, the previous eleven items applied specifically to the monks of Mount Sinai. The seven items which follow are applicable to Christians as a whole. Item twelve deals once again with the issue of taxation. These were not black-taxes or extortion as existed and continue to exist in many parts of the world. These were government taxes used to provide services to all the inhabitants of the Islamic *ummah* regardless of their religion. For those who argue that the Prophet Muhammad was merely a religious leader, that "there are no politics in Islam," or that "politics has always been secondary in Islam," the evidence shows that they are far afield of the historic reality. These erroneous beliefs may cause them to act in clear contravention of authoritative and unquestionable testimony. Politics is what propelled Islam into the broader global arena. The aim of Islam was not only a promising berth in the hereafter as well as a deepening sense of the presence of Allah in this life but also the creation of a just, ethically-based socio-economic system on earth which would help cultivate the best of human and spiritual values. It is this expansive and humanitarian system that helps the spirit to soar. Corrupt systems are corrupting. Immoral systems are demoralizing. It is only through a righteous Islamic Republic that Muslims can reach their highest potential securing what is best in both worlds: this life, and the Hereafter. The Messenger of Allah made sure, through such documents as these, that all People of the Book were invited into this balanced political body.

Fearing, once again, that his followers might eventually impose excessive taxation upon the People of the Book, the Prophet specified a limit. As item twelve establishes, "Those Christians who are inhabitants, and with their riches and traffic are able to pay the poll-tax, shall pay no more than twelve drachms." Clearly, this limit was not set in stone and could be changed in the future are a result of inflation. However, any increase would have to be justified. In other words, any future taxes would have to represent the equivalent of what 12 drachms were for the economy of the time. There is little doubt that the Prophet acknowledged a possible change in situation, society, and cultures. Unlike many nations, such as the United States, which provides the rich with many tax loopholes not available to the middle class, the Islamic State created by the Prophet taxed all parties equally. It should be noted, however, that although this is not mentioned in the covenant, Islamic law does not tax the poor. And the definition of poor determined by Islamic law is most generous. People are considered poor if they do not have enough savings to survive for an entire year without working. In the United States, that would represent an income of less than $20,000.00 per year in 2013 depending on where one resides. This does not have to be cash in hand. It could also be collateral as in the partial payment of a home mortgage and the value of vehicles. Still, people who live pay-check to pay-check are not obliged to pay taxes under Islamic rule. If post-medieval Europe was infamous for taxation which oppressed the poor (the Jews were crushed by these onerous taxes; large numbers of Christians from throughout Europe immigrated to the Americas to escape them), Islamic rule represented liberation. Although a great deal of fuss is made, by the foes of Islam, about the poll-tax imposed on *dhimmis* or Muslim subjects, the truth eludes most people. The poll-tax required of non-Muslims is actually much lower than the 2.5% *zakat* paid by Sunni Muslims and vastly less than the 20% of *khums* paid by Shi'ite Muslims. Non-Muslims are actually taxed far less than Muslims in an Islamic State. Such is the price Muslims are prepared to pay for peace. As for the political pundits who decry the "crushing taxes" that Muslims imposed on *dhimmis*, some economic contextualization is in order. What exactly did ten *dirhams* represent in the time of the Prophet? According to Muhammad Hamidullah (1908–2002 CE), the sum "represented the expenses of an average family for ten days" (Introduction 149). This is far from being the "exorbitant annual poll-tax" denounced by Habib Levy (165).

Some may claim that the poll-tax was discriminatory since it targeted only Jews and Christians and excluded other non-Muslims. They fail to note that the *jizyah* did not exist in the early days of Islam and that many jurists believe that it can legally be discontinued (Hamidullah 149–150). Hence, it is not an issue that any non-Muslim can hold over the heads of Muslims in good faith. In truth, the poll-tax was eventually abolished. What was never abolished, though, was the protection granted, not only to Jews and Christians, but to all other citizens of the Islamic State. While conservative clerics insisted that only Jews and Christians were People of the Book entitled to the status of *dhimmah* or protected people, others argued that it also embraced Zoroastrians, Manicheans, Buddhists, and even Hindus. Scholars like al-Biruni (937–1048 CE), Jamal al-Din al-Afghani (1837–1897 CE), Muhammad 'Abduh (1849–1905 CE), and Rashid Rida (1865–1935 CE) all believed in expanding the bounds of those considered as protected subjects. Their arguments were based on the Qur'an and the Sunnah. They claimed that followers of other cosmogonies followed "hidden scriptures" (56: 77–80) from prophets of the past. They pointed to the example of Imam 'Ali ibn Abi Talib (d. 661 CE), who required his governor in Egypt to treat all of his subjects with mercy, love, and kindness, as they were "equals in creation" (278). In Moghul India, for example, "the emperors and their officers gave like justice to all; they permitted every man to worship according to the rites of his forefathers" (Lybyer 298). The arguments of Muslim Modernists, however, are not without flaws, for the Vedas, the Zend Avesta, and the Buddhist scriptures were not hidden. Furthermore, as "liberal" and "progressive" as they may have been, it is seriously doubtful that they ever accepted these as valid Books. If Muslims grant rights to the followers of other religions, it is in the guise of *human* as opposed to religious rights. All of the children of Adam are entitled to dignity.

Item thirteen is a continuation of the Prophet's policy of promoting peace and prosperity. He warns Muslims not to bother believers be they Jews or Christians:

> Excepting this, nothing shall be required of them, according to the express order of God, that says, 'Do not molest those that have a veneration for the books that are sent from God, but rather in a kind manner give of your good things to them, and converse with them, and hinder everyone from molesting them.'

Not only must Muslims be kind and considerate to them, they must also prevent others from indulging in any form of harassment. If nobody is to make a mockery of Islam and the Prophet, nobody is permitted to make a mockery of Judaism and Christianity. As the Prophet taught, to insult one divinely-revealed religion is to insult them all. He who opposes one religion opposes all religion. Embracing the principle that the sacred is superior to the profane, Islam outlaws abuse towards God, His Messengers, and revealed religions, as well as anything that believers hold sacred. Islam's respect for the People of the Book applies to all domains of social co-existence, even into the context of marriage. As the Prophet professed in item fourteen,

> If a Christian woman shall happen to marry a Muslim, the Muslim shall not cross the inclination of his wife, to keep her from her church and prayers, and the practice of her religion.

While Twelver Shi'ite Islam prohibits permanent marriages between Muslims and the People of the Book, it does allow for fixed-term marriage, which can legally apply for a lifetime. Though some Westerners would view this as a "double-standard" and a form of discrimination, the same types of marriages, both permanent and fixed-term, are routinely entered into by Muslim couples. If True Islam requires that a Muslim man and a Christian woman contract a fixed-term marriage, it is because this form of marriage provides the non-Muslim woman with a greater degree of rights, liberties, and protections. Although the Muslim community may hope and wish for the Christian woman to eventually embrace Islam, she is free to remain faithful to the faith of her forefathers. True Islam is actually tolerant to the extreme. While a Muslim is categorically prohibited from consuming wine or pork, Islamic law allows a Christian wife to do so. Though a Muslim wife would be expected to wear the *hijab*, the Christian woman is allowed to dress as she pleases, according to the standards of her own religious community. However, for the purpose of self-preservation, Islam requires that any child produced by mixed unions be raised in the Muslim faith. The same rule applies to Roman Catholics who enter into mixed marriages: all children are to be raised as Catholics. Strictly speaking a marriage between a Catholic of either sex and any non-Catholic is against Canon Law, which is more restrictive than the *shari'ah* in this regard. However, Bishops regularly grant permission for such marriages as long as the promise to raise all children as Catholics is made. And if Islam does not allow Muslim women to marry non-Muslim men, the reason is obvious. As a man, and head of the household, a faithful Muslim would never dishonor or disgrace Jesus Christ, Moses or Abraham. No such assurances could ever be provided by a Jewish or Christian man, who may be intolerant, or consider Muhammad as a false prophet and a charlatan.

When the Prophet provided for the protection of churches and monasteries, he also ensured that they would be regularly maintained. As item fifteen declares "that no person hinder them from repairing their churches." Some misguided Muslims, though they might refrain from destroying churches, would have simply allowed them to fall into decay and disuse. Through this edict, the Prophet arranged for the continuity of the Christian community. As far as Islam is concerned, the greater the number of people who worship the one God, the better humanity will be served. Islam views religion as a positive social force. While there might be differences in certain theological matters, all monotheistic religions share the same guiding principles. Islam, under the leadership and divine guidance of the Prophet, focused on similarity as opposed to difference, seeking to unite Judaism and Christianity under the protective cover of Islam, as one cohesive monotheistic movement. By protecting other religions, Islam also protects itself from the cancerous spread of secularism, liberalism, and materialism.

If the earlier warnings were not sufficiently clear, the Prophet intensifies his admonition in item sixteen. He decrees that "Whosoever acts contrary to my grant, or gives credit to anything contrary to it, becomes truly an apostate to God, and to his divine apostle, because this protection I have granted to them according to this promise." He reiterates his pledge to exclude the Christians from military service. While Christians are not required to protect the Islamic State, the Islamic State is required to protect them. As the Prophet establishes in item seventeen, "No one shall bear arms against them, but, on the contrary, the Muslims shall wage war for them." The Prophet closes the covenant with authority in item eighteen: "And by this I ordain, that none of my nation shall presume to do or act contrary to this my promise, until the end of the world." It bears noticing that the phrase "none of my nation shall presume to do or act contrary to this my promise" lays a charge on all Muslims everywhere, yet many millions of believers have no knowledge of this covenant or its intentions.

Doubtless, the promise of protection until the Day of Judgment was contingent upon the Christians upholding their side of the bargain. If they rebelled against Islamic rule, if they aided and abetted the enemies of Islam, such as the Crusaders, or, more recently, European colonizers, and American imperialists, the covenant would no longer apply to them and would be effectively annulled. This is not to suggest that the covenant is currently null and void or that it represents a missed opportunity which cannot be recovered; the fact is, it has been largely adhered to for more than a millennium. Nor does this imply that the Prophet was oblivious to the flaws and devilish nature of men. It remains, as always, a model for relations between Muslims and Christians and the basis on which to build bridges. It is the foundational stepping-stone for all negotiations, treaties, and accords between Muslims and Christians.

Although many Christian communities violated their oaths, the monks of Mount Sinai have always maintained the utmost respect for Muhammad. Not only have they upheld the covenant made with the Prophet, they have cherished it always as their most valued possession. In a recent statement, the Monastery of Saint Catherine had this to say about the Prophet Muhammad, his contacts with the monks of Mount Sinai, and the covenant he concluded with them:

> According to the tradition preserved at Sinai, Muhammad (AS) both knew and visited the monastery and the Sinai fathers. The Koran makes mention of the Sinai holy sites. In the second year of the Hegira, corresponding to AD 626, a delegation from Sinai requested a letter of protection from Muhammad (S). This was granted, and authorized by him when he placed his hand upon the document. In AD 1517, Sultan Selim I confirmed the monastery's prerogatives, but took the original letter of protection for safekeeping to the royal treasury in Constantinople. At the same time, he gave the monastery certified copies of this document, each depicting the hand print of Muhammad (S) in token of his having touched the original. (Sinai Monastery)

Considering that the Monastery of Saint Catherine contains the largest collection of Christian documents and codices after the Vatican Library, and is described as a "veritable conservatory of the Christian Orient" (Géhin 163), the library at Mount Sinai is precisely the place where one would expect to find a priceless document like the *Patent* or *Covenant of Muhammad.*

While Muslims and Christians may differ on certain issues, they largely agree on the content of the covenant. Besides the monks of Mount Sinai, the authenticity of the *Patent of Muhammad* has been attested to by John Davenport in his *Apology for Mohammed and the Koran* (148). For Davenport, "[t]he . . . facts and arguments" contained in the covenant "will, it is presumed, suffice to convince every candid and unprejudiced mind that this second charge against Mohammed," namely, the allegation that Islam was propagated by the sword, causing an enormous waste of human blood, and a vast amount of human misery, "being utterly devoid of foundation, is, therefore, both false and scandalous" (151). In fact, the authenticity of *The Covenant of the Prophet Muhammad with the Monks of Mount Sinai* has been recognized by a long list of Muslim scholars, including, Dr. A. Zahoor, Dr. Z. Haq, Dr. Muqtedar Khan, Dr. Reza Shah-Kazemi, and endorsed by numerous Islamic associations such as the Islamic Supreme Council of Canada. Such is the example of true Christian-Muslim relations.

If the content of the *Covenant of the Prophet Muhammad with the Monks of Mount Sinai* provides a rich source for academic exegesis, so do the notes found in the various copies of the treaty. The copy of the covenant that has been commented upon in this book is the one which is on display in the Holy Monastery of Saint Catherine at Mount Sinai and which was copied by Moritz. The covenant in question notes that

> This promise of protection [*'ahd*] was written in his own hand by 'Ali ibn Abi Talib in the Mosque of the Prophet, may the peace and blessings of Allah be upon him, on the third of Muharram in the second year of the Prophet's Hegira.

Although it is accurate that 'Ali acted as the Prophet's scribe, as he did on many occasions, the year of composition may be a later addition. Until the time of 'Umar (r. 634–644 CE), the Arabs simply used to sign documents mentioning the day and month, but not the year. This explains why the dates of certain documents appear to be off. However, such a shortcoming is not grounds to dismiss the documents themselves. The scribe notes that

> A copy of this covenant has been deposited in the treasury [*khizanah*] of the Sultan. It was signed with the seal of the Prophet, peace be upon him. It was written on a piece of leather from Ta'if.

This copy of the covenant is not dated but this could easily be done by determining the lifespan of the scribe and judge who are signatories. It appears, at this point, to date from 1800/01 CE. The meaning of "seal" here is somewhat ambiguous. Does it refer to the palm-print of the Prophet or to the actual seal from his ring which he would dip in ink and use to mark documents? The Arabic version in my possession clearly states that the covenant was written on *jild* or leather which is consistent with early prophetic practice. The surviving segments of the Qur'an, which were written by the scribes of Revelation, are all found on leather. Sidney H. Griffith, however, has translated the word as "parchment" (63). While it is possible that the original was written on parchment, this is not the accurate rendition of the Arabic word found on the covenant. The scribe in question clearly believed that the covenant was authentic. Otherwise, there would be no placed for the pious formula: "Blessed be he who abides by its contents. Blessed be he for he belongs to those who can expect the forgiveness of Allah." The document mentions that

> This copy, which is copied from the original, is sealed with the signature of the noble Sultan [*sharif al-Sultani*]. This reproduction was copied from the copy that was copied from the copy written in the handwriting of the Leader of the Believers, 'Ali ibn Abi Talib, may Allah bless his countenance.

This confirms that the first official copy, provided by Selim I to the monks of Mount Sinai in 1517 CE, was sealed with his signature. The meaning of the following sentence is ambiguous. Does it indicate that the copy in question was the third copy of the original which had been written in the hand of Imam 'Ali (d. 661 CE)? Or does it indicate that the copy taken by Sultan Selim I was the third copy of the original document? Although the document provides more indications, they do not necessarily help to elucidate this mystery. It reads:

> With the order of the noble Sultan [*sharif al-Sultani*], that is still in effect, with the help of Allah, which was given to a community of monks who inhabit the Mountain of Tur-Sina'i because the copy, which was copied from the copy written by

the Leader of the Believers, was lost, in order that his document be a support of the Sultan's royal decrees which are evidenced by the records in the hands of the community in question.

Since the name of the Sultan is not stipulated, it is unclear if it refers to Selim I or the Sultan who reigned when this copy, dating from the 1800s was made. The Arabic, as far as I understand, states that the original covenant was lost, and that the copy was provided by the Sultan to replace it. Was it not simply taken by the Sultan as opposed to lost? While a true *muhaddith* or *hadith* scholar focuses on the *isnad-cum-matn*, namely, the chain of authorities and the content of the tradition, this is clearly not possible in the case of a document purporting to be a copy of an original dictated by the Prophet himself; we are no longer dealing with hearsay, no matter how well-attested, but with documentary evidence. With the *Covenant of the Prophet Muhammad with the Monks of Mount Sinai*, its authority, or lack thereof, must be exclusively determined on the basis of content analysis. In this regard, the covenant has passed the test. Notes found on other copies of the covenant convey even more confidence. One copy of the covenant, written in Turkish Arabic script, which was made in 1858 and bears the seal of the Sinai dependency of Canea, Crete, contains the following heading: "Here is the reason for the writing of this document of eloquent language and the condition that necessitated the formulation of this document of true statements" (Griffith 63–64). That "[t]he Testament was confirmed by Sultan Selim, and by subsequent rulers, to the time of Sultan Abdul Hamid II in 1904" (64) should therefore suffice to ease the qualms of most scholars.

Conclusions

While there will always be those who seek to cast doubt on anything and everything that might reveal Islam as a positive force, most academics not bound to "the hermeneutics of suspicion" have good grounds for considering *The Covenant of the Prophet Muhammad with the Monks of Mount Sinai* to be authentic in the absence of definitive evidence of forgery. To date, no scholar has presented any solid proof that the covenant is a fake. On the contrary, Muhammad's extensive travels throughout the Greater Levant, his confirmed contacts with Christians in various regions, the remarkable stability of the account of his contact with the Monastery of Saint Catherine, the historic recognition of the *achtiname* by both the monks of Mount Sinai and Muslim scholars from all schools of jurisprudence, the discovery of the *firman* of Selim I in a Turkish collection, and the comparative study of the Prophet's numerous treaties and covenants, all seem to support the authentic nature of the *Covenant of the Prophet Muhammad with the Monks of Mount Sinai.*

Chapter 3

The Prophet Muhammad and the Christians of Persia

Introduction

While only a small number of scholars and educated readers are cognizant of the covenants the Prophet concluded with the Monastery of Saint Catherine and the Christians of Najran, far fewer are familiar with those he concluded with the Armenian Christians, the foremost of which is the *Covenant of the Prophet Muhammad with the Christians of Persia*. The covenant in question is strikingly similar to the *Covenant of the Prophet Muhammad with the Monks of Mount Sinai*, so much so that some scholars assert it to be a Persian translation of the same. This Persian-language covenant, however, which survives only in English translation, contains components not found in the Arabic-language covenant from which it is said to originate. The possibilities are three-fold: 1) the Persian version is the product of a very free translation of the Arabic original; 2) the Persian version has been tampered with by Shiʿite scholars; or, as far-fetched as it may seem, 3) the Arabic version of the *Covenant of the Prophet Muhammad with the Monks of Mount Sinai* is actually a translation from the original Persian.

Issues of Authenticity

It is related by Girangos Vartabed, an Armenian writer from the second half of the 13th century, that the Messenger of Allah granted the Armenians Christians residing in Persia the freedom to preserve their Christian faith on the condition that they pay "four dirhams in money, three measures of wheat, a saddle-bag, a rope of hair, and a towel" (qtd. Arpee 355). According to Leon Arpee (1877–1947 CE), an American Presbyterian pastor and historian who was born in Turkey to an Armenian family, the *Covenant of the Prophet Muhammad with the Christians of Persia*, which I have included in this work, "reproduces a charter, purporting to be . . . originally granted by Mohammed . . . to the Monastery of St. Catherine, at Mount Sinai, and intended by the Prophet to be valid for Christians everywhere" (355). As Arpee explains, "New Julfa . . . was the seat of a Bishop recognized as the spiritual head of all the Armenians of Persia, India and Java, and holding a charter after the Prophet's reputed original defining the rights and obligations of a Christian community under Shiite law" (235). To all evidence, Arpee was operating on assumptions. As a result of my intimate knowledge of the *Covenant of the Prophet Muhammad with the Monks of Mount Sinai*, I can confirm that the *Covenant of the Prophet Muhammad with the Christians of Persia* is not a complete and accurate translation of the former document.

At the time of publication, namely, 1946, Arpee reported that the *Covenant of the Prophet Muhammad with the Christians of Persia* "was preserved in the archives of the Armenian Bishop of New Julfa" (355). The document, he reports, was granted to the Armenian Bishop of New Julfa in the 17th century by the Shah of Persia (355). The Shah in question was ʿAbbas I, who, according to American and European accounts, had relocated over 150,000 Armenians in 1606 from Julfa, also known as Jugha or Djugha in Nakhichevan, to New Julfa, an Armenian quarter established in Isfahan by edict of the Safavid leader. According to Persian accounts, the Armenians were not forcibly uprooted from historic Armenia; on the contrary, they were fleeing persecution at the hands of the Ottomans (Bournoutian 206). "The Shah was greeted as a liberator by the Armenians," writes George A. Bournoutian, "who could no longer endure heavy Ottoman taxes" (208). In New Julfa, ʿAbbas the Great built them a new cathedral, granted them religious liberties, offered them interest-free loans, and allowed them to elect their own mayor. As far as A. Christian Van Gorder is concerned, "It is probable that Safavids treated Armenians better than Ottomans [did] and were thus seen as allies, if not liberators" (63). In the view of Persian Jews, "Christians—especially the Armenians—lived in comfort" under the protection of Shah 'Abbas (Levy 265). George A. Bournoutian describes the founding of New Julfa in the following terms:

> Persian masons, together with Armenian craftsmen, built the new settlement. Many churches were constructed, thirteen of which survive today. Armenians had rights that were denied other minorities. They elected their own mayor . . . rang church bells, had public religious processions, established their own courts, and had no restrictions on clothing or the production of wine. No Muslims could reside in New Julfa. The Armenian mayor was given one of the shah's royal seals in order to by-pass bureaucratic tangles and had jurisdiction over the two-dozen Armenian villages around Isfahan. (209)

For Arpee, explains Seta B. Dadoyan, "the Safavid Shah 'Abbas made a Medinan-style commitment to the Armenians," an agreement that was "ratified by a copy of an old Medinan oath allegedly given to the Syrian Christians" (60–61). How and where the Shah obtained this covenant is unclear. Although I have access to virtually every Shi'ite source in existence, I failed to locate the *Covenant of the Prophet Muhammad with the Monks of Mount Sinai* in any of them. While I may have missed it, since it is like searching for a needle in a hundred acre hay-field, it may also have existed in a Shi'ite work which is no longer extant. Since the *Covenant of the Prophet Muhammad with the Monks of Mount Sinai* is not found in any Sunni sources either, the same explanation applies. This leaves the Christian community as a source of origin. Either the Shah obtained it from another Christian community in his empire, or he obtained it from somewhere in the Arabic-speaking world, most likely the Monastery of Saint Catherine. The possibilities I can envision are as follows: 1) The Armenian Christians of Julfa provided Shah 'Abbas with a copy of the covenant in an attempt to dissuade him from uprooting them; while it may not have prevented him from relocating them, it did convince him to grant them special rights; 2) The Armenian Christians, seeking refuge and safety in the Safavid Empire, presented Shah 'Abbas with a copy of the covenant as part of their attempt to receive special refugee status; 3) the Safavids had obtained a copy of the covenant from Christian monks; 4) the Safavids obtained a copy of the covenant from Arab Shi'ite scholars from the Levant who moved to Persia in masse during the rule of Shah 'Abbas.

The Armenian Christians, it is possible, had received a covenant from the Prophet which they passed down from generation to generation until the 20th-century when the original, or copy of the original, apparently went missing. It is also possible that they had a copy of the *Covenant of the Prophet Muhammad with the Monks of Mount Sinai* under the authority of which they claimed protection since it was addressed to "the Christians of the world." Since the Armenians from Julfa, and then New Julfa, controlled an extensive international trading network, they were in close contact with other Armenian Christians throughout the world, including those in Europe, including France (Bournoutian 209). A copy of the *Covenant of the Prophet Muhammad with the Monks of Mount Sinai* may have reached the Christians of Persia through these Armenian trade routes. The Safavid Shahs may also have received a copy of the covenant directly from Christian monks through diplomatic channels. As George A. Bournoutian observes, most Western diplomats, visitors, and merchants who visited Persia were housed in New Julfa (209). If the *Covenant of the Prophet* does not trace back to Julfa, it may have been brought to New Julfa by Christian monks or emissaries from abroad.

Shah Isma'il (r. 1501–1524 CE) sent Persian envoys to Hungary and Egypt (Levy 277). It is possible that a Persian envoy brought back a copy of a covenant from Egypt. Shah Isma'il also received many ambassadors from abroad, including Petrus de Monte, a Maronite monk from Mount Lebanon who arrived in Persia in 1516 as an ambassador from Louis II from Hungary. The Shah also received an envoy from Charles V, king of Spain, during the same period. The Maronite monk, in particular, stands out as a prime suspect. The year 1516/1517 marks the transfer of the *Covenant of the Prophet Muhammad with the Monks of Mount Sinai* to the Treasury of the Ottoman Empire. It seems like quite a coincidence that both the Ottoman Sultan and the Safavid Shah would receive copies of the covenant of the Prophet at the same precise period. The fact that Petrus del Monte was from Mount Lebanon, the very same region where Father Scaliger was given a copy of the *Covenant of the Prophet Muhammad with the Christians of the World* by Arab Capuchin monks seems quite curious as well. While he had little love for Christians, Shah Tahmasp (r. 1524–1576) has received Anthony Jenkinson, an English ambassador who was sent by Queen Elizabeth (Levy 263).

Since Shah ʿAbbas ruled from 1587 to 1629 CE, and Father Scaliger was in Persia in 1628–1629 CE, could this French missionary have provided the Safavid leader with a copy of the covenant of the Prophet he had discovered? While possible, this scenario seems unlikely due to its late nature. Still, Mount Carmel stands out as a source of diffusion. The various Christian denominations were extremely active in the political matters of the time. They operated large diplomatic networks and were represented in most Muslims governments. The purpose of these networks was to advocate for the interests of their communities. By the time of Shah ʿAbbas II, French Capuchin missionaries had grown even more influential (Levy 288). Since they were operating openly rather than covertly, the possibility that they were perpetrating a fraud, in the full light of day, seems slim. After all, they were not disseminating new documents; they were simply circulating covenants of the Prophet that had been known since the early days of Islam.

If Shiʿite clerics ruled at home, ʿAbbas the Great employed Christians to represent him abroad. He appointed Robert Sherley—who, along with his brother joined the Safavid court in 1598—as his ambassador to the kings of Europe, sending him to Germany, Italy, Spain, England, and Rome on his behalf (Levy 266). Shah ʿAbbas also received delegations from Spain and Portugal (Jurdi Abisaad 80), among other nations. As Habib Levy describes, Persia had become a "circus of European spies" (259). "It was not long," he writes, "before European spies and agitators disguised as merchants, travelers, painters, artists, ambassadors, princes, advisors, representatives, functionaries, missionaries, and teachers descended upon Iran" (Levy 263). Any of these could have provided the Shah with a copy of the *Covenant of the Prophet* as a gesture of good-faith.

If anything, ʿAbbas the Great appears to have obtained the covenant from Safavid state archives. It may have been given to Ismaʿil by a Christian monk a century before; however, the covenant fits perfectly well into the imperial agenda of ʿAbbas the Great whose tolerance of Christians formed part of his policy of establishing ties with European powers in order to combat the Ottomans, their common enemy. Ironically, if the Safavids were trying to convince the Spaniards that the Shiʿites treated their Christian subjects kindly, the Ottomans were doing the very same with the French. Both Sunnis and Shiʿites were brandishing copies of the *Covenant of the Prophet* to win the sympathy and support of antagonistic Western Christian powers. Oddly enough, the Spanish Christians may have reciprocated by supporting the spread of Shiʿism among the North African Moriscos in an attempt to destabilize the Ottomans who ruled there (Cutillas Ferrer 49–64). Since both the Ottomans and the Safavids held up variants of what may originally have been the same covenant, the question of which is the most authentic begs to be answered.

Considering that numerous prominent Twelver Shiʿite scholars relocated to the Safavid Empire during the rule of Shah ʿAbbas, it is possible that a copy of the *Covenant of the Prophet* accompanied them. If this document is not found in surviving Shiʿite sources, this may be due in part to the fact that it was destroyed when Jamal Pasha, the Ottoman ruler, burned thousands of books authored by Shiʿite scholars from Jabal ʿAmil in Syria (Jurdi Abisaad 218, note 12). If the covenant was authenticated by Imam Jaʿfar al-Sadiq, and contains clear

Shiʿite elements, it may have been brought to the Safavid Empire by Twelver Shi'ite scholars, as opposed to Christian monks. This does not exclude the possibility that the ʿAmili Shiʿite scholars had obtained copies of it from Christian clerics. Since scholars at the service of the Shah, such as Ahmad ibn Zayn al-ʿAbidin al-ʿAlawi al-ʿAmili (d. 1644 CE), produced polemical literature in order to induce Christians to embrace Islam, the covenant may have played a part in appealing to the followers of Christ and encouraging them to convert to the Shiʿite faith. There also exists the remote possibility that the *Covenant of the Prophet* was the property of the Shiʿite Muslims from Julfa. According to George A. Bournoutian, Shah ʿAbbas was greeted as a liberator by both the Christians and the Shiʿites of Nakhichevan province (208). As such, a certain Shiʿite-Christian solidarity seems to have existed under Ottoman rule.

For readers prone to jumping to conclusions, the answer may be simple: since the *Covenant of the Prophet Muhammad with the Christians of Persia* was supposedly written in Persian, and the *Covenant of the Prophet Muhammad with the Monks of Mount Sinai* is in Arabic, the Persian version must naturally be a translation of the Arabic original. For a scholar, however, the situation is far more complex as some of the Arabic versions of the *Covenant of the Prophet Muhammad with the Monks of Mount Sinai* are actually translations of the Turkish copies of the covenant. For example, Anton F. Haddad's *Oath of the Prophet Mohammed* is an English translation made on the basis of an Arabic translation by Naufal Effendi Naufal, a Christian from Tripoli, Syria. This Arabic translation, which is found in a book written by him and known as *Sunnajat al-tarab*, was based on a Turkish copy of the *Covenant of the Prophet Muhammad with the Monks of Mount Sinai*. The Arabic versions of the *Covenant of the Prophet* also contain many mistakes. A case could be made that the original Arabic document was translated into Turkish or Persian, that the original Arabic was lost, and that some of the Arabic versions in existence were poor translations from Turkish or Persian translations completed by persons for whom Arabic was a second or third language. Otherwise, the mistakes in the Arabic might be explained as the errors of non-Arab scribes.

Though it may appear overly speculative to many, it could be argued that the original *Covenant of the Prophet* was written in Persian, and the mistakes found in the Arabic are the result of a poor translation. Linguistic issues aside, what might explain the differences in content between the Arabic and Persian versions? In other words, why are there Shiʿite elements in the covenant with the Persians? Again, the answer is easy to some: Shah ʿAbbas Shiʿitized the *Covenant of the Prophet* in the same fashion that he imposed Shiʿism as the official religion of his empire. This would be a clear case of Shiʿite *tahrif* or manipulation of sources. The Shiʿites, however, might respond that it was the Turks or the Arabs who had purged the covenant of any ʿAlid elements. In fact, evidence of Umayyad tampering appears evident in many covenants, at least where the list of witnesses are concerned. Why is Muʿawiyyah ibn Abi Sufyan, a die-hard enemy of Islam, listed as the scribe of the Prophet on documents which date prior to his professed conversion?

In the opinion of Dadoyan, Arpee's claim concerning the *Covenant of the Prophet Muhammad with the Christians of Persia* is "highly dubious yet intriguing" (60). Although the American missionary claims to have taken it from the *History of New Julfa at Isfahan*, Dadoyan asserts that "[n]o such document exists in this book, and no record exists of any such document in the archives of the Prelacy of New Julfa" (64, note 56). What is more, "[n]o documents that he refers to are found in the archives of the Armenian Bishopric of New Julfa" (61). The allegations made by Dadoyan seem absolute and factually-based. Upon closer examination, however, they are seen to be grounded on assumptions. "The present document," writes Arpee, is rendered "from the version of Johanianz (New Julfa, 1881)" (355). In fact, at least half a dozen books on Armenian history were published in Armenian in 1880 and 1881. The *Covenant* may actually be included in another Armenian history.

If the allegations made by Seta B. Dadoyan are

indeed correct, why did it take over sixty years for any historian to call him out on his claims? If it was relatively easy to falsify prophetic sayings under the Umayyads and the 'Abbasids, introducing a fabricated *Covenant of the Prophet* in 1948 would have been scholarly suicide. Arpee, to begin with, did not have sufficient linguistic proficiency as to replicate a 17th-century Persian edict nor did he have enough knowledge of Shi'ism to produce a convincing product. Furthermore, he had nothing to gain by perpetrating a historical fraud: no fame or fortune could possibly come his way and actual harm could have been directed towards him. Having read Arpee's works, he comes across as a serious historian and his own works are often cited by specialists in the field. What would motivate him to undermine his entire academic edifice by inserting a dubious document? The explanation might be simple. Most scholars in the 1950s did not type. Secretaries would type their manuscripts. End notes were particularly problematic. It is possible that Arpee, a typist, an editor, or a printer made a mistake in referencing the *Covenant of the Prophet Muhammad with the Christians of Persia.* As for Dadoyan's claim that the covenant is not found in the archives of the Armenian Bishopric of New Julfa, it is of little import. As Arpee wrote, "[t]he Convent of New Julfa, residence of the Bishop, once had a Library (now robbed of its most valued treasures)" (235). When he wrote that the covenant "was preserved in the archives of the Armenian Bishop of New Julfa" he may have meant that *it had been* preserved prior to the convent being sacked. In any event, this issue remains unclear and requires further investigation. Many archives contain works in their collections that are not listed in their catalogue.

If the copy of the *Covenant* that was stored in the archives of the Bishop of New Julfa dates from the 17th century, it was evidently based on a much more ancient version. As Arpee reports, "Ja'far, sixth Shi'ite Imam (8th century), testifies to its authenticity after comparing the text with the original in his own hand" (355). This is probably the single most important endorsement any covenant of the Prophet can receive. For Shi'ites, Imam Ja'far al-Sadiq is an infallible, divinely-guided and inspired Imam, and the rightful successor of the Prophet. His authority is unquestionable. If Imam Ja'far al-Sadiq stated that the *Covenant of the Prophet Muhammad with the Christians of Persia* was genuine to the letter, and that it was identical to the copy which he himself possessed, and which had been passed down from his forefathers, Imam Muhammad al-Baqir, Imam 'Ali Zayn al-'Abidin, Imam Husayn, Imam Hasan, Imam 'Ali, and the Prophet Muhammad, then it is this version that is the original while the *Covenant of the Prophet with the Monks of Mount Sinai* is either a translation, a derivative or a unique document in its own right.

According to Giragos Vartabed, "the Catholicos, John of Otzun, at the close of his audience of the Arab Caliph (whom he identifies with Hisham), made and was granted for his people a threefold petition, viz., for 1) freedom of private conscience, 2) freedom of public worship, and 3) freedom of churches and clergy from taxation" (Arpee 355). In Arpee's estimation, "[t]he granting, or rather the confirming, of these rights by Omar II, or by Hisham, may very well be historical. The Caliph Omar II (717–20), the Caliph Hisham (724–43), the Catholicos John of Otzun (717–28), and the authenticator of the ensuing document, the Imam Mohammed Jafar [Ja'far ibn Muhammad] (711–36), were all contemporaries" (355). So, although the existing copy of the *Covenant of the Prophet Muhammad with the Christians of Persia* dates from the 17th century, we have documented evidence that it was being adhered to and emulated in the 8th century and that a leading religious authority, Imam Ja'far al-Sadiq, has authenticated it. That the Prophet Muhammad was making treaties with Persian Christians is not problematic in the least. As Arpee explains, "it was not an uncommon thing for Mohammed to enter into correspondence with nations and rulers with whom he had not as yet come into close quarters" (355). What he was doing was brilliant and visionary from a strategic point of view. He was actually preparing the ground for the future conquest of Persia by aligning the oppressed Christians with the Muslims against the pagan oppressors.

Commentary on the Content of the Covenant

The *Covenant of the Prophet Muhammad with the Christians of Persia* commences, as is fitting, in the name of Allah, the Most Merciful: "By the will of God! In the name of God Merciful!" Unlike some of the others covenants of the Prophet, which focus on the obligations of Muslims towards Christians first and which finish with the obligations of Christians towards Muslims last, the *Covenant of the Prophet Muhammad with the Christians of Persia* begins by establishing the obligation of obedience imposed on "all Christian nations . . . throughout the world" who live in eastern Arabia and Persia, regardless of whether they are directly or indirectly in contact with Muslims. Not only is the covenant binding upon Christians, but "it behooves all Moslems also to observe its provisions." Whoever obeys it, says the Prophet, had perfect faith. Whoever corrupts it or annuls it, however, will be worthy of punishment regardless of his religion, social status, or political rank. For those who might give secondary status to the Word of the Prophet when compared to the Word of Allah, the Messenger of Allah insists that the words of this covenant were divinely inspired. The covenant is thus of divine, as opposed to human, origin, the weight of which is so heavy that no prophet of the past nor angels standing nigh was ever burdened with its like. As such, "[t]he words . . . of this covenant . . . must be obeyed" by all of the Prophet's people. While Moses may have been granted a covenant from God, it applied to the Children of Israel. Unlike Muhammad, he was not burdened with the obligation of protecting the members of other religious communities outside of his own.

"All pious believers," proclaims the Prophet, "shall deem it their bounden duty to defend believers and to aid them wheresoever they may be, whether far or near." Treating Christians as *mu'minin* or believers is consistent with the *Constitution of Medina*, one of the earliest documents in the history of Islam and a sure sign of the antiquity of the *Covenant of the Prophet Muhammad with the Christians of Persia*. The obligation of Muslims to defend the Christians extends beyond *dar al-islam* or Muslim majority lands, into Christendom, where the followers of the Prophet are obliged to protect churches, monasteries, as well as monks and priests. Regardless of where Christians are found, Muslims are duty bound to protect them. The Christians referred to, of course, are those who are friends of Islam, the brothers and sisters of the believers, and not Crusaders, colonizers or imperialists. This principle, one can only expect, will be met with outrage by Salafis, Wahhabis, and Takfiris. As preposterous, inconceivable and unpractical as it may seem for many people today, this injunction was actually observed by early Muslims rulers. As Muhammad Hamidullah writes, "A document of the time of the Umayyad caliph 'Umar ibn 'Abd al-'Aziz (reported by Ibn Sa'd), says, that the payment of the ransoms by the Muslim government includes liberating even the non-Muslim subjects who . . . have been made prisoners by the enemy" (*Introduction* 127). Even the Umayyads, the greatest liars in the history of Islam, would never have come up with such a thing. 'Umar ibn 'Abd al-'Aziz, who was the only righteous ruler the Umayyads ever produced, could only have been following a precedent set by the Prophet, most probably, his covenant with the Christians of Persia. According to traditional Islamic political theory, a citizen is a citizen, regardless of religion. It was the obligation of the Islamic State to protect its citizens, whether they were Jews, Christians, Muslims, or otherwise, not only within its borders, but beyond them as well. In the 21st century, this standard of commitment of a state towards its subjects is only met by the most powerful and developed nations of the world.

As far as the Prophet is concerned, caring for the *ahl al-dhimmah* or People of Protection is part of the Golden Rule: do unto others as you would have them do unto you. However, this is taken up a notch by the Messenger of Allah who enjoins Muslims to care for Christians to the same extent that they honor and respect the Prophet himself. The Christians are to be taxed fairly. And while there were some instances in which Muslims overtaxed Christians, these were exceptions to the rule. As we will see, the idea that Islamic rulers routinely imposed oppressive taxes on Christians or prohibited the construction of churches or monasteries is not accurate. As the Prophet decrees:

> their building enterprises shall not be interfered with; their priests shall not be molested in the performance of their task; they shall not be persecuted for their faith or their customs, but shall be allowed to pray as they will in their own places of worship and according to their own rites; neither shall their churches be dismantled or destroyed, or their homes and mansions confiscated by Moslems, for mosques or residences, without their consent. Whosoever shall not do as is here prescribed, but shall do contrary to my behests; the same shall be held a despiser of this Compact, and a gainsayer of the word of God and of his Prophet.

Christians were taxed at a rate of four dirhams per adult male, which could be paid in cash or goods. This money was not to be the personal property of some lord, governor, or Sultan, but was to be placed in the Treasury for public use. As for merchants, the wealthy, pearl divers, mine operators or owners of large estates, the rate of taxation was not to exceed twelve dirhams. Despite allegations that only the People of the Book had limited rights, while other "infidels" were denied rights altogether, the Prophet states that non-Christians would be taxed at four dirhams per year. In other words, Jews, Zoroastrians, polytheists, animists, or even atheists had the same rights as Christians. Land taxes, of course, apply only to sedentary populations, not to nomads. If some of the other covenants of the Prophet use the term *Sultan*, the *Covenant of the Prophet Muhammad with the Christians of Persia* employs the term *Imam*, when referring to the ruler. In all honesty, this appears to have been the term originally employed by the Prophet and which was modified to *Sultan* to suit Arab and Ottoman Sunni sentiment. It is the term *Imam*, and not *Sultan*, that is employed in the Qur'an and most of the Sunnah.

While Christians have no military obligations towards the Islamic State—they pay taxes in lieu of service—Muslims are obliged to protect them. "No Christians shall be brought by force to confess Islam," commands the Prophet, and relations between both parties must remain kind and cordial. So long as Christians observe their obligations towards the Islamic State, "no Christians shall be tyrannized over or oppressed." Importantly, however, the Christians shall not "on their part tyrannize over Moslems or oppress them, from this time forth even until such time as God shall ordain." Peace is not a one-way street. Christians are prohibited from oppressing Muslims as well as siding with and supporting the enemies of Islam. This sentence seems to foreshadow the final conflict between the followers of Christ and Imam Muhammad al-Mahdi against the Anti-Christ in which all human beings will be forced to select a side.

"Moslems shall not take the women and maidens of the Christians by force," decrees the Prophet, proving categorically that the crimes committed towards Berber women by early Muslim conquerors and later slave-hunters and traders are outlawed in Islam. They are heinous crimes punishable in this life and the next. Most interestingly, the Prophet says that Christian women, out of their own free will, and motivated out of love, may marry Muslim men "permanently or only for a time."

The reference is indubitably to both permanent [*nikah*] as well as fixed-term marriage [*muta'h*]. As all honest Muslim scholars are aware, temporary marriage was not only permitted during the time of the Prophet but actually promoted to prevent incidents of fornication, adultery, and sexual assault, particularly when men were away from their wives for extended periods of time, as in the case of war. Some Sunnis contend that the practice was prohibited by the Prophet; however, the dates they provide, such as the Conquest of Khaybar (629 CE), the Battle of Awtas (630 CE) or the Conquest of Mecca (January 11, 630 CE) are all contradictory. Furthermore, none of the traditions prohibiting fixed-term marriages have sound chains of narration (Kashif al-Ghita' 84). Companions of the Prophet such as 'Abd Allah ibn 'Abbas, Mujahid, 'Ata', Jabir ibn 'Abd Allah al-Ansari, Salmah ibn al-Akwa', Abu Sa'id al-Khudri, Mughirah ibn Sha'hab, Sa'id ibn Jarir, and Ibn Jarih all insisted that *muta'h* was permissible (Kashif al-Ghita' 85).

Imam 'Ali and his eleven descendants from the Household of the Prophet always insisted that *mut'ah* was Islamically sanctioned and pointed at Caliph 'Umar as the cause of its prohibition. The tradition of the Prophet prohibiting fixed-term marriage was thus forged to support this post-prophetic prohibition. As all sources agree, 'Umar ibn al-Khattab was the first to ban fixed-term marriages (Kashif al-Ghita' 80–83; Husayn 304; Tatabataba'i 227; Rizvi 74–75). As the second Caliph admitted that "[t]here are two *mut'ahs* which existed in the time of the Prophet of God and Abu Bakr which I have banned, and I will punish those who disobey my orders. These two *mut'ahs* are the *mut'ah* concerning the pilgrimage and the *mu'tah* concering women" (qtd. Tabataba'i 227).

This prohibition has no binding value as it contradicts the Qur'an, which is eternal in application. "And those of whom ye seek content [*istamta'tum*, from the same root as *mut'ah*] (by marrying them)," explains Allah, "give unto them their portions as a duty" (4:24). Some Sunnis argue that this verse was actually abrogated; however, the Companions of the Prophet would not have continued to perform *mut'ah* had that been the case. Even some eminent Sunni scholars, such as Zamakhshari and Hakam ibn 'Ayniyah, report that the verse of *mut'ah* was not abrogated (Kashif al-Ghita' 79). In recent decades, the Takfiris have embraced *mut'ah* while violating all of its legal tenets. As is customary, they simply make a mockery of Islam through their twisted misinterpretations, in the same way that they have made the *takbir* ["*Allahu Akbar*"] a synonym for death, destruction, and terror.

In the event a Christian woman marries a Muslim man by her free will, she is free to continue in her Christian faith. Hence, the custom of requiring Christian women to convert, prior to marrying a Muslim man, is unfounded. If any Muslim actually pressures a Christian woman into a "conversion of convenience," he has committed a serious sin. In clear contradiction of Muslim cultural customs, where arranged marriages are often imposed on women against their will, the Prophet mentions that the main criteria for marriage is love and that there can be no marriage for a woman who does not want it. While Muslim scholars are well aware of these prophetic sayings, there is a chasm the size of the Grand Canyon between the theory of Islam and its actual practice. In many instances, the customs of cultural Muslims stand in clear contradiction to the Qur'an, the Sunnah, and the *shari'ah*.

If Christians are allowed to repair their churches, chapels, and monasteries, and Muslims are free to help, Christians are also encouraged to help Muslims in their construction projects as an expression of friendship and good will. So long as Christians submit to Islamic rule and seek Muslim protection, all help given to them by Muslims is in every way legitimate. Unlike the *Covenant of the Prophet Muhammad with the Monks of Mount Sinai*, in which the monks were not expected to act as scouts, spies, or agents for the Muslims, the Prophet lifts this restriction from lay Christians: "If any one of them shall be sent as an envoy to negotiate peace between Moslems and Infidels, no one shall prevent his going, and if he should prove of service to our cause, let the service be accepted."

In 650 CE, Mu'awiyyah, the governor of Syria, penetrated most of Armenia with a large army (Bournoutian 72). Not only did he exempt the Armenians from taxes for a number of years, he agreed to maintain their cavalry so long as the Arabs could rely upon them in times of war (72). Granting the Armenians autonomy, Mu'awiyyah, who was under the command of Caliph 'Uthman, posted no governor in Armenia yet promised that Arab troops would protect this Christian country if Byzantium attacked (72). As Bournoutian notes, Theodore Rshtuni, who had been appointed prince of Armenia by Emperor Heraclius, "managed to obtain something from the Muslim ruler, which he had been unable to wrest from the Christian emperor of Byzantium" (73). The

Caliphs, writes Malachia Ormanian, "had an interest in seeing the Armenians regulate their own religious affairs in a spirit which was opposed to Greek ideas" (44). Rather than impose their religion on conquered peoples, they preferred to grant them administrative and social autonomy. When the Byzantines attacked, and ousted Rshtuni, "Mu'awiyyah dispatched a new army, which then forced the Byzantines to retreat, and reinstated Rshtuni" (73). This is a clear case of Muslim forces coming to the rescue of autonomous Christian allies in order to defend them from their Christian foes.

The Christians under the protection of Islam, once again, are implicitly counted among the believers and distinct from the infidels. In order to belong to the Community of Believers and the Family of Abraham, Christians are required to do as follows:

> [T]hey shall give no aid to infidels, whether openly or surreptitiously, neither receive into their houses enemies of Moslems lest at a convenient opportunity they attack them. They shall not permit enemy men to stop at their houses or churches, neither shall they harbor enemy troops, or aid them with spear, arrow, sword or horse, or with aught else.
>
> They shall not act as guides to them, or show them how to ambush the enemy. They shall not commit to them their possessions for safe-keeping; they shall not communicate with them, or aid them by word or deed, or afford them shelter except only under duress.
>
> If a Moslem shall chance at a Christian's house, he may there be entertained three days and three nights; more than that is unnecessary. Christians shall avert from Moslems the abuse and oppressions of tyrants.
>
> In the event that it becomes necessary for them to hide Moslem in their own mansions or houses, they shall give him a place to lie, and take care of him, neither forsaking him, nor leaving him without food, so long as he shall be in hiding. Women and children of Moslems shall not be betrayed or shown to the enemy; neither shall Christians deviate from these orders.

Any Christian who acts contrary to the covenant or ignores it, warns the Prophet, "shall be accounted as annulling the same." Such a person "is loathsome to God, and the Prophet shall visit upon him his just retribution." The Prophet concludes the covenant stating that it is binding on Christians so long as God wills. In another example of its 'Alid elements, the name of Muhammad is followed by "blessings of God rest upon him and his posterity." While Sunni Muslims simply send peace and blessings upon the Prophet, Shi'ite Muslims typically bless both the Messenger of Allah and his Holy Household, the *ahl al-bayt*. For example, the name of 'Ali, in the list of witnesses of the *Covenant of the Prophet Muhammad with the Assyrian Christians* is followed by the formula *'alayhi al-salam* or "peace be upon him." While some early Sunni authorities occasionally used this pious phrase after the mention of 'Ali, the practice eventually became solely associated with Shi'ism. Finally, like some other covenants of the Prophet, this with the Persians is also dated on the fourth year of the *hijrah*, a date that was probably included by a scribe at one point during the document's transmission and which is unlikely to have been found on the original.

Conclusions

The *Covenant of the Prophet Muhammad with the Christians of Persia* is a document of great historical interest that is not without its problems; its origin and evolution should be subject to continued scholarly scrutiny. At this current juncture, writes Seta B. Dadoyan, the covenant's authenticity "cannot be established" (61). I would counter with "neither can it be disproved." As much doubt as Seta B. Dadoyan may have cast on this covenant and Arpee's explanation of its origin, she admits that "the history of New Julfa in an Islamic state somehow proves this extravagant hypothesis" (61). While the covenant in question appears to have gone missing, it may simply have been misplaced or it may have been stolen. One can only hope that it will be rediscovered, enabling scholars to examine it in greater detail. As Dadoyan intimates, the *Covenant of the Prophet Muhammad with the Christians of Persia* must have existed at some point. "[O]ver 250 years later," she writes, "and despite great differences in circumstances, the two rescripts of the Ottoman *Tanzimat* or reforms (1839, 1856) were not more than modernized versions of the early Islamic or Medinan system of regulating the status of non-Muslims or *dhimmi* subjects" (61). "At present, in many Muslim countries," she continues, "the status of the Christian minorities is not very different from this early Islamic tradition, surely with clear improvements on the civil rights level" (61). Once again, we are faced with a clear-cut case of continuity in the legal canon. Tolerance of Christians who are at peace with Muslims forms an intrinsic part of the Islamic tradition.

Chapter 4

The Prophet Muhammad and the Christians of Najran

Introduction

If the *Covenant of the Prophet Muhammad with the Monks of Mount Sinai* is relatively unknown, the *Covenant of the Prophet Muhammad with the Christians of Najran* is virtually unheard of outside a small circle of mostly non-Muslim Orientalists. If the covenant concluded between the Prophet and the Christians from Sinai has received mixed reviews, with some scholars attesting to its authenticity and others considering it spurious, the *Covenant of the Prophet Muhammad with the Christians of Najran* has been castigated by both the Orientalist who brought it to light and by the few others who are familiar with it.

Issues of Authenticity

The *Covenant of the Prophet Muhammad with the Christians of Najran* came to light when the Arabic/French edition of the *Histoire nestorienne inédite: Chronique de Séert,* by Addai Scher (1867–1915 CE), the Assyrian Chaldean Catholic archbishop of Siirt, a city in southeastern Turkey, was published posthumously in *Patrologia Orientalis,* five years after his death at the hands of the Young Turks. According to the chronicle itself, the copy of the covenant was made on the basis of a document found in the year 265 AH (878/879 CE) in the possession of Habib, the Monk, in the city of Birmantha (Scher 281/601). According to the testimony of Habib, the copy he had was made on the basis of an original found in the Library of Philosophy where he was the curator prior to becoming a monk (281/601). According to him, the pact or patent was written on cow-hide which had turned yellow with age and bore the seal of the Prophet Muhammad, upon whom be peace and blessings (281/601). Despite the inestimable discovery that he made, Archbishop Addai Scher duly dismissed it concluding that:

> This covenant is certainly apocryphal. It was forged by the Christians so that the Muslims would spare them. Every Christian sect in the Orient possesses a copy which is more or less different one to the other. . . . This one is written in a language which is unsure and incorrect. (282 /602)

Considering the categorical nature of his claims, it would have been particularly crucial for Scher to support these assertions as sound scholarship requires. The onus of proof lies on the person making the claim. As the Qur'an says, "Produce your proof if ye are truthful" (2:111). The Archbishop, however, did not advance a single argument to support his allegations and did not present a shred of proof to demonstrate that the covenant in question was counterfeit. He simply claimed that the covenant was apocryphal. On what basis, may we ask? He claimed that it was forged by Christians so that they would be spared by the Muslims. Yet, history has shown that Muslims generally respected the rights of other religious communities. Since they were interested in territorial expansion and taxation it was not to their benefit to massacre subject populations.

Scher also claimed that every Christian congregation in the Orient possesses similar covenants which are more or less different. This is simply not true. The covenant which is in circulation among the Greek Orthodox is identical. If other Christian communities, such as those in Najran, Iraq, and Syria, had covenants that were more or less different, it was because the Prophet made different accords with different denominations. Since these were different covenants from the onset, uniformity is no proof of authenticity or inauthenticity. The Archbishop also alleges a fantastic conspiracy among diverse and often mutually antagonistic Christian denominations of the Middle East; that they all contrived to produce covenants that they then falsely attributed to the Prophet Muhammad.

Had they all done so independently, the results should have been radically different for surely none of them had the same level of understanding of the Qur'an, the Sunnah, and early Islamic history. Had they done so collaboratively, then, surely, all of the covenants would have been identical. The only thing that explains both the consistency and subtle differences in style and structure between the covenants of the Prophet with the monks of Mount Sinai, Najran, Assyria, Persia, Armenia, and the World is that they were authored by the same individual: Muhammad, the Messenger of Allah. These are exactly the same type of variations found in the various treaties that the Prophet made with different peoples.

In addition to accusing all Christian churches of perpetrating an appalling fraud, the Archbishop portrays Muslims as imbeciles, a people who are so ignorant of their own tradition that they could easily be deceived by forged documents. It is as if the Muslim *ummah* were devoid of scholars who could evaluate the authenticity of serious claims of prophetic composition. The fact, which Scher does not mention, is that the Muslims actually abide by the dictates of such covenants. To insist that the Prophet could never have composed or delivered generous terms of submission is to allege that the early Muslims lacked basic civility, when, in truth, Islam is all about civility. Issues of authenticity aside, these documents and the Muslims' respect for them demonstrate a people's nobility of spirit and chivalry. Finally, Scher asserts that the *Covenant* is written in flawed Arabic, yet does not avail himself of his linguistic expertise to support the supposition. It is an ironic and unfortunate twist of fate that the person who insisted so much that Muhammad never provided any charter of protection and privileges to the Christians was actually put to death by the Young Turks during the Assyrian atrocities of 1915 CE.

Rather than hold up the *Covenant of the Prophet Muhammad with the Christians of Najran*, and admonish Westernized Turks for failing to adhere to Islamic norms of moral and military conduct, what could he possibly have told them? That they were evil Muslims acting exactly as expected? By lowering expectations with regard to Islamic practice and disregarding the principles of the Prophet, Archbishop Addai Scher (1867–1915 CE) refused to avail himself of a document that might have saved him. His death at the hands of deviants is a lesson to both Christians and Muslims: namely, that denigrating Islamic ethics or even denying their existence may contribute to a self-fulfilling prophecy.

To understand this phenomenon better, it is necessary to analyze the elements that led to the fall of the Ottoman Empire. The last Muslim Empire collapsed due to a combination of incompetence, corruption, and ignorance. As a result of these three factors, Western powers were able to move in swiftly, planning, organizing, and implementing plans aimed at destroying a deeply decayed Caliphate which, despite its flaws, was the last bastion of pan-Islamic political power. The Western world, which viewed Islam as the greatest threat to European expansion and hegemony, employed, among others, the infamous military officers from the "Young Turk Movement." Despite the fact that they were members of the Ottoman Army, these Westernized atheists represented a Fifth Column at the core of the Caliphate. Inspired by European ideas, the "Young Turks" set out to destroy the Ottoman Empire so as to impose a secular state.

After organizing themselves as a political party in 1906, these "young Turkish officers" organized a *coup d'état* in July of 1908 and forced the Sultan to accept the Constitution of 1876. Consequently, they were able to manipulate the Sultan like a puppet. It was these officers and the Western powers that supported them, that perpetrated the massacres against the Assyrians in 1915. By the next year, in 1916, they had acquired so much power that they were able to proclaim the Turkish Republic. It was these West-worshipping secular atheists who committed the mass murder of Armenians. In 1922, Kemal Atatürk (1881–1938 CE) went down in the annals of infamy by abolishing the Caliphate, giving the *coup de grâce* to the only surviving symbol of the Ottoman Empire. It must be made clear, then, that it was not the Muslims who were responsible for the crimes committed against the Assyrians and the Armenians; but the "Young Turks" who were Westernized anti-Islamic atheists. And as Wilhem von Pressel, the "Father of the Baghdad Railway," observed circa 1876, "[Ottoman Muslims] treat Christians with mildness and friendliness, as long as their religious fanaticism is not urged on" (qtd. McMeekin 232).

The Fatwa of Husayn ibn 'Ali, the Sharif of Mecca, Commanding Muslims to Protect the Armenian Christians
[3 illustrations on this page]

As Vahakn N. Dadrian argues in *German Responsibility in the Armenian Genocide: A Review of the Historical Evidence of German Complicity*, the massacres of Christians in the Ottoman Empire were, to a large extent, the product of German policy. If the British had created, encouraged, and exploited Islamic extremism in order to support their agenda, so had the Germans, laying the foundations of modern-day Islamic terrorism. Rather than blame Islam and the Qur'an, a close examination of "Islamic fundamentalism" reveals an ideology rooted in ideas disseminated by the West in colonialist times. It is an interpretation of Islam devised by imperialists in order to incite the ignorant Muslim masses to fight on their behalf. It is also important to recall that "[t]he Armenian community in Turkey was not simply 'an unarmed Christian minority'" and that "it is not acceptable to discuss the events of 1915–16 without mentioning the fifth-column role of the Armenian revolutionaries" (Lewy 268–269). Comparing the disputed Armenian Genocide with the Jewish Holocaust is simplistic, factually inaccurate, and

العرب

فوز عظيم للحلفاء

misleading. The European powers of the time were eager to partition the Muslim world, promising homelands for European Jews, Arabs, Kurds, Assyrians, and Armenians, all at the expense of the Ottoman Empire (Bournoutian 301). The Turks may have committed massacres; however, there is no evidence that they intended to exterminate entire groups of people. Their plan, as desperate, ill-conceived, and disastrously implemented as it may have been, was to relocate potentially dangerous and disloyal Christians from strategically sensitive areas to places of lesser geo-political risk (Lewy 150–161).

Since history is our greatest teacher, and history repeats itself, it is important to learn lessons from the past. As such, it is important to note that the methods employed by these young secular military officers were the same as the techniques used by Western powers in Bosnia-Herzegovina, Palestine, and Nigeria, as well as India, Pakistan, and Iraq. They organize attacks against Christians, Sunnis, and Shi'ites, and then present them as "confessional," "sectarian," or "inter-religious" attacks in order to foment dissent and discord. Duped and deceived, the masses denounce such hideous crimes as "Islamic terrorism" caused by "Muslim fundamentalists" and get drawn into an artificial conflict. In the meantime, the foreign powers that set up these conflicts in the first place use them as justification for covert or overt intervention and the imposition of puppet governments. This does not mean that Muslim extremists do not exist as independent actors or never operate on their own initiative; I only wish to point out that the use of such fanatics by Western powers has a long and well-documented history. Mahmood Mamdani's *Good Muslim, Bad Muslims: America, the Cold War, and the Root of Terror* (97, 108–109, 121, 123, 126–137, 140–144, 156.-158, 160, 163, 165, 177, 210–211, 235–237), Richard Labevière's *Dollars for Terror: The United States and Islam* (99, 387, 390, and all of chapter 5 and 6), Loretta Napoleoni's *Terror Incorporated: Tracing the Dollars Behind the Terror Networks* (72–73, 81–85, 87, 118, 138), and Peter Lance's 1000 *Years of Revenge: International Terrorism and the FBI: The Untold Story* (25, 39, 42) are all required reading in this regard.

If, as we have seen, the views of Archbishop Addai Scher (1867–1915 CE) regarding the origin of the covenants carry little weight, they are the least of the problems faced by scholars. The strongest argument that can be made against the *Covenant of the Prophet Muhammad with the Christians of Najran* resides in the fact that mention of this document appears to be completely absent in the classical Islamic sources which have survived to the present. It is on this basis that most scholars dismiss it as dubious. However, when viewed in a broader context, such a position seems eminently reactionary and intransigent. Like the *Covenant of the Prophet Muhammad with the Monks of Mount Sinai*, the *Covenant of the Prophet Muhammad with the Christians of Najran* does not appear in a vacuum. In fact, the Messenger of Allah met with delegations of Christians from Najran on numerous occasions. He received the first such delegation in Mecca before his Night Journey or *Mi'raj*, namely, prior to 621 CE. Ibn Ishaq (704–761/770 CE) reports that:

> When the Messenger was in Mecca some twenty Christians came to him ... when they heard news of him. They found him in the mosque and sat and talked with him, asking him questions, while some Qurayshites were in their meeting round the Ka'bah. When they had asked all the questions they wished, the Messenger invited them to come to God and read the Qur'an to them. When they heard the Qur'an, their eyes flowed with tears, and they accepted God's call, believed in him, and declared his truth. They recognized in him the things which had been said of him in their scriptures. ... It is said that these Christians came from Najran, but God knows whether that was so. (179)

Clearly, the Prophet seems to have been in contact with the Christians of Najran as early as the second year before the *hijrah*. Muhammad continued communicating with the Christians of Najran after the Islamic State was established in Medina, and he received a delegation in the year 630 CE, namely, in the year 8 after the *hijrah*. The details of this delegation, which included sixty riders, led by fourteen nobles, have been described in detail in Ibn Ishaq's *Sirah* or *Life of Muhammad*. The Messenger of Allah was so tolerant, hospitable, and accommodating, towards his Christian visitors that he allowed them to perform their liturgy in his own mosque in Medina (Shah- Kazemi 125; Khan 247; Ibn Kathir, qtd. Haya 5). As Ibn Ishaq reports,

> [W]hen they came to Medina they came into the Messenger's mosque as he prayed the afternoon prayer clad in Yamani garments, cloaks, and mantles, with the elegance of men of B. al-Harith b. Ka'b. The Prophet's Companions who saw them that day said that they never saw their like in any

> deputation that came afterwards. The time of their prayers having come they stood and prayed in the Messenger's mosque, and he said that they were to be left to do so. They prayed towards the east. (271)

The Prophet and the Bishop from Najran engaged in a detailed debate concerning Christian dogma which resulted in an impasse. The Messenger of Allah then received revelation instructing him to invite the Christians to mutually invoke imprecations in order to determine the truth of the matter. The next morning, at the Event of *Mubahalah*, the Prophet arrived in the presence of 'Ali, Fatimah, Hasan, and Husayn. The aura of sanctity that surrounded the Prophet and his *ahl al-bayt* was so intense that their bishop, Abu Haritha ibn 'Alqama, concluded that attempting to curse such saintly figures would be an act of suicide. After discussing the matter, the Christians of Najran decided to make peace with the Prophet and leave on good terms. The Prophet granted them a treaty and bid them farewell (Mufid 118).

When the Christians of Najran did not honor their accord with the Prophet, the Messenger of Allah sent them a stern, clear warning in his Letter to the People of Najran: "In the Name of Allah, the God of Abraham, Isaac, and Jacob. I invite you to worship God instead of men. If you refuse, you must pay *jizyah*. Otherwise, I will declare war on you. And peace be upon you" (qtd. Qureshi 54). The Christians of Najran contracted to pay the *jizyah* in the year 9 AH and were granted a treaty which stipulated:

> They will give two thousand [suits of] clothes annually to the Muslims in two installments, one in the month of Safar and the other in Rajab. If there is any rebellion or disturbance in Yemen, they will send thirty [suits of] armor, thirty horses, thirty camels, and thirty weapons of all kind. The Muslims will be responsible for their return. In return, neither will their churches will be demolished nor their priests be ousted. Moreover, they will not be converted from their religion, provided they do not engage in usury or commence a rebellion. (qtd. Qureshi 117)

The Christians, however, were not entirely satisfied with the first treaty they had signed. As such, they sent a delegation to Medina to meet with the Prophet in the year 10 AH. The purpose was to negotiate a more extensive understanding. Known as *The Treaty of Najran*, it establishes the following rights and obligations between Christians and Muslims:

The Treaty of Najran

In the Name of Allah, the Most Compassionate, the Most Merciful.

This is a writ of protection between Muhammad, the Messenger of Allah, and the People of Najran. Although he has the power to take his share from their fruit, gold, silver, iron (arms), and slaves, he has left all of these things for them provided that they pay two thousand garments of stipulated value every year, one thousand in Rajab, and the other one thousand in Safar. Each garment will be equal to one *awqiyyah* [measure of weight]. Anything below or above this number will be calculated. The [suits of] armor, horse or carriages offered will be calculated as well. It is the obligation of the people of Najran to lodge and board my messengers. No messenger will remain for more than one month. If there is disorder in the Yemen, the people of Najran commit to lending thirty [suits of] armor, thirty horses, and thirty camels. In the event of any casualty or destruction of private property, the people of Najran will be compensated. To the Christians of Najran and its neighboring territories, God's protection and the pledge of His Prophet extend to their lives, their religion, and their property. It applies to those who are present as well as those who are absent. There shall be no interference

with the practice of their faith or their religious observances. There will be no change to their rights and privileges. No bishop shall be removed from his bishopric; no monk from his monastery, and no priest from his parish. They shall all continue to enjoy everything they previously enjoyed great or small. No image or cross shall be destroyed. They will not oppress or be oppressed. They shall not practice blood-vengeance as they did in the Days of Ignorance. No tithe shall be levied from them nor shall they be required to furnish provisions for the Muslim troops. If anyone demands his right from you, justice will be maintained between you. You will not be oppressed nor will you be allowed to oppress others. Whoever from among you engages in usury after this will be excluded from my protection. No one shall be held responsible for another's crime. Whatever is mentioned in this treaty is from Allah and Muhammad is responsible for it until Allah sends a new command. This treaty is binding so long as they are loyal, fulfill their obligations, and avoid what is wrong. (qtd. Qureshi 182-183)

The *Treaty of Najran*, which was written by 'Abd Allah ibn Abu Bakr (1st half of the 7th century CE), and witnessed by Abu Sufyan ibn Harb, Ghilan ibn 'Amr, Malik ibn Awf, Aqra ibn Habis, Mughira ibn Shu'ba, represents a remarkable degree of tolerance. As Qureshi explains,

> It conferred on the non-Muslims, living in the Islamic State, autonomy, both religious and administrative. It is an unforgettable milestone, in early Muslim history, for tolerance and high-mindedness. 'This document,' observes Syed Amir 'Ali, 'has furnished the guiding principle to all Muslim rulers in their mode of dealing with their non-Muslim subjects, and if they have departed from it in any instance the cause is to be found in the character of the particular sovereign.' (183)

Since the Christians of Najran had concluded several treaties with the Prophet, granting them unprecedented rights and liberties, there exists no logical reason for them to falsify a covenant which is essentially the same as the ones that were granted to them previously. Despite Philip Khuri Hitti's (1886–1978 CE) claim to the contrary, in which he alleges that "in pursuance of his predecessor's nationalistic policy, 'Umar expelled the Christians from Najran" (28), compensating them and allowing them to migrate to Syria (28), the Christian community of Najran resided there for centuries after (Goddard 42–43). It may be that 'Umar exiled only the hierarchs and nobles, like the Babylonians did in the case of the Jews.

It is also possible that 'Umar (r. 634–644 CE) offered the Christians the option to pay the *jizyah* or relocate to Syria with monetary compensation. It seems that some Christians immigrated to Syria at the time while the majority of the migrants relocated to Kufah, a stronghold of the partisans of 'Ali. They may have opted to move there feeling that their rights would be better respected among the followers of the Household of the Prophet. Still, the historicity of these documented events has been called in to question. According to some sources, the Christians of Najran continued to exert significant influence well into the late 9th century (Goddard 42–43). The first Zaydi Imam of Yemen, al-Hadi (r. 897–911 CE), is reported to have concluded a treaty with the People of the Book of the oasis in 897 CE (Dobson 90). A second Yemeni source from the year 999/1000 CE alludes to the continued Christian presence in Najran (Grabar, Brown, and Bowerstock 753). The Persian traveler, Yusuf ibn Ya'qub ibn al-Mujawir (13th century CE), described the oasis as one third Jewish and one third Christian. Evidence of Christians in Najran thus extends as late as the 13th century CE (753). As an Arab Christian, Hitti's (1886–1978 CE) scholarship is noted for its subjectivity and his persistent attempt to present Muslims in a poor light. Considering the objective evidence, Jafri appears to have come to the correct conclusion: the Christian tribes in question "had been accorded special terms and privileges by the

Prophet, which were maintained by Abu Bakr and 'Umar" (113).

If the fabrication of a covenant supposedly by the Prophet Muhammad was not dangerous enough, the alleged forgers of the *Covenant of the Prophet Muhammad with the Christians of Najran* would certainly have risked their very lives through the inclusion of a long list of witnesses. If these supposed charlatans knew anything about the treaties of the Prophet Muhammad, they would know that, with rare exceptions, they were not signed by witnesses. These treaties were short dispatches sent by the Prophet. Thus, noting the names of thirty-two witnesses from the Companions of the Prophet is anomalous. If a valid document would not be likely to have a long list of witnesses, the existence of such a list could be presented as proof of forgery. The monks, or whoever else was responsible for this possible addition, may not have known that attaching a long list of witnesses would make the document look forged as opposed to authentic. Since the movements of the Prophet's Companions were well-known and duly documented, the forgers would have been running a huge risk to assume that all of them were present in Medina at the same time on the same date. Many Companions traveled or participated in military campaigns; therefore, there is no guarantee that all of them would be together. Scholars who have superficially perused the *Covenant* contend that neither Abu Hurayrah nor Mu'awiyyah ibn Abi Sufyan (602–680 CE) were Muslims at the time, that Sa'd ibn Mu'adh was dead, and that Ja'far ibn Abi Talib was in exile in Ethiopia.

Surprisingly, what initially appears to be a major error may actually act as confirmation of the *Covenant*'s authenticity if a case can be made that the witnesses to it were all present at its signing. In fact, it is possible that the *Covenant of the Prophet Muhammad with the Monks of Mount Sinai*, the *Covenant of the Prophet Muhammad with the Christians of Najran*, and the *Covenant of the Prophet Muhammad with the Christians of the World*, were designed to be anomalous. Unlike the Prophet's other treaties, which were generally short and concise, these covenants were long and detailed. Perhaps they were supposed to serve as models for millennia to come. This would explain the long lists of witnesses for the purpose of authentication. Ironically, though, what might well have been intended to convince readers of their authenticity has caused critics to question their credibility. As with the case of the *Covenant of the Prophet Muhammad with the Monks of Mount Sinai*, there also exists the possibility that the chain of authorities was appended at a later date. But let us return to the question at hand.

Based on the Qur'anic verses referred to in the *Covenant of the Prophet Muhammad with the Christians of Najran*, and the allusions to historical events, it appears initially that the document was concluded during the period of Jewish opposition, most probably in the immediate aftermath of the Battle of the Trench or the Battle of Khaybar. Although it is alleged that Abu Hurayrah (603–681 CE) only embraced Islam two years prior to the Prophet's passing, he actually was one of the first converts to Islam. Known originally as 'Abd al-Shams, the Sun-Worshipper, he was a Yemenite from the tribe of Banu Daws who had embraced Islam through Tufayl ibn 'Amr, the leader of his tribe, who had met Muhammad in Mecca. After embracing Islam, the man who would become known as Abu Hurayrah accompanied Tufayl to Mecca in order to meet the Prophet Muhammad. It was the Messenger of Allah himself who renamed him 'Abd al-Rahman. After returning to his tribe for several years, Abu Hurayrah migrated to Medina in 628/629 CE where he spent three years in the company of the Prophet, living in and around his Mosque. Since Abu Hurayrah was known to visit the Prophet, he may very well have been present when the *Covenant of the Prophet Muhammad with the Christians of Najran* was signed.

As for Sa'd ibn Mu'adh, it is reported that he died from his wounds in Medina after returning from the Battle of the Trench. If the covenant was concluded after the Battle of the Trench, Sa'd ibn Mu'adh may still have been in a position to ratify it. It should be recalled that in medieval times, most deaths did not take place on the battlefield:

they took place weeks or months later as a result of infections and gangrene. There also exists the possibility that the *Sirah* [biographical] literature has not accurately recorded the year of Sa'd ibn Mu'adh's death as his name appears in other traditions and treaties referring to events that took place as late at the Battle of Khaybar. Furthermore, the entire scope of events surrounding the supposed slaughter of the Banu Qurayzah has been called into question by historians. If the story of the extermination of the Banu Qurayzah is false, all related details concerning it, including Sa'd ibn Mu'adh's role, and his death, might therefore be fabrications.

While it is true that Ja'far ibn Abi Talib led a group of Muslim refugees into exile in Abyssinia in 616 CE, critics of the *Covenant* ignore the fact that he returned to Medina in 626 CE at the very moment that Muhammad was returning from the Battle of Khaybar. As for Mu'awiyyah ibn Abi Sufyan (d. 680 CE), he might not yet have been a Muslim at the moment. However, along with his father, Abu Sufyan, he used to regularly travel back and forth between Mecca and Medina on diplomatic missions. As a prominent figure in Arab society, it would not be surprising if Mu'awiyyah (d. 680 CE) had been asked by the Prophet or the Christians of Najran to act as a witness to the covenant.

Finally, as mentioned earlier in this work, there remains the possibility that the accepted chains of narration were actually added centuries after the fact when such tracking devices became a requirement for *hadith* scholarship. As Mahmud Abu Riyya explains in *Light on the Muhammadan Sunnah or Defense of Hadith*, there "were those who would not fabricate text of *hadith*, but would bring in a correct authentic chain of transmission" (144) for a text that was lacking it, whether authentic or not. There is no denying that the Umayyads and 'Abbasids opened wide the doors of innovation and creative editing and wasted no opportunity when it came to falsifying the prophetic *sunnah*. They were not the only ones, of course, as "[t]he heyday of *hadith* forgery was the first four hundred years of Islamic history" (Brown 71).

According to Imam Abu Zakariyyah Muhyi al-Din Yayha ibn Sharaf al-Nawawi (1234–1278 CE), traditions were falsified by the *zanadiqah* or heretics who hated God and Islam, out of favoritism, religiosity, rebellion, bigotry, partisanship, or fanaticism, as well as a desire for fame or for monetary reward (Abu Riyya 144). Abu Riyya lists many other reasons that caused people to falsely attribute sayings to the Prophet Muhammad, including: a desire to create conflict and disunity between Muslims; to promote schools or schism; neglect; to please persons in positions of power; error and inadvertence; faulty memory; mental confusion; ego; and popularity. Although some Jewish people were notorious for forging false *ahadith*, creating an entire genre of *Isra'iliyyat*, Christians appear to have played a very minor role in trafficking these false truths. If Christian concepts were introduced into Islam, it was mostly by means of some misguided Sufi Muslims who admired monasticism and who cited Biblical and apocryphal sayings of Jesus Christ on the authority of the Prophet Muhammad (Rizvi 41).

While most critics believe that the *Covenant of the Prophet Muhammad with the Christians of Najran* dates from the early years after the *hijrah*, they have done so on the basis of the chronology found in Sunni sources which place the deputation from the Christians of Najran prior to the Battle of Badr. In reality, this makes little sense as the Prophet was still relatively unknown in Arabia. He did not, at that time, represent any threat to the tribes and there would have been no reason for the Christians of Najran to request or have been granted a treaty of any kind. The most sensible chronology comes from Shi'ite sources which state that the deputation of Christians and the contest of prayer [*mubahalah*] took place "after the conquest (of Mecca)" (116). As Shaykh al-Mufid relates in his *Kitab al-irshad*:

> When Islam had spread after the conquest (of Mecca) and the raids . . . which followed it, and its authority had become strong, delegations began to visit the Prophet, may Allah bless him and his family. Some of them submitted to Islam while others sought protection so that they might return to their

people (to tell) their people about his view towards them. Among those who came in a delegation to him were Abu Haritha, the bishop of Najran, with thirty of the Christians who included the deputy (*al-'aqib*), the chief (*al-sayyid*) and 'Abd al-Masih. They arrived at Medina at the time of the afternoon prayer. They were wearing robes of silk and crosses.

The Jews approached them and they began to interrogate each other. The Christians said: 'You are not believing in anything (correctly).' And the Jews replied to them: 'You are not believing in anything (correctly).' Concerning that, Allah, may He be praised, revealed: The Jews say that the Christians are not believing in anything (correctly) and the Christians say that the Jews are not believing in anything (correctly) . . . etc. To the end of the verse (2:113).

When the Prophet had prayed the afternoon prayer, they came forwards. At their head was the bishop. He said to him: 'Muhammad, what do you say about the Lord, the Messiah?'

'He is a servant of Allah,' replied the Prophet, 'whom Allah chose and he answered Him.'

'Do you know, Muhammad, whether a father caused him to be born?' asked the bishop.

'He was not born as a result of intercourse so he could not have a father,' answered the Prophet.

'How can you say that he is a servant who has been created, when you can only consider a servant who has been created to be born as a result of intercourse and so to have a father?' he asked.

Allah, may He be praised and exalted, revealed these verses in *Surat Al 'Imran* (3) in answer to him: *The likeness of Jesus according to Allah is like the likeness of Adam. Allah created him from earth. Then Allah said to him: 'Be.' That is the truth from your Lord. Therefore do not be one of those who go beyond the bounds (of reason). If anyone disputes with you concerning him, after knowledge has been given to you, say to him: 'Come, let us call our sons and your sons, our women and your women, and ourselves and yourselves. Then let us call on Allah to witness against each other and let us make the curse of Allah fall on those who lie* (3:61).

The Prophet, may Allah bless him and his family, recited it to the Christians and challenged them to a contest of prayer to Allah (*mubahalah*). He said: 'Allah, the Mighty and High, has informed me that dread torment will come down on him who has spoken falsely after the contest of prayer (*mubahalah*). By this the truth will be distinguished from the false.'

The Bishop held a meeting of consultation with 'Abd al-Masih and the deputy. Their unanimous view was to wait until the early morning of the next day. When they both returned to their men, the bishop told them: 'Watch Muhammad tomorrow morning. If he comes out with his children and his family, then be warned against the contest of prayer (*mubahalah*) with him. However, if he comes out with his Companions, then make the contest of prayer with him, for he believes in something other (than the true religion).'

On the next morning, the Prophet, may Allah bless him and his family, came and took 'Ali ibn Abi Talib by the hand, while al-Hasan and al-Husayn, peace be upon them, were walking in front of him and Fatimah, peace be on her, walked behind him. The Christians came out, at their head their bishop. When the bishop saw that the Prophet, may Allah bless him and his family, was advancing with those who were with him, he asked about them. He was told: 'That is his cousin 'Ali ibn Abi Talib, who is his son-in-law and the father of his two grandsons and the most lovable of creatures to him. Those children are the sons of his daughter by 'Ali, peace be on him. They are the most lovable of creatures to him. That girl is his daughter, Fatimah, peace be on her, the dearest of people to him and the closest to his heart.'

The bishop looked at the deputy, the chief and 'Abd al-Masih, and said: 'Have you seen that he has come with the special members of his children and his family so that he may make the contest of prayer with them, trusting in his truthfulness. By Allah, he would not have come with them while he was afraid that the proof would be against him. Therefore be warned against the contest of prayer with him. By Allah, if it was not for the position of Caesar (i.e. the Byzantine emperor), I would submit to him. But (now) make peace with him on what can be agreed between you and him. Return to your land and think about it yourselves.

'Our view conforms with your view,' they replied.

'Abu al-Qasim,' the bishop called out, 'we will not make a contest of prayer with you but we will make peace with you. Therefore make peace with us as we propose.'

So the Prophet made peace with them on the condition (of the payment) of two thousand protective breastplates, each breastplate being forty stan-

> dard dirham (in value). If they varied in value, it would be taken into account. The Prophet, may Allah bless him and his family, had a document written (laying out the terms) by which he had made peace with them. The document is as follows:
>
> In the Name of Allah, the Most Compassionate, the Most Merciful.
>
> In terms of gold and silver, produce and slaves, nothing will be taken from them except two thousand protective breastplates, each breastplate being worth forty dirhams. If they vary in value, it will be taken into account. They will pay one thousand of them in the month of Safar and one thousand of them in the month of Rajab. (In addition), they will provide forty dinars for a dwelling house for my agent (*rasul*), not more than that. Also in every incident that occurs in Yemen, it will be required of them, (that is) of everyone who lives in a permanent settlement (*dhi'adan*), to pay as guaranteed equally (by both parties) thirty breastplates, thirty horses and thirty camels as guaranteed equally (by both parties). They will have the neighborly protection of Allah (*jiwar Allah*) and the protection (*dhimmah*) of Muhammad ibn 'Abd Allah. Whoever of them takes interest after this year will be denied my protection.
>
> This is a document made on behalf of Muhammad, the Prophet, the Messenger of Allah, may Allah bless him and his family, and the people of Najran and their followers. (116–118)

As with any other historical event, there are minor differences in detail between accounts. Fakhr al-Din al-Razi (1149–1209 CE), in his commentary, cites the Archbishop as saying: "O Christians! I surely see faces of men who, if they were to ask Allah to move a mountain, He would surely do it. Do not hold a meeting or you will be destroyed and no Christian will remain on Earth until the Day of Resurrection" (qtd. Ordoni 158). After the delegation asked to be relieved from the mutual invocation of curses, the Messenger of Allah said: "Indeed I will; but the One who sent me with righteousness is my witness that had I cursed you, Allah would not have left a Christian on the fact of the earth" (qtd. Ordoni 158).

It is interesting how biographers like Ibn Ishaq and al-Waqidi, who worked under the watchful eye of the oppressive rulers of the age, skipped or glossed over the identification and spiritual status of the *ahl al-bayt* which, besides the head of the family, Muhammad, included Fatimah, 'Ali, Hasan, and Husayn, all of whom comprise the Purified Five. It is equally interesting how Shi'ite biographers, like Shaykh Mufid, summarize the theological debate between the Prophet and the People of the Book, which is much stressed by Ibn Ishaq (270–277). The debate between the Jews and Christians, which took place in the presence of the Prophet, is not mentioned by Ibn Ishaq, and is shortened to two sentences by Shaykh al-Mufid. The *Covenant of the Prophet Muhammad with the Christians of Najran*, however, deals with this issue in much greater length. For Sunni scholars like Ibn Ishaq, Shi'ite sympathies were to be suppressed. For Shi'ite scholars like Shaykh al-Mufid, they were to be emphasized. They were all clearly relying on the same complete sources which they altered to serve their own ideological interests. This is another reason why no complete picture of early Islam can be derived solely from Sunni, or even Shi'ite, sources, for that matter. It is only when we combine all accounts passed down by Sunnis, Shi'ites, and Christians, as with the case of the covenants, that we can obtain all of the relevant details.

Since Fatimah would have been far too young to participate in the mutual casting of curses in the early years of the *hijrah*, the *Covenant of the Prophet Muhammad with the Christians of Najran* must necessarily date from the last year of the Prophet's life. It is thus technically possible that most of the witnesses listed on the covenant were present at its signing. Admittedly, this could only have happened during a brief window of time, but it still remains within the realm of the possible. Since the letters, treaties, and the covenants of the Prophet grew steadily longer over the course of the years, this might explain the length of the *Covenant of the Prophet Muhammad with the Christians of Najran*. Most of the Prophet's earliest communications were not witnessed; thereafter the number of witnesses also increased exponentially over time from a couple to over thirty. This may also be explained by the increase in the literacy rate among the Companions of the Prophet.

After Scher, the most prominent opponent of the *Covenant of the Prophet Muhammad with the Christians of Najran* was Claude Cahen (1909–1991 CE), the French Marxist Orientalist and historian, who dismissed it as "a pious fraud of Nestorian monks of the 9th century" (qtd. Nercessian). This opinion, which is unsubstantiated by evidence, has been blindly accepted by Vrej Nerses Nersessian. Despite the fact that the *Covenant* is preserved by two oriental Christian sources, the *Chronicle of Séert* and the Ecclesiastical chronicle of Bar Hebraeus, Nersessian declares it to be "a patent fabrication, probably the work of some Nestorian priest or monk" without adding anything to support his argument. Such simple parroting contributes nothing to scholarly debate and discussion and does nothing to advance knowledge in the field.

As for the most recent attacks upon the authenticity of the *Covenant of the Prophet Muhammad with the Christians of Najran*, they come from Brandie Ratliff—who relies on Scher (1867–1915 CE) (602, note 1) and Louis Massignon (1883–1962 CE) (250–257)—and from Barbara Roggema. In "The Monastery of Saint Catherine at Mount Sinai and the Christian Communities of the Caliphate," she observes that "[a]spects of this letter have also been questioned; it seems to have been produced by viziers of the 'Abbasid period, who were of Nestorian origin and wanted protection for their community" (17, note 11). This claim, however, was advanced by Massignon, a man whose sympathy towards Islam was ambivalent (Irwin 224). In fact, he once wrote that he studied the language of the Qur'an in order to demolish it (225). As for Ratliff, she provides no new evidence of her own and simply relies on the speculative notions of other Orientalists. The Christians in the Islamic world did not have a history of falsifying prophetic traditions or documents. Since their rights were enshrined in the Qur'an, the Sunnah, and the *shari'ah*, there was no real benefit in forging a letter of privileges, as real risks were involved. As prevalent as spreading false sayings may have been, many a forger and falsifier was executed in exemplary fashion during the 'Abassid Caliphate. Furthermore, virtually all falsifications originated from the center of power. In other words, the traditions that were forged supported the political, ideological, and religious views of the administration. The 'Abbasids had no need to falsify a pact from the Prophet since the rights of minorities had already been protected in the Qur'an, Sunnah, and *shari'ah*.

Although she only mentions the *Covenant of the Prophet Muhammad with the Christians of Najran* in passing as part of her study on the story of Bahira, Barbara Roggema is adamant in her opinions. In her estimation, the declaration of the Prophet which precedes the pact is "clearly fictitious" (116). The idea of the Prophet praising the Christians and condemning Jews and polytheists simply does not sit well with her. As for the piece that follows, namely, the pact proper, she states that it was also "certainly penned by Christians" (117). She cautions, however, that the covenant itself "should not be dismissed as an absolute forgery, because it includes a list of obligations for Christians known also from the *Pact of 'Umar*; and it also echoes some of the Prophet's demands and promises to the people of Najran as contained in Muslim sources" (117). As she admits, the covenant found in the *Chronicle of Séert*

> contains obligations similar to the *Pact of 'Umar*, such as having to provide hospitality to Muslims for three days and not giving shelter to enemies of the Muslims; Abu Yusuf Ya'qub and al-Baladhuri also include an agreement between the Prophet and the Christians of Najran in their works; comparing their texts with the one in the *Chronicle of Séert* one finds in the same wording the pledge that there will be no Muslim interference in monastic and church affairs, while the supposed agreement in the *Chronicle of Séert*'s version that if one does not have the capacity to provide the Muslims with a garment one can instead pay its value in money . . . is in all likelihood a response to the stipulation by the Prophet that the community of Najran must pay 2000 garments each year as contained in the Muslim sources concerned. . . . (117)

In order to support her claim that Christians forged documents, and falsely attributed them to the Prophet, Roggema points out that some Jews were accused of doing the same thing (118, note 68). "Did the Christian authors of these edicts want to prescribe, once and for all, a policy which in reality did not exist in such clear-cut terms," wonders the author, "[o]r did the authors of the texts . . . consider the rule a historical given, despite some variations in its application?" (118). Answers to these questions have already been provided. While one may question citations of covenants found in historical sources which date centuries after the fact, one may not question original, authenticated documents: namely, the existing copies of similar pacts sealed by the Prophet himself. This hard evidence gives credence to the covenants found in early historical sources. As for the supposed forgeries that the People of the Book brought forth when the tax collector came knocking on the door or to stop the destruction of their places of worship that had been illegally built, namely, without proper permits or on lands which they did not own, where is the evidence that the documents in question were actually forged? The Prophet, it is well known, sent in excess of one hundred letters to religious communities in the known world. These may have remained in the hands of Jewish and Christian community leaders for centuries. As for taking the liberty of giving new life to long-established precedents through deception, it eludes reason. If the Christians, for example, had copies of the agreements the Prophet had made with their communities, why would they need to "forge" new ones? For Roggema, the *Covenant of the Prophet Muhammad with the Christians of Najran* is a cut and paste job drawn from previous prophetic agreements and the *Pact of 'Umar* with new elements included. She comes to this conclusion, not only on the basis of similarity in content, but on the basis of identical wording. But if all of these sources are so similar and, in many cases, identical, would it not be simpler, and more sound, to attribute them to the same single author?

While interpolation is a possibility, it is not necessarily a reality. In fact, when we compare the various versions of the treaties, and agreements, that the Prophet concluded with the Christians of Sinai and Najran, we find many minor differences. These are exactly the types of small variations found in the *hadith* literature and which occur naturally, but inadvertently, through the process of oral transmission. They can also be caused by transcription of primitive, unvocalized Arabic script, to clearer, more complete, and fully vocalized Arabic script. Like all documents of the time, the letters of the Prophet Muhammad were written in a very elementary form of Arabic script. The *Covenant of the Prophet Muhammad with the Monks of Mount Sinai* and the *Covenant of the Prophet Muhammad with the Christians of Najran* were copied from early Arabic script into the more expressive 'Uthmani script. Due to the nature of primitive Arabic script, its lack of vowels and even of dots above and below the letters, texts could be difficult to decipher. The situation could be aggravated by the poor condition of a manuscript.

When compared, the variants between the various covenants appear to be the result of different readings of the unvocalized and unpunctuated Arabic original. The differences between the *Covenant of the Prophet Muhammad with the Christians of Najran* and the *Covenant of the Prophet Muhammad with the Christians of the World* appear similar in nature to those found in the two variants of the *Treaty of Maqnah* found in Ibn Sa'd (d. 845 CE) and Baladhuri (d. c. 892 CE). As Moshe Gil (b. 1921 CE) explains, "Certain expressions were already unfamiliar in Ibn Sa'd's time, and he tried to explain them in the continuation to the version of the treaty, not quite accurately" (29–30, note 27). At times, to improve comprehension, transmitters attempted to modernize the language of their narrations. If Baladhuri's version indicates that the tribe was the Habibah, Ibn Sa'd's says that it was the Janbah. However, both readings are possible when the Arabic letters *ha*, *jim*, and *kha* were indistinguishable due to the absence of dots as were the letters *ba*, *ta*, *tha*, and *nun*. Furthermore, as Baladhuri explained, he obtained a copy of the document from an Egyptian who had seen the original in Maqnah (Gil 29–30, note 27). According to Baladhuri's Egyptian informant, the letter of protection was written on red parchment, the script of which was already faded (Gil 29–30, note 27). Based on this information, it seems that the variants between some of the covenants under study were the result of different possible readings of the consonantal script. It also appears that the original covenants were in poor condition when they were copied into ʿUthmani script. Some words, sentences or entire paragraphs may have been unclear while others may have been missing completely, leaving the scribe with two options: skip the section or attempt to reconstruct it to the best of his ability. If this is what happened, there is no question of interpolation as any mistakes were made in good faith. Finally, when one considers the similarities shared by these various covenants, and the fact that they are found in different geographic domains, it can be concluded that they all came from a single source. In *hadith* studies, such a phenomenon is known as proliferation of transmitters and is considered a mode of authentication (Azami 33–42). The covenants of the Prophet are found in various regions with more or less the same form or meaning in all versions. This suggests that they share a common origin.

Commentary on the Content of the Covenant

The *Covenant of the Prophet Muhammad with the Christians of Najran* is the longest of all the accords concluded by the Messenger of Allah. Unlike the other two, which proceed directly to the issues at hand, the document in question commences with the more traditional *basmallah*, specifically, in the name of Allah, the Most Compassionate, the Most Merciful. Unlike the covenants concluded with the monks of Mount Sinai and the Assyrian Christians, the document in question actually consists of two distinct sections: an exordium, which contextualizes the coming into being of the covenant, and the covenant itself.

The exordium to the treaty clearly stipulates its purpose from the onset, affirming that it is a "covenant of protection granted by Allah and His Messenger to the People of the Book, the Christians, who belong to the religion of Najran or any other Christian sect." Like the Qur'an and Sunnah, which contained time-bound instructions combined with eternal principles, the *Covenant of the Prophet* applied to the Christians of Najran in particular, as well as the broader Christian community as a whole, so long as they submitted to Islamic authority in the same manner as the Christians from southern Arabia.

The document asserts that it was "written by Muhammad, the Messenger of Allah to all of humanity, as a guarantee of protection on the part of Allah and His Messenger, and made it binding upon the Muslims who will come after him, which they have to be aware of, recognize as authentic, believe in, and preserve it in their favor." The use of the verb *kataba* was, and continues to be, cause for consternation for the majority of Muslims who piously believe that the Prophet Muhammad was illiterate. They generally argue that, as an unlettered individual, the Messenger of Allah could never have written the covenant in question. The issue, however, has been adequately addressed in my study on the "Pre and Early Islamic Period" found in a *Cultural History of Reading*:

> According to the Qur'an, the Prophet was *ummi* (7:157–58), a term interpreted by most Sunni scholars as meaning 'illiterate.' Although the word *ummi*, in its modern usage, includes the definition of illiterate, it also means 'an inhabitant of Mecca, known as *Umm al-Qura*, the Mother of all Cities,' 'Gentile,' in the sense of not belonging to the People of the Book, the Jews and the Christians, and 'unlettered,' in the sense of not having received a formal education. According to the Prophet's Family, Muhammad could read and write in seventy languages. They always insisted that the title of '*ummi* Prophet' referred to that fact that he was from Mecca.
>
> According to many orientalists, such as Maxine Rodinson, W. Montgomery Watt, and Albert Guillaume, the Prophet was indeed literate before Islam, a skill required of any businessman of the period. In some Shiʿite sources, the Prophet is said to have been literate prior to receiving the revelation, while others argue that he became literate upon receiving the revelation. Although the literacy of the Prophet prior to the Qur'anic revelation is subject to specu-

lation, the fact that Muhammad wrote and signed letters during his lifetime is sufficient proof that he practiced what he preached.

Appreciating the importance of literacy, the Prophet embarked on a campaign to alphabetize the Arabic world. The core of Muhammad's literacy campaign was the Qur'an, which continues to act as the primary text for alphabetization in the Muslim world to the present day. The Prophet's many sayings promoting education include: 'Knowledge is worship;' 'Seek knowledge from the cradle to the grave;' 'The seeking of knowledge is obligatory for every Muslim, male or female;' 'Acquire knowledge and share it with the people;' and 'Seek knowledge, even in China.'

The Prophet encouraged his literate Companions to teach his illiterate Companions how to read. Due to a lack of teachers, he even enlisted prisoners of war as teachers. So long as prisoners taught two Muslims how to read, they would be set free. Although the Prophet only ruled in Medina for ten years, he created legions of literate and learned Muslims who would rise to the most sublime of scholarly ranks. (526)

When the Imams were asked whether the Prophet was illiterate, they would respond: "By Allah, he could read and write in seventy languages" (Majlisi). This miraculous ability is said to have been passed down to each of the Twelve Imams. As Imam 'Ali said in *Hadith al-tariq*: "The Imam is blessed in his majesty with the knowledge of all languages spoken by all living things." As many traditions demonstrate, the Prophet and the Imams had knowledge of all languages. There are Sunni traditions which demonstrate that the Prophet, Hasan, and Husayn used to speak Persian. Many of the Imams are cited speaking Hebrew. Imam 'Ali al-Rida (765–818 CE) was well-known for being fluent in all the languages spoken in his part of the world. In fact, the very first command received by the Prophet was "Read!" (96:1); thus, it seems scandalous to suggest that he did not practice what he preached. While the imperative *iqra* is sometimes translated as "recite" in English, which can either mean "read out loud from a text" or "recite from memory," the Arabic verb *qara* means "to read" while other verbs such as *sama'*, *alqa*, and *sarada* mean "to recite." While it is possible that the Prophet was illiterate during the pre-Islamic period, thus proving that he could not have forged the Qur'an (Saleh 33), and explaining why he signed an early engagement with the monks of Mount Sinai with his palm-print, it is improbable that he remained so after receiving the revelation. After all, it is reported in *Bihar al-anwar* that the Prophet was granted knowledge of all languages when Gabriel descended upon him for the first time and that he subsequently taught 'Ali the different scripts employed by previous prophets (xviii, 266, 278–282). And *Surah al-'Alaq* or The Clot describes Allah as the One who "teacheth by the pen, teacheth man that which he knew not (96:4–5) implying that the Prophet was taught to read and write, or inspired to learn to read and write, by Allah through the intermediary of Gabriel.

When the Holy Qur'an says: "Read: In the name of thy Lord who createth, / createth man from a clot. / Read: And they Lord is the Most Bounteous, / Who teacheth by the pen, / Teacheth man that which he knew not" (96: 1–5), the development of the human being from fertilized egg to full adult form, and the motion from hearing and listening to reading and writing, are presented as strictly equivalent. In a single flash, on that day, in that moment, Muhammad understood the relationship of speech to writing, of hearing to reading, of the immediate response to the Command of Allah to the full assimilation and establishment of that Command in the human heart. In the science of *tasawwuf*, this motion from the spoken to the written word is understood as the passage from *hal* or state to *maqam* or station. Muhammad, as Prophet, learned to read as Allah had commanded him and also to write, a skill he taught his Companions, the foremost of which was 'Ali ibn Abi Talib. The Messenger of Allah stood as the Speaker vis-à-vis the scribe as Listener so as to maintain the hierarchy of revelation and keep the Word of Allah fresh, alive, and resonant. So, the Holy Qur'an was his grammar school; that is where he learned his alphabet.

Esoterically speaking, to be "unlettered" is to be

perfectly receptive to the words of Allah, like a blank sheet of paper ready to be written on by the Pen. The hearts of most of us are covered over with scribbles, doodles, and half-erased sentences, leaving God little space to write, but the Heart of the Prophet was "virgin." Not for nothing did Gabriel appear both to Muhammad and the Virgin Mary, announcing the advent of a Divine revelation. And *ummi* might also be an allusion to the kind of knowledge we get "with our mother's milk," i.e., from the Original Source, through direct revelation or perception. That Original Source is of course Allah; both *al-Rahmah* and *al-Dhat*, are feminine nouns. And the language we learn by listening, not by reading, is still called our "mother-tongue."

Whether it was written by the hand of the Prophet or that of one of his scribes, the exordium to the *Covenant* with the Christians from Najran warns that "it is forbidden for any man, whether he is a governor or holder of authority, to revoke it or infringe upon it." As a contract between communities, the document is legally binding: it was very much a treaty concluded by the Prophet as a sovereign political authority and popularly acclaimed leader. The exordium to the *Covenant* stipulates that "the Believers must not charge them with other conditions than those which are included in this document," thus preventing any future attempts to modify the terms in a fashion which was detrimental to the Christians. "He who preserves it, respects it, and abides by its dictates," reads the document, "will have fulfilled his obligations and will have adhered by the covenant of the Messenger of Allah." Obeying the covenant is obedience to God and His Messenger. "He, however, who breaks it, opposes it or changes it," warns the *Covenant*, "will carry his crime on his head; for he will have betrayed the Covenant of Allah, broken his faith, resisted His Authority and contravened the will of His Messenger: he will thus be an imposter in the eyes of Allah." The expression, "to carry his crime on his head," seems consistent with Qur'anic rhetoric which speaks of sinners being seized by their forelocks: "(For) the sinners will be known by their marks: and they will be seized by their forelocks" (55:41; see also 96:15–16).

As the Prophet professes, "the religion of Allah has been imposed and the covenant which he has made has rendered protection obligatory." The Messenger of Allah clearly speaks from a position of power. The *Covenant* has not been concluded by equal parties. The Islamic State is the ultimate authority. However benevolent the terms may have been, they were terms of surrender and submission. This covenant was not simply a goodwill gesture on behalf of the Prophet towards the Christian community, but a document commanding submission to his sovereignty as the rightful ruler of the physical world. Consequently, "He who does not abide by this covenant will have violated his sacred obligations, and he who violates his sacred obligations is unfaithful and will be rejected by Allah and by all sincere Believers." As the Qur'an states, "Those who conceal the clear (Signs) We have sent down, and the Guidance, after We have made it clear for the people in the Book,-on them shall be Allah's curse, and the curse of those entitled to curse" (2:159).

The exordium to the *Covenant* goes on to explain why the Prophet has granted such generous terms to the Christians of Najran. As the document relates, the rewards they received were not unwarranted; they were duly earned and deserved: "The reason for which the Christians have been found worthy of this covenant of protection from Allah, His Messenger, and the Believers, is because it is a right they have earned." As such, it is a covenant "to which every Muslim is bound . . . and which obliges every Muslim to respect it, to defend it, to conserve it, to protect it perpetually, and to live up to it." The following rationale is especially revealing. As the Prophet explains,

> Verily, the people who followed the ancient religions and the ancient Books expressed hostility towards Allah and His Messenger and loathed them by denying the mission of the Prophet which Allah, the Most High, has clearly proclaimed in His Book. This demonstrates the crookedness of their breasts, the wickedness of their intentions, and the hardness of their hearts. They themselves prepared the burden of the crime they bore while hiding the one which Allah wanted to impose upon them, by pro-

claiming it instead of hiding it and by testifying instead of denying it.

This section sheds light on how the Prophet's message was received by the early Arabs. The reference to the followers of "the ancient religions" appears to allude to the Sabians, to the Magians, and perhaps even to the polytheists. As for the followers of "the ancient Books," this would seem to refer to the *ahl al-kitab*, the People of the Book, unanimously agreed upon to include the Jews and the Christians, and extended to the Zoroastrians and even Hindus and Buddhists by a minority of scholars. The words in question appear to include echoes of the Qur'an, which warns that: "Those who believe (in the Qur'an), those who follow the Jewish (scriptures), and the Sabians, Christians, Magians, and Polytheists, Allah will judge between them on the Day of Judgment: for Allah is witness of all things" (22:17). While there was some debate as to who fits into the category of "People of the Book," "the practice of the Prophet and that of the Orthodox Caliphs has . . . decided that all non-Muslims may be tolerated as subjects" (Hamidullah, *Muslim Conduct* 112–13). Such was the opinion of Muhammad al-Shaybani (749/50–805 CE), Muhammad ibn Ahmad al-Sarakhsi (d. c. 1096 CE), Abu Hanifah (699–767 CE), and Abu Yusuf (d. 798 CE) (113). As for the hardness of hearts and the sickness of souls, such metaphors are used repeatedly in the Qur'an, in verses such as: "In their hearts is a disease; and Allah has increased their disease: And grievous is the penalty they (incur), because they are false (to themselves)" (2:10; see also 2:74; 3:7; 5:13; 5:52; 6:43; 8:49; 9:77; 9:125; 22:53; 24:50; 33:12; 33:60; 39:22; 47:20; 47:29; 74:31; 83:14 . . .).

As the Messenger of Allah explains, his message was not received with open arms. He certainly could not expect a warm reception. After all, the Qur'an relates how the Jewish people "slew the prophets in defiance of right" (3:112; 4:155). As the Prophet continues,

> These people acted in opposition to the obligation that was imposed upon them, did not observe it as they should have, did not follow the clearly marked paths, and agreed only to show their hostility towards Allah and His Messenger, to attack them, and to persuade people by means of imposture and false arguments, that Allah could not have sent him to humanity to proclaim, to preach, and to call to Allah by His Permission, to be a shinning lamp, and to promise Paradise to those who obeyed him and portend fire for those who disobeyed him.

While he does not mention them by name, the Prophet seems to be alluding quite clearly to the Jews of Medina. Historical accounts are consistent that both the Jews and Christians were eagerly awaiting the arrival of a long-awaiting prophet and messenger. Sources like *Hayat al-qulub*, by 'Allamah Majlisi (1616–1689 CE), include a large number of prophecies concerning the birth, status, and signs of Muhammad, the Messenger of Allah (Chapter 2). Although they recognized Muhammad for what he was, they rejected him on the basis that he was an Arab rather than a Jewish person. As many scholars have shown, however, there is ample evidence in both the Old Testament and the New Testament to support the claim that Muhammad was indeed the final Messenger of Allah foretold by prophets past. Works like *Muhammad in the Bible* by 'Abdul 'Ahad Dawud (1867– c. 1940 CE), formerly Rev. David Benjamin Keldani, Bishop of Urmia, *What the Bible Says about Muhammad* by Ahmed Deedat (1918–2005 CE), and *Muhammad in the Bible* by Jamal Badawi serve as essential starting points for any research on the subject. According to Abraham Isaac Katsh (Katz) (c. 1908–1998 CE), a Jewish scholar, the Prophet was so profoundly influenced by Judaism that he was "almost Judaized" (xxv). Nonetheless, he claims that there is nothing that the Prophet could have possibly done to convince the Jews to embrace Islam (xvii). For Heribert Busse, another Jewish academic, "[i]t was a hopeless venture to want to convert the Jews to Islam" (19).

This view is clearly false, however, as many Jews have embraced Islam from the time of the Prophet to the present. Some of the Companions of the Prophet, such as 'Abd Allah ibn Sallam, were converts from Judaism, as were many prominent figures in Islamic history, including Hibat Allah Abu al-Barakat al-Baghdadi, Ibn Yahya al-Maghribi, Rashid al-Din al-Hamadani, Ya'qub ibn Killis, Ibn Yayha of Seville, Shabbetai Zevi, and Jacob Querido. The twentieth century saw the conversion of Leopold Weiss (1900–1992 CE), Youssef Darwish, Lev Nussimbaum (1905–1942 CE), Abdullah Schleifer, and Moustafa Mould, along with Maryam Jameelah (1934–2012 CE), Michael Wolfe (b. 1945 CE), Samuel L. Lewis (1896–1971 CE), Leonard Lewisohn, and Kabir Helminski, among many others. Disappointed with Judaism, and disillusioned with Zionism, an increasing number of Israeli Jews have been embracing Islam over the past decades (Palter), the most famous of which is Tali Fahima (b. 1976), a pro-Palestinian activist. *Jews for Allah* is a good starting point for anyone interested in studying this fascinating phenomenon. It is true, however, that the Jews of Medina, were mostly hostile towards the Prophet Muhammad's revival of what he presented as pure Judaism and Christianity.

As Almighty Allah explained to the Prophet in the Holy Qur'an, "It is never the wish of those without Faith among the People of the Book, nor of the Pagans, that anything good should come down to you from your Lord" (2:105). In fact, "Quite a number of the People of the Book wish they could Turn you (people) back to infidelity after ye have believed, from selfish envy, after the Truth hath become Manifest unto them" (2:109). In the Qur'an, Almighty Allah accused the Jews not only of concealing the truth (2:146); He warns that "it is the wish of a section of the People of the Book to lead you astray" (3:69). The allusion made by the Messenger of Allah to the "shining lamp," namely, the light of truth which the infidels seek to extinguish with their mouths (9:32), seems to come straight for "The Chapter of the Light:"

> Allah is the Light of the heavens and the earth. The Parable of His Light is as if there were a Niche and within it a lamp: the lamp enclosed in Glass: the glass as it were a brilliant star: Lit from a blessed Tree, an Olive, neither of the east nor of the west, whose oil is well-nigh luminous, though fire scarce touched it: Light upon Light! Allah doth guide whom He will to His Light: Allah doth set forth Parables for men: and Allah doth know all things. (24:35)

Besides trying to confuse and confound the early Muslims, the Jews went beyond pointless polemics to seditious plotting. As the exordium explains,

> They exceeded the bounds of opposition by inciting others to do what they themselves would never have dared to do: to deny his revelation, to reject his mission, and to seek, through cunning, to make him succumb to pitfalls.

Not only did they betray the covenants which they concluded with the Prophet, they aided and abetted the idol-worshipping enemies and even attempted, on several occasions, to assassinate the Messenger of Allah. In the words of the exordium,

> They targeted the Prophet of Allah and decided to kill him. They reinforced the Party of the Polytheists of the Tribe of Quraysh as well as others in order to fight him, to dispute his doctrine, to force it back, and to contradict it.

One Jewish woman threw a stone at his head in an attempt to kill him. Another Jewish woman actually poisoned him but the morsel of meat spoke to the Prophet, warning him that it was poisoned. He spit the meat out at the very last moment, barely saving his life. The effect of the poison, however, damaged his internal organs and the Messenger of Allah suffered from severe stomach pains for several years prior to succumbing. It is for this reason that many Muslims historians and theologians consider that Muhammad was not only a Prophet and a Messenger, but a martyr as well. "For this reason," continued the exordium to the *Covenant*, "they deserved to be deprived of the Alliance of Allah and His Protection." The Prophet then proceeds to allude to the treacherous machinations of the Jews of Medina during many difficult moments for the Muslims:

> Their behavior during the days of Hunayn, the battles against the Bani Qaynuqah, the tribe of Qurayzah and Nadhar, is well-known. Their leaders lent support to the inhabitants of Mecca, the enemies of Allah, against the Messenger of Allah, and

> supported them, by means of troops and weapons, against the Prophet, out of hatred for the Believers.

This explains why hostile Jewish populations were deprived of writs of protection on the part of the Prophet. Evidently, this did not apply to Jewish communities that made peace with the Prophet, such as the inhabitants of Maqnah. "The Christians," however, "refused to wage war against Allah and His Messenger. Allah, as well, has declared that their tenderness towards to the followers of this faith and their affection for Muslims were sincere." As evidence that the Christians of Najran were acting in good faith at the time, the Prophet points out the words of praise they received in the Holy Qur'an:

> Among other words of praise which Allah has bestowed upon them in His Book and His Revelations, after having been convinced of the hardness of heart of the Jews, He recognizes their inclination and affection towards the Believers: *Certainly you will find,* He says, *the most violent of people in enmity for those who believe (to be) the Jews and those who are polytheists, and you will certainly find the nearest in friendship to those who believe (to be) those who say: 'We are Christians;' this is because there are priests and monks among them and because they do not behave proudly. And when they hear what has been revealed to the messenger you will see their eyes overflowing with tears on account of the truth that they recognize; they say: 'Our Lord! We believe, so write us down with the witnesses (of truth). And why should we not believe in God and what has come down to us of the truth? And we hope to be admitted by our Lord among those who are upright and do good?'*

As Ahmad Shboul summarizes, "the Qur'anic attitude towards Christian piety and spirituality is essentially one of recognition and respect" (123). Going over and beyond the call of duty, the Prophet explains, "some Christian, who were worthy of trust and who knew the divine religion, helped us to proclaim this religion and came to the help of Allah and His Messenger, by preaching to men according to His Will and to help him accomplish his mission." In other words, some Christians, who sympathized with the Prophet and Islam, actually assisted the Messenger of Allah in refuting the arguments advanced by the Jewish adversaries. This certainly seems to have occurred during some of the encounters between the Prophet and Christians from Najran.

If detailed accounts of these events have not reached us, it may be due to the fact that the hostility of Christian Crusaders had left such a bad taste in the mouth of Muslim scholars that they had no interest in highlighting the bright, but brief, moment of congenial Christian-Muslim coexistence. With the Christians eventually expelled or exiled from Arabia, and the world divided between *dar al-islam*, the land of Islam, and *dar al-kufr*, the land of the disbelief, the very idea that Judaism, Christianity, and Islam could live side by side in peace and harmony must have escaped many Muslims. It was simply not something to which they could relate to experientially during the Crusades and colonialism. Eventually, congenial relations between Jews, Christians, and Muslims did return to many parts of the Muslim world, only to be shattered, once again, by the creators of more contemporary conflicts. The Prophet then proceeds to explain the nature of his early encounter with the Christians of Najran,

> The Sayyid 'Absiso, Ibn Hijrah, Ibrahim the monk, and 'Isa the Bishop, came to see me, accompanied by forty horsemen from Najran along with others who, like them, profess the Christian religion in the lands of Arabia as well as foreign lands. I informed them of my mission and asked them to help reinforce it, to proclaim it, and to assist it.
>
> And since the cause of Allah appeared evident to them, they did not turn back on their steps nor did they turn their backs. On the contrary, they drew close, remained firm, consented, assisted, confirmed, made generous promises, gave good advice, and assured me by means of oaths and covenants that they would support the truth which I brought and that they would repel those who refused and contradicted it.

The preceding account appears to agree with the historical record. According to early Islamic sources, the Christians of Najran sent two delegations to Medina. The first deliberations resulted in a standstill that was to be resolved by the mutual invocation of curses. After the Christians backed down, the Prophet prepared a peace treaty for them (Qureshi 85). After this deputation returned, a second larger one arrived. According to Qureshi, "[i]t consisted of sixty persons. Prominent among them were Abu al-Harith al-Ayham and 'Abd al-Masih. In addition to them, twenty-four famous chiefs were also included in this deputation" (85). Qureshi, it is clear, has confused the names of the participants. According to both Sunni and Shi'i sources, the leaders of the Christians were 'Abd al-Masih, who was the *'Aqib*, deputy or leader, of the delegation; the Sayyid, their administrator, whose name was al-Ayham; and their Bishop and scholar, known as Abu Haritha ibn 'Alqama (Ibn Ishaq 271; Mufid 116). The Sayyid 'Absiso, mentioned in the *Covenant of the Prophet Muhammad with the Christians of Najran*, may be al-Ayham, whose father is not identified in the *Sirat Rasul Allah* or *Kitab al-irshad*. The patronymic Ibn Hijrah may have belonged to 'Abd al-Masih. 'Isa may have been the first name of Abu Haritha b. 'Alqamah who is only referred to by his *kunyah* in Islamic sources. These variations in names are thus a non-issue. The same applies with the precise number of Christians. Ibn Ishaq speaks of "sixty riders, fourteen of them from their nobles" (270), Shaykh al-Mufid talks of thirty Christians (116), while the *Covenant* mentions forty. It should be recalled that in Semitic languages, such numbers are simply used to symbolize a large amount. Hence, the account in the *Chronicle of Séert* agrees with early Islamic sources.

It was the Christians of Najran who sought out the Prophet as many other communities did and had done during the early decades of Islam. In a tribal society, based on the rule of force and fear, alliances meant everything. Among the Arabs, as among the Amerindians, the isolated individual could not exist. The smallest entity was the immediate family. The immediate family belonged to an extended family of connected family clans. These family clans operated within the confines of a larger tribal organization which, as much as possible, attempted to function as part of a broader confederation of tribes. How the Prophet was perceived in the early days of Islam is difficult to ascertain. Was he simply seen as a rising warlord? Or was he seen as a socio-spiritual and political revolutionary who offered the opportunity of a new system, a new society, and a new and better order? As more and more tribes concluded alliances with the Prophet, it seems that it was this latter understanding that prevailed. What the Messenger of Allah offered was as simple as it was utterly revolutionary: a superior way of life in every aspect. Most tribal members joined the Islamic Alliance, not out of fear, but out of hope, with the firm conviction that justice could actually prevail.

Unlike many others, this particular group of Christians from Najran had not betrayed the trust of the Prophet. As the Messenger of Allah explains,

> After they rejoined their co-religionists, they did not break their covenant nor did they change their opinion. On the contrary, they observed what they had promised to me when they left me and I learned, to my great pleasure, that they proved their devotion, united to wage war against the Jews, and that they came to an understanding with the People of the Vocation, to publicize the cause of Allah, to support it, and to defend its apostles, and that they had debunked the evidence which the Jews had relied upon in order to deny and hinder my mission and my word. The Christians sought to prop up my action and waged war against those who hated my doctrine and who wanted to rebut it, alter it, repudiate it, change it, and overturn it.

In light of the above, it is important to clarify a few points. In the explication provided by the Messenger of Allah above, as well as many other places in this work, the reader comes across two very different attitudes towards the Prophet and Islam on the part of Christians and Jews. According to historical records, it is indicated that the Christians had a friendly, understanding, harmonious, loyal, honest, social, and sympathetic relationship with the Muslims, something which was noticeably absent with regards to the Jewish community. When reading about such events in the 21st century, as opposed to witnessing them in the 7th century, the connotations, deductions, analysis, implications, and interpretations are necessarily quite different. In that distant past, it would never have occurred to anyone to speak of "anti-Semitism" or anything similar. In our own time, it is practically impossible to avoid such value judgments which, when applied to the distant past, result in grotesque absurdities. And, it is but a small step for people with unbalanced minds to claim that the Messenger of Allah was "anti-Semitic" after which any criticism of the poor relations between different parties is placed under the banner of "racism." However, as George F. Nafziger and (b. 1949 CE) Mark W. Walton observe: "It is apparent to Western readers [of the Old Testament] that these were not the first Hebrews to have trouble with a prophet" (4).

Any conflict between the Muslims and Jews of Medina was not racial as all parties were Semites. Although we know little about the Jews of Arabia, and scholars are not even certain if they were actual Hebrews or simply Arab converts to Judaism, the Jews and Muslims shared the same Arabic language and culture. Regarding allegations of anti-Semitism on the part of the Prophet, nothing can be further from the truth. In that period, cursing, combating, killing, and enslaving people were considered normal. It did not matter if those who suffered were Muslims, Christians, Jews, pagans, polytheists, or atheists. These were common, deeply-rooted, and socially-accepted daily practices.

In relatively recent times, however, anything that is critical of "Jews" or "Judaism" is considered an act of "anti-Semitism" even if what is being analyzed took place one or two thousand years ago. Obviously, it is important to stress that such attitudes do nothing but impede the critical analysis of events, both past and present. While Muslims are customarily accused of being anti-Jewish in the mass media, "Anti-Semitism is a Christian vice" (21). As Karen Armstrong (b. 1944) rightly recognizes,

> Hatred of Jews became marked in the Muslim world only after the creation of the state of Israel in 1948 and the subsequent loss of Arab Palestine. It is significant that Muslims were compelled to import anti-Jewish myths from Europe, and translate into Arabic such virulently anti-Semitic texts as the *Protocols of the Elders of Zion*, because they had no such traditions of their own. Because of this new hostility towards the Jewish people, some Muslims now quote the passages in the Qur'an that refer to Muhammad's struggle with the three rebellious Jewish tribes to justify their prejudices. By taking these verses out of context, they have distorted both the message of the Qur'an and the attitude of the Prophet, who himself felt no such hatred of Judaism. (2000: 22)

If we look at Islamic history as a whole, we can see that some religious and political leaders oppressed the Jews; this mistreatment, however, was sporadic and not normative. The regulations restricting the Jews promulgated by Muhammad Taqi Majlisi in the 17th century (Levy 293–295) violate both the letter and the spirit of Islam. Habib Levy, a Persian Jew, has the perspicacity to distinguish between real Muslim leaders and pseudo-mullahs. As he explains, "We say 'pseudo-mullahs' and do not include the few discerning leaders who correctly understood the concept of religion and sought the protection of the followers of all religions, especially the monotheistic religions" (Levy 288). He proudly points out the *fatwa* of five Iranian jurists in 1842 in favor of the Jews as an example of the true nature of Islam (Figure 11, 390–391). Islam, it cannot be stressed enough, is not opposed to Judaism. In fact, Muslims are closer to Jews in belief than they are to Christians and the differences between the Law of Moses and the Law of Muhammad are slight. Jews and Muslims lived together harmoniously for most of Islamic history. This relationship, however, was virtually ruined by the establishment of the State of Israel. But even so, Muslims differentiate between Jews, as followers of Abraham, with whom they have no problems, and Zionists, whom they oppose vehemenently as usurpers and oppressors.

Returning to the analysis of the cited segment, the emphasis on the unity between Christians and Muslims during the early days of Islam seems to support the contention of Fred Donner (b. 1945) that Islam began as a broader movement of monotheistic believers, which was comprised of committed Muslims, as well as righteous Jews and

Christians, who, though distinct, all agreed upon universal principles. As a result of the activities of pro-Islamic Christian missionaries, the message of Muhammad was spread far and wide and the results were remarkable. As the Messenger of Allah acknowledges,

> All of the Arab chiefs, all of the leading Muslims, and all the People of the Vocation, from around the world sent me letters expressing the fondness of Christians towards my cause, their zeal to push back the incursions made along the fortified borderlines of their region, their determination to observe the treaty which they contracted with me when they met with me and which I granted them. For, truly, the bishops and the monks showed an unshakable loyalty in their attachment to my cause and the devotion of their persons to confirm and support the spread of my mission.

These words of the Prophet appear to support Donner's claim that the Prophet Muhammad's Believer's Movement included, not only Muslims, but Jews and Christians as well (68–74). These Jewish and Christian believers fought alongside the Muslims and also played important roles in early Islamic administration (176, 177, 181–183). Christians, in particular, were closely connected to the Household of the Prophet, the Umayyads, and the 'Abbasids. In Morocco, the Alawite kings tended to have Jewish advisors. Take the case of John ibn Hawai, known as John the Black, who was a Christian from Abyssinia. A former slave of Abu Dharr al-Ghiffari (d. 652 CE), the famous Companion of the Prophet, he became a Follower of Imam 'Ali, Imam Hasan, and Imam Husayn, and met martyrdom in Karbala' in the year 680 CE. There are many other instances of devout Christians who were so deeply committed to the cause of Islam that they devoted their lives, and often offered them, to defend it. I suppose this is similar to Catholics who supported atheistic leftist movements in Latin America and atheist Marxists who sided with Islamists against the Shah of Iran. It might also be compared to Jews, Muslims, and Christians, who support Western-style secular, liberal, democracy. It is also reminiscent of the supporters of the *teología islamo-cristiana de la liberación* or Islamo-Christian Liberation Theology which consists primarily of former leftist revolutionaries who view Islam as the sole force capable of confronting globalized capitalism. While some of these activists are *bona fide* Muslim converts, others embrace Islam as a political ideology without becoming observant in any manner. There are others who simply support "revolutionary Islam" while remaining atheists, Christians, or whatever they were before converting to the Islamist cause. This is a topic I have tackled in *Religion and Revolution: Spiritual and Political Islam in Ernesto Cardenal*. It is also possible that some of the Christians and Jews who made common cause with Islam recognized it not only as a political force, to which accommodations would have to be made, or which might be useful to them in certain ways, but as a kindred revelation of the One God which was not only politically but spiritually supportive of their own. Islam, then, represented some sort of Abrahamic socio-political and spiritual alliance.

The role of these early Christians who supported Muhammad and acted as representatives and emissaries of Islamic power to their people merits detailed study. It may be that they did not attempt to directly convert Christians to the Muslim cause; however, they most certainly softened their attitude towards Islamic rule. While they still maintained their beliefs, these "Christian Islamists" agreed with Islam on most theological points and probably agreed with Islam in totality when it came to socio-political and economic issues. Plus, they must have been particularly pleased that the Prophet, and Imam 'Ali, among others, judged Jews according to the Torah, and Christians according to the Gospel. These Christian partisans of the Muslim movement must have presented some interesting arguments to members of their religious community: the Prophet of Islam promises to do what Christians have very often failed to do: rule according to the teachings of Christ. It was a win-win situation for all believers.

Unlike the Jews, who sided with the polytheists, the Christians of Najran sided with the Muslims. Nearly a millennium and a half of anti-Jewish sentiment among the Christians may have played a role in the matter. Since Arabia was the refuge for every "heterodox" and "heretical" Christian sect, who did nothing but dispute among each others on matters of doctrine, Islam encouraged them to agree upon the essentials and not allow theological discrepancies to jeopardize this agreement. Since the Qur'an expresses love and admiration for Jesus and Mary, and Muslims believe that Jesus was both a prophet and the Messiah, who was born to a virgin mother, the issue of his divinity and crucifixion seemed minor in comparison to the Jews' rejection of Jesus. The Christians of the time were well aware of the atrocious allegations that some Jews made about Jesus and his mother (Qur'an 4:156). Not only did they view Jesus as a false prophet and false Messiah, they accused his mother of playing the harlot with Roman soldiers. Jesus, for many Jews of the time, was simply the bastard son of a whore; a slander openly asserted in the Talmud. According to the Prophet, his early Christian supporters zealously defended his efforts at revolutionary religious reform:

> I want my mission to be spread. I ask them to join together in support of this goal against those who would deny and reject aspects of my doctrine, who would want to destroy and ruin it, by blaming them and abasing them [i.e., these enemies].
>
> They acted according to my instructions and abased them. They worked so hard to bring them to confess to the truth with submission, to respond to the call of Allah, by will or by force, allowing them to be drawn (into Islam) as conquered people. They Christians acted this way in observance of the treaties contracted between them and me, in order that they fail not to fulfill the obligations to which they had committed themselves during their meeting with me and through a spirit of zeal to support my cause and to make my mission known.

The Christians of Najran, it would appear, came to the Prophet's defense in a theological dispute with the Jews. Ibn Ishaq mentions that a dispute between Christians and Jews took place in the presence of the Prophet (258). Since the Jews rejected Jesus and the Gospel, the Christians were much closer to the Prophet's position. Hence, their arguments might have been viewed as generally supportive of the claims made by Muhammad. Besides siding with the Prophet against the Jews on certain theological issues, the Christians of Najran also provided him with military support. While rarely recognized, and generally ignored for reasons mentioned before, Christian knights and warriors participated in several battles fighting the polytheists alongside the Army of Muhammad. As the Prophet acknowledges, "It was as a result of their faithful devotion that they waged war against the Jews, the Qurayshites and the other polytheists." Showing the highest degree of selflessness and self-sacrifice, the Christians "demonstrated no desire for worldly gain for which the Jews seek and yearn by practicing usury, looking for money, and selling the law of God for a miserable price. Woe to those who work for such a gain. Woe to those for what they write, and woe to them for what they gain by such means." As the Messenger of Allah to all of humanity, the Prophet Muhammad came to reiterate the prohibition of usury. He warned that

> Those who devour usury will not stand except as stand one whom the Evil one by his touch Hath driven to madness. That is because they say: 'Trade is like usury,' but Allah hath permitted trade and forbidden usury. Those who after receiving direction from their Lord, desist, shall be pardoned for the past; their case is for Allah (to judge); but those who repeat (The offence) are companions of the Fire: They will abide therein (for ever). (2:275)

He taught that "Allah will deprive usury of all blessing, but will give increase for deeds of charity: For He loveth not creatures ungrateful and wicked" (2:276). He urged people to "Fear Allah, and give up what remains of your demand for usury, if ye are indeed believers" (2:278) and warned them "Devour not usury, doubled and multiplied; but fear Allah. that ye may (really) prosper" (3:130). In spite of all his admonitions, "they took usury, though they were forbidden; and that they devoured men's substance wrongfully" (4:161). Since God had written them off as unbelievers for whom "a grievous punishment" (4:161) awaited, the Prophet wasted no more time attempting to appeal to their heart of hearts. As such, explains the Prophet,

> the Jews and the polytheists of Quraysh along with others deserved to be treated as the enemies of Allah and His Messenger due to their treacherous plans, their enmity, the plots they devised (against me), and the fierce, intermittent war they waged in support of my enemies. Thus did they become the enemies of Allah, His Messenger, and the good Believers.

Unlike the Jews and the polytheists, the Prophet reports that "the Christians . . . behaved in the very opposite way." He goes to great detail in describing their honorable actions,

> They respected my alliance. They recognized my rights. They fulfilled the promises that they had made during our meeting. They assisted the lieutenants that I had sent to the frontiers. They earned my concern and my affection by fulfilling the obligations that I had contracted with them spontaneously in the name of all of the Muslims spread from East to West, my protection during my life and after my passing, when Allah will make me die. So long as Islam will spread and my true mission and faith will grow, this covenant will be obligatory for all Believers and Muslims, so long as water fills the ocean floor, rain falls from the sky, the earth produces plants, the stars shine in the firmament, and the dawn appears to the traveler nor will it be permitted for anyone to break this treaty, alter it, add to it, delete from it, for such additions infringe upon my covenant and suppressions weaken my protection.

Having contextualized his dealings with the Christians of Najran, and having explained the reasons for contracting the covenant in question, the Prophet insists on the binding nature of the treaty: "This covenant, which I wish to accord myself, binds me. Anyone from my *ummah* who, after me, breaks this Covenant of Allah, Glorified and Exalted be He, the Proof of Allah will be raised against him, and Allah is sufficient as a Witness." "What drives me to act this way," explains the Messenger of Allah, "is that three people (from Sayyid Ghassani) asked me for a document that would act as a safe-conduct, a treaty which recognized their fidelity to their promises towards the Muslims and to the treaty which I voluntarily concluded with them." The request, of course, was most reasonable as traveling the desert dunes and rocky volcanic mountain ranges of Arabia was a perilous endeavor. If the terrain and climate were dangerous, they paled in comparison to the murderous and blood-thirsty tribes that awaited any opportunity to pounce upon unexpected prey. With a writ of protection from the Prophet, which could be shown to both friends and foes of the Messenger of Allah, the Christian riders could reach their destination in safety and security.

Despite the number of different denominations among the Christians, each accusing the other of heterodoxy and heresy, the Prophet adopted an admirable stance: he recognized all of them. As the Messenger of Allah explains, the *Covenant* was ratified, not only with the Nestorian Christians, but with all "the different Christians sects." It was thus "inviolable, solemn, and obligatory for all Muslims and Believers." The application of the term "Believers" to both the Muslims and the righteous People of the Book is consistent with the language used in *The Constitution of Medina* demonstrating that, in the early days of Islam, the term *mu'minun* or "believers" applied to any members of Muhammad's monotheistic movement whereas *muslimun* or "submitters" was used specifically for the Muslims. Seeking to set a clear precedent for future generations, and to ensure that the historicity of the event never be called into question, the Prophet made sure that the *Covenant* was witnessed by his closest Companions as well as the leaders of the Christians. "I . . . called the leaders of the Muslims and my main Companions," declares the Messenger of Allah, "and having stood surety to the demand of the Christians, I prepared this document, which Muslims, whether or not they hold power, are obliged to preserve from generation to generation." In power or out of power, whether they were ruling or ruled over, the Muslims were bound to treat their Christian brothers and sisters with compassion. As the Prophet continues,

> To carry out my orders in order to abide by the obligation of loyalty and respect towards those who requested this covenant of me, and to be faithful to

> the obligations which I have contracted, so that they not be reproached for having disobeyed my order.

The obligation of justice is demanded, not only of the ruling authorities, but of the Muslim community in its entirety. If the Muslim rulers go astray, the Muslim masses are obliged to promote the good and prohibit the wrong. If the Muslim masses go astray, it is the obligation of the Muslim authorities to make them behave in a way that is befitting of them. Whether they are the majority or the minority, Muslims must not cause injury to the Christians. In the words of the Messenger of Allah,

> The people, as well, must abstain from harming them, and abide by the covenant that I have made with them so that they can enter along with me by the gates of faithfulness, and contribute to the good that I have done to those who have earned it for having supported my mission and enraged the deniers and the skeptics.

The Prophet closes his exordium to the *Covenant*, reminding all Believers to be benevolent, encourage good will, command charity, deter evil, be sincere, and seek justice. Thus concludes the exordium and thus commences the *Covenant* itself.

The *Covenant of the Prophet Muhammad with the Christians of Najran* commences in the traditional formulaic fashion: "In the Name of Allah, the Most Compassionate, the Most Merciful." With unabashed authority, and complete conviction, the Prophet proclaims that he is "the Messenger of Allah to all of humanity, who was sent to preach and to warn," and "who has been entrusted the Trust of Allah among His Creatures so that human beings would have no pretext before Allah, after his messengers and manifestation, before this Powerful and Wise Being." Muhammad was not merely the ruler of Medina. He was not only the ruler of Arabia. He had eyes on the entire globe. He was not, however, a cynical and self-serving imperialist, as his intention was not enslaving but liberating.

The *Covenant of the Prophet* is concluded with Sayyid Ibn Harith ibn Ka'b, "his co-religionists, and all those who profess the Christian religion, be they in East or West, in close regions or faraway regions, be they Arabs or foreigners, known or unknown." A true internationalist, and most certainly not an imperialist according to the modern meaning of the term, the Prophet issued a decree which applied universally to all Christians, regardless of their country of origin, their nationality, their ethnicity or their linguistic association. The Messenger of Allah describes the document as "an authoritative contract" and "authentic certificate" established "on the basis of convention and justice" as well as an "inviolable pact." Readers familiar with the period in question—namely, the ruthlessness of the Roman Empire, the rise of Attila the Hun, and the depredations of the Vandals—will know that the world was very much deprived of charity and justice. In fact, the social conditions of the day were vastly unjust, atrociously immoral, and egregiously unethical. For the bulk of the population of Europe in that age, speaking of "charity" and "justice" would make one a laughing-stock. The powerful man crushed and destroyed his enemies, while enslaving, torturing, abusing, and eventually murdering their family members. Despite the teachings of Jesus in the Gospels relating to charity and love of enemies, which were not yet socially dominant, all of this was considered completely normal conduct. And while the *Covenant* in question was based on compassion, the Prophet also conveys the seriousness of his intent:

> Whoever abides by this edict, shows his attachment to Islam, will be worthy of the best that Islam has to offer. On the contrary, any man who destroys it, breaks the pact which it contains, alters it, disobeys my commandments, will have violated the pact of Allah, transgresses his alliance, and disdained his treaty. He will merit his malediction, whether he is a sovereign or someone else.

Rather than distancing himself from this entente, and protecting himself behind the power of the establishment, the Prophet assumes personally responsibility for the covenant in question. As the Messenger of Allah, the rightful ruler over Allah's creation, and as the Vicegerent of Almighty God, the Prophet speaks as the ultimate authority. As such, he bears ultimate responsibility for the action of his people.

> I commit myself to an alliance and a pledge with them on behalf of Allah and I place them under the safeguard of His Prophets, His Elect, His Saints, the Muslims and the Believers, the first of them and the last of them. Such is my alliance and pact with them.

The reference to Allah's Elect appears to be an allusion to the *ahl al-bayt*, the Members of the Prophet Household, and the Twelve Imams from the Prophet's Purified Progeny. While "His Saints" or the *awliyya' al-salihin* may refer to the saintly Companions of the Prophet, the term is equally applicable to the People of the House of Prophecy. Since, at least according to the Shi'ah, the *imamah* [Imamate] was the divinely-ordained extension of the *nubuwwah* [Prophethood], the inclusion of the *ahl al-bayt* in the *Covenant* seems consistent with other treaties concluded by the Prophet. For example, in *The Treaty of Maqnah*, the Prophet insisted that "Nobody will rule over you but a person from among yourselves or a member of the Household of the Prophet." In short, whether they had home-rule or not, the inhabitants of the region would be bound to the overarching authority of *ahl al-bayt* after the passing of the Prophet. Not only was the Messenger of Allah establishing Prophetic Rule; he was actively involved in setting the groundwork for the Imamate. From a Sufi point of view, the *awliyya' al-salihin* could also refer to the great mystics and gnostics of Islam who embody the spiritual authority of the Prophet.

Demonstrating, once again, and for all to see and hear, that Islam was not a new religion, but the culmination of prophecy, deeply rooted in the monotheistic religions that preceded it, the Prophet extends a hand to the *Bani Isra'il* or Children of Israel, confirming the continuation of the Law of Moses, and calling upon Christians to return to the Law of Allah: "I proclaim once again the obligations that Allah imposed on the Children of Israel to obey Him, to follow His Law, and to respect His Divine Alliance." If some Jews obsessed about the law, and some Christians ignored the law with an overemphasis on faith, the Prophet Muhammad stressed that salvation was based both on faith [*iman*] and adherence to the Divine Law [*shari'ah*] of Islam. The Messenger of Allah was not rejecting Judaism; he was embracing it by purifying and updating the *halakha*. The Messenger of Allah was not rejecting Christianity; he was embracing the true historical religion of Jesus Christ while rejecting certain extraneous elements it had absorbed through Greco-Roman contact. The Prophet Muhammad was not demythologizing Christianity, like the most faithless secularizing "Christians" of today, in order to complete the destruction of the Christian tradition. On the contrary, the virgin birth, the characterization of Jesus as "a spirit of Allah," the prophecy that he will return to earth before the Hour to slay al-Dajjal [the Anti-Christ], are all intrinsic to Islam, and all are the very kind of "mythological mysteries" that faithless modern critics want to dismiss. The Prophet Muhammad was calling the Jews toward piety and faith and the acceptance of Jesus as the Prophet and Messiah while calling upon Christians to return to elements of the Jewish law, including circumcision, ritual prayer, fasting, and abstinence from forbidden foods—although Pauline Christianity, from which the main line of Christian history and theology sprang, held that Christians were no longer under "the curse of the law" (cf. Galatians 3:10–13).

Islam, when properly understood, was not a new religion. It was the same movement for social justice, the same school for the development of human character, and the same call to constant remembrance of Allah, that was taught by the prophets and messengers of God from the time of Adam, something which is shown by 'Abdul Ahad Dawud in his chapters on "Muhammad in the Old Testament" and "Muhammad in the New Testament" which are found in his book on *Muhammad in the Bible*. It is for this reason that Dr. Robert F. Shedinger affirms that Jesus was a Muslim, in a generic as opposed to specific sense, as were all the prophets of God that came before him.

In concluding a covenant with the Christians, the Prophet was not relegating them to the status of second class citizens. He was not subjecting them to a life of servitude. On the contrary, he was treating them as citizens of the Universal Islamic Order. As members of the Muslim *ummah*, the Christians were entitled to rights and protections. As the Messenger of Allah proclaims in the *Covenant*,

> I hereby declare that my horsemen, my foot-soldiers, my armies, my resources, and my Muslim partisans will protect the Christians as far away as they may be located, whether they inhabit the lands which border my state, in any region, close or far, in times of peace as much as in times of war.
>
> I commit myself to support them, to place their persons under my protection, as well as their churches, chapels, oratories, the monasteries of their monks, the residences of their anchorites wherever they are found, be they in the mountains or the valleys, caves or inhabited regions, in the plains or in the desert.
>
> I will protect their religion and their Church wherever they are found, be it on earth or at sea, in the West or in the East, with utmost vigilance on my part, the People of my House, and the Muslims as a whole.
>
> I place them under my protection. I make a pact with them. I commit myself to protect them from any harm or damage; to exempt them for any requisitions or any onerous obligations and to protect them myself, by means of my assistants, my followers and my nation against every enemy who targets me and them.

If individual rights were virtually non-existent in Europe, where entire countries, their populations and their resources were considered the exclusive domain of the ruling power, the Prophet acknowledged his obligation to rule over all of his subjects equitably. "Having authority over them," he writes, "I must govern them, protecting them from all damage and ensuring that nothing happens to them that does not happen to me and my Companions who, along with me, defend the cause of Islam."

Since the Army of Islam was actively engaged in campaigns of liberation throughout Arabia and the Levant, Muhammad, the Messenger of Allah, placed prohibitions upon his military commanders with respect to the Christians. "I forbid any conquerors of the faith to rule over them during their invasions or to oblige them to pay taxes unless they themselves willingly consent. Never should any Christian be subjected to tyranny or oppression in this matter." This prohibition of taxing the Christians of Najran may apply only to clerics as was the case with the monks of Mount Sinai. Alternatively, the Christians may have had the option to pay taxes or participate in military service. Echoing the covenant with the Monastery of Saint Catherine, the Prophet provided protection for the Christian religious establishment:

> It is not permitted to remove a bishop from his bishopric, a monk from his monastic life, or anchorite from his vocation as a hermit. Nor is it permitted to destroy any part of their churches, to take parts of their buildings to construct mosques or the homes of Muslims. Whoever does such a thing will have violated the pact of Allah, disobeyed his Messenger, and become estranged from the Divine Alliance.

Since the Christians of Najran entered freely into the *ummah* of Islam, which was established by the Messenger of Allah as a multi-ethnic, multi-religious, multicultural, and multilingual mosaic that fostered unity through diversity, the Prophet was generous in matters of taxation. To commence with, clerics were excluded: "It is not permitted to impose a capitation or any kind of tax on monks or bishops nor on any of those who, by devotion, wear woolen clothing or live alone in the mountains or in other regions devoid of human habitation." As for Christians who were not clerics, a tax-cap was established: "Let there be a limit set of four *dirhams* per year that all other Christians, who are not clerics, monks, or hermits, need to pay." Accommodating as always, the Prophet provided Christians the option to pay in cash or in goods. Instead of paying the tax of four *dirhams* per year, they could "provide one outfit of stripped material or one embroidered turban from Yemen." It should also be recalled that, according to Islamic law, only able-bodied adults are subject to taxation. Khalid ibn al-Walid (592–642 CE), a Companion of the Prophet, stressed this fact in his pact with the Christians of Iraq saying that:

> Any Christian who cannot provide for himself due to old age, along with any sick or poor people who depend on the charity of their co-religionists, are exempted from paying the *jizyah* [tax] and will be provided for by the Muslim Treasury. This applies to the exempted person and to all those who depend upon him. (qtd. Haya 5)

With a transparency never seen in the Western world, the Prophet could account for every penny entrusted to the Islamic State. The cash and goods collected were "to help Muslims and to contribute to the growth of the Public Treasury." Rather than living in a permanent present, with no thought for the future, the Prophet actually established a National Reserve and a governmental budget.

If the tax of four *dirhams* per year was directed towards the working class, the Prophet envisaged higher taxes for landowners, owners of large enterprises and mines, as well as those with inherited wealth. Although the rich were to pay more, a limit was set to how much they had to contribute: in this case, a maximum of twelve *dirhams* per year. In others words, the wealthy were to pay three times the amount of taxes paid by the lower and middle classes. These numbers were not random. They did not come out of thin air. They were the product of much thought and contemplation inspired by revelation. The Messenger of Allah was very much establishing the bases of the Islamic economic system.

If citizens and residents of the Islamic State were to be taxed, no such taxes were to be levied on "travelers, who are not resident of the country, or wayfarers whose country of residence is unknown." During medieval times, people did not have freedom of movement. Travel was perilous. Wayfarers could be robbed, enslaved or slaughtered. The Prophet, ever the visionary that he was, not only granted freedom of movement to the citizens of his state, but permission to non-residents to travel through Islamic lands.

During his travels through the Ottoman Empire between 1655 and 1663, Jean de Thévenot (1633–1667 CE) confirmed that all Christian and Jewish males paid four and a half *piastres* per year in taxes which they were required to pay from the age of nine and up (159). He points out that the priests and clerics of the Christians, along with the rabbis of the Jews, were excluded from taxation as was the case with women (159). The French Orientalist also observed that only Jews and Christians who were citizens of the Islamic State and subjects of the Caliph had to pay such taxes (159). Jews and Christians who came from Christian lands were granted a travel or trade visa which excluded them from taxation (159). Such accounts confirm that the prophetically-prescribed treatment of the People of the Book was still in practice in Ottoman times. The moderate tax rate paid by the People of the Book is startling considering the crushing taxes often imposed, not only on Jews and Muslims, but on Christians as well, in lands that claimed to follow the teachings of Christ.

The Prophet did not believe in multiple taxes. Either people pay the capitation tax or they pay the land tax. The Islamic State, however, reserves the right to tax inherited property. The reason for this is that stagnant money is detrimental to the economy. For the economy to be healthy, money must circulate. It should not, and cannot, be held captive. Landowners, like workers, must contribute their share to the tax pool; however, once again, they are only required to pay their fair share. And if the landowners are not to be oppressed neither are those who work the land: peasants, farmers, and laborers. They are to be taxed, but never excessively. As the Prophet says, "Let them pay in the same fashion that was imposed on other similar tributaries."

While Muslims do not pay the *per capita* tax, they do pay two obligatory religious taxes, and have the obligation to protect and defend the Islamic State. In return for capitation, the Christians of Najran were not required to enlist for military service. As the Prophet explains,

> The men who belong to our alliance will not be obliged to go to war with the Muslims in order to combat their enemies, to attack them, and to seize them. Indeed, the members of the alliance will not engage in war. It is precisely to discharge them of this obligation that this pact has been granted to them as well as to assure them the help and protec-

> tion on the part of the Muslims. No Christian is to be constrained to provide equipment to a single Muslim, in money, in arm or in horses, in the event of a war in which the Believers attack their enemies, unless they contribute to the cause freely. Whoever does so, and contributes spontaneously, will be the object of praise, reward, and gratitude, and his help will not be forgotten.

Since the Muslims were most often confronted by belligerent Christians from Europe, Muhammad did not want to compel Christians to kill other Christians. From a military perspective, the presence of Christians among the Muslim ranks could cause some concern as they could conceivably form a fifth column. In some exceptional circumstances, Christians who preferred military service as opposed to taxation could integrate into the Islamic Army and fight side by side with their Muslim brothers against those who opposed the Islamo-Christian Confederacy.

If kings of other countries felt it within their right to impose a religion upon their subjects by decree or force, and slaughter all those who objected, the Prophet insisted upon freedom of religion. As he stressed,

> No Christian will be made Muslim by force: *And dispute ye not with the People of the Book, except with means better* [29:46]. They must be covered by the wing of mercy. Repel every harm that could reach them wherever they may find themselves and in any country in which they are.

Since believers are expected to hide the sins and shortcomings of other believers, the Prophet urged Muslims to provide the same cover for Christians. This was not to make sure that they escape justice and retribution, but to protect them from revenge and to discourage the Arab custom of blood feuds. Muslims were expected to help, defend, and protect their Christian associates. In the event of misdemeanors, Muslims were urged to be forgiving. In the instance of more serious, but unintentional offences, like involuntary homicide, Muslims were to promote pardon and to encourage the settlement of grievances by means of monetary compensation. Muslims and Christians were supposed to support each other in good times and in bad, like partners in a marriage. As the Prophet explains,

> The Muslims must not abandon the Christians, neglect them, and leave them without help and assistance since I have made this pact with them on behalf of Allah to ensure that whatever good befell Muslims it would befall them as well and that whatever harm befell Muslims would befall them as well. In virtue of this pact, they have obtained inviolable rights to enjoy our protection, to be protected from any infringement of their rights, so that they will be bound to the Muslims both in good and bad fortune.

At a time when girls were routinely and customarily forced into arranged marriages against their will, the Prophet provided protection, not only to Muslim women, but to women as a whole. Two thousand years ahead of his time, the Messenger of Allah decreed that

> Christians must not be subjected to suffer, by abuse, in the matter of marriages which they do not desire. Muslims should not take Christian girls in marriage against the will of their parents nor should they oppress their families in the event that they refused their offers of engagement and marriage. Such marriages should not take place without their desire and agreement and without their approval and consent.

In the event of a mixed marriage, between a Muslim man and a Christian woman, respect was the requirement:

> If a Muslim takes a Christian woman as a wife, he must respect her Christian beliefs. He will give her freedom to listen to her [clerical] superiors as she desires and to follow the path of her own religion. Whoever, despite this order, forces his wife to act contrary to her religion in any aspect whatsoever he will have broken the alliance of Allah and will enter into open rebellion against the pact of His Messenger and Allah will count him among the impostors.

Echoing the conditions established in his covenants with the Christians from the Sinai and Assyria, the Prophet ordered his followers to aid Christians as an act of charity:

> If the Christians approach you seeking the help and assistance of the Muslims in order to repair their churches and their convents, or to arrange matters pertaining to their affairs and religion, these must help and support them. However, they must not do so with the aim of receiving any reward. On the contrary, they should do so to restore that religion, out of faithfulness to the pact of the Messenger of Allah, by pure donation, and as a meritorious act before Allah and His Messenger.

Returning to the issue of war, the Prophet prohibited his commanders from obliging Christians to act as secret agents of the Islamic State. While it may have been convenient to do so, as the Christians could more readily infiltrate the enemy, the Prophet viewed it as a distasteful and potentially dangerous approach to take. And in reality, any such effort could easily have backfired. As a result, he decreed that

> In matters of war between them and their enemies, the Muslims will not employ any Christian as a messenger, scout, guide or spy or for any other duty of war. Whoever obliges one of them to do such a thing will harm the rights of Allah, will be a rebel against His Messenger, and will cast himself out of His Alliance. Nothing is permitted to a Muslim [with regards to the Christians] outside of obeying these edicts which Muhammad ibn 'Abd Allah, the Messenger of Allah, has passed in favor of the religion of the Christians.

If all of this seems very one-sided, and leads certain Islamists to denounce these covenants as Christian fabrications which present the Prophet as some soft leader as opposed to a true man, the treaty in question imposed an important list of obligations upon the Christians as well. Since rights come with obligations, the Prophet proffered the following,

> He is also placing conditions [upon the Christians] and I demand that they promise to fulfill and satisfy them as commands their religion, among which, among other things, none of them may act as a scout, spy, either overtly or covertly, on behalf of an enemy of war, against a Muslim. None of them will shelter the enemies of the Muslims in their homes from which they could await the moment to launch an attack. May these enemies [of the Muslims] never be allowed to halt in their regions, be it in their villages, their oratories, or in any other place belonging to their co-religionists. They must not provide any support to the enemies of war of the Muslims by furnishing them with weapons, horses, men, or anything else, nor must they treat them well. They must host for three days and three nights any Muslims who halt among them, with their animals. They must offer them, wherever they are found, and wherever they are going, the same food with which they live themselves, without, however, being obliged to endure other annoying or onerous burdens.
>
> If a Muslim needs to hide in one of their homes or oratories, they must grant him hospitality, support him, and provide him with their food during the entire time he will be among them, making every effort to keep him concealed and to prevent the enemy from finding him, while providing for all of his needs.
>
> Whoever contravenes or alters the ordinances of this edict will be cast out of the alliance between Allah and His Messenger.

As the Prophet makes explicitly clear, no Christian will aid and abet the enemies of Islam. They must not shelter the enemies of Islam. They must not, at any time, allow the forces of the enemy to occupy their lands or buildings. Hence, allowing foreign infidel forces to use one's military, air or naval bases or to set up bases of their own is categorically prohibited in Islam. To help the enemy is to be the enemy. Providing supplies to the enemies of Islam is also outlawed. They are not to receive weapons, food or supplies. The Christian allies of Islam are even prohibited from providing the Christian enemies of Islam with good-treatment. If Muslims are not allowed to assist the armed forces of the enemy in any way, shape or form, imagine, then, how serious it is for a nominal Muslim to join the military of a nation that wages war against Islam, occupies Muslim countries, and kills innocent Muslim civilians, men, women, and children. Such an act is nothing less than infidelity [*kufr*].

The Christian associates of the Muslims were also expected to provide temporary room and board to any Muslim passing through their region. This sort of obligation, which was grossly abused in Europe and the Americas, was so offensive in practice that it was outlawed in the US Bill of Rights. British soldiers who found themselves in English colonies could occupy individual dwellings, eat everything while the owners and the children went malnourished, and abuse of the female inhabitants of the household. The Prophet put clear limits to the quartering of Muslim soldiers in private homes and prohibited them from behaving in any fashion which was unbecoming of a believer. Speaking of the Christian hosts, the Messenger of Allah, as we have seen above, said the following:

> They must host for three days and three nights any Muslims who halt among them, with their animals. They must offer them, wherever they are found, and wherever they are going, the same food with which they live themselves, without, however, being obliged to endure other annoying or onerous burdens.
>
> If a Muslim needs to hide in one of their homes or oratories, they must grant him hospitality, give him help, and provide him with their food during the entire time he will be among them, making every effort to keep him concealed and to prevent the enemy from finding him, while providing for all of his needs.

If the Prophet warned Muslims at some length of the wrath of Allah if they betrayed the covenants he had concluded with them, his words to the Christians were blunt: "Whoever contravenes or alters the ordinances of this edict will be cast out of the alliance between Allah and His Messenger." In other words, if the Christians betray the Islamic State, they will be at the mercy of the unbelievers who, unlike the Muslims, were not especially well-known for their justice and compassion towards conquered populations. In other words, if the Christians did not hold up their side of the bargain, the Muslims would not protect any frontier populations from the invasions of other armies. Treacherous Christians could also be exiled from *dar al-islam* and forced to live under Christian rule, a terrible punishment indeed. The living conditions in Muslim Spain were like heaven compared to those in Christian Spain.

The Prophet closes the *Covenant* with genuine good-wishes:

> May everyone abide by the treaties and alliances which have been contracted with the monks, and which I have contracted myself, and every other commitment that each prophet has made with his nation, to assure them safeguard and faithful protection, and to serve them as a guarantee.

He also stresses that his actions are consistent with those of previous prophets who concluded similar covenants with various nations. The Prophet's closing words are categorical: "This must not be violated or altered until the hour of the Resurrection, Allah-willing." The caveat, however, is clear. If the Christians betray the Muslims, aid and abet their enemies, and attack the Muslims, they will be cast out of the Islamic Alliance. Unlike most of the treaties concluded by the Prophet, the *Covenant of the Prophet Muhammad with the Christians of Najran* was witnessed, in this case by thirty prominent Companions of the Prophet.

Conclusions

The *Covenant of the Prophet Muhammad with the Christians of Najran* represents a historical find of momentous importance. Since it was first published in an obscure Orientalist journal in 1919, and the editor and translator himself slandered it as spurious, one can understand why the document has remained virtually unknown outside of a handful of Arabists and Islamicists. Although it was reprinted in 1956 in Muhammad Hamidullah's *Majmu'ah al-watha'iq al-siyasiyyah li al-'ahd al-nabawi wa al-khilafah al-rashidah* and in 2002 in Muhammad 'Amarah's *al-Islam wa al-akhar*, the work has not reached the wide audience that it merits. In the Muslim world, which has only recently started to recover from centuries of scholarly stagnation, the overwhelming majority of *'ulama'*, professors, intellectuals, and educated readers, remain oblivious to the very existence of the covenant in question and those who have heard of it have showed no interest in subjecting it to further scholarly analysis, much less sharing it with the Muslim masses who could greatly benefit from its content.

Chapter 5

The Prophet Muhammad and the Christians of the World

Introduction

Known in Arabic as *al-'Ahd wa al-shurut allati sharataha Muhammad rasul Allah li ahl al-millah al-nasraniyyah*, literally, the *Treaty and Covenant which Muhammad, the Messenger of Allah, Concluded with the Christian Community*, the *Covenant of the Prophet Muhammad with the Christians of the World* is of obscure origin. Like the *Covenant of the Prophet Muhammad with the Monks of Mount Sinai*, and the *Covenant of the Prophet Muhammad with the Christians of Najran* (with which it shares remarkable similarities), the *Covenant of the Prophet Muhammad with the Christians of the World* does not exist in any extant Islamic sources. While its early trajectory is unknown, what is certain is that reproductions and translations of the *Covenant* were circulating throughout the Ottoman Empire and Europe in the early 17th century.

Issues of Authenticity

The *'Ahd wa al-shurut*, known in Latin as the *Testamentum et pactiones*, *Testamentum Muhammedis*, *Muhammedis Testamentum*, and *Testamentum Mahometi*, is referred to in English as the *Treaty of Muhammad* or the *Patent of Muhammad*. These English titles are a source of confusion as they are identical to those applied to the *Pactum Muhammedis* which the Prophet Muhammad concluded with the monks of Mount Sinai. For the sake of clarity, I refer to the covenant with the monastery of Saint Catherine as the *Covenant of the Prophet Muhammad with the Monks of Mount Sinai*, the covenant with the Christians of Southern Arabia as the *Covenant of the Prophet Muhammad with the Christians of Najran*, and the current document, which is addressed to all Christians, as opposed to a specific community, as the *Covenant of the Prophet Muhammad with the Christians of the World*.

Unlike the first two covenants, the origin of the *Covenant of the Prophet with the Christians of the World* is more obscure. According to Fortescue, "Yeshu'yab II was said to have gone to see Mohammed, and to have obtained from him a document granting privileges to Nestorians" (92). In his estimation, "This is the famous *Testament of Mohammed*, published by Gabriel Sionita (Paris, 1630)" (92, note 5). According to 17th- and 18th-century sources, the original was brought to Europe by Father Pacifique Scaliger (d. 1648), known in Latin as Pacificus Scaliger, a Capuchin monk (Dollinger 291; Goujet 100; Mosheim 255; Basnage de Beauval 82; Gieseler 563, note 7; Bayle, 1735: 241). According to Bayle, the covenant was "found in a monastery at Mount Carmel" (Bayle 241). This would mean that the document was uncovered in Palestine in close proximity to Lebanon.

The Carmelites, one of the oldest orders of Catholic monks in the Holy Land, were founded by Berthold, a Frenchman, who died in 1188. Since there were no Carmelite monks in Palestine in the 7th century, the Prophet Muhammad could not conceivably have granted them a covenant. According to the Carmelite Constitution of 1281, however, the site has been occupied, uninterruptedly, first by Jewish prophets, and then by Christian monks and priests, from the time of Elijah and Elisha until the founding of the monastery. The Carmelites, then, may have obtained a copy of a covenant concluded by the Prophet with their predecessors. During the Crusades, the site changed hands frequently. While it was a monastery during some periods it was a mosque during others. Chronologically, the claim is correct that there was a Catholic monastery at Mount Carmel during the time of Scaliger.

According to several sources from the 17th, 18th, and 19th centuries, Father Pacifique Scaliger (1588–

1648 CE) discovered the covenant in a convent or monastery belonging to Carmelite monks (Van Dyke 85; Bayle 241). As Sir Paul Ricaut (1629–1700 CE) relates in his *Histoire de l'état présent de l'empire Ottoman* (1670),

> The *Treaty*...was found in a convent belonging to the monks of Mount Carmel, close to Mount Lebanon, and at one day's journey from Mecca, where Muslim pilgrims perform their Qurban, or sacrifice, prior to entering the City. It is said that the original was brought to the Library of the King of France. (320)

If this is the case, the *Covenant of the Prophet Muhammad with the Christians of the World* was discovered in Arabia as opposed to Palestine. After all, it takes approximately forty days to go from the Hijaz to Syria or Iraq by caravan. Evidently, this poses a series of problems. Was the convent or monastery located one day's journey north of Mecca or one day's journey south of the sacred city? Either way, this leads to absolutely nowhere of significance. Even the fastest of travelers would only reach caravan stops. It is virtually inconceivable to make it to Ghadir Khumm, a marsh or pond in the Wadi Rabigh, in a span shorter than three days. Ta'if is within one's day of travel of Mecca. However, there is no record of Christians living there. The only major town north of Mecca is Medina. The only major town south of Mecca is Najran. As for the place, within one day of travel from Mecca, where Muslims perform the sacrifice, that is the tent city of Mina, which is really but a neighborhood of the sacred city. There were never any Christian monasteries in Mina. Did Ricaut make a miscalculation? This most certainly seems to be the case. Was he simply wrong about the distance? Or was he also wrong about the religious order? While it is possible that Scaliger (1588–1648 CE) located the covenant in a monastery that belonged to the Carmelites, it may have been in a Greek Orthodox monastery, such as Mar Saba, the longest continually inhabited monastery in the Middle East. It also so happens that it was often described as a convent. Like the Monastery of Saint Catherine, the Monastery of Mar Saba contains many ancient manuscripts, one of which may have been a copy of a covenant granted by the Prophet Muhammad.

While I have some doubts about the details provided by Ricaut, so did the author himself. After all, he stated that "On dit," which means, "It is said," or "It is alleged" that the document was taken from the Convent of Mount Carmel to the Library of the King of France (320). This is immediately followed by "quoiqu'il en soit" which means, "whatever the truth may be," it is an "ancient and curious" document (320). It is astonishing that so many scholars have repeated details from Ricaut as if they were fact when the author himself clearly had doubts about them. Although they quoted Ricaut out of context for centuries, scholars never considered tracking down the source of this story, Father Pacifique Scaliger himself, for a most revealing surprise.

Although author after author has insisted that Father Pacifique Scaliger discovered the *Testament of the Prophet* in the Monastery of Mount Carmel, the priest and missionary makes no such mention in his *Relation du voyage de Perse* (1631). In the final chapter of his travel journal, titled "Pièce très rare et curieuse qui est le *Testament de Mahomet*," [The *Testament of Muhammad*, a Very Rare and Curious Document], the cleric states the following:

> I did not want to finish this account without sharing with you something very rare which fortuitously fell into my hands, as a result of my spirit of curiosity, and which is the *Testament of Muhammad*. In order for you to understand how and why said *Testament* was made, you should know that this past year, 1628, there was a violent, but passing, persecution including economic persecution against ecclesiastics and Christian merchants, that was as such: It was under the pretext of their need to live in those countries that they were each required to pay certain sums of dinars according to their financial standing. In order to reward said Christians, taking them under his protection and leadership, he made the following pacts and contracts with them. (405–406)

As readers will recognize, no mention is made of any discovery. Scaliger (1588–1648 CE) simply says that the manuscript "fortuitously fell into his hands" as a result of his curiosity. Obviously, this does not exclude a discovery. However, it makes one wonder why he insisted on implication as opposed to indication. The scarce information provided by Scaliger suggests that the *Covenant* was given to him. E. Rehatsek, for example, affirms that "[t]he first copy of this diploma was brought to Europe by Pacificus Scaliger, who had obtained it from Arab Capuchin monks" (97, note 141a). As for Scalinger's attempt to elucidate the origin of the piece, it causes more confusion than clarity. It almost seems like he provides a justification for its falsification. While he speaks of a brief period of Christian persecution in 1628, he affirms that "he" took them under his protection and made a testament with them. Who does the "he" refer to? Is it the Sultan or is it the Prophet? And why this gigantic jump back in time? Rather than cast doubt on the covenant, which does not appear to be his intent, was Father Scaliger simply trying to explain why the covenant came to the surface? In other words, when persecution raised its ugly head, the Christians resorted to their time-honored tradition: bringing forth a covenant of the Prophet in order to vindicate their rights.

As for the covenant itself, Father Scaliger describes it as the "*Testament of Muhammad* which the Turks call his hand or signature, which he made in favor of the Christians before dying, and in the presence of the witnesses who have signed below, who were his disciples, & authenticated by the Secretary or Notary Public as you will see" (407). This information, it appears, implies that there was no discovery at all and that the covenant that the Christians brought to the fore was famous among the Turks. Curiously, Scaliger (1588–1648 CE) says that the Turks referred to it as the "Hand of Muhammad" or the "Signature of Muhammad." Did the document "rediscovered" by the French father feature a hand-print of the Prophet similar to the one found at the Monastery of Saint Catherine? Could the Messenger of Allah have signed a series of covenants in the same fashion? Or did the Christians of the Levant follow the example of the monks of Mount Sinai down to the hand-print? The Turks, it would seem, never doubted the document. And by the Turks, I refer to their administrators, religious scholars, and even the Sultan. When pressured by European diplomats to grant the keys of the Holy Sepulcher of Jerusalem to the Roman Catholic Church, Sultan Ibrahim I responded that the possession of these sacred sites had been granted in time immemorial by Muhammad, himself, to the Greek Christians, and that he would never violate the clauses of that treaty at any price (Lamartine 356). The Sultan, who ruled from 1640 to 1648 CE, did not refer to a recently rediscovered covenant attributed to the Prophet which had just been published in Paris in 1630. He spoke of one which was as old as historical memory itself. Not only were the Ottomans familiar with the covenant in question, it is possible that it was them, and not the Christians, who provided Scaliger with a copy.

Scaliger, whose full French name was René de l'Escale dit Pacifique de Provins, was born in France in 1588. He arrived in Constantinople in 1622 and traveled through Egypt, the Holy Land, and Syria prior to returning to Italy in 1623. There, he met with Pope Gregory XV in order to discuss establishing Capuchin missions in the Middle East. After going to Paris, where he organized the missionary network, he headed to Syria and Mount Lebanon in 1628 where he obtained the authorization of the Ottomans to establish convents and monasteries. After founding missions in Aleppo and Cyprus, he set off for Persia where he founded missions in Baghdad and Isfahan, and established diplomatic ties between the French and the Persians. He finally returned to Europe in 1629 and spent several years in Paris. In 1645, he embarked for the New World, specifically the French Antilles. He returned briefly to Paris in 1646 and, after a short span of time, decided to spread the Gospel in French Guiana, only to die during the voyage in 1648 (Pouillon 734).

If I have provided this brief chronological sketch, it is for a precise purpose. Based on the information he provides, we can infer that Father Pacifique de Provins came across the covenant between 1627 and 1628. This coincides with the period of time he spent in the Levant in the vicinity of Mount Lebanon. Thus the claim that the covenant came from a monastery at Mount Carmel could in fact be correct. However, this was also the time when Scaliger (1588–1648 CE) obtained permission from the Ottomans to establish Capuchin missions, monasteries, and convents, throughout their empire. As he cites in his *Relation du voyage de Perse*, Sultan Murad IV (r. 1623–1640 CE) issued two edicts in favor of the Capuchin monks in April of 1627; the first, which authorized them to establish themselves in Aleppo; and the second one, which authorized them to establish themselves throughout the entire Ottoman Empire (233–236). These documents, which contain echoes of the covenant of the Prophet, provide protection to the Capuchin fathers, freedom of movement and religious practice, along with liberty to preach and teach in their churches, on grounds that they belong to an allied nation (236). Could Father Scaliger have presented the covenant to the Ottomans in order to support the case of the Capuchins who wished to establish themselves in the Middle East? Or was it the other way around? Did the Ottomans provide Father Scaliger with a copy of the *Testament of Muhammad* as an act of good will towards the Christians of France? As religious as they were, the Capuchins acted as diplomats, ambassadors, and even covert operatives and spies on behalf of the French King. Is it not significant that Father Scaliger left the Ottoman Empire in 1629 and headed directly to Paris where he provided the document to the King of France? Could the copy of the covenant have been a gift of Sultan Murad to the French King?

What we do know is that the covenant was in the hands of François Hotman almost immediately. Schefer alleges that "a copy of this act of Muhammad was sent from the East to François Hotman, Counselor in the parliament of Paris by father Pacifique" (Thenaud 72, note 2). Since Father Pacifique Scaliger personally traveled from the Levant to Paris there would have been no need for him to send the covenant by courier. If anything, he would have personally delivered it to Hotman since he was the personal representative of the King of France to the Parliament of Paris. As fate would have it, François Hotman was the host of Gabriel Sionita, a Professor of Arabic and Syriac at the *collège Royale* since 1618 (Bernard 43; Thenaud 72, note 2), to whom he entrusted the task of translating it from Arabic into Latin. Unless he were pulling a prank of enormous proportions, Scaliger was convinced of the covenant's authenticity. Whether he received it from Carmelite or Capuchin monks or from the Sultan himself matters little. The King appears to have accepted it as authentic. His representative, François Hotman, believed that it was such. And so did Gabriel Sionita (1577–1648 CE). Most importantly, Father Pacifique de Provins was present in Paris from 1629 to 1645 and witnessed edition after edition of the *Testamentum et pactiones* starting in 1630. If most of these editions were in Arabic and Latin, and some simply in Latin, Father Pacifique published his own French translation of the *Testament of Muhammad* in 1631 as the last section of his *Relation du voyage de Perse*. In fact, from the moment he brought the covenant to light to the moment he died in 1648, Pacifique de Provins never disavowed this document.

I remain convinced that Father Pacifique Scaliger (1588–1648 CE) did indeed discover the covenant in a monastery in the Middle East, most probably in the Levant. However, since he traveled from the Levant to Persia, he may have come across it anywhere along the way. I am equally convinced Father Scaliger brought it to France, a fact which all scholars agree upon (Bayle 1737: 38; Bayle, 1735, 241), where it was eventually entered into the library of the French King (Goujet 100). Recognizing the importance of the covenant, "François Hotman, Counselor in the Parlement of Paris . . . hired Sionita to put it into Latin" (Goujet 100). According to Goujet, "this erudite Maronite was well liked by this magistrate who housed him in his home for a long time" (Goujet 100). I also refuse to accept the allegation that Father Pacifique Scaliger had personally forged the manuscript (Bayle, 1735: 241). First of all, there is no evidence whatsoever that Father Scaliger was sufficiently proficient in Classical Arabic and adequately well-versed in Islamic Studies to successfully undertake such a task. Secondly, Father Scaliger was not only a scholar but a saintly figure renowned for his sincerity and piety. A friar from the Capucin Order of Monks described him in the following terms:

> Father Pacific Scaliger, from the noble and ancient family which bears this name, dedicated himself to the elevated paths of evangelical perfection by joining the Capuchins of the province of French Guiana. He distinguished himself by his acts of mortification, his fasts, and his other austerities. These practices were accompanied by fervent prayer, and a vast knowledge of theology, so much so that he was charged with teaching. Burning with zeal to save souls, he traveled to Persia and America in order to spread knowledge of the true God. As a result, his apostolic efforts lead to numerous conversions. (un religieux du même ordre 433–434)

For some, I must admit, this "zeal to save souls" might suggest that Father Scaliger could have been capable of pious fraud; but for what conceivable purpose? The *Covenant of the Prophet Muhammad with the Christians of the World* could not conceivably contribute to the conversion of Muslims to Christianity. On the contrary, it seems better suited to attract Christians to Islam. Was he simply seeking to protect fellow Christians in the lands of Islam? But during the period, which coincides with Ottoman rule, the Christians had never had it better. Not only were they tolerated, some would say that they were favored over other minorities. Still, since Scaliger was very much a man of God, he simply does not, in my opinion, fit the profile of a person who would perpetuate a religious fraud. It should be remembered that the King of France, and the impressive body of scholars and specialists who surrounded him, were no fools. The French sovereign was actively engaged in acquiring ancient manuscripts from the Middle East. Father Scaliger had no motive to dupe and deceive the King of France and the scholarly community centered in Paris. It would have been totally out of character for the pious priest.

If the *Covenant of the Prophet Muhammad with the Christians of the World* is known to the world today, it is because of the efforts of Gabriel Sionita (1577–1648 CE). Known in Arabic as Jibra'il al-Sahyuni, this learned Maronite priest is famous for publishing the Parisian polyglot of the Bible. He is also responsible for presenting an Arabic edition of the *Covenant of the Prophet Muhammad with the Christians of the World* along with a Latin translation. Savary de Brèves, the former French ambassador to Turkey, who happened to have an interest in Oriental Studies, may have played a role in bringing the Arabic version of the *Covenant* to France. When recalled from Rome, where he was stationed, Savary de Brèves "took two Maronites with him to Paris to assist in the publication of the polyglot under the auspices of de Thou, the royal librarian, and Cardinal Duperron. The two Maronites were Gabriel Sionita and John Hesronita" (Catholic Encyclopedia). Evidently, other parties may have been involved. As Fatma Müge Göçek has shown, "[m]anucripts on Christianity and Greek civilization, along with those in Ottoman, Persian, and Arabic were collected avidly" (98) in France during the period of the Franco-Ottoman Alliance. As Göçek explains, "[t]his combination of religious and cultural interests supported by the King led to the development of large royal collections and libraries" (Göçek 98). In the words of the protagonist of Giovani Paolo Marana's novel, *L'Espion dans les cours des princes chrétiens*, "Cardinal de Richelieu . . . had a large quantity of Persan, Syrian, and Arabic books" (155). Since the French King commissioned travelers to "search for rarities" (Göçek 98), it is quite possible that an especially gifted or lucky literary explorer obtained a copy of the *Covenant of the Prophet with the Christians of the World.*

Convinced that only the source covenant could provide answers to the many questions concerning its origin, I proceeded to follow the chain of possession: Scaliger to the King, the King to Hotman, Hotman to Sionita, but then what? Was it returned to the King's library? Was it placed in the library of a Catholic monastery? Was it lost or destroyed during the French Revolution? I was well aware that "the accumulation of Arabic and other oriental manuscripts in the collections of the King's ministers and other wealthy and influential men" was "a prominent phenomenon in seventeenth-century France" (Toomer 34). The question, of course, was, where did the *Covenant* end up? "Almost all such manuscripts," explains Toomer, "eventually ended up in major libraries in France, the majority in the Royal Library, thus forming the basis of the splendid collection of Arabic manuscripts in the *Bibliothèque nationale*" (35). Unless he immediately returned the manuscript of the *Testament of Muhammad* to the King's Library by means of François Hotman or Du Ryer, Sionita was the last person to have it in his possession. That places the manuscript in his hands in 1630. "When Sionita was arrested in 1640," write Hamilton and Richard, "his lodgings were searched and his manuscripts confiscated" (46). Once again, the trail leads to the King's collection which eventually ended up in the *Bibliothèque nationale.* It is unlikely, however, that the King would have allowed the manuscript to remain outside of his reach for long. He had, after all, obliged Mr. de Brèves to sell him the Turkish, Arabic, and Persian manuscripts he had brought back from his embassy in Constantinople (Bernard 45, note 1). A true collector, the King was actively engaged in acquiring ancient and unique manuscripts. The *Testament of Muhammad* must have been considered a crown jewel and one of the finest pieces in his collection.

Despite centuries of speculation concerning the origin of the *Testament of Muhammad*, it was only M. J. Guillaume who actually bothered to check the catalog of the *Bibliothèque nationale de France* for further information. In his notes to the *Procès-verbaux du Comité d'instruction publique de la Convention nationale,* he had this to say:

> The *Pact of Muhammad in Favor of the Christian* is an apocryphal document of which the Department of Manuscripts of the National Library possesses a copy, which forms part of a voluminous Arabic manuscript of 262 sheets. The *Catalogue des manuscrits arabes*, by the Baron de Slane (Paris, 1883–1895), provides the following details concerning this manuscript (pages 54–55): It is also catalogued under number 214 and contains copies of several works; the document in question is the twelfth and last of these works and takes up folios 245–246. The manuscript is dated from the year 1254 of the martyrs (1538 CE). Two notes, one to folio 114 and the other to folio 125, inform us that the copyist of the manuscript was named George, that he belonged to the Jacobite religion, and that he was of European origin. With regards to the text translated by Lefèbvre de Villebrune, the catalog says the following:
>
> "N° 214... 12° (Fol. 245). Copy of the charter granted by Muhammad, the son of 'Abd Allah, and grand-son of 'Abd al-Muttalib, to all Christians, featuring the signatures of approximately thirty Companions. It is one of many redactions of this apocryphal document." (831, B)

While Guillaume is to be commended for actually going to the *Bibliothèque nationale* and looking up the manuscript in the catalog, no scholar actually bothered to examine the actual document until I came to the scene. Currently, the complete catalog listing reads as follows:

> Anthology
> Arabic 214 (serial number)
> 385 (Regius) (old serial number)
> Ancient Arab Collection 88 (old serial number)
> 1538
> 17 lines per page. Written surface: 210 x 135 mm. Western paper. 262 fol. (f. 261 v., 262 v left blank). Paginated using Coptic numerals. Oriental writing (Egyptian). – Title headings. 285 x 210 mm. Binding made of reddish brown calf leather; back made of red Moroccan with the numbers of Napoleon the 1st. Manuscript in Arabic
>
> National Library of France. Department of Manuscripts
>
> *Presentation of Content*
>
> Copy made for the library of Yuhanna ibn Ishaq al-Batanuni (f. 256 v), by Girgis al-Ifrangi (f. 114, 125) and completed successively on the 26th (f. 220) and 28th of Basnas (f. 231 v) and the 3 Ba'una 1254 of the Martyrs (f. 256 v).
>
> *History of Conservation*
>
> A note by Renaudot.
> Purchased by Vansleb in the Orient. Seals with the

numbers of Vansleb. — Pen marks (f. 1); marks of readers, including one by Girgis ibn Yuhanna al-Tamawi (f. 1 v); reading mark belonging to Butrus ibn Diyab al-Halabi, dated 1673 CE, and of Mansur ibn Sulayman Sahyun al-Ramadi, dated 14 Baba 1336 of the Martyrs (1620 CE) (f. 2); mention of the arrival of a missionary to Old Cairo on the 9th of Hatur 1380 of the Martyrs (1592 CE) and mark belonging to Gabriyal Sahyun al-Ziftawi (f. 2 v); mark of ownership of Sim'an ibn Fadl Allah al-Barallusi (f. 262).

As for the actual covenant itself, it is indexed by the *Bibliothèque national* under the title: *Charte accordée à tous les chrétiens, par Muhammad ibn 'Abd Allah ibn 'Abd al-Muttalib* 12. F. 257–261 (foliotation) or *Charter Accorded to all Christians by Muhammad ibn 'Abd Allah ibn 'Abd al-Muttalib.*

For an astute observer, a series of errors and anomalies immediately come to light. For starters, Guillaume's rendition is incomplete. After indicating that the copyist named George was of European origin, the Baron de Slane notes that "nothing in his writing indicates that he was a French writer" (55). His handwriting was not that of a European. Slane, however, seems to take the family name, al-Ifrangi or the Frenchman too literally for in Arabic *ifranj*, like *rumi*, is applied indiscriminately to all Europeans. The notice by Eusèbe Renaudot (1646–1720 CE) also contains inaccuracies. He alleges that the manuscript was purchased by Johann Michael Vansleb (1635–1676 CE) in the East. He deduced this by the fact that the manuscript contains Vansleb's seal. This is chronologically incorrect for several reasons.

To begin with, this German theologian, linguist, and explorer, who travelled to Egypt on two occasions in search of ancient manuscripts, made his two trips in 1671 and in 1672. Since the *Testament of the Prophet* was published in 1630 by Gabriel Sionita, Vansleb could not possibly have purchased it in Egypt forty years later. Furthermore, the manuscript contains the mark of Gabriyal Sahyun al-Ziftawi, namely, that of Gabriel Sionita himself! So, clearly, the document in question is the one that was used by Sionita to prepare his Arabic/Latin edition. While Father Pacifique Scaliger (1588–1648 CE) left no mark on the manuscript, there is no question that this is the actual document that he brought back from the Middle East. As such, it is the answer to many allegations. Father Scaliger absolutely and categorically did not forge the *Testament of Muhammad.* The document he brought to France in 1629, and which had fortuitously fallen into his hands between 1627 and 1628, dates from 1538. It was already nearly one hundred years old. Prior to reaching Scaliger and Sionita, the document had been read, in 1620, by Mansur ibn Sulayman Sahyun al-Ramadi, mentions the arrival of a missionary to Old Cairo in 1592, and indicates that it was owned at one point by Sim'an ibn Fadl Allah al-Barallusi. While this does not prove that the *Testament of Muhammad* was not forged at some point in the distant past, it does prove that Father Scaliger did not falsify it himself. Not only did Father Scaliger consider the manuscript to be genuine, the document itself bears every indication that all of its previous owners did so as well.

The year 1538 is not without significance. Ever since 1536, when Sieur Forêt, the representative of King Francis I of France, signed a series of capitulations with Sultan Suleiman I, "[t]he French had secured in the Levant a position of absolute preeminence" (Hadjiantonious 53). As a result of one particular clause, "[t]he French were granted the right of religious liberty and France was given the right of the protection of the Holy Sites in Palestine, which with the passing of time was interpreted to mean the right of the protection of all Christians living in the Ottoman Empire and generally in the Levant" (53). If, previously, it had been the Greek Orthodox, the Armenians, and the Assyrians who claimed special privileges granted by the Prophet, to the exclusion of the Byzantines, the French were now asserting these rights in the name of the Roman Catholic Church. This does not suggest that the French fabricated the *Covenant of the Prophet Muhammad with the Christians of the World*, as this document had been in circulation, with minor differences, for centuries. It was, however, the opportune moment for French Catholics to stake their claims to the Holy Land with a covenant of the Prophet in hand. By 1580, however, the Ottomans had granted the very same rights to the English (Hadjiantonious 53). The English, however, would wait until 1688 before circulating an English translation of the *Covenant* to support their Christian claims.

The *Covenant of the Prophet Muhammad with the Christians of the World* occupies sheets 257 to 262, that is, the last eleven pages, of an Arabic Christian anthology. The work appears to have been a *mushaf* or stack of sheets. The copy in question was bound on April 13, 1872. The table of contents, which is written in Latin, at the beginning of the book, says that it contains a variety of theological treatises and commentaries from the Eastern Church, an anonymous doctrinal exposition, a debate with a certain ʿAbd al-Rahman concerning the truth of the Christian religion, an epistle, a debate with a Jew concerning the truth of the Christian religion, a work on the wisdom of Solomon, a debate between Christians and Jews, an exposition of the Nicene Creed, an exposition of Sunday prayers, extracts from various authors, along with various questions and responses. Though the *Covenant of the Prophet Muhammad with the Christians of the World* forms an integral part of the work, no mention of it is made in the table of contents which means that it could easily have been overlooked, lost, and locked away, hidden in the final pages of an obscure manuscript of which but a single copy remains in existence. Although the book has no title, its objective is clear: it is a work of Christian apologetics, the goal of which was to prepare monks, priests, and missionaries to defend Christianity when confronting Jews and Muslims. Does this make the *Covenant* a fake? No, not any more than it makes the other works it contains false. If it was included in the anthology, it was because it served the interests of the Christian community. These covenants had been circulating for a millennium, from the time of the Prophet into the 16th and 17th centuries, and provided Christians with safety and security. Its inclusion thus makes perfect rational sense.

Although the *Covenant of the Prophet Muhammad with the Christians of the World* which dates from 1538 seems to be the source of the *Covenant of the Prophet Muhammad with the Christians of World* which was published by Gabriel Sionita in Paris in 1630, the issue is not cut and dry. The chronology, of course, seems sound. The covenant that Father Scaliger revealed to the world was already old when he came across it. That the 1630 covenant was based on the covenant of 1538 is logical. Furthermore, the covenant of 1538 contains the reading marks of Gabriel Sionita. The problem, though, is that the covenants of 1538 and 1630 have different beginnings and ends. The Arabic in the former is superior to that in the latter when the opposite would have been expected. While documents have a tendency to improve with time, the covenants of the Prophet appear to have been subjected to the opposite process. Sionita, it should be stressed, published the *Covenant* without full vocalization and case endings. Johann Georg Nissel (1621–1662) was critical of this fact and republished the work with all of the *tashkil* and *ʿirab* in order to return it to its original glory. One would assume that Nissel relied on the copy from 1538 which contains all of the symbols required for proper pronunciation and complete comprehension. If this is actually the case, why did Nissel fail to call Sionita out for having modified the manuscript from 1538? In the hope of uncovering clues, I will now examine the covenants, commencing with the first that was published in 1630 and then followed by the one I located in the Arabic archives at the National Library of France, which dates from nearly a century earlier, and which has never been previously published.

Published in Paris by Antoine Vitray in 1630 CE under the title *al-ʿAhd wa al-shurut allati sharataha Muhammad rasul Allah li ahl al-millah al-nasraniyyah* or *The Covenant which Muhammad, the Messenger of Allah, Concluded with His Christian Subjects*, the content corresponds closely with the *Covenant of the Prophet Muhammad with the Christians of Najran* which is found in the *Chronicle of Séert*, an ancient history compiled by Nestorian Christians. While not identical, the *Covenant of the Prophet Muhammad with the Christians of the World*, which was published in 1630 CE, is strikingly similar to the *Covenant of the Prophet Muhammad with the Christians of Najran*, discovered in a monastery in Iraq in 878 CE. While an obsessive skeptic could argue that the version from 1630 was simply forged on the basis of another forgery from 878 CE, a more open intellect would find evidence supporting the general stability of the same text over the course of nearly a millennium. Are we dealing with the same original document to which modifications were made later? Or are we dealing with the same covenant which was re-issued on more than one occasion thus explaining the disparities? If so, this would be consistent with the practice of the Prophet. Alternatively, one could argue, as I do, that these are, in reality, two different patents of protection.

Unlike the *Covenant of the Prophet Muhammad with the Monks of Mount Sinai*, the *Covenant of the Prophet Muhammad with the Christians of Najran* and the *Covenant of the Prophet Muhammad with the Christians of the World* were both written in the hand of Mu'awiyyah ibn Abi Sufyan (d. 680 CE). While the *Covenant of the Prophet Muhammad with the Christians of Najran* does not bear a date, the *Covenant of the Prophet Muhammad with the Christians of the World* dates from the second day of the month of Rabi' Ashar of the fourth year after the *hijrah*. This is also the same year in which the *Covenant of the Prophet Muhammad with the Assyrian Christians* was signed. In fact, both covenants date from a time in which the Messenger of Allah was actively engaged in diplomatic efforts. While the *Covenant of the Prophet Muhammad with the Christians of Najran* and the *Covenant of the Prophet with the Christians of the World* address many similar issues, concede similar rights, and demand similar obligations, they are not identical in structure, vocabulary, and content. Furthermore, they contain two different lists of witnesses; the former featuring thirty, and the latter featuring thirty-six.

The date, as mentioned before, poses a series of problems, since, according to Islamic biographical sources, Mu'awiyyah only embraced Islam prior to the Conquest of Mecca in the year 8 AH or 630 CE. However, the date could have been wrongly appended at a later time or the name of the original scribe was altered. Since Selim I was a *nasibi*, namely, one who is hostile towards the Household of the Prophet, it is possible that the Sultan himself modified the name of the scribe for religious and political purposes, replacing the name of Imam 'Ali (d. 661 CE) with that of Mu'awiyyah ibn Abi Sufyan. Support for this contention lies in the Sultan's actions. After all, Selim I ordered the massacre of forty thousand Anatolian Shi'ites, not to mention the imprisonment and deportation of many more (Somel 262, Eversley 105). As Gábor Ágoston explains,

> Ottoman propaganda justified Selim's campaigns against the Safavids by portraying the Shi'ite enemy and its . . . allies . . . as 'heretics' and even 'infidels,' whose revolts hindered the Ottoman's struggle against the Christian adversaries of the Empire. . . . Since the Sunni Mamluks cooperated with the 'heretic' Safavids, the war against them was also justifiable. Before the Sultan could turn against the empire's Christian enemies, claimed Ottoman propagandists, these rebel Muslims had to be dealt with. (93)

In the eyes of Selim I, the Shi'ite Empire of the Safavids was "worse than the infidel" (Wheatcroft 50). Hence, "its subjects more worthy of death than any number of Christians" (50). Since the Mamluks were allies of the Safavids, Selim I's Egyptian campaign was endorsed by the Ottoman religious establishment on the grounds that "he who aids a heretic is himself a heretic" (Finkel 109).

As we have seen, many of the other covenants which remain in existence include Imam 'Ali (d. 661 CE) as the scribe and primary witness. With this consideration in mind, it seems quite possible that the other covenants of the Prophet which bear the signature of Mu'awiyyah were actually written by Imam 'Ali. Such a "textual modification" could have been perpetrated by the Ottomans, but most probably by the Umayyads. And there exists a more sinister possibility; namely, that Mu'awiyyah himself, God forbid, forged the covenants in question. Al-Mada'ini (d. 225/840), an early historian, reported that Muʿawiyyah encouraged the systematic forging and circulation of traditions (Brown 70). Ignác Goldziher, among others, "argues that many *hadiths* and the nature of the early *hadith* tradition as a whole leaves no doubt that the Umayyad dynasty actively pursued a program of political propaganda in which *hadith* forgery played an important role" (Brown 206). Still, the forgeries perpetrated by the Umayyads revolved around their conflict with the partisans of Imam ʿAli and did not necessarily extend to issues of foreign policy and the treatment of minorities.

If the identity of the scribe and the date of the *Covenant of the Prophet Muhammad with the Christians of the World* are controversial, another issue that arises is: why would the French have disseminated the content of the covenant in the first place—an interesting topic altogether. Despite its long history of animosity and aggression towards the Islamic world, both past and present, from medieval Crusades to modern-day imperialism, there was a period of history in which France was actually at peace with Muslims. Known as the Franco-Ottoman Alliance or the Franco-Turkish Alliance, the accord was concluded in 1536, causing great scandal in the rest of the Western world. Denounced as "the impious alliance" or "the sacrilegious union of the Lily and the Crescent," the alliance lasted from the 16th to the 19th century since it served the ongoing interests of both parties. The Sultan who set the stage for the alliance was Selim I (r. 1512–1520 CE) who succeeded in uniting the Middle East through his conquest, from 1516 to 1517 CE, of the Mamluk Sultanate of Egypt, which encompassed Greater Syria, the Hijaz, and Egypt. His successor, Sulayman the Magnificent (r. 1520–1566 CE), established the Franco-Ottoman Alliance with King Francis I of France (r. 1515–1547 CE) in 1536. Beyond commercial considerations, Francis I was also eager to ensure the protection of the Christians living in the Ottoman Empire through a series of *Capitulations*. Ambassadors were ex-changed. Trade, religious, military and financial agreements were concluded and joint campaigns were conducted. What is significant, as far as Islam is concerned, is that "[t]he alliances that Sulayman cemented with the Catholic French did not lead anyone to question his bona fides as a Muslim" (179). Tolerance and co-existence with members of other religions was not aberrant or abnormal in Islam: it was normative. For Issa Boullata, the root cause of this attitude is clear: "the Qur'an has specifically prescribed kindness and tact and gracious manners for Muslims when dealing with people of other faiths" (51)

The *Capitulations*, of course, were not one-sided; the French reciprocated the favors of the Ottomans. If the Turks provided churches to Christians, the Christians provided mosques for Muslims. In fact, when Barbarossa wintered in Toulon, France, from 1543–1544 CE, King Francis I (r. 1515–1547 CE) had the city's cathedral converted into a mosque. If French influence was paramount in Istanbul, Turkish influence was equally important in Paris where coffee drinking and Ottoman clothing were all the rage, including the turban and the caftan, along with the practice of reclining on Persian rugs.

Since the printing press was banned in the Ottoman Empire from 1483 to 1729 CE, due to pressure exerted by obscurantist *ʿulama*, much Islamic literature was printed in Europe, particularly in Italy and France. Bayazid II, Selim I, and their successors, all stood behind an edict which ruled that "occupying oneself with the science of printing was punishable by death" (Göçek 112). As Chejne explains, "[t]he first known Arabic press was installed in the Vatican in the early part of the sixteenth century" (*The Arabic Language* 191, note 3). "It was not," however, "until the eighteenth century that it was introduced to the Arab world: in Aleppo (1702), Egypt (1798), and Lebanon (1834)" (191, note 3), and, typically, at the hands of the French (101). While they had led the Western world into the Renaissance, the Muslims were now centuries behind European Christians.

For ultra-conservative clerics, the printing press was a prohibited innovation which was to be vehemently opposed (83–84). Ibrahim Muteferrika, who founded the Ottoman printing press in 1726, explained that the influential religious dignitaries had insistently forbidden this new invention (Göçek 113). They feared that placing more than the minimum necessary amount of books in circulation would pose a threat to public order and the conduct of religion (Göçek 113). In an effort to maintain Muslims in a state of ignorance, only minorities were allowed to print books and, even then, only in Hebrew or Latin characters (111). Supposedly, since Muslims were only familiar with the Arabic script, they would not be corrupted by works in other alphabets. By the time of Murad III, in 1587/1588 CE, imperial decrees were passed allowing printed books, in all languages and scripts, for trade purposes (Göçek 110). After some Arabic, Persian, and Turkish books were seized by religious fanatics, the Sultan ordered that they be returned to their rightful owners (110). Although Muslims could not print books, "[t]he Ottoman state was favorable to the trade and printing of books by foreigners in the Ottoman empire" (111).

If Muslims missed out on a major method of information dissemination, the Christians took full advantage of it, publishing books in a large number of languages, including the spiritual and scholarly language of Islamic civilization and culture. As Fatma Müge Göçek explains,

> In the sixteenth and seventeenth centuries, three noted Arabic printers existed in Italy. The Medici Press published Gospels, Arabic grammar, Greek authors in Arabic translation, and a number of Islamic scientific works. The Arabic printing press founded by the Congregation for the Propagation of the Faith printed Arabic translations of the Bible and other Christian works. The outstanding product of Tipografia del Seminario in Padua was the publication of the Qur'an with an Arabic text and a Latin translation. These books were marketed in the Ottoman Empire. (110)

If printing the Qur'an was cause for capital punishment in the Ottoman Empire so was the publication of any other works since nothing but the Word of God was worthy of being read. In light of this, it is less surprising to learn that the first machine-printed Arabic Qur'an was produced in Europe. It is generally believed that it was first printed in Venice by Paganino and Alessandro Paganini in 1537/1538 for export to the Ottoman Empire. However, since it contained many mistakes, and had been printed by "impure infidels," their attempts were met with hostility and the entire run was apparently condemned to flames.

It appears that the French may actually have preceded the Italians in mass-producing the Qur'an. In fact, a copy of the Qur'an, printed circa 1536 CE, was bound in 1549 according to regulations set in place under Francis I (r. 1515–1547 CE). The volume, which bears the arms of Henri II (r. 1547–1559 CE), can be found in the *Bibliothèque nationale de France*. That the French were the first to machine press the Qur'an is indicative of their interest in Islam. Besides printing the holy book of Islam, 16th- and 17th-century French society was simply teeming with interest in all things Islamic. Orientalists like Guillaume Postel (1510–1581 CE) advocated a universalistic world religion which would integrate Jews, Muslims, and Christians of all denominations, into a broader, and more inclusive, Christian creed. Jean Bodin (1530–1596 CE), the French jurist, professor of law, and politician who was opposed any aspect of compulsion in relation to religion, recognized that various religions could co-exist in a single state, and advocated religious pluralism and universalism. Other works that were published included a bilingual, French-Turkish, edition of the 1604 Franco-Ottoman *Capitulations* between Sultan Ahmed I (r. 1603–1617 CE) and Henry IV, King of France, (r. 1589 to 1610 CE), published by François Savary de Brèves (1560–1627 CE) in 1615. The publication of *al-'Ahd wa al-shurut allati sharataha Muhammad rasul Allah li ahl al-millah al-nasraniyyah* or *The Covenant which Muhammad, the Messenger of Allah, Concluded with the Christian Community* in an Arabic and Latin version in 1630 was motivated by political, economic, military, religious, and cultural considerations. As Josée Balagna acknowledges,

> It is very interesting that the *Testament* was edited in Paris in 1630 by Antoine Vitray by Louis XIII with the collaboration of Gabriel Sionite who was a friend of Savary de Brèves. Louis III still maintains the policy of Henri IV and Savary, pro-Ottoman

friendship, support for Eastern Christians, and this *Testament* acts as a proof of Muslim tolerance towards Christians. In Vitray's preface, we learn that thanks to the generosity of Michel Le Jay, the king's printer for Oriental languages, he obtained some very elegant Arabic, Syriac, and Samaritan characters. The Arabic ones were those of Savary. (67)

But who, then, was the intended audience of the *Covenant of the Prophet Muhammad with the Christians of the World*? As Fatma Müge Göçek explains, "[t]he printing presses in the West started printing religious books in Arabic script by the sixteenth century for religious and trade purposes" (110). Surprisingly, "[t]he first known Islamic book printed in the West was an Arabic book on the canonical times of prayer; this book was printed in 1514 at Fano (Italy) under the patronage of Pope Julius II" (110). For many Muslims familiar with the history of Islamo-Christian conflict, this fact is simply stunning. While religion played a role in the printing of Arabic books in Europe, money was a major motivating factor. As professionals, Christian printers were prepared to print anything that was profitable. Considering the size of the Muslim market, this explains their eagerness to mass produce the Qur'an. Evidently, they also printed material that was of interest to Christians. In 1516 CE, for example, "an edition of the Psalms of David was printed in Hebrew, Greek, Arabic, Aramaic, and Latin" in Genoa (110). "These books," explains Göçek, "served to maintain the faith among Arabic-speaking Christian communities in the Middle East and to help spread Christianity among other groups" (110). If this is the case, then, perhaps, the publication of the *Covenant of the Prophet Muhammad with the Christians of the World* was aimed primarily at the Christians who inhabited the Ottoman Empire. After all, Sionita printed a Syriac and Latin prayer book, at his own expense, in 1625 CE, which was intended to be used by the Christians of the Levant (Bernard 44). So, clearly, Sionita had the Christians of the Arab world in mind when he published the *Testamentum et pactiones*. However, since it was also translated into Latin, French, and German, there must also have been a market for such a work among European Christians. It must also be recalled that Paris in the 1600s was a very cosmopolitan city. As André Du Ryer (c. 1580–1660 CE) wrote, there were many people who lived in Paris who understood and spoke the languages of Asia, Africa, and even the Americas (Bernard 54). Hence, there was a market both at home and abroad for the *Testament of Muhammad*.

As Norman Daniel explains in *Islam in the West*, political ideas of friendship with Muslims were popular in Europe during the 1600s CE something which is evidenced by the numerous editions of Muhammad's *Testamentum* (406). If Maronites like Sionita, and his Catholic patrons, were interested in such ideas, so were the Protestants of the time. Referring to Theodore Buchmann Bibliander, the publisher, and J. Fabricius, the compiler, Santiago-Otero observes that "Both the editor, and the compiler, were Calvinists, a fact that demonstrates the increased importance of the study of Islam among the reformists" (Santiago Otero 409). Claudius Salmasius (d. 1653 CE) was also a Protestant as was Abraham Hinckelmann (1652–1695 CE). If the Moriscos of the time were using Protestant arguments to antagonize their Catholic persecutors, Protestants were employing Islamic arguments against them as well.

If European Christians wanted to remind Ottoman Christians of their rights under Islam, this increased information about the Muslim legal system appears to have impacted their rulers at home. Islamic ideas of religious tolerance seem to have influenced a series of French kings, such as Henri IV, le Grand (r. 1589–1610 CE), who guaranteed religious liberties to Protestants by means of the *Edict of Nantes* (1598 CE). Not surprisingly, following this ecumenical move, Henry IV was assassinated by François Ravaillac (1578–1610 CE), a Catholic fanatic. Eventually, over the span of the centuries covered by the Franco-Ottoman Alliance, many leading figures in French society embraced Islam. Viewed myopically, cases of French Christians becoming practicing Muslims have often been dismissed as "conversions of convenience," acts which formed part of various imperial agendas. However, in light of the open attitude towards the Ottomans, the positive light in which Muslims were presented, and the availability of Islamic literature, including a French translation of the Qur'an completed by André du Ryer (c. 1580–1660 CE) in 1647, it seems plausible that some French Christians would have been convinced of the Islamic cause. Could this have been the case with one of the former owners of the Sionita's edition of the *Covenant*? The edition I consulted includes the invocations: *Ya Allah*, *Ya Muhammad*, *Ya Abu Bakr*, *Ya 'Umar*, *Ya 'Uthman*, *Ya 'Ali*, *Ya Hasan*, and *Ya Husayn*. These were handwritten by Valerianus Oserole in 1659 CE. Could he have been a convert to Islam? Otherwise, why would a Christian write these traditional Islamic invocations? In any event, now that we understand better the geo-political importance of the *Covenant of the Prophet Muhammad with the Christians of the World*, let us turn to the response it received.

As we have seen, the *Testamentum et pactiones* or *al-'ahd wa al-shurut* was first published in 1630 CE. The work was an immediate scholarly success, causing a great deal of controversy, and eliciting a significant degree of debate and discussion. Since the work sold out almost immediately, and bookstores could not meet the demand, the work was re-published four times during the first year of publication. It was republished in various editions and languages by other translators and publishers in 1655, 1638, 1668, 1690, and as late as 1888 CE. It also appeared in French translations in historical works, such as Sir Paul Ricaut's (1629–1700 CE) *History of the Ottoman Empire*, and even in diplomatic reports. While the work aroused much interest for over two centuries, the covenant was shrouded in silence during the twentieth century and early 21st century.

While the *Testament et pactiones* or *al-'Ahd wa al-shurut* was rejected by many authorities, it was defended by even larger numbers of them, the first of whom were Muslims. As Mosheim explains, "There is . . . extant an injunction or *Testament*, as it is commonly called, that is, a diploma of Mohammed himself, in which he promises full security to all Christians living under his dominion; and though some learned men doubt the authenticity of this instrument, yet the Mohammedans do not call it in question" (254). While Layard points out that the covenant "has been rejected as a forgery by several European critics" he also observes that "its authenticity is admitted by early Mohammedan and Eastern Christian writers" (207). Although Luke states that the covenant was "generally regarded in the West as of dubious authenticity," he also recognizes that it was "accepted by early Moslem writers as genuine" (Luke 68). As Louis-Joseph-Delphin Féraud-Giraud admits, "the authenticity of this document is called into question" (36). He points out, however, that the *Treaty of 'Umar* alludes to a previous covenant concluded by the Prophet with the Christians (36, note 1).

Not only was the covenant recognized by early Muslim authorities, it was also defended by early Christian writers. As Layard (1817–1894 CE) points out, "[t]he substance of this treaty is given by three Syriac authors—Bar Hebreaus, Maris, and Amrus (Assemani, vol. iv, p. 59). It was first published in Arabic and Latin by Gabriel Sionita, Paris, 1630, and is usually called the 'Testamentum Mahometi'" (207). Gregory Bar Hebraeus (1226–1286 CE), it should be stressed, was a bishop in the Syriac Orthodox Church in the 13th century CE. He has been described as the most learned and versatile man from the Syriac Orthodox Church. Edward Rehatsek (1819–1891 CE) summarizes the account of Bar Hebraeus in the following terms:

> About this time Muhammad began to propagate Islam with all his might, and is by Barhebraeus stated to have received a visit from the patriarch Jesujab in company with Sa'yd, the chief of the Christians of Najran, who brought him enormous gifts, with the intention of establishing a treaty between the Christians and the Arabs. Muhammad agreed and gave them a diploma, in which he recommended to the Arabs to protect Christians, and neither to attack them nor force them to change their religion. He altogether prohibited the raising of tribute from priests and monks, and allowed only four coins to be taken from the poor, but twelve from the rich. He moreover gave permission to

Christians to repair their churches, and desired the Arabs to aid them in the work. Lastly, Christian men and women might serve in Arab houses without any detriment to their religion. (97)

While Matthaei Amrus, who lived in the 14th century CE, does not allude to an actual visit, he generally agrees with the earlier account of Bar Hebraeus. In the words of the former,

> Islam made its appearance, and this patriarch [Jesujab] wrote letters to the lord of the law of Islam [Muhammad], sent him presents, and asked him to protect his flock dwelling there, and he agreed thereto. Then Jesujab wrote numerous excellent letters to his Companions [the Sahabah], and the lord of the law presented him with gifts, among which there were a number of camels and 'Aden garments. This was brought to the notice of the king of Persia, who manifested his displeasure at the patriarch's doings and correspondence, but especially when then presents arrived. Accordingly Jesujab excused himself till he was delivered from his anger, and lived till the time of Omar Ben Al-Khetab, who wrote him a powerful letter of protection, promising that no tax should be taken from his brother's servants and partisans likewise; and the letter is preserved to this day. (qtd. Rehatsek 98)

The writings of Bar Hebraeus, Amrus, and Maris, are another reason why Father Scaliger (1588–1648 CE) cannot be accused of concocting a covenant. He could not have invented something that already existed and the content of which had been acknowledged from the earliest of days by Syriac Christian authorities. In fact, Christian and Muslim Arabs had upheld the *Covenant of the Prophet Muhammad with the Christians of the World* for centuries prior to its rediscovery by Father René de l'Escale Pacifique de Prouins (1588–1648 CE), known by the name of Scaliger.

Arabs aside, the first European scholar to stand behind the covenant was Father Pacificus Scaliger. I have no doubt that he discovered what he believed, or what he was told, was a true covenant of the Prophet Muhammad (570–632 CE) with the Christians of the world. He sent this covenant to the King of France in good faith so that it could be preserved for posterity. François Hotman de Marfontaine, a Magistrate who was close, not only to Du Ryer (c. 1580–1660 CE), the translator of the Qur'an, and his circle of Islamologists, but to the King of France, was provided with the manuscript which had been discovered by Scaliger. Hotman knew Sionita well. In fact, Sionita had long lived as an esteemed guest in his home. As such, he called upon Sionita, as Professor of Arabic, to translate the work into Latin. Although he has been criticized for "correcting" what appeared to him as the bad Arabic of the New Testament (M 254), and had some conflicts with some of his colleagues, Sionita was also the object of a great deal of praise (Goujet 100). After Scaliger, then, it was Sionita, and Hotman, his host and patron, who argued in favor of the covenant's authenticity.

Scaliger, Sionita, and Hotman, who were all associated with the discovery and dissemination of the covenant, were soon followed by outside authorities. Claudius Salmasius (1588 or 1596–1653 CE), for example, wrote that:

> I lately saw Mahomet's *Testament*: I have no doubt of its being genuine. But I wish the translator had not given it that name; for it is nothing like a Testament. It is a league and a covenant, by which he made the Christians secure; of which Elmacin in the Life of Mahomet, seems to make mention; where he relates out of the Christian histories, that that imposter favored the Christians, and, when some Christians came to him, desiring safe-guards, imposed a tax on them, and entered into covenant with them. (qtd. Bayle 1737: 38)

The classical scholar, Salmasius, whose French name was Claude de Saumaise, was described as a "person of considerable learning" who had an "extensive acquaintance" with Hebrew, Arabic, and Persian (Society for the Diffusion of Useful Knowledge 362). In light of his erudition, the professional opinion of this famous philologist is not without weight. Professor Jacobo Nagy de Harsany (b. 1615 CE), who included a French translation of the *Testament de Mahomet* in his *Colloquia familiar turco-latina*, treated the covenant as trustworthy. Like Saumaise, Nagy de Harsany was also well-versed in Oriental languages. In fact, this Hungarian scholar had perfected his knowledge of Turkish and Arabic in the Ottoman Empire where he was the representative of the prince of Transylvania.

As Pierre Bayle (1647–1706 CE) explains, "Mr. Hinkleman, is of the same opinion with Salmasius; and so was also Sir Paul Ricaut" (38). After relating the origin of the covenant, Ricaut (1629–1700 CE) explains that "there are very good authors, who, believe it to be genuine, and that it was made at the time set down at the end of it . . . when the empire of Mahomet was yet very weak, and in its infancy; for at that time he was at war with the Arabians, and feared lest the Christians should declare against him; wherefore, to prevent this being attacked by two enemies at once, he made this treaty with them in the monastery of the monks of Mount Carmel, from whence these austere friars derive their name" (qtd. Bayle 1737: 38). It was also accepted as genuine by Eusèbe Renaudot (1646–1720), the French theologian and Orientalist (Rehatsek 98). Unlike virtually every other scholar, who passed judgment on the basis of published copies of the covenant, Renaudot, who was perfectly proficient in Arabic—a language he learned in his youth—actually went to the *Bibliothèque nationale*, where he examined the original manuscript. We know this because he actually left notes to this effect on the manuscript itself.

The *Covenant of the Prophet Muhammad with the Christians of the World* is also treated as factual by Henri Layard (1817–1894 CE), Pedro de Madrazo (1816–1898 CE), and the Societé d'Amis de la Religion et de la Patrie, as well as James Thayer Addison (1887–1953 CE). Pedro de Madrazo considers the covenant to be authentic. In order to support their views, Layard and Madrazo point to the fact that the writings of three early Syriac authors, Bar Hebraeus, Maris, and Amrus, confirmed its substance. For Madrazo, the covenant was an example of Islamic tolerance towards Christians (Layard 207; Madrazo 123). In *Annales de la Religion*, the Societé d'Amis de la Religion et de la Patrie remark that "history has preserved a treaty of Muhammad with the Christians which protects their religious property for he was less cruel in establishing his false religion than our persecutors have been to destroy the true one" (112–113). A detailed defense of the covenant was also made by Dr. Addison whose arguments were summarized by Bayle as follows:

> Dr Addison . . . mentions the treaty of *Alliance*, which is reported to have been made between Mahomet and the Christians; and takes notice afterwards of the different opinions of learned men concerning that piece. . . . Dr. Addison says, that we may consider it as one of Mahomet's artifices to support his authority, which was then in its infancy; but when he afterwards saw it sufficiently established, he changed his language, and added several chapters to his Koran, where he denounces death, imprisonment and slavery against the infidels, by which expression he particularly meant the Christians. (241)

In the 18th, 19th, and early 20th century, the *Testament of Muhammad* or *Covenant of the Prophet Muhammad with the Christians of the World* acquired a great deal of importance in Western diplomacy. In 1826, M. Grassi (Alfio) included a detailed commentary of the *Traité de Mahomet avec les Chrétiens* in his *Charte Turque ou Organisation religieuse, civile et militaire de l'empire ottoman* (75–89). His work, which is filled with freshness and objectivity, provides a praise-filled presentation of the Prophet, whom he describes as the greatest of geniuses (66), and describes his *Testamentum et pactiones* as a political and moral masterpiece (75). Grassi also offers an honest exposé of Western scholarly subjectivity. As he recognizes, "Most historians, all of whom are Christian, have viewed Muhammad with the kind of contempt that only an impostor and a sectarian persecutor of Christian belief can inspire, have attempted less to appreciate the truth than to diminish the marvelous nature of his achievements" (66). Following in the footsteps of his predecessors, Alexandre de Miltitz, the former minister of the Prussian king to the Ottoman Porte, included a copy of the *Privilège accordé par Mahomet aux Chrétiens* in his famous *Manuel des Consuls*, which was published in 1838, (496–499). This was not a new translation, but rather, the French translation of the English translation of the original Arabic that had been included in Ricaut's

(1629–1700 CE) *Histoire de l'état présent de l'empire ottoman* (316–358).

In 1881, Edward A. Van Dyke, a consular clerk of the United States at Cairo, also included an English translation and short commentary of the *Treaty of Muhammad* in his *Capitulations of the Ottoman Empire*. The translation, however, was made on the basis of the French translation found in Ricaut. Although Van Dyke observed that "[t]his treaty is considered by many as apocryphal" (87), he himself believed that it was genuine. Van Dyke, however, believed that the covenant represented an early strategy of the Prophet which later evolved. As this diplomat explains,

> In the beginning of his rule Mahommed, either out of real feelings of toleration and moderation or through adroit and well-calculated hypocrisy, everywhere proclaimed the principles of toleration toward every kind of religion, and particularly toward that of the Christians.... The first chapters of his Koran are filled with the praises of Jesus Christ and the Virgin Mary his mother. By this adroit policy he wished to conciliate the Christians in his favor, and assure them that he did not threaten their religion.... It is true that Mahommed afterwards changed the tone of his language toward the Christians, and made fearful laws against them. (Van Dyke 85)

The views of Dr. Addison and Van Dyke are evidently incorrect. While Ibn Ishaq and other traditionists have reported that the Prophet's last injunction was his words: "Let not two religions be left in the Arabian Peninsula" (689), I have little doubt that the saying was attributed to him *post-factum* in response to the apostasy of the Arabs and the treachery of some Christian and Jewish tribes who betrayed the trust of the Muslims. Muhammad Hamidullah, however, accepted the tradition as authentic but insists that it was limited to certain insubordinate populations and that it was not a general prohibition (*Introduction* 150). History confirms that Jews and Christians continued to live in the Hijaz for centuries after the fact even in such sacred sites such as Medina and Mecca (150). As for their interpretation of the Qur'an, the views of Addison and Van Dyke are self-serving, chronologically incorrect, and exegetically unsound. The term *kuffar* or infidels, as employed in the Qur'an, applies to polytheists and not Christians.

Van Dyke, it seems, was not acting but reacting; in other words, his interpretation of early Islamic history responded to developments in Turkey. In the same way that many non-Muslims interpret Islam on the basis of the actions of modern-day terrorists, Van Dyke was projecting the alleged Turkish oppression of the Greeks back to the Prophet. As such, he cites Qur'anic verses out of context to explain why "the Turks behaved with such cruelty in the war of Greek Independence" (85). He also refers readers to Muir's *Life of Mahommed* "[f]or other treaties with the Christians, and Mahommed's system of subjugating them to a humiliating tribute" (87). While Van Dyke believes that it was limited in time and scope, he remains thoroughly impressed by the *Covenant of the Prophet Muhammad with the Christians of the World*. Plagiarizing Grassi (75), Van Dyke writes that "[t]his treaty should be considered as a masterpiece of political forethought and as a rare monument of wisdom, morality, and toleration" (85).

If the French monarchy and many of their diplomats had insisted upon the authenticity of the *Covenant of the Prophet Muhammad with the Christians of the World* during the 16th and 17th centuries, they maintained the same position during the 18th and early 19th centuries. The four hundred and forty first séance of the *Comité d'instruction publique de la Convention nationale* [National Convention's Committee for Public Instruction], which took place on June 22nd, 1795, included the following motion:

> The Committee, having read a letter from citizen Lefèbvre-Villebrune, considering that it would be beneficial towards the dialogue between the French and the Turks to make public, by means of printing, the pact made between Muhammad and the Christians, which dates from the 4th year of the *hijrah*, motions that said pact be printed by the printing press of the Republic, in Arabic, along with the French translation which citizen Lefèbvre-Ville-

> brune remains in charge, and that it will be published in large enough numbers for it to be distributed to the consuls of the Republic in the Ports of the Levant and who will be invited to circulate it in the Ottoman Empire. (Guillaume 320)

The French, as they admit themselves, believed that the diffusion of the *Pact of Muhammad* would help encourage dialogue with the Turks. They wanted all French consuls to familiarize themselves with the document and attempt to disseminate it throughout the Ottoman Empire. In the five hundred and eleventh séance of the *Comité d'instruction publique de la Convention nationale* [National Convention's Committee for Public Instruction] which was held on October 23, 1795, the following motion was passed:

> The Committee motions that the translation made by citizen Lefèbvre-Villebrune of the *Pact of Muhammad in Favor of the Christians* be published by the printing press of the legal office in the amount of one thousand copies to be distributed to the members of the Committee, sent to all of the libraries in the Republic, in the Ports of the Levant, and addressed to various scholars from Europe. Citizen Grégoire is assigned [the completion] of the final article of this motion. (Guillaume 827)

Within several months, the project, which was aimed initially at diplomats, was expanded to include all of the libraries in France and the Levant. Copies of the covenant were also going to be sent to all the leading scholars in Europe. This ambitious plan to promote the *Covenant of the Prophet with the Christians of the World* came to an abrupt end during the five hundred and fourteenth séance when Mr. Lefèbvre-Villebrune was suddenly removed from the project and replaced by a certain Mr. Legrand (Guillaume 858). Apparently, the Committee reproached him for having removed a manuscript from the National Library (Guillaume 858, note 4). To the best of my knowledge, the translation, publication, and dissemination of the *Pact of Muhammad* envisaged by the Committee never saw the light of day. What is interesting is the difference in discourse between the National Convention's Committee for Public Instruction who gathered in 1795 and M.J. Guillaume, the editor of the *Procès-Verbaux*. If the French politicians from the late 18th century treated the *Covenant of the Prophet with the Christians of the World* as factual and historical, the editor, writing in the early 20th century, treats the treaty with disdain. "The *Pact of Muhammad in Favor of the Christians*," he writes, "is an apocryphal Arab document" (Guillaume 831, B). In another place, Guillaume speaks of the "the so-called *Treaty* or *Pact of Muhammad with the Christians*" (858, note 4). Rather than merely a personal difference, Guillaume seems to embody a shift of conscience that took place during the transition from Catholic kingdom to secular French Republic. The Western world, which once viewed the *Testament of the Prophet* as an awe-inspiring masterpiece of diplomacy and tolerance to be emulated, commenced to view Islamic institutions with contempt. If the *shari'ah* is slandered on a daily basis by the enemies of Islam in the Western world and their allies in the Eastern world, it was once a source of inspiration in Europe and the Americas. Writing in 1826, M. Grassi (Alfio) spoke of the superiority of the *shari'ah* in the following terms:

> The *Charter of Muhammad* only is inviolable: it only exists, without modification, for a number of centuries, since the time of its founder. Its laws govern immense population of our globe. The Turkish government, and the other governments that have adopted it, owe their stability and power to its inviolability. None has the right to undermine it, to change it, to add to it, or to remove a single page from it, a single line, a single word, without incurring the death penalty. The laws of this Charter are obligatory for the rich, for the poor, and even for the prince himself. (front page)

When considering the ideal legal system to implement in the Americas after independence, both Simón Bolívar (1783–1830 CE) and José Martí (1853–1895 CE) spoke of the superiority of the Qur'an over the American Constitution. It seems that so long as Muslims were powerful, they were treated with respect and their legal systems were regarded with reverence. However, as the last Islamic Superpower, the Ottoman Empire, started to wane, admiration turns into disdain as the Western world attempted to assert its dominance over the final, unconquered, remains of the Muslim world. Weakness is not a source of admiration; in both politics and economics, it is power and wealth that inspire respect.

If many scholars defended the *Covenant of the Prophet Muhammad with the Christians of the World*, there are some that remained neutral. Based on the limited amount of information available at the time, Johann Heinrich Hottinger (1620–1667 CE) adopted a cautious attitude and remained neutral on the subject. He could not confidently claim that the covenant was authentic. Nor did he feel that there was sufficient evidence to dismiss it as a forgery. While he admits that a treaty was made between the Prophet and the Nestorians, Layard (1817–1894 CE) points out that the actual covenant that has reached us "has been rejected as a forgery by several European critics, whilst its authenticity is admitted by early Mohammedan and Eastern Christian writers" (Layard 207). This statement, however, is slanted. As true as it may be that several European critics have rejected the covenant as a forgery, it is equally true that a large number of Western scholars have also recognized it as genuine. Hence, Layard does not provide a complete picture of the scholarly debate on the subject. Luke also reports that the Prophet "is said to have been visited by Ishu-yahb II, who was Patriarch of the Nestorians at the time of the Arab conquest and to have granted him the charter of privileges known as the *Testamentum Mahometi*" (68). While he notes that this document was "accepted by early Moslem writers as genuine" (68), he alleges that it is "now generally regarded in the West as of dubious authenticity" (68). This claim, once again, is factually incorrect. The covenant in question continues to cause controversy between those who oppose it and those who recognize it.

If the authors who attempted to be objective have fallen short, the situation with scholars who oppose the covenant is all the more serious. This opposing camp includes Hugo Grotius (1583–1645 CE), Gisbertus Voëtius (1589–1676 CE), Johannes Hoornbeek (1617–1666 CE), Bespier, Dean Humphrey Prideaux (1648–1724 CE), Pierre Bayle (1647–1706 CE), Ignaz von Döllinger (1799–1890 CE), and Johann Lorenz von Mosheim (1693–1755 CE). As this latter explains,

> Those who with Grotius reject this *Testament*, suppose it was fabricated by the monks living in Syria and Arabia, to circumvent their hard masters, the Mohammedans. Nor is the supposition incredible. For the monks of Mount Sinai formerly showed a similar edict of Mohammed, which they said he drew up while a private man; an edict exceedingly favorable to them, and beyond all controversy fraudulently drawn up by themselves. The fraud was sufficiently evident; yet the Mohammedans, a people destitute of all erudition believed it was a genuine ordinance of their prophet, and they believe so still. This imposition is treated by Cantemir, *Hist. de l'Empire Ottoman*, tome ii, p. 269 &c. The argument therefore which Renaudot and others draw in favor of the *Testament* in question, from the acknowledgement of its authenticity by the Mohammedans, is of little weight; because in things of this nature, no people could be more easily imposed upon than the rude and illiterate Mohammedans. Nor is the argument of more force which the opposers of the *Testament* draw from the difference of its style from that of the *Koran*. For it is not necessary to suppose that Mohammed himself composed this *Testament*; he might have employed his secretary. But however dubious the *Testament* itself may be, the subject matter of it is not doubtful. For learned men have proved by powerful arguments, that Mohammed originally would allow no injury to be offered to the Christians and especially to the Nestorians. (255)

The arguments of Mosheim and his predecessors are all based on prejudice. For them, the Prophet could never have conceivably offered such an "exceedingly favorable" edict. Muhammad, in their minds, was not a man capable of such mercy. Mosheim and his associates express overtly racist and prejudiced views of Arabs and Turks. Muslims, after all, are far too stupid and ignorant to differentiate between a genuine and fraudulent ordinance of the Prophet Muhammad. For Mosheim, Muslims are illiterate, primitive people.

Of course, most Muslims feel the same about Mosheim and his ilk. Then, in a startling *volte-face*, Mosheim undermines his own arguments and admits that while the *Testament* in question is false, its content is correct; namely, that Muhammad would never allow the Christians, and especially the Nestorians, to suffer any injury at the hands of Muslims. In an additional blow, a footnote was added by an editor which further emasculates his arguments. It reads:

> This testament is a formal compact between Mohammed on the one part, and the Nestorians and Monophysites on the other. He promises to them his protection, and they promise to him loyalty and obedience. He promises them entire religious freedom; and they promise him support against his enemies. Mohammed might have deemed it sound policy to conclude such a treaty with these sectaries; that by their aid he might subdue the countries of Asia subject to the Greek emperors. (254–255)

The same two-pronged offensive is undertaken by Dollinger. He argues that "The so-called *Testament of Muhammad*, which was brought by Pacifique Scaliger, a Capuchin missionary, and printed in Paris since 1630, as well as another document supposedly granted by the Prophet to the monks of Mount Sinai, all shows signs of being fictitious" (291). Despite the fact that they contain rights similar to those granted to the Christians of Najran, Dollinger alleges that these two other testaments "would have placed Christians in a better position than the Muslims themselves as Tychsen observes in his dissertation: *De Muhammoede aliarum religionum sectatores tolerantes* (T. XV des Mémoires de la société de Goettingue)" (291). In what can only be described as a self-defeating argument, Dollinger admits that the Prophet made a covenant with the Christians of Najran and other religious communities (291). To all evidence, Dollinger was ignorant of the text of the *Covenant of the Prophet Muhammad with the Christians of Najran*. While he may have read summaries of it in Abu Dawud (d. 889 CE), for example, or al-Tabari (d. 923 CE), he clearly did not read the covenant itself. Had he done so, he would have realized that it is almost identical in content to the *Testament of Muhammad*. Hence, if he recognizes that the *Covenant of the Prophet Muhammad with the Christians of Najran* is authentic, he is admitting, by default, that the *Covenant of the Prophet Muhammad with the Christians of the World* is equally authentic.

When Addison asked a person who was very skilled in the Arabic language what he thought of the treaty of Muhammad with the Christians, the individual replied that, when he read it, he had the sense that it was spurious (Bayle 241). The individual in question argued that the covenant in question did not resemble the Qur'an in the least bit (241). He also pointed out that the preface mentioned that it has been brought from the East by Pacifique Scaliger (241). The reader concluded that it was very probable that the covenant had been forged by the missionary in question (Bayle 241).

These arguments, however, are amateurish. If there is one thing that is clear to any scholar of the Arabic language it is that the Qur'an was positively not the product of Muhammad's mind and pen. In fact, there is nothing at all like it in the entire body of Arabic literature. It is a unique and inimitable work which stands alone. If we cast aside weak traditions, and focus on the select group of sayings which are admitted as authentic by both Muslim and non-Muslim authorities, the style of the Qur'an and the *hadith* are as different as day and night. The Prophet Muhammad was a man of masterful eloquence. However, his words cannot compare to those of the Creator. The Qur'an has a style of its own and Muhammad had a voice of his own. In fact, he was the master of many modes of delivery. His covenants, treaties, and pacts are written in a characteristic style; his sermons, in a different style; his wisdom sayings in still another. Like any talented soul, he modified his delivery depending on genre and target audience. So, to claim that the *Covenant of the Prophet Muhammad with the Christians of the World* is forged simply because it differs from the Qur'an in style is based on a fundamentally false premise—as if Shakespeare could never have written both tragedies and comedies, both short poems and epic-length poems, or William Blake have composed not only epics and lyric poems, but also satires, letters, exegetical commentaries, etc. Furthermore, the fact that Father Scaliger brought the manuscript back to Europe does not constitute proof of forgery. These conclusions are all the result of a reading of the testament rooted in ignorance and prejudice.

Since many scholars operate on the basis of a negative view of the Prophet Muhammad and are inherently hostile towards Islam, any evidence that would call into question their stereotypes is immediately rejected. Edwin E. Jacques, for example, seeking to kill two birds with one stone, confidently claims that "both the existing documents, the *Testamentum* and the *Pactum Muhammedis*, assuring liberal privileges to all Christians, are spurious" (203). In his mind, it is inconceivable that Muhammad would grant any such rights to Christians. The same can be said of Johann Karl Ludwig Gieseler (1792–1854 CE) who equally asserts that "both the *Testamentum et pactiones initae inter Mohammedem et Christiana fidei cultores* . . . and the *Pactum Muhammedis, quod indulsit Monachis mentis Siani et Christianis in universum* . . . in which distinguished privileges are secured to all Christians, are spurious" (563, note 7).

If many of the earliest scholars to study the *Covenant of the Prophet with the Christians of the World* were divided when it came to issues of authenticity, the situation soon seems to have changed. In this regard, a review of the 1690 Hamburgh edition of the *Testamentum et pactiones* is especially revealing. Henri Basnage de Beauval (1657–1710 CE) has the following to say about this intriguing work:

> This is quite a singular work. It is a type of contract between Muhammad and the Christians. It is true that Grotius doubted it and that it looks like pious fraud. However, Mr. Hinkleman assures us that scholars have set aside their suspicions since the Arabic text was first brought from the East by Father Pacifique Scaliger. Mr. Hinkleman is himself a just judge. He is far too well-versed in Oriental languages to be duped. The date, which belongs to the fourth year of the *hijrah*, and which corresponds to the 626th year of the Christian era, is, for him, a strong indication of the document's authenticity. For, as Abu al-Faraj reports, the Jews had some major conflicts with Muhammad at that time. This skilled Imposter, who did not want Christians to turn against him, and who wanted to cause anguish to the Jews by means of this preference, declared himself the protector of the Christians. He also attempted to appear gentle and peaceful in order to avoid inciting individuals, thereby establishing his domination more securely by tenderness as opposed to force. This is why he inserted in his Qur'an favorable sentiments for all religions, declaring that all people without distinction, whether or not they were Jews and Christians, who believed in God, the Day of Judgment, and who did good deeds, had nothing to fear from divine justice. Let us see what this *Patent of Muhammad* contains.
>
> At the beginning, Muhammad describes himself as the *Messenger of God* who was sent to instruct people and to announce the truth that was entrusted to him. He then promises the Christians, on his behalf and that of his followers, to defend them against everything; to protect their churches and their monasteries; to help rebuild them; and to exempt them from taxes on the condition that Christians do not provide the enemies of Muhammad with weapons or an escape route. And, in order to ensure that the validity of this *Testament* is not revoked, it is signed by thirty-three Muslims. Perhaps Muslims will not find the full force of Asiatic style nor the hyperboles of their so-called Prophet. (Basnage de Beauval 81–82)

This book review, which was printed in *Histoire des ouvrages des savans*, is remarkable in many regards. To commence, it insists that Hinkleman was perfectly proficient in the Arabic language. In other words, unlike some of the scholars who dismissed the covenant as being of dubious authenticity, Hinkleman could actually read it in its original. He was thus a scholar operating within his area of expertise, which was not the case with others. Evidently, the opinion of a specialist far outweighs the opinion of one who is not an expert. While the printed opinions of many of these early critics have been cited for centuries, Hinkleman, who was their contemporary, affirms that they changed their minds. While they initially believed that the *Testamentum et pactiones* was a fraud, Hinkleman states that they eventually overcame their doubts. While there was much debate and discussion, and the scholarly community was divided, Hinckleman affirms that they eventually came to a consensus concerning the covenant's authenticity. Hinkleman also provides some important insight into the timing of the covenant in question. As much as he had hoped that the Jews would recognize and follow him, the violent reaction of the Jewish community, and their betrayal of the covenant in which they had entered with the Prophet obliged him to explore an alternative strategy. Turning away from the Jews, as he turned away from Jerusalem in favor of Mecca for the purpose of prayer, the Prophet sought the support and solidarity of the Christian community. Since he was struggling against internal enemies, namely, the Jews that lived in and around Medina, the Prophet's position was potentially precarious: an attack by outside enemies, Christians in this case, could have caused the fledgling Islamic State to collapse. As such, the Messenger of Allah established, and in some cases re-established, treaties with the surrounding Christian communities. These, in turn, acted as buffers between the Islamic State and the Byzantine Empire. The Prophet had seen how the polytheists had attempted to turn the Abyssinian Christians against the Prophet. The Messenger of Allah, and his Companions, acted swiftly and efficiently in establishing ties of friendship with this regional superpower. The Prophet was also aware of the machinations between Abu Sufyan with Heraclius. Consequently, the Messenger of Allah was wise to win the favor of the oppressed Monophysite Christians who lived on the margins of the Byzantine Empire. Well aware of the divisions which existed in Christianity, and the polemics that fomented them, the Prophet used these weaknesses to his advantage, making friends out of those who could have been foes. Nowadays, we imagine that strategic intelligence is inseparable from unprincipled duplicity and hypocrisy, as if Jesus' "render unto Caesar the things that are Caesar's and to God the things that are God's" were an example of prevarication and low cunning, not a brilliant escape from a trap laid for him by the Scribes and Pharisees that also gave him the chance to illustrate important principles. Likewise, Allah granted Muhammad an unprecedented ability, and opportunity, to express spiritual realities in terms of social and political action.

Unlike other critics, who only focus on the generous concessions granted by the Prophet in his covenant, Basnage de Beauval (1657–1710 CE) has the good sense to recognize what he received in return. With only some semi-autonomous statelets separating the Muslims from the Byzantines, the Prophet wanted to slow any major movement of Christian troops from the northern empire. Without shelter, support, or supplies from the Christian communities on the way, the Byzantine army could never enter the Hijaz and engage the Army of Muhammad. Tax exemptions, as with the monks of Mount Sinai, and limited taxes, as with other Christian communities, were a small price to pay to slow down the potential progress of enemy forces. Plus, it was a necessary diplomatic step in the preparation of an Islamic advance into the Levant, Egypt, and beyond. Basnage de Beauval refers to the fact that the *Testamentum et pactiones* does not share the same style as the Qur'an. However, he seems to realize that this is an unpretentious treaty written in the legal style of the time and not a document, like the Qur'an, which burst upon the scene as a divine literary miracle.

In the late 19th century, Sir Travers Twiss (1809–1897 CE) made some interesting comments concerning the *Covenant of the Prophet Muhammad with the Christians of the World*. He points out, for example, that Murad III (1546–1595) employed the term "conditions" to describe the twenty-two privileges he granted to Queen Elizabeth of England (1533–1603 CE) (431). As Twiss observes, this is the identical term used by the Prophet Muhammad in his pact with Christians in general and which dates from the fourth year of the *hijrah* (625 CE) (431). While he admits that its authenticity is called into question, he observes that this ancient document uses the term "conditions" in a manner that is perfectly harmonious with the

Qur'an (431). Twiss also stresses that the term "conditions" is also found in the second oldest Islamic covenant, namely, the *Capitulations of Caliph 'Umar*, known as the *Treaty of 'Umar* (432). The implications are clear. The *Treaty of 'Umar* speaks of "conditions" imposed on the Christians. The *Testament of Muhammad* speaks of "conditions" imposed on the Christians. And the Qur'an itself speaks of the "conditions" for granting *aman* or security to treaty-bound Christians. In other words, the *Treaty of 'Umar* was influenced by the *Testament of Muhammad* which, in turn, was influenced by the Qur'an. Speaking of the *Capitulations of Caliph 'Umar*, Twiss has this to say:

> The authenticity of this document has also been called into question. However, its ancient nature is indisputable. Furthermore, it is reasonable to suppose that if the so-called testament of the Prophet Muhammad (which dates from the year 625) and the so-called capitulations of the Caliph 'Umar (which date from the year 636) were both unauthentic then the monks who would have invented them would have been more careful in their redaction to employ a language that was not of the sort that would astonish their contemporaries by being in disagreement with Muslim laws and, consequently, inadmissible in their Muslim courts. (432)

The arguments made by Twiss are impressive. If the *Treaty of 'Umar* was falsified under Umayyad or 'Abbasid times, why would the Christians have included elements which were in contradiction to the legal code that was currently in place? If the *Testament of Muhammad* was falsified under Fatimid rule, why would the monks have included as witnesses Companions who were viewed unfavorably by the authorities? Why not concoct a covenant signed and witnessed by the Sahabahs who were staunch supporters of Imam 'Ali's (d. 661 CE) right to succession? And why ask for tax exemptions when most of the other treaties concluded by the Prophet required allies to pay tribute? As Twiss argues, it was not necessary for the privileges accorded to the People of the Book take the form of a unilateral concession on the part of the Caliph (432) [or even the Prophet for that matter]. It could have been a treaty between two parties (432). So, according to the analysis of Twiss, both the form and content of the *Testament of Muhammad* and the *Treaty of 'Umar* show clear signs of authenticity.

In "Lettre XLI" of Giovanni Paolo Marana's (1642–1693 CE) epistolary novel, *L'Espion dans les cours des princes chrétiens*, his protagonist, a Turkish spy working for the count of the Ottoman Empire in the courts of Europe, particularly France, mentions that he used to regularly visit the Royal Library. He relates that during the time of Cardenal Mazari, he came across a manuscript on which was written: *Original du traité de Mahomet, prophète des Arabes avec ceux qui font profession de la foi de Jésus* (156). The purpose of the novel, it must be mentioned, was to present European Christian readers with a Turkish Muslim view of both Europe and the Orient. The author, Marana, was a Marrano or a Jewish person who had been compelled to convert to Christianity. While he probably could not express his appreciation for Muslims and Turks openly, his ingenious literary device allowed him unprecedented freedom to share his sympathies. This fourth volume, which was published in 1697, demonstrates intimate familiarity with the *Testament of Muhammad* and its content, so much so that the author may actually have seen the original copy in the Royal Library. Speaking of the manuscript of the covenant, he writes that: "There was a note in Latin on the bottom stated that 'this document was found in the Convent of the Christian brothers of Mount Carmel.'" (156) The spy, who is supposedly writing to Abrahim Eli Zeid, the "predicateur du Serrail" or Imam of the Ottoman Porte, explains that:

> I have copies of this parchment & I sent it to you here enclosed, so that you can judge whether it is authentic or counterfeit. The Christians affirm that this covenant was truly made by the Ambassador of God, and, consequently, they reproach us claiming that we are all disobeying our Legislator, & violating the treaty which was signed and sealed by the one we call the Seal of the Prophets; a treaty which was witnesses by our four main legal authorities, Abu Bakr, 'Uthman, and 'Ali. (156)

If Marana was actually reflecting the attitude of

the time, which he appears to be deliberately doing, some Christians may have upheld the *Testament of the Prophet* and attempted to hold it over the heads of the Turks. It also suggests that some Turks were not certain whether the covenant was genuine; hence, the need for the spy to send it to Istanbul for the purpose of authentication. While there are some scattered references to the possibility that the Turks rejected the covenant as a fraud, such as Ricaut (1629–1700 CE), who claims that "the Turks deny that this *Treaty* was made Muhammad with the Christians," (332) the vast majority of sources insist that they recognized it as trustworthy. Marana's fictional Turkish spy, however, proceeds to address the pertinent question of who actually broke the covenant? As he explains to the religious authority he is supposedly addressing,

> If you take the time to examine this manuscript, you will certainly know whether it was us or them who violated this law. Supposing that it was, as they allege, the testament of the Prophet, it is certain that it grants various advantages to the partisans of Jesus, like leaving them in peace, protecting them, loving them, exempting them from taxes and tribute, giving them freedom of conscience, and permission to marry as they see fit, etc. It is no less certain, however, that he only granted them these things under certain conditions, that they were obliged to observe on their part, like, for example, that none of them would provide shelter to the enemies of the true Believers, engage in correspondence with them, furnish them directly with arms, horses, money, or other things required for war; but, on the contrary, they would receive Muslims in their homes, would grant them shelter for three days, & would defend them against their enemies. If the Christians have contravened any of these articles, the Prophet declares the treaty null and void & destitutes them from the advantages which were provide to them therein. You will see that the parties solemnly and mutually engage themselves to religiously observe the content of the treaty until the very end.
>
> The question, which needs to be asked, is whether it was us or the Christians who first violated these articles? For, if it can be proved that the Christians are the aggressors, then they have no grounds to complain of their misfortune or to accuse the true Believers, as they ordinarily do through their oppression & tyranny, since it is manifest that the only harm that has befallen them results from their violation of the law that had been given to them. Their infidelity has annulled the covenant of God & His Prophet and removed them from the advantages they could have claimed for themselves had they only faithfully observed it on their part. Be that as it may, the Prophet is not to blame in the least: may the guilt rest upon those who have committed the crime. (156–157)

The arguments of Giovani Paolo Marana's protagonist are not without resonance. If there were, and continue to be, unbelievers who wish to co-opt the covenants of the Prophet in order to shame Muslims into submission or to convince them to support their geo-political plans for the Islamic world, the treaties of Muhammad apply only and exclusively to People of the Book who are peaceful. "But we are the good ones!" some Westerners will say; "We only seek to bring you the benefits of freedom, liberty, and democracy" as they invade, occupy, and exploit oppressed Muslim nations. Hence comes the "good Muslim" versus "bad Muslim" dichotomy which has been so eloquently exposed by Mahmoud Mamdani. The "good Muslim" is the one who supports Western imperialism while the "bad Muslim" is the one who opposes such an agenda. Repeating the errors they made in the past, namely, siding with Christian powers against Muslim political entities, only to find themselves betrayed by their former allies, the so-called Muslim rulers of Saudi Arabia, Jordan, Egypt, Kuwait, Qatar, Oman, and the United Arab Emirates, side with secularized Christians from the United States and Western Europe to overthrow and destroy any Muslim nation that attempts to assert even a minimal degree of independence and sovereignty. This is not to say that the covenants of the Prophet are null and void. On the contrary, I am convinced that they remain authoritative and applicable until the Day of Judgment. However, they apply exclusively to peaceful Christian communities, whether they live as minorities in the midst of Muslim majorities or share the same country with a more or less equal number of non-Muslims, or they live abroad, in their own independent nations, where they are the overwhelming majority. In the last case, Muslims would expect, and, in fact, they would demand, that Muslim minorities living in Christian or secular liberal nations receive the same or similar rights as the People of the Book receive under an Islamic State where the *Covenant of the Prophet* is recognized and applied.

Commentary on the Content of the Covenant (1630)

Contrary to convention, the *Covenant of the Prophet Muhammad with the Christians of the World* does not commence with the *basmallah*, the traditional invocation of Islam which appears at the beginning of documents. If anything, its suppression was an editorial decision of Gabriel Sionita. After all, one can only assume that the *Covenant* was preceded by "In the Name of Allah, the Most Compassionate, the Most Merciful," or one of its many variants involving other attributes of the Divinity. The author of the *Covenant* immediately identifies himself, established his authority, and explains the reason for which he writes:

> It was written by Muhammad, the Messenger of Allah, the proclaimer and warner [*bashiran wa nadhiran*], to all the people [*al-nas kaffah*], [Muhammad], who is entitled to the protection of Allah [*wadi'at Allah*] in truth, and as a proof [*hujjah*] of Allah for the Christian religion [*din al-nasraniyyah*] in the eastern land and its west, its Arabs and non-Arabs [*fasihiha wa 'ajamiha*], near or far, known or unknown.

Muhammad is the Messenger of Allah who was sent as a proclaimer and warner, not only to the Arabs, but rather to humanity as a whole. Since it is not always clear to which noun the indirect object pronoun refers to in Arabic, this sentence could be interpreted in many ways. Is it the people who are entitled to the protection of Allah or is it the Prophet? Is the *Covenant* a proof of Allah or is the Messenger of Allah? The reading I have provided represents one possibility. Other translators may offer other readings. The expression *wadi'at Allah*, for example, is a challenge to translate. The translation provided by Van Dyke gives "emanated from God" and makes it refer to the Christian religion. Pococke provides "careful guardian of the whole world" while Arundale writes "confidant of God, and charged with the keeping of all created beings." The English translation in M. Mauchin's rendition which appears in Baron Marie-Joseph de Géramb offers "the friend of God, and that he is charged with the care of all his creatures." The translation that appears in Skrobucha gives "promises of God" while Anton F. Haddad writes "as a trust on the part of God." While it may convey a wide range of meanings, I am relatively secure that *wadi'at Allah*, in this case, signifies that the Christians are Allah's trust among His Creations. The Prophet then proceeds to describe the nature of the *Covenant* and what it constitutes:

> This document [*kitaban*], which has been prepared for them, constitutes an authoritative covenant [*'ahdan mariyyan*], a well-known certificate [*sijlan manshuran*], and a testament [*wasiyyah*] from him which must be respected and which will protect them.

The *Covenant* is a legal document, a binding covenant, edict, contract, and decree; a certificate, as well as a testament, a last will, and a final set of counsels. The use of the word *wasiyyah*, which means "a final will and testament," conveys that this covenant was not a fleeting, politically-motivated document, an accord that was time-bound and easily revocable. If we are dealing with the definitive will of the Prophet, it must be respected by Muslims and only major violations on the part of Christians could justify breaking it. These are not my words, but those of the Messenger of Allah himself:

> Whoever holds to Islam, abides by it, and whoever breaks the covenant contained in this testament, and transgresses [*khalafahu*] it among the non-Muslims, and contradicts what I commanded in it, he has violated the covenant of Allah [*'ahd Allah*], denies the oath of Allah [*mithaq Allah*] and has disdained his protection [*dhimmah*] whether he is a

Sultan or anyone else among the believers and the Muslims.

Abiding by the *Covenant of the Prophet* is equated with faith and attachment to Islam while violating it implies the opposite. Christians, as well, are warned that any discord or disobedience with regard to the terms of the Covenant would effectively exclude them therefrom. If the Prophet many times took the initiative to contact other communities, the Covenant in question was actually the response to a request as we read below:

> I started by committing myself to the Covenant, granted alliances [*'uhud*] and pledges [*mawathiq*] to those who requested it from me and from all of my Muslim Community [*millati min al-muslimin*]. I gave them the Covenant of Allah [*'ahd Allah*] and His Pledge [*mithaq*] and I placed them under the safeguard of His Prophets, His Chosen Ones [*asfiya*], His Friends [*awliyya'*] from among all the Believers [*mu'minin*] and the Muslims over time. My protection [*dhimmati*] and my security [*mithaqi*] represent the most solid covenant that Allah, the Most Exalted, has given a prophet sent in truth to demand obedience, to give obligations [*farida*], and to respect the covenant [*'ahd*].

A curious feature of this covenant includes the use of the word *ahli* or "families" which suggests a Shi'ite reading. The partisans of 'Ali always associate the Prophet with his *ahl al-bayt*. As such, when they bless the Messenger of Allah, they customarily bless his family as well. While Sunnis include all Muslims in the family of the Prophet, the Shi'ites are very precise as to those who are included in the People of the House (33:33); they are the Purified Five: the Prophet, Fatimah, 'Ali, Hasan, and Husayn. The Messenger of Allah proceeds to place the Christians under the protection of the Prophets and Messengers, of whom he is the last, as well as his Elect and his Saints. For Wahhabis, this would be tantamount to heresy. For those Sunnis who have not morphed into Salafis as a result of immense Saudi propaganda funds, the *awliyya' al-salihin* would encompass an important group of saintly figures, past and present. For Shi'ites, the Saints and Elects are none other than Fatimah al-Zahra, 'Ali, and the eleven successive Imams from among their offspring. If this is the right reading, and the Prophet did grant this covenant in both his name and the name of his Progeny, this could serve as further evidence of the legitimacy of the Imamate. The Prophet then pledges to:

> protect their judges in my fortified borderlines [*fi thughuri*] with my horses and my men, my helpers, and my followers, from among the Believers, from every region among the regions of the enemy, whether they be far away or close by, whether they be at peace or at war, I safeguard them. I grant security to their churches, their places of pilgrimage [*siyahah*] wherever they are and wherever they may be found, be they in the mountains or the valleys, in the caves or the inhabited regions, in the plains or the desert, or in buildings; and that I protect their religion and their property wherever they are and wherever they may be found in land or at sea, in the East or West, the same way that I protect myself, my successors [*khatimi*], and the People of my Community [*ahl al-millati*] among the Believers and the Muslims.

When the Prophet promises to protect specific Christian groups such as the Greek Orthodox Church, Assyrians, Armenians, and others, his commitment was not limited to the lands of Islam but extended to any place where his allies were found. For example, if the Armenians were attacked by the Byzantines, the Prophet would have sent his troops to protect and defend them. The Islamic State thus protects its citizens, regardless of their religion, both at home and abroad. This segment also contains an unusual choice of words: specifically, the term *khatimi*. Although I have translated it as "successors," based on the context, the word literally means "rings" or "seals" and appears in the Qur'an, which reads: "Muhammad is not the father of any of your men, but he is the Messenger of Allah, and the seal of the Prophets and God has full knowledge of all things" (33:40). There are also a large number of traditions to this effect. If the Prophet actually spoke of his seals, they may have been the Seals of the Imamate as opposed to the Seals of Prophecy. According to

Shiʿite beliefs, the door of divine guidance has never closed. When the prophethood came to an end, the gate of the Imamate was opened, the first Imam being ʿAli and the final Imam, being Muhammad al-Mahdi, the last of twelve. This, of course, is simply one reading. The words that were written as *ahli* and *khatimi* may have been misread. If so, this might help us pin-point the geographic location from which this copy of the *Covenant* originates. It may have passed through the hands of Levantine Shiʿites from what is now current-day Lebanon or Syria. Despite the possibility of Shiʿite, Sunni, Sufi, and Christian readings, which may be perceived from the selection of words used to transcribe ambiguous combinations of consonants, the command of the Prophet is clear:

> I place them under my protection from any damage or harm [*makruh*]; to exempt them from any requisitions or any onerous obligations. I am behind them, protecting them myself, by means of my followers, my helpers, and the members of my religious community [*ahl al-millati*].

Since it is the Prophet Muhammad himself who protects his Christian allies, to oppose his accord would be an act of apostasy. By adhering to the *Covenant*, however, and protecting peaceful Christians who live under the protection of Islam, Muslims act as representatives of the Prophet for the world. If the Prophet Muhammad was a mercy to humankind, it was because he was a reflection of the Most Merciful. As the walking Qur'an, he embodied all of the attributes of Allah. Muslims, however, seem to forget, or simply not care, that their every actions reflect upon the Prophet. They can thus be the pride of the Prophet or his crying shame. The Prophet explains his obligations as such:

> Having authority over them, I must govern them, protecting them from all damage and ensuring that no harm happens to them that does not happen to me and my Companions who, along with me, protect this ascribed authority [*nisbatu al-amr*].

This is the Golden Rule which is shared by all major religious traditions. The meaning of the expression *nisbatu al-amr* elicited a great deal of debate and discussion among the Arabic linguists I consulted. After much research, they concluded that it derives from *nasaba/yansubu*, which means "to ascribe"; the meaning thus being "the ascribed authority." As my colleagues observed, this expression was mostly used in Shi'ite texts, a fact that may shed some light on the "coded" expression. The first stipulation provided by the Prophet pertains to the economic realm since the economy is the basis of a sound society.

> I remove from them the harm from taxes and loans in the supplies borne to the People of the Pact [*ahl al-ʿahd*] from loan [*ʿariyah*] and land tribute [*kharaj*] except what they themselves consent to give. They should not be compelled in this matter.

What the Messenger of Allah meant by loan is unclear. In the past however, citizens were often obliged to lend man-power, horses, and arms, among other items, to the State under certain circumstances. They also had to pay land tribute. The Prophet, as a gesture of good-will, opposed both measures. Moving from the economic, the Prophet promises both freedom of movement and freedom of religion:

> It is not permitted to remove a bishop from his bishopric or a Christian from his Christianity, a monk from his monastic life, or a pilgrim from his pilgrimage, or a hermit monk from his tower. Nor is it permitted to destroy any part of their churches, to take parts of their buildings to construct mosques or the homes of Muslims. Whoever does such a thing will have violated the pact of Allah, disobeyed his Messenger, and betrayed the Divine Alliance.

Since the covenant in question was made with a religious community, supposedly the Monastery of Mount Carmel in the Holy Land, "[i]t is not permitted to impose a capitation [*jizyah*] or any kind of tax on monks or bishops only that which they are prepared to give willingly." This tax exemption, however, is limited to religious establishments. And while taxed, laypeople are protected from over-taxation:

> The capitation [*jizyah*] upon owners of large businesses, and divers, and those who exploit mines for

precious stones, gold and silver, and those who are wealthy, and powerful, among those who have professed Christianity, may not surpass more than twelve *dirhams* per year, so long as they are inhabitants of these countries or residents, and not travelers.

Taxation, in the Prophet's plan, is limited to sedentary populations and does not extend to travelers and nomads unless they inherit land over which the ruler has a right:

> The traveler, or the resident whose place [of residence] is unknown, is not obliged to pay the land tribute [*kharaj*] or the poll-tax [*jizyah*] unless he has inherited land over which the ruler [*sultan*] has a monetary right. He must pay the money [*mal*] as others without, however, the charges unjustly exceeding the measure of their means [or strength].

Workers are of particular concern to the Prophet. While he does not wish to suffocate landowners, neither does he desire to oppress workers by means of heavy taxation.

> As for the labor force which the owners spend upon to cultivate these lands, to render them fertile, and to harvest them, they are not to be taxed excessively. Let them pay in the same fashion that was imposed on other similar tributaries.

Turning to military matters, the Messenger of Allah explains that non-Muslims under Muslim protection are not subject to compulsory service.

> The free non-Muslims enjoying Muslim protection [*ahl al-dhimmah*] will not be obliged to go to war with the Muslims in order to combat their enemies, to attack them, and to seize them. Indeed, such free non-Muslims [*ahl al-dhimmah*] will not engage in war along with the Muslims. It is precisely to discharge them of this obligation that this pact has been granted to them as well as to assure them the help and protection on the part of the Muslims. They will not be obliged to go out with the Muslims to meet their enemies or be forced to give their horses, their arms, unless they contribute to the cause freely. Whoever does so will be recognized for his action.

The method of *da'wah* or the dissemination of the Islamic faith is not one of force but one of example and eloquent and intelligent exposition. The position of the Prophet regarding religious rights sets a historical precedent:

> No Christian will be made Muslim by force: *And dispute ye not with the People of the Book, except with means better* [29:46]. They must be covered by the wing of mercy. Repel every harm that could reach them wherever they may find themselves and in any country in which they are.

In an Islamic society, human beings have freedom of conscience: "[t]here is no compulsion in religion" (2:256). Christians, as all other individuals, are to be treated kindly, gently, and with affection. They are to be protected from enemies both foreign and domestic. And that is not all:

> If a Christian were to commit a crime or an offense, Muslims must provide him with help, defense, and protection. They should pardon his offense and encourage his victim to reconcile with him, urging him to pardon him or to receive compensation in return.

If the member of a minority makes a mistake, this is not a call to arms or an excuse to organize a pogrom. This is a call for calm, reason, and reconciliation, not a pretext to "cleanse" a community from those who are different. Muslims, Jews, and Christians, in fact all believers, must understand that they should stand as one in opposition to atheism. As the Prophet explains, those who believe form but a single body:

> The Muslims must not abandon the Christians and leave them without help and assistance since I have made this pact with them on behalf of Allah to ensure that whatever good befell Muslims it would befall them as well and that whatever harm befell Muslims would befall them as well. In virtue of this pact, they have obtained inviolable rights to enjoy our protection, to be protected from any infringement of their rights, so that they will be bound to the Muslims both in good and bad fortune.

Although there is unity in religious diversity, there is no place for syncretism. Equality does not mean that all are identical. Each religious system is coherent within itself. Each religion is an ecosystem. Combining two ecosystems would ruin the fragile ecological balance. There are barriers in nature and the universe. There are also certain boundaries within religious that need to be respected. This includes, for example, certain types of mixed marriages which can cause conflict within families and society. Thus, the Prophet has decreed that:

> Christians must not be subject to suffer, by abuse, on the subject of marriages which they do not desire. Muslims should not take Christian girls in marriage against the will of their parents, nor should they oppress their families in the event that they refused their offers of engagement and marriage. Such marriages should not take place without their desire and agreement and without their approval and consent.
>
> If a Muslim takes a Christian woman as a wife, he must respect her Christian beliefs. He will give her freedom to listen to her [clerical] superiors as she desires, to follow the path of her own religion, and he will not force her to leave it. Whoever, despite this order, forces his wife to act contrary to her religion in any aspect whatsoever he will have broken the alliance of Allah and will enter into open rebellion against the pact of His Messenger, and Allah will count him among the impostors.

While Muslims may not agree with Christians on all matters doctrinal, they must respect Christianity as a crystallization of the divine message. Although, from a Muslim perspective, certain Christian beliefs and practices are incorrect, many Christian beliefs are correct from an Islamic standpoint. The same can be said of Judaism. The similarities between Islam, Christianity, and Judaism far outweigh any differences. To disrespect Christianity it to disrespect Christ in the same fashion that disrespecting Judaism is to disrespect Moses. Muslims do not have *carte blanche* to denigrate divinely revealed religions and then cry bloody murder when Islam is attacked. Jews, Christians, and Muslims must defend each other from the onslaught of the secular New World Order which is deeply committed to destroying them all. Christians, teaches the Prophet, are the neighbors of Muslims. Not only must Muslims grant Christians freedom of religion and provide them with protection, they must treat them in a neighborly fashion. As the Prophet sets forth:

> If the Christians seek the help and assistance of the Muslims in order to repair their churches and their convents or to arrange matters pertaining to their affairs and religion, they, [the Muslims], must help and support them. However, they must not do so with the aim of receiving any reward. On the contrary, they should aim to restore that religion, out of faithfulness to the pact of the Messenger of Allah, by pure donation, and as a meritorious act before Allah and His Messenger.

Despite the fact that this injunction was observed during the days of the Rightly-Guided Caliphs, it was soon abandoned until the end of Ottoman times. Muslims were not only obliged to protect Christian churches, convents, and monasteries, they were supposed to help to build them. Although rulers from the Umayyads to the Ottomans prohibited the destruction of churches, they also prohibited their repair and construction, hoping that Christians would gradually be absorbed into the Muslim community. It may have been a slow, gradual, and gentle process; however, its aim was the eventual assimilation of Christians. This policy was un-Islamic and in clear contradiction of the covenants of the Prophet. It is the product of human weakness and not infallible inspiration. The following clause, though generally observed, was modified by Mu'awiyyah during the early days of Islam:

> In matters of war between them and their enemies, the Muslims will not employ any Christian as a messenger, scout, guide or spy or for any other duty of war. Whoever obliges one of them to do such a thing is an oppressor [*zalim*], a rebel against the Messenger of Allah, and has differed over his testament [*wasiyyah*].

Mu'awiyyah, history informs us, organized the first Muslim navy during the rule of Caliph 'Uthman. In order to do so, he sought the service of Christian sailors and mariners. Such Christians, however, were not obliged to serve in the Muslim forces. They were allies of the Muslims. They were loyal to Islam. And they were hired for their skills. Mu'awiyyah also allowed the Armenians to keep their cavalry, which Caliph 'Uthman maintained, so that the Christian allies of the Muslims could defend themselves from the Byzantines. It was only after the Armenians proved they were incapable of protecting themselves that Mu'awiyyah sent Arab forces to the region. The clause, it appears, prohibits coercion and allows for exceptions in case of voluntary service.

The *Covenant*, the Prophet stresses, was not single-sided. It was not an imposition of Muslims on non-Muslims. It was a settlement which the Christians requested, which they negotiated, and which they agree upon. As such, "[t]hey must hold fast to this covenant [*'ahd*] and respect what they have agreed upon." While the Prophet has granted the Christians many liberties, they have many obligations in return:

> Among other things, none of them may act as a scout, spy, either overtly or covertly, on behalf of an enemy of war, against a Muslim. None of them will shelter the enemies of the Muslims in their homes from which they could await the moment to launch an attack. May these enemies [of the Muslims] never be allowed to halt in their regions, be it in their villages, their oratories, or in any other place belonging to their co-religionists. They must not provide any support to war enemies of the Muslims by furnishing them with weapons, horses, men, or anything else, including greeting them. They must host for three days and three nights any Muslims who halt among them, with their animals. They must offer them, wherever they are found, and wherever they are going, the same food with which they live themselves, without, however, being obliged to endure other annoying or onerous burdens.
>
> If a Muslim needs to hide in one of their homes or oratories, they must grant him hospitality, give him help, and provide him with their food during the entire time he will be among them, making every effort to keep him concealed and to prevent the enemy from finding him, while providing for all of his needs.

"Whoever contravenes or alters the ordinances of this edict," states the Prophet, "will be cast out of the alliance between Allah and His Messenger." "May everyone abide by the treaties and alliances which have been contracted with the kings, the monks [*ruhban*], and the Christians [*nasara*] from the People of the Book," continues the Messenger of Allah, "and every other commitment that each prophet has made with his nation, to assure them safeguard and faithful protection, and to serve them as a guarantee." As final evidence of the *Covenant*'s binding nature, the Prophet states that "[t]his must not be violated or altered until the hour [of the Resurrection] and the end of the world [*dunya*]." This differs from other covenants of the Prophet which include the expression *insha' Allah* or "God willing" which some ill-intended individuals might use to violate its provisions.

The *Covenant* closes with a list of witnesses that, with a few exceptions, seems reasonably sound, but which was probably appended to it to appease *hadith* scholars. While an in-depth analysis of these authorities would be in order, it would be a lengthy endeavor best suited for a subsequent study. The identity of the scribe, Mu'awiyyah, and the date, the fourth year of the *hijrah*, are almost certainly Umayyad additions. Perhaps sensing that the list of witnesses might pose potential problems, the scribe writes that "Allah suffices as a Witness for what is contained in this document [*kitaban*]." The implication, in my opinion, is that the document is authentic regardless of the chain of authorities. The *Covenant* then closes with praises to Allah, the Lord of the Worlds, drawn from *Surah al-Fatihah*, the Opening Chapter of the Qur'an.

Commentary on the Content of the Covenant (1538)

The *Covenant of the Prophet Muhammad with the Christians of the World*, which was published by Gabriel Sionita in Paris in 1630, was said to have been based on a copy uncovered in the Monastery of Mount Carmel in the Holy Land. This document, which was brought to France by Father Pacifique Scaliger, was already said to be old. By following the chain of custody, I was able to locate a copy of this covenant in the National Library of France. The document I found dates to 1538 CE and features marks by Gabriel Sionita. This must, of course, be the source covenant that was published by this Maronite priest in 1630. The problem, however, is that the document contains some marked differences. For reasons which are difficult to explain, the edition printed by Sionita is actually inferior to the source covenant. While most of the body of the work is the same, both the beginning and the end differ substantially. Many words which were completely clear in the source covenant were modified, thus completely changing the meaning of certain sentences. Either Sionita's Arabic was not up to par and his editorial skills were sloppy or he attempted to "improve" and "correct" the text with the opposite result. If this is the actual source covenant, which was allegedly found in the vicinity of Mount Carmel and Mount Lebanon, why does it trace back to Cairo? Was the covenant that Scaliger obtained in Palestine simply copied in Egypt? Or are we dealing with a totally different covenant? Rather than the original *Covenant of the Prophet Muhammad with the Christians of the World* from Palestine, which was printed in 1630, the 1538 document may represent a *Covenant of the Prophet Muhammad with the Christians of Egypt*. Since both covenants have a logical connection, I have opted to include it in this section as opposed to treating it as a totally different manuscript.

Like the *Covenant of the Prophet Muhammad with the Christians of Najran*, which was found in a Nestorian chronicle from the 9th century, the *Covenant of the Prophet Muhammad with the Christians of the World* is the last folio in an Arab Christian anthology of apologetic literature which was copied in 1538. Curiously, whoever indexed the work in Latin, failed to mention it. As such, it could easily be overlooked. The work, written in beautiful Arabic handwriting, is vocalized, a feature typically reserved for religious works like the Qur'an. This is not the case with the *Covenant* alone, but with all the documents found in the book. The *Covenant of the Prophet Muhammad with the Christians of the World* commences "In the Name of Allah, the Creator [*al-Khaliq*], the Living [*al-Hayy*], the Speaking [*al-Natiq*], the One who Remains after the Annihilation of Creation [*al-Baqi ba'd fana' al-khaliq*]." Far from a traditional "In the Name of Allah, the Most Compassionate, the Most Merciful," this covenant commences in a fancier form, calling upon some of the favorite divine attributes of the Sufis. The name *al-Hayy* or the Living is a common *dhikr* or invocatory prayer for Muslim mystics. This formulaic invocation, of course, was probably absent from the original *Covenant of the Prophet*, and was included as a header by some scribe. The scribe then explains that "This is a copy [*nuskhah*] of the covenant [*'ahd*] which was written by Muhammad ibn 'Abd Allah ibn 'Abd al-Muttalib for all the Christians [*nasara*]." After the subtitle, "Copy [*nuskhah*] of the Covenant [*kitab al-'ahd*]," the actual covenant commences:

> This covenant of Allah [*'ahd Allah*] was ordered to be written by Muhammad ibn 'Abd Allah ibn 'Abd al-Muttalib, the Messenger of Allah, Allah's peace and blessings be upon him and his family [*alihi*], to all the Christians and all the monks, to guard and protect them, because [*wadi'at Allah fi khalqihi*] in order for the covenant to be a proof [*hujjah*] against them and there would be no claim against Allah after the Messenger. He made this a protection [*dhimmah*] from him and a protection for them by the authority of Allah, for Allah is All-Mighty [*'Aziz*] and All-Wise [*Hakim*]. It was written by the Lion [*asad*] and the People of His Vocation [*ahl al-millati*] to all those who profess the Christian religion [*da'wat al-nasraniyyah*] in the Eastern lands and its West, near and far, be they Arabs or non-Arabs [*'ajami*], known or unknown, as a covenant [*'ahd*] from him, a justice [*'adl*] and tradition [*sunnah*] to be preserved.

Unlike some other covenants, which simply speak of Muhammad ibn 'Abd Allah, this one provides the names of both father and grandfather. Rather than simply blessing the Prophet, as is customary among Sunnis, the *Covenant* blesses both the Messenger of Allah and his family [*alihi*] as is common among Sufis, be they Sunnis or Shi'is. If the covenant of 1630 is addressed to all the Christians, the covenant of 1538 addresses all Christians and all monks. In this instance, the expression *wadi'at Allah* appears to refer, not to the Prophet, but to the Christians, who are entrusted with Allah's creations, which is a most unusual reading. This implies that it is the Christians, and not the Prophet, who are the Proofs of Allah for His Creation. The use of expressions like *hujjat Allah* or Proof of Allah is consistent with Shi'ite usage and applied to the Twelve Imams but also appears in Sufi works. As is the case with some Sufi works, the *Covenant* makes greater use of divine attributes, such as *al-'Aziz* and *al-Hakim*. It also states that it was written by *al-asad* or the Lion. The latter is positively bizarre since it was 'Ali, and not Muhammad, who bore the title the Lion of Allah. It was as such that he was referred to in the *Covenant of 'Ali, Fourth Caliph, of Baghdad, Granting Certain Immunities and Privileges to the Armenian Nation*, the earliest copies of which date to the 18th century.

Whoever transcribed this covenant into 'Uthmani script from its primitive predecessor had interesting lexical inclinations. Instead of *din al-nasraniyyah* or the Christian religion, he opts for *da'wat al-nasraniyyah*, which is broader in meaning. The language of the covenant of 1538 is also more elaborate and tends to accumulate more adjectives. Unlike the covenant from 1630, the one from 1538 says that it is a justice [*'adl*] and a tradition [*sunnah*]. These terms have their surface meaning; however, they also convey matters of doctrine. The Shi'ites, for example, treat *al-'adl al-ilahi* or *'adl* as the second pillar of Islam after *tawhid* or divine unity. Yes, God is One; however, Shi'ites insist that God is also Just to differentiate them from those Sunni philosophers who believe that God's omnipotence allows him to place a good person in hell and an evil person in heaven. For Shi'ites, such a belief is totally untenable. This stress on justice in the *Covenant* seems to echo this Shi'ite article of faith. The mention of *sunnah*, however, comes as a surprise. Shi'ites certainly follow the Sunnah and, in fact, argue that they are the true Sunnis. The term Sunni, however, was only coined during the conflict between Mu'awiyyah and Imam Hasan. In order to differentiate themselves from the followers of the grandson of the Prophet, who were known as *ahl al-bayt* or the People of the House of Prophecy, Mu'awiyyah identified his partisans as *ahl al-sunnah wa al-jama'at* or the People of Tradition and the Community. If Sunnis tend to be Sunnis and Shi'ites tend to be Shi'ites, it is the Sufis who tend to combine aspects from both of the major divisions in Islam.

The segment that follows stresses that he who adheres to the covenant is worthy of Islam while he who violates it is damned:

> He who observes it holds to his Islam and is worthy of his religion [*din*]. He who breaks it [*nakatha*] and jeopardizes the covenant [*'ahd*] which was ordered by the Messenger of Allah, and changes it, and transgresses what has been commanded, has rejected the Covenant of Allah [*'ahd Allah*], denies the Oath of Allah [*mithaq Allah*], disdains his religion, and merits His Maledictions, whether he is a Sultan or anyone else among the believers [*mu'minin*] and the Muslims.

These words are not hyperbolic in meaning for, according to Islam, the breaking of oaths and covenants is a mortal sin which merits eternal damnation. The Qur'an speaks of "those who are keepers of their trusts and covenants" (28:8). Allah commands those who believe to fulfill their obligations (5:1). Almighty Allah expresses love for those who fulfill their promises (3:76). He reminds Muslims to "fulfill the covenant of Allah when you have made a covenant, and do not break the oaths after making them firm, and you indeed made Allah a surety for you. Surely Allah knows what you do" (16:91). As Almighty Allah asks, "O you who believe! Why do you say that which you do not do? It is most hateful to Allah that you should say that which you do not do" (61: 2–3). As Allah warns, "every promise shall be questioned about" (17:34). As for covenant breakers, the curse of Allah is upon them and Hell will be their abode (13:25).

The Prophet proceeds to explain that the *Covenant* was requested of him and the Muslim Community as a whole and that he placed the Christians under the protection of Prophets, Chosen Ones, and Friends of Allah, terminology which is consistent with Sufi tradition.

> I commit myself to grant alliance [*'uhud*] and pledges [*mawathiq*] to those who requested them from me and from all of my Muslim Community [*millati min al-muslimin*] to give them the covenant of Allah [*'ahd Allah*] and His Pledge [*mithaq*] and I place them under the safeguard of His Prophets, His Chosen [*asfiya*], His Friends [*awliya*] from the Believers [*mu'minin*] and the Muslims, among the first of them and the last of them. And my protection [*dhimmati*] and my security [*mithaqi*] represent the most solid covenant that Allah, the Most High, has given a prophet which was sent in truth to demand obedience, to give obligations [*farida*], and the demand respect of the covenant [*'ahd*].

The protection the Prophet promised includes:

> The covenant of Allah [*'ahd Allah*] is that I should protect their land [*ard*], their monasteries [*al-diyar*], with my power [*qudrah*], my horses, my men, my weapons [*silahi*], my strength [*quwwati*], and my Muslim followers [*atba'i*] in any region, far away or close by, and that I should protect their businesses. I grant security to them, their churches, their businesses, their houses of worship [*buyut salawatihim*], the places of their monks, the places of their pilgrims, wherever they may be found, be they in the mountains or the valleys, caves or inhabited regions, the plains or the desert and that I should protect their *dhimmah*, their faith [*millah*], and their religion [*din*], wherever they may be found in the East or West, in the sea or on land, the same way that I protect myself, my entourage [*khassati*], and the People of my Community [*ahl al-millati*] among the Muslims.

This segment is lexically richer and more descriptive than the covenant of 1630. The choice of words is more precise and of greater lucidity. For example, where the covenant of 1630 speaks of *khatimi* or seals, which seems strange and out of place, and even contrary to Islamic custom, which considers the Prophet the final *khatim*, the covenant of 1538 offers *khasati* which means "my entourage" which makes much more sense. The word also has a secret sense, largely unknown to Sunnis, which indicates Shi'ites. The Shi'ites refer to the Sunnis as the *'ammah* or common people and to themselves as the *khassah*, the special or chosen people. When the Prophet speaks of protecting his *khassati* as he protects himself, he may mean the Members of his Household. The Messenger of Allah continues describing the nature of his protection in the following terms:

> I place them under my protection [*dhimmah*], my security [*mithaq*], and my trust [*aman*] at every moment. I defend them from any damage, harm [*makruh*] or retribution [*tabi'a*]. I am behind them, protecting them from every enemy or anyone who wishes them harm [*muhdi*]. I sacrifice myself for them by means of my helpers [*a'wani*], my followers [*atbai*], and the People of my Community [*ahl al-millah*] because they are my flock [*ra'iyyah*] and the people under my protection [*ahl al-dhimmati*], I extend [*amudu*] my authority [*sultah*], my care [*ri'ayyah*], and my protection over them from every harm [*makruh*] so that it does not reach them. No harm will reach them unless it reaches my Companions [*ashabi*] who [are there to] protect them and assist Islam [*nusrat*].

The choice of terms is, once again, interesting. The Prophet refers to his followers as *atba'i*. Typically, the people who came into direct contact with the Messenger of Allah were known as *ashab* or Companions. It was the followers of the Companions who were known as *atba* or *tabi'in*. Scribes always run the risk of applying later meanings to earlier terms; all kinds of extraneous elements can color the content of a covenant. Take, for example, the presentation of the Prophet as a shepherd whose flock consists of both Muslims and Christians. It is conceivable that the Messenger of Allah described himself in such terms; however, it may also be the gloss of a Christian scribe. The rest of the *Covenant*, with the exception of the conclusion, is virtually identical to that of 1630, with a few notable exceptions. It reads:

> I remove from them the harm from taxes and loan in the supplies borne to the People of the Pact [*ahl al-'ahd*] except what they themselves consent to give. They should not be compelled or unfairly treated in this matter.

> It is not permitted to remove a bishop from his bishopric, a monk from his monastic life, a Christian from his Christianity, an ascetic [*zahid*] from his tower, or a pilgrim from his pilgrimage. Nor is it permitted to destroy any part of their churches or their businesses or to take parts of their buildings to construct mosques or the homes of believing Muslims [*mu'minin al-muslimin*]. Whoever does such a thing will have violated the covenant of Allah [*'ahd Allah*], disobeyed [*khalafa*] his Messenger, and deviated [*hadha*] from His Divine Alliance.
>
> It is not permitted to impose a capitation [*jizyah*] or any kind of land tribute [*kharaj*] on monks, bishops or those who are worshippers among them, who, by devotion, wear woolen clothing [*al-suf*] or live alone in the mountains or in other regions secluded from human presence.

The elements that stand out include the use of the term *zahid* or "ascetic" rather than monk. If there were ever ascetics in Islam, they were the Sufis, and the Sufis often spoke of themselves in such terms. Instead of speaking simply of Muslims, this covenant emphasizes believing Muslims as it wishes to distinguish between those who claim to be Muslims, but are really disbelieving hypocrites, and the true, *bona fide*, Muslims, who actually believe in Allah and Islam. If this covenant was transcribed during Umayyad times, it may have been read in light of actual conditions. If the Shi'ites rose up and broke away from the major body of Muslims, and the Sufis adopted a form of passive, spiritual, resistance, these factors may have had an impact on how the *Covenant* was interpreted. The reference to "worshippers . . . who . . . by devotion wear woolen clothing [*al-suf*]" almost appears like an allusion to the Sufis, "those who wear woolen clothing." It is as if the *Covenant* were foreshadowing the unfortunate series of events that took place after the passing of the Prophet, a time of decline during which the light of Islam became progressively dimmer and the spirituality of Islam gave way to the materialism and imperialism of the Banu Umayyah, the heirs of whom are the present-day Gulf Arabs. The *Covenant* continues dealing with issues of capitation and taxation:

> The capitation [*jizyah*] will be applied to those Christians who are not clerics [*man la yataabad*] with the exception of the monk and the pilgrim in the amount of four dirhams per year or an inexpensive cloak [*tawb*]. He who does not have the money or the food with which to feed himself, the Muslims will help him by means of the savings stored in the Treasury [*bayt al-mal*]. If they find difficulties in securing food, the Muslims will also help them, provided they willingly accept.
>
> May the land tribute [*jizyah al-kharaj*] on big business by land or sea, pearl-diving, mining for precious stones, gold and silver, or those who are wealthy among those who profess the Christian faith, not exceed twelve *dirhams* [*fiddah*] per year, so long as they are inhabitants and residents in these countries.
>
> May nothing similar be demanded of travelers, who are not residents of the country or wayfarers whose country of residence is unknown. There shall be no land tax with capitation for others than those who own land as will the other occupants of lands over which the ruler has a right. They will pay taxes as others pay them without, however, the charges unjustly exceeding the measure of their means. As for the labor force which the owners spend upon to cultivate these lands, to render them fertile, and to harvest them, they are not to be taxed excessively. Let them pay in the same fashion and justly that was imposed on other similar tributaries.

Another sign of updating of information appears in the amount of *jizyah*. If other covenants merely mention the sum of twelve dirhams, the covenant of 1538 specifies that they are twelve silver dirhams. As regards military service, the *Covenant* stipulates the following:

> The people under our protection [*ahl al-dhimmah*] will not be obliged to go to war with the Muslims in order to combat their enemies and to attack them. Indeed, the people under our protection [*ahl al-dhimmah*] are not to engage in war. It is precisely to discharge them of this obligation that this pact has been granted to them as well as to assure them the help and protection of the Muslims. They will not be constrained to provide equipment to any of the Muslims, in arms or horses, in the event of a war in which the Muslims attack their enemies, unless they contribute to the cause freely. And what the Mus-

> lims have borrowed will be guaranteed by the [State] Treasury [*bayt al-mal*] until it is returned to them. If they die or are damaged, the [State] Treasury [*bayt al-mal*] will provide monetary compensation.

If the covenant of 1630 merely states that Christians are not obliged to provide arms and horses to the Muslim war effort, while promising recognition to those who help, the covenant of 1538 provides specific protections, assurances, and guarantees to those who lend their property to the Muslims. Not only are the goods guaranteed by the State Treasury, the National Bank so to speak, lenders are assured that if their property is not returned, or returned in a damaged state, the *bayt al-mal* will provide them with its monetary value. As for issues of freedom of religion, reconciliation, mixed marriages, repairing church property and employing Christians in Muslim wars, the covenant of 1538 coincides with that of 1630 with some minor variations in vocabulary:

> No one who practices the Christian religion will be forced to enter into Islam. *And dispute ye not with the People of the Book, except with means better* [29:46]. They must be covered by the wing of mercy and all harm that could reach them—wherever they may find themselves and wherever they may be—must be repelled.
>
> If a Christian were to commit a crime or an offense, Muslims must provide him with help, defense, and protection, as well as pay his penalty for him. They should encourage reconciliation between him and the victim, to help or save him.
>
> The Muslims must not abandon him or leave him without help and assistance because I have given them a covenant of Allah which is binding upon the Muslims.
>
> In virtue of this pact, they have obtained inviolable rights to enjoy our protection, to be protected from any infringement of their rights, and they are not to be disputed, rejected, or ignored so that they will be bound to the Muslims both in good and bad fortune.
>
> The girls of the Christians must not be subject to suffer, by abuse, on the subject of marriages which they do not desire. Muslims should not take Christian girls in marriage against the will of their parents nor should they oppress their families in the event that they refused their offers of engagement and marriage. Such marriages should not take place without their desire and agreement and without their approval and consent.
>
> If a Muslim takes a Christian woman as a wife, he must respect her Christian beliefs. He will give her freedom to listen to her [clerical] superiors as she desires and to follow the path of her own religion. Whoever, despite this order, forces his [Christian] wife to act contrary to her religion, he will have broken the alliance of Allah and broken the promise [*mithaq*] of His Messenger and he will be counted, by us, among the liars [*kadhibin*].
>
> If the Christians approach you seeking the help and assistance of the Muslims in order to repair their churches and their convents, or to arrange matters pertaining to their affairs and religion, these [Muslims] must help and support them. However, they must not do so with the aim of receiving any reward or debt. On the contrary, they should do so to restore that religion, out of faithfulness to the pact of the Messenger of Allah, by pure donation, and as a meritorious act before Allah and His Messenger.
>
> In matters of war between them and their enemies, the Muslims will not employ any Christian as a messenger, scout, guide, to show power, or for any other duty of war. Whoever obliges one of them to do such a thing will be unjust [*zaliman*] towards Allah, disobedient [*'asiyan*] to His Messenger, and will be cast out [*mutakhalliyan*] from his religion. Nothing is permitted to a Muslim [with regards to the Christians] outside of obeying these edicts which Muhammad ibn 'Abd Allah, the Messenger of Allah, has passed in favor of the religion of the Christians.

The adjectives in this covenant are stronger than those found in 1630, describing those who break it as liars, unjust oppressors, and disobedient outcasts. The demands made of Christians are also more emphatic:

> I am also placing conditions [upon the Christians] and I demand that they promise to fulfill and satisfy them as commands their religion. Among other things, none of them may act as a scout, spy, either overtly or covertly, on behalf of an enemy of war, against a Muslim. None of them will shelter the ene-

mies of the Muslims in their homes from which they could await the moment to launch an attack. May these enemies [of the Muslims] never be allowed to halt in their regions, be it in their villages, their oratories, or in any other place belonging to their co-religionists. They must not provide any support to the war enemies of the Muslims by furnishing them with weapons, horses, men, or call for unnecessary things. They must not annoy them and they should be honored as long as they persist in their religion and their care for their pact. They must grant Muslims three days and three nights when they halt among them. They must offer them, wherever they are found, and wherever they are going, the same food with which they live themselves, without, however, being obliged to endure other annoying or onerous burdens.

If a Muslim needs to hide in one of their homes or oratories, they must grant him hospitality, give him help, and provide him with their food during the entire time he will be among them, making every effort to keep him concealed and to prevent the enemy from finding him, while providing to all of his needs.

The final warnings found in the covenant of 1538 are almost identical to those found in 1630:

> Whoever contravenes or alters the ordinances of this edict will be cast out of the alliance between Allah and His Messenger.
>
> May everyone abide by the treaties and alliances which have been contracted with the monks, and which I have contracted myself, wherever they may be.
>
> The Messenger of Allah, may the peace and blessings of Allah be upon him, must respect what he has granted, on his authority and all the Muslims, to guard them and have mercy on them until the end, until the Hour of [Resurrection] arrives, and the world comes to an end.

The *Covenant*, however, includes one interesting addition: the integration of a prophetic tradition or *hadith* in defense of Christians: "Whoever is unjust after this towards a [Christian] subject [*dhimmi*], breaks the covenant and rejects it, I will be his enemy on the Day of Judgment among all the Muslims." This is virtually identical to the saying of the Prophet cited in the *Sunan* of Abu Dawud, which reads: "Whoever oppresses non-Muslim subjects shall find me to be their advocate on the Day of Judgment [against the Muslim oppressors]." If the *Covenant* is in agreement with the Qur'an, and skillfully integrates verses from the Holy Book, it also interweaves and paraphrases prophetic traditions with great agility.

If there is any major difference between the covenants of the Prophet of 1538 and 1630, it involves the list of thirty witnesses. As Arabic readers can certify by examining the scanned copy from 1538, a large number of the names are misspelled, something quite odd coming from such a skillful scribe. Were these mistakes made by a Frenchman or European who, while proficient in Arabic, was weak in spelling? Or was he faithfully transcribing the manuscript that he was copying, even reproducing the mistakes found on the original? The witnesses include: Abu Bakr al-Siddiq, 'Umar ibn al-Khattab, 'Uthman ibn 'Affan, 'Ali ibn Abi Talib, Abu Dharr, Abu al-Darda', Abu Hurayrah, 'Abd Allah ibn Mas'ud, al-'Abbas ibn 'Abd al-Malik, Fadl ibn al-'Abbas al-Zahri, Talhah ibn 'Abd Allah, Sa'd ibn Mu'adh, Sa'd ibn Ubadah, Thabit ibn Qays, Yazid ibn Talit, 'Abd Allah ibn Yazid, Farsus ibn Qasim ibn Badr ibn Ibrahim, Amir ibn Zarib, Sahl ibn Tamim, and 'Abd al-'Azim. Then, the handwriting changes, and the list continues with 'Abd al-'Azim ibn Husayn, 'Abd Allah ibn 'Amr ibn al-'As, 'Ammar ibn Yasir, Mu'azzam ibn Musa, Hassan ibn Thabit, Abu Hanifah, 'Ubayd ibn Mansur, Hashim ibn 'Abd Allah, Abu al-'Azir, Hisham ibn 'Abd al-Muttalib.

If the list of witnesses on the *Covenant of the Prophet Muhammad with the Monks of Mount Sinai* and the 1630 copy of the *Covenant of the Prophet Muhammad with the Christians of the World* pose more than a few problems, this list of authorities is more difficult to digest. Curiously, though, there seems to be an overlap with the Sinai and Najran covenants. In all instances, the scribes seemed to have struggled to make sense out of certain names. If the presence of many of these Companions of the Prophet is possible, some are unlikely, and other individuals named are unknown. There may be a logical explanation for this. Some of the witnesses may have been Jews or Christians who accompanied delegations to Medina in order to submit to the Prophet. This would explain why they do not appear in any books on narrators of *hadith*. While the issue of authorities deserves more detailed study, it seems relatively certain that these signatories were attached posthumously. This is not at all unusual. There are many instances in which traditions were passed without chains of narration only to suddenly appear in later works with complete *isnads*. Since the events were so close to memory, early scholars saw no need to cite chains of narration. They had witnessed the events themselves or else their fathers or grandfathers had been present. It was only later, when the distance between narrator and eyewitness became greater, and after the Umayyads had devoted themselves to distort, corrupt, and destroy the message of Muhammad, that scholars developed a system of authentication which required unbroken references back to the Prophet.

Fortunately, this copy of the *Covenant* provides some details as to its origin. It states that "'Ali ibn Abi Talib, may Allah be pleased with him, wrote this covenant." The identity of the scribe, that of Imam 'Ali, agrees with the historical record unlike the 1630 copy of the *Covenant* which attributes it to Mu'awiyyah, a claim that is as unlikely as it is unpalatable. Could Gabriel Sionita have changed the name of the scribe in order to appease the Ottomans who were at war against the Shi'ite Safavids? It seems that anything is possible at this point. The scribe also states that "[t]he manuscript [*sijl*] was written on a piece of leather [*jild*] that was not small. It remained at the Sultan's authority and was sealed by the Prophet, peace and blessings be upon him." These details are very similar to those found on the *Covenant of the Prophet Muhammad with the Monks of Mount Sinai*. The *Covenant of the Prophet Muhammad with the Christians of Najran* also states that it was written on leather. This would suggest that it was authored during the early Islamic period, prior to the availability of parchment. This marks the end of the *Covenant* but not the end of the book. The scribe provides the following concluding remarks:

> This blessed book [*kitab al-mubarak*] was completed on the holy day of Monday, in the last month of Ba'una, the blessed, in the year of our Masters the Martyrs, the Pure Ones, the Felicitous, the Satisfied [*abrar*], may Allah grant us their intercession and may their intercession be with us. Amen!
>
> This corresponds to the 27th of the sacred [*haram*] month of Muharram of the year 945 of the Arabic *hijrah*. May Allah make its end good! Amen!
>
> This blessed book [*kitab al-mubarak*] belongs to the great soul [*al-mubajjal*], the master [*al-mawla*], the leader [*al-ra'is*], the elder [*al-shaykh*], the scholar [*al-'alim*], Sim'an, the son of [*najl*], the source of greatness [*al-mu'azzam*] Fadl Allah, may Allah rest his soul in peace [*nayaha allah nafsahu*], known as [*al-ma'ruf*] al-Barallusi.
>
> The writer of these words is the humble [*miskin*], full of faults and sins [*khataya wa al-dunub*], asking the brothers who read these words [lit. letters] to mention them in their prayers [*salawat*] and the Messiah [*masih*] will reward them one hundred and sixty three times.

Some myopic Muslims may see the date of 945 AH [1538 CE] and cry foul. How can a document which dates from nearly one thousand years after the Prophet conceivably be trustworthy? More rational readers will understand that this is simply a copy from 1538 CE. There is no reason to believe that it does not trace back to the time of the Prophet. If we center solely on dates, then a 2013 edition of *Sahih Bukhari* should be treated as a forgery unless we have an original of the work. And even then, we are dealing with a work compiled over two centuries after the death of the Prophet. Hence, without a text of traditions compiled during the Prophet's actual lifetime, anything else must be treated as a fabrication. If we applied the same criteria to the Qur'an, we would destroy the Islamic faith as there is currently no complete copy of the Qur'an which dates to the time of the Prophet.

The scribe then identifies the owner of the book: Sim'an ibn Fadl Allah al-Barallusi. Although the long list of honorifics makes him sound like a Muslim scholar, perhaps of the Shi'ite persuasion, Arab Christians are also fond of such displays of pious pomposity. Considering the nature of the book as a whole, and not solely the *Covenant*, the owner was almost certainly a Christian. Clues to the history of the Covenant may also come from other individuals identified in the book. The book makes mention of a certain Yuhanna ibn Ishaq al-Batanuni, the owner of the library for which the manuscript was copied. Did Sim'an ibn Fadl Allah al-Barallusi commission a copy from the library? Other individuals associated with the copy include were Girgis ibn Yuhanna al-Tamawi, Butrus ibn Diyab al-Halabi, and Mansur ibn Sulayman Sahyun al-Ramadi. A note in the book also mentions the arrival of a missionary to Old Cairo in 1592. Perhaps this person brought the book from Egypt to Mount Carmel. Finally, the book reveals that it was copied by Girgis al-Ifrangi, namely, George the Frenchman or George the European. The librarians at the National Library of France have noted that the style of the Arabic script shows no signs that it was written by a European. Although they have the right to be skeptical, it is possible that a European, who had studied and served in the Middle East for an extended period of time, could acquire enough skills to copy Arabic manuscripts.

The final note at the end of the *Covenant*, and at the end of the book in which it is found, appears to be addressed to a monk by the name of Michel: "Michel: the brothers who read these words [lit. letters] must mention them in their prayers [*salawat*] and the Messiah [*masih*] will reward them one hundred and sixty three times." Where some of my Arab colleagues read "Michel" others read *yasilu* or "ask" which is equally possible. If it is an Arabic verb, and not a French surname, the French connection can be downplayed by a degree. It could be argued that the scribe is referring to the words found in the entire book; however, a whole manuscript cannot reasonably be recited in one's prayers. No. This word of advice applies specifically to the *Covenant of the Prophet Muhammad with the Christians of the World* (1538) and its implications are startling. Here, we have a Christian cleric, a mysterious Michel, who urges monks and priests to mention the *Covenant of the Prophet* in their prayers. While I suppose that it could include personal prayers, the command appears aimed at congregational prayers: mass and liturgy. We can imagine that, at one point, in the early 16th century, Christian clerics in Egypt and the Levant recited the *Covenant of the Prophet* during church services. Since Christians were granted the liberty to preach, and Muslim rulers did not generally interfere in Church affairs, this was clearly not a command from the Ottoman authorities. The *Covenant*, which was copied in 1538 from an older copy, coincided with the rule of Sulayman the Magnificent who ruled from 1520 to 1566 CE. This was an age of peace and prosperity for Christians. It was clearly not crafted during a period of persecution in order to assuage the oppressive authorities. Uncovering the identity of Michel would help us comprehend the socio-historical context in which the *Covenant* was copied and spread. As can be appreciated, our understanding of the covenants of the Prophet is only barely beginning.

Conclusions

While it shares similarities with the *Covenant of the Prophet Muhammad with the Christians of Najran*, the *Covenant of the Prophet Muhammad with the Christians of the World* is a distinct treaty which was apparently produced during the same period of time. Due to differences in content, structure, language, and witnesses, we can be confident that the covenant in question was not a simple copy of a standard treaty sent to Christian communities. As with the patents the Prophet provided to different Jewish communities, no two treaties were identical, though they shared a large number of common elements and conditions. These minor differences, I contend, are evidence of authenticity as opposed to forgery as they point to a common origin, the Messenger of Allah, who was expressing the same ideas in slightly divergent forms. Like the *Covenant of the Prophet Muhammad with the Monks of Mount Sinai*, the *Covenant of the Prophet Muhammad with the Christians of the World* is not directly addressed to a particular community. If these were forgeries, why would the falsifiers fail to be more specific? And why would they ask for so little when the sky could have been the limit? If the

Christians were not so ambitious, the reason seems quite simple: the authentic covenants of the Prophet were well-known and any such interpolations would have been detected, denounced, and duly punished in due course. Consequently, they limited themselves to preserving, protecting, and circulating the existing covenants that they had received from the Prophet Muhammad himself. Mistakes may have been made by scribes; however, most of them appear unintentional. Whether the *Covenant of the Prophet Muhammad with the Christians of the World* from 1538 is the forerunner of the *Covenant of the Prophet Muhammad with the Christians of the World* from 1630, remains to be determined. The former may have been directed to the Coptic Christians from Egypt and the latter to the Maronites from Palestine. It would be premature to come to any definitive conclusions at this early point.

Chapter 6

The Prophet Muhammad and the Assyrian Christians

Introduction

If the *Covenant of the Prophet Muhammad with the Christians of Najran* was unknown to Muslims until its rediscovery, almost one hundred years ago, the *Covenant of the Prophet with the Assyrian Christians* has long been known to the Muslims from upper Mesopotamia or what is now south-eastern Turkey and part of northern Iraq. Unlike most of the other covenants of the Prophet, the original of the agreement was allegedly composed in the Persian language (Brevick 114), something that will come as a surprise to most Muslims. While this is one of the major issues that need to be addressed, it is not one that should provoke any *a priori* claims of forgery. On the contrary, it is one that compels the scholar and critic to conduct a more in-depth analysis of the claims made concerning this curious covenant.

Issues of Authenticity

According to George David Malech, the origin of the *Covenant of the Prophet Muhammad with the Assyrian Christians*, which he describes as the *Agreement between Prophet Mohammed and Nazarene Christians of the East*, is as follows:

> Mohammed wrote an epistle to Said, head of the Nazarene tribe, who were Christians, and asked him and his people to accept the teachings of Islam. Together Jahb Alahah, their bishop, Said appeared before the Prophet and agreed to pay him tribute for enjoying the liberty to worship in their own way unharmed by the Islamites. The document was signed by Mohammed himself and a number of the leading Islamites. It is written in the Persian language and has been preserved among the Christians for many centuries. (221)

The original document is said to have been preserved by the Assyrian Christians throughout the centuries until the time of Selim I (r. 1512–1520 CE) only to be seized by the Sultan. As we read in Malech's *History of the Syrian Nation and the Old Evangelical-Apostolic Church of the East*:

> In 1517 Sultan Selim came from Constantinople to Bag[h]dad, and it is said, that Shimon the fourth, the patriarch, visited the sultan and showed him the precious document. And the sultan said that it was so valuable, that it ought to be preserved in the royal treasury of Constantinople. The patriarch had to give it up, but Selim gave him a copy of the document, signed by himself. The copy is kept by the patriarch; it is still extant—the original is in Constantinople. (Malech 221)

This account of events is strangely similar to the stories shared by the Christians of Najran. Jahb Alahah may be a corruption of Abu Haritha while Said could be the Sayyid 'Absiso, the leaders of the delegation from Najran which met with the Prophet Muhammad. As to its fate, the original *Covenant of the Prophet Muhammad with the Assyrian Christians* seems to have suffered the same fate as the *Covenant of the Prophet Muhammad with the Monks of Mount Sinai.* In both instances, the same protagonist is at play, the Sultan Selim I, and the year is identical: 1517 CE. For some scholars, these shared characteristics may point to appropriation. In other words, the Christians of Assyria may have claimed the *Covenant of the Prophet Muhammad with the Monks of Mount Sinai* as their own since it addressed "all Christians." If it applied to the Christians from Mount Sinai, then, it applied to all other Christians as well. They might merely have obtained or made a copy of the original covenant and, over the years, came to believe that they had been granted their own individual charter of protection and privileges when, in fact, they had simply adopted the document that was originally directed to the Monastery of Saint Catherine. This remains within the realm of possibility. These suspicious similarities, however, have other explanations that are equally legitimate.

The similarities in names are of little significance as the repertoire of personal names among the Christians of the time was very limited in scope. Large numbers of delegations met with the Prophet during his final two years of life; hence, he may very well have entertained Christians, not only from Najran, but from Egypt, the Levant, Persia, and beyond. As to the claim that it was Selim I who, in 1517, insisted that the *Covenant of the Prophet Muhammad with the Assyrian Christians* be preserved in the Treasury in Istanbul, it makes perfect chronological sense. Of all the Caliphs, Selim I was of the most relentless in his search for religious relics. Both he and his agents scoured the lands of Islam in search of ancient copies of the Qur'an, letters of the Prophet, and any items that belonged to the Messenger of Allah, his Companions, or previous prophets. The year 1517 coincides with the culmination of Selim's wars of expansion, first in Persia, and then in Palestine and Egypt, which rendered the Ottoman Empire, with its nearly one billion acres, one of the most powerful political players in the world. As is customary, conquered communities often approach their new rulers to express their submission, to convey their loyalty, and to request protection or privileges. This would have been the ideal time for the Assyrian or Armenian Christians to show their copies of their respective covenants of the Prophet.

Skeptics will surely suggest that it was the ideal time to forge false charters of protection, and poor ones at that, since they were not even in Arabic, but in Persian. For those who believe that the Prophet could speak Persian, as demonstrated by traditions in Muslim and Bukhari, this poses no problem. For those who doubt that he could do so, they should be reminded that one of his closest companions was Salman the Persian (d. 654 CE), who was perfectly proficient, not only in Persian but in Aramaic, and possibly Greek as well. Salman al-Farsi, as he is known in Arabic, was not only literate, he was the first person to translate part of the Qur'an into the Persian language, *Surah al-Fatihah* to be precise, with the authorization of the Prophet (Hamidullah, *Introduction* 210). Hence, he could easily have acted as the Prophet's scribe when it came to composing letters or covenants in Farsi. Furthermore, the fact that the *Covenant* was written in Persian does not appear to have surprised Selim I or any of his scholars. Had the Ottoman authorities concluded that the *Covenant* was a fake, it would have been destroyed and the perpetrators of the fraud would have been put to the sword. The *Covenant* would not have been placed in the Treasury nor would a certified copy been granted to the Christians to take its place.

As for the issue of language, it is odd that academics would argue that the *Covenant of the Prophet Muhammad with the Assyrian Christians* was written originally in Farsi when the document itself commences with the words: "The translation of the holy messenger's treaty, peace be upon him and his family." This initial section, which appears in the covenant presented by Malech, was not translated into English. While it is plausible that Salman al-Farsi could have written the covenant on behalf of the Prophet, the scribe is said to have been Mu'awiyyah ibn Abi Sufyan. This makes one wonder. If the Safavids produced a Shi'ite recension of the *Covenant of the Prophet*, why did they fail to remove the name of Mu'awiyyah? Since the language itself may hold clues, I had several professors of religious studies, who are native speakers of Persian, peruse the document. They were of the opinion that the language was consistent with that used in 17th-century Persia. One colleague felt, however, that the language was so archaic that it could conceivably have been written during the time of the Prophet. The fact remains that Persian prose writers were able to write in that style into the early twentieth century. Still, none of these scholars were able to see anything that indicated it was a forgery. As for the writing itself, it might provide evidence; however, it has not yet been established whether the version in Malech's text was transcribed in modern or ancient times. Although I am told that the English translation is good, it is not perfectly accurate, particularly when it comes to the list of witnesses at the end. Hence, a new, complete, translation would most certainly be in order. And if this Persian covenant is a translation of the covenant of Sinai, why does it have twenty-seven witnesses when two of the Sinai covenants have sixteen signatories and four have twenty-two? Was this an attempt to give the covenants the highest *hadith* grade, that of *muttawatir*, indicating that it was passed down by a large number of narrators?

The existence of the *Covenant of the Prophet Muhammad with the Assyrian Christians* has been long attested. As William Ainser Wigram relates, "Assyrian tradition declares that special privileges were given to their church and their patriarch, by a *firman* of the Prophet himself" (Wigram, *An Introduction* 310). As Brigadier General J.G. Browne acknowledged, "[t]he Prophet Mohammed . . . gave the Assyrians a written *firman* . . . according them permission to carry out their own religious observances without interference" (n.p.). As her Ladyship Surma D'Bait Mar Shimum (1883–1975 CE) wrote, "It is a thing of common knowledge among the Mussalmans of Hakkiari that there was a special *firman* granted by the Prophet to our house, and therewith, as the universal belief went, a certain special knife of his giving" (n.p.). According to this member of the Patriarchal House,

> This *firman* was embossed in letters of gold, on parchment, and was written 'circle wise,' with the print of a hand in the middle. (This is an ancient type of Arab script. The print of the hand of the donor of the grant was impressed in the middle of the parchment, and the substance of the decree written around it, in one continuous spiral.) The knife had a shaft of silver, with a piece of red coral set in the pommel, and an inscription inlaid in gold on the blade. (n.p.)

As Surma D'Bait Mar Shimum further explains, the *Firman of the Prophet Muhammad* which was granted to the Patriarchal House was the center of religious devotion. "Once in the year," she relates, "a selected Mollah of Julamerk used to come up and read that document in the public assembly" (n.p.). In such a manner, the memory of the *Covenant of the Prophet Muhammad with the Assyrian Christians* was maintained alive among both Muslims and Christians. The fact that her family had been granted a special status from the Prophet Muhammad was recognized and respected by the Muslims of the region. "[T]he strictest Moslems," she writes, "who will not, as a rule, eat anything that has been slaughtered by a Christian, will eat without hesitation of any animal slaughtered by a member of the Patriarchal family" (n.p.). As Wigram confirms, "It is an undoubted fact that the patriarchal house, as such, is regarded with a respect among the Moslems, which they do not show to other Christian bishops" (Wigram, *An Introduction* 310).

"In Jelu," writes the Right Honorable Earl Percy, "one of the most treasured relics of the great church of Mar Zaia" was "a handkerchief covered with Arabic writing which the natives believe to be a *firman* of the Prophet himself according sanction and protection to their worship" (645). As Percy explains,

> A similar tradition asserts that the substance of the *firman* given by the Porte to each successive occupant of the Patriarchal See, confirming his spiritual authority over the Nestorians of the Empire, was originally accorded by Mahomet to Ishy Yau, the then Patriarch of the East, residing at Bag[h]dad; and Assemani, in his Bibliotheca Orientalis compiled for Clement XI, gives the Latin text of Bar Hebraeus' account of this extraordinary transaction. The treaty, he says, was negotiated by the help of large presents through the agency of Said the Christian Prince of Najran (Nagranensium). By its terms Mahomet gave the Christians a 'diploma' commending them to the protection of the Arabs, safeguarding their religion and laws, and exempting them from military service. If they entered a Moslem household they were to be shielded from insults to their faith, they were to be allowed to erect churches as they pleased, and the Arabs were even enjoined to assist them in the work; and finally the amount which might be raised in taxes from the rich and poor was laid down with strict and minute precision. (645–646)

While it may be that various Christian communities contended for the honor of having been accorded an agreement by the Messenger of Allah, it is clear that many clerics had come to Muhammad seeking charters. If his actions are any indication, Caliph 'Umar entertained few doubts as to the claims of the Assyrian Christians. The rights confirmed by 'Umar are clearly the very same granted in the *Covenant of the Prophet Muhammad with the Assyrian Christians.* As William Ainser Wigram relates in *The Assyrians*:

> The Arab leaders, representing Omar the Khalif, made no difficulty . . . Christians of the Assyrian Church were to have full security as a 'millet' in the land, on practically the same terms, as they had received under the Persian. That is to say, those born in the nationality had the right to remain in it and practice their religion, with exemption from military service. They might repair their churches, but might not erect new ones without permission; they had, of course, to pay ordinary taxes, with the 'kharj' in addition, in substitution for the military service that they could not render and Musulmans would not accept, though monks were declared to be exempt from this burden. Finally, it was specially laid down that Christian girls who were taken in marriage by Moslems might keep their religion's rule, excellent in intent, but hard to execute in fact. (33)

The fact that the Assyrian Christians had been granted a charter of protection from the Messenger of Allah was well-known among Muslims. Assyrian tradition relates that a Sunni Muslim, from the Hanbali *madhhab*, had plotted to usurp a piece of land which belonged to the Jacobite church in Baghdad. When his plan was frustrated, he obtained the body of a Muslim, and paraded it through the streets of the city, crying out: "The Christians have killed this man." This was all that was necessary to incite Muslim mobs to rise up against the Christian community, robbing and killing at will. They surrounded a church in which five hundred Christians had taken refuge, set it on fire, thus burning to death all those that were in it. After the church was burned to the ground, some Muslims were surprised to find a copy of the Gospel that had survived the flames, undamaged. "Verily, this is a true religion," a Muslim said in dismay, "we are doing wrong in not obeying the command of our Prophet who gave these people a *firman* not to be molested" (Yohannan 98–99).

In fact, a copy of the *firman* of the Prophet Muhammad had been preserved by the Patriarch of the Assyrian Church (Stafford 95). The covenant in question granted the Assyrian Church rights to freedom of religion and administration as well as the right to be a millet, namely, a protected community presided over by its chief Bishop who was authorized to represent them in dealings with the Muslim sovereigns (Stafford 95). This treasured relic was stored in the great church of Mar Zaia in Jilu, a district located in the Hakkari region of upper Mesopotamia which consisted of some twenty Assyrian Christian villages. It is reported that the *Covenant of the Prophet Muhammad with the Assyrians Christians* was both a shield and a protection to the followers of Christ. So powerful was the patent that whenever it was raised, Muslims would drop their weapons, obey the Prophet, and leave the Assyrian Christians unharmed. The Muslims, it is evident, were all familiar with the warning contained in the *Covenant* that he who disobeyed it would be excluded from the blessings of heaven forever.

If the original copy of the *Covenant of the Prophet Muhammad with the Assyrian Christians* was taken to Istanbul, where, unfortunately, it has yet to be located; what happened, then, to the certified copy left behind by Sultan Selim I? Well, according to George David Malech, the original was taken to Istanbul in 1517. This is also the opinion of William Chauncey Emhardt and George M. Lamsa, who write that:

> A documentary decree was issued by Mohammed and written by Ali, his son-in-law, in which he promises to the Nestorians protection and privileges at the hands of his followers. This document was given to the Nestorian Patriarch Essvo Yabh toward the end of the seventh, and was treasured by the Patriarchal family until the end of the last century [19th century CE]. It is now said to be in the Ottoman Museum in Constantinople. (75–76)

It may be, however, that these authors are confusing the *Covenant of the Prophet Muhammad with the Assyrians Christians* with the *Covenant of the Prophet Muhammad with the Monks of Mount Sinai*, neither of which, by the way, are currently in the catalog of the collection housed in the famous Turkish museum.

The actual owners of the document make no mention of any such transfer and, to all appearances, indicate that the *firman* held by Patriarchal family was the original and also included a dagger that was given by the Prophet as a gift. Since Surma D'Bait Mar Shimum was the sister of Mar Shimun XXI Benyamin, the Patriarch of the Assyrian Church of the East (1887–1918 CE), her testimony must take precedence over the scholarly speculations of a person like Percy. After all, the sacred relics of the Prophet actually belonged to her family and she relates accounts from people who had actually seen them.

Whether it was the original, or a certified copy thereof, what, then, was the fate of this treasured relic? According to Wigram, "a document, purporting to be the grant in question, was actually preserved until the middle of the 19th century, when Kurdish hatred of Christians overcame their reverence for the Prophet, and the grant perished in the 'Massacres of Bedr Khan Beg'" (*An Introduction* 310). According to Stafford, this catastrophic event took place in 1847 and resulted in the destruction of the *firman* (95). Brigadier General JG Browne also identifies 1847 as the year in which the *Covenant of the Prophet* was destroyed. As we read in "The Assyrians: A Debt of Honor:"

> About 170 years ago, part of the people living in the (Mosul) plains broke away from the Patriarch (the Mar Shimun) and formed the Chaldean Church. Otherwise there is little to note until the year 1847, when the Wali of Mosul, frightened by the tales that reached him of the increasing strength of the Assyrians, organized what is called a political massacre. Instigated by him, and helped by Turkish troops, a powerful Kurdish chief called Bedir Khan Beg attacked the Assyrians. A horrible massacre followed, much destruction was done, and the *firman* of Mohammed (the permission for the Assyrians to carry out their own religious observances without interference, granted by the Prophet Mohammed) was destroyed. (n. p.)

As for Surma D'Bait Mar Shimum, who was closely connected to the events, as opposed to a distant observer from abroad, the "*firman*...was preserved to the time of Bedru Khan Beg (1845)" (n. p.). Her Ladyship insists that the *firman* was stolen, not destroyed, at that time, along with the dagger of the Prophet:

> These things were kept among the treasures of the Patriarchate till the day of the massacre, and when the *firman*, which was then captured, was brought and shown to Bedru Khan, he exclaimed, 'The curse of Allah be upon Nurullah Beg of Julamerk, for he it was who stirred me up against the *firman* of the Prophet. Had I known that this house possessed this *firman*, I should never have dared to go against them. May God requite this war of you.'

Theodore D'Mar Shimun (1906–2001 CE), another member of the Patriarchal House, confirms this fact:

> When we went to Dizan, this decree, always in a satchel, was hung on a cottage post, during midday meal. When the Kurds attacked, our men went to fight in Mar Shalita Church. Amidst the confusion caused by the attack, the satchel containing the dagger and decree was left behind and latter stolen by the Kurds and taken to Bedr Khan Beg. We know this because it was later told to us that Bedr Khan had said if he had known that such a thing existed in our house, he would not have fought against it. My uncle Hormizd, while at school in Istanbul, wrote to his sister, Lady Surma, saying that he had overheard the son of Bedr Khan Beg in a coffeehouse saying, 'Our family possess something that is invaluable among the Muslim world.' A similar statement was repeated by Bedr Khan Beg's great-grandson to an Armenian of Bohtan, who lived in Cyprus. The great-grandson lived in Damascus, Syria, and was vacationing on Cyprus during the summer holiday. There is no doubt that they were speaking about the *firman* stolen from Qudshanis. (*The History* 38)

Percy, however, claims that "when the Turkish troops occupied the village at the time of my visit in 1899, this [ie. the *Covenant of the Prophet*] was the only article which they apparently thought it worth their while to carry away" (645). This date, of course, seems off by nearly half a century. However, it does suggest that the *Covenant of the*

Prophet with the Assyrians Christians was not destroyed in 1845 or 1847 during the massacre of Bedr Khan, but at some later point prior to the Assyrian atrocities of 1915.

Bedir (Badr) Khan Beg (c. 1800–1868 CE), for those who are not familiar with the name, was a Kurdish leader who became the first leader of the Emirate of Botan in what is now southeastern Turkey around 1820. Under his rule, his breakaway Kurdish state even encompassed the Bahdinan part of northern Iraq. Exploiting the weakness of the Ottoman Empire, he attempted to forge an independent Kurdistan. Since European powers had been spreading discontent and encouraging dissent among the Christians of the Ottoman Empire, the Assyrians, like the Armenians, were viewed as a source of sedition, namely, as a sort of fifth column. "Eastern Christians," write William Chauncey Emhardt and George M. Lamsa, "were told that the whole world was dominated by Christian nations and that its inhabitants who lived under Christian rule lived on a much higher plane of life" (83); consequently, "[t]his caused discontent toward Mohammedan rulers" (83). While some placed their hopes in America and Western Europe, others prayed that the Russians would save them, only to become seriously disillusioned (88).

Bedir Khan, in an attempt to create a homogeneous homeland composed of Kurdish Muslims, set out to exterminate the Christians of the region. These massacres, which took place in the middle of the 19th century, were eventually brought to an end by the Turks who were pressured by the British and the French to intervene in the region. Defeated by the Ottomans in 1847, Bedir Khan was exiled to Crete, where the Ottomans used his skills to crush a rebellion of Cretan Greeks in 1856. As a reward for his service, he was allowed to move to Damascus, where he died in 1868. While it is alleged that he had forty to ninety sons, only twenty-two are actually confirmed, many of whom continued to play an important role in Ottoman and Kurdish affairs. If the *Covenant of the Prophet Muhammad with the Assyrian Christians* was indeed stolen by the family of Bedir Khan Beg, there exists the distinct possibility that it may have survived in private hands to this day. Locating and retrieving this covenant would be the work of a modern-day James Bond / Indiana Jones.

Percy's claim, however, that the *Covenant* was only seized by Turkish troops in 1899 should not be so easily dismissed. Since the Patriarchal Family had to flee the region in the mid-19th century after the Massacres of Bedir Khan, the document may very well have remained in the hands of the local thieves until it was confiscated by the Young Turks. Albert Yelda, the former Christian representative in the Iraqi National Congress, explains that while the *firman* disappeared without a trace in 1847, it was later destroyed by the Turkish rulers before they set out to kill 30,000 Christians (Siemon-Netto). While his chronology is unclear, it appears that Yelda was referring to the Assyrian Genocide of 1915 in which Turkish troops, and neighboring Kurdish tribes, slaughtered scores of Christians in the region of Jilu, in the Hakkari region of upper Mesopotamia, forcing the surviving Assyrians to flee to Salmas in Iran, from where they spread as refugees around the world. The claim that the *Covenant of the Prophet Muhammad with the Assyrian Christians* was destroyed prior to a major massacre makes a great deal of sense, whether it was in 1845, 1847 or even 1915. The perpetrators of this crime against humanity could not have been Muslims according to any stretch of the imagination, but rather, the Young Turks: a movement of secular revolutionaries who wished to emulate the West in all matters: even massacres.

The Christians, it is imperative to point out, were always safe under true Islamic rule. As Emhardt and Lamsa have noted, "[t]he Assyrians as well as other Christians in the Near East have never realized the value of those sacred privileges bestowed on them by their Mohammedan neighbors. The trouble with these Christians was that they were left too free" (82). "At first the Mahometans appear to have treated the Christians in a friendly manner," observed Percy when speaking of the relations between Muslim Turks and Kurds and Assyrian Christians (645). "[A]nd when their attitude changed," he stresses, "the change, as at the present day, was due not to religious antagonism but to jealousy of their superior wealth" (645). If the Kurds and the Turks targeted the Assyrians, and later the Armenians, as they did do and which no honest individual can deny, it was not the result of Islamic inspiration: it was due to nationalistic, secular, political, and economic considerations. In fact, in order to do so, the Kurds and Turks had to effectively apostatize, as marked symbolically by the physical destruction of the *firman* of the Prophet Muhammad.

The vast majority of scholars who have written about the Assyrian Christians treat the *Covenant of the Prophet* granted to the Patriarchal House as a historical fact. Wigram, however, writes that "the claim of a special position is one that can hardly be substantiated under present conditions" (*An Introduction* 310). Simply because the *Covenant of the Prophet with the Assyrian Christians* does not presently exist does not mean that it never existed. After all, translations of the document were made, which we are fortunate to have. If the original *Declaration of Independence* were destroyed in a fire, and all we are left with are copies in other books, does that give any scholar grounds to question its existence?

The major problem caused by the *Covenant of the Prophet Muhammad with the Assyrian Christians* lies with the identity of the scribe who wrote it: Mu'awiyyah ibn Abi Sufyan (602–680 CE). According to most Islamic sources, Mu'awiyyah only embraced Islam prior to the Conquest of Mecca in the year 8 AH or 630. Why, critics will naturally ask, was Mu'awiyyah acting as the Prophet's scribe? While it may come as a surprise to some Shi'ites, Mu'awiyyah did indeed act as Muhammad's scribe during the final two years of his life: from the year 630 to the year 632 CE. However, the *Covenant of the Prophet Muhammad with the Assyrian Christians* dates from two years before. If the document is not a forgery, three other explanations are possible: 1) That the date on the document is mistaken as in many documents dating from the period, and thus that it actually dates from the final two years of the Prophet's life, or 2) that Mu'awiyyah had actually embraced Islam at an earlier date as some Sunni scholars have suggested, or 3) that Mu'awiyyah was simply present in Medina at the time and asked to act as an intermediary between the Muslims and the Christians. As a polytheist, he would have been perceived as a more objective outside party. But, most importantly, he belonged to the tiny group of Arabs who were actually literate. As al-Baladhuri (d. c. 892 CE) has explained, there were only seventeen members from the tribe of Quraysh who could read and write (see Chejne, *The Arabic Language* 59; 189, note 14). Hafsah, 'A'ishah, and Umm Kulthum numbered among the literate women while the literate men included 'Ali, 'Umar, 'Uthman, Abu 'Ubaydah, Talhah, Abu Sufyan, and Mu'awiyyah (189, note 14). Certainly there were more. The Prophet, for example, sent his adopted son, Zayd, to learn Hebrew and Syriac, in order to minimize his dependency on the Jewish secretaries he had used prior to the conflict with the Medinan Jews (Zeitlin 131). In total, the Prophet is reported to have had at least forty-five scribes who wrote on his behalf at one time or another (Azami 10).

Commentary on the Content of the Covenant

The *Covenant of the Prophet Muhammad with the Assyrian Christians* shares many similarities with the treaty concluded with the monks of the Monastery of Saint Catherine in the Sinai. Still, it contains numerous elements not seen in the prior and various aspects are expanded upon. Like any of his other documents, speeches, sermons or declarations, the Prophet invariably commences his covenant with a reference to God and his personal role as His Final Messenger. "God has told me in a vision what to do," he proclaims, "and I confirm His Command by giving my solemn promise to keep this agreement." In other words, the Prophet is not acting upon his own volition. He is merely the receptacle of Revelation, its conduit, and its embodiment. Not only is Muhammad in the Qur'an; the Qur'an was also in Muhammad.

"To the followers of Islam," commences the first item, "Carry out my command, protect and help the Nazarene nation in this country of ours in their own land." These words are important for the sense they convey. The Christians, known in Arabic as the Nazarenes, that is, the followers of Jesus of Nazareth (7–2 BCE to 30–36 CE), are recognized as a people and a nation of their own, a people and a nation existing within the confines of the Greater Islamic *ummah*. "As late as the thirteenth century," writes Philip Jenkins (b. 1952), the Christians of the East "still called themselves *Nasraye*, 'Nazarenes,' a form that preserves the Aramaic term used by the apostles; and they knew Jesus as Yeshua. Monks and priests bore the title *rabban*, teacher or master, which is of course related to the familiar *rabbi*" (7).

Rather than try to homogenize the Islamic world, making it all Arabic-speaking Muslims, the Prophet recognized that there were nations and peoples within the Muslim *ummah*. Such a concept never materialized in the West until the end of the twentieth century when countries like Canada finally recognized that Quebec was a nation within the country of Canada or when Spain recognized Cataluña, Galicia, and the Basque Country as autonomous regions within the country of Spain. Whether they were Jews or Christians, and later Hindus and Buddhists, these communities represented a kind of United Nations under Islamic rule.

In item two, the Prophet provides for the protection of places of worship: "Leave their places of worship in peace." It was never the practice of true Muslims to destroy the places of worship of monotheistic believers or even those who were not monotheistic. In zones which were governed or continue to be governed by the commands of the Messenger of Islam, attacks against sites holy to the Buddhist, Shintō, and even Hindu faiths have never taken place. It is only in very recent times that such shameful actions have been perpetrated, the most notorious of which was the destruction of the Buddhas of Bamiyan by the Taliban of Afghanistan in March 2001. It should also be stressed that the individuals involved in such actions were inspired by Salafism and not the Islam of the Prophet Muhammad. Not only did the Prophet protect churches, he commanded his followers to "help and assist their chief and their priests when in need of help, be it in the mountains, in the desert, on the sea, or at home." Far from treating Christian clerics as conquered subjects, the Prophet ordered his followers to serve them, help them, and assist them in all matters. The Islamic State under Muhammad was not one in which preferential treatment was given to Muslims while Jews and Christians were marginalized. As friends and allies of the Muslims, the Christians were granted special treatment. They may have had some obligations towards the State, such as paying certain taxes; however the Islamic Government recognized that it also had responsibilities towards its citizens regardless of their religion. If mosques were to be built and repaired, so were churches, monasteries, and synagogues.

In item four, the Prophet advises his followers to "Leave all their possessions alone, be it houses or other property, do not destroy anything of their belongings." He stresses that "the followers of Islam shall not harm or molest any of the members of this nation because the Nazarenes are my subjects, pay tribute to me and will help the Muslims." Since the Prophet was dealing with what previously was a vassal kingdom of the Byzantines, the Assyrians were not granted the tax-free status that the Monastery of Saint Catherine received; this was due to the fact that the Assyrians represented a fully-functioning economic hub as opposed to a monastic community. Unlike the monks, who could not be compelled to kill and wage war, the Christians of Assyria committed to pay taxes to the Islamic State and help the Muslims when called to do so.

As for taxation, the rate was negotiable. "No tribute, but what is agreed upon, shall be collected from them," decided the Prophet in item five, recognizing that economies rise and fall and that taxation should not be fixed, but rather adjusted, according to circumstances. During times of prosperity, taxation may be increased. During recessions or depressions, people should be granted tax-breaks in order to help stimulate the economy through increased spending. Item four also decrees that "their churches and buildings shall be left as they are, they shall not be altered." In other words, they cannot be destroyed, modified or replaced by other buildings. Destroying Sufi centers and turning them into parking lots as happened in Qum, Iran, during the early 21st century, would only have incensed the Messenger of Allah. The Prophet also promised not to interfere in religious matters: "their priests shall be permitted to teach and worship in their own way—the Nazarenes have full liberty of worship in their churches and homes." This right to worship freely has been denied to most Muslims since the days of European colonization. The oppressive dictatorships and pseudo-democracies ruling in the Muslim world have fundamentally failed to protect freedom of worship. In Malaysia, the Shi'ite school of Islam is outlawed and those who practice it are punished by imprisonment. In Saudi Arabia, Shi'ite centers, be they Twelver, Isma'ili and Zaydi, have been closed and quite often destroyed. In many Muslim countries, mosques only open briefly for prayers and study circles are prohibited. Religious gatherings in homes are also outlawed. And, in many Muslim countries, the sermons of Imams are censored or imposed by the Ministry of Religious Guidance which should really be renamed the "Ministry of Religious Misguidance." It goes without saying that if this happens with Muslims who do not follow "the official line," the same thing happens with other religions, such as Christianity. In short, the Prophet granted Christians more rights than Muslims themselves now receive in much of the Islamic world. If Muslims are deprived of their rights in their own countries, one can only image the situation for adherents of other religions. To cite a single example, one only has to look to Saudi Arabia where the construction of Christian churches is against the law. In clear contradiction with the words and practice of the Prophet Muhammad, the Grand Mufti of the of Saudi Arabia, Shaykh 'Abd al-'Aziz al-Shaykh, the highest ranking religious leader of the country, ruled in March of 2012 that "All churches in the Arabian Peninsula must be destroyed" (Asia News). In Iraq, a Shi'ite "ayatullah" by the name of Ahmad al-Hasani al-Baghdadi issued an edict in 2012 against Christians in Iraq, labeling them as "polytheists" and "friends of the Zionists" who must choose "Islam or death" while their women may be legitimately taken as "wives" by the Muslims (Mahmoud).

The issue of church property continues in item five, where the Prophet decrees that "None of their churches shall be torn down, or altered into a mosque, except by the consent and free will of the Nazarenes." He also warns that "If anyone disobeys this command, the anger of God and His Prophet shall be upon him." The presence of churches, mosques, monasteries, and synagogues are the pride of the Prophet and proof that he was sent as a mercy to all of humankind. The destruction of religious edifices and the persecution of religious groups from the People of the Book or the various Islamic schools bring shame to the Prophet's good name. If Muslims are prohibited from belittling the People of the Book and destroying their property, what are we to make, then, of so-called Islamists who insult and abuse them and destroy, not only their material belongings, but their lives as well? Such people do not speak for Islam, act for Islam, or represent Islam in any fashion or form. They are, in most instances, conscious or unconscious agents of the enemies, not only of Islam, but of religion as a whole. If the imperialists used Islamic extremists for their own ends during the colonialist period, spreading Salafism and concocting Arab nationalism in order to undermine the Ottoman Empire, it would be naïve to believe that neo-imperialists of the 20th and 21st century are not doing the same. While most of their rank and file are unaware of this reality, many, if not most of the world's militant Muslim movements were created and remain under the control of US, British, French, and Israeli secret services. They are used as agents of instability to justify continued occupation or to justify intervention and invasion. They are used to soil the image of Islam, discredit the Islamic political option, and ensure that no

Muslims in their right mind would ever want to live under what is falsely presented as *shari'ah* law. For the powers that be, "Islamists" are a convenient enemy. So long as the collective consciousness remains concerned with "terrorists," the people's attention is distracted from the crimes committed by those who actually dominate the world.

In item six, the Prophet specifies that the tribute paid by the Christians will be dedicated to promoting the spread of Islam and shall be deposited in the *bayt al-mal*. This ensured that the money would not be pocketed by immoral administrators. It also demonstrates that the Prophet was not a king and did not consider the income generated by the Islamic State as his personal possession. The *bayt al-mal*, literally "the House of Money," was a Public Treasury, the sole purpose of which was to provide government services. As such, it was spent on education, infrastructure, social services, and military expenses, among other things. There was a gradation in the tax rate. As the Messenger of Allah explained, "A common man shall pay one dinar (piece of money), but the merchants and people who own mines of gold and silver and are rich shall pay twelve dinars." Hence, as it is logical to any intelligent person, the rich were taxed at a higher rate than the middle and lower classes. As we saw in the *Covenant of the Prophet Muhammad with the Monks of Mount Sinai*, the Islamic economic system does not tax the poor. As the Prophet determined, "Strangers and people who have no houses or other settled property shall not have taxes levied upon them." Inheritance of property, however, is taxable in Islam. As the Prophet established, "If a man inherits property he shall pay a settled sum to the *bayt al-mal* treasury." In Islam, as in other systems, commercial transactions can be subject to taxation.

In item seven, we see, once again, how different terms were applied to different populations. If monks are not expected to join the military, as it might conflict with their vows and vocation, the Christians from Assyria were allowed to help the Muslims, although they were under no obligation to do so. As the Prophet explained,

> The Christians are not obliged to make war on the enemies of Islam, but if an enemy attacks the Christians, the Muslims shall not deny their help, but give them horses and weapons, if they need them, and protect them from evils from outside and keep the peace with them.

Manifesting his opposition to coerced conversions, the Prophet decrees that "The Christians are not obliged to become Muslims, until God's will makes them believers." In other words, it is up to God to guide non-Muslims towards Islam. Muslims may help facilitate this journey; through example and education but never through imposed indoctrination. The claim of Karen Armstrong (b. 1944) that "Muhammad never asked Jews or Christians to accept Islam" (2000: 10) is thus factually incorrect. The Messenger of Allah may not have forced the People of the Book to embrace Islam; however, he always invited them to do so. "While Muslims did not require the people they conquered to convert to Islam," writes Rollin Armour, "they presumed their subjects would eventually do so, and they believed, furthermore, that Islam would eventually cover the entire world" (32). While the result was not immediate, the strategy was sound and "more Christians embraced the faith of Muhammad of their own will than were ever forcibly converted under threat of death" (Betts 10). While Muslims remained a minority during the first few centuries of Islamic rule, "it is obvious that the great majority of Christians ultimately turned to Islam" (Humphreys 261).

Although women were considered the property of their husbands or fathers for much of recorded history, to the extent that they could sell them and even execute them at will, the Prophet's attitude towards women was remarkably "modern." But in reality, it was traditional; namely, it followed the true teachings of previous prophets and messengers of God. Even in the best of instances, a wife did not generally have an independent existence or will outside of that of her husband in the Prophet's time. For the Arabs of that period, and this even appears in the rules of Arabic grammar, the masculine predominates over the feminine. Hence, to address the male is to address the female. The Qur'an, however, does not always speak simply of "believers," which would include both male and female, it emphasizes the use of "believing males" and "believing females" (3:195; 4:124; 16:97; 33:35; 40:40). The presence of gender-inclusive language in a scripture from then 7th century is totally unique and the specific defense of women's rights found in the items eight and nine is nothing short of astounding.

"The Muslims shall not force Christian women to accept Islam," stresses the Prophet, "but if they themselves wish to embrace it, the Muslims shall be kind to them." The onus here is on women. It does not say that women can only become Muslim if their fathers or uncles allow them to do so. It does not say that they need their husband's permission. Women are thus recognized as fully independent individuals with reasoning capacity equal (and sometimes superior) to those of men. If other religions expect women to follow the religions of their husbands, no such requirement is made in Islam. "If a Christian woman is married to a Muslim and does not want to embrace Islam," says item nine, "she has liberty to worship at her own church according to her own religious belief, and her husband must not treat her unkindly on account of her religion." Such tolerance has rarely been seen, much less contemplated, in many societies.

As an expression of the seriousness of the covenant, item ten warns that "If anyone disobeys this command, he disobeys God and His Prophet and will be guilty of a great offense." In Islam, the greatest sins are not crimes against persons or property but firstly offenses against God, and secondarily, those against His Prophet. The rights of God and His Prophets, Messengers, and Friends come first. The covenants that the Prophet made with the Christians are not simple business contracts. They are not accords between two equal and self-determined parties. They are covenants concluded between God's Messenger and the Christian People with Allah as their Witness. The consequences of disobeying such orders could only be dire.

If the Prophet urged Muslims to allow Christians to renovate their churches in the *Covenant with the Monks of Mount Sinai*, he is even more explicit in stipulating such obligations in his *Covenant with the Assyrian Christians*. Not only must Muslims allow Christians to preserve their churches, they are required to help build them. As item eleven states, "If the Nazarenes wish to build a church, their Muslim neighbors shall help them. This shall be done, because the Christians have obeyed us and have come to us and pleaded for peace and mercy." If Jews and Christians destroy the holy sites of Muslims, Muslims are not to retaliate by destroying their holy sites as revenge. Muslims are not supposed to succumb to the wicked ways of their enemies. They should not lower themselves to the level of the transgressors. They should always emulate the example of Muhammad, the Messenger of Allah. Hence, unlike the Franks who sacked Constantinople in 1204, Mehmet II (r.1444–1446 and 1451–1481 CE), the Conqueror, insisted that artistic and archeological treasures of the city be protected and preserved (Lunde 85). While he was wrong to convert the Hagia Sofia into a mosque in 1453, at least he protected it, and treated all of the Christian symbols within it with respect. In fact, the Sultan allowed the icons of Jesus, the Virgin Mary, and a host of saints to remain in the mosque alongside newly-added Islamic calligraphy. While it took time, the Turkish State attempted to redress their historical wrong by converting the mosque into a museum in 1935. By treating Christian icons with respect, the Sultan was emulating the Sunnah of the Prophet Muhammad. However, the secularization of a holy site is as bad, if not worse, than its appropriation by a different religion.

After the conquest of Mecca, and the triumph of monotheism over polytheism, the Messenger of Allah ordered the destruction of all idols and images in and around the Ka'bah. Among the images of pagan deities were paintings of Abraham, the Virgin Mary and the infant Jesus, along with a picture of angels. As Ibn Ishaq (704–761/70 CE) reports, "Quraysh had put pictures in the Ka'bah including two of Jesus son of Mary and Mary (on whom be peace).... The apostle ordered that the pictures should be erased except those of Jesus and Mary" (552). Al-Waqidi (747–823 CE) and al-Azraqi are even more descriptive. They both relate that the Messenger of Allah placed his hand protectively over the icon of Jesus and Mary, and ordered all the other pictures, except that of Abraham, be erased (Waqidi 411; Azraqi 111). Another tradition, however, states that the image of Abraham was also erased because it portrayed him as an old man casting lots (Waqidi 411). As Omid Safi explains,

> As had been the case with Judaism, Islamic teachings did not approve of graven images in places of worship. Yet Muhammad's action demonstrates that he and his followers could and did distinguish between idols devoted to polytheistic deities and icons of previous revelations, such as Christianity. (151)

If the earliest surviving biographies of the Prophet mention the fact that he protected the images of the infant Jesus, the Virgin Mary, and perhaps even that of Abraham, Ibn Hisham's (d. 834) mutilated version of Ibn Ishaq's *Sirah* makes no such mention. As Alfred Guillaume (1888–1966 CE) observes, "Apparently I. H. has cut out what I. I. wrote and adopted the later tradition that all the pictures were obliterated" (552). According to G. R. D. King, these images survived until the destruction of the Ka'bah by the Umayyads in 683 CE (219–220). There is no doubt that the biographers of the Prophet and the collectors of *hadith* were biased, both religiously and politically. It is equally evident that the suppression of material that was favorable towards Christians took place at a time when ties between the followers of Christ and the followers of Muhammad had degenerated. It appears that a hardening of positions seems to have developed between the two communities with Muslim scholars becoming increasingly intransigent in their interpretations of Islam rendering the Muslim religion increasingly intolerant, puritanical, and exclusivist.

Regardless of the reasons that motivated such manipulations of sacred history, Muslims are duty-bound to abide by the example of the Prophet Muhammad as opposed to the ideologically-inspired misinterpretations of misguided mullahs. The teachings and actions of the Messenger of Allah speak for themselves. Not only should Muslims respect holy sites, they must respect holy people, regardless of whether or not they belong to the Islamic faith. Piety is piety. Righteousness is righteousness. Love of God and devotion are universal. Nobody has a monopoly on goodness. Until the rise of iconoclastic Salafism, which aims to destroy all historical and archeological remnants of Islamic history, Muslims showed a great deal of reverence for sacred sites and the resting places of pious and saintly people. The Mamluk dynasty (1250–1517), for example, "made heroic efforts to create a whole new landscape of Muslim devotion and pilgrimage" (Jenkins 217). In and around Damascus alone, writes, Bethany J. Walker,

> One could visit a variety of shrines, revered by Muslims and Christians alike: the Mosque of Moses' Footprints, the birthplace of Abraham, the Cave of [Abel's] Blood, Adam's Cave, the Hunger Cave, the refuge of Mary and Jesus, Elias' oratory, and the Cemetery of the Prophets. Within four miles of the city were the cemeteries of holy men and numerous mausolea of multifarious venerable, such as ... various Companions of the Prophet ... and 'People of the House' of the Prophet (Umm Kulthum, 'Ali Talib's daughter; the children of Hasan and Husayn, the sons of 'Ali, son-in-law of the Prophet); the 'Martyrs' ... Seth, Noah, and Moses, and numerous other luminaries. (qtd. Jenkins 217–218)

In 1912, American archeologist Frederic Jones Bliss observed how Muslims and the People of the Book shared the same sacred spaces in greater Syria:

> Christians, Moslems, Jews and Nuseiriyeh [Alawites] visit each other's shrines. The Moslems take their insane, or 'possessed' to get rid of their evil spirits in the cave of Saint Anthony, belonging to the Maronite convent of Qozhayya in the Lebanon. Christians go on a similar errand to the well at the

> shrine of Sheikh Hassan er Rai (the Shepherd) near Damascus.... During the procession of Good Friday, barren Moslem women pass under the cloth on which is stamped the figure of Christ, in hopes that they may bear children. Christian women in Hums consult Dervish diviners. The Nuseiriyeh observe Christmas, though they subordinate Jesus to Ali.... Instances of Moslems seeking baptism for their children as a sort of charm have been reported from all parts of Syria and Palestine. (qtd. Jenkins 205)

"Even at the start of the twentieth century," reports Jenkins, "Muslims requested Christians to parade the relics of their saints as a means of driving off an epidemic" (205). In the 1990s, Muslims continued to visit the famous church of the Virgin of Seidnaya in Syria in order to ask for the intercession of Mary, the Mother of Jesus (205). Syria, which was a symbol of spiritual symbiosis, has since been shattered by outside forces which seek to cause chaos and destruction through division.

Since Muslims are commanded in the Qur'an to respect the signs of Allah (Qur'an 22:32; 40:81; 5:29; 31:32), they must respect the righteous servants of God among the People of the Book. As such, item eleven states that "If there be among thc Christians a great and learned man the Muslims shall honor him and not be envious of his greatness." To do injustice to any treaty-bound Christian is an act of insubordination towards the Seal of the Prophets. As item thirteen states, "If anyone is unjust and unkind to the Christians he will be guilty of disobeying the Prophet of Allah."

Like the Christians from Mount Sinai, the Assyrian Christians also had certain obligations towards the larger Islamic Community. "The Christians should not shelter an enemy of Islam or give him horse, weapon or any other help" stipulates item fourteen. In the same spirit, item fifteen stresses that "If a Muslim is in need, the Christians shall for three days and nights be his host and shelter him from his enemies." If they are to be friends and allies of the Muslims, the Christians must not aid and abet the enemies of Islam. Considering that they had greater protection, rights and liberties, under Islamic rule, many Christians could scarcely conceive of siding with rough-hewn Christian Crusaders from a less refined, civilized, and culturally-advanced Europe. The Jews of al-Andalus, for example, actually invited the Muslims of North Africa to liberate them from the yoke of oppression of the Christian Visigoths prior to 711 CE (Levy 169). This was not the first time that Jews sided with Muslims in confrontations with Christians. Jewish people are reported to have aided the Arabs in capturing Byzantine cities during the early Muslim conquests (Armour 27). In any event, the minuscule Muslim army met very little resistance from the Spanish Catholic masses who loathed their Germanic overlords and oppressors. As Ahmad Thomson writes, "The oppressed majority of this corrupt and decaying society regarded the Muslims not so much as conquerors but as saviors. The Muslims ended their slavery and gave them freedom to practice their religion" (88).

As allies of the Muslims, the Christians of Assyria were expected to provide protection to Muslims in times of war and peace. In nomadic societies, hospitality cannot be denied. Even warring Arab tribes would never deny hospitality to an enemy in need of shelter. With the sweltering heat of the day, which can kill without access to shade and ample water, and the blistering cold of the night, which can kill quickly as the temperature drops to below freezing, denying hospitality means death. If even enemies granted each other temporary protection from the elements and basic nourishment, friends and allies were expected to treat each other with still greater kindness. Insisting on the rights of women and children, rights which were not recognized by the dominant cultures of the day who treated them like chattel to be bought and sold, Muhammad, the Messenger of Allah—who ended the practice of female infanticide among the Arabs—demanded guarantees of their protection. "The Christians," declares the Prophet, "shall protect the Muslim women and children and not deliver them up to the enemy or expose them to view."

If the Muslims were repeatedly warned of the wrath of God if they failed to fulfill their obligations towards the Christians, the Prophet is subtle, yet stern, regarding any failure of the Christians to abide by their agreement: "If the Nazarenes fail to fulfill these conditions," states item seventeen, "they have forfeited their right to protection, and the agreement is null and void." If they betrayed the Muslims, the Christians would no longer be granted protection from their enemies. The Muslims would not come to their aid if they were attacked by others. Furthermore, if they broke the treaty by actually attacking the Muslims, they would suffer the military consequences. If the path of peace did not content the Christians, then, according to their wishes, they would face the path of war. Their combatants would be killed and the rest of the population would suffer the consequences of armed conflict. Their properties would be confiscated. And any survivors would be subjected to military occupation and denied any taxation privileges. As the Messenger of Allah made manifest throughout his life, the true Muslim is a lamb towards the believers and the friends of the believers, but he is a lion towards the enemies of Allah.

For the sake of posterity and to ensure continued protections during successive rulers, the Prophet made every effort possible to preserve the *Covenant*. As item eighteen expresses, "This document shall be entrusted to the Christian chief and head of their church for safe keeping." It was thanks to such actions that the different covenants of the Prophet were preserved in various churches throughout the greater Middle East. While many Muslims refuse to return the greetings of peace towards People of the Book, the Prophet sent them his most sincere salutations as a sign of the bonds between both communities. He concluded the covenant with "The peace of God be over them all," hoping for peace, prosperity, and enduring good relations.

Unlike some Christian communities, who hid their covenants of the Prophet and kept them out of the public eye, where they did little good, the Assyrian Christians of Turkey and Iraq made sure that the words of the Messenger were well-known to Christians and Muslims alike. As a result, the existence of this covenant, as well as its content, remained common knowledge well into the 19th century. After this its memory began to fade among the lay people, but it remained well-known to Assyrian clerics and community leaders. "The lethal attacks on . . . churches in Iraq" in the early 21st century, writes Uwe Siemon-Netto, "violated the stated will of the Prophet Muhammad, who in the 7th century issued a *Firman*—or letter of protection—for Assyrian Christians." According to Albert Yelda, the Messenger of Allah had granted the Assyrians protection out of respect for their knowledge of medicine and science and decreed that that they be left in peace (Siemon-Netto). Joseph Yacoub, a professor of political science at the Catholic University of Lyon, fears that terrorist bombings of Christian churches may accomplish what the Messenger of Allah attempted to prevent: the complete de-Christianization of Iraq.

Conclusions

The authenticity of the Prophet's patents with the people of the Sinai and Najran has been questioned by some scholars; so has that of the *Covenant of the Prophet Muhammad with the Assyrian Christians*. As readers will readily acknowledge, the content of the covenants with the Christians of Mount Sinai and Najran is completely compatible with that of the covenant concluded with the Assyrian Christians. In style and substance, the works all appear to be the work of the same genius. They show a side of Muhammad which has rarely been shared with the world: the role of the Prophet as statesmen and as master politician, diplomat, and tactician. The spiritual Muhammad is shown to some. The military Muhammad is shown to others. And the historical Muhammad is shown to most. Few, however, have glimpsed the intellectual inner workings of Muhammad's mind and the failure to do so has produced catastrophic results. To this day, some scholars persist in their erroneous view that the spread of Islam was a form of imperialism rooted in religious zeal and Arab nationalism when, in reality—though rigorous in some aspects—it was an opening of hearts and minds and the acceptance of a new culture and civilization which was far superior to the oppressive ideologies of the time.

Chapter 7

The Prophet Muhammad and the Armenian Christians of Jerusalem

Introduction

As part of what can only be described as a concerted campaign to establish alliances with Christian communities, the Messenger of Allah reached out, not only to the Greek Orthodox Christians from Mount Sinai, the Coptic Christians of Egypt, the Assyrian Christians of upper Mesopotamia, and the Christians of Persia, but to the Armenian Christians of Jerusalem. He had, of course, sent word to the Byzantine Christians; however, they had rebuked his offers. Since the Eastern Roman Empire had expressed hostility towards him, Muhammad's strategy seems to have been to create a buffer zone of Greek, Assyrian, Armenian, and Persian Christian sympathizers, to help protect the Muslim homeland from any attacks from the Byzantine Christians and Western Roman Catholics.

Issues of Authenticity

The *Covenant of the Prophet Muhammmad with the Armenian Christians*, known as the *Firman Attributed to the Prophet Muhammad, Confirming the Rights of the Armenians in the Holy Places of Jerusalem* (Narkiss 11, figure 2) has received little circulation and is generally unknown among both Armenians and Muslims. The scroll, which is made of paper on a silk backing, measures 327 x 21.5 cm and is housed at the St. James Library in the Armenian Patriarchate of Jerusalem. According to Armenian historians, "Patriarch Abraham [I] of Jerusalem traveled to Mecca in the seventh century to secure special privileges for the Patriarchate from the Prophet Mohammed himself" (Azadian). As Haig Krikorian, author of *Lives and Times of the Armenian Patriarchs of Jerusalem*, explains: "Abraham [I] (638–669), regarded by many as the first Armenian Patriarch of Jerusalem, had trekked all the way to Mecca, to plead with the Prophet Mohammed for protection for his flock" (Hagopian). Yet another Armenian source writes that "[t]he first Armenian Patriarch of Jerusalem was Abraham who, according to the Arab historian Zeki al-Din, seeing the that the influence of Muhammad was growing stronger, went to him personally in 626 and received and official document regarding the safety of the Armenian Church and her possessions in Jerusalem" (Belleville Armenian Church). Unlike some of the other Christian figures that appear in the *hadith* and *sirah* literature, and whose historicity cannot always be confirmed, Abraham I appears in the full light of history. Since he was Patriarch from 638 to 669 CE, he had two full years in order to obtain a *firman* or covenant from the Prophet Muhammad. This may very well have been in Mecca, right after its conquest, but most likely in Medina, after his return, when large numbers of leaders from lands far and near came to the Messenger of Allah to offer their submission and to seek special rights and privileges.

The authenticity of the *Oath*, *Pact*, *Firman* or *Covenant of the Prophet* has been challenged by Father Jerôme Golubovich's *I Frati Minori nel possesso de'luoghi santi di Gerusalemme (1333) e i falsi firmani posseduti dai Greo-Elleni: Note e documenti per la soluzione della questione de'luoghi santi* which was published in 1921. Manifesting a complete lack of objectivity, the Franciscan sets off with a singular purpose; namely, to prove that the documents presented by the Greek Orthodox Church in support of their exclusive possession of the holy sites in Palestine are spurious. According to the anonymous academic who reviewed Father Jerôme Golubovich's *I Frati Minori* in the *Revue Biblique*, "we are faced with a fraud built like a war

The Firman of 'Umar ibn al-Khattab with the Armenian Christians of Jerusalem

machine at the peak of the controversy over the sanctuaries of Palestine" (L'École Pratique d'Études Bibliques 637). As Golubovich conveniently concludes, the *Pact* or *Testament of Muhammad* with the monks of Mount Sinai, the *Treaty of 'Umar*, and the *firman* of Selim I, among many others, are all fake (L'École Pratique d'Études Bibliques 637). He alleges that most of these forgeries date to 1630–1634, namely, the tyrannical rule of Murad IV (637). The length to which this Catholic cleric is willing to go in his attempt to strip the Greek Orthodox Church of the holy sites is startling. Rather than content himself with the fact that they are in Christian hands, he produces research that, if it were true, would leave their ownership up in the air. Rather than be turned over to the Catholics, the sites would be returned to their earlier guardians: the Muslims.

Although Father Golubovich cannot prove that they are guilty beyond a reasonable doubt, he does not hesitate to accuse distinguished leaders of the Greek Orthodox Church. To be precise, the Franciscan friar alleges that the frauds in question were authored by Cyril Lucaris (1572–1638 CE), born Kyrillos Lukaris, the Greek Patriarch of Alexandria, and later, Ecumenical Patriarch of Constantinople; by the Father Lambrinos; by his *procureur*, Théophane, the Patriarch of Jerusalem; as well as by his arch-deacon, Grégoire, who is described by the anonymous critic as a "former Jew who, on a spite-filled day, sold the pot to the roses" (L'École Pratique d'Études Bibliques 637). Evidently, in the eyes of this extreme reviewer, corrupt Greek Orthodox Christians conspired with Jews, Muslims, and Turks to prevent a relatively powerless Catholic Church from taking possession of the property rights to the holy sites in Palestine—a rather far-fetched notion to say the least, given that Jews, Muslims, and Greek Orthodox do not even associate with one another in Jerusalem. The Latins, of course, were not the only Christians who attempted to expropriate Armenian properties and subjugate the Armenian Church; the Greeks made similar efforts (Hagopian).

Despite his "firm command" of history, the arguments of Golubovich are as unconvincing as they are historically inaccurate. He claims, for example, that the *Pact of Muhammad* appeared around 1569 CE (L'École Pratique d'Études Bibliques 636). But while the original is reported to have been taken to Istanbul by Selim I in 1517, the covenant itself had been endorsed by religious authorities at regular intervals over the previous five hundred years. To claim that the covenant was concocted by the monks is one thing; to claim that they faked five centuries of *fatwas* from several Muslim dynasties is another. And while it might be convenient for some to assert that the *Covenant of the Prophet Muhammad with the Monks of Mount Sinai* only dates to 1569, or even 1517 for that matter, how then could it have been seen by Jean Thenaud, the guardian of the Convent of the Cordeliers of Angoulême during this pilgrimage to St. Catherine's Monastery in 1512? In fact, in his *Voyage d'outremer (Égypte, Mont Sinay, Palestine)*, he stated that there was a Muslim mosque next to the Church of Saint Catherine in which were preserved the privileges that Muhammad gave to the monks, namely, freedom from taxation and obligations, which were signed by his palm-print (Thenaud 72). In other words, the *Covenant* or *Pact of Muhammad* could not have been crafted by means of the combined efforts of Greek Orthodox Christians, Cryptic Jews, and Turkish Muslims in the late 16th century or early 17th century as its existence predates the Ottoman Conquest of the Sinai.

Father Jerôme Golubovich concluded that the *Covenant of the Prophet Muhammad with the Armenian Christians* was a fake, along with every other document that supports their claims to the title of the holy sites under their jurisdiction. The *Firman Attributed to 'Umar ibn al-Khattab, the Conqueror of Jerusalem in* 638, however, which is housed in the St. James Library in the Armenian Patriarchate of Jerusalem, and of which a handwritten Arabic copy is kept at the National Library in Paris, seems to indicate otherwise. Known also as the *Achtiname* or *Ahtiname of Caliph 'Umar ibn al-Khattab*, it was delivered to Sophronios, the Greek Orthodox Patriarch of Jerusalem, on the 20th of Rabi' al-Awwal of the 15th year of the *hijrah*. It reads:

The Firman of 'Umar ibn al-Khattab with the Armenian Christians of Jerusalem

In the name of the good and merciful God of whom we invoke His understanding, Omar Ibn al-Khattab, glory be to God, who has reared us in Islam and who has honored us through Faith, who through compassion on us, sent us His Prophet Mohammed, may the peace and blessings of the Lord be with him who led us from deceit to the truth and has gathered us where before we were scattered. Glory to Him who joined our hands, who ran to our help against our enemies, who placed under our rule countries, and has joined us with true bonds of brotherhood.

Let us give to the Lord thanks, for all the benefits to those who are servants of the Lord. The present decree of Omar Ibn al-Khattab, is a contract and a pact delivered to the distinguished and most reverent Sophronios, Patriarch of the Imperial Nation, on Mount of Olives, in Jerusalem. It includes as well the laity, clergy, monks and nuns and I grant to them full security wherever they wish to be.

Because when a citizen fulfills his duties to the Authorities punctually, we the Faithful as well as our posterity, owe in turn to grant him the necessary security. Therefore, let them stop reproaching them for their faults for they already declared submission and obedience.

Let them have therefore full and absolute security as concerns their life, their Churches, their beliefs and all places of pilgrimage which they now have within or without the city, namely the Kamame (the Church of the Resurrection), the Church of Bethlehem, where Jesus, may peace be on him, was born, the Great Church and the Cave with the three gates, the southern, northern and western ones. They together with the rest of the Christians who reside here, Georgians, Abyssinians (Ethiopians), as well as Franks, Copts, Syrians, Armenians, Nestorians, Jacobians and Maronites, who will come as simple pilgrims and will belong to said Patriarch.

They may have the primacy above all the others according to what was granted to them from the part of the Prophet and dear Messenger of the Lord, who honored them with the sign of his gracious hand and ordered they be granted protection and security. Similarly we too, the true faithful, owe to behave, honoring the example of him who acted beneficially towards them.

All the Christian pilgrims to the All Holy Tomb, should give the Patriarch one drachma and 1/3 of a silver drachma. Every genuine faithful, man or woman, judge or Governor, who exercises duties as a judge on earth, must respect whatever we have granted by warrant, whether rich or poor, Muslim or Muslimist disciple of the Prophet. For this reason we have granted for their sake the present Decree. Let everybody act accordingly towards what is contained therein and have this, obtained in their hands continual authority. Glory be to God of the people and suffice for us God, the Protector and Graceful One.

Executed on the 20th of Rabi' al-Awwal of the 15th year of the departure of the Prophet.

Let him be transgressor of the Agreement of God and hateful against the beloved Prophet, he who acts contrary to the content of this Decree. (Jerusalem Patriarchate)

Politically, religiously, and economically motivated skeptics claim that Sophronios is not a historical figure, which is false. There were literally hundreds of patriarchs in Jerusalem at the time, one of which was most certainly Sophronios. No forger would have been careless enough to invent a figure that never existed. When the *Firman of 'Umar* speaks of "what was granted to them from the part of the Prophet," the document clearly alludes to a previous agreement. The original, it should be noted, was also stamped with the print of the Prophet's hand, a feature found on other covenants concluded by the Messenger of Allah. Besides the Second Caliph, 'Umar ibn al-Khattab, the covenant of the Prophet with the Armenian Christians was also confirmed by the Fourth Caliph, 'Ali ibn Abi Talib, in a decree that dates from the year 660 CE, just one year prior to his martyrdom.

Known as the *Covenant of 'Ali, Fourth Caliph, of Baghdad, Granting Certain Immunities and Privileges to the Armenian Nation*, it was translated into Armenian by Gregor Campan in 1767, and afterwards by M. Saragian. The covenant was authenticated by Joakim Gregor Bagratuni of Constantinople in the year 1804. Johannes Avdall reported in 1869 that he had been "in possession of a copy of the original document, written in Cufic characters" which he had lent to Henry Torrens, Vice-President of the Asiatic Society, for translation and insertion in the Journal. "It appears," continues Avdall, "that this rare piece of antiquity was lost or mislaid among his unpublished papers." If Henry Torrens was so negligent, they could crucify him one thousand times and that would not suffice considering his crime against history. Although the ancient Arabic copy of the *Covenant of 'Ali* was lost, Johannes Avdall was able to complete a correct and faithful translation into English on the basis of the Armenian translation. Published in the *Journal of the Asiatic Society of Bengal* in 1870, it reads: [see next page]

The Covenant of 'Ali with the Armenian Christians of Jerusalem

In the Name of God, the Beneficent and Merciful from whom we solicit help.

Praise and thanksgiving to the Creator of the Universe, and blessings upon the great and benign Muhammed and his sacred tribe.

[After all this, it is the purport of the translation of the Covenant which was written by Hashim, the son of Athap, the son of Valas, according to the command of the blessed chief of the Arabians, and of the Lion, of the holy of the holies, of 'Ali, the grandson of Abu Talib, the exalted, in Cufic character, in the celebrated domicile of Kharanthala, in the magnificent palace, in the month of Safar, in the fortieth year of the *hijrah*.]

Whereas certain of the Armenian nation, men of distinction, famous for their erudition and honored for their dignity, namely, Jacob Sayyid 'Abdul-Shuyukh and the son of Saha, and Abraham the Priest, Bishop Isaiah, and several others, forty in number, having communicated with me, and being present in the enactment of this Covenant, solicited me to this, and have rendered every assistance in their power to our agent whom we had sent [to] our forts and frontiers, (which was the occasions of our conference and the enactment of this Covenant). Therefore, I have made this Covenant with them on my behalf, as well as on behalf of all the tribes of Islam [so that Islam] shall prevail, and the doctrine of Christianity shall continue. It shall be the duty of all potentates and of all princes, and of all men to carry out our Covenant, by the help of God, so long as the sea shall be capable of wetting wool, tufts from the earth, and stars shall give light, and the moon shall rise upon aliens and strangers. No man shall dare to violate or alter this Covenant, nor increase and decrease or change the same; because he that increases it, increases his punishment, and decreases our patience.

And those who violate this Covenant, shall be considered intriguing infringers of that which I have bestowed on them (the Armenians), and in league with those who do not profess loyalty to me. They also become transgressors against the divine ordinance, and thus incur the just indignation of the only God.

Moreover, the testimony of Sayyid (Arch) Bishop and of the others, whose names have written before, is a binding and sufficient authority. Because the principal followers of Christ requested me to establish a Covenant and a treaty among all the Christians, placed under the shadow of the rule of the Musulmans, now, by virtue of this Covenant, there shall be perpetual peace and tranquility between Christians and Musulmans. The contents of this Covenant are indubitable and true, and I have given to them (the Armenians) of my accord and with a cheerful countenance. I shall abide by this Covenant and act accordingly, so long as the Armenians shall be faithful to me and continue in their loyalty to my government, and take no part in opposing the religion of my people. If they remain steadfast in the observance of this Covenant, they shall resemble the Musulmans and the Mumins.

Moreover, I have convened together the grandees of the Musulmans and the leading men of my elders and dignitaries and in their presence have established this Covenant, which the Christian nation requested of me and desired to possess. I have written down and recorded for them conditions and stipulations, which are hereafter to stand firm and remain in force. Should, in future, any monarch or prince, or any person of rank and authority, oppress them and treat them with cruelty, they should produce and present this record of my Covenant, because it is incumbent on monarchs, and on all Musulmans to act according to our behests; but the Armenians also, by acts of fidelity and loyalty, should comply with our mandates and obey our will, in conformity with the contents of the treaty which I have made and established with them. There shall be no disobedience or opposition to my commands and wishes. Moreover, it is politic and expedient, not to molest and oppress the Christians, so that by the adoption of conciliatory course, they might be induced to comply with the stipulations contained in this my Covenant.

Thus my Covenant is a burden and an obligation to its recipients, and wearisome and irksome to maliciously disposed and evil-minded persons, and I desire that there should be no contention between the Christians and my exalted nation. But if any one shall act against all that I have written concerning the Christians, who have proved themselves worthy of my favor and benevolence, such a person acts against the will of God, who inspired me with grace to do this act of goodness to that nation and to save them from troubles and vexations; for I have entered into a Covenant of patriarchs, of prophets, which was brought down from heaven by an angel, enjoins obedience to the laws and performance of duties, and also faithfulness to my divine Covenant. Because the Christians under my authority are my subjects, and I am ruler over them, it is my duty to have a paternal eye over them and to protect them from all evils and troubles; and thus a good reward shall be given to me and to my nation which is scattered in different parts of the world.

And the scale of taxation fixed by me for those nobles should be strictly adhered to. No demand should be made beyond what was already written down and sanctioned. They should not be molested or oppressed. Their country should not be taken from them. They should not be alienated from their country. The priests should not be converted from Christianity. The monks and hermits should not be disturbed in their solitudes, nor removed from their monasteries. Their preachers should not be prohibited to preach. Their habitations and their hereditary lands should not be devastated. Nobody should remove or pull down the bells from the steeples of their churches. This is the law which I have made for them. But, those who shall infringe my Covenant, by disobeying my behests, shall be transgressors of the ordinance of God, and shall suffer severe punishments and eternal penalties.

Let no crowned head or man of authority of the Musulmans or believers compel the Christians to profess the religion of the Musulmans. Nor let them hold any controversies with them on matters of religion, but let them treat them with kindness and tenderness; and under the shadow of their mercy and clemency, protect them from all sorts of oppression and tribulations, wherever they may be found and wherever they may reside. And if the Christian people be in want of money or in need of pecuniary help for the building of churches or monasteries, for their national and social assemblies, and for their civil and domestic purposes, the Musulmans ought to assist them and supply them with the necessary means, by granting them a portion of their superabundant and disowned property. And they should also aid them by good advice and suggestions in

their transactions, because doing so is pleasing and acceptable in the sight of God and His Apostle. But, if any one should infringe the contents of this my Covenant, he is an unbeliever and an apostate from the divine prophet, and he will assuredly be deprived of his merits, and the Prophet shall look upon him with anger and displeasure. If the stubborn and refractory shall prove themselves unfaithful and disobedient to the Covenant which I have established, they cannot remain faithful and obedient to the son of Abu Talib, the exalted. For, whatever he may command and ordain, it is the duty of Musulmans to carry out his orders, by succoring and commiserating them (the Armenians) at all times, so long as this world shall last.

Glory to the Creator of the Universe!

The Covenant of ʿAli with the Armenian Christians of Jerusalem

This *Covenant of ʿAli*, which merits a major study in itself, shows many similarities with the covenants of the Prophet Muhammad with various Christian communities and denominations. While the exordium of the *Covenant of ʿAli*, which was written by a later scribe, contains some misunderstandings, the content of the charter itself is in full conformity with the previous covenants of the Prophet. The fact that it was originally written in Kufic script is sound and consistent with the custom of Imam ʿAli. The claim that the Christians had come to the aid of Imam ʿAli is correct. The Imam, it is reported, was well-loved by the Christians. In many places, the *Covenant* appeals to Muslims who were disloyal to the Imam. This could only refer to the seditious Muʿawiyyah and his turn-coat followers. One of the reasons for protecting the Christians was to ensure that, although Islam would prevail, Christianity would continue. This clearly indicates that the triumph of Islam does not rest in the eradication and annihilation of other religions. The Imam envisages a pluralistic Islamic society which encompasses members of other faiths. As such, the *Covenant* establishes that "there shall be perpetual peace and tranquility between Christians and Musulmans." Evidently, such a clause could never apply to Christians who are at war against Islam and Muslims. Still, it would continue to be applicable to Christians who live as *ahl al-dhimmah* or Protected People in the Muslim world. So long as they fulfill their obligations, Imam ʿAli asserts that the Christians "shall resemble the Musulmans and the *Muʾmins*." They are not, under any circumstances, to be considered second-class citizens. So long as they abide by the conditions of the *Covenant*, and are law-abiding citizens, the Christians are just like the Muslims as far as the Islamic State is concerned. A wise politician, Imam 'Ali warns that it is expedient that Muslims not molest and oppress the Christians. Poor treatment, understood the Imam, would only turn Christians against the Muslims. Conciliation, he comprehended, was always the key to peaceful relations. If any Christians were to be brought into the fold of Islam, it would be through love, kindness, charity, and exemplary actions. The duty of the true Imam, Caliph or Sultan, explains 'Ali, is to protect his subjects: all of them, regardless of their religion, due to the simple fact that they are all creatures of Almighty Allah.

Most interestingly, the *Covenant of 'Ali* contains subtle traits of Shi'ism. The Imam, for example, speaks of divine inspiration, something Sunnis would never attribute to anyone but the Prophet. 'Ali, however, clearly states that he issued the covenant to the Armenians Christians as a result of divine inspiration; that the covenant he entered into was a covenant of patriarchs and prophets; and that the covenant was brought down from heaven by an angel. Most Sunnis will claim that these are signs that the covenant is a Shi'ite forgery. Sufis would generally maintain a more open-mind while Shi'ites might readily embrace it, viewing these features as evidence of the covenant's authenticity. It takes an objective observer to point out that genuine Sunni traditions confirm the reality of divine inspiration (as distinguished from revelation which is exclusive to prophets and messengers) which is granted to pure and pious Muslims by means of dreams and visions. So, from a doctrinal point of view, a Sunni scholar cannot deny the possibility that Imam 'Ali was inspired by Allah by the intermediary of angels. Another strong sign of Shi'im can be seen in Imam 'Ali's stern warning that anyone who disobeyed his commands and was disloyal to him was an unbeliever and an apostate. The *Covenant of 'Ali*, claims the Imam, was divine in nature and obligatory until the end of time.

Since Shi'ites have always been a minority, a mere ten percent of the Muslim world population, and ruled only on rare occasion—the Idrisids, the Fatimids, the Safavids, and the post-1979 Iranians—why would a Christian concoct a *Covenant of 'Ali* that contained so many 'Alid elements? Why not assume the attitude of the Sunni majority and present the image of the Caliph 'Ali as one of the rightly-guided Companions and a faithful follower of the Sunnah? Had a Christian presented the *Covenant of 'Ali* to radical Sunnis, he could have been beheaded. So, this covenant cannot have been concocted by some creative Christian who wanted to protect his community. How would he even have known that Shi'ites believe their Imams are divinely-inspired by angels? How would he know that those who fought the Fourth Caliph, namely, the Khawarij and the Umayyads, were considered apostates and infidels? And why come up with a *Covenant from 'Ali* when the *Firman of 'Umar* already protected the rights of Christians and would undoubtedly have received a better reception among Sunni rulers? What we have here is an example of the long-honored tradition of Muslim rulers of confirming the rights granted by their predecessors. Following in the footsteps of 'Ali, 'Umar, and the Prophet, Caliph Muktafi II of Baghdad issued a *Charter of Protection* to the Nestorian Church in the year 1138 CE. While it is too long to reproduce here, the Caliph confirms that he is following the precedent of the imams and predecessors, and acting in conformity with the method adopted by the Orthodox Caliphs, in granting protection to the Christians (6). The rights he grants are the same mentioned by Imam 'Ali, Caliph 'Umar, and the various covenants of the Prophet. As A. Mingana, the editor of the *Charter of Protection*, stresses:

> The need has always been felt for an authoritative statement throwing light on the relations between official Islam and official Christianity at the time when Islam had power of life and death over millions of Christian subjects. Individual Christians may have suffered persecution at the hand of individual Muslims; isolated cases of Christian communities suffering hardship through the fanaticism of a provincial governor, or a jurist, or the hallucinations of a half-demented Sheikh or Mullah are also recorded in history; a Caliph or two—such as Mutawwakil—did, certainly, subject the Christians

> to some vexatious measures; but such incidents, however numerous, are to be considered as infractions of the law, and the men who brought them about were breakers of the law, as all criminals are breakers of the law. The statutory attitude of Islam laid down in the present document proves beyond the possibility of doubt that, however imperfect official Islam may have been in some social aspects, statutory intolerance was not among its defects. The charter emanates from the chancery of an 'Abassid Caliph, but could an English King, a Dutch Queen or a French President write in the twentieth century a more tolerant charter in favor of their numerous Muslim subjects? It is not the Kur'an that was the cause of persecution of Christians in early times, nor of their wholesale massacre in contemporary history, any more than the Gospel was the inspiring factor of the barbarities of the Inquisition. Politics, personal ambitions, or economic expediency should not be confused with religion. (1–2)

Salah al-Din al-Ayyubi (c. 1138–1193 CE), a notorious *nasibi* [hater of the Household of the Prophet and their partisans], was famous for his tolerance and nobility of character when confronting Christian Crusaders. When he conquered Jerusalem, he emulated the example of previous Muslim rulers and granted special protections to the Armenian Christians of the Holy Land.

The Firman of Salah al-Din with the Armenian Christians of Jerusalem

The Firman of Salah al-Din with the Armenian Christians of Jerusalem

While most authorities treat the *Edict of Salah al-Din* as historically genuine, Roman Catholic clergymen, Western Orientalists, and even Armenian Orthodox authorities question the *Covenant of the Prophet with the Armenian Christians of Jerusalem*. Avedis K. Sanjian, for example, speaks of "[t]he *Firman* attributed to the Prophet Mohammed, confirming the rights of the Armenians in the Holy Places of Jerusalem" (Narkiss 11), "[t]he *Firman* attributed to Omar Ibn al-Khattab [sic]" (11), and "[t]he *Firman* attributed to Caliph 'Ali" (13). Seta B. Dadoyan also refers to "[t]he [a]lleged 'Prophet's Oath to the Armenians'" (60). Dadoyan summarizes the early history of Muslim-Armenian contacts as follows:

> In Armenian histories the earliest context and occasion of Islamic-Armenian contacts was the status of the Armenians and Eastern Christians of Jerusalem.

What is known in Armenian histories as the 'Prophet's Oath' was considered an actual oath allegedly granted to a Christian deputation from Jerusalem in Medinah, headed by the Armenian Patriarch, during early 630s, if not earlier.

According to the Armenian tradition of oaths, this legend marks the first phase of interactions with Islam. In line with the tradition of the Prophet and in the same spirit, a similar arrangement was said to have been made by 'Ali ibn Abi Talib in 626/4H (future caliph in 656–661...), and a little later by Caliph 'Umar Ibn al-Khattab (634–644). The core of these initial 'oaths' was tolerance toward and protection of Christian communities by their Muslim rulers in return for their absolute submission and payment of taxes. In line with this tradition, the treatises of Mu'awiyah and Ibn Maslamah were 'reconfirmations' of the so-called 'Prophet's Oath.' This is how Armenians viewed their relations with the Islamic Caliphate at the time. In their opinion, the Umayyads simply 'renewed'—as it was often said—the 'Prophet's Oath' in 703 and 719. Much later, in 1187 when Ayyubid Salah ed-Din entered Jerusalem, the Armenians saw another 'renewal' of the initial oath to Armenians for protection in return for their subjection and tribute. In fact, Salah ed-Din himself established this in his oath, which is accepted as authentic. Armenians were said to have shown Salah ed-Din the oaths of 'Ali and 'Umar.... It does indeed support the Armenian tradition of tracing all oaths as continuations of what they called the Prophet's Oath. (60)

As far as Robert W. Thomson is concerned, "Muhammad himself was credited with an arrangement only worked out under his successors" (842). As much as Dadoyan may doubt the *Prophet's Oath with the Armenians* or what we call the *Covenant of the Prophet Muhammad with the Armenian Christians of Jerusalem*, she recognizes that a long succession of Muslim rulers, the Ayyubids, the Umayyads, and the Rightly-Guided Caliphs, all renewed the edict of the Prophet Muhammad. Whether the copy currently housed at the Library of St. James at the Armenian Patriarchate of Jerusalem is the original Prophet's oath, a copy thereof, or a transcription of an oral promise, is immaterial. The longer we look back in time, the more difficult it is to see clearly. What matters is that we have an unbroken chain guiding us through the mist. Salah al-Din accepted the edicts of 'Ali and 'Umar as authentic. These Companions had personal knowledge of the Prophet's words and actions. This chain is solid and sound and traces back to the Truth: the fundamental fact that the Prophet Muhammad granted protection and privileges to the Armenian Christians of Jerusalem.

It is not only Muslims, but Christians, who have stood behind the covenant of the Prophet with the Armenian Christians. Samuel of Ani, Mxit'ar of Ani, Kirakos, and Juanser all confirm that "Muhammad himself made a pact with the Armenians, guaranteeing the free observance of Christianity" (Thomson, "Muhammad" 842). As Samuel wrote in the 13th century,

> Mahmet stayed the sword, and by the word of his instruction they subjected themselves the greater part of the universe. With an eternal oath he sealed a deed for the land of Armenia, (that) they could freely observe Christianity. And he sold them ... their faith, taking from every household four drachmas, three bushels of xorbal, one nose-bag, one cord of hair, and one gauntlet. But from the priests, nobles and cavalry he ordered tax to be taken. (qtd. Thomson, "Muhammad" 843)

The argument that the covenants of the Prophet Muhammad, 'Umar, and 'Ali are forgeries is feeble. As Robert W. Thomson's study on Muhammad in the Armenian tradition demonstrates, the Armenians did not have a precise and coherent understanding of the Islamic religion (858). Armenian sources which deal with Islam are filled with absurdities and misunderstandings of all kinds. These doctrinal and historical misunderstandings would have come through in the content of a forged covenant. If the covenants in question are in agreement with the Qur'an, the Sunnah, and the *shari'ah*, this suggests that their authorship has been rightly attributed, and that the chain of confirmation and renewal traces back to the Prophet Muhammad.

While I have not mentioned many other Caliphs and Sultans who confirmed the rights of the Armenian Christians, this tradition continued into the 20th century. In 1917, the Sharif of Mecca, al-Husayn ibn 'Ali, issued an edict which was aimed at all Muslims. In his *fatwa*, the Head of the Royal Hashimite Court, commanded the following of all Muslims:

> You are asked to protect and take great care of the entire Armenian, Jacobite, community, living in your territories, within your borders, and within your tribes; to help them in all of their affairs; and to defend them like you would defend yourselves, your property, and your children; to furnish them with everything they may need, whether they are sedentary or nomads, for they are a Protected People of the Muslims [*ahl al-dhimmah al-muslimin*], about whom the Prophet Muhammad, may peace and blessings be upon him, said: 'Whoever takes even a string from them, I will be his adversary on the Day of Judgment.' This is among the most important things that I ask you to do, which I hope you will fulfill, on the basis of the noble character and determination with which you act.

What we are witnessing is a clear case of covenantal continuity: from the Prophet to 'Umar, from 'Umar to 'Ali, from 'Ali to Muktafi II, Caliph of Baghdad, all the way to the *Firman of the Sharif of Mecca and Custodian of the Holy Sites*, al-Husayn ibn 'Ali (1854–1931 CE). As Mingana explains, "[t]he praiseworthy keynote of tolerance that runs through" the *Firman* "is that of all the Muslim Caliphs, and not only one of them" (2). While Muslim rulers may have had their political and doctrinal differences, they clearly agreed upon one thing: the prophetic command to protect the Christians living under Islamic rule.

As for the Takfiris who spread terror among Christians and Muslims in Syria, Iraq, Pakistan, and elsewhere, they are, according to the covenants of the Prophet, the Caliphs, the Imams, and the Sultans, apostates and infidels. They are truly those who wage war against Allah and His Messenger and all of the values and ethics which true Islam teaches. But unlike the followers of this heretical cult, Muslims, be they Sunni, Shi'i or Sufi, do not declare their blood to be *halal* nor would they condemn unarmed Salafi civilians to death. As for armed Wahhabi terrorists, whether they are individual actors, guerrilla groups, or State players like Saudi Arabia, it is the obligation of all believers to oppose them in the same manner that it is imperative to oppose their Western backers, be they American, British, French, or Israeli, by any means necessary, as long as these are consonant with the traditions and laws of Islam. Takfirism is the polar opposite of Islam. Where true Islam unites Muslims and non-Muslims in a humanitarian spirit, Takfirism divides by means religious racism, hatred, and intolerance. Radical Salafism has nothing to offer to the world besides spite and violence. Rather than preach peace, its leaders promote bigotry. They promise nothing but despotism, tyranny, and treachery, and do nothing but advance the interests of infidels. While weak, exploited, and oppressed, the Muslim *ummah* had maintained a sense of unity within diversity. Acting in accordance with Western plans, the Wahhabis seek to dislocate, divide, and dismember the Islamic world. In short, they seek to destroy Muslim collective identity. Without a sense of self and without any semblance of Islam remaining to serve as a cause, there will be no grounds on which to build a Muslim future. If there are Imams who lead to heaven, there are Imams who lead to hell while promising paradise. "And We made them (but) Imams inviting to the Fire; and on the Day of Judgment no help shall they find. In this world We continued to curse them; and on the Day of Judgment they will be among the hateful" (Qur'an 28:41–42).

Conclusions

The Armenian Patriarchate has always been careful to speak of the *firman* attributed to the Prophet as opposed to the *firman* of the Prophet; in the same spirit of caution they have so far shown an understandable reluctance to expose this precious relic to public view and scholarly appraisal. However, were I or another academic to find definitive proof that the *Covenant of the Prophet Muhammad with the Armenian Christians of Jerusalem* was forged—and it would be extremely difficult to establish such a proof—the Christians in the Middle East would not suffer as a consequence. The Church, as a whole, could not be blamed for the mistake of a misguided, but well-intentioned, Christian who attempted to protect his community over a thousand years ago. However, if the document is indeed genuine, as I believe both it and the other covenants presented in this book most likely are, and if scholars could provide solid evidence supporting its authenticity, it would confirm the rights of the Armenians to the sacred sites in the Holy Land, and could be held high as evidence of the protection granted to them by the Prophet. Keeping such covenants under lock and key, hidden away in the archives of churches, monasteries, and libraries, is of no benefit to anyone. After perusing this book, if the Patriarchate were to accept it as an honest attempt to demonstrate the Prophet's great admiration for the Christian religion, and his commands directed to all Muslims to respect the rights and guard the security of peaceful Christians everywhere, we may yet hope they will decide to make their *firman* available for further study.

Part II

TEXTS

It is He Who sent down to thee (step by step), in truth, the Book, continuing what went before it; and He sent down the Law (Of Moses) and the Gospel (of Jesus)

Before this, as a guide to mankind, and he sent down the Criterion (of right and wrong). Then those who reject faith in the Signs of Allah will suffer the severest penalty, and Allah is Exalted in Might, Lord of Retribution. (3:3–4)

Chapter 8

Text of the Covenant of the Prophet Muhammad with the Monks of Mount Sinai (I)

[*By the Prophet Muhammad*]
Translation cited by Pococke (1809) "Chapter XIV: The *Patent of Mahomet*, which he granted to the Monks of Mount Sinai; and to Christians in General" 389–391; qtd. Davenport 147–151

As God is great and governs, from whom all the prophets are come, for there remains no record of injustice against God; through the gifts that are given unto men, Muhammad the son of 'Abd Allah, the Messenger of Allah, and careful guardian of the whole world; has wrote the present instrument to all those who are in his national people, and of his own religion, as a secure and positive promise to be accomplished to the Christian nation, and relations of the Nazarene, whosoever they may be, whether they be the noble or the vulgar, the honorable or otherwise, saying thus.

I. Whosoever of my nation shall presume to break my promise and oath, which is contained in this present agreement, destroys the promise of God, acts contrary to the oath, and will be a resister of the faith, (which God forbid) for he becomes worthy of the curse, whether he be the King himself, or a poor man, or whatever person he may be.

II. That whenever any of the monks in his travels shall happen to settle upon any mountain, hill, village, or other habitable place, on the sea, or in deserts, or in any convent, church, or house of prayer, I shall be in the midst of them, as the preserver and protector of them, their goods and effects, with my soul, aid, and protection, jointly with all my national people; because they are a part of my own people, and an honor to me.

III. Moreover, I command all officers not to require any poll-tax on them, or any other tribute, because they shall not be forced or compelled to anything of this kind.

IV. None shall presume to change their judges or governors, but they shall remain in their office, without being deported.

V. No one shall molest them when they are travelling on the road.

VI. Whatever churches they are possessed of, no one is to deprive them of them.

VII. Whosoever shall annul any of one of these my decrees, let him know positively that he annuls the ordinance of God.

VIII. Moreover, neither their judges, governors, monks, servants, disciples, or any others depending on them, shall pay any poll-tax, or be molested on that account, because I am their protector, wherever they shall be, either by land or sea, east or west, north or south; because both they and all that belong to them are included in this my promissory oath and patent.

IX. And of those that live quietly and solitary upon the mountains, they shall exact neither poll-tax nor tithes from their incomes, neither shall any Muslim partake of what they have; for they labor only to maintain themselves.

X. Whenever the crop of the earth shall be plentiful in its due time, the inhabitants shall be obliged out of every bushel to give them a certain measure.

XI. Neither in time of war shall they take them out of their habitations, nor compel them to go to the wars, nor even then shall they require of them any poll-tax.

[In these eleven chapters is to be found whatever relates to the monks, as to the remaining seven chapters, they direct what relates to every Christian.]

XII. Those Christians who are inhabitants, and with their riches and traffic are able to pay the poll-tax, shall pay no more than twelve drachms.

XIII. Excepting this, nothing shall be required of them, according to the express order of God, that says, 'Do not molest those that have a veneration for the books that are sent from God, but rather in a kind manner give of your good things to them, and converse with them, and hinder everyone from molesting them' [29:46].

XIV. If a Christian woman shall happen to marry a Muslim man, the Muslim shall not cross the inclination of his wife, to keep her from her church and prayers, and the practice of her religion.

XV. That no person hinder them from repairing their churches.

XVI. Whosoever acts contrary to my grant, or gives credit to anything contrary to it, becomes truly an apostate to God, and to his divine apostle, because this protection I have granted to them according to this promise.

XVII. No one shall bear arms against them, but, on the contrary, the Muslims shall wage war for them.

XVIII. And by this I ordain, that none of my nation shall presume to do or act contrary to this my promise, until the end of the world.

Witnesses,
Ali, the son of Abu Thaleb; Homar, the son of Hattavi; Ziphir, the son of Abuan; Saith, the son of Maat; Thavitt, the son of Nesis; Amphachin, the son of Hassan; Muathem, the son of Kasvi; Azur, the son of Jassin; Abombaker, the son of Ambi; Kaphe Ottoman, the son of Gafas; Ambtelack, the son of Messutt; Phazer, the son of Abbas; Talat, the son of Amptolack; Saat the son of Abbatt; Kasmer the son of Abid; Ambtullack the son of Omar

This present was written by the leader, the successor, 'Ali the son of Abu Talib; the Prophet marking it with his hand at the mosque of the Prophet (in whom be peace) in the second year of the Hegira, the third day of the month of Muharram.

Text of the Covenant of the Prophet Muhammad with the Monks of Mount Sinai (II)

[*By the Prophet Muhammad*]
Arundale's (1837) English translation of M. Mauchin's French translation cited in his *Illustrations of Jerusalem and Mount Sinai*: 28–29

In the Name of God, Merciful and Compassionate.

Mohammed-ebn-Abdallah, gives this Edict for all the world in general. He announces and proclaims that he is the confidant of God, and charged with the keeping of all created beings. And in order that no one, under pretext of ignorance, may err, I have written this letter in the form of an ordinance, for my nation, and for all those who are Christians; from the east and from the west, far and near; for all those that are eloquent and not eloquent, the learned and the ignorant. Those who do not follow that which is related, and do not execute what which I ordain, will act contrary to the will of God and merit to be cursed, whoever they are, Sultan or other Musulman.

If a father or a hermit retire into any mountain, grotto, plain, desert, town, village, or church, I will be behind him as his protector against all enemies, myself in person, my forces and my subjects, although these priests are cancelled by me. I will avoid doing them any hurt. No contributions must be taken from them, unless voluntarily. It is not permitted to change a bishop from his bishopric, nor a priest from his priesthood, nor a hermit from his hermitage,—none of the objects in their churches must enter into the construction of the mosques; not even into the habitation of Musulmen. Those who do not conform to this will act contrary to the law of God and his Prophet.

It is forbidden to exact contributions from the priests, the bishops, and the devotees. I will preserve their prerogatives everywhere; wherever they are, by land and by sea, in the east and in the west, in the south and in the north. They shall enjoy my privileges against everything disagreeable. Those who sow and plant in the mountains and places scattered about, shall not pay tithes or contributions; not even voluntarily, when it is destined for their nourishment. If they want corn, every house shall assist them with a measure; and they shall not be obliged to serve in the wars or pay imposts. Those who possess goods or merchandise shall not give more than twelve drachms of silver every year. No one must be molested; it is forbidden to enter into discussion with them by soft measures, putting aside everything disagreeable, and preserving the wing of compassion.

If a Christian woman shall go to the house of a Musulman, she must be well treated, and allowed to perform her prayer in a church, without any obstacle against her or her religion. He who acts contrary to this, will be regarded as a rebel against God and his Prophet.

The Christians shall be assisted to preserve their churches and houses; those who assist them to keep their own religion, they shall not be obliged to carry arms; but the Musulmen shall bear them for them; and they shall not disobey this ordinance to the end of the world.

The testimonies which attest the truth of this Edict, which has been given by Mohammed-ebn-Abdallah, envoy of God for all the Christians, and which are the accomplishment of that which they have agreed are *Ali-ebn-Taleb, Aboubek-rebu-Aby-Kohafey, Omar ebn-el-Khattal, Otman-ebn-Assan, Abou-el-Daida, Abou-Horeyrah, Abdallah-Abou-Massaoud, Abbat-ebn-Abdel-Motbb, Fodeyl-ebn-Abbas, Zobeir-ebn-Aouan, Talhat-ebn-Obeydallah, Saad-ebn-Maoz, Saad-ebn-Obadey, Thabet-ebn-Keys, MonKayetmeth, Hachem-ebn-Ommyeh, Hareth-ebn-Thabet, Abdallah-ebn Amrou, Ebn-el-Ass, Amer-ebn-Yassin, Moazzam-ebn-Kerachy, Abdel-Azim-ebn-Hassan.*

This Edict was written by the hand of Aby-Taleb, the 3 Moharran, the second year of the Hegira, and of J.C. the 1st of August, 622. It is signed by the Prophet himself. Happy he who confirms.

Text of the Covenant of the Prophet Muhammad with the Monks of Mount Sinai (III)

[*By the Prophet Muhammad*]
English translation of M. Mauchin's French translation as cited in Baron Marie-Joseph de Géramb's (1840) *Pilgrimage to Jerusalem and Mount Sinai*: 246–247

In the name of God, clement and merciful.

Mohamed ebn Abdallah has issued this edict for the whole world in general. He proclaims that he is the friend of God, and that he is charged with the care of all his creatures. In order that none may plead ignorance, I have written this dispatch in the form of an ordinance, for my nation and for all those who are in Christendom, in the East, or in the West, near and afar off, for all who are eloquent and not eloquent, known and unknown. He who shall not follow what it contains, and will not do what I enjoin, will act contrary to the will of God, and will deserve to be cursed, be he who he may be, sultan or any other Musulman.

If a priest or a hermit retires to a mountain, cavern, plain, desert, town, village, or church, I shall be behind him as his protector from all enemies, I myself in person, my forces, and my subjects; as those priests are my rayas [Christian subjects], I shall avoid doing them any injury. Voluntary contributions only shall be taken from them, and they shall not be constrained to pay any. It is not lawful to drive a bishop from his bishopric, nor a priest from his religion, nor a hermit from his hermitage: nothing belonging to their churches shall be used in the building of mosques, or even in the building of the dwellings of Musulmans. He who shall not conform to this will violate the law of God and that of his Prophet.

It is forbidden to impose contributions upon priests, bishops, and religious men. I will maintain their privileges, wherever they may be, on land or on sea, in the east or in the west, in the south or in the north: they shall enjoy my privileges and my safeguard against all disagreeable things. Those who shall sow or plant in the mountains and in the sequestered places, shall pay neither tithes nor contributions, not even voluntarily, when the produce is destined for their own subsistence. If they are in want of corn, they shall be assisted with one measure for each house, and they shall not be obliged to go forth to war, or to pay any taxes.

Those who possess immoveable property or merchandise shall not give more than twelve silver drachmas per year. None shall be molested; neither shall any enter into strife with those who follow the precepts of Gospel, but behave mildly towards them, avoiding all disagreeable things.

When a Christian woman shall join the Musulmans, they shall treat her well, and permit her to go and pray in a church, without placing any obstacle between her and her religion. He who does the contrary shall be regarded as a rebel against God and his Prophet.

The Christians shall be assisted to preserve their churches and their houses, which will assist them to preserve their religion: they shall not be obliged to bear arms, but the Musulmans shall bear arms for them, and they shall not disobey this ordinance until the end of the world.

The witnesses who attest the truth of this edict, which has been issued for all the Christians, and which is the complement of what has been granted to them, are:

Aly ebn Taleb, Aboubekr Aly Kohafey, Omar ebn el-Khattab, Otman ebn Hassan, About el Darda, Abou Horeyrah, Abdallah Abou Massaoud, Abbas ebn Abdel Motteb, Fodeyl ebn Abbas, Zobeir ebn Aouan, Talhat ebn Obeydallah, Saad ebn Maoz, Saad ebn Obadey, Thabet ebn Kays Mou Khayetmeth, Hachem ebn Omyeh, Hareth ebn Thabet, Abdallah ebn Amrou, Ebn el Ass, Amer ebn Yassin, Meazzam ebn Kerachy, Adel Azim eben Hassan.

This edict was written by the hand of Aly ebn Taleb, the 3rd of Mohanam, in the second year of the Hegira, and of Jesus Christ, the 1st of August, 622: it is signed by the Prophet himself. Happy he who shall do, and woe to him who shall not do according to its contents.

Text of the Covenant of the Prophet Muhammad with the Monks of Mount Sinai (IV)

[*By the Prophet Muhammad*]
Translation cited by Skrobucha in *Sinai* (1966): 58
By permission of Oxford Universtiy Press

To all whom it may concern this letter is addressed by Muhammad, son of Abdullah, he who proclaims and admonishes men to take knowledge of the promises of God to his creation, in order that men may raise no claim or right against God or against the Prophet, for God is almighty and all-wise. It is written to people of this faith and to all in the world who profess the Christian religion in East and West, near and far, whether they are Arabs or non-Arabs, unknown or known, as writ which he has issued for their protection. If any person henceforth violates the protection hereby proclaimed, or contravenes it or transgresses the obligations imposed by it, he forgoes the protection of God, breaks his covenant, dishonors his religion and deserves to be accursed, whether he be a sultan or any one so ever of the faithful of Islam.

If a monk or pilgrim seeks protection, in mountain or valley, in a cave or in tilled fields, in the plain, in the desert, or in a church, in such case I am with him, and defend him from everyone who is his enemy—I, my helpers, all men of my faith, and all my followers, for these people are my followers and my protégés. I wish to protect them from interference with the supply of victuals, which my protégés have procured for themselves, and also from the payment of taxes over and above what they themselves approve. On none of these accounts shall either compulsion or constraint be used against them.

A bishop shall not be removed from his bishopric, nor a monk from his monastery, nor a hermit from his tower, nor shall a pilgrim be hindered from his pilgrimage. Moreover, no church or chapel shall be destroyed, nor shall the property of their churches be used for the building of mosques or houses for the Muslims. Whoever offends against this rule forfeits God's protection and is insubordinate to his Messenger.

Neither poll-tax nor impost shall be laid on monks, bishops, or hermits, for I wish to extend protection to them, wherever they are, in East or West, in North or South, for they are under my protection, within my covenant, and under my security against every injury. Those also who go to the solitude of the mountains, or to the holy places, shall be free from poll-tax, and from tithe or duty on whatever they grow for their own use, and they shall be assisted in raising a corn-crop by a free allowance of one *qadah* [unit of dry measure] in every *ardabb* [= 6 *waybah* = 24 *rub'a*] for their personal use.

They shall be not obliged to serve in war, or to pay the poll-tax; even those for whom an obligation to pay land-tax exists, or who possess resources in land or from commercial activity, shall not have to pay more than ten *dirhams* a head a year. On no one shall an unjust tax be imposed, and with these people of the Book there is to be no strife, unless it be over what is for the good. We wish to take them under the wing of our mercy, and the penalty of vexation shall be kept at a distance from them, wherever they are and wherever they may settle.

If a Christian woman enters a Muslim household, she shall be received with kindness, and she shall be given opportunity to pray in her church; there shall be no dispute between her and a man who loves her religion. Whoever contravenes God's protection and acts to the contrary is a rebel against his covenant and his Messenger. These people shall be assisted in the improvement of their churches and religious dwellings; thus they will be aided in their faith and kept true to their allegiance. None of them shall be compelled to bear arms, but the Muslims shall defend them; and they shall not contravene this promise of protection until the hour comes and the last day breaks upon the world.

As witnesses to this letter of protection, written by Muhammad, son of Abdullah, God's Messenger, and as sureties for the fulfillment of all that is prescribed herein, the following persons set their hands

Ali the son of Abu Thaleb; Homar, the son of Hattavi; Ziphir, the son of Abuan; Saith, the son of Maat; Thavitt, the son of Nesis; Amphachin, the son of Hassan; Muathem, the son of Kasvi; Azur, the son of Jassin; Abombaker, the son of Ambi Kaphe; Ottoman, the son of Gafas; Ambtelack, the son of Messutt; Phazer, the son of Abbas; Talat, the son of Amptolack; Saat the son of Abbatt; Kasmer the son of Abid; Ambtullack the son of Omar

This promise of protection was written in his own hand by Ali bin Abu Talib in the Mosque of the Prophet on the third of Muharram in the year 2 of the Prophet's Hegira…

Praise be to all you abide by its contents, and cursed be all who do not observe it.

Text of the Covenant of the Prophet Muhammad with the Monks of Mount Sinai (V)

[*By the Prophet Muhammad*]
Translated by Anton F. Haddad in 1902

This is a letter which was issued by Mohammed, Ibn Abdullah, the Messenger, the Prophet, the Faithful, who is sent to all the people as a trust on the part of God to all His creatures, that they may have no plea against God hereafter. Verily God is the Mighty, the Wise. This letter is directed to the embracers of Islam, as a covenant given to the followers of Nazarene in the East and West, the far and near, the Arabs and foreigners, the known and the unknown.

This letter contains the oath given unto them, and he who disobeys that which is therein will be considered a disobeyer and a transgressor to that whereunto he is commanded. He will be regarded as one who has corrupted the oath of God, disbelieved His Testament, rejected His Authority, despised His Religion, and made himself deserving of His Curse, whether he is a Sultan or any other believer of Islam.

Whenever monks, devotees and pilgrims gather together, whether in a mountain or valley, or den, or frequented place, or plain, or church, or in houses of worship, verily we are [at the] back of them and shall protect them, and their properties and their morals, by Myself, by My Friends and by My Assistants, for they are of My Subjects and under My Protection.

I shall exempt them from that which may disturb them; of the burdens which are paid by others as an oath of allegiance. They must not give anything of their income but that which pleases them—they must not be offended, or disturbed, or coerced or compelled. Their judges should not be changed or prevented from accomplishing their offices, nor the monks disturbed in exercising their religious order, or the people of seclusion be stopped from dwelling in their cells.

No one is allowed to plunder the pilgrims, or destroy or spoil any of their churches, or houses of worship, or take any of the things contained within these houses and bring it to the houses of Islam. And he who takes away anything therefrom, will be one who has corrupted the oath of God, and, in truth, disobeyed His Messenger.

Poll-taxes should not be put upon their judges, monks, and those whose occupation is the worship of God; nor is any other thing to be taken from them, whether it be a fine, a tax or any unjust right. Verily I shall keep their compact, wherever they may be, in the sea or on the land, in the East or West, in the North or South, for they are under My Protection and the testament of My Safety, against all things which they abhor.

No taxes or tithes should be received from those who devote themselves to the worship of God in the mountains, or from those who cultivate the Holy Lands. No one has the right to interfere with their affairs, or bring any action against them. Verily this is for aught else and not for them; rather, in the seasons of crops, they should be given a Kadah for each *Ardab* of wheat (about five bushels and a half) as provision for them, and no one has the right to say to them this is too much, or ask them to pay any tax.

As to those who possess properties, the wealthy and merchants, the poll-tax to be taken from them must not exceed twelve Dirhams a head per year (*i.e.* about 45 cents).

They shall not be imposed upon by anyone to undertake a journey, or to be forced to go to wars or to carry arms; for the Islams have to fight for them. Do no dispute or argue with them, but deal according to the verse recorded in the Koran, to wit: 'Do not dispute or argue with the People of the Book but in that which is best' [29:46]. Thus they will live favored and protected from everything which may offend them by the Callers to religion (Islam), wherever they may be and in any place they may dwell.

Should any Christian woman be married to a Musulman, such marriage must not take place except after her consent, and she must not be prevented from going to her church for prayer. Their churches must be honored and they must not be withheld from building churches or repairing convents.

They must not be forced to carry arms or stones; but the Islams must protect them and defend them against others. It is positively incumbent upon every one of the Islam nation not to contradict or disobey this oath until the Day of Resurrection and the end of the world.

This is the oath which Mohammed Ibn Abdullah gave to the Christian nation, the fulfillment and promulgation of which has been agreed upon by all the witnesses who have hitherto attached their names. It was signed by the great Assistants of Mohammed, as follows.

Ali Ibn Abi Talib; Abou Bekr Ibn Kahafat; Omar Ibn El-Khattab; Ottman Ibn Affan; Aboul Darda; Abou Harirat; Abdullah Ibn Masood; Abbas Ibn Abdoul Mottaleb; El-Fadhl Ibn Abbas; Ezzobier Ibn El-Awam; Talhat Ibn Abdullah; Said Ibn Maath; Said Ibn Abada; Thabit Ibn Nafees; Zied Ibn Thabit; Abou Hanifa Ibn Attaba; Hashim Ibn Obied; Maazam Ibn Kariesh; El-Harith Ibn Thabit; Abdoul Azim Ibn Haasan; Abdullah Ibn Omar Ibn El-Aas; Aamir Ibn Yasir

This oath was written by the hand of Ali ibn Abi Talib in the worship place of the Prophet on the third day of Moharram in the second year of El-Hajrih.

Text of the Covenant of the Prophet Muhammad with the Monks of Mount Sinai (VI)

[*By the Prophet Muhammad*]
Translated by John Andrew Morrow in 2013

In the Name of Allah, the Most Compassionate, the Most Merciful.

(A copy of the manuscript of the covenant [*'ahd*] written by Muhammad, the son of 'Abd Allah, may the peace and blessings of Allah be upon him, to all the Christians.)

This covenant [*kitabun*] was written by Muhammad, the son of 'Abd Allah, the proclaimer and warner [*bashiran wa nadhiran*], trusted to protect Allah's creations [*wadi'at Allah fi khalqihi*], in order that people may raise no claim [*hujjah*] against Allah after [the advent of] His Messengers [*rusul*] for Allah is Almighty, Wise.

He has written it for the members of his religion [*ahl al-millatihi*] and to all those who profess the Christian religion in East and West, near or far, Arabs or non-Arabs [*'ajami*], known or unknown, as a covenant of protection.

If anyone breaks the covenant [*'ahd*] herein proclaimed, or contravenes or transgresses its commands, he has broken the Covenant of Allah, breaks his bond, makes a mockery of his religion, deserves the curse [of Allah], whether he is a sultan or another among the believing Muslims.

If a monk or pilgrim seeks protection, in mountain or valley, in a cave or in tilled fields, in the plain, in the desert, or in a church, I am behind them, defending them from every enemy; I, my helpers [*a'wani*], all the members of my religion [*ahl al-millati*], and all my followers [*atba'i*], for they [the monks and the pilgrims] are my protégés and my subjects [*ahl al-dhimmati*].

I protect them from interference with their supplies and from the payment of taxes save what they willingly renounce. There shall be no compulsion or constraint against them in any of these matters.

A bishop shall not be removed from his bishopric, nor a monk from his monastery, nor a hermit from his tower [*sawma'ah*], nor shall a pilgrim be hindered from his pilgrimage. Moreover, no building from among their churches [*bayt min buyut kanaisihim*] shall be destroyed, nor shall the money [*mal*] from their churches be used for the building of mosques or houses for the Muslims. Whoever does such a thing violates Allah's covenant [*'ahd Allah*] and dissents from the Messenger of Allah.

Neither poll-tax [*jizyah*] nor fees [*gharamah*] shall be laid on monks [*ruhban*], bishops [*asaqifah*], or worshippers for I protect them, wherever they may be, on land or sea, in East and West, in North and South. They are under my protection, within my covenant [*mithaqi*], and under my security [*amani*], against all harm [*makruh*].

Those who also isolate themselves in the mountains or in sacred sites shall be free from the poll-tax [*jizyah*], land tribute [*kharaj*] and from tithe [*'ushr*] or duty on whatever they grow for their own use, and they shall be assisted in raising a crop by a free allowance of one *qadah* [unit of dry measure] in every *ardabb* [= 6 *waybah* = 24 *rub'a*] for their personal use.

They shall be not obliged to serve in war, or to pay the poll-tax [*jizyah*]; even those for whom an obligation to pay land tribute [*kharaj*] exists, or who possess resources in land or from commercial activity, shall not have to pay more than twelve *dirhams* a head per year.

On no one shall an unjust tax be imposed, and with the People of the Book there is to be no strife, unless it be over what is for the good [5:48]. We wish to take them under the wing of our mercy, and the penalty of vexation shall be kept at a distance from them, wherever they are and wherever they may settle.

If a Christian woman enters a Muslim household, she shall be received with kindness, and she shall be given opportunity to pray in her church; there shall be no dispute between her and a man who loves her religion. Whoever contravenes the covenant of Allah [*'ahd Allah*] and acts to the contrary is a rebel against his covenant [*mithaqahu*] and his Messenger.

These people shall be assisted in the maintenance of their religious buildings and their dwellings [*mawadi'*]; thus they will be aided in their faith and kept true to their allegiance.

None of them shall be compelled to bear arms, but the Muslims shall defend them; and they shall never contravene this promise of protection until the hour comes and the world ends.

As witness to this covenant, which was written by Muhammad, son of 'Abd Allah, the Messenger of Allah, may the peace and blessings of Allah be upon him, to all the Christians.

As sureties for the fulfillment of all that is prescribed herein, the following persons set theirs hands.

The names of the witnesses:

'Ali ibn Abi Talib; Abu Bakr ibn Abi Quhafah; 'Umar ibn al-Khattab; 'Uthman ibn 'Affan; Abu al-Darda'; Abi Hurayrah; 'Abd Allah ibn Mas'ud; 'Abbas ibn 'Abd al-Muttalib; Harith ibn Thabit; 'Abd al-'Azim ibn Hasan; Fudayl ibn 'Abbas; al-Zubayr ibn al-'Awwam; Talhah ibn 'Abd Allah; Sa'd ibn Mu'adh; Sa'd ibn 'Ubadah; Thabit ibn Nafis; Zayd ibn Thabit; Bu Hanifah ibn 'Ubayyah; Hashim ibn 'Ubayyah; Mu'azzam ibn Qurayshi; 'Abd Allah ibn 'Amr ibn al-'As; 'Amir ibn Yasin

This covenant [*'ahd*] was written in his own hand by 'Ali ibn Abi Talib in the Mosque of the Prophet, may the peace and blessings of Allah be upon him, on the third of Muharram in the second year of the Prophet's Hegira.

A copy of this covenant has been deposited in the treasury [*khizanah*] of the Sultan. It was signed with the seal of the Prophet, peace be upon him. It was written on a piece of leather from Ta'if.

Blessed be he who abides by its contents. Blessed be he for he belongs to those who can expect the forgiveness of Allah.

This copy, which is copied from the original, is sealed with the signature of the noble Sultan [*sharif al-Sultani*]. This reproduction was copied from the copy that was copied from the copy written in the handwriting of the Leader of the Believers, 'Ali ibn Abi Talib, may Allah bless his countenance.

With the order of the noble Sultan [*sharif al-Sultani*], that is still in effect, with the help of Allah, which was given to a community of monks who inhabit the Mountain of Tur-Sina'i because the copy, which was copied from the copy written by the Leader of the Believers, was lost, in order that his document be a support of the Sultan's royal decrees which are evidenced by the records in the hands of the community in question.

This is a reproduction of the original [*'asl*] without adapation [*fadl wa wasl*].

Written by the weakest of slaves,
al-Bari Nuh ibn Ahmad al-Ansari
The judge from Egypt, the Safeguarded [*mahrusah*], has pardoned them.

Sealed with the round seal and certified.
Nuh Ahmad ibn al-Ansari
[signature]

Modeled on a seal whose original [*mahar*] is signed with this signature.

Written by the poor [*faqir*], Muhammad al-Qadi, from Ancient Egypt, may he be forgiven!

Text of the *Covenant of the Prophet Muhammad with the Monks of Mount Sinai*

(Corrected Arabic Original[1])

بِسْمِ اللهِ الرَّحْمنِ الرَّحِيمْ

نُسْخَةُ سِجِلِّ العَهْدِ كَتَبَهُ مُحَمَّدٌ بْنُ عَبْدِ اللهِ، صَلَّى اللهُ عَلَيْهِ وَسَلَّمْ، إِلَى كَافَّةِ النَّصَارَى.

هَذَا كِتَابٌ كَتَبَهُ مُحَمَّدٌ بْنُ عَبْدِ اللهِ إِلَى كَافَّةِ النَّاسِ أَجْمَعِينَ بَشِيرًا وَنَذِيرًا وَمُؤْتَمَنًا عَلَى وَدِيعَةِ اللهِ فِي خَلْقِهِ لِئَلاَّ يَكُونَ لِلنَّاسِ عَلَى اللهِ حُجَّةٌ بَعْدَ الرُّسُلِ، وَكَانَ اللهُ عَزِيزًا حَكِيمًا.

كَتَبَهُ لِأَهْلِ مِلَّتِهِ وَلِجَمِيعِ مَنْ يَنْتَحِلُ دِينَ النَّصْرَانِيَةِ مِنْ مَشَارِقِ الْأَرْضِ وَمَغَارِبِهَا، قَرِيبِهَا وبَعِيدِهَا، فَصِيحِهَا و عَجَمِيهَا، مَعْرُوفِهَا وَمَجْهُولِهَا، كِتَابًا جُعِلَ لَهُمُ عَهْدًا.

فَمَنْ نَكَثَ العَهْدَ الَّذِي فِيهِ وَخَالَفَهُ إِلَى غَيْرِهِ وتَعَدَّى مَا أَمَرَهُ كَانَ لِعَهْدِ اللهِ نَاكِثًا وَلِمِيثَاقِهِ نَاقِضًا وَبِدِينِهِ مُسْتَهْتِرًا و لِلَّعْنَةِ مُسْتَوْجِبًا، سُلْطَانًا كَانَ أَمْ غَيْرُهُ مِنَ الْمُسْلِمِينَ الْمُؤْمِنِينَ.

وَإِذَا احْتَمَى رَاهِبٌ أَوْ سَائِحٌ فِي جَبَلٍ أَوْ وَادٍ أَوْ عُمْرَانٍ أَوْ سَهْلٍ أَوْ رَمْلٍ أَوْ رَدْنَه أَوْ بِيْعَةٍ وَأَنَا أَكُونُ مِنْ وَرَائِهِمْ ذَابًّا عَنْهُمْ مِنْ كُلِّ عَدُوٍّ لَهُمْ بِنَفْسِي وَأَعْوَانِي وَأَهْلِ مِلَّتِي وَأَتْبَاعِي، لِأَنَّهُمْ رَعِيَتِي وَأَهلُ ذِمَّتِي.

وَأَنَا أَعْزِلُ عَنْهُمُ الْأَذَى فِي المُؤَنِ الَّتِي تَحْمِلُ أَهْلَ العَهْدِ مِنَ الْقِيَامِ بِالْخَرَاجِ، إِلاَّ مَا طَابَتْ نُفُوسُهُمْ وَلَيْسَ عَلَيْهِمْ جَبْرٌ وَلاَ إِكْرَاهٌ عَلَى شَيْءٍ مِنْ ذَلِكَ.

1. In presenting this and following covenants in modern Arabic script, spelling and grammatical anomalies have been corrected, punctuation marks have been inserted, and, to facilitate reading, the text has been fully vocalized and case endings included.

وَلاَ يُغَيِّرُ أُسْقُفٌّ مِنْ أُسْقُفِيَّتِهِ وَلاَ رَاهِبٌ مِنْ رَهْبَانِيَّتِهِ وَلاَ جَلِيسٌ مِنْ صَوْمَعَتِهِ وَلاَ سَائِحٌ مِنْ سِيَاحَتِهِ. وَلاَ يُهَدَّمُ بَيْتٌ مِنْ بُيُوتِ كَنَائِسِهِمْ وَبِيَعِهِمْ وَلاَ يَدْخُلُ شَيْءٌ مِنْ مَالِ كَنَائِسِهِمْ فِي بِنَاءِ مَسْجِدٍ وَلاَ فِي مَنَازِلِ الْمُسْلِمِينَ. وَمَنْ فَعَلَ ذَلِكَ فَقَدْ نَكَثَ عَهْدَ اللهِ وَخَالَفَ رَسُولَ اللهِ.

وَلاَ يُحْمَلَ عَلَى الرُّهْبَانِ وَالأَسَاقِفَةِ وَلاَ مَنْ يَتَعَبَّدُ جِزْيَةٌ وَلاَ غَرَامَةٌ، وَأَنَا أَحْفَظُ ذِمَّتَهُمْ أَيْنَمَا كَانُوا مِنْ بَرٍّ أَوْ بَحْرٍ، فِي الْمَشْرِقِ وَالْمَغْرِبِ، وَالشَّمَالِ وَالْجَنُوبِ، وَهُمْ فِي ذِمَّتِي وَمِيثَاقِي وَأَمَانِي مِنْ كُلِّ مَكْرُوهٍ.

وَكَذَا مَنْ يَنْفَرِدُ فِي الْجِبَالِ وَالْمَوَاضِعِ الْمُبَارَكَةِ لاَ يَلْزَمُهُمْ مِمَّا يَزْرَعُونَ، لاَ خَرَاجَ وَلاَ عُشْرَ وَلاَ يُشَاطَرُونَ لِكَوْنِهِ بِرَسْمِ أَفْوَاهِهِمْ، وَيُعَانُوا عِنْدَ إِدْرَاكِ الْغَلَّةِ بِإِطْلاَقِ قَدْحٍ وَاحِدٍ مِنْ كُلِّ إِرْدَبٍّ بِرَسْمِ أَفْوَاهِهِمْ.

وَلاَ يُلْزَمُوا بِخُرُوجٍ فِي حَرْبٍ وَلاَ قِيَامٍ بِجِزْيَةٍ وَلاَ مِنْ أَصْحَابِ الْخَرَاجِ وَذَوِي الأَمْوَالِ وَالْعَقَارَاتِ وَالتِّجَارَاتِ مِمَّا أَكْثَرَ مِنِ اثْنَيْ عَشَرَ دِرْهَمًا بِالْحَجْمَةِ فِي كُلِّ عَامٍ.

وَلاَ يُكَلَّفُ أَحَدٌ مِنْهُمْ شَطَطًا وَلاَ يُجَادَلُ أَهْلُ الْكِتَابِ "إِلاَّ بِالَّتِي هِيَ أَحْسَنُ"، وَنَحْفَظُ لَهُمْ جَنَاحَ الرَّحْمَةِ، وَيُكَفُّ عَنْهُمْ أَذَى الْمَكْرُوهِ حَيْثُمَا كَانُوا وَحَيْثُمَا حَلُّوا.

وَإِنْ صَارَتِ النَّصْرَانِيَّةُ عِنْدَ الْمُسْلِمِينَ فَعَلَيْهِ "رِضَاهَا" وَتَمْكِينِهَا مِنَ الصَّلاةِ فِي بِيعَتِهَا وَلاَ يُحِيلُ بَيْنَهَا وَبَيْنَ مَنْ هَوَى دِينِهَا وَمَنْ خَالَفَ عَهْدَ اللهِ وَاعْتَمَدَ بِالضِّدِّ مِنْ ذَلِكَ فَقَدْ عَصَى مِيثَاقَهُ وَرَسُولَهُ.

وَيُعَانُوا عَلَى مَرَمَّةِ بِيَعِهِمْ وَمَوَاضِعِهِمْ وَيَكُونُ ذَلِكَ مَعُونَةً لَهُمْ عَلَى دِينِهِمْ وَفَعَالِهِمْ بِالْعَهْدِ.

وَلاَ يُلْزَمُ أَحَدٌ مِنْهُمْ بِثِقْلِ سِلاَحٍ بَلِ الْمُسْلِمِينَ يَذِبُّوا عَنْهُمْ وَلاَ يُخَالِفُوا هَذَا الْعَهْدَ أَبَدًا إِلَى حِينِ تَقُومُ السَّاعَةُ
وَتَمْضِي الدُّنْيَا.

وشَهِدَ بِهَذَا العَهْدِ الَّذِي كَتَبَهُ مُحَمَّدٌ بْنُ عَبْدِ اللهِ رَسُولُ اللهِ صَلَّى اللهُ عَلَيْهِ لِجَمِيعِ النَّصَارَى وَالوَفَاءِ بِجَمِيعِ مَا شَرَطَ لَهُمْ عَلَيْهِ مَنْ أَثْبَتَ اسْمَهُ وشَهَادَتَهُ آخِرَهُ.

أَسْمَــــــــــاءُ الشُّهُودِ:

عليٌّ ابنُ أبِي طَالِبْ أَبُو بَكْرِ بْنُ أبِي قُحَافَة عمرُ بنُ الخَطَّاب عُثْمَانُ بْنُ عَفَّان أَبُو الدَّرْدَاءْ

أَبُو هُرَيْرَة عبدُ الله بْنُ مَسعُود عَباس بْنُ عَبدِ المُطَّلب حَارِثُ بْنُ ثَابِتْ عَبْدُ العَظِيم بنُ حَسَن

فُضَيْل بْنُ عَبَّاس الزُّبَيْر بْنُ العَوَّام طَلَحَة بْنُ عَبْدِ الله سَعْد بْنُ مُعاذ سَعْد بْنُ عُبادَه ثَابِتُ بْنُ نَفِيس زَيْدُ بنُ ثَابِت بُوحَنيفَة بنُ عُبَيَّه هَاشِم بْنُ عُبَيَّه مُعظَّم بْنُ قُرَشِي عَبْدُ اللهِ بْنُ عَمْرُو بْنُ العَاصْ عَامِر بنُ يَاسِين

وَكَتَبَ عَلِيٌّ بْنُ أَبِي طَالِبْ هَذَا العَهد بَخطِّهِ فِي مَسْجِد النَّبِيِّ صَلَّى اللهُ عَلَيْهِ وَسَلَّمَ بِتَارِيخِ الثَّالِثِ مِنَ المُحَرَّمِ ثَانِي سَنَةٍ مِنَ الهِجرْةِ النَّبَوِيَةِ.

وَأُودِعَتْ نُسْخَتُهُ فِي خِزَانَةِ السُّلْطَانِ. وخُتِمَ بِخَتمِ النَّبِيِّ عَلَيْهِ السَّلاَمُ وَهُوَ مَكْتُوبٌ فِي جِلْدٍ أَدِيمٍ طَائِفِي.

فَطُوبَى ثُمَّ طُوبَى لِمَنْ عَمِلَ بِهِ وَبِشُرُوطِهِ، ثُمَّ طُوبَى وَهُوَ عِنْدَ اللهِ مِنَ الرَّاجِينَ عَفْوَ رَبِّهِ.

وَفِي الْأَصْلِ المَنْقُولِ مِنْهُ هَذِهِ النُّسْخَةُ المُتَوَّجَةُ بِالنِّيشَانِ الشَّرِيفِ السُّلْطَانِي مَا صُورَتُهُ. نُقِلَتْ هَذِهِ النُّسخَةُ مِنَ النُّسْخَةِ الَّتِي نُقِلَتْ مِنَ النُّسْخَةِ الْكَائِنَةِ بِخَطِّ أَمِيرِ الْمُؤْمِنِينَ عَلِيٍّ ابْنِ أَبِي طَالِبْ كَرَّمَ اللهُ وَجْهَهُ.

بِالْأَمْرِ الشَّرِيفِ السُّلْطَانِي لاَ زَالَ نَافِذًا بِعَونِ المُعِينِ السُّبْحَانِي ووُضِعَتْ بِأَيْدِ طَائِفَةِ الرُّهْبَانِ القَاطِنِينَ بِجَبَلِ طُورِ سِينَا لِكَوْنِ النُّسْخَةِ المَنْقُولَةِ مِنْ نُسْخَةٍ بِخَطٍّ أَمِيرِ المُؤْمِنِينَ ضَائِعَةٌ ولَيكُونَ سَنَدًا عَلَى مَا تَشْهَدُ بِهِ المَرَاسِيمُ السُّلْطَانِيَةُ والمُرَبَّعاتُ والسِّجِلاَّتُ الَّتِي فِي أَيْدِي الطَّائِفَةِ المَزْبورَةِ.

صُورَةٌ نُقِلَتْ عَنِ الْأَصْلِ بِدُونِ الفَصْلِ وَالوَصْلِ.

نَمَّقَهُ أَضْعَفَ عِبادَ البَارِي نُوحٌ بْنُ أَحْمَدِ الْأَنْصَارِي.

القَاضِي بِمِصْرَ المَحْروسَةِ عَفَا عَنْهُمَا،

مَخْتُومٌ بِخَتْمٍ مُسْتَدِيرٍ ثِقَتُهُ هَكَذَا

نُوحٌ أَحْمَدُ الأَنْصَـــارِي

عَلَى شَاكِلَةِ مَهَرٍ أَصْلُهُ المُمْضَى هَذَا الإِمْضَاءُ

نَمَّقَهُ الفَقِيرُ مُحَمّدُ الْقَاضِي بِمِصْرَ الْقَدِيمَةِ غُفِرَ لَهُ.

Turkish language copy of the *Achtiname* or *Covenant of the Prophet Muhammad with the Monks of Mount Sinai* from 1638 (by permission of St. Catherine's Monastery, Sinai, Egypt)

Chapter 9

Text of the Covenant of the Prophet Muhammad with the Christians of Persia

[*By the Prophet Muhammad*]
Cited in Arpee, 1946: 355–360

By the will of God! In the name of God Merciful!

Be this Writ known to all in the handwriting, and the style, a Compact firm, a Treaty that must be obeyed by all Christian nations, such as dwell throughout the world toward the eastward of Arabia and Persia, or within the bounds of them, whether they be in immediate contact with the Faithful or whether they be distant, and whether or not they have acquaintanceship with the Faithful. This Covenant and Compact is worthy of obedience, and it behooves all Moslems also to observe its provisions. Whosoever shall esteem it his bounden duty to obey the words of this Covenant, his faith is perfect after the manner of men who do well, as such a one [who] shall be esteemed worthy of a reward; but those who shall willfully pervert the words of this Covenant, annul it or do despite to it, or shall disobey the commands of this Compact, persisting in their contrary way, such shall be deemed nullifiers of the Covenant or Compact of God. Whosoever also shall irreverently despise this Writ, the same shall be held worthy of punishment, whether he be a king, or one of the people, whether he be a pious believer (*sc.*, a Moslem), or only a believer (*sc.*, a Christian).

Now: to begin the words of this Compact, in accordance with the prompting of God vouchsafed to me in authentication. With a firm bond do I bind this Compact, the like of which no prophets of the past ever have bound, and as no angels standing before God have found it easy to command. The words, therefore, of this Covenant, which I am about to lay down, must be obeyed by all who are my people.

All pious believers shall deem it their bounden duty to defend believers and to aid them wheresoever they may be, whether far or near, and throughout Christendom shall protect the places where they conduct worship, and those where their monks and priests dwell. Everywhere, in mountains, on the plains, in towns and in waste places, in deserts, and wheresoever they may be, that people shall be protected, both in their faith and in their property, both in the West and in the East, both on sea and land.

And even as they honor and respect Me, so shall Moslems care for that people as being under our protection, and whensoever any distress or discomfort shall overtake them, Moslems shall hold themselves in duty bound to aid and care for them, for they are a people subject to my Nation, obedient to their word, whose helpers also they are.

It therefore is proper for my sake to attend to their comfort, protection and aid, in face of all opposition and distress, suppressing everything that becomes a means to their spoliation. In the levying of taxes, it is necessary not to exact more than they are able to pay, but to adjust matters with their consent, without force or violence. Their building enterprises shall not be interfered with; their priests shall not be molested in the performance of their task; they shall not be persecuted for their faith or their customs, but shall be allowed to pray as they will in their own places of worship and according to their own rites; neither shall their churches be dismantled or destroyed, or their homes and mansions confiscated by Moslems, for mosques or residences, without their consent. Whosoever shall not do as is here prescribed, but shall do contrary to my behests; the same shall be held a despiser of this Compact, and a gainsayer of the word of God and of his Prophet.

No land taxes shall be exacted from them in excess of the value of four *dinars*, or one linen sheet, which shall be applied for the benefit of the Moslems and held as a sacred trust for public use. Nothing more also shall be exacted from them (*scil.*, by way of a poll-tax) than what we here prescribe. Whether they be merchants and wealthy, or whether they live in the open country, whether they fish for pearls in the sea, or own mines of precious stones, or of gold, or of silver, or possess other rich estates, they shall not be made to pay more than twelve *dirhams*.

Of those who are not of the Christian faith [and] neither conduct worship according to the Christian rite, four *dirhams* shall be exacted. But of those who conform to that people and are obedient to their word, not more shall be demanded than the aforementioned Twelve Dirhams, provided that they dwell where all their people are resident. Those who travel, and being without a place of permanent abode are constantly on the move, shall not be subject to land taxes, except that in the event any of them shall fall heirs to property on which the Imam has a legal claim, the lawful tax shall be exacted, yet even so the taxpayer shall not be made the victim of violence or of unlawful exactions in excess of his ability to pay. His mansions, his produce, and his fruits shall not be made to objects of avarice.

Christians shall not be asked to fight for Moslems against the enemies of the Faith, neither shall Moslems at war with foreign nations or engaged in massacre constrain Christians to make common cause with them against the enemy. But if the enemy shall attack the Christians, then the Moslems shall not spare the use against him or their horses, their swords and their spears. In so doing they will perform a pleasant deed.

No Christians shall be brought by force to confess Islam, and no disputes except over the better things shall be envisaged in with them. Moslems shall extend over the Christians everywhere the arm of mercy and kindness, protecting them from the exactions of oppressors. If any Christian shall be found inadvertently offending, Moslems shall deem it their duty to assist him, accompanying him to the law-courts, so that not more may be exacted of him than is prescribed by God, and peace may be restored between the parties to the dispute according to the Scripture.

All conditions previously named being observed, and the capitation tax being paid by them, no Christians shall be tyrannized over or oppressed by my people. Neither shall they on their part tyrannize over Moslems or oppress them, from this time forth even until such time as God shall ordain. Moslems shall not take the women and maidens of the Christians by force, but only with the consent of their lords, except in the event that they by free choice shall desire to be united to Moslems and married to them whether permanently or only for a time, when this shall be permitted to them out of respect to the freewill of women who should be at liberty to marry whom they love and choose. And if any Christian women shall marry a Moslem, it shall be permitted to her to continue in the Christian faith, attending the churches of the Christians without let or hindrance, and she shall live at her pleasure according to her own faith and laws. No obstacle shall be placed in the way of her communicating with her own spiritual advisers; neither shall she, forcibly and against her will, be made to forsake her own faith and laws. Whosoever shall do despite the words of this Contract, the same shall be accounted as having done despite God, and shall be held guilty in the Prophet's sight of annulling the words of the Covenant of the Prophet of God. Such a one shall be numbered among sinners before God.

Christians must attend to all repairs on their own churches, chapels and monasteries. If in the interest of the benevolent Moslem public, and of their faith, Moslems shall ask of the Christians for assistance, the latter shall not deny them what help, as an expression of friendship and goodwill, they are able to render. Seeing that the Christians have submitted to us, implored our protection and taken refuge with us, we deem all help and succor rendered to them every way legitimate. If any one of them shall be sent as an envoy to negotiate peace between Moslems and Infidels, no one shall prevent his going, and if he should prove of service to our cause, let the service be accepted; but whosoever shall despise him, the same shall be numbered among the wicked, guilty before the Prophet of God, and an enemy of his revealed word.

[Here also follows a Treaty of Mohammed, the Great Prophet of God (may the blessings of God rest upon him and his posterity!), with the Christian people, a Treaty which His Majesty after the foregoing words commanded and established with the Christians relative to their faith and laws, embracing a few commandments by which Christians shall regard themselves as being bound. Let them do nothing contrary to the previous words, and everything in harmony with those following.]

One of the commandments is this; that they shall give no aid to infidels, whether openly or surreptitiously, neither receive into their houses enemies of Moslems lest at a convenient opportunity they attack them. They shall not permit enemy men to stop at their houses or churches, neither shall they harbor enemy troops, or aid them with spear, arrow, sword or horse, or with aught else.

They shall not act as guides to them, or show them how to ambush the enemy. They shall not commit to them their possessions for safe-keeping; they shall not communicate with them, or aid them by word or deed, or afford them shelter except only under duress.

If a Moslem shall chance at a Christian's house, he may there be entertained three days and three nights; more than that is unnecessary. Christians shall avert from Moslems the abuse and oppressions of tyrants.

In the event that it becomes necessary for them to hide a Moslem in their own mansions or houses, they shall give him a place to lie, and take care of him, neither forsaking him, nor leaving him without food, so long as he shall be in hiding. Women and children of Moslems shall not be betrayed or shown to the enemy, neither shall Christians deviate from these orders.

And if any Christian shall do contrary to this Treaty, or ignore it, he shall be accounted as annulling the same. Such a one is loathsome to God, and the Prophet shall visit upon him his just retribution.

Wherefore let all Christians deem it both binding and proper to observe the words of this Treaty even until such time as God shall ordain.

In witness whereof is attached the Signature that in the presence of the Clergy and the Lords of the Nation, the Holy, Great Prophet, Mohammed, affixed, confirming the foregoing Treaty.

God Omnipotent and Lord of All!

In pursuance of the Command of the Great Prophet of God, Mohammed, the Lord's Chosen (may the blessing of God rest upon him and upon his posterity!), this Treaty was drawn up on the Monday following the first four months of the Fourth Year of the Hegira.

Chapter 10

Text of the Covenant of the Prophet Muhammad with the Christians of the World (I)

[*By the Prophet Muhammad*]
[1630]
Translation cited by Sir Paul Rycaut in 1668: 99–102

Mahomet sent from God to teach mankind, and declare the Divine Commission in truth, wrote these things. That the cause of Christian religion determined by God, might remain in all parts of the East, and of the West, as well amongst the inhabitants, as strangers, near and remote, known, and unknown: to all these people I leave this present writing, as an inviolable league, as a decision of all farther controversies, and a law whereby justice is declared, and strict observance enjoined. Therefore, whosoever of the Moselmans Faith shall neglect to perform these things, and violate this league, and after the manner of Infidels break it, and transgress what I command herein, he breaks the Compact of God, resists his agreement, and condemns his Testament, whether he be a King, or any other of the faithful. By this agreement, whereby I have obliged myself, and which the Christians have required of me, and in my Name, and in the name of all my Disciples, to enter into a Covenant of God with them, and League and Testament of the Prophets, Apostles elect, and faithful Saints, and blessed of times past and to come. By this Covenant I say, and Testament of mine (which I will have maintained with as much Religion, as a Prophet Missionary, or as an Angel next to the Divine Majesty, is strict in his obedience towards God, and in observance of his Law and Covenant) I promise to defend their Judges in my Provinces, with my Horse and Foot, Auxiliaries, and other my faithful followers; and to preserve them from their enemies, whether remote or near, and secure them both in peace and war: and to protect their Churches, Temples, Oratories, Monasteries, and places of Pilgrimage, wheresoever situated, whether in Mountain or Valley, Cavern or House, a Plain, or upon the Sand, or in what sort of edifice soever: also to preserve their Religion and their goods in what part soever they are, whether at Land or Sea, East or West, even as I keep myself and my Scepter, and the faithful believers of my own people. Likewise, to receive them into my protection from all harm, vexation, offence, and hurt. Moreover, to repel those enemies which are offensive to them and me, to stoutly oppose them both in my own person, by my servants, and all others of my people of Nation. For since I am over them, I ought to preserve and defend them from all adversity, and that no evil touch them before it first afflict mine, who labor in the same work. I promise farther to free them from those burdens which confederates suffer, either by loans of money or impositions; so that they shall be obliged to pay nothing but what they please, and no molestation or injury shall be offered them herein. A Bishop shall not be removed from his Diocese, or a Christian compelled to renounce his faith, or a

Monk his profession, or a Pilgrim disturbed in his Pilgrimage, or a Religious man in his Cell: Nor shall their Churches be destroyed, or converted into Mosques: for whosoever doth so break this Covenant of God, opposes the Messenger of God, and frustrates the Divine Testament. No imposition shall be laid upon Friars or Bishops, nor any of them who are not liable to Taxes, unless it be with their own consent. And the Tax which shall be required from rich Merchants, and from Fishermen of their Pearl, from Miners of their Precious Stones, shall not exceed above 12 shillings yearly; and it shall also be from them who are constant inhabitants of the place, and not from Travelers, and Men of uncertain abode; for they shall not be subject to impositions or contributions, unless they are possessors of inheritance of Land or Estate; for he which is lawfully subject to pay money to the Emperor, shall pay as much as another, and not more; nor more required from him, above his faculty and strength. In like manner, he that is taxed for his Land, Houses or Revenue, shall not be burdened immoderately, nor oppressed with greater Taxes then any others that pay contribution: Nor shall the confederates be obliged to go to War with the Moselmans against their enemies, either to fight or discover their Armies, because it is not of duty to a confederate, to be employed in Military affairs; but rather this Compact is made with them, that they may be the less oppressed; but rather the Moselmans shall watch, and ward, and defend them: And therefore, that they shall not be compelled to go forth to fight, or encounter the enemy, or find Horse of Arms, unless they voluntarily furnish them; and he who shall thus willingly contribute, shall be recompensed and rewarded. No Moselman shall insult the Christians, nor contend with them in anything but in kindness, but treat them with all courtesy, and abstain from all oppression or violence towards them. If any Christian commit a crime or fault, it shall be the part of the Moselman to assist him, intercede and give caution for him, and compound for his miscarriage; liberty shall also be given him to redeem his life, nor shall he be forsaken, nor be destitute of help, because of the Divine Covenant which is with them, that they should enjoy what the Moselmans enjoy, and suffer what they suffer: and on the other side, that the Moselmans enjoy what they enjoy, and suffer what they suffer. And according to this Covenant, which is by the Christians just request, and according to that endeavor which is so required for confirmation of its Authority, you are obliged to protect them from all calamity, and perform all offices of good will towards them, so that the Moselmans may be sharers with them in prosperity and adversity. Moreover, all care ought to be had, that no violence be offered to them, as to matters relating to marriage, *viz.* That they compel not the Parents to match their Daughters with Moselmans: Nor shall they be molested for refusal, either to give a Bridegroom or a Bride; for this is an act wholly voluntary, depending on their free-will and pleasure. But if it happen that a Christian Woman shall join with a Moselman, he is obliged to give her liberty of conscience in her Religion, that she may obey her Ghostly Father, and be instructed in the Doctrines of her Faith without impediments; therefore he shall no disquiet her, either by threatening divorce, or by solicitations to forsake her Faith: but if he shall be contrary thereunto, and molest her herein, he despises the

Covenant of God, and is entered into the number of liars. Moreover, when Christians would repair their Churches or Convents, or anything else appertaining unto their Worship, and have need of the liberality and assistance of the Moselmans hereunto, they ought to contribute, and freely to bestow according to their ability; not with intention to receive it again, but *gratis*; and as a good will towards their Faith, and to fulfill the Covenant of the Messenger of God, considering the obligation they have to perform the Covenant of God, and the compact of the Messenger or God. Nor shall they oppress any of them living amongst the Moselmans, nor hate them, nor compel them to carry Letters, or show the way, or any other manner forces them: for he which exercises any manner of this Tyranny against them, is an oppressor, and an adversary to the Messenger of God, and refractory to his Precepts. These are the covenants agreed between Mahomet the Messenger of God, and Christians. But the conditions on which I bind these covenants on their Consciences, are these: That no Christian give any entertainment to a Soldier, enemy to the Moselmans, or receive him in his house publicly or privately; that they receive none of the enemies of the Moselmans, as sojourners into their Houses, Churches or religious Convents; nor under-hand furnish the Camp of their enemies with Arms, Horse, Men, or maintain any intercourse or correspondence with them, by contracts or writing; but betaking themselves to some certain place of abode, shall attend to the preservation of themselves, and to the defense of their Religion. To any Moselman and his Beasts, they shall give three days entertainment with variety of Meat; and moreover, shall endeavor to defend them from all misfortune and trouble; so that if any Moselman shall be desirous, or be compelled to conceal himself in any of their houses or habitations, they shall friendly hide him, and deliver him from the danger he is in, and not betray him to his enemy: and in this manner the Christians performing Faith on their side, whosoever violates any of these conditions, and doth contrarily, shall be deprived of the benefits contained in the Covenant of God and his Messenger; nor shall he deserve to enjoy these privileges indulged to Bishops and Christian Monks, and to the believers of the contents of the *Achoran.* Wherefore I do conjure my people by God and his Prophet to maintain these things faithfully, and fulfill them, in what part soever of the world they are. And the Messenger of God shall recompense them for the same; the perpetual observation of which he seriously recommends to them, until the Day of Judgment, and dissolution of the world. Of these conditions which Mahomet the Messenger of God hath agreed with the Christians, and hath enjoined, the witnesses are:

Abu-Bacre Assadiqu, Ombar ben-alcharab, Ithman ben Afaw, Ati ben abi-taleb…

With a number of others; the Secretary was Moavia ben abi Sofian, a Soldier of the Messenger of God, the last day of the Moon of the fourth Month, the fourth year of Hegira in Medina. May God remunerate those who are witnesses to this writing. Praise be to God the Lord of all creatures.

Text of the Covenant of the Prophet Muhammad with the Christians of the World (II)

[*By the Prophet Muhammad*]
[1630]
Translation cited by Edward A. Van Dyck in 1881

Mahommed, messenger of God, sent to teach men and declare to them his Divine mission, has written the following things, to wit: That the matter of the Christian religion, emanated from God, can remain free in all parts of the East and of the West, both among those who are [natives] of the country and among those who are neighbors to it, both among those who are strangers and among those who are not; and I leave to all these people this present writing as an inviolable treaty and as a perfect [rule of] decision in all differences and contestations to come hereafter, and as a law by which justice is shown, and the observation of which is strictly enjoined. Wherefore every man, professing the faith of the Moslems, who shall neglect to fulfill these things, and who shall violate or break this agreement, after the manner of unbelievers, and shall transgress the things I herein command, breaks the covenant of God, resists His Will, and despises his testament, be he king, prince, or other unbeliever. By this agreement, whereto I have bound myself, on the prayers of the Christians, both in my name and in the name of my followers, to enter with them into the covenant of God and into the peace of the prophets, the chosen apostles, the faithful saints, and the blessed of times past and of times to come; by this my covenant, which I wish to be executed as religiously as a prophet sent of God or an angel who draws nigh to the Divine Majesty, is exact and regular in the obedience that he owes to His law and commandments, I promise to protect their magistrates in my provinces with my foot and horse, with my auxiliaries, and with the believers that follow me. I promise also to defend them against their enemies, be they far or near, to guard them in peace and in war, to keep their churches, their temples, their oratories, their convents, and the places to which they make pilgrimages, wherever they be situated, upon mountains or in valleys, in caverns or in houses, in the fields or in the deserts, or in any other sort of building whatsoever, and to preserve also their religion and their goods in whatever place they be, whether on land or on the sea, in the East or in the West, in the same way that I preserve myself and my scepter and the faithful believers who are my people. I promise also to take them under my protection and to guarantee them from all violence and vexation that shall be committed against them, and to repulse the enemies who might wish to harm them and me, and to resist such rigorously, both in my own person and by my servants and by those who are my people and my nation; for, whereas I am set over them, I ought to and must defend them and guarantee them from all adversity and prevent any harm from befalling them that does not first befall my own who labor with me in the same work.

I also promise to exempt them from all the burdens that confederates are bound to bear, whether loan of silver or imports, so that they shall not be held to pay but that which they please, without any harm or punishment being inflicted upon them for so doing. Their bishop shall not be taken away from his diocese nor shall any Christian be constrained to renounce his faith, nor any workman his profession, nor shall any pilgrim be troubled while making his pilgrimage, nor any monk in his cell; neither shall their temples be torn down or converted into mosques, for he who does this breaks the present covenant of God, opposes His Message, and renders null the Divine Testament. No impost shall be put upon the monks or the bishop nor upon any of those who are not subject to taxes, unless it be with their consent. The tax to be demanded of rich merchants, of pearl-fishers, and of the miners who mine precious stones, gold and silver, as well as that to be demanded of other wealthy Christians, domiciled and established in fixed places, and not upon travelers or those who have no fixed dwelling place; these shall not be subjected to any impost nor to the ordinary contributions, if they have no goods or heritage; for he who is held to pay, legitimately, and according to the law, money to the ruler, shall pay as much as another and no more, and nothing shall be required of him beyond his strength and ability; so also he who taxed for his land, his houses and his income, shall not be overburdened or oppressed with greater taxes than those who pay the contributions. The confederates shall in no way be obliged to go to war along with the Moslems against their enemies either to fight or to discover their armies; for allies are not to be employed in military expeditions, this treaty having been made with them only to relieve them and prevent them from being crushed.

Still more, the Moslems will watch over them, guard them and defend them. They shall not, therefore, be obliged to go to fight and oppose the enemy, nor to furnish horses or arms, unless of their own free will; and those who shall furnish anything of the sort, shall be compensated and thanked therefore. No Moslem shall torment the Christians, nor dispute with them unless it be with civility; he shall treat them kindly and shall abstain from doing them violence of any sort. If it happen that some Christian commit a crime or fall into some error, the Moslem is bound to help him, intercede for him and become his surety and settle his matter; he can even redeem his life; and he shall not be abandoned or deprived of succor, because of the godly covenant made with him, and for that he ought to enjoy that which the Moslems enjoy and suffer that which they suffer; and, on the other hand, that the Moslems enjoy what he enjoys and suffer what he suffers. And in conformity with this treaty, which is made upon the just prayers of the Christians, and in conformity with the diligence that is required in obeying its authority, ye are bound to protect them and guarantee them from all calamity and render them all possible good offices, and so to do that all, Moslems shall share with them both good and bad fortune. Furthermore, particular care shall be had that no violence be done to them in the matter of marriage; that is to say, that the fathers and mothers shall not be forced to give their daughters in marriage to Moslems, and that they shall be in no way troubled for having refused theirs sons or their daughters in marriage, for this act is purely voluntary, and ought to be done with a good heart and with joy. That if it comes to pass that a Christian woman unites herself to a Moslem, he shall leave her liberty of conscience and suffer her to obey her spiritual father and be instructed in the doctrine of her faith without any hindrance. He shall, therefore, leave her in quiet, and shall in no way torment her by threatening to divorce her or by pressing her to renounce her religion; and if he does otherwise on this head, he despise the covenant of God, he rebels against the treaty made by his apostle, and becomes one of the liars. If the Christians wish to repair their churches, their monasteries, or other places where they perform divine service, and stand in need of the help and liberality of Moslems, the latter are bound to contribute thereto with all their power and grant what they ask, not with the design of asking it again or of deriving benefit therefrom, but gratuitously as a token of good will toward their religion, and in obedience to the treaty made by the apostle of God, and in view of the obligation they are under to execute and fulfill it. They shall oppress none of them, living among the Moslems; they shall not in any way hate them, or oblige them to carry letters or serve as guides, and shall do them no violence whatsoever; for he who often practices these kinds of tyranny is an oppressor, an enemy of God's apostle, and a rebel against his commands.

Behold the things that have been laid down between Mahommed, God's apostle, and the Christians: The conditions to which I bind them in conscience are that no Christian shall entertain a soldier who is an enemy of the Moslems, nor receive him into his house, be it publicly or secretly; that they shall give no shelter to an enemy of the Moslems, and that they shall not suffer such to dwell in their houses, churches, or convents; that they shall in no way furnish underhand the camp of the enemy with men, with arms, or with horses, and that they shall have no correspondence or intercourse with the enemy, be it by writing or otherwise; but that by withdrawing to some place of security they look to their own preservation and the defense of their religion; that they furnish during three days to every Moslem things necessary for his subsistence and that of his beast, and this properly and in different kinds of goods; that they also do their utmost to defend them if attacked, and to guard them against every unhappy accident; for this reason, if any Moslem wishes to hide himself in any of their houses, they shall hide him, with a good will and deliver him from the danger in which he is placed without discovering him to his enemy; if the Christians keep faith on their part, those who shall violate some of these conditions, whichever they may be, and shall do any to the contrary, shall be deprived—the Christians of the advantages contained in the covenant of God and His Apostle, and shall be unworthy of enjoying the privileges granted to bishops and other monks; and the believers of that which is contained in the Qur'an.

Wherefore I do conjure my people, in the name of God and by his prophet, to keep faithfully all these things, and fulfill them in whatever part of the earth they may be; and the messenger of God will recompense them provided that they inviolably observe them till the day of judgment and till the dissolution of the world.

The witnesses of the present conditions to which Mahommed, the apostle of God, has agreed are:

Abu Bakr es-Suddik; Omar Ibn-el-Khattab; Othman Ibn 'Affan; 'Ali Ibn Abi Talib and several others; the scribe who has drawn them up in Mu'awiyyah Ibn Abi Safian, the soldier of the apostle of God, the last day of the moon of the fourth month, the fourth year of the flight to Medina. May God recompense those who are witnesses to this writing. Praise be to the God of all creatures.

Text of the Covenant of the Prophet Muhammad with the Christians of the World (III)

[*By the Prophet Muhammad*]
[1630]
Translation cited by John Andrew Morrow in 2013

[In the Name of Allah, the Most Compassionate, the Most Merciful.]

It was written by Muhammad, the Messenger of Allah, the proclaimer and warner [*bashiran wa nadhiran*], to all the people [*al-nas kaffah*], [Muhammad], who is entitled to the protection of Allah [*wadi'at Allah*] in truth, and as a proof [*hujjah*] of Allah for the Christian religion [*din al-nasraniyyah*] in the eastern land and its west, its Arabs and non-Arabs [*fasihiha wa'ajamiha*], near or far, known or unknown.

This document [*kitaban*], which has been prepared for them, constitutes an authoritative covenant [*'ahdan mariyyan*], a well-known certificate [*sijlan manshuran*], and a testament [*wasiyyah*] from him which must be respected and which will protect them.

Whoever holds to Islam, abides by it, and whoever breaks the covenant contained in this testament, and transgresses [*khalafahu*] it among the non-Muslims, and contradicts what I commanded in it, he has violated the Covenant of Allah [*'ahd Allah*], denies the Oath of Allah [*mithaq Allah*] and has disdained His Protection [*dhimmah*] whether he is a Sultan or anyone else among the believers and the Muslims.

I commit myself to grant alliances [*'uhud*] and pledges [*mawathiq*] to those who requested them from me and from all of my families [*ahli*] from among the Muslims to give them the covenant of Allah [*'ahd Allah*] and His Pledge [*mithaq*] and I place them under the safeguard of His Prophets, His Messengers, His Elect, His Saints, from the Muslims and the Believers, among the first of them and the last of them. And my protection [*dhimmati*] and my pact [*mithaq*] the most solid covenant that Allah has given a prophet sent or an angel [or sovereign] drawn near, [namely], the right to demand obedience, to give obligations [*farida*], and respect of Allah's Covenant [*ahad Allah*].

That I protect their judges in my fortified borderlines [*fi thughuri*] with my horses and my men, my helpers, and my followers, from among the Believers, from every region among the regions of the enemy, whether they be far away or close by, whether they be at peace or at war, I safeguard them. I grant security to their churches, their places of pilgrimage [*siyahah*] wherever they are and wherever they may be found, be they in the mountains or the valleys, in the caves or the inhabited regions, in the plains or the desert, or in buildings; and that I protect their religion and their property wherever they are and wherever they may be found in land or at sea, in the East or West, the same way that I protect myself, my successors [*khatimi*], and the People of my Community [*ahl al-millati*] among the Believers and the Muslims.

I place them under my protection from any damage or harm [*makruh*]; to exempt them from any requisitions or any onerous obligations. I am behind them, protecting them myself, by means of my followers, my helpers, and the members of my religious community [*ahl al-millati*].

Having authority over them, I must govern them, protecting them from all damage and ensuring that no harm happens to them that does not happen to me and my Companions who, along with me, protect this noble command.

I block from them the harm in the supplies which obliges the people of the pact [*ahl al-'ahd*] from loan [*'ariyah*] and land tribute [*kharaj*] except what they themselves consent to give. They should not be compelled in this matter.

It is not permitted to remove a bishop from his bishopric or a Christian from his Christianity, a monk from his monastic life or a pilgrim from his pilgrimage or a hermit monk from his tower. Nor is it permitted to destroy any part of their churches, to take parts of their buildings to construct mosques or the homes of Muslims. Whoever does such a thing will have violated the pact of Allah, disobeyed his Messenger, and betrayed the Divine Alliance.

It is not permitted to impose a capitation [*jizyah*] or any kind of tax on monks or bishops only that which they are prepared to give willingly.

The capitation [*jizyah*] upon owners of large businesses, and divers, and those who exploit mines for precious stones, gold and silver, and those who are wealthy, and powerful, among those who have professed Christianity, may not surpass more than twelve *dirhams* per year, so long as they are inhabitants of these countries or residents, and not travelers.

The traveler, or the resident whose place [of residence] is unknown, is not obliged to pay the land tribute [*kharaj*] or the poll-tax [*jizyah*] unless he has inherited land over which the ruler [*sultan*] has a monetary right. He must pay the money [*mal*] as others without, however, the charges unjustly exceeding the measure of their means [or strength].

As for the labor force which the owners spend upon to cultivate these lands, to render them fertile, and to harvest them, they are not to be taxed excessively. Let them pay in the same fashion that was imposed on other similar tributaries.

The free non-Muslims enjoying Muslim protection [*ahl al-dhimmah*] will not be obliged to go to war with the Muslims in order to combat their enemies, to attack them, and to seize them. Indeed, such free non-Muslims [*ahl al-dhimmah*] will not engage in war along with the Muslims. It is precisely to discharge them of this obligation that this pact has been granted to them as well as to assure them the help and protection on the part of the Muslims. They will not be obliged to go out with the Muslims to meet ltheir enemies or be forced to give their horses, their arms, unless they contribute to the cause freely. Whoever does so will be recognized for his action.

No Christian will be made Muslim by force: *And dispute ye not with the People of the Book, except with means better* [29:46]. They must be covered by the wing of mercy.

Repel every harm that could reach them wherever they may find themselves and in any country in which they are.

If a Christian were to commit a crime or an offense, Muslims must provide him with help, defense, and protection. They should pardon his offense and encourage his victim to reconcile with him, urging him to pardon him or to receive compensation in return.

The Muslims must not abandon the Christians and leave them without help and assistance since I have made this pact with them on behalf of Allah to ensure that whatever good befell Muslims it would befall them as well and that whatever harm befell Muslims would befall them as well. In virtue of this pact, they have obtained inviolable rights to enjoy our protection, to be protected from any infringement of their rights, so that they will be bound to the Muslims both in good and bad fortune.

Christians must not be subject to suffer, by abuse, on the subject of marriages which they do not desire. Muslims should not take Christian girls in marriage against the will of their parents, nor should they oppress their families in the event that they refused their offers of engagement and marriage. Such marriages should not take place without their desire and agreement and without their approval and consent.

If a Muslim takes a Christian woman as a wife, he must respect her Christian beliefs. He will give her freedom to listen to her [clerical] superiors as she desires, to follow the path of her own religion, and he will not force her to leave it. Whoever, despite this order, forces his wife to act contrary to her religion in any aspect whatsoever he will have broken the alliance of Allah and will enter into open rebellion against the pact of His Messenger, and Allah will count him among the impostors.

If the Christians seek the help and assistance of the Muslims in order to repair their churches and their convents or to arrange matters pertaining to their affairs and religion, they, [the Muslims], must help and support them. However, they must not do so with the aim of receiving any reward. On the contrary, they should aim to restore that religion, out of faithfulness to the pact of the Messenger of Allah, by pure donation, and as a meritorious act before Allah and His Messenger.

In matters of war between them and their enemies, the Muslims will not employ any Christian as a messenger, scout, guide or spy or for any other duty of war. Whoever obliges one of them to do such a thing is an oppressor [*zalim*], a rebel against the Messenger of Allah, and has differed over his testament [*wasiyyah*].

These are the conditions that Muhammad, the Messenger of Allah, has placed upon the Christian community [*ahl al-millah al-nasraniyyah*], with regard to their religion and their community [*dhimmah*]. They must hold fast to this covenant [*'ahd*] and respect what they have agreed upon.

Among other things, none of them may act as a scout, spy, either overtly or covertly, on behalf of an enemy of war, against a Muslim. None of them will shelter the enemies of the Muslims in their homes from which they could await the moment to launch an attack. May these enemies [of the Muslims] never be allowed to halt in their regions, be it in their villages, their oratories or in any other place belonging to their co-religionists. They must not provide any support to war enemies of the Muslims by furnishing them with weapons, horses, men, or anything else, including greeting them. They must host for three days and three nights any Muslims who halt among them, with their animals. They must offer them, wherever they are found, and wherever they are going, the same food with which they live themselves without, however, being obliged to endure other annoying or onerous burdens.

If a Muslim needs to hide in one of their homes or oratories, they must grant him hospitality, give him help, and provide him with their food during the entire time he will be among them, making every effort to keep him concealed and to prevent the enemy from finding him, while providing for all of his needs.

Whoever contravenes or alters the ordinances of this edict will be cast out of the alliance between Allah and His Messenger.

May everyone abide by the treaties and alliances which have been contracted with the kings, the monks [*ruhban*], and the Christians [*nasara*] from the People of the Book, and which I have contracted myself, and every other commitment that each prophet has made with his nation, to assure them safeguard and faithful protection, and to serve them as a guarantee.

This must not be violated or altered until the hour [of the Resurrection] and the end of the world [*dunya*].

This document [*kitaban*], which was written by Muhammad, the Messenger of Allah, for the Christians who had written to him and requested from him this covenant, was witnessed by:

Abu Bakr al-Siddiq; ʿUmar ibn al-Khattab; ʿUthman ibn ʿAffan; ʿAli ibn Abi Talib; Muʿawiyyah ibn Abi Sufyan; Abu al-Darda'; Abu Dharr; Abu Hurayrah; ʿAbd Allah ibn Masʿud; ʿAbd Allah ibn al-ʿAbbas; Hamzah ibn ʿAbd al-Muttalib; Fadl; Zayd ibn Thabit; ʿAbd Allah ibn Zayd; Harfus ibn Zayd; al-Zubayr ibn al-ʿAwwam; Saʿd ibn Muʿadh; Thabit ibn Qays; Usamah ibn Zayd; ʿUthman ibn Matʿun; ʿAbd Allah ibn ʿAmr al-ʿAs; Abu Rabiʿah; Hassan ibn Thabit; Jaʿfar ibn Abi Talib; Ibn al-ʿAbbas; Talhah ibn ʿAbd Allah; Saʿd ibn ʿUbadah; Zayd ibn Arqam; Sahl ibn Bayda'; Da'ud ibn Jubayr; Abu al-ʿAliyyah; Abu Ahrifah; Ibn ʿUsayr; Hashim ibn ʿAsiyyah; Zayd ibn Arqam; ʿUmar ibn Yamin; Kaʿb ibn Malik; Kaʿb ibn Kaʿb. May Allah be pleased with all of them!

Written [down] by Muʿawiyyah ibn Abi Sufyan, and dictated by the Messenger of Allah on the second day of the month of Rabiʿ Ashar during the fourth year of the Hegira in Medina.

Allah suffices as a Witness for what is contained in this document [*kitaban*].

Praise be to Allah, the Lord of the Worlds!

Text of the Covenant of the Prophet Muhammad with the Christians of the World (IV)

[*By the Prophet Muhammad*]
[1538]
Translation by John Andrew Morrow in 2103

In the Name of Allah, the Creator [*al-Khaliq*], the Living [*al-Hayy*], the Speaking [*al-Natiq*], the One who Remains after the Annihilation of Creation [*al-Baqi ba'd fana' al-khaliq*].

This is a copy [*nuskhah*] of the covenant [*'ahd*] which was written by Muhammad ibn 'Abd Allah ibn 'Abd al-Muttalib for all the Christians [*nasara*].

Copy [*nuskhah*] of the Covenant [*kitab al-'ahd*]

This covenant of Allah [*'ahd Allah*] was ordered to be written by Muhammad ibn 'Abd Allah ibn 'Abd al-Muttalib, the Messenger of Allah, may Allah's peace and blessings be upon him and his family [*alihi*], to all the Christians and all the monks, to guard and protect them, because they are Allah's trust among His Creations [*wadi'at Allah fi khalqihi*] in order for the covenant to be a proof [*hujjah*] against them and there would be no claim against Allah after the Messenger. He made this a protection [*dhimmah*] from him and a protection for them by the authority of Allah, for Allah is All-Mighty [*'Aziz*] and All-Wise [*Hakim*]. It was written by the Lion [*asad*] and the People of His Vocation [*ahl al-millati*] to all those who profess the Christian religion [*da'wat al-nasraniyyah*] in the Eastern lands and its West, near and far, be they Arabs or non-Arabs [*'ajami*], known or unknown, as a covenant [*'ahd*] from him, a justice and tradition to be preserved.

He who observes it holds to his Islam and is worthy of his religion [*din*]. He who breaks it [*nakatha*] and jeopardizes the covenant [*'ahd*] which was ordered by the Messenger of Allah, and changes it, and transgresses what has been commanded, has rejected the Covenant of Allah [*'ahd Allah*], denies the Oath of Allah [*mithaq Allah*], disdains his religion, and merits His Maledictions, whether he is a Sultan or anyone else among the believers [*mu'minin*] and the Muslims.

I started by committing myself to the covenant, granted alliances [*'uhud*] and pledges [*mawathiq*] to those who requested them from me and from all of my Muslim Community [*millati min al-muslimin*]. I gave them the Covenant of Allah [*'ahd Allah*] and His Pledge [*mithaq*] and I placed them under the safeguard of His Prophets, His Chosen Ones [*asfiya*], His Friends [*awliyya'*] from among all the Believers [*mu'minin*] and the Muslims over time. My protection [*dhimmati*] and my security [*mithaqi*] represent the most solid covenant that Allah, the Most Exalted, has given a prophet sent in truth to demand obedience, to give obligations [*farida*], and to respect the covenant [*'ahd*].

The covenant of Allah [*'ahd Allah*] is that I should protect their land [*'ard*], their monasteries [*al-diyar*], with my power [*qudrah*], my horses, my men, my weapons [*silahi*], my strength [*quwwati*], and my Muslim followers [*atba'i*] in any region, far away or close by, and that I should protect their businesses. I grant security to them, their churches, their businesses, their houses of worship [*buyut salawatihim*], the places of their monks, the places of their pilgrims, wherever they may be found, be they in the mountains or the valleys, caves or inhabited regions, the plains or the desert and that I should protect their *dhimmah*, their faith [*millah*], and their religion [*din*], wherever they may be found in the East or West, in the sea or on land, the same way that I protect myself, my entourage [*khasati*], and the People of my Community [*ahl al-millati*] among the Muslims.

I place them under my protection [*dhimmah*], my security [*mithaq*], and my trust [*aman*] at every moment. I defend them from any damage, harm [*makruh*] or retribution [*tabi'a*]. I am behind them, protecting them from every enemy or anyone who wishes them harm [*muhdi*]. I sacrifice myself for them by means of my helpers [*a'wani*], my followers [*atba'i*], and the People of my Community [*ahl al-millah*] because they are my flock [*ra'iyyah*] and the people under my protection [*ahl al-dhimmati*], I extend [*amudu*] my authority [*sultati*], my care [*ri'ayyah*], and my protection over them from every harm [*makruh*] so that it does not reach them. No harm will reach them unless it reaches my Companions [*ashabi*] who [are there to] protect them and assist Islam [*nusrat*].

I remove from them the harm from taxes and loan in the supplies borne to the People of the Pact [*ahl al-'ahd*] except what they themselves consent to give. They should not be compelled or unfairly treated in this matter.

It is not permitted to remove a bishop from his bishopric, a monk from his monastic life, a Christian from his Christianity, an ascetic [*zahid*] from his tower, or a pilgrim from his pilgrimage. Nor is it permitted to destroy any part of their churches or their businesses or to take parts of their buildings to construct mosques or the homes of believing Muslims [*mu'minin al-muslimin*]. Whoever does such a thing will have violated the covenant of Allah [*'ahd Allah*], disobeyed [*khalafa*] his Messenger, and deviated [*hadha*] from His Divine Alliance.

It is not permitted to impose a capitation [*jizyah*] or any kind of land tribute [*kharaj*] on monks, bishops or those who are worshippers among them, who, by devotion, wear woolen clothing [*al-suf*] or live alone in the mountains or in other regions secluded from human presence.

The capitation [*jizyah*] will be applied to those Christians who are not clerics [*man la yattabad*] with the exception of the monk and the pilgrim in the amount of four dirhams per year or an inexpensive cloak [*tawb*]. He who does not have the money or the food with which to feed himself, the Muslims will help him by means of the savings stored in the Treasury [*bayt al-mal*]. If they find difficulties in securing food, the Muslims will also help them, provided they willingly accept.

May the land tribute [*jizyah al-kharaj*] on big business by land or sea, pearl-diving, mining for precious stones, gold and silver, or those who are wealthy among those who profess the Christian faith, not exceed twelve *dirhams* [*fiddah*] per year, so long as they are inhabitants and residents in these countries.

May nothing similar be demanded of travelers, who are not residents of the country or wayfarers whose country of residence is unknown. There shall be no land tax with capitation for others than those who own land as will the other occupants of lands over which the ruler has a right. They will pay taxes as others pay them without, however, the charges unjustly exceeding the measure of their means. As for the labor force which the owners spend upon to cultivate these lands, to render them fertile, and to harvest them, they are not to be taxed excessively. Let them pay in the same fashion and justly that which was imposed on other similar tributaries.

The people under our protection [*ahl al-dhimmah*] will not be obliged to go to war with the Muslims in order to combat their enemies and to attack them. Indeed, the people under our protection [*ahl al-dhimmah*] are not to engage in war. It is precisely to discharge them of this obligation that this pact has been granted to them as well as to assure them the help and protection of the Muslims. They will not be constrained to provide equipment to any of the Muslims, in arms or horses, in the event of a war in which the Muslims attack their enemies, unless they contribute to the cause freely. And what the Muslims have borrowed will be guaranteed by the [State] Treasury [*bayt al-mal*] until it is returned to them. If they die or are damaged, the [State] Treasury [*bayt al-mal*] will provide monetary compensation.

No one who practices the Christian religion will be forced to enter into Islam. *And dispute ye not with the People of the Book, except with means better* [29:46]. They must be covered by the wing of mercy and all harm that could reach them, wherever they may find themselves and wherever they may be, must be repelled.

If a Christian were to commit a crime or an offense, Muslims must provide him with help, defense, and protection, as well as pay his penalty for him. They should encourage reconciliation between him and the victim, to help or save him.

The Muslims must not abandon him or leave him without help and assistance because I have given them a covenant of Allah which is binding upon the Muslims.

In virtue of this pact, they have obtained inviolable rights to enjoy our protection, to be protected from any infringement of their rights, and they are not to be disputed, rejected, or ignored so that they will be bound to the Muslims both in good and bad fortune.

The girls of the Christians must not be subject to suffer, by abuse, on the subject of marriages which they do not desire. Muslims should not take Christian girls in marriage against the will of their parents nor should they oppress their families in the event that they refused their offers of engagement and marriage. Such marriages should not take place without their desire and agreement and without their approval and consent.

If a Muslim takes a Christian woman as a wife, he must respect her Christian beliefs. He will give her freedom to listen to her [clerical] superiors as she desires and to follow the path of her own religion. Whoever, despite this order, forces his [Christian] wife to act contrary to her religion, he will have broken the alliance of Allah and broken the promise [*mithaq*] of His Messenger and he will be counted, by us, among the liars [*kadhibin*].

If the Christians approach you seeking the help and assistance of the Muslims in order to repair their churches and their convents, or to arrange matters pertaining to their affairs and religion, these [Muslims] must help and support them. However, they must not do so with the aim of receiving any reward or debt. On the contrary, they should do so to restore that religion, out of faithfulness to the pact of the Messenger of Allah, by pure donation, and as a meritorious act before Allah and His Messenger.

In matters of war between them and their enemies, the Muslims will not employ any Christian as a messenger, scout, guide, to show power, or for any other duty of war. Whoever obliges one of them to do such a thing will be unjust [*zaliman*] towards Allah, disobedient [*'asiyan*] to His Messenger, and will be cast out [*mutakhalliyan*] from his religion. Nothing is permitted to a Muslim [with regards to the Christians] outside of obeying these edicts which Muhammad ibn 'Abd Allah, the Messenger of Allah, has passed in favor of the religion of the Christians.

I am also placing conditions [upon the Christians] and I demand that they promise to fulfill and satisfy them as commands their religion. Among other things, none of them may act as a scout, spy, either overtly or covertly, on behalf of an enemy of war, against a Muslim. None of them will shelter the enemies of the Muslims in their homes from which they could await the moment to launch an attack. May these enemies [of the Muslims] never be allowed to halt in their regions, be it in their villages, their oratories, or in any other place belonging to their co-religionists. They must not provide any support to the war enemies of the Muslims by furnishing them with weapons, horses, men or call for unnecessary things. They must not annoy them and they should be honored as long as they persist in their religion and their care for their pact. They must grant Muslims three days and three nights when they halt among them. They must offer them, wherever they are found, and wherever they are going, the same food with which they live themselves, without, however, being obliged to endure other annoying or onerous burdens.

If a Muslim needs to hide in one of their homes or oratories, they must grant him hospitality, give him help, and provide him with their food during the entire time he will be among them, making every effort to keep him concealed and to prevent the enemy from finding him, while providing to all of his needs.

Whoever contravenes or alters the ordinances of this edict will be cast out of the alliance between Allah and His Messenger.

May everyone abide by the treaties and alliances which have been contracted with the monks, and which I have contracted myself, wherever they may be.

The Messenger of Allah, may the peace and blessings of Allah be upon him, must respect what he has granted, on his authority and all the Muslims, to guard them and have mercy on them until the end, until the Hour of [Resurrection] arrives, and the world comes to an end.

Whoever is unjust after this towards a [Christian] subject [*dhimmi*], breaks the covenant and rejects it, I will be his enemy on the Day of Judgment among all the Muslims.

As witness to this covenant [*kitab*]—which was written by Muhammad ibn 'Abd Allah, the Messenger of Allah, may the peace and blessings of Allah be upon him, to all the Christians [*jami'*] to whom he put conditions in it, and for whom he wrote the following covenant [*'ahd*]—there are thirty witnesses:

Abu Bakr al-Siddiq; 'Umar ibn al-Khattab; 'Uthman ibn 'Affan; 'Ali ibn Abi Talib; Abu Dharr; Abu al-Darda'; Abu Hurayrah; 'Abd Allah ibn Mas'ud; al-'Abbas ibn 'Abd al-Malik; Fadl ibn al-'Abbas al-Zahri; Talhah ibn 'Abd Allah; Sa'id ibn Mu'azz; Sa'id ibn Ubadah; Thabit ibn Qays; Yazid ibn Talit; 'Abd Allah ibn Yazid; Farsus ibn Qasim ibn Badr ibn Ibrahim; Amir ibn Yazid [Imam ibn Yazid?]; Sahl ibn Tamim; 'Abd al-'Azim ibn al-Najashi

[different handwriting]:
'Abd al-'Azim ibn Husayn; 'Abd Allah ibn 'Amr ibn al-'As; 'Amr ibn Yasir; Mu'azzam ibn Musa; Hassan ibn Thabit; Abu Hanifah; 'Ubayd ibn Mansur; Hashim ibn 'Abd Allah; Abu al-'Azar; Hisham ibn 'Abd al-Muttalib

'Ali ibn Abi Talib, may Allah be pleased with him, wrote this covenant, and the manuscript [*sijl*] was written on a piece of leather [*jild*] that was not small. It remained at the Sultan's authority and was sealed by the Prophet, peace and blessings be upon him. All praise be to Allah.

This blessed book [*kitab al-mubarak*] was completed on the holy day of Monday, in the last month of Ba'una, the blessed, in the year of our Masters the Martyrs, the Pure Ones, the Felicitous, the Satisfied [*abrar*], may Allah grant us their intercession and may their intercession be with us. Amen!

This corresponds to the 27th of the sacred [*haram*] month of Muharram of the year 945 of the Arabic *hijrah*. May Allah make its end good! Amen!

This blessed book [*kitab al-mubarak*] belongs to the great soul [*al-mubajjal*], the master [*al-mawla*], the leader [*al-ra'is*], the elder [*al-shaykh*], the scholar [*al-'alim*], Sum'an, the son of [*najl*], the source of greatness [*al-mu'azzam*] Fadl Allah, may Allah rest his soul in peace [*nayaha allah nafsahu*], known as [*al-ma'ruf*] al-Barallusi.

The writer of these words is the humble [*miskin*], full of faults and sins [*khataya wa al-dunub*], asking the brothers who read these words [lit. letters] to mention them in their prayers [*salawat*] and the Messiah [*masih*] will reward them one hundred and sixty-three times.

[The writer of these words is the humble [*miskin*], full of faults and sins [*khataya wa al-dunub*]. Michel: the brothers who read these words [lit. letters] must mention them in their prayers [*salawat*] and the Messiah [*masih*] will reward them one hundred and sixty-three times.] (translator's note: this is an alternate reading)

Text of the *Covenant of the Prophet Muhammad with the Christians of the World*

(Corrected Arabic Original from 1630 CE)

الْعَهْدُ وَالشُّرُوطُ الَّتِي شَرَطَهَا مُحَمَّدٌ رَسُولُ الله لأَهْلِ الْمِلَّةِ النَّصْرَانِيَّةِ

كَتَبَهُ مُحَمَّدٌ رَسُولُ الله إِلَى النَّاسِ كَافَّةً بَشِيراً وَ نَذِيراً، عَلَى وَدِيعَةِ اللَّهِ فِي حَقِّهِ، لِتَكُونَ حُجَّةَ اللَّهِ سِجِلَّ دِينِ النَّصْرَانِيَّةِ فِي مَشْرِقِ الْأَرْضِ وَمَغْرِبِهَا، وفَصِيحِها وأعجَمِها، قَرِيبِهَا وبَعِيدِهَا، ومَعْرُوفِها ومَجْهُولِها، كِتَاباً جَعَلَهُ لَهُمْ عَهْداً مَرعِيّاً، وسِجِلّاً مَنْشُوراً، وَصِيَّةً مِنْهُ تُقِيمُ فِيهِ عَدْلَهُ، وَذِمَّةً مَحْفُوظَةً. فَمَنْ كَانَ بِالْإِسْلَامِ مُتَمَسِّكًا، وَلِما فِيهِ مُتَسَاهِلًا مِنْ صَنِيعِهَا، وَنَكَثَ الْعَهْدَ الَّذِي فِيهَا وَخَالَفَهُ إِلَى غَيْرِ الْمُؤْمِنِينَ، وَتَعَدَّى فِيهِ مَا أَمَرْتُ بِهِ، كَانَ لِعَهْدِ اللَّهِ نَاكِثاً، ولمِيثاقِه نَافِياً، وبذِمَّتِهِ مُسْتَهِينًا، سُلْطَانًا كَانَ أَوْ غَيْرَهُ مِنْ الْمُؤْمِنِينَ وَالْمُسْلِمِينَ، فبدأتُ بِإِعْطَاءِ الْعُهُودِ عَلَى نَفْسِي، وَ الْمَوَاثِيقَ الَّتِي يَسْأَلونَها عَنِّي وَ عَنْ جَمِيعِ أَهَالِيَّ مِنْ الْمُسْلِمِينَ، بِأَنْ أُعْطِيَهُمْ عَهْدَ اللَّهِ وَمِيثَاقَهُ، وَ ذِمَّةَ أَنْبِيَائِهِ وَ رُسُلِهِ وَ أَصْفِيَائِهِ وَ أَوْلِيَائِهِ مِنَ الْمُؤْمِنِينَ وَ الْمُسْلِمِينَ، فِي الْأَوَّلِينَ وَ الْآخِرِينَ، وَ ذِمَّتِي وَ مِيثَاقِي أَشَدُّ ما أَخَذَ اللَّهُ عَلَى نَبِيٍّ مُرْسَلٍ، أَوْ مَلَكٍ مُقَرَّبٍ، مِنْ حَقِّ الطَّاعَةِ وَ إِيتَاءِ الْفَرِيضَةِ وَ الْوَفَاءِ بِعَهْدِ اللَّهِ، أَنْ أَحْفَظَ قَاصِيَهِمْ فِي ثُغُورِي بِخَيْلِي وَ رِجَالِي وَ أَعْوَانِي وَ أَتْبَاعِي مِنَ الْمُؤْمِنِينَ، فِي كُلِّ نَاحِيَةٍ مِنْ نَوَاحِي الْعَدُوّ، بَعِيدًا كَانُوا أَمْ قَرِيبًا، سِلْماً كَانُوا أَمْ حَرْباً، وَ أَومِنَهُمْ وَ أَذُبَّ عَنْهُمْ وَ عَنْ كَنَائِسِهِمْ وَ بِيَعِهِمْ وَ مُصَلَّاهُمْ وَ مَوَاضِعِ الرُّهْبَانِ مِنْهُمْ وَ مَوَاطِنِ

السِّيَاحَةُ حَيْثُ كَانُوا وَ أَيْنَما وَجَدُوا، فِي جَبَلٍ اَوْ وَادٍ، اَوْ مَغارَةٍ اَوْ عُمْرَانٍ، اَوْ سَهْلٍ أَوْ رَمْلٍ أَوْ بِنَاءٍ، وَ أَنْ أَحُوطَ دِينَهُمْ وَ مُلْكَهُمْ حَيْثُ كَانُوا وَ أَيْنَ وُجِدُوا، فِي بَرٍّ أَوْ بَحْرٍ، فِي شَرْقٍ اَوْ غَرْبٍ، بِمَا أَحُوطُ بِهِ نَفْسِي وَ خَلَّتِي وَ أَهْلَ مِلَّتِي مِنَ الْمُؤْمِنِينَ وَ الْمُسْلِمِينَ، وَ أَنْ أُدْخِلَهُمْ فِي أَمَانِي مِنْ كُلِّ أَذًى وَ مَكْرُوهٍ وَ سَوْءَةٍ وَ تَبِعَةٍ، وَ أَنْ أكونَ مِنْ وَرَائِهِمْ دَارِئاً عَنْهُمْ كُلَّ عَدُوٍّ يُرِيدُنِي وَ إِيَّاهُمْ بِنَفْسِي وَ أَتْبَاعِي وَ أَعْوَانِي وَ أَهْلِ مِلَّتِي، وَ أَنَا ذُو سُلْطَةٍ عَلَيْهِمْ، وَ بِذَلِكَ يُوجِبُ عَلَيَّ رَعْيَهُم وَ حِفْظَهُمْ مِنْ كُلِّ مَكْرُوهٍ، وَ أَنْ لاَ يَصِلَ إِلَيْهِمْ حَتَّى يَصِلَ إِلَيَّ و أَصْحَابِي الذّابّينَ عَنْ نصيبة الْأَمْرِ، وَ أَنْ أَعْزِلَ عَنْهُمْ الْأَذَى فِي الْمَوَادِّ الَّتِي تَحْمِلُ أَهْلَ الْعَهْدِ مِنْ الْعَارِيَّةِ وَ الْخَراجِ، إِلَّا مَا طَابَتْ بِهِ أَنْفُسُهُمْ، وَ لَا يَكُونُ عَلَيْهِمْ جَبْرٌ وَ لاَ إِكْرَاهٌ فِي ذَلِكَ، وَ لاَ يُنْفَى أُسْقُفٌ عَنْ اسقفيّتِهِ، وَ لَا نَصْرَانِيٌّ عَنْ نَصْرَانِيَّتِهِ، وَ لاَ رَاهِبٌ عَنْ رُهْبَانِيَّتِهِ، وَ لاَ سَائِحٌ عَنْ سِيَاحَتِهِ، وَ لاَ رَاهِبٌ عَنْ صَوْمَعَتِهِ، وَ لَا يُهْدَمُ بَيْتٌ مِنْ بُيُوتِ كَنَائِسِهِمْ، وَ لاَ يَدْخُلُ شَيْئٌ فِي بِنَاءِ الْمَسَاجِدِ وَ لاَ فِي مَنَازِلِ الْمُسْلِمِينَ، فَمَنْ فَعَلَ ذَلِكَ فَقَدْ نَكَثَ وَعَدَ اللَّهِ، وَ خَالَفَ رَسُولَ اللَّهِ، وَ خَانَ ذِمَّةَ اللَّهِ، وَ أَنْ لاَ يُحَمَّلُ الرُّهْبَانُ وَ لاَ الْأَسَاقِفَةُ وَ لاَ جَمِيعُ مَنْ لَمْ يُلْزَمْ بِثَمَنِهِ، إِلَّا أَنْ تَطِيبَ بِذَلِكَ أَنْفُسُهُمْ، وَ لاَ يُجَاوِزُوا الْجِزْيَةَ عَلَى أَصْحَابِ التِّجَارَاتِ الْعِظَامِ، وَ الْغَوّاصِينَ، وَ الَّذِينَ يُخْرِجُونَ مَعَادِنَ الْجَوْهَرِ وَ الذَّهَبِ وَ الْفِضَّةِ، وَ ذَوِي الْأَمْوَالِ الْجَمَّةِ وَ الْقُوَّةِ، مِمَّنْ انْتَحَلَ النَّصْرَانِيَّةَ أَكْثَرَ مِنْ اثْنَيْ عَشَرَ دِرْهَمًا فِي كُلِّ عَامٍ، إِذَا كَانُوا فِي الْمَوْضِعِ قَاطِنِينَ وَ بِهِ مُقِيمِينَ، وَ أَنَّهُ لَيْسَ لِعَابِرِ سَبِيلٍ وَ لَيْسَ هُوَ مِنْ قاطني الْبَلَدِ مِمَّنْ لَا يُعْرَفُ مَوْضِعُهُ الْخَرَاجَ وَ لاَ الْجِزْيَةَ، إِلَّا أَنْ يَكُونَ فِي يَدِهِ مِيرَاثُ الْأَرْضِ مِمَّنْ يَجِبُ عَلَيْهِ مَالُ السُّلْطَانِ مِنْ حَقٍّ، فَيُؤَدِّي ذَلِكَ عَلَى مَا يُؤَدِّي غَيْرُهُ، وَ لَا يُتَجَاوَزُ عَلَيْهِ وَ لاَ يُحْمَلُ مِنْهُ إِلَّا مِقْدَارُ طَاقَتِهِ وَ قُوَّتِهِ، و عَلَى مَنْ يَجُوزُ مِنَ الْأَرْضِ وَ عِمَارَتِهَا وَ إِقْبَالِ ثَمَرِهَا لاَ يُكَلَّفُ شَطَطاً وَ

لَا يُجَازُ بِهِ عَنْ حَدِّ أَصْحَابِ الْخَرَاجِ مِنْ نُظَرَائِهِ، وَلَا يُكَلَّفُ أَهْلُ ذِمَّةِ الْخُرُوجَ مع الْمَلَإِ مِنَ الْمُسْلِمِينَ إِلَى عَدُوِّهِمْ لِمُلَاقَاةِ الْحَرْبِ وَ مُكَاشَفَةِ الْأَقْرَانِ، لِأَنَّهُ لَيْسَ عَلَى أَهْلِ الذِّمَّةِ مُبَاشَرَةُ الْقِتَالِ، وَإِنَّمَا أُعْطُوْا الذِّمَّةَ عَلَى أَنْ لَا يُكَلَّفُوا، وَ أَنْ يكونَ المسلِمون ذبّابينَ عَنْهُمْ مُحرزِينَ مِنْ دُونِهِمْ، وَ لَا يُكْرَهُونَ عَلَى الْخُرُوجِ مَعَ الْمُسْلِمِينَ لِلْحَرْبِ الَّتِي يلْقونَ فِيهَا عَدُوَّهُمْ، وَ لَا بِقُوَّةٍ مِنْ خَيْلٍ وَ سِلَاحٍ إِلَّا أَنْ يَتَبَرَّعُوا، فَيُحْمَلُ عَلَى ذَلِكَ مِنْ تَبَرَّعَ بِهِ وَ عُرِفَ لَهُ ذَلِكَ وَ كُفِيَ عَلَيْهِ، وَ لَا يُجبَرُ أَحَدٌ مِمَّنْ كَانَ عَلَى مِلَّةِ النَّصْرَانِيَّةِ مِنَ الْإِسْلَامِ كُرْهًا، وَ لَا يُجَادِلُ إِلَّا بِالَّتِي هِيَ أَحْسَنُ، وَ يخفِضُ لَهُمْ جَنَاحَ الرَّحْمَةِ، وَ يَكُفُّ عَنْهُمْ الْأَذَى وَ الْمَكْرُوهَ حَيْثُ كَانُوا وَ أَيْنَ وُجِدُوا، و إِنْ جَرأَ أَحَدٌ مِنْ النَّصَارَى جَرِيرَةً اَوْ جَنَى جِنَايَةً، فَعَلَى الْمُسْلِمِينَ نَصْرُهُ وَ مَنْعُهُ وَ الذَّبُّ عَنْهُ وَ الغَرْمُ عَنْ جَرِيرَتِهُ وَ الدُّخُولُ فِي الصُّلْحِ بَيْنَهُ وَ بَيْنَ مَا أَصَابَ مِنَّا عَلَيْهِ، وَ أَمّا فِدَاءً يُفَادى بِهِ، وَ لاَ يُخْذَلوا وَ لا يُرْفَضُوا، بَلْ أَعْطَيْتُهُمْ عَهْدَ اللهِ عَلَى أَنَّ لَهُمْ مَا لِلْمُسْلِمِينَ، وَ عَلَيْهِمْ مَا عَلَى الْمُسْلِمِينَ، وَ لِلْمُسْلِمِينَ مَا لَهُمْ وَ عَلَى الْمُسْلِمِينَ مَا عَلَيْهِمْ، بِالْعَهْدِ الَّذِي استوْجَبهُ حَقُّ الرِّعَاءِ وَ الذَّبُّ عَنْ الحرمةِ، بِهِ اسْتَوْجَبُوا بِذَبٍّ عَنْهُمْ كُلَّ مَكْرُوهٍ، وَ يَدْخُلُ لَهُمْ فِي كُلِّ مِرْفَقٍ، حَتَّى يكونَ المسلِمونَ شِرْكًا فِيمَا لَهُمْ وَ فِيمَا عَلَيْهِمْ، وَ لَهُمْ أَنْ تَحمِلَ مِنْ أَمْرِ النِّكَاحِ شَطَطاً، وَ لَا يُكْرِهُوا أَهْلَ الْبِنْتِ مِنْهُمْ عَلَى تَزْوِيجِ الْمُسْلِمِينَ، وَ لَا يُضَارُّوا فِي ذَلِكَ إِنْ مَنَعوا خاطِباً وأَبوا تَزْوِيجاً، فإِنَّ ذلكَ لاَ يَكُونُ إِلَّا بِطِيبِ أَنْفُسِهِمْ وَ مُسَامَحَةِ أَهْوَائِهِمْ إِنْ أَحَبُّوهُ وَ رَضَوْهُ، وَ إِذَا صَارَتْ النَّصْرَانِيَّةُ فِي بَيْتِ الْمُسْلِمِ، فَعَلَيْهِ أَنْ يُرْضِيَ هوَاهَا فِي دِينِهَا مِنْ الاقْتِدَاءِ بِرُؤَسَائِهَا وَالْأَخْذِ بِمَعَالِمِ دِينِهَا، وَلَا يَمْنَعُهَا فِي ذَلِكَ وَ لاَ يُكْرِهُهَا عَلَى تَرْكِهَا وَ لَا يُضَارَّهَا فِي تَرْكِ دِينِهَا، فَإِنْ فَعَلَ ذَلِكَ وَ أَكْرَهَهَا عَلَيْهِ، فَقَدْ أَخْلَفَ عَهْدَ اللَّهِ وَ عَصَى مِيثَاقَ رَسُولِ اللَّهِ، وَهُوَ عِنْدَ اللَّهِ مِنَ الْكَاذِبِينَ. ولَهُمْ إِنْ احْتَاجُوا إِلى مَرَمَّةِ

كَنَايِسِهِمْ اَوْ صَوَامِعِهِمْ اَوْ شَيْءٍ مِنْ مَصْلَحَةِ دِينِهِمْ إِلَى مَرْفَدٍ مِنَ الْمُسْلِمِينَ اَوْ مَعُونَةٍ

عَلَى مَرَمَّةٍ، أَنْ يَرْفُدُوا عَلَيْهِ وَ يُعَاوِنُوا وَ لَا يَكُونَ ذَلِكَ دَيْنًا، بَلْ مَعُونَةً لَهُمْ عَلَى

مَصَالِحِ دِينِهِمْ، وَ وَفَائِهِمْ بِعَهْدِ رَسُولِ اللَّهِ هِبَةً مُوْهَبَةً لَهُمْ، ذِمَّةَ اللَّهِ وَ ذِمَّةَ رَسُولِ

اللَّهِ عَلَيْهِمْ وَ لَهُمْ. وَ لَا يَكُونُ أَحَدٌ مِنْهُمْ أَنْ يَكُونَ بَيْنَ الْمُسْلِمِينَ وَ لَهُمْ عَدُوٌّ وَ قَالُوا:

كُنْ رَسُولًا اَوْ دَلِيلًا اَوْ مُسَخَّرًا اَوْ فِي شَيْءٍ مِمَّا يَقُومُ الْحَرْبُ، فَمَنْ فَعَلَ ذَلِكَ بِأَحَدٍ

كَانَ ظَالِماً وَ لِرَسُولِ اللَّهِ عَاصِيًا وَ مِنْ وَصِيَّتِهِ مُخْتَلِفًا.

هَذِهِ الشُّرُوطُ الَّتِي شَرَطَ مُحَمَّدٌ رَسُولُ اللَّهِ لِأَهْلِ الْمِلَّةِ النَّصْرَانِيَّةِ، وَ أَشْرَطَ عَلَيْهِمْ

فِي دِينِهِمْ أُمُورًا فِي ذِمَّتِهِمْ، عَلَيْهِمِ التَّمَسُّكُ بِهَا وَ الْوَفَاءُ بِمَا عَاهَدَ عَلَيْهِمْ، وَ مِنْهَا أَنْ

لَا يَكُونَ أَحَدٌ مِنْهُمْ عَيْنًا لِأَحَدٍ مِنْ أَهْلِ الْحَرْبِ عَلَى أَحَدٍ مِنَ الْمُسْلِمِينَ فِي سِرٍّ وَ لَا

عَلَانِيَةٍ، وَ لَا بِوَفَاءٍ فِي مَنَازِلِهِمْ وَ لَا يَأْوُوا عَدُوًّا لِمُسْلِمٍ، وَ لَا يَنْزِلُ أَوْطَانَهُمْ وَ لَا فِي

مَسَاكِنِ عِبَادَتِهِمْ، وَ لَا يَرْفُدُوا أَحَداً مِنْ أَهْلِ الْحَرْبِ عَلَى الْمُسْلِمِينَ بِقُوَّةٍ مِنْ عَارِيَّةِ

السِّلَاحِ وَ لَا الْخَيْلِ وَ لَا الرِّجَالِ، وَ لَا يَسْتَوْدِعُوا لَهُمْ مَالًا، وَ لَا يُكَاتِبُوهُمْ، وَلَا

يُصَافِحُوهُمْ، إِلَّا أَنْ يَكُونَ فِي دَارٍ يَذِبُّونَ فِيهَا عَنْ أَنْفُسِهِمْ يَدْرَؤُونَ عَنْ دِمَائِهِمْ وَ

رِعَايَةِ دِينِهِمْ، وَ لَا يَمْنَعُونَ أَحَداً مِنَ الْمُسْلِمِينَ قِرَايَةَ ثَلَاثَةِ أَيَّامٍ وَ لَيَالِيهَا لِأَنْفُسِهِمْ وَ

لِدَوَابِّهِمْ حَيْثُ كَانُوا وَأَيْنَ وُجِدُوا، وَ يَبْذِلُونَ لَهُمُ الْقِرَى الَّذِي مِنْهُ يَأْكُلُونَ، وَ لَا يُكَفُّوا

عَلَى ذَلِكَ فَيحْمِلُوا الْأَذِيَّةَ عَنْهُمْ وَ الْمَكْرُوهَ، فَإِنْ احْتِيجَ إِلَى اخْتِفَاءِ أَحَدٍ مِنَ الْمُسْلِمِينَ

فِي مَنَازِلِهِمْ وَ مَوَاطِنَ إِعْمَارِهِمْ، أَنْ يُوَدّوهُمْ وَ يَرْفِدوهُمْ وَ يُوَاسوهُمْ عَمَّا شَقَّ بِهِ مَا

كَانُوا مُخْتَفِينَ، إِذَا كَتَمُوا عَنْهُمْ وَلَمْ يُظْهِروا الْعَدوَّ عَلى عَوْرَتِهِمْ وَلَمْ يُخْلُوا مِنَ

الْوَاجِبِ عَلَيْهِمْ فِي ذَلِكَ، فَمَنْ نَكَثَ مِنْهُمْ شَيْئاً مِنْ هَذِهِ الشُّرُوطِ وَ تَعَدَّاهَا إِلَى غَيْرِهِ،

فَبَرِئَ مِنْ ذِمَّةِ اللَّهِ وَ ذِمَّةِ رَسُولِ اللَّهِ، عَلَيْهِمْ بِذَلِكَ الْعُهُودَ وَ الْمَوَاثِيقَ الَّتِي أُخِذَتْ

عَنِ الْأَحْبَارِ وَ الرُّهْبَانِ وَ النَّصَارَى مِنْ أَهْلِ الْكِتَابِ، وَ أَشَدُّ مَا أَخَذَ اللَّهُ وَ النَّبِيُّ

عَلَى أُمَّتِهِ مِنْ الْأَيْمَانِ، وَ الْوَفَاءِ بِمَا جَعَلَ لَهُمْ عَلَى نَفْسِهِ وَ عَلَى الْمُسْلِمِينَ، رِعَايَةُ ذَلِكَ لَهُمْ وَ وعِزَّتُهُم بِهِ وَ الِانْتِهَاءُ إِلَيْهِ أَبَداً حَتَّى تَقُومَ السَّاعَةُ وَ تَنْقَضِيَ الدُّنْيَا، وَاشْهَدُوا عَلَى هَذَا الْكِتَابِ الَّذِي كَتَبَهُ مُحَمَّدٌ رَسُولُ اللَّهِ بَيْنَ النَّصَارَى الَّذِي أَشْرَطَ عَلَيْهِمْ وَ كَتَبَ لَهُمْ هَذَا الْعَهْدَ.

أَبُو بَكْرٍ الصِّدِّيقُ   عُمَرُ بْنُ الْخَطَّابِ   عُثْمَانُ بْنُ عَفَّانَ   عَلِيُّ بْنُ أَبِي طَالِبٍ   مُعَاوِيَةُ بْنُ أَبِي سُفْيَانَ   أَبُو الدَّرْدَاءِ   أَبُو ذَرٍّ   أَبُو هُرَيْرَةَ   عَبْدُ اللَّهِ بْنُ مَسْعُودٍ   عَبْدُ اللَّهِ بْنُ عَبَّاسٍ   حَمْزَةُ بْنُ عَبْدِ الْمُطَّلِبِ   فُضَيْلٌ   زَيْدُ بْنُ ثَابِتٍ   عَبْدُ اللَّهِ ابْنُ زَيْدٍ   حرفوس بْنُ زَيْدٍ   الزُّبَيْرُ بْنُ الْعَوَّامِ   سَعْدُ بْنُ مُعَاذٍ   ثَابِتُ بْنُ قَيْسٍ   أُسَامَةُ بْنُ زَيْدٍ   عُثْمَانُ بْنُ مَظْعُونٍ   عَبْدُ اللَّهِ بْنُ عَمْرِو بْنِ الْعَاصِ   ابْنُ رَبِيعَةَ   حَسَّانُ بْنُ ثَابِتٍ   جَعْفَرُ بْنُ أَبِي طَالِبٍ   ابْنُ الْعَبَّاسِ   طَلْحَةُ بْنُ عُبَيْدِ اللَّهِ   سَعْدُ بْنُ عُبَادَةَ   زَيْدُ بْنُ أَرْقَمَ   سَهْلُ بْنُ بَيْضَا   داود بْنُ جُبَيْرٍ   أَبُو الْعَالِيَةِ   أَبُو حُذَيْفَةَ بْنُ عَسِير هَاشِمُ بْنُ عسيه   عَمَّارُ بْنُ يَاسِرٍ   كَعْبُ بْنُ مَالِكٍ   كَعْبُ بْنُ كَعْبٍ رِضْوَانُ اللَّهِ عَلَيْهِمْ أَجْمَعِينَ.

وَ كَتَبَهُ مُعَاوِيَةُ بْنُ أَبِي سُفْيَانَ مِنْ إِمْلَاءِ رَسُولِ اللَّهِ يَوْمَ الِاثْنَيْنِ تَمَامَ أَرْبَعَةِ أَشْهُرٍ مِنْ السَّنَةِ الرَّابِعَةِ مِنْ الْهِجْرَةِ بِالْمَدِينَةِ وكَفَى بِاللَّهِ شَهِيداً عَلَى مَا فِي هَذَا الْكِتَابِ وَالْحَمْدُ لِلَّهِ رَبِّ الْعَالَمِينَ.

Text of the *Covenant of the Prophet Muhammad with the Christians of the World*

(Corrected Arabic Original from 1538 CE)

بِاسْمِ اللهِ الْخَالِقِ الْحَيِّ النَّاطِقِ الْبَاقِي بَعْدَ فَنَاءِ الْخَلاَئِقِ

هذا نسهة الْعَهْدِ الَّذِي كَتَبَهُ مُحَمَّدٌ ابْنُ عَبْدِ اللهِ ابْنُ عَبْدِ الْمُطَّلِبِ لِكَافَّةِ النَّصَارَى

نُسْخَةُ كِتَابِ الْعَهْدِ

هَذَا عَهْدُ اللهِ أَمَرَ بِكِتَابَتِهِ مُحَمَّدٌ ابْنُ عَبْدِ اللهِ ابْنُ عَبْدِ الْمُطَّلِبِ رَسُولُ اللهِ صَلَّى اللهُ عَلَيْهِ وَعَلَى آلِهِ لِكَافَّةِ النَّصَارَى وَسَائِرِ الرُّهْبَانِ حِفْظًا مِنْهُ لَهُمْ وَرِعَايَةً، لِأَنَّهُمْ وَدِيعَةُ اللهِ فِي خَلْقِهِ لِيَكُونَ الْحُجَّةَ عَلَيْهِمْ وَلاَ يَكُونُ لِلنَّاسِ عَلَى اللهِ حُجَّةٌ بَعْدَ الرَّسُولِ. وَجَعَلَ ذَلِكَ ذِمَّةً مِنْهُ وَحِفْظًا لَهُمْ بِأَمْرِ اللهِ وَكَانَ اللهُ عَزِيزًا حَكِيمًا كَتَبَهُ الْأَسَدُ وَأَهْلُ مِلَّتِهِ لِكُلِّ مَنْ يَنْتَحِلُ دَعْوَةَ النَّصْرَانِيَّةِ مِنْ مَشْرِقِ الْأَرْضِ وَمَغْرِبِهَا، وَقَرِيبِهَا وَبَعِيدِهَا، عَرَبِيِّهَا وَعَجَمِيِّهَا، مَعْرُوفًا وَمَجْهُولاً، عَهْدًا مِنْهُ وَعَدْلاً لَهُمْ سُنَّةً مِنْهُ تُحْفَظُ. مَنْ رَعَاهَا كَانَ بِالإِسْلاَمِ مُتَمَسِّكًا، وَلِدِينِهِ مُسْتَأْهِلاً. وَمَنْ نَكَثَهَا وَضَيَّعَ الْعَهْدَ الَّذِي أَمَرَ بِهِ رَسُولُ اللهِ وَغَيَّرَهُ وَتَعَدَّى فِيهِ مَا أَمَرَ بِهِ، كَانَ لِعَهْدِ اللهِ نَاكِثًا وَلِمِيثَاقِهِ نَاقِضًا وَبِدِينِهِ مُسْتَهِينًا وَلِلَعْنِهِ مُسْتَوْجِبًا، سُلْطَانًا كَانَ أَوْ غَيْرِهِ مِنَ الْمُؤْمِنِينَ وَالْمُسْلِمِينَ.

فَبَدَأْتُ فِيهِ بِإِعْطَاءِ الْعَهْدِ عَلَى نَفْسِي وَالْمَوَاثِيقَ الَّتِي سَأَلُوا عَنِّي وَعَنْ جَمِيعِ مِلَّتِي مِنَ الْمُسْلِمِينَ بِأَنْ أُعْطِيهِمْ [عَهْدَ] اللهِ وَمِيثَاقِهِ وَذِمَّةَ أَنْبِيَائِهِ وَأَصْفِيَائِهِ وَأَوْلِيَائِهِ مِنَ الْمُؤْمِنِينَ وَالْمُسْلِمِينَ فِي الْأَوَّلِينَ وَالْآخِرِينَ وَذِمَّتِي وَمِيثَاقِي وَأَشَدَّ مَا أَخَذَهُ اللهُ تَعَالَى عَلَى نَبِيٍّ مُرْسَلٍ مِنْ حَقِّ الطَّاعَةِ وَإِتْيَانِ الْفَرِيضَةِ وَالْوَفَاءِ بِالْعَهْدِ.

عَهْدُ اللهِ أَنْ أَحْفَظَ أَرْضَهُمْ وَأَدْيَانَهُمْ بِقُدْرَتِي وَخَيْلِي وَرِجَالِي وَسِلَاحِي وَقُوَّتِي وَأَتْبَاعِي مِنَ الْمُسْلِمِينَ فِي كُلِّ نَاحِيَةٍ مِنْ نَوَاحِي الْقَرِيبِ وَالْبَعِيدِ، وَأَنْ أَحْمِيَ بِيَعَهُمْ وَأَذِبَّ عَنْهُمْ وَعَنْ كَنَائِسِهِمْ وَبِيَعِهِمْ وَبُيُوتِ صَلَوَاتِهِمْ مَوَاضِعَ لِلرُّهْبَانِ مِنْهُمْ وَمَوَاضِعَ لِلسُّوَّاحِ حَيْثُ كَانُوا مِنْ جَبَلٍ أَوْ وَادٍ أَوْ مَغَارَةٍ أَوْ عُمْرَانٍ أَوْ سَهْلٍ أَوْ رَمْلٍ، وَأَنْ أَحْفَظَ ذِمَّتَهُمْ وَمِلَّتَهُمْ وَدِينَهُمْ أَيْنَ كَانُوا شَرْقِيًا أَوْ غَرْبِيًّا أَوْ بَحْرِيًا أَوْ قِبْلِيًّا بِمَا أَحْفَظُ بِهِ نَفْسِي وَخَاصَّتِي وَأَهْلِ مِلَّتِي مِنَ الْمُسْلِمِينَ.

وَأَنْ أُدْخِلَهُمْ فِي ذِمَّتِي وَمِيثَاقِي وَأَمَانِي فِي كُلِّ حِينٍ وَمَوَدَّةٍ وَأَصُدَّ عَنْهُمْ كُلَّ أَذاً أَوْ مَكْرُوهٍ أَوْ تَبِعَةٍ، وَأَنْ أَكُونَ مِنْ قُوَّاتِهِمْ ذَابًّا عَنْهُمْ كُلَّ عَدُوٍّ أَوْ مُؤْذِي وَأَفْدِيهِمْ بِنَفْسِي وَأَعْوَانِي وَأَتْبَاعِي وَأَهْلِ مِلَّتِي لِأَنَّهُمْ رَعِيَّتِي وَأَهْلُ ذِمَّتِي [وأبيد؟] السُّلْطَةَ عَنْهُمْ وَكَذَلِكَ عَلَيَّ رِعَايَتُهُمْ وَحِفْظُهُمْ مِنْ كُلِّ مَكْرُوهٍ، وَلَا يَصِلُ ذَلِكَ إِلَيْهِمْ وَلَا يَصِلُ شَيْءٌ مِنْ ذَلِكَ إِلَيْهِمْ حَيْثُ يَصِلُ إِلَى أَصْحَابِي الذَّابِّينَ عَنْهُمْ وَعَنْ نُصْرَةِ الْإِسْلَامِ.

وَأَنْ أَعْزِلَ عَنْهُمُ الْأَذَى فِي الْمُؤَنِ الَّتِي تُحَمَّلُ لِأَهْلِ الْعَهْدِ مِنَ الْعَارِيَةِ بِالْخَرَاجِ إِلَّا مَا طَابَتْ بِهِ نُفُوسُهُمْ وَلَيْسَ عَلَيْهِمْ جُورٌ وَلَا إِكْرَاهٌ عَلَى شَيْءٍ مِنْ ذَلِكَ.

وَلَا تَغْيِيرُ أُسْقُفٍ عَنْ أُسْقُفِيَّتِهِ وَلَا رَاهِبٍ مِنْ رَهْبَانِيَتِهِ وَلَا نَصْرَانِيٍّ مِنْ نَصْرَانِيَّتِهِ وَلَا زَاهِدٍ مِنْ صَوْمَعَتِهِ وَلَا سَائِحٍ مِنْ سِيَاحَتِهِ، وَلَا يُهْدَمُ بَيْتٌ مِنْ بُيُوتِ كَنَائِسِهِمْ وَبِيَعِهِمْ، وَلَا يَدْخُلُ شَيْءٌ مِنْ مَنْزِلِهِمْ فِي شَيْءٍ مِنَ الْمَسَاجِدِ وَلَا مَنَازِلِ الْمُؤْمِنِينَ الْمُسْلِمِينَ، فَمَنْ فَعَلَ ذَلِكَ فَقَدْ نَكَثَ عَهْدَ اللهِ وَخَالَفَ رَسُولَهُ وَحَادَ عَنْ ذِمَّتِهِ.

وَلَا تُحَمَّلُ الرُّهْبَانَ وَلَا الْأَسَاقِفَةَ وَلَا مَنْ تَعَبَّدَ مِنْهُمْ وَكَافَّةَ لَابِسِي الصُّوفِ أَوْ يُوجَدُ فِي الْجِبَالِ وَالْمَوَاضِعِ الْمُعْتَزِلَةِ عَنِ الْأَبْصَارِ شَيْءٌ مِنَ الْجِزْيَةِ وَالْخَرَاجِ.

وَأَنْ يَقْتَصِرَ بِغَيْرِهِمْ مِنَ النَّصَارَى مِمَّنْ لَا يَتَعَبَّدُ وَلَا رَاهِبٍ وَلَا سَائِحٍ مِنَ الْجِزْيَةِ عَلَى أَرْبَعَةِ دَرَاهِمَ فِي كُلِّ عَامٍ أَوْ ثَوْبٍ لَطِيفِ الثَّمَنِ، وَمَنْ عَدِمَ الثَّمَنَ وَالْقُوتَ

أَعَانوهُ الْمُسْلِمُونَ مِنْ قُوتِ بَيْتِ المَالِ، فَإِنْ لَمْ يُسَهَّلْ عَلَيْهِمُ القُوتُ حُمِلَ عَنْهُمْ وَلاَ يَقُومُ ذَلِكَ عَلَيْهِمْ إِلاَّ بِمَا طَابَتْ بِهِ أَنفُسُهُمْ.

وَلاَ يُتَجَاوَزُ بِجِزْيَةِ الْخَرَاجِ مِنَ الْعِمَارَاتِ وَالتِّجَارَاتِ الْعِظَامِ فِي الْبَحْرِ وَالْغَوْصِ وَفِي اسْتِخْرَاجِ الْمَعَادِنِ مِنَ الْجَوَاهِرِ وَالذَّهَبِ وَالْفِضَّةِ وَذَوِي الْأَمْوَالِ وَغَيْرِهِمْ مِنْ مُنْتَحِلِي النَّصْرَانِيَّةِ اثْنَا عَشَرَ فِضَّةً جِزْيَةٌ فِي كُلِّ عَامٍ إِذَا كَانُوا بِالْمَوَاضِعِ قَاطِنِينَ مُقِيمِينَ.

وَلاَ يُعْتَرَضُ عَابِرُ طَرِيقٍ وَلَيْسَ مِنْ أَقْطَارِ الْبِلاَدِ وَلاَ مِنْ أَهْلِ الاِخْتِيَارِ مِمَّنْ لاَ يُعْرَفُ مَوْضِعُهُ بِخَرَاجٍ وَلاَ جِزْيَةٍ إِلاَّ أَنْ يَكُونَ فِي يَدِهِ مِيزَانٌ مِنْ مَوَازِينِ الْأَرْضِ يَجِبُ عَلَيْهِ فِيهِ مَالُ السُّلْطَانِ مِنْ حَقٍّ فَيُؤَدِّي ذَلِكَ مَا يُؤَدِّي مِثْلَهُ، وَلاَ يُجَارُ عَلَيْهِ وَلاَ يَحْمِلُ فِيهِ إِلاَّ عَلَى قَدْرِ طَاقَتِهِ وَقُوَّتِهِ عَلَى تَحْوِيطِ الْأَرْضِ وَعِمَارَتِهَا وَأَقْبَلَ ثَمَرَتُهَا. وَلاَ يُكَلَّفُ شَطَطًا وَلاَ يُتَجَاوَزُ حَدُّ أَصْحَابِ الْخَرَاجِ مِنْ نُظَرَائِهِ.

وَلاَ يُكَلَّفُ أَهْلُ الذِّمَّةِ مِنْهُمْ الْخُرُوجَ مَعَ الْمُسْلِمِينَ إِلَى عَدُوِّهِمْ لِمُلاَقَاةِ الْحَرْبِ وَمُكَاشَفَةِ الْأَبْرَارِ لِأَنَّهُ لَيْسَ عَلَى الذِّمَّةِ مُبَاشَرَةُ الْقِتَالِ، وَأُعْطُوا الدِّيَةَ عَلَى أَنْ لاَ يُكَلَّفُوا ذَلِكَ. وَأَنْ تَكُونَ لِلْمُسْلِمِينَ دَفْعًا عَنْهُمْ وَجَزَرًا مِنْ دُونِهِمْ وَلاَ يُكْرَهُوا عَلَى تَجْهِيزِ أَحَدٍ مِنَ الْمُسْلِمِينَ إِلَى الْحَرْبِ الَّذِي يَكُونُ فِيهِ عَدُوُّهُمْ بِقُوَّةٍ مِنَ السِّلاَحِ وَلاَ خَيْلٍ إِلاَّ أَنْ يَكُونَ يَسْتَبْرِعُ مُتَبَرِّعٌ مِنْ تِلْقَاءِ نَفْسِهِ فَيَكُونُ مَا تَقَوَّى الْمُسْلِمُونَ مِنْ ذَلِكَ عَارِيَةٌ مَضْمُونَةٌ يَضْمَنُهُ بَيْتُ الْمَالِ إِلَى أَنْ تُرَدَّ إِلَيْهِمْ، فَإِنْ تُوُفِّيَ أَوْ غِيرَ عَلَيْهِ غُرِمَ لَهُ قِيمَةُ ذَلِكَ مِنْ صُلْبِ بَيْتِ مَالِ الْمُسْلِمِينَ وَأُدِّيَ إِلَيْهِ وَحُمِلَ إِلَى مَنْ يَتَبَرَّعُ وَغُرِمَ لَهُ وَأُوفِيَ عَلَيْهِ.

وَلاَ يُجْبَرُ عَلَى مَنْ كَانَ فِي مِلَّةِ النَّصرَانِيَةِ كُرْهًا عَلَى الإِسْلاَمِ وَلاَ يُجَادَلُوا إِلاَّ بِالَّتِي هِيَ أَحْسَنُ وَيُحْفَظُ لَهُمْ جَنَاحُ الرَّحْمَةِ وَيُكَفُّ عَنْهُمُ الْأَذَى وَالْمَكْرُوهُ حَيْثُ مَا كَانُوا وَأَيْنَ مَا حَلُّوا.

وَإِنْ أَجْرَمَ أَحَدٌ مِنَ النَّصَارَى أَوْ جَنَا جِنَايَةً فَعَلَى الْمُسْلِمِينَ نُصْرَتُهُ وَمَعُونَتُهُ وَمُسَاعَدَتُهُ وَالذَّبُّ عَنْهُ وَالْمَغْرَمَةُ عَنْهُ وَعَنْ جَزِيرَتِهِ وَالدُّخُولُ فِي الصُّلْحِ بَيْنَهُ وَبَيْنَ مَنْ جَنَا عَلَيْهِ أَوْ بِمُسَاعَدَتِهِ أَوْ بِإِنْقَاذِهِ.

وَلاَ يُجَادَلُوا وَلاَ يُرْفَضُوا وَلاَ يُتْرَكُوا هَمَلاً لِأَنِّي أَعْطَيْتُهُمْ عَهْدَ اللهِ، عَلَى الْمُسْلِمِينَ بِمَا عَلَيْهِمْ بِالْعَهْدِ الَّذِي اسْتَوْجَبُوا حَقَّ الذِّمَامِ وَالذَّبِّ عَنِ الْجِزْيَةِ. وَاسْتَوْجَبُوا أَنْ يُذَبَّ عَنْهُمْ كُلُّ مَكْرُوهٍ وَيُدْخَلَ بِهِمْ تَحْتَ كُلِّ تَرَفُّقٍ وَيَكُونُوا لِلْمُسْلِمِينَ شُرَكَاءَ بِمَا عَلَيْهِمْ وَلَهُمْ.

وَلاَ يُحَمَّلُوا مِنَ النِّكَاحِ شَطَطًا إِلاَّ مَا يُرِيدُوهُ، وَلاَ تُكْرَهُ الْبَنَاتُ مِنْهُمْ عَلَى تَزْوِيجِ الْمُسْلِمِينَ، وَلاَ يُضَادُّوا بِذَلِكَ أَنْ مَنَعُوا خَاطِبًا أَوْ بِزِيجَةٍ تَزْوِيجًا لِأَنَّ ذَلِكَ لاَ يَكُونُ إِلاَّ بِطِيبَةِ أَنْفُسِهِمْ وَأَهْوَائِهِمْ إِنْ أَحَبُّوهُ وَرَضُوا بِهِ.

وَإِنْ صَارَتِ النَّصرَانِيَةُ عِنْدَ الْمُسْلِمِ فَعَلَيْهِ أَنْ يَرْضَى بِنَصْرَانِيتِهَا وَيُعِينُهَا عَلَى هَوَاهَا مِنَ الاقْتِدَاءِ بِرُؤَسَائِهَا وَالْأَخْذِ بِمَعَالِمِ دِينِهَا، فَمَنْ أَكْرَهَهَا عَلَى شَيْءٍ مِنْ أَمْرِ دِينِهَا فَقَدْ خَالَفَ عَهْدَ اللهِ وَعَصَى مِيثَاقَ رَسُولِهِ وَهُوَ عِنْدَنَا مِنَ الْكَاذِبِينَ.

وَلَهُمْ إِنْ اِحْتَاجُوا إِلَى مَرَمَّةِ بِيَعِهِمْ وَمَوَاضِعِ صَلَوَاتِهِمْ أَوْ شَيْءٍ مِنْ مَصْلَحَةِ دِينِهِمْ إِلَى تَعَهُّدِ الْمُسْلِمِينَ بِتَقْوِيَةِ مَوَاضِعِهِمْ لَهُمْ عَلَى مَرَمَّتِهَا، أَنْ يَزِيدُوا عَلَى مَرَمَّتِهَا وَيُعَاوِنُوا وَلاَ يَكُونُ الآنَ عَلَيْهِمْ دَيْنًا بَلْ تَقْوِيَةً لَهُمْ عَلَى دِينِهِمْ وَذِمَّتِهِمْ وَفَاءً لَهُمْ بِالْعَهْدِ عَهْدِ رَسُولِ اللهِ وَهِبَةً لَهُمْ مِنْهُمْ لِلَّهِ وَلِرَسُولِهِ.

وَلاَ يُكْرَهُ أَحَدٌ مِنْهُمْ عَلَى أَنْ يَكُونَ فِي الْحَرْبِ عَنِ الْمُسْلِمِينَ لِعَدُوِّهِمْ رَسُولاً وَلاَ عَوْنًا وَلاَ مُتَجَبِّرًا وَلاَ فِي شَيْءٍ مِمَّا يَلِيقُ بِالْحَرْبِ، فَمَنْ فَعَلَ ذَلِكَ بِأَحَدٍ مِنْهُمْ كَانَ لِلَّهِ ظَالِمًا وَلِرَسُولِهِ عَاصِيًا وَمِنْ دِينِهِ مُنْخَلِعًا إِلاَّ تَمَامَ الْوَفَاءِ بِهَذِهِ الشُّرُوطِ الَّتِي أَشْرَطَهَا مُحَمَّدٌ ابْنُ عَبْدِ اللهِ ابْنُ عَبْدِ الْمُطَّلِبِ رَسُولُ اللهِ صَلَّى اللهُ عَلَيْهِ لِأَهْلِ مِلَّةِ النَّصْرَانِيَةِ.

وَأَشْتَرِطُ عَلَيْهِمْ أُمُورًا فِي دِينِهِمْ وَذِمَّتِهِمْ عَلَيْهِمْ التَّمَسُّكُ بِهَا وَالْوَفَاءُ بِمَا عَاهَدَهُمْ عَلَيْهِ، مِنْهَا أَنْ لاَ يَكُونَ أَحَدٌ مِنْهُمْ عَيْنًا لِأَحَدٍ مِنْ أَهْلِ الْحَرْبِ عَلَى أَحَدٍ مِنَ الْمُسْلِمِينَ فِي سِرٍّ وَلاَ فِي عَلاَنِيَّةٍ، وَلاَ يَأْوُوا فِي مَنَازِلِهِمْ عَدُوَّ الْمُسْلِمِينَ يَرُدُّ، وَأَوْفَى بِهَذِهِ الْوَصِيَّةِ، وَلاَ بَيْتِهِ وَلاَ أَوْطَانِهِمْ وَلاَ أَضْيَاعِهِمْ وَلاَ شَيْءَ مِنْ مَسَاكِنِ عِبَادَتِهِمْ وَلاَ غَيْرِهِمْ مِنْ أَهْلِ الْمِلَّةِ، وَلاَ يَزِيدُوا أَحَدًا مِنْ أَهْلِ الْحَرْبِ عَلَى الْمُسْلِمِينَ لَهُمْ بِسِلاَحٍ وَلاَ خَيْلٍ وَلاَ رِجَالٍ، وَلاَ يَسْتَدْعُوا مَا لاَ بِهِ حَاجَةٌ وَلاَ غَيْرُ ذَلِكَ، وَلاَ يُضَايِقُوهُمْ وَلْيُكَرِّمُوا فِي الْأَرْضِ بَقِيَّةَ مَا يَدُومُونَ فِيهَا عَلَى نُفُوسِهِمْ وَيَدُومُونَ عَلَى أَدْيَانِهِمْ بِرِعَايَةِ ذِمَّتِهِمْ، وَأَنْ يُقِرُّوا مَنْ يَنْزِلُ عَلَيْهِمْ مِنَ الْمُسْلِمِينَ ثَلاَثَةَ أَيَّامٍ بِلَيَالِيهَا فِي أَنْفُسِهِمْ وَدِيَانَتِهِمْ حَيْثُ مَا كَانُوا وَأَيْنَ مَا حَلُّوا، وَأَنْ يَبْذُلُوا لَهُمْ الْقِرَى الَّذِي مِنْهُ يَأْكُلُونَ وَلاَ يَفْعَلُونَ شَيْئًا سِوَى ذَلِكَ وَيَحْمِلُونَ الْأَذَى عَنْهُمْ وَالْمَكْرُوهَ.

وَإِنْ اِخْتَفَى أَحَدٌ مِنَ الْمُسْلِمِينَ عِنْدَهُمْ فِي مَنَازِلِهِمْ وَمَوَاطِنِ رَهْبَانِيَتِهِمْ فَعَلَيْهِمْ أَنْ يَأْوُوهُمْ وَيُوَاسُوهُمْ حَيْثُ مَا كَانُوا مَخْفِيِينَ إِذَا كَتَمُوا عَنْهُمْ وَعِنْدَهُمْ، وَلاَ يُظْهِرُوا الْعَدُوَّ عَلَى أَحَدِهِمْ وَلاَ يَحْمِلُوا شَيْئًا مِنَ الْوَاجِبِ عَلَيْهِمْ فِي ذَلِكَ.

فَمَنْ نَكَثَ شَيْئًا مِنْ هَذِهِ الشُّرُوطِ وَتَعَدَّى إِلَى غَيْرِهَا فَقَدْ نَقَضَ عَهْدَ اللهِ وَرَسُولِهِ.

وَعَلَيْهِمْ بِذَلِكَ الْعَهْدِ وَالْمِيثَاقِ الَّتِي أَخَذْتُ عَلَى الرُّهْبَانِ وَالْإِيمَانِ مِنِّي عَلَى نَفْسِي لَهُمْ أَيْنَ مَا كَانُوا وَحَلُّوا.

وَعَلَى رَسُولِ اللهِ صَلَّى اللهُ عَلَيْهِ وَسَلَّمَ الْوَفَاءُ بِمَا جَعَلَ لَهُمْ عَلَى نَفْسِهِ وَعَلَى جَمِيعِ الْمُسْلِمِينَ مِنْ رِعَايَةِ ذَلِكَ لَهُمْ وَالرَّأْفَةِ بِهِمْ إِلَى الانْتِهَاءِ حَتَّى تَقُومَ السَّاعَةُ وَتَنْقَضِي الدُّنْيَا.

وَمَنْ ظَلَمَ بَعْدَ ذَلِكَ ذِمِّيًا وَنَقَضَ الْعَهْدَ وَرَفَضَهُ كُنْتُ خَصْمَهُ يَوْمَ الْقِيَامَةِ مِنْ جَمِيعِ الْمُسْلِمِينَ كَافَّةً.

وَشَهِدَ فِي هَذَا الْكِتَابِ الَّذِي كَتَبَهُ مُحَمَّدٌ ابْنُ عَبْدِ اللهِ رَسُولُ اللهِ صَلَّى اللهُ عَلَيْهِ لِجَمِيعِ النَّصَارَى الَّذِي اِشْتَرَطَ لَهُمْ عَلَيْهِ، إِذْ كَتَبَ لَهُمْ هَذَا الْعَهْدَ ثَلاثُونَ شَاهِدًا وَهُمْ:

الْعَبَّاسُ ابْنُ عَبْدِ الْمَلِكِ فَضْلُ ابْنُ الْعَبَّاسِ الزَّهْرِي طَلْحَةُ ابْنُ عَبْدِ اللهِ

سَعِيدُ ابْنُ مُعَاذٍ سَعِيدُ ابْنُ عُبَادَةَ ثَابِتُ ابْنُ قَيْسٍ يَزِيدُ ابْنُ تَلِيتٍ

عَبْدُ اللهِ ابْنُ يَزِيدَ فَرْصُوصَ ابْنُ قَسِيمٍ ابْنُ بَدْرٍ ابْنُ إِبْرَاهِيمَ إِمَامُ ابْنُ يَزِيدَ

سَهْلُ ابْنُ تَمِيمٍ عَبْدُ الْعَظِيمِ النَّجَشِي عَبْدُ الْعَظِيمِ ابْنُ حُسَيْنْ عَبْدُ اللهِ ابْنُ عَمْرُ

ابْنُ الْعَاصْ عَمْرُ ابْنُ يَاسِرْ مَعَظَّمُ ابْنُ مُوسِي حَسَّانُ بْنُ ثَابِتْ

أَبُو حَنِيفَةَ عُبَيْدُ ابْنُ مَنْصُورْ هَاشِمُ ابْنُ عَبْدِ اللهِ أَبُو الْعَازَرْ

هِشَامُ ابْنُ عَبْدِ الْمُطَّلِب

وَكَتَبَ عَلِيٌّ ابْنُ أَبِي طَالِبِ رَضِيَ اللهُ عَنْهُ هَذَا الْعَهْدَ، وَالسِّجِلُّ مَكْتُوبٌ فِي جِلْدٍ غَيْرِ صَغِيرٍ وَخُلِّدَ بِتَثْبِيتِ حُكْمِ السُّلْطَانِ وَهُوَ مَخْتُومٌ بِخَاتَمِ النَّبِيِّ صَلَّى اللهُ عَلَيْهِ، وَالْحَمْدُ لِلَّهِ.

كَمُلَ هَذَا الْكِتَابُ الْمُبَارَكُ، وَكَانَ الْفَرَاغُ مِنْهُ فِي يَوْمِ الاثْنَيْنِ الْمُبَارَكِ آخِرَ شَهْرِ بؤُونه الْمُبَارَكِ سَنَةَ سَادَتِنَا الشُّهَدَاءَ الْأَطْهَارِ السُّعَدَاءِ الْأَبْرَارِ رَزَقَنَا اللهُ شَفَاعَتَهُمْ، تَكُونُ مَعَنَا آمِينْ.

الْمُوَافِقِ ذَلِكَ لِلسَّابِعِ وَالْعِشْرِينَ مِنْ شَهْرِ اللهِ الْمُحَرَّمِ الْحَرَامِ سَنَةَ خَمْسَةٍ وَأَرْبَعِينَ وَتِسْعُمِائَةٍ لِلْهِجْرَةِ الْعَرَبِيَّةِ، أَحْسَنَ اللهُ عَاقِبَتَهَا إِلَى خَيْرٍ، آمِينْ.

هَذَا الْكِتَابُ الْمُبَارَكُ مِلْكُ الْمُبَجَّلِ النَّفْسَ الْمَوْلَى الرَّئِيسُ الشَّيْخُ الْعَالِمُ سِمْعَانَ نَجْلُ الْمُعَلِّمِ فضْلُ اللهِ الْمُتَنَيِّحِ نَيَّحَ اللهُ نَفْسَهُ الْمَعْرُوفِ بِالْبَرْلُسِي.

وَنَاقِلُ هَذِهِ الْأَحْرُفِ الْمِسْكِينُ الْمَمْلُوءِ الْخَطَايَا وَالذُّنُوبِ يَسْأَلُ الْإِخْوَةَ الَّذِينَ يَقِفُونَ عَلَى هَذِهِ الْحُرُوفِ أَنْ يَذْكُرُوهُ فِي صَلَوَاتِهِمْ وَالْمَسِيحُ يُعَوِّضُهُمْ عَنْ ذَلِكَ عِوَضَ الْوَاحِدِ ثَلَاثِينَ وَسِتِّينَ وَمِائَةَ.

They do not observe toward a believer any pact of kinship or covenant of protection. And it is they who are the transgressors. (9:10)

Reproduction of Original

al-'Ahd allati kataba Muhammad ibn 'Abd Allah ibn 'Abd al-Muttalib li kafah al-nasraniyya

[The Covenant which Muhammad ibn 'Abd Allah 'Abd al-Muttalib Wrote to all the Christians]

(Ms Arabe 214)

1538

Reproduced from the original held by the Bibliotéque Nationale de France

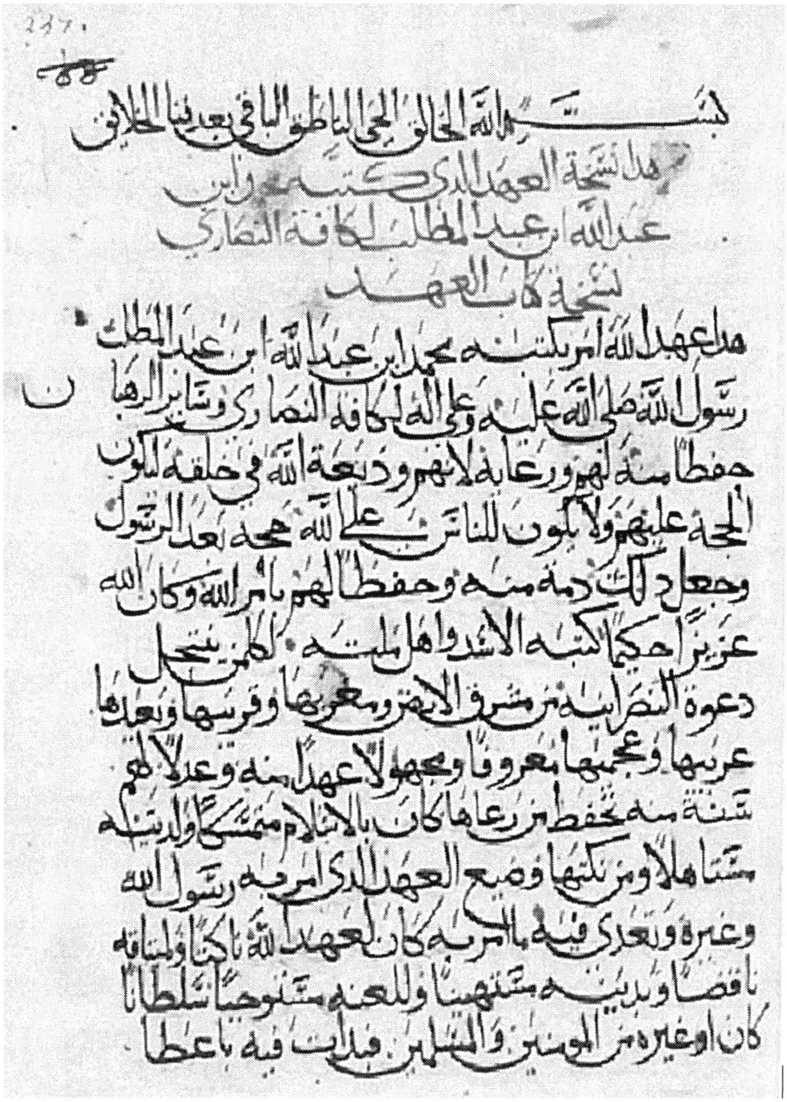

بسم الله الخالق الحي الناطق الباقي بعد فنا الخلايق

هذا نسخة العهد الذي كتبه محمد ابن

عبد الله ابن عبد المطلب لكافة النصارى

نسخة كتاب العهد

هذا عهد الله امر بكتبه محمد ابن عبد الله ابن عبد المطلب

رسول الله صلى الله عليه وعلى آله لكافة النصارى وسائر الرهبان

حفظا منه لهم ورعاية لانهم وديعة الله في خلقه لتكون

الحجة عليهم ولا يكون للناس على الله حجة بعد الرسول

وجعل ذلك ذمة منه وحفظا لهم بامر الله وكان الله

عزيزا حكيما كتبه الاشد واهل ملته لكل من ينتحل

دعوة النصرانية من شرق الارض ومغربها وقريبها وبعيدها

عربها وعجميها معروفها ومجهولها عهدا منه وعدلا لهم

سنة منه تحفظ من رعاها كان بالاسلام متمسكا ولدينه

مستاهلا ومن نكثها وضيع العهد الذي امر به رسول الله

وغيره وتعدى فيه بالتربه كان لعهد الله ناكثا ولميثاقه

ناقضا وبدينه مستهينا وللعنة مستوجبا سلطانا

كان او غيره من المومنين والمسلمين فذلك فيه ناعطا

العهد على نفسي والمواثيق التي سألوا عني وعن جميع ملتي
من المسلمين بأن أعطيهم الله وميثاقه وذمة أنبيائه
وأصفيائه وأوليائه من المؤمنين والمسلمين في الأولين
والآخرين وذمتي وميثاقي وأشد ما أخذ الله تعالى على نبي
مرسل من حق الطاعة وإيثار الفريضة والوفاء بالعهد
عهد الله أن أحفظ أرضهم وأذب عنهم بقدرتي وخيلي ورجالي
وسلاحي وقوتي وأتباعي من المسلمين في كل ناحية من نواحي
القريب والبعيد وأن أحمي بيعهم وأذب عنهم وعن كنائسهم
وبيعهم وبيوت صلواتهم ومواضع الرهبان منهم ومواضع
السواح حيث كانوا من جبل أو واد أو مغارة أو عمران أو سهل
أو رمل وأن أحفظ دينهم وملتهم ودينهم أين كانوا شرقا
أو غربا أو بحرا أو برا مما أحفظ به نفسي وخاصتي وأهل
ملتي من المسلمين وأن أدخلهم في ذمتي وميثاقي وأماني
من كل غبن ومؤونة وأصد عنهم كل أذى ومكروه أو تبعة
وأن أكون من ورائهم ذابا عنهم كل عدو أو مؤذي وأنهم
نفسي وأعواني وأتباعي وأهل ملتي لأنهم رعيتي
وأهل ذمتي وأبعد السلطنة عنهم وكذلك على رعاياتهم

وهو مطهرهم من كل مكروه ولا ينال ذلك الظلم ولا ينال شيئا من
ذلك الظلم حتى يصل الى اصحابى الذابين عنهم وعن
نصرة الاسلام وان اعتزل عنهم الاذى فى المؤن التى تحمل
اهل العهد من القاربة بالخراج الا ما طابت به نفوسهم
وليس عليهم جور ولا اكراه على شئ من ذلك ولا تغيير
اسقف عن اسقفيته ولا راهب من رهبانيته ولا
نصرانى من نصرانيته ولا زاهد من صومعته ولا سائح
من سياحته ولا يهدم بيت من بيوت كنائسهم وبيعهم
ولا يدخل شئ من منازلهم فى شئ من المساجد ولا منازل المسلمين
المسلمين فمن فعل ذلك فقد نكث عهد الله وخالف
رسوله وحاد عن ذمته ولا يحمل الرهبان ولا الاساقفة
ولا من تعبد منهم وكافة لا يلبس الصوف او يوحد فى
الجبال والمواضع المعتزلة عن الامصار شيئا من الجزية
والخراج وان يقتصر بغيرهم من النصارى ممن لا يتعبد ولا
راهب ولا سائح من الجزية على اربعة دراهم فى
كل عام او ثوب لطيف اليمن وعن عدم اليمن والعون
اعانوه المسلمون من قوة بيت المال وان لم يسهل عليهم

العوت حمل عنهم ولا نقوم ذلك عليهم الا بما طابت به انفسهم
ولا يتجاوز بجزيته الخراج من العمارات والتجارات العظام
في البحر والغوص في استخراج المعادن من الجواهر والذهب
والفضة وذوي الاموال وغيرهم من منتحلين النصرانية يكون
اثنى عشر درهما الجزية في كل عام اذا كانوا بالمواضع قاطنين
مقيمين ولا يعترض عابر طريق ولس من اقطار البلاد ولا من
اهل الاخيار من لا يعرف موضعه بخراج ولا جزية الا ان
يكون في يده ميراث من مواريث الارض تجب عليه فيه
مال السلطان من حق فيودي ذلك ما يودي مثله
ولا يجار عليه ولا يحمل فيه الا على قدر طاقته وقوته على
عمل الارض وعمارتها واقبال ثمرتها ولا يكلف شططا
ولا يتجاوز حد اصحاب الخراج من نظرائه ولا يكلف اهل الذمة
منهم الخروج مع المسلمين الى عدوهم لملاقاة الحرب
ومكاشفة الاقران لانه ليس على اهل الذمة مباشرة القتال
واعطوا الذمة على ان لا يكلفوا ذلك وان تكون المسلمين
ذوبعا عنهم وجوارا من دونهم ولا يكرهوا على تجهيز احد
من المسلمين الى الحرب الذي يكون فيه علاوهم بقوة من السلاح

ولا يحل الا ان يكون لشيء شرع شرع من تلقاء نفسه فيكون
ما تقوى المسلمون من ذلك عارية مضمونة يضمنه بيت
المال الى ان ترد اليهم فان توى او عيب عليه غرم له قيمة
ذلك من صلب بيت مال المسلمين واذا اليه وعمل الى من
شرع وغرم له واوفى عليه ولا يجبر على من كان في ملة النصرانية
كرها على الاسلام ولا يجادلوا الا بالتي هي احسن ويخفض
لهم جناح الرحمة ويكف عنهم الاذى او المكروه حيث ما كانوا واين
ما حلوا وان اجرم احد من النصارى او جنى جناية فعلى
المسلمين نصرته ومعونته ومساعدته والذب عنه
والغرية عنه وعن جريرته والدخول في الصلح بينه
وبين من جنى عليه او مساعدته او بانفاده ولا يخذلوا
ولا يرفضوا ولا يتركوا اهملا لاني اعطيتهم عهد الله على المسلمين
بما عليهم بالعهد الذي استوجبوا من الذمام والذب
عن الحرمة واستوجبوا ان يذب عنهم كل المكروه ويصل
بهم بحيث كل مرفق ويكونوا للمسلمين شركا بما عليهم
ولهم ولا يحملوا من النكاح شططا لا يريدوه ولا يكره
البنات منهم على تزويج المسلمين ولا يضادوا ابدا لك ان

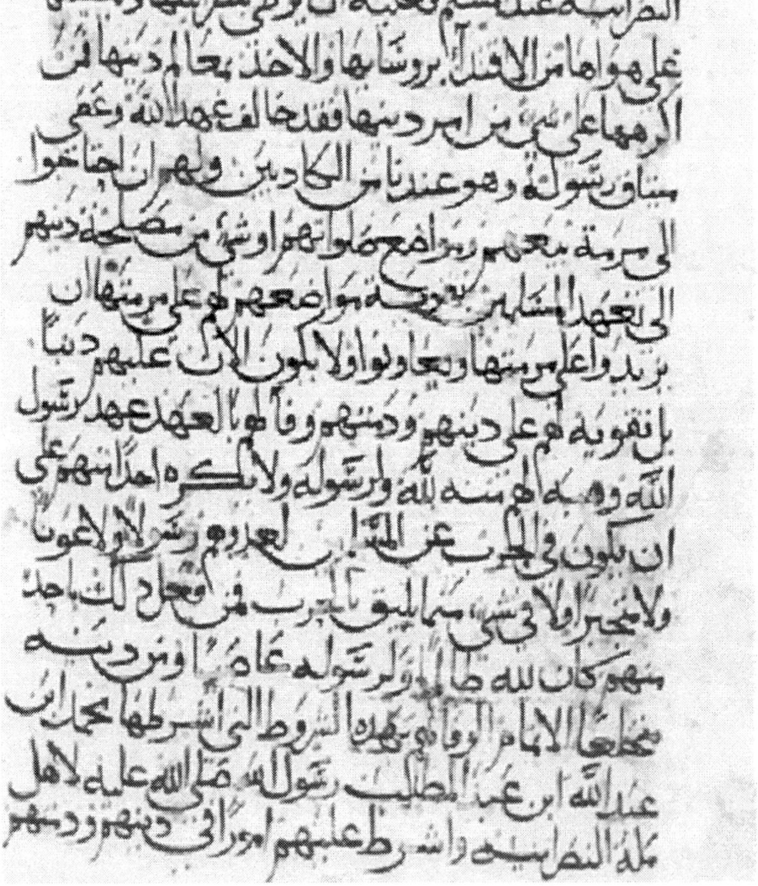
منعوا منها الا [illegible] او برغبة ورضا الا ان ذلك لا يكون الا
بطيبة انفسهم واهوائهم ان احبوه ورضوا به وان صارت
النصرانية عند المسلم فعليه ان يرضى بنصرانيتها ويتبعها
على هواها من الاقتداء برؤسائها والاخذ بمعالم دينها فان
اكرهها على شيء من امر دينها فقد خالف عهد الله وعصى
ميثاق رسوله وهو عند الله من الكاذبين ولهم ان احتاجوا
الى مرمة بيعهم وصوامعهم او شيء من مصلحة دينهم
الى العهد المسلمين [illegible] على مرمتها ان
يرفدوا على مرمتها ويعاونوا ولا يكون ذلك عليهم دينا
بل تقوية لهم على دينهم ووفاء بالعهد عهد رسول
الله وهبة لهم ومنة لله ولرسوله ولا يكره احد منهم على
ان يكون في الحرب عن المسلمين لعدوهم رسولا ولا عونا
ولا مخبرا ولا في شيء مما يليق بالحرب فمن فعل ذلك باحد
منهم كان لله ظالما ولرسوله عاصيا ومن ذمته
متخليا الا بالوفاء بهذه الشروط التي شرطها محمد بن
عبد الله بن عبد المطلب رسول الله صلى الله عليه لاهل
ملة النصرانية واشترط عليهم امورا في دينهم ودينهم

عليهم التمسك بها والوفا بما عاهدهم عليه منها ان لا يكون
لاحد منهم عينا لاحد من اهل الحرب على احد من المسلمين
في سر ولا في علانيه ولا ياووا في منازلهم عدو المسلمين يريد
وا وفا بهذه الوصيه ولا ببينته ولا اوطانهم ولا اضاعفهم
ولا شي من مساكن عبادهم ولا غيرهم من اهل الملة ولا
يريدوا احدا من اهل الحرب على المسلمين لهم بسلاح ولا
خيل ولا رجال ولا يستدعوا اماله به حاجه ولا غير ذلك ولا
يصانعوهم وليكرموا في الارض بقيه ما يدومون فيها على
نفوسهم ويدومون على اديانهم برعايه ديتهم وان
يقروا من نزل عليهم من المسلمين ثلثه ايام بلياليها في انفسهم
ودياتهم حيث ما كانوا وان ما حلوا وان يبذلوا لهم القرا الذي
منه ياكلون ولا يفعلون شيا سوى ذلك ويحملون
الاذا عنهم المروه وان اختفى احد من المسلمين عندهم
في منازلهم ومواطن رهبانيتهم فعليهم ان ياووهم ويومنوهم
حيث ما كانوا مختفين اذا التموا [illegible] وعندهم ولا يظهروا
العدو على احدهم ولا يحملوا اشيا من [illegible] عليهم في
ذلك فمن نكث شيا من هذه الشروط وتعدى الى

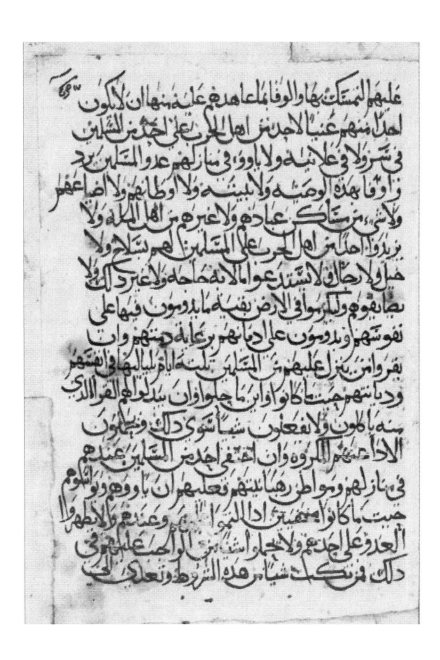

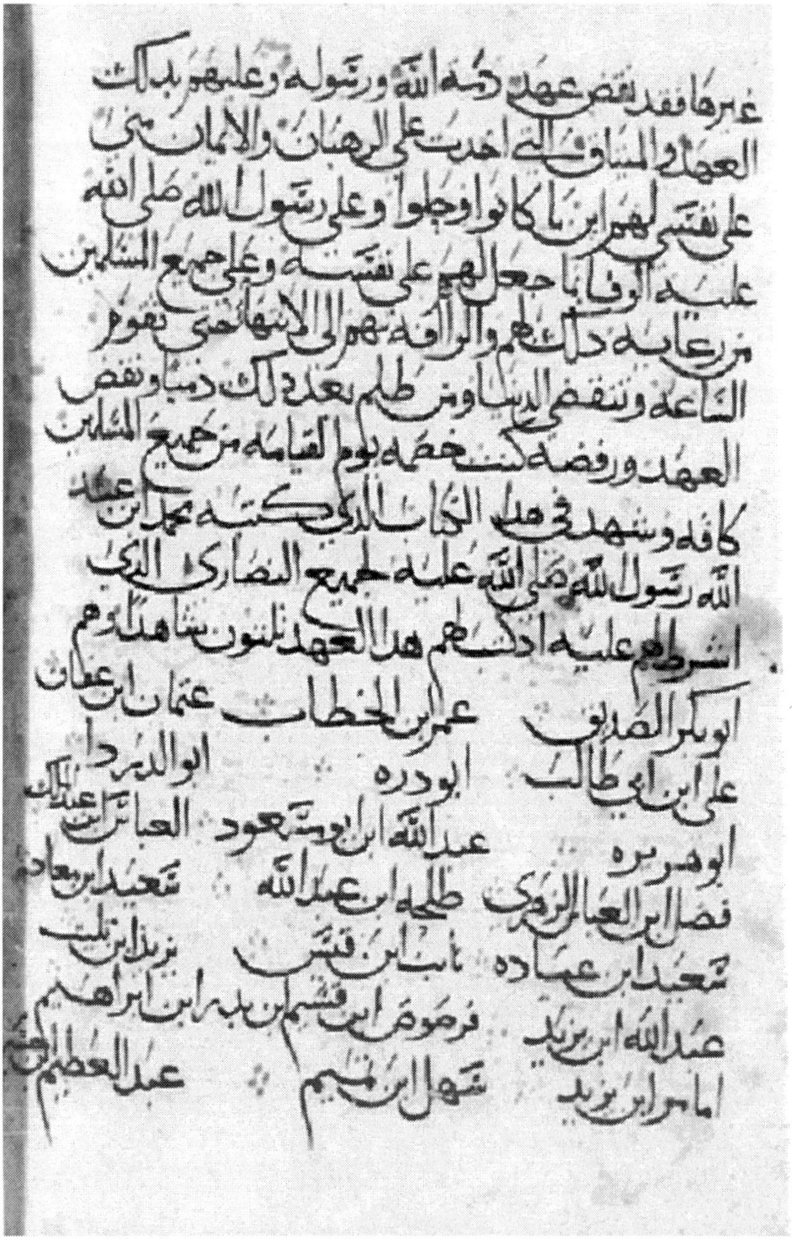

غيرها فقد نقض عهد ذمة الله ورسوله وعليهم بذلك
العهد والميثاق التي اخذت على الرهبان والايمان مني
على نفسي لهم اين ما كانوا وحلوا وعلى رسول الله صلى الله
عليه الوفا بما جعل لهم على نفسه وعلى جميع المسلمين
من رعاية ذلك لهم والرافه بهم الى الانتهاء حتى تقوم
الساعة وتنقضي الدنيا ومن ظلم بعد ذلك ذميا ونقض
العهد ورفضه كنت خصمه يوم القيامة من جميع المسلمين
كافة وشهد على هذا الكتاب الذي كتبه محمد ابن عبد
الله رسول الله صلى الله عليه لجميع النصارى الذي
اشترط لهم عليه اذ كتب لهم هذا العهد ثلثون شاهدا وهم

ابو بكر الصديق — عمر ابن الخطاب — عثمان ابن عفان
علي ابن ابي طالب — ابو ذره — ابو الدردا
ابو هريره — عبد الله ابن مسعود — العباس ابن عبد المطلب
فضل ابن العباس الزبير — طلحه ابن عبد الله — سعيد ابن معاذ
سعد ابن عباده — ثابت ابن قيس — يزيد ابن ثابت
عبد الله ابن يزيد — فرصوم ابن قشيم ابن نبيه ابن ابراهيم
امامه ابن يزيد — سهل ابن تميم — عبد العظيم

عبد العظيم ابن حنين ❁ عبد الله ابن عمر ابن العاص
عمر ابن ياسر ❁ معظم ابن موسى ❁ حسان ابن ثابت
ابو حنيفه ❁ عبيد ابن منصور ❁ هاشم ابن عبد الله
ابو العازر ❁ هشام ابن عبد المطلب ❁ وكتب على
ابن ابي طالب رضي الله عنه هذا العهد والسجل
مكتوب في جلد غير صغير وخاتم تثبيت حكم السلطان
وهو مختوم بخاتم النبي صلى الله عليه والحمد لله
تما
هذا الكتاب المبارك
وكان الفراغ منه في يوم الاثنين المبارك اخر شهر
بوونه المبارك سنه لنا دانا ا الشهدا
الاطهار السعدا الابرار رزقنا الله شفاعتهم
تكون معنا امين

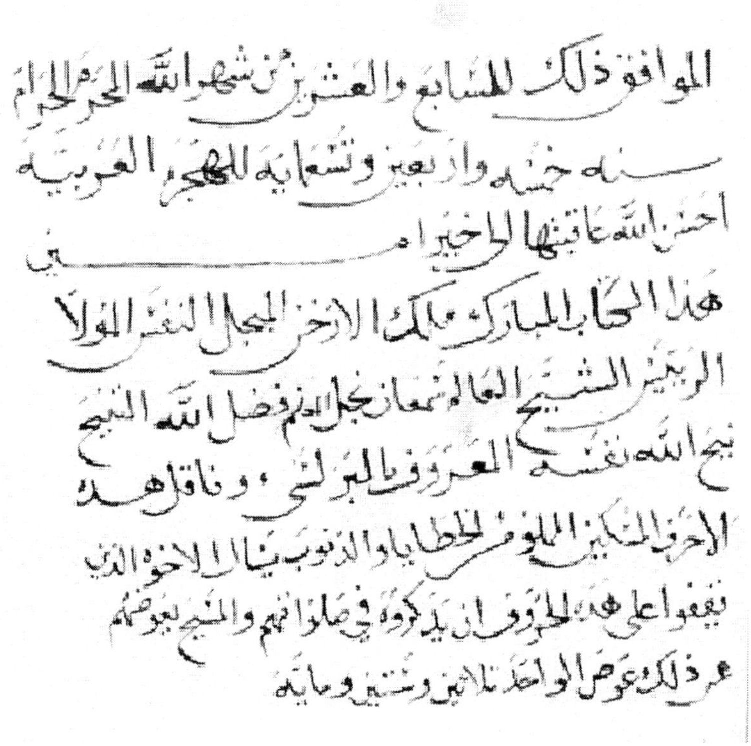
الموافق ذلك للسابع والعشرين من شهر الله المحرم الحرام
سنه خمسه واربعين وتسعمايه للهجرة العربيه
احسن الله عاقبتها الى خير امين
هذا الكتاب المبارك ملك الاخ المبجل النفس المولا
الربيبن الشيخ العالم سمعان نجل المرحوم فضل الله النيح
نيح الله نفسه المعروف بالبرلسي ، وانا قارى هذه
الاحرف المسكين الملوم من الخطايا والذنوب يسال الاخوه الذين
يقفوا على هذه الحروف ان يذكروه في صلواتهم والمسيح يعوضهم
عن ذلك عوض الواحد ثلاثين وستين ومايه

Reproduction of Original

al-'Ahd wa al-shurut allati sharataha Muhammad Rasul Allah li ahl al-millah al-nasraniyyah:

Testamentum et pactiones initae inter Mohamedem Apostolum Dei, et Christianae fedei cultores

[The Covenant of the Prophet Muhammad with the Christians of the World]

Editor: Gabriel Sionita

Publisher: Paris: Antoine Vitré, 1630

Reproduced from the original held by the Department of Special Collections of the Hesburgh Libraries of the University of Notre Dame

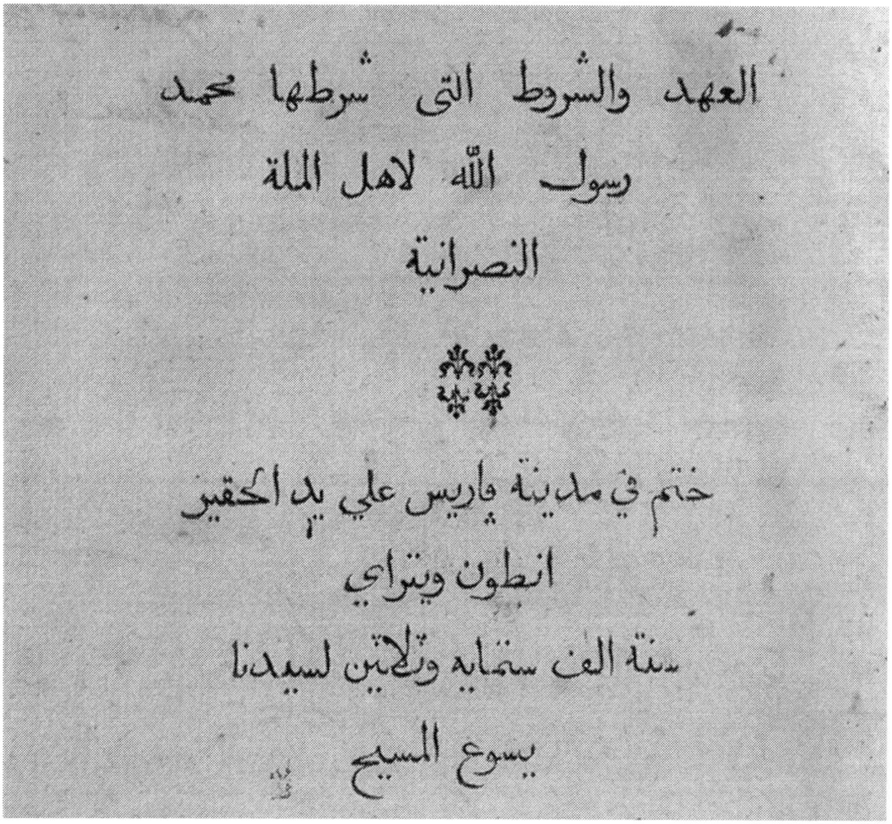

العهد والشروط التى شرطها محمد

رسول الله لاهل الملة

النصرانية

ختم في مدينة باريس علي يد الحقير

انطون ويتراي

سنة الف ستمايه وثلاثين لسيدنا

يسوع المسيح

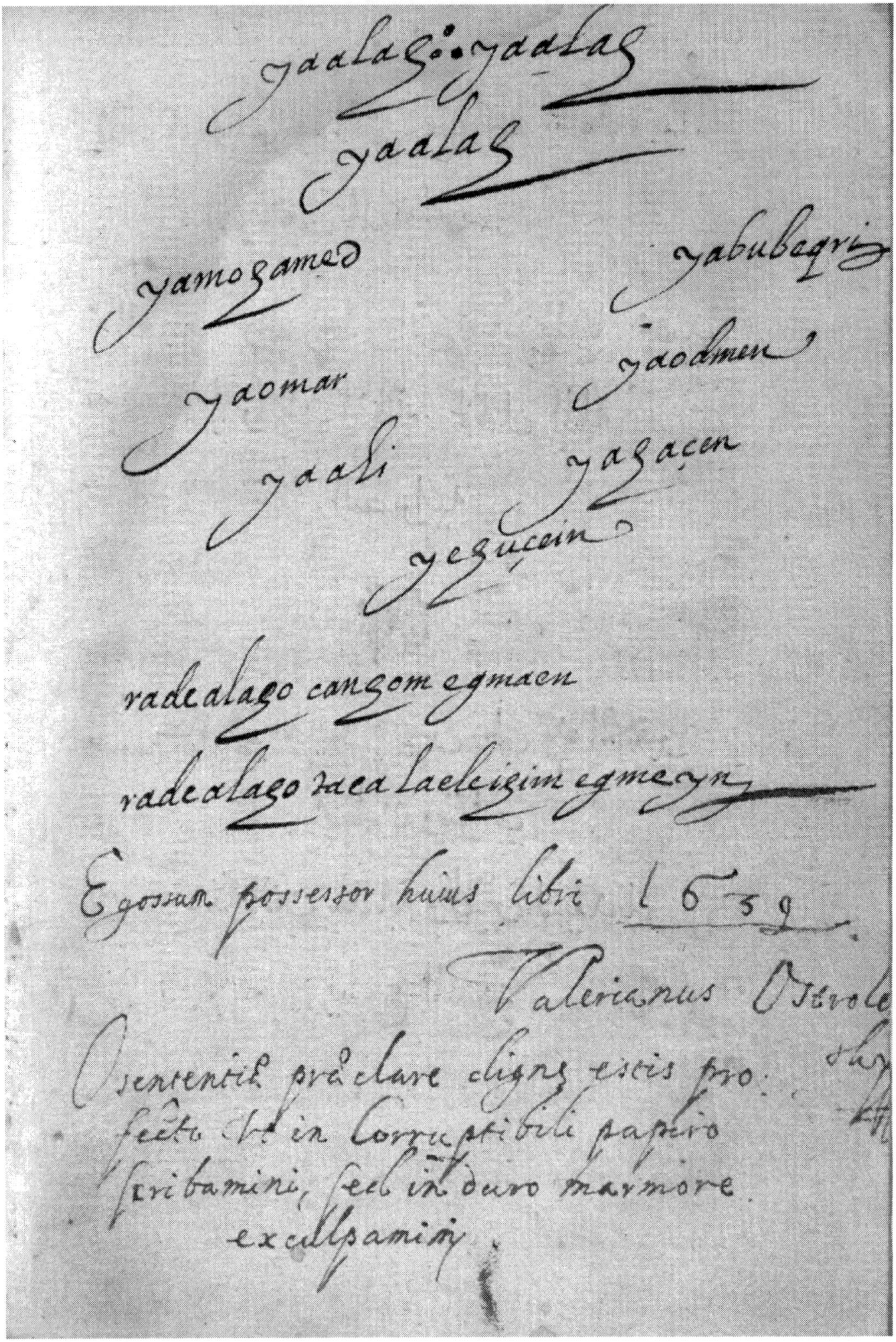

yaalaz . yaalaz

yaalaz

yamozamed yabubeqri

yaomar yaodmen

yaali yazaçen

yezuçein

radealazo canzom egmaen

radealazo zaca laelezim egmeyn

Ego sum possessor huius libri 1659

Valerianus Ostrole

O sententiæ præclare digne essetis pro-
fecto ut in corruptibili papiro
scribamini, sed in duro marmore
excalpamini

ج

العهد والشروط التي شرطها محمد رسول
الله لاهل الملة النصرانية

كتبه محمد رسول الله الي الناس كافة بشيرًا
ونديرًا علي وديعة الله في حقه ليكون حجة
الله سجل دين النصرانية في مشرق الارض
ومغربها وفصيحها واعجمها وقريبها
وبعيدها ومعروفها ومجهولها كتابا جعله
لهم عهدًا مرعيا وسجلاً منشورًا وصية
منه تقيم فيه عدله وذمة محفوظة فمن
كان بالاسلام متمسكا ولما فيه متساهلاً من
صنيعها ونكث العهد الذي فيها وخالفه
الي غير المومنين وتعدي فيه ما امرت به

A ij

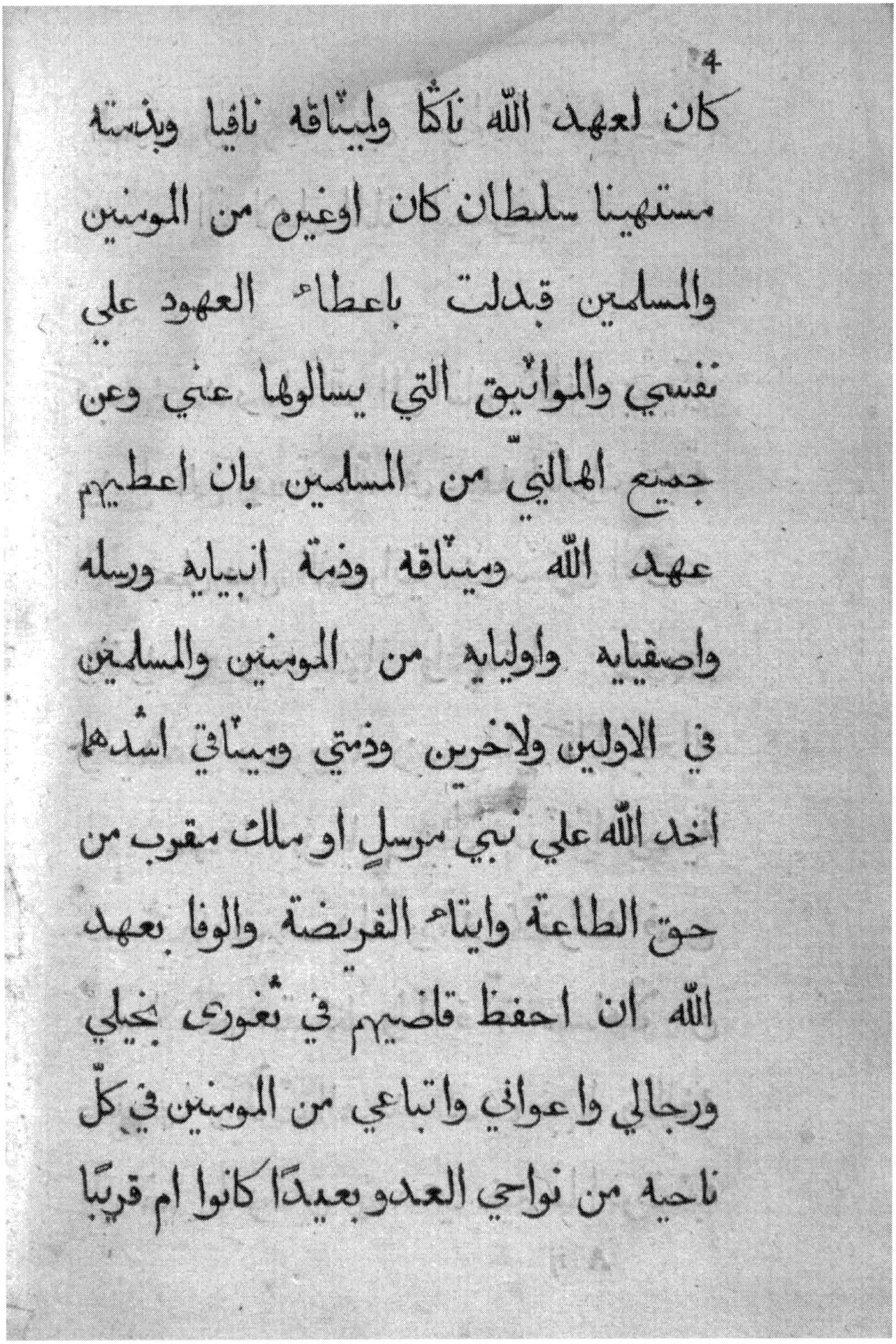

4

كان لعهد الله ناكثا ولميثاقه نافيا وبذمته
مستهينا سلطان كان اوغيره من المومنين
والمسلمين فبذلت باعطاء العهود علي
نفسي والمواثيق التي يسالوها عني وعن
جميع اهالي من المسلمين بان اعطيهم
عهد الله وميثاقه وذمة انبيايه ورسله
واصفيايه واوليايه من المومنين والمسلمين
في الاولين ولاخرين وذمتي وميثاقي اشدها
اخذ الله علي نبي مرسلٍ او ملك مقرب من
حق الطاعة وايتاء الفريضة والوفا بعهد
الله ان احفظ قاصيهم في ثغوري بخيلي
ورجالي واعواني واتباعي من المومنين في كل
ناحيه من نواحي العدو بعيدًا كانوا ام قريبًا

سلما كانوا ام حربا وامنهم وادب عنهم وعن
كنايسهم وبيعهم ومصلاهم ومواضع الرهبان
منهم ومواطن السياحة حيث كانوا واين
وجدوا في جبل او واد او مغارة او عمران او
سهل او رمل او بناء وان احوط دينهم
وملكهم حيث كانوا واين وجدوا في بر او بحر
في شرق او غرب بما احوط به نفسي وخاصتي
واهل ملتي من المومنين والمسلمين وان
ادخلهم في اماني من كل اذى ومكروه ومونة
وتبعة وان اكون من ورايهم دار عنهم كل
عدو يريدني واياهم بنفسي واتباعي واعواني
واهل ملتي وانا ذو سلطة عليهم وبذلك
يوجب علي رعيهم وحفظهم من كل

A iij

6

مكروه وان لايصل اليهم حتي يوصل الي
اصحابي الدابين عن نصيبة الامروان اعزل
عنهم الاذي في المواد التي تحمل اهل
العهد من العارية والخراج الا ما طابت به
انفسهم ولايكن عليهم جبر ولا اكراه في ذلك
ولا ينفي اسقف عن اسقفيته ولا نصراني
عن نصرانيته ولاراهب عن رهبانيته ولا
سايح عن سياحته ولا راهب عن صومعته
ولا يهدم بيتاً من بيوت كنايسهم ولا يدخل
شي في بنا المساجد ولا في منازل المسلمين
فمن فعل ذلك فقد نكث عهد الله وخالف
رسول الله وخان ذمة الله وان لايحمل الرهبان
ولا الاساقفه ولا جميع من لم يلزم بثمنه الا ان

7

تطيب بذلك انفسهم ولا يجاوزوا الجزيه علي
اصحاب التجارات العظام والغواصين والذين
يخرجون معادن الجوهر والذهب والفضه
وذوي الاموال الجمة والقوة ممن ابتجل
النصرانيه اكثر من اثني عشر درهما في كل عام
اذا كانوا في الموضع قاطنين وبه مقيمين وانه
ليس لعابر سبيل وليس هو من قاطني
البلد ممن لايعرف موضعه الخراج ولا الجزية
الا ان يكون في يده ميراث الارض ممن
يجب عليه مال السلطان من حق فيودي
ذلك علي ما يودي غيره ولايتجاوز عليه
ولايحمل منه الا مقدار طاقته وقوته وعلي
من يحوز من الارض وعمارتها واقبال ثمرها لا

8

يكلف شططا ولا يجازبه عن خد اصحاب
الخراج من نظرايه ولا يكلف اهل ذمة
الخروج مع الملا من المسلمين الي عدوهم
لملاقات الحرب وكاشفة الاقران لانه ليس
علي اهل الذمة مباشرة القتال وانما اعطوا
الذمة علي ان لا يكلفوا وان يكونوا المسلمين
دبابون عنهم محرزون من دونهم ولا يكرهون
علي الخروج مع المسلمين الحرب التي
يلقون فيها عدوهم ولا بقوة من خيل وسلاح
الا ان يتبرعوا فيحمل علي ذلك من تبرع
به وعرف له ذلك وكفي عليه ولا يجبر احدا
ممن كان علي ملة النصرانيه من الاسلام كرها
ولا يجادل الا بالتي هي احسن ويخفض لهم

9

جناح الرحمة ويكف عنهم الاذي والمكروه
حيث كانوا واين وجدوا وان جرا احدا من
النصاري جريرة او جني جناية فعلي
المسلمين نصره ومنعه والذب عنه والغرم
عن جريرته والدخول في الصلح بينه وبين ما
اصاب منا عليه واما فداء يفادي به ولا يخذلوا
ولا يرفضوا بل اعطيتهم عهد الله علي ان
لهم ما للمسلمين وعليهم ما علي المسلمين
وللمسلمين ما لهم وعلي المسلمين ما عليهم
بالعهد الذي استوجبه حق الرعا والذب عن
الحرمة به استوجبوا بذب عنهم كل مكروه
ويدخل لهم في كل مرفق حتي يكونوا
المسلمين شركا فيما لهم وفيما عليهم ولهم ان

B

١٥

تحمل من امر النكاح شططاً ولا يرادونهم ولا
يكرهوا اهل البنت منهم علي تزويج المسلمين
ولا يضاروا في ذلك ان منعوا خاطبا وابوا تزويجاً
فان ذلك لا يكون الا بطيب انفسهم ومسامحة
اهوايهم ان احبوه ورضوه واذا صارت
النصرانية في بيت المسلم فعليه ان يرضي
هواها في دينها من الاقتدا بروسايها والاخذ
بمعالم دينها ولا يمنعها في ذلك ولا يكرهها
علي تركها ولا يضاراها في ترك دينها فان
فعل ذلك وكرهها عليه فقد اخلف عهد
الله وعصي ميثاق رسول الله وهو عند الله
من الكاذبين ولهم ان احتاجوا الي مرمة
بيعهم او صوامعهم او شي من مصلحة
كنا

دينهم الي سوفدٍ من المسلمين او معونة علي
مومنةٍ ان يرفدوا عليه ويعاونوا ولا تكونوا
ذلك دينا بل معونة لهم علي مصالح دينهم
ووفايهم بعهد رسول الله هبة موهبة لهم ذمة
الله وذمة رسول الله عليهم ولهم ولا يكون احد
منهم ان يكون بين المسلمين ولهم عدو
وقالوا كن رسولا او دليلا او مسخرا اوفي شي
مما يقوم الحرب فمن فعل ذلك باحدٍ كان
ظالما ولرسول الله عاصيا ومن وصيته مختلفا
هذا شروط الذي شرط محمد رسول الله لاهل
الملة النصرانيه واشرط عليهم في دينهم اموراً
في ذمتهم عليهم التمسك بها والوفا بما عاهد
عليهم ومنها ان لايكون احد منهم عينا لاحد

B ij

٤٤

من اهل الحرب علي احد من المسلمين في
سر ولا علانية ولا يوفا في منازلهم ولا ياوا عدوا
لمسلم ولا ينزل اوطانهم ولا في مسا كن
عبادتهم ولا يوفدوا احد من اهل الحرب علي
المسلمين بقوة من عارية السلاح ولا الخيل ولا
الرجال ولا يستودعوا لهم مالا ولا يكاتبوهم ولا
يصافحوهم الاان يكون في دار يدبون فيها عن
انفسهم يدرون علي دمايهم ورعاية دينهم ولا
يمنعون احد من المسلمين قراة ثلاثة ايام
ولياليها لانفسهم ولدوابهم حيث كانوا واين
وجدوا ويبدلون لهم القوي الذي منه
ياكلون ولا يكلفوا علي ذلك فيحملوا الاذية
عنهم والمكروه فان احتيج الي اختفا احد من

13

المسلمين في منازلهم ومواطن اعمارهم ان
يودوهم ويرفدوهم ويساوهم عمّا شق به ما كانوا
محتفين اذا كتموا عنهم ولم يظهروا العدو
علي عورتهم ولم يخلوا من الواجب عليهم في
ذلك فمن نكث منهم شيا من هذه الشروط
وتعداها الي غيره فبري من ذمة الله وذمة
رسول الله عليهم بذلك العهود والمواثيق التي
اخذت عن الاحبار والرهبان والنصاري من
اهل الكتاب واشد ما اخذ الله النبي علي
امته من الايمان والوفا بذلك اين كانوا وحيث
وجدوا وعلي رسول الله الوفا بما جعل لهم علي
نفسه وعلي المسلمين رعاية ذلك لهم وسعتهم به
والانتها اليه ابدا احتي تقوم الساعة وتنقضي

B iij

14

الدنيا واشهدوا علي هذا
الكتاب الذي كتبه محمد رسول الله بين
النصاري الذي اشرط عليهم ولقب لهم هذا
العهد

ابو بكر الصديق — عمر بن الخطاب
عثمان بن عفان — علي بن ابي طالب
معاويه بن سفيان — ابو الدردا
ابو اذر — ابو هريرة
عبد الله بن مسعود — عبد الله بن العباس
حمزة بن عبد المطلب — فضيل
زيد بن ثابت — عبد الله ابن زيد
حرقوس بن زيد — الزبير بن العوام

٤٥

سعد بن معاذ ثابت بن قيس

اسامة بن زيد عثمان بن مطعون

عبدالله بن عمر العاص ابن ربيعة

حسن بن ثابت جعفر بن ابي طالب

ابن العباس طلحة بن عبدالله

سعد بن عباده زيد بن ارقم

سهل بن بيضا داود بن جبير

ابو العاليه ابو احريفة بن عسيد

هاشم بن عسبه عمار بن ياسين

كعب بن مالك كعب بن كعب

رضوان الله عليهم اجمعين

وكتب معاويه بن ابي سفيان من املا رسول الله يوم الاثنين تمام اربعة اشهر من السنة

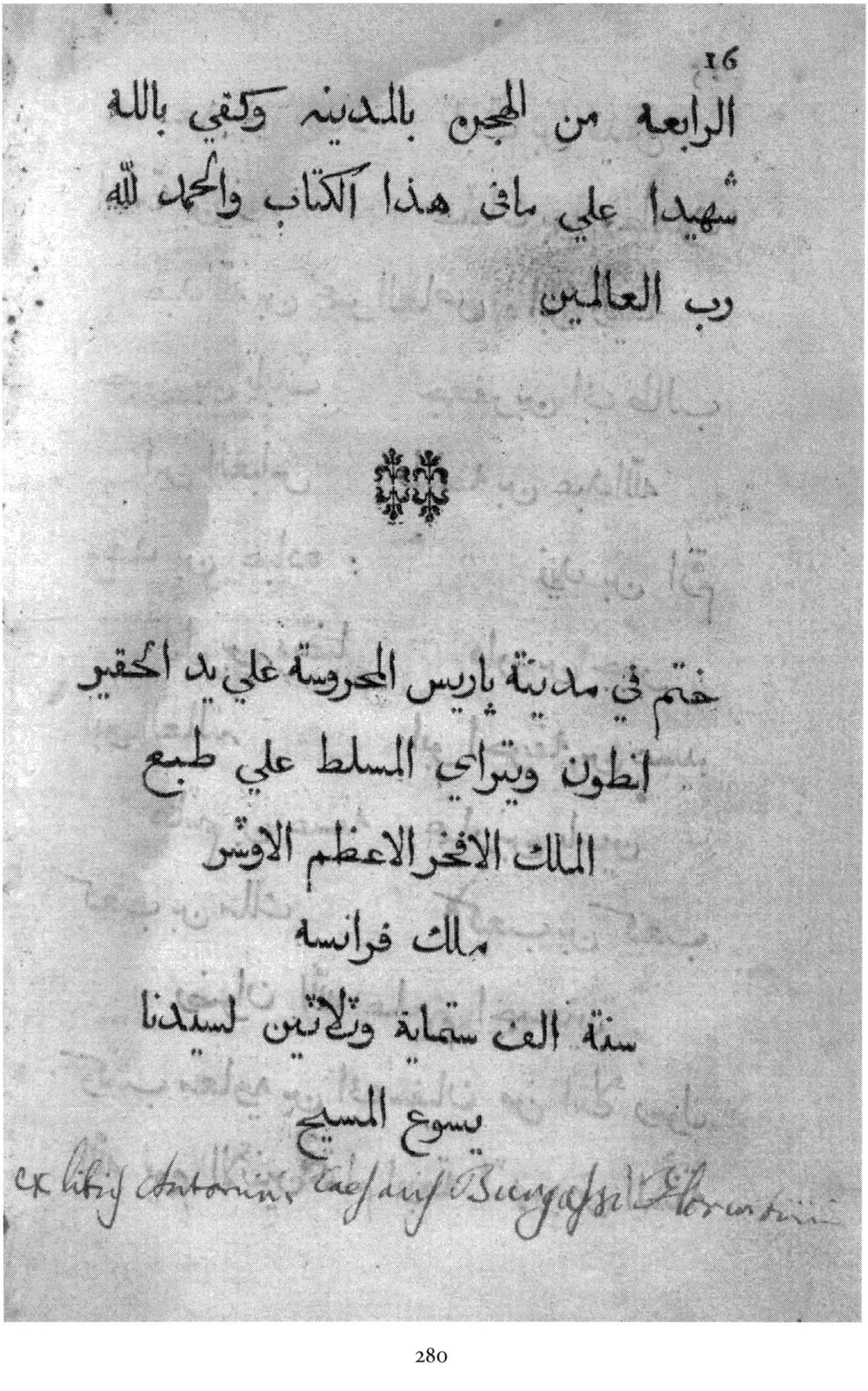

16

الرابعة من الهجرة بالمدينة وكفي بالله
شهيدا علي ماقي هذا الكتاب والحمد لله
رب العالمين

ختم في مدينة باريس المحروسة علي يد الحقير
انطون ويتراي المسلط علي طبع
الملك الافخر الاعظم الاوفر
ملك فرانسه
سنة الف ستماية وثلاثين لسيدنا
يسوع المسيح

ex libris Antonii Caesaris Burgassi Florentini

Reproduction of Original

al-'Ahd wa al-shurut allati sharataha Muhammad Rasul Allah li ahl al-millah al-nasraniyyah:

Testamentum et pactiones initae inter Mohamedem Apostolum Dei, et Christianae fedei cultores

[The Covenant of the Prophet Muhammad with the Christians of the World]

Editor: Johann Georg Nissel

Publisher: Elsevier: Lugduni Batavorum, 1655

اَلْعَهْدُ وَٱلشُّرُوطُ ٱلَّتِي شَرَطَهَا مُحَمَّدٌ رَسُولُ
ٱللَّهِ لِأَهْلِ ٱلْمِلَّةِ ٱلنَّصْرَانِيَّةِ ۞

SIVE

TESTAMENTUM,

INTER MUHAMEDEM, ET CHRISTIANÆ RELIGIONIS POPULOS INITUM.

Cujus

Textus Authenticus hìc noviter recusus, à mendis quàm plurimis probè castigatus, nunc primùm figuris vocalium nobilitatus, nec non è regione versione Latinâ adornatus.

Quô

Pariter Editionis Parisiensis multivaria hinc indè, eaque grandia errata deteguntur, loca corrupta debitæ integritati restituuntur, totiusque hujus memorabilis facti cognitio dilucida atque plana redditur.

Operâ & studio

JOANNIS GEORGII NISSELII, LL. Oriental. Cultoris.

LUGDUNI BATAVORUM,

Ex Officina JOANNIS ELZEVIER, Acad. Typogr.

Sumptibus Authoris.

Anno cIↃ IↃC LV.

العهد والشروط التي شرطها محمد رسول
الله لاهل النصرانية *

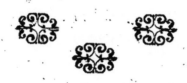

ختم في مدرسة الشريفة لبدأ علي يد
الحقير الفقير
يوحنا غورغيوس نهليوس

سنة الف وسبعماية خمس وخمسين لسيدنا
يسوع المسيح

(2)

العهد والشروط التي شرطها محمد رسول الله لأهل النصرانية

كتبه

محمد رسول الله إلي الناس كافة بشيرا ونذيرا علي وديعة الله في خلقه لتكون حجة الله سجل دين النصرانية في مشرق الأرض ومغربها وفصيحها وأعجمها وقريبها وبعيدها ومعروفها ومجهولها كتابا جعله لهم عهدا مرعيا وسجلا منشورا وصية منه تقيم فيهم عدله وذمة لمحفوظه فمن كان بالإسلام متمسكا ولما فيه متساهلا من صنيعها ونكث العهد الذي فيها وخالفه إلي غير المؤمنين وتعدي فيه ما أمرت به كان لعهد الله ناكثا ولميثاقه نافيا وبذمته مستهينا سلطان كان أو غيره من المؤمنين والمسلمين فبذلت باعطاء العهود علي نفسي والمواثيق التي يسألوها عني وعن جميع أهاليّ من المسلمين بأن أعطيهم عهد الله وميثاقه وذمة أنبيائه ورسله وأصفيائه وأوليائه من المؤمنين والمسلمين في الأولين والآخرين وذمتي وميثاقي أشدها أخذ الله علي نبي مرسل أو ملك مقرب

(4)

مُقْرِبٍ مِنْ حَقِّ ٱلْمَنَعَةِ وَإِيتَاءِ ٱلْفَرِيضَةِ وَٱلْوَفَا بِعَهْدِ ٱللَّهِ أَنْ
أَحْفَظَ قَاصِيَهُمْ فِي ثُغُورِي بِخَيْلِي وَرِجَالِي وَأَعْوَانِي
وَٱلدَّانِي مِنَ ٱلْمُؤْمِنِينَ فِي كُلِّ نَاحِيَةٍ مِنْ نَوَاحِي ٱلْعَدُوِّ
بَعِيدًا كَانُوا أَمْ قَرِيبًا سِلْمًا كَانُوا أَمْ حَرْبًا وَأُؤْمِنُهُمْ
وَأَذِبُّ وَعَنْ كَنَائِسِهِمْ وَمَوَاطِنَ ٱلسِّيَاحَةِ حَيْثُ كَانُوا وَأَيْنَ
وُجِدُوا فِي جَبَلٍ أَوْ وَادٍ أَوْ مَغَارَةٍ أَوْ عُمْرَانٍ أَوْ سَهْلٍ أَوْ رَمْلٍ
أَوْ بِنَاءٍ وَأَنْ أَحُوطَ دِينَهُمْ وَمِلَّتَهُمْ حَيْثُ كَانُوا وَأَيْنَ وُجِدُوا
فِي بَرٍّ أَوْ بَحْرٍ فِي شَرْقٍ أَوْ غَرْبٍ بِمَا أَحُوطُ بِهِ نَفْسِي
وَخَاتِمِي وَأَهْلَ مِلَّتِي مِنَ ٱلْمُؤْمِنِينَ وَٱلْمُسْلِمِينَ وَأَنْ أُدْخِلَهُمْ
فِي أَمَانِي مِنْ كُلِّ أَذًى وَمَكْرُوهٍ وَمَؤُونَةٍ وَتَبِعَةٍ وَأَنْ
أَكُونَ مِنْ وَرَائِهِمْ ذَابًّا عَنْهُمْ بِرَدِّي وَإِيَّاهُمْ بِنَفْسِي وَأَتْبَاعِي
وَأَعْوَانِي وَأَهْلِ مِلَّتِي وَأَنَا ذُو سُلْطَةٍ عَلَيْهِمْ وَبِذَلِكَ يُوجَبُ
عَلَيَّ رَعِيَّتُهُمْ وَحِفْظُهُمْ مِنْ كُلِّ مَكْرُوهٍ وَأَنْ لَا يَصِلَ إِلَيْهِمْ
حَتَّى يَصِلَ إِلَى أَصْحَابِي ٱلذَّابِّينَ عَنْ نَصِيبَةِ ٱلْأَمْرِ وَأَنْ
أَعْزِلَ عَنْهُمُ ٱلْأَذَى فِي ٱلْمُؤَنِ ٱلَّتِي تَحْمِلُ أَهْلَ ٱلْعَهْدِ
مِنَ ٱلْعَارِيَةِ وَٱلْخَرَاجِ إِلَّا مَا طَابَتْ بِهِ أَنْفُسُهُمْ وَلَا يَكُونَ عَلَيْهِمْ
جَبْرٌ وَلَا إِكْرَاهٌ فِي ذَلِكَ وَلَا يُنْفَى أُسْقُفٌ عَنْ أُسْقُفِيَّتِهِ وَلَا
نَصْرَانِيٌّ عَنْ نَصْرَانِيَّتِهِ وَلَا رَاهِبٌ عَنْ رَهْبَانِيَّتِهِ وَلَا سَائِحٌ عَنْ
سِيَاحَتِهِ وَلَا رَاهِبٌ عَنْ صَوْمَعَتِهِ وَلَا يُهْدَمُ بَيْتًا مِنْ بُيُوتِ
كَنَائِسِهِمْ

كَنَائِسِهِمْ وَلَا يَدْخُلَ شَيْءٌ مِنْ بِنَاءِ ٱلْمَسَاجِدِ وَلَا فِي مَنَازِلِ
ٱلْمُسْلِمِينَ فَمَنْ فَعَلَ ذَلِكَ فَقَدْ نَكَثَ عَهْدَ ٱللَّهِ وَخَالَفَ رَسُولَ
ٱللَّهِ وَخَانَ ذِمَّةَ ٱللَّهِ وَأَنْ لَا يُحْمَلَ ٱلرُّهْبَانُ وَلَا ٱلْأَسَاقِفَةُ
وَلَا جَمِيعَ مَنْ لَمْ يَلْزَمْ بِثَمَنٍ إِلَّا أَنْ تَطِيبَ بِذَلِكَ أَنْفُسُهُمْ وَلَا
يُجَاوِرُوا ٱلْجِزْيَةَ عَلَى أَصْحَابِ ٱلتِّجَارَاتِ ٱلْعِظَامِ وَٱلْغَوَّاصِينَ
وَٱلَّذِينَ يُخْرِجُونَ مَعَادِنَ ٱلْجَوْهَرِ وَٱلذَّهَبِ وَٱلْفِضَّةِ وَذَوِي
ٱلْأَمْوَالِ ٱلْجَمَّةِ وَٱلْقُوَّةِ مِمَّنْ إِنْتَحَلَ ٱلنَّصْرَانِيَّةَ أَكْثَرَ مِنْ
إِثْنَيْ عَشَرَ دِرْهَمًا فِي كُلِّ عَامٍ إِذَا كَانُوا فِي ٱلْمَوْضِعِ
قَاطِنِينَ وَبِهِ مُقِيمِينَ وَإِنَّهُ لَيْسَ لِعَابِرِ سَبِيلٍ وَلَيْسَ هُوَ مِنْ
قَاطِنِي ٱلْبَلَدِ مِمَّنْ لَا يُعْرَفُ مَوْضِعُهُ ٱلْخَرَاجَ وَلَا ٱلْجِزْيَةَ إِلَّا أَنْ
يَكُونَ فِي يَدِهِ مِيرَاثُ ٱلْأَرْضِ مِمَّنْ يَجِبُ عَلَيْهِ مَالُ ٱلسُّلْطَانِ
مِنْ حَقٍّ فَيُؤَدِّي ذَلِكَ عَلَى مَا يُؤَدِّي غَيْرُهُ وَلَا تَجَاوُزَ عَلَيْهِ
وَلَا يُحْمَلُ مِنْهُ إِلَّا مِقْدَارَ طَاقَتِهِ وَقُوَّتِهِ وَعَلَى مَنْ يَجُوزُ مِنَ
ٱلْأَرْضِ وَعِمَارَتِهَا وَإِقْبَالِ ثَمَرِهَا لَا يُكَلَّفُ شَطَطًا وَلَا
يُجَازَى بِهِ عَنْ حَقِّ أَصْحَابِ ٱلْخَرَاجِ مِنْ نُظَرَائِهِ وَلَا يُكَلَّفُ أَهْلَ
ذِمَّةِ ٱلْخُرُوجَ مَعَ ٱلْمَلَأِ مِنَ ٱلْمُسْلِمِينَ إِلَى عَدُوِّهِمْ لِمُلَاقَاتِ
ٱلْحَرْبِ وَكَاشِفَةِ ٱلْأَقْرَانِ لِأَنَّهُ لَيْسَ عَلَى أَهْلِ ٱلذِّمَّةِ مُبَاشَرَةُ
ٱلْقِتَالِ وَإِنَّمَا أُعْطُوا ٱلذِّمَّةَ عَلَى أَنْ لَا يُكَلَّفُوا وَأَنْ يَكُونُوا
لِلْمُسْلِمِينَ ذَبَّابُونَ عَنْهُمْ مُحْرِزُونَ مِنْ دُونِهِمْ وَلَا يُكْرَهُونَ عَلَى
ٱلْخُرُوجِ

(٥)

ٱلْخُرُوجِ مَعَ ٱلْمُسْلِمِينَ ٱلْحَرْبِ ٱلَّتِي يَلْقَوْنَ فِيهَا عَدُوَّهُمْ وَلَا بِقُوَّةٍ مِنْ خَيْلٍ وَسَلَاحٍ إِلَّا أَنْ يَتَبَرَّعُوا فَيَحْمِلُ عَلَي دَلِكَ مَنْ تَبَرَّعَ بِهِ عَرَفَ لَهُ دَلِكَ وَكَفَي عَلَيْهِ وَلَا يُجْبِرُ أَحَدًا مِمَّنْ كَانَ عَلَي مِلَّةِ ٱلنَّصْرَانِيَّةِ مِنَ ٱلْإِسْلَامِ كُرْهًا وَلَا يُجَادِلُ إِلَّا بِٱلَّتِي هِيَ أَحْسَنُ وَيُخْفَضُ لَهُمْ جَنَاحَ ٱلرَّحْمَةِ وَيُكَلِّفُ عَنْهُمْ ٱلْأَدَي وَٱلْمَكْرُوهَ حَيْثُ كَانُوا وَأَيْنَ وُجِدُوا وَأَنْ جَرَا أَحَدًا مِنَ ٱلنَّصَارَي جَرِيرَةً أَوْ جَنَي جِنَايَةً فَعَلَي ٱلْمُسْلِمِينَ نَصْرَهُ وَمَنْعَهُ وَٱلدَّبُّ عَنْهُ وَٱلْغُرْمَ عَنْ جَرِيرَتِهِ وَٱلدُّخُولُ فِي ٱلصُّلْحِ بَيْنَهُ وَبَيْنَ مَا أَصَابَ مِنَّا عَلَيْهِ وَأَمَّا فِدَاءٌ يُفَادِي بِهِ وَلَا يُخْذَلُوا وَلَا يُرْفَضُوا بَلْ أَعْطَيْتُهُمْ عَهْدَ ٱللَّهِ عَلَي أَنْ لَهُمْ مَا لِلْمُسْلِمِينَ وَعَلَيْهِمْ مَا عَلَي ٱلْمُسْلِمِينَ وَلِلْمُسْلِمِينَ مَا لَهُمْ وَعَلَي ٱلْمُسْلِمِينَ مَا عَلَيْهِمْ بِٱلْعَهْدِ ٱلَّذِي إِسْتَوْجَبَهُ حَقَّ ٱلرَّعَا وَٱلدَّبَّ عَنِ ٱلْحُرْمَةِ بِهِ إِسْتَوْجَبُوا بِدَبٍّ عَنْهُمْ كُلَّ مَكْرُوهٍ وَيَدْخُلُ لَهُمْ فِي كُلِّ مَرْفَقٍ حَتَّي يَكُونُوا ٱلْمُسْلِمِينَ شُرَكَا فِيمَا لَهُمْ وَفِيمَا عَلَيْهِمْ وَلَهُمْ أَنْ تَحْمِلَ مِنْ أَمْرِ ٱلنِّكَاحِ شِطَطًا وَلَا بَرًّا دُونَهُمْ وَلَا يُكْرِهُوا أَهْلَ ٱلْبِنْتِ مِنْهُمْ عَلَي تَزْوِيجِ ٱلْمُسْلِمِينَ وَلَا يُضَارُّوا فِي دَلِكَ إِنْ مَنَعُوا خَاطِبًا وَأَبَوْا تَزْوِيجًا فَإِنَّ دَلِكَ لَا يَكُونُ إِلَّا بِطِيبِ أَنْفُسِهِمْ وَمُسَامَحَةِ أَهْوَائِهِمْ أَحَبُّوهُ وَرَضُوهُ وَإِدَا صَارَتْ ٱلنَّصْرَانِيَّةُ

فِي

فِي بَيْتِ ٱلْمُسْلِمِ فَعَلَيْهِ أَنْ يُرْضِيَ هَوَاهَا فِي دِينِهَا مِنَ ٱلْإِقْتِدَاءِ بِرُؤَسَائِهَا وَٱلْأَخْذِ بِمَعَالِمِ دِينِهَا وَلَا يَمْنَعُهَا فِي ذَلِكَ وَلَا يُكْرِهُهَا عَلَى تَرْكِهَا وَلَا يُضَارُّهَا فِي تَرْكِ دِينِهَا فَإِنَّ فَعَلَ ذَلِكَ وَكَرِهَهَا عَلَيْهِ فَقَدْ أَخْلَفَ عَهْدَ ٱللَّهِ وَعَصَى مِيثَاقَ رَسُولِ ٱللَّهِ وَهُوَ عِنْدَ ٱللَّهِ مِنَ ٱلْكَاذِبِينَ وَلَهُمْ أَنْ إِحْتَاجُوا إِلَى مَرَمَّةٍ كَنَائِسِهِمْ أَوْ صَوَامِعِهِمْ أَوْ شَيْءٍ مِنْ مَصْلَحَةِ دِينِهِمْ إِلَى مُرْفِدٍ مِنَ ٱلْمُسْلِمِينَ أَوْ مَعُونَةٍ عَلَى مَرَمَّةٍ أَنْ يُرْفِضُوا عَلَيْهِ وَيُعَانُوا وَلَا تَكُوِّنُوا ذَلِكَ دِينًا بَلْ مَعُونَةٌ لَهُمْ عَلَى مَصَالِحِ دِينِهِمْ وَوَفَائِهِمْ بِعَهْدِ رَسُولِ ٱللَّهِ هِبَةً مَوْهِبَةً لَهُمْ ذِمَّةَ ٱللَّهِ وَذِمَّةَ رَسُولِ ٱللَّهِ عَلَيْهِمْ وَلَهُمْ وَلَا يَكُونُ أَحَدٌ مِنْهُمْ أَنْ يَكُونَ بَيْنَ ٱلْمُسْلِمِينَ وَلَهُمْ عَدُوٌّ وَقَالُوا كُنْ رَسُولًا أَوْ دَلِيلًا أَوْ مُسَخَّرًا أَوْ فِي شَيْءٍ مِمَّا يَقُومُ ٱلْحَرْبُ فَمَنْ فَعَلَ ذَلِكَ بِأَحَدٍ كَانَ ظَالِمًا وَرَسُولِ ٱللَّهِ عَاصِيًا وَمِنْ وَصِيَّتِهِ مُخْتَلِفًا هَذَا شُرُوطُ ٱلَّذِي شَرَطَ مُحَمَّدٌ رَسُولُ ٱللَّهِ لِأَهْلِ ٱلْمِلَّةِ ٱلنَّصْرَانِيَّةِ وَٱشْتَرَطَ عَلَيْهِمْ فِي دِينِهِمْ أُمُورًا فِي ذِمَّتِهِمْ عَلَيْهِمْ ٱلتَّمَسُّكُ بِهَا وَٱلْوَفَاءُ بِمَا عَاهَدَ عَلَيْهِمْ وَمِنْهَا إِنْ لَا يَكُونُ أَحَدٌ مِنْهُمْ غَبِيًّا لِأَحَدٍ مِنْ أَهْلِ ٱلْحَرْبِ عَلَى أَحَدٍ مِنَ ٱلْمُسْلِمِينَ فِي سِرٍّ وَلَا عَلَانِيَةٍ وَلَا يُوَفَّاءٍ فِي مَنَازِلِهِمْ وَلَا يَأْوُوا عَدُوًّا لِلْمُسْلِمِ وَلَا يُنْزِلُ أَوْطَانَهُمْ وَلَا فِي مَسَاكِنِ عِبَادَاتِهِمْ وَلَا يَرْفُضُوا

(١٤)

يُرْفِضُوا أَحَدَ مِنْ أَهْلِ ٱلْحَرْبِ عَلَي ٱلْمُسْلِمِينْ بِقُوَّةٍ مِنْ عَارِيَةٍ
ٱلسِّلَاحِ وَلَا ٱلْخَيْلِ وَلَا ٱلرِّجَالِ وَلَا يَسْتَوْدِعُوا لَهُمْ مَالًا وَلَا
يُكَاتِبُوهُمْ وَلَا يُصَافِحُوهُمْ إِلَّا أَنْ يَكُونَ فِي دَارٍ يَدَبُّونَ
فِيهَا عَنْ أَنْفُسِهِمْ يَذُبُّونَ عَلَي دِمَائِهِمْ وَرِعَايَةِ دِينِهِمْ وَلَا
يَمْنَعُونَ أَحَدَ مِنَ ٱلْمُسْلِمِينَ قِرَاةٍ ثَلَاثَةِ أَيَامٍ وَلَيَالِيهَا لِأَنْفُسِهِمْ
وَلِدَوَابِهِمْ حَيْثُ كَانُوا وَأَيْنَ وُجِدُوا وَيُبْذِلُونَ لَهُمْ ٱلْقِرَي
ٱلَّذِي مِنْهُ يَأْكُلُونَ وَلَا يُكَفُّوا عَلَي ذَلِكَ فَيَحْمِلُوا ٱلْأَذِيَّةَ
عَنْهُمْ وَٱلْمَكْرُوهَ فَإِنَّ إِحْتِيجَ إِلَي إِخْتِفَا أَحَدَ مِنَ ٱلْمُسْلِمِينَ فِي
مَنَازِلِهِمْ وَمَوَاطِنِ أَعْمَارِهِمْ أَنْ يُؤْوُوهُمْ وَيُرْفِضُوهُمْ وَيُسَاوُهُمْ
عَمَّا شَقَّ بِهِ مَا كَانُوا مُخْتَفِينَ إِذَا كَتَمُوا عَنْهُمْ وَلَمْ يُظْهِرُوا
ٱلْعَدُوَّ عَلَي عَوْرَتِهِمْ وَلَمْ يُخَلُّوا مِنَ ٱلْوَاجِبِ عَلَيْهِمْ فِي ذَلِكَ
فَمَنْ نَكَثَ مِنْهُمْ شَيًّا مِنْ هَذِهِ ٱلشُّرُوطِ وَتَعَدَّاهَا إِلَي غَيْرِهِ
فَبَرِّي مِنْ ذِمَّةِ ٱللَّهِ وَذِمَّةِ رَسُولِ ٱللَّهِ عَلَيْهِمْ بِذَلِكَ ٱلْعُهُودُ
وَٱلْمَوَاثِيقِ ٱلَّذِي أَخَذَ عَنِ ٱلْأَحْبَارِ وَٱلرُّهْبَانِ وَٱلنَّصَارَي مِنْ
أَهْلِ ٱلْكِتَابِ وَآشَدُّ مَا أَخَذَ ٱللَّهِ وَٱلنَّبِيُّ عَلَي أُمَّتِهِ مِنَ
ٱلْأَيْمَانِ وَٱلْوَفَا بِذَلِكَ أَيْنَ كَانُوا وَحَيْثُ وُجِدُوا وَعَلَي
رَسُولِ ٱللَّهِ ٱلْوَفَا بِمَا جَعَلَ لَهُمْ عَلَي نَفْسِهِ وَعَلَي ٱلْمُسْلِمِينَ
رِعَايَةِ ذَلِكَ لَهُمْ مُعِزَّتِهِمْ بِهِ وَٱلْإِنْتِهَا إِلَيْهِ أَبَدًا حَتَّي تَقُومَ
ٱلسَّاعَةَ وَتَنْقَضِي ٱلدُّنْيَا وَٱشْهَدُوا *

عَلَي

عَلَي هٰذَا ٱلْكِتَابْ ٱلَّذِي كَتَبَهُ مُحَمَّد
بَرَسُولُ ٱللّٰهِ بَيْنَ ٱلنَّصَارَي ٱلَّذِي أَشْرَطَ
عَلَيْهِمْ وَلَقَّبَ لَهُمْ هٰذَا ٱلْعَهْد *

أَبُو بَكْرٍ ٱلصِّدِيقِ	Abu Bakri Affadick.
عُثْمَانُ بَنْ عَفَّانٍ	Othman ben-affan.
مُعَاوِيَةُ بَنْ أَبِي سُفِيَانٍ	Moavia ben-abi Sofian.
أَبُو أَنِي	Abu adrin.
عَبْدُ ٱللّٰهِ بَنْ مَعْسُودٍ	Abdalla ben-mafud. ٧
حَمْزَةُ بَنْ عَبْدِ ٱلْمُطَّلَبِ	Hamza ben-abdi-lmottaleb.
زَيْدٌ بَنْ ثَابِتٍ	Zaido ben-thabet. ۱٥
حَرْفُوس بَنْ زَيْدٍ	Harfus ben-zaid. —
سَعْدٌ بَنْ مَعَاذٍ	Saad ben-moad. ۱۲
أَسَامَةُ بَنْ زَيْدٍ	Afamet ben-zaid. -
عَبْدُ ٱللّٰهِ بَنْ عَمْرُ ٱلْعَاصِ	Ab dalla ben-omar-alas.
حَسَنٌ بَنْ ثَابِتٍ	Hafan ben-thabet. ۲٥
إِبَنْ ٱلْعَبَّاسِ	Iben alabbas. —
سَعْدٌ بَنْ عَبَادَةٍ	Saad ben-abade. ۱۳
سَهْلٌ بَنْ بَيْضَا	Sahal ben-baida.

Abu

(15)

أبو العالية	Abu aliah.
هاشم بن عسية	Haſſchem ben-aſſia.
كعب بن ملك	Caab ben-malc.
ثابت بن قيس	Thabet ben-cais.
عثمان بن مظعون	Othman ben-matun.
ابن ربيعة	Aben rabiah.
جعفر بن أبي طالب	Giafar ben-abidaleb.
طلحة بن عبد الله	Talla ben-ab-dalla.
زيد بن أرقم	Zaida ben-arcam.
داود بن جبير	Dauid ben-giobair.
أبو أحريفة بن عسير	Abu ahrifa ben-oſair.
عمار بن يامين	Omar ben-jamin.
كعب بن كعب	Caab ben-caab.

D 2 Qui

رضوان الله عليهم أجمعين
وكتب معاوية بن أبي
سفيان من أملاء رسول الله
يوم الاثنين تمام أربعة أشهر
من السنة الرابعة من الهجرة
بالمدينة وكفي بالله شهيدا
علي مـــا في هذا
الكتاب *

والحمد لله رب
العالمين ۞

Qui omnes gratioſi ſunt apud Deum: Secretarius autem fuit Moavia ben abi Sofian, miles Nuncii Dei, die Lunæ ultimi menſis quarti, anni quarti Hegiræ, in Medina Remuneretur autem Deus omnes qui huic Scripturæ ſunt atteſtati:

Laus Deo Domino
Creaturarum.

Fulfill the Covenant of Allah when ye have entered into it, and break not your oaths after ye have confirmed them; indeed ye have made Allah your surety; for Allah knoweth all that ye do. (16:91)

Chapter 11

Text of the Covenant of the Prophet Muhammad with the Christians of Najran

[*By the Prophet Muhammad*]
Translation by John Andrew Morrow in 2013

[Exordium]

In the Name of Allah, the Most Compassionate, the Most Merciful.

A covenant of protection granted by Allah and His Messenger to the People of the Book, the Christians, who belong to the religion of Najran or any other Christian sect.

It has been written by Muhammad, the Messenger of Allah to all of humanity, as a guarantee of protection on the part of Allah and His Messenger, and made it binding upon the Muslims who will come after him, which they have to be aware of, recognize as authentic, believe in it, and preserve it in their favor.

It is forbidden for any man, whether he is a governor or holder of authority, to revoke it or infringe upon it.

The Believers must not charge them with other conditions than those which are included in this document.

He who preserves it, respects it, and abides by its dictates, will have fulfilled his obligations and will have adhered by the covenant of the Messenger of Allah.

He, however, who breaks it, opposes it or changes it, will carry his crime on his head for he will have betrayed the Covenant of Allah, broken his faith, resisted His Authority and contravened the will of His Messenger: he will thus be an imposter in the eyes of Allah. For protection is obligatory in Allah's religion and the covenant confirmed. He who does not abide by this covenant will have violated his sacred obligations, and he who violates his sacred obligations is unfaithful and will be rejected by Allah and by all sincere Believers.

The reason for which the Christians have been found worthy of this covenant of protection from Allah, His Messenger, and the Believers, is because it is a right they have earned, to which every Muslim is bound, to obtain this covenant established in their favor by the men of this Religion, and which obliges every Muslim to respect it, to defend it, to conserve it, to protect it perpetually, and to live up to it.

Verily, the people who followed the ancient religions and the ancient Books expressed hostility towards Allah and His Messenger and loathed them by denying the mission of the Prophet which Allah, the Most High, has clearly proclaimed in His Book. This demonstrates the crookedness of their breasts, the wickedness of their intentions, and the hardness of their hearts. They themselves prepared the burden of the crime they bore while hiding the one which Allah wanted to impose upon them, by proclaiming it instead of hiding it, and by testifying instead of denying it.

These people acted in opposition to the obligation that was imposed upon them, did not observe it as they should have, did not follow the clearly marked paths, and agreed only to show their hostility towards Allah and His Messenger, to attack them, and to persuade people by means of imposture and false arguments that Allah could not have sent him to humanity to proclaim, to preach, and to call to Allah by His Permission, to be a shinning lamp, and to promise Paradise to those who obeyed him, and portend fire for those who disobeyed him.

They exceeded the bounds of opposition by inciting others to do what they themselves would never have dared to do: to deny his revelation, to reject his mission, and to seek, through cunning, to make him succumb to pitfalls.

They targeted the Prophet of Allah and decided to kill him. They reinforced the Party of the Polytheists of the Tribe of Quraysh as well as others in order to fight him, to dispute his doctrine, to force it back, and to contradict it.

For this reason, they deserved to be deprived of the Alliance of Allah and His Protection. Their behavior during the days of Hunayn, the battles against the Bani Qaynuqah, the tribe of Qurayzah and Nadir, is well-known. Their leaders lent support to the inhabitants of Mecca, the enemies of Allah, against the Messenger of Allah, and supported them, by means of troops and weapons, against the Prophet, out of hatred for the Believers.

The Christians, on the contrary, refused to wage war against Allah and His Messenger. Allah, as well, has declared that their tenderness towards the followers of this faith and their affection for Muslims were sincere.

Among other words of praise which Allah has bestowed upon them in His Book and His Revelations, after having been convinced of the hardness of heart of the Jews, He recognizes their inclination and affection towards the Believers: *Certainly you will find,* He says, *the most violent of people in enmity for those who believe (to be) the Jews and those who are polytheists, and you will certainly find the nearest in friendship to those who believe (to be) those who say: 'We are Christians;' this is because there are priests and monks among them and because they do not behave proudly. And when they hear what has been revealed to the messenger you will see their eyes overflowing with tears on account of the truth that they recognize; they say: 'Our Lord! We believe, so write us down with the witnesses (of truth). And why should we not believe in God and what has come down to us of the truth? And we hope to be admitted by our Lord among those who are upright and do good?"* [5:82–83]

In fact, some Christians, who were worthy of trust and who knew the divine religion, helped us to proclaim this religion and came to the help of Allah and His Messenger, by preaching to men according to His Will, and to help him accomplish his mission.

The Sayyid 'Absiso, Ibn Hijrah, Ibrahim the monk, and 'Isa the Bishop, came to see me, accompanied by forty horsemen from Najran, along with others who, like them, profess the Christian religion in the lands of Arabia, as well as foreign lands. I informed them of my mission and asked them to help reinforce it, to proclaim it, and to assist it.

And since the cause of Allah appeared evident to them, they did not turn back on their steps nor did they turn their backs. On the contrary, they drew close, remained firm, consented, assisted, confirmed, made generous promises, gave good advice, and assured me, by means of oaths and covenants, that they would support the truth which I brought and that they would repel those who refused and contradicted it.

After they rejoined their co-religionists, they did not break their covenant nor did they change their opinion. On the contrary, they observed what they had promised to me when they left me and I learned, to my great pleasure, that they proved their devotion, united to wage war against the Jews, and that they came to an understanding with the People of the Vocation, to publicize the cause of Allah, to support it, and to defend its apostles, and that they had debunked the evidence which the Jews had relied upon in order to deny and hinder my mission and my word. The Christians sought to prop up my action and waged war against those who hated my doctrine and who wanted to rebut it, alter it, repudiate it, change it, and overturn it.

All of the Arab chiefs, all of the leading Muslims, and all the People of the Vocation, from around the world sent me letters expressing the fondness of Christians towards my cause, their zeal to push back the incursions made along the fortified borderlines of their region, their determination to observe the treaty which they contracted with me when they met with me and which I granted them. For, truly, the bishops and the monks showed an unshakable loyalty in their attachment to my cause and the devotion of their persons to confirm and support the spread of my mission.

I want my mission to be spread. I ask them to join together in support of this goal against those who would deny and reject aspects of my doctrine, who would want to destroy and ruin it, by blaming them and abasing them.

They acted according to my instructions and abased them. They worked so hard to bring them to confess to the truth with submission, to respond to the call of Allah, by will or by force, allowing them to be drawn (into Islam) as conquered people. The Christians acted this way in observance of the treaties contracted between them and me, in order that they fail not to fulfill the obligations to which they had committed themselves during their meeting with me and through a spirit of zeal to support my cause and to make my mission known.

They were different in their faithful devotion from the Jews, the Qurayshites, and the other polytheists. They demonstrated no desire for worldly gain for which the Jews seek and yearn by practicing usury, looking for money, and selling the law of God for a miserable price. Woe to those who work for such a gain. Woe to those for what they write, and woe to them for what they gain by such means.

As such, the Jews and the polytheists of Quraysh along with others deserved to be treated as the enemies of Allah and His Messenger due to their treacherous plans, their enmity, the plots they devised (against me), and the fierce, intermittent war they waged in support of my enemies. Thus did they become the enemies of Allah, His Messenger, and the good Believers.

The Christians, however, behaved in the very opposite way. They respected my alliance. They recognized my rights. They fulfilled the promises that they had made during our meeting. They assisted the lieutenants that I had sent to the frontiers. They earned my concern and my affection by fulfilling the obligations that I had contracted with them spontaneously in the name of all of the Muslims spread from East to West, my protection during my life and after my passing, when Allah will make me die. So long as Islam will spread and my true mission and faith will grow, this covenant will be obligatory for all Believers and Muslims, so long as water fills the ocean floor, rain falls from the sky, the earth produces plants, the stars shine in the firmament, and the dawn appears to the traveler nor will it be permitted for anyone to break this treaty, alter it, add to it, delete from it, for such additions infringe upon my covenant and suppressions weaken my protection.

This covenant, which I wish to accord myself, binds me. Anyone from my *ummah* who, after me, breaks this Covenant of Allah, Glorified and Exalted be He, the Proof of Allah will be raised against him, and Allah is sufficient as a Witness.

What drives me to act this way is that three people (from Sayyid Ghassani) asked me for a document that would act as a safe-conduit, a treaty which recognized their fidelity to their promises towards the Muslims and to the treaty which I voluntarily concluded with them.

I wanted that the details of the alliance be ratified in the eyes of whoever follows in my path in all Arab regions, and that I and those of my vocation be bound to abstain from responsibility over those who called themselves Christians and who follow any of the different Christian sects and that this treaty be inviolable, solemn, and obligatory for all Muslims and Believers.

I therefore called the leaders of the Muslims and my main Companions and having stood surety to the demand of the Christians, I prepared this document, which Muslims, whether or not they detain power, are obliged to preserve from generation to generation, to carry out my orders in order to abide by the obligation of loyalty and respect towards those who requested this covenant of me, and to be faithful to the obligations which I have contracted, so that they not be reproached for having disobeyed my order.

The people, as well, must abstain from harming them, and abide by the covenant that I have made with them so that they can enter along with me by the gates of faithfulness, and contribute to the good that I have done to those who have earned it for having supported my mission and enraged the deniers and the skeptics.

In order that there be no proof on the part of those who are the object of this covenant against the partisans of Islam, if these were to act against the content of this document, failing to recognize the rights that they have earned from me and which they deserved to obtain.

Finally, this covenant reminds [Believers] to be benevolent; encourages good will; commands charity; deters evil; and is the path of sincerity and the way which leads to justice, Allah willing.

[*The Covenant of the Prophet Muhammad with the Christians of Najran*]

In the Name of Allah, the Most Compassionate, the Most Merciful.

This document has been provided by Muhammad ibn 'Abd Allah ibn 'Abd al-Muttalib, the Messenger of Allah to all of humanity, who was sent to preach and to warn, who has been entrusted the Trust of Allah among His Creatures so that human beings would have no pretext before Allah, after his messengers and manifestation, before this Powerful and Wise Being.

To Sayyid Ibn Harith ibn Ka'b, his co-religionists, and all those who profess the Christian religion, be they in East or West, in close regions or faraway regions, be they Arabs or foreigners, known or unknown.

This document which has been prepared constitutes an authoritative contract, an authentic certificate established on the basis of convention and justice, as well as an inviolable pact.

Whoever abides by this edict, shows his attachment to Islam, will be worthy of the best that Islam has to offer. On the contrary, any man who destroys it, breaks the pact which it contains, alters it, disobeys my commandments, will have violated the pact of Allah, transgresses his alliance, and disdained his treaty. He will merit his malediction, whether he is a sovereign authority or someone else.

I commit myself to an alliance and a pledge with them on behalf of Allah and I place them under the safeguard of His Prophets, His Elect, His Saints, the Muslims and the Believers, the first of them and the last of them. Such is my alliance and pact with them.

I proclaim, once again, the obligations that Allah imposed on the Children of Israel to obey Him, to follow His Law, and to respect His Divine Alliance. I hereby declare that my horsemen, my foot-soldiers, my armies, my resources, and my Muslim partisans will protect the Christians as far away as they may be located, whether they inhabit the lands which border my state, in any region, close or far, in times of peace as much as in times of war.

I commit myself to support them, to place their persons under my protection, as well as their churches, chapels, oratories, the monasteries of their monks, the residences of their anchorites, wherever they are found, be they in the mountains or the valleys, caves or inhabited regions, in the plains or in the desert.

I will protect their religion and their Church wherever they are found, be it on earth or at sea, in the West or in the East, with utmost vigilance on my part, the People of my House, and the Muslims as a whole.

I place them under my protection. I make a pact with them. I commit myself to protect them from any harm or damage; to exempt them for any requisitions or any onerous obligations and to protect them myself, by means of my assistants, my followers and my nation against every enemy who targets me and them.

Having authority over them, I must govern them, protecting them from all damage and ensuring that nothing happens to them that does not happen to me and my Companions who, along with me, defend the cause of Islam.

I forbid any conquerors of the faith to rule over them during their invasions or to oblige them to pay taxes unless they themselves willingly consent. Never should any Christian be subjected to tyranny or oppression in this matter.

It is not permitted to remove a bishop from his bishopric, a monk from his monastic life, or anchorite from his vocation as a hermit. Nor is it permitted to destroy any part of their churches, to take parts of their buildings to construct mosques or the homes of Muslims. Whoever does such a thing will have violated the pact of Allah, disobeyed his Messenger, and become estranged from the Divine Alliance.

It is not permitted to impose a capitation or any kind of tax on monks or bishops nor on any of those who, by devotion, wear woolen clothing or live alone in the mountains or in other regions devoid of human habitation.

Let there be a limit set of four *dirhams* per year that all other Christians who are not clerics, monks, or hermits need to pay. Otherwise, let them provide one outfit of stripped material or one embroidered turban from Yemen. This is to help Muslims and to contribute to the growth of the Public Treasury. Were cloth difficult for them, they should provide its equivalent price, if they themselves willingly consent.

May the capitation of the Christians who have income, who own land, who engage in an important amount of commerce by land or by sea, who exploit mines for precious stones, gold and silver, who are wealthy, not surpass, as a whole, twelve *dirhams* per year, so long as they are inhabitants of these countries and are residents there.

May nothing similar be demanded of travelers, who are not residents of the country or wayfarers whose country of residence is unknown.

There shall be no land tax with capitation for others than those who own land as with the other occupants of inherited properties over which the ruler has a right. They will pay taxes as other pay them without, however, the charges unjustly exceeding the measure of their means. As for the labor force which the owners spend upon to cultivate these lands, to render them fertile, and to harvest them, they are not to be taxed excessively. Let them pay in the same fashion that was imposed on other similar tributaries.

The men who belong to our alliance will not be obliged to go to war with the Muslims in order to combat their enemies, to attack them, and to seize them. Indeed, the members of the alliance will not engage in war. It is precisely to discharge them of this obligation that this pact has been granted to them as well as to assure them the help and protection on the part of the Muslims. No Christian is to be constrained to provide equipment to a single Muslims, in money, in arm or in horses, in the event of a war in which the Believers attack their enemies, unless they contribute to the cause freely. Whoever does so, and contributes spontaneously, will be the object of praise, reward, and gratitude, and his help will not be forgotten.

No Christian will be made Muslim by force: *And dispute ye not with the People of the Book, except with means better* [29:46]. They must be covered by the wing of mercy. Repel every harm that could reach them wherever they may find themselves and in any country in which they are.

If a Christian were to commit a crime or an offense, Muslims must provide him with help, defense, and protection. They should pardon his offense and encourage his victim to reconcile with him, urging him to pardon him or to receive compensation in return.

The Muslims must not abandon the Christians, neglect them, and leave them without help and assistance since I have made this pact with them on behalf of Allah to ensure that whatever good befell Muslims it would befall them as well and that whatever harm befell Muslims would befall them as well. In virtue of this pact, they have obtained inviolable rights to enjoy our protection, to be protected from any infringement of their rights, so that they will be bound to the Muslims both in good and bad fortune.

Christians must not be subjected to suffer, by abuse, on the subject of marriages which they do not desire. Muslims should not take Christian girls in marriage against the will of their parents nor should they oppress their families in the event that they refused their offers of engagement and marriage. Such marriages should not take place without their desire and agreement and without their approval and consent.

If a Muslim takes a Christian woman as a wife, he must respect her Christian beliefs. He will give her freedom to listen to her [clerical] superiors as she desires and to follow the path of her own religion. Whoever, despite this order, forces his wife to act contrary to her religion in any aspect whatsoever he will have broken the alliance of Allah and will enter into open rebellion against the pact of His Messenger and Allah will count him among the impostors.

If the Christians approach you seeking the help and assistance of the Muslims in order to repair their churches and their convents or to arrange matters pertaining to their affairs and religion, these must help and support them. However, they must not do so with the aim of receiving any reward. On the contrary, they should do so to restore that religion, out of faithfulness to the pact of the Messenger of Allah, by pure donation, and as a meritorious act before Allah and His Messenger.

In matters of war between them and their enemies, the Muslims will not employ any Christian as a messenger, scout, guide or spy or for any other duty of war. Whoever obliges one of them to do such a thing will harm the rights of Allah, will be a rebel against His Messenger, and will cast himself out of His Alliance. Nothing is permitted to a Muslim [with regard to the Christians] outside of obeying these edicts which Muhammad ibn 'Abd Allah, the Messenger of Allah, has passed in favor of the religion of the Christians.

He is also placing conditions [upon the Christians] and I demand that they promise to fulfill and satisfy them as commands their religion, among which, among other things, none of them may act as a scout, spy, either overtly or covertly, on behalf of an enemy of war, against a Muslim. None of them will shelter the enemies of the Muslims in their homes from which they could await the moment to launch an attack. May these enemies [of the Muslims] never be allowed to halt in their regions, be it in their villages, their oratories, or in any other place belonging to their co-religionists. They must not provide any support to the enemies of war of the Muslims by furnishing them with weapons, horses, men, or anything else, nor must they treat them well. They must host for three days and three nights any Muslims who halt among them, with their animals. They must offer them, wherever they are found, and wherever they are going, the same food with which they live themselves without, however, being obliged to endure other annoying or onerous burdens.

If a Muslim needs to hide in one of their homes or oratories, they must grant him hospitality, guide him help, and provide him with their food during the entire time he will be among them, making every effort to keep him concealed and to prevent the enemy from finding him, while providing for all of his needs.

Whoever contravenes or alters the ordinances of this edict will be cast out of the alliance between Allah and His Messenger.

May everyone abide by the treaties and alliances which have been contracted with the monks, and which I have contracted myself, and every other commitment that each prophet has made with his nation, to assure them safeguard and faithful protection, and to serve them as a guarantee.

This must not be violated or altered until the hour of the Resurrection, Allah-willing.

This document, by Muhammad ibn 'Abd Allah which contains the covenant he concluded with the Christians and which includes the conditions imposed upon these latter, has been witnessed by:

'Atiq ibn Abi Quhafah; 'Umar ibn al-Khattab; 'Uthman ibn 'Affan; 'Ali ibn Abi Talib; Abu Dharr; Abu al-Darda'; Abu Hurayrah; 'Abd Allah ibn Mas'ud; al-'Abbas ibn 'Abd al-Muttalib; al-Fadl ibn al-'Abbas; al-Zubayr ibn al-'Awwam; Talhah ibn 'Ubayd Allah; Sa'd ibn Mu'adh; Sa'd ibn 'Ubadah; Thumamah ibn Qays; Zayd ibn Thabit and his son 'Abd Allah; Hurqus ibn Zuhayr; Zayd ibn Arqam; Usamah ibn Zayd; 'Umar ibn Mazh'un 'Ammar; Mus'ah ibn al-Zubayr ibn Jubayr; Abu al-Ghaliyyah; 'Abd Allah ibn 'Amr ibn al-'As; Abu Hudayfah; Ka'b ibn Malik; Hasan ibn Thabit; Ja'far ibn Abi Talib

[Written by Mu'awiyyah ibn Abi Sufyan]

Text of the *Covenant of the Prophet Muhammad with the Christians of Najran*

(Corrected Arabic Original from the 9th century CE)

نُسْخَتُهُ

بِسْمِ اللهِ الرَّحْمنِ الرَّحِيمِ

هَذَا كِتَابُ أَمَانٍ مِنَ اللهِ وَرَسُولِهِ، لِلَّذِينَ أُوتُوا الْكِتَابَ مِنَ النَّصَارَى، مَنْ كَانَ مِنْهُمْ عَلَى دِينِ نَجْرَانَ، وَإِنْ عَلَى شَيْءٍ مِنْ نِحَلِ النَّصْرَانِيَةِ،

كَتَبَهُ لَهُمْ مُحَمَّدٌ بْنُ عَبْدِ اللهِ، رَسُولُ اللهِ إِلَى النَّاسِ كَافَّةً ذِمَّةً لَهُمْ مِنَ اللهِ وَرَسُولِهِ، وَعَهِدَ عَهْدَهُ إِلَى الْمُسْلِمِينَ مِنْ بَعْدِهِ عَلَيْهِمْ أَنْ يَعُوهُ وَيَعْرِفُوهُ وَيُؤْمِنُوا بِهِ وَيَحْفَظُوهُ لَهُمْ.

لَيْسَ لِأَحَدٍ مِنَ الْوُلَاةِ وَلَا لِذِي شِيعَةٍ مِنَ السُّلْطَانِ وَغَيْرِهِ نَقْضُهُ وَلَا تَعَدِّيهِ إِلَى غَيْرِهِ، وَلَا حَمْلُ مُؤُونَةٍ مِنَ الْمُؤْمِنِينَ عَلَيْهِمْ سِوَى الشُّرُوطِ الْمَشْرُوطَةِ فِي هَذَا الْكِتَابِ.

فَمَنْ حَفِظَهُ وَرَعَاهُ وَوَفَّى بِمَا فِيهِ فَهُوَ عَلَى الْعَهْدِ الْمُسْتَقِيمِ وَالْوَفَاءِ بِذِمَّةِ رَسُولِ اللهِ.

وَمَنْ نَكَثَهُ وَخَالَفَهُ إِلَى غَيْرِهِ وَبَدَّلَهُ فَعَلَيْهِ وِزْرُهُ وَقَدْ خَانَ أَمَانَ اللهِ وَنَكَثَ عَهْدَهُ وَعَصَاهُ وَخَالَفَ رَسُولَهُ وَهُوَ عِنْدَ اللهِ مِنَ الْكَاذِبِينَ، لِأَنَّ الذِّمَّةَ وَاجِبَةٌ فِي دِينِ اللهِ الْمُفْتَرَضِ وَعَهْدِهِ الْمُؤَكَّدِ. فَمَنْ لَمْ يَرْعَ خَالَفَ حَرَمَهَا وَمَنْ خَالَفَ حَرَمَهَا فَلَا أَمَانَةَ لَهُ وَبَرِئَ اللهُ مِنْهُ وَصَالِحُ الْمُؤْمِنِينَ.

فَأَمَّا السَّبَبُ الَّذِي اِسْتَوْجَبَ لِأَهْلِ النَّصْرَانِيَةِ الذِّمَّةَ مِنَ اللهِ وَرَسُولِهِ وَالْمُؤْمِنِينَ فَحَقٌ لَهُمْ لاَزِمٌ لِمَنْ كَانَ مُسْلِمًا وَعَهْدٌ مُؤَكَّدٌ لَهُمْ عَلَى أَهْلِ هَذِهِ الدَّعْوَةِ يَنْبَغِي لِلْمُسْلِمِينَ رِعَايَتُهُ وَالْمَعُونَةُ بِهِ وَحِفْظُهُ وَالْمُوَاظَبَةُ عَلَيْهِ وَالْوَفَاءُ بِهِ،

إِذْ كَانَ جَمِيعُ أَهْلِ الْمِلَلِ وَالْكُتُبِ الْعَتِيقَةِ أَهْلَ عَدَاوَةٍ لِلَّهِ وَرَسُولِهِ وَإِجْمَاعٍ بِالْبَغْضَاءِ وَالْجُحُودِ لِلصِّفَةِ الْمَنْعُوتَةِ فِي كِتَابِ اللهِ مِنْ تَوْكِيدِهِ عَلَيْهِمْ فِي حَالِ نَبِيِّهِ، وَذَلِكَ يُؤْذِنُ عَنْ غِشِّ صُدُورِهِمْ وَسُوءِ مَأْخَذِهِمْ وَقَسَاوَةِ قُلُوبِهِمْ بِأَنْ عَمِلُوا أَوْزَارَهُمْ وَحَمَلُوهَا وَكَتَمُوا مَا أَكَّدَهُ اللهُ عَلَيْهِمْ فِيهَا بِأَنْ يُظْهِرُوهُ وَلاَ يَكْتُمُوهُ وَيَعْرِفُوهُ وَلاَ يَجْحَدُوهُ.

فَعَمِلَتِ الْأُمَمُ بِخِلاَفِ مَا كَانَتِ الْحُجَّةُ بِهِ عَلَيْهِمْ، فَلَمْ يَرْعَوْهُ حَقَّ رِعَايَتِهِ وَلَمْ يَأْخُذُوا فِي ذَلِكَ بِالآثَارِ الْمَحْدُودَةِ وَأَجْمَعُوا عَلَى الْعَدَاوَةِ لِلَّهِ وَرَسُولِهِ وَالتَّأْلِيبِ عَلَيْهِمْ والراس لِلنَّاسِ بِالتَّكْذِيبِ وَالْحُجَّةِ لاَ يَكُونُ اللهُ أَرْسَلَهُ إِلَى النَّاسِ بَشِيرًا وَنَذِيرًا وَدَاعِيًا إِلَى اللهِ بِإِذْنِهِ وَسِرَاجًا مُنِيرًا يُبَشِّرُ بِالْجَنَّةِ مَنْ أَطَاعَهُ وَيُنْذِرُ بِالنَّارِ مَنْ عَصَاهُ.

فَقَدْ حَمَلُوا مِنْ ذَلِكَ أَكْثَرَ مَا زَيَّنُوا لِأَنْفُسِهِمْ مِنَ التَّكْذِيبِ، وَزَيَّنُوا لِلنَّاسِ فِعْلَهُ وَدَفْعَ رِسَالَتِهِ وَطَلَبَ الْغَائِلَةِ لَهُ وَالْأَخْذَ عَلَيْهِ بِالْمِرْصَادِ،

فَهَمُّوا بِرَسُولِ اللهِ وَأَرَادُوا قَتْلَهُ وَأَعَانُوا الْمُشْرِكِينَ مِنْ قُرَيْشٍ وَغَيْرِهِمْ عَلَى عَدَاوَتِهِ وَالْمُمَارَاةِ فِي نَقْضِهِ وَجُحُودِهِ،

وَاسْتَوْجَبُوا بِذَلِكَ الانْخِلاَعَ مِنْ عَهْدِ اللهِ وَالْخُرُوجَ مِنْ ذِمَّتِهِ، وَكَانَ مِنْ أَمْرِهِمْ فِي يَوْمِ حُنَيْنٍ وَبَنِي قَيْنُقَاعَ وَقُرَيْظَةَ وَالنَّضِيرِ وَرُؤَسَائِهِمْ وَمَا كَانَ مِنْ مُوَالاَتِهِمْ أَعْدَاءَ اللهِ مِنْ أَهْلِ مَكَّةَ عَلَى حَرْبِ رَسُولِ اللهِ وَمُظَاهَرَتِهِمْ إِيَّاهُمْ بِالْمَادَّةِ مِنَ الْقُوَّةِ وَالسِّلاَحِ إِعَانَةً عَلَى رَسُولِ اللهِ وَعَدَاوَةً لِلْمُؤْمِنِينَ.

خَلاَ مَا كَانَ مِنْ أَهْلِ النَّصْرَانِيَةِ، فَلَمَّا لَمْ يُجِيبُوا إِلَى مُحَارَبَةِ اللهِ وَرَسُولِهِ لِمَا وَصَفَهُمُ اللهُ مِنْ لِينِ قُلُوبِهِمْ لِأَهْلِ هَذِهِ الدَّعْوَةِ وَمُسَالَمَةِ صُدُورِهِمْ لِأَهْلِ الْإِسْلاَمِ،

وَكَانَ فِيمَا أَثْنَى اللهُ عَلَيْهِ فِي كِتَابِهِ وَمَا أَنْزَلَهُ مِنَ الْوَحْيِ أَنْ وَصَفَ الْيَهُودَ وَقَسَاوَةَ قُلُوبِهِمْ وَرِقَّةَ قُلُوبِ أَهْلِ النَّصْرَانِيَةِ إِلَى مَوَدَّةِ الْمُؤْمِنِينَ، فَقَالَ ﴿لَتَجِدَنَّ أَشَدَّ النَّاسِ عَدَاوَةً لِلَّذِينَ آمَنُوا الْيَهُودَ وَالَّذِينَ أَشْرَكُوا وَلَتَجِدَنَّ أَقْرَبَهُمْ مَوَدَّةً لِلَّذِينَ آمَنُوا الَّذِينَ قَالُوا إِنَّا نَصَارَى ذَلِكَ بِأَنَّ مِنْهُمْ قِسِّيسِينَ وَرُهْبَاناً وَأَنَّهُمْ لاَ يَسْتَكْبِرُونَ. وَإِذَا سَمِعُوا مَا أُنْزِلَ إِلَى الرَّسُولِ تَرَى أَعْيُنَهُمْ تَفِيضُ مِنَ الدَّمْعِ مِمَّا عَرَفُوا مِنَ الْحَقِّ يَقُولُونَ رَبَّنَا آمَنَّا فَاكْتُبْنَا مَعَ الشَّاهِدِينَ. وَمَا لَنَا لاَ نُؤْمِنُ بِاللهِ وَمَا جَاءَنَا مِنَ الْحَقِّ وَنَطْمَعُ أَنْ يُدْخِلَنَا رَبُّنَا مَعَ الْقَوْمِ الصَّالِحِينَ.﴾

وَذَلِكَ أَنَّ أُنَاساً مِنَ النَّصَارَى وَأَهْلِ الثِّقَةِ وَالْمَعْرِفَةِ بِدِينِ اللهِ أَعَانُونَا عَلَى إِظْهَارِ هَذِهِ الدَّعْوَةِ وَأَمَدُّوا اللهَ وَرَسُولَهُ فِيمَا أَحَبَّ مِنْ إِنْذَارِ النَّاسِ وَإِبْلاَغِهِمْ مَا أُرْسِلَ بِهِ.

وَأَتَانِي السَّيِّدُ عَبْدُ يَشُوعَ وَابْنُ حِجْرَةَ وَإِبْرَاهِيمُ الرَّاهِبُ وَعِيسَى الْأُسْقُفُ فِي أَرْبَعِينَ رَاكِبًا مِنْ أَهْلِ نَجْرَانَ وَمَعَهُمْ مِنْ مِلَّةِ أَصْحَابِهِمْ مِمَّنْ كَانَ عَلَى مِلَّةِ النَّصْرَانِيَةِ فِي أَقْطَارِ أَرْضِ الْعَرَبِ وَأَرْضِ الْعَجَمِ فَعَرَضْتُ أَمْرِي عَلَيْهِمْ وَدَعَوْتُهُمْ إِلَى تَقْوِيَتِهِ وَإِظْهَارِهِ وَالْمَعُونَةِ عَلَيْهِ.

وَكَانَتْ حُجَّةُ اللهِ ظَاهِرَةً عَلَيْهِمْ فَلَمْ يَنْكُصُوا عَلَى أَعْقَابِهِمْ وَلَمْ يُوَلُّوا مُدْبِرِينَ وَقَارَبُوا وَلَبِثُوا وَرَضُوهُ وَأَرْفَدُوا وَصَدَّقُوا وَأَبْدَوْا قَوْلاً جَمِيلاً وَرَأْيًا مَحْمُودًا وَأَعْطَوْنِي الْعُهُودَ وَالْمَوَاثِيقَ عَلَى تَقْوِيَةِ مَا أَتَيْتُهُمْ بِهِ وَالرَّدِّ عَلَى مَنْ أَبَى وَخَالَفَهُ.

وَانْقَلَبُوا إِلَى أَهْلِ دِينِهِمْ وَلَمْ يَنْكُثُوا عَهْدَهُمْ وَلَمْ يُبَدِّلُوا أَمْرَهُمْ بَلْ وَفَّوْا بِمَا فَارَقُونِي عَلَيْهِ وَأَتَانِي عَنْهُمْ مَا أَحْبَبْتُ مِنْ إِظْهَارِ الْجَمِيلِ وَحِلْفِهِمْ عَلَى حَرْبِهِمْ مِنَ الْيَهُودِ وَالْمُوَافَقَةِ لِمَنْ كَانَ مِنْ أَهْلِ الدَّعْوَةِ عَلَى إِظْهَارِ أَمْرِ اللهِ وَالْقِيَامِ بِحُجَّتِهِ وَالذَّبِّ عَنْ رَسُولِهِ فَكَسَّرُوا مَا احْتَجَّ بِهِ الْيَهُودُ فِي تَكْذِيبِي وَمُخَالَفَةِ أَمْرِي وَقَوْلِي. وَأَرَادَ

النَّصَارَى مِنْ تَقْوِيَةِ أَمْرِي وَنَصَبُوا لِمَنْ كَرِهَهُ وَأَرَادَ تَكْذِيبَهُ وَتَغْيِيرَهُ وَنَقْضَهُ وَتَبْدِيلَهُ وَرَدَّهُ.

وَبَثَّ الْكُتُبَ إِلَيَّ كُلُّ مَنْ كَانَ فِي أَقْطَارِ الْأَرْضِ مِنْ سُلُطَاتِ الْعَرَبِ مِنْ وُجُوهِ الْمُسْلِمِينَ وَأَهْلِ الدَّعْوَةِ بِمَا كَانَ مِنْ تَجْمِيلِ رَأْيِ النَّصَارَى لِأَمْرِي وَذَبِّهِمْ عَنْ غُزَاةِ الثُّغُورِ فِي نَوَاحِيهِمْ وَالْقِيَامِ بِمَا فَارَقُونِي عَلَيْهِ وَقَبِلْتُهُ إِذْ كَانَ الْأَسَاقِفَةُ وَالرُّهْبَانُ لِذَلِكَ مِنَّةٌ قَوِيَّةٌ فِي الْوَفَاءِ بِمَا أَعْطَوْنِي مِنْ مَوَدَّتِهِمْ وَأَنْفُسِهِمْ وَأَكَّدُوا مِنْ إِظْهَارِ أَمْرِي وَالإِعَانَةِ عَلَى مَا أَدْعُو إِلَيْهِ،

وَأُرِيدُ إِظْهَارَهُ، وَأَنْ يَجْتَمِعُوا فِي ذَلِكَ عَلَى مَنْ أَنْكَرَ أَوْ جَحَدَ شَيْئًا مِنْهُ وَأَرَادَ دَفْعَهُ وَإِنْكَارَهُ، وَأَنْ يَأْخُذُوا عَلَى يَدَيْهِ وَيَسْتَذِلُّوهُ.

فَفَعَلُوا وَاسْتَذَلُّوا وَاجْتَهَدُوا حَتَّى أَقَرَّ بِذَلِكَ مُذْعِنًا وَأَجَابَ إِلَيْهِ طَائِعًا أَوْ مُكْرَهًا وَدَخَلَ فِيهِ مُنْقَادًا أَوْ مَغْلُوبًا، مُحَامَاةً عَلَى مَا كَانَ بَيْنِي وَبَيْنَهُمْ وَاسْتِقَامَةً عَلَى مَا فَارَقُوا عَلَيْهِ وَحِرْصًا عَلَى تَقْوِيَةِ أَمْرِي وَمُظَاهَرَتِي عَلَى دَعْوَتِي.

وَخَالَفُوا فِي وَفَائِهِمْ الْيَهُودَ وَالْمُشْرِكِينَ مِنْ قُرَيْشٍ وَغَيْرِهِمْ، وَنَزَّهُوا نُفُوسَهُمْ عَنْ رِقَّةِ الْمَطَامِعِ الَّتِي كَانَتِ الْيَهُودُ تَتْبَعُهَا وَتُرِيدُهَا مِنَ الْأَكْلِ لِلرِّبَا وَطَلَبِ الرَّشَا وَبَيْعِ مَا أَخَذَهُ اللهُ عَلَيْهِمْ بِالثَّمَنِ الْقَلِيلِ، ﴿فَوَيْلٌ لَهُمْ مِمَّا كَتَبَتْ أَيْدِيهِمْ وَوَيْلٌ لَهُمْ مِمَّا يَكْسِبُونَ.﴾ فَاسْتَوْجَبَ الْيَهُودُ وَمُشْرِكُو قُرَيْشٍ وَغَيْرُهُمْ أَنْ يَكُونُوا بِذَلِكَ أَعْدَاءَ اللهِ وَرَسُولِهِ لِمَا نَوَوْهُ مِنَ الْغِشِّ وَزَيَّنُوا لِأَنْفُسِهِمْ مِنَ الْعَدَاوَةِ وَصَارُوا إِلَى حَرْبٍ عَوَانٍ مُغَالِبِينَ مَنْ عَدَانِي وَصَارُوا بِذَلِكَ أَعْدَاءَ اللهِ وَرَسُولِهِ وَصَالِحِ الْمُؤْمِنِينَ.

وَصَارَ النَّصَارَى عَلَى خِلَافِ ذَلِكَ كُلِّهِ رَغْبَةً فِي رِعَايَةِ عَهْدِي وَمَعْرِفَةِ حَقِّي وَحِفْظًا لِمَا فَارَقُونِي عَلَيْهِ وَإِعَانَةً لِمَنْ كَانَ مِنْ رُسُلِي فِي أَطْرَافِ الثُّغُورِ فَاسْتَوْجَبُوا بِذَلِكَ رَأْفَتِي وَمَوَدَّتِي وَوَفَائِي لَهُمْ بِمَا عَاهَدْتُهُمْ عَلَيْهِ وَأَعْطَيْتُهُمْ مِنْ نَفْسِي عَلَى جَمِيعِ

أَهْلِ الْإِسْلَامِ فِي شَرْقِ الْأَرْضِ وَمَغَارِبِهَا وَذِمَّتِي مَادُمْتُ وَبَعْدَ وَفَاتِي إِذَا مَا أَمَاتَنِي

اللهُ مَا نَبَتَ الْإِسْلَامُ وَمَا ظَهَرَتْ دَعْوَةُ الْحَقِّ وَالْإِيمَانِ لِأَنَّ ذَلِكَ مِنْ عَهْدِي لِلْمُؤْمِنِينَ

وَالْمُسْلِمِينَ مَا بَلَّ بَحْرٌ صُوفَةً وَمَا جَادَتِ السَّمَاءُ بِقَطْرَةٍ وَالْأَرْضُ بِنَبَاتٍ وَمَا

أَضَاءَتْ نُجُومُ السَّمَاءِ وَتَبَيَّنَ الصُّبْحُ لِلسَّارِينَ مَا لِأَحَدٍ نَقْضُهُ وَلاَ تَبْدِيلَهُ وَلاَ الزِّيَادَةَ

فِيهِ وَلاَ الِانْتِقَاصُ مِنْهُ لِأَنَّ الزِّيَادَةَ فِيهِ تُفْسِدُ عَهْدِي وَالِانْتِقَاصَ مِنْهُ يَنْتَقِصُ ذِمَّتِي،

وَيُلْزِمُنِي الْعَهْدُ بِمَا أَعْطَيْتُ مِنْ نَفْسِي وَمَنْ خَالَفَنِي مِنْ أَهْلِ مِلَّتِي وَمَنْ نَكَثَ عَهْدَ اللهِ

عَزَّ وَجَلَّ وَمِيثَاقَهُ صَارَتْ عَلَيْهِ حُجَّةُ اللهِ وَكَفَى بِاللهِ شَهِيدًا.

وَإِنَّ السَّبَبَ فِي ذَلِكَ ثُلُثُ نَفَرٍ مِنْ أَصْحَابِهِ سَأَلُوا كِتَابًا لِجَمِيعِ أَهْلِ النَّصْرَانِيَةِ أَمَانًا

مِنَ الْمُسْلِمِينَ وَعَهْدًا يُنْجِزُ لَهُمُ الْوَفَاءَ بِمَا عَاهَدُوهُمْ وَأَعْطَيْتُمُوهُ إِيَّاهُ مِنْ نَفْسِي،

وَأَحْبَبْتُ أَنْ أَسْتَتِمَّ الصَّنْعَةَ فِي الذِّمَّةِ عِنْدَ كُلِّ مَنْ كَانَتْ حَالُهُ حَالِي وَكَفَّ الْمَؤُونَةَ

عَنِّي وَعَنْ أَهْلِ دَعْوَتِي فِي أَقْطَارِ أَرْضِ الْعَرَبِ مِمَّنْ انْتَحَلَ اسْمَ النَّصْرَانِيةِ وَكَانَ

عَلَى مِلَلِهَا، وَأَنْ أَجْعَلَ ذَلِكَ عَهْدًا مَرْعِيًّا وَأَمْرًا مَعْرُوفًا يَمْتَثِلُهُ الْمُسْلِمُونَ وَيَأْخُذُ بِهِ

الْمُؤْمِنُونَ.

فَأَحْضَرْتُ رُؤَسَاءَ الْمُسْلِمِينَ وَأَفَاضِلَ أَصْحَابِي، وَأَكَّدْتُ عَلَى نَفْسِي الَّذِي أَرَادُوا

وَكَتَبْتُ لَهُمْ كِتَابًا يُحْفَظُ عِنْدَ أَعْقَابِ الْمُسْلِمِينَ مَنْ كَانَ مِنْهُمْ سُلْطَانًا أَوْ غَيْرَ سُلْطَانٍ،

إِنْفَاذَ مَا أَمَرْتُ بِهِ لِيَسْتَعْمِلَ بِمُوَافَقَةِ الْحَقِّ الْوَفَاءَ وَالتَّخَلِّي إِلَى مَنِ الْتَمَسَ عَهْدِي

وَإِنْجَازَ الذِّمَّةِ الَّتِي أَعْطَيْتُ مِنْ نَفْسِي لِئَلَّا تَكُونَ الْحُجَّةُ عَلَيْهِ مُخَالَفَةً أَمْرِي،

وَعَلَى السُّوقَةِ أَنْ لاَ يُؤْذُوهُمْ وَأَنْ يُكَمِّلُوا لَهُمُ الْعَهْدَ الَّذِي جَعَلْتُهُ لَهُمْ لِيَدْخُلُوا مَعِي فِي

أَبْوَابِ الْوَفَاءِ وَيَكُونُوا لِي أَعْوَانًا عَلَى الْخَيْرِ الَّذِي كَافَيْتُ بِهِ مَنِ اسْتَوْجَبَ ذَلِكَ مِنِّي

وَكَانَ عَوْنًا عَلَى الدَّعْوَةِ وَغَيْظًا لِأَهْلِ التَّكْذِيبِ وَالتَّشْكِيكِ،

وَلِئَلاَّ تَكُونَ الْحُجَّةُ لِأَحَدٍ مِنْ أَهْلِ الذِّمَّةِ عَلَى أَحَدٍ مِمَّنْ انْتَحَلَ مِلَّةَ الْإِسْلَامِ مُخَالَفَةً لِمَا وَضَعْتُ فِي هَذَا الْكِتَابِ وَالْوَفَاءِ لَهُمْ بِمَا اسْتَوْجَبُوا مِنِّي وَاسْتَحَقُّوا،

إِذْ كَانَ ذَلِكَ يَدْعُو إِلَى اسْتِتْمَامِ الْمَعْرُوفِ وَيَجُرُّ إِلَى مَكَارِمِ الْأَخْلَاقِ وَيَأْمُرُ بِالْحُسْنَى وَيَنْهَى عَنِ السُّوءِ، فِيهِ اِتِّبَاعُ الصِّدْقِ وَإِيثَارُ الْحَقِّ إِنْ شَاءَ اللهُ تَعَالَى.

وَكُتِبَ سِجِّلاً نُسْخَتُهُ

بِسْمِ اللهِ الرَّحْمنِ الرَّحِيمِ

هَذَا كِتَابٌ كَتَبَهُ مُحَمَّدٌ بْنُ عَبْدِ اللهِ بْنُ عَبْدِ الْمُطَّلِب رَسُولُ اللهِ إِلَى النَّاسِ كَافَّةً بَشِيرًا وَنَذِيرًا وَمُؤْتَمَنًا عَلَى وَدِيعَةِ اللهِ فِي خَلْقِهِ وَلِئَلاَّ يَكُونَ لِلنَّاسِ عَلَى اللهِ حُجَّةٌ بَعْدَ الرُّسُلِ وَالْبَيَانِ وَكَانَ عَزِيزًا حَكِيمًا.

لِلسَّيِّدِ ابْنِ الْحَارِثِ بْنِ كَعْبٍ وَلِأَهْلِ مِلَّتِهِ وَلِجَمِيعِ مَنْ يَنْتَحِلُ دَعْوَةَ النَّصْرَانِيَةِ فِي شَرْقِ الْأَرْضِ وَغَرْبِهَا، قَرِيبِهَا وَبَعِيدِهَا، فَصِيحِهَا وَأَعْجَمِهَا، مَعْرُوفِهَا وَمَجْهُولِهَا،

كِتَابًا لَهُمْ عَهْدًا مَرْعِيًّا وَسِجِلاًّ مَنْشُورًا سُنَّةً مِنْهُ وَعَدْلاً وَذِمَّةً مَحْفُوظَةً،

مَنْ رَعَاهَا كَانَ بِالْإِسْلَامِ مُتَمَسِّكًا وَلِمَا فِيهِ مِنَ الْخَيْرِ مُسْتَأْهِلاً، وَمَنْ ضَيَّعَهَا وَنَكَثَ الْعَهْدَ الَّذِي فِيهَا وَخَالَفَهُ إِلَى غَيْرِهِ وَتَعَدَّى فِيهِ مَا أَمَرْتُ كَانَ لِعَهْدِ اللهِ نَاكِثًا وَلِمِيثَاقِهِ نَاقِضًا وَبِذِمَّتِهِ مُسْتَهِينًا وَلِلَعْنَتِهِ مُسْتَوْجِبًا سُلْطَانًا كَانَ أَوْ غَيْرَهُ،

بِإِعْطَاءِ الْعَهْدِ عَلَى نَفْسِي بِمَا أَعْطَيْتُهُمْ عَهْدَ اللهِ وَمِيثَاقَهُ وَذِمَّةَ أَنْبِيَائِهِ وَأَصْفِيَائِهِ وَأَوْلِيَائِهِ مِنَ الْمُؤْمِنِينَ وَالْمُسْلِمِينَ فِي الْأَوَّلِينَ وَالْآخِرِينَ ذِمَّتِي وَمِيثَاقِي.

وَأَشَدُّ مَا أَخَذَ اللهُ عَلَى بَنِي إِسْرَائِيلَ مِنْ حَقِّ الطَّاعَةِ وَإِيثَارِ الْفَرِيضَةِ وَالْوَفَاءِ بِعَهْدِ اللهِ أَنْ أَحْفَظَ أَجَاصِيهِمْ فِي ثُغُورِي بِخَيْلِي وَرَجْلِي وَسِلَاحِي وَقُوَّتِي وَأَتْبَاعِي فِي كُلِّ نَاحِيَةٍ مِنْ نَوَاحِي الْعَدُوِّ، بَعِيدًا كَانَ أَوْ قَرِيبًا، سِلْمًا كَانَ أَوْ حَرْبًا،

وَأَنْ أَحْمِيَ جَانِبَهُمْ وَأَذِبَّ عَنْهُمْ وَعَنْ كَنَائِسِهِمْ وَبِيَعِهِمْ وَبُيُوتِ صَلَوَاتِهِمْ وَمَوَاضِعِ الرُّهْبَانِ وَمَوَاطِنِ السُّيَّاحِ حَيْثُ كَانُوا مِنْ جَبَلٍ أَوْ وَادٍ أَوْ مَغَارٍ أَوْ عُمْرَانٍ أَوْ سَهْلٍ أَوْ رَمْلٍ،

وَأَنْ أَحْرُسَ دِينَهُمْ وَمِلَّتَهُمْ أَيْنَمَا كَانُوا مِنْ بَرٍّ أَوْ بَحْرٍ شَرْقًا أَوْ غَرْبًا بِأَنْ أَحْفَظَ بِهِ نَفْسِي وَخَاصَّتِي وَأَهْلَ الإِسْلاَمِ مِنْ مِلَّتِي،

وَأَنْ أُدْخِلَهُمْ فِي ذِمَّتِي وَمِيثَاقِي وَأَمَانِي مِنْ كُلِّ أَذًى وَمَكْرُوهٍ أَوْ مؤُونَةٍ أَوْ تبِعَةٍ، وَأَنْ أَكُونَ مِنْ وَرَائِهِمْ ذَابًّا عَنْهُمْ كُلَّ عَدُوٍّ يُرِيدُنِي وَإِيَّاهُمْ بِسُوءٍ بِنَفْسِي وَأَعْوَانِي وَأَتْبَاعِي وَأَهْلِ مِلَّتِي.

وَأَنَا ذُو السَّلْطَنَةِ عَلَيْهِمْ وَلِذَلِكَ يَجِبُ عَلَيَّ رِعَايَتُهُمْ وَحِفْظُهُمْ مِنْ كُلِّ مَكْرُوهٍ وَلاَ يَصِلُ ذَلِكَ إِلَيْهِمْ حَتَّى يَصِلَ إِلَى أَصْحَابِي الذَّابِّينَ عَنْ بَيْضَةِ الإِسْلاَمِ مَعِي،

وَأَنْ أَعْزِلَ عَنْهُمُ الْأَذَى فِي الْمُؤَنِ الَّتِي يَحْمِلُهَا أَهْلُ الْجِهَادِ مِنَ الْغَارَةِ وَالْخَرَاجِ إِلاَّ مَا طَابَتْ بِهِ أَنْفُسُهُمْ وَلَيْسَ عَلَيْهِمْ إِجْبَارٌ وَلاَ إِكْرَاهٌ عَلَى شَيْءٍ مِنْ ذَلِكَ،

وَلاَ تَغْيِيرُ أُسْقُفٍ عَنْ أُسْقُفِيَتِهِ وَلاَ رَاهِبٍ عَنْ رَهْبَانِيَتِهِ وَلاَ سَائِحٍ عَنْ سِيَاحَتِهِ وَلاَ هَدْمُ بَيْتٍ مِنْ بُيُوتِ بِيَعِهِمْ وَلاَ إِدْخَالُ شَيْءٍ مِنْ بِنَائِهِمْ فِي شَيْءٍ مِنْ أَبْنِيَةِ الْمَسَاجِدِ وَلاَ مَنَازِلِ الْمُسْلِمِينَ، فَمَنْ فَعَلَ ذَلِكَ فَقَدْ نَكَثَ عَهْدَ اللهِ وَخَالَفَ رَسُولَهُ وَحَادَ عَنْ ذِمَّةِ اللهِ.

وَأَنْ لاَ يُحَمَّلُ الرُّهْبَانُ وَالْأَسَاقِفَةُ وَلاَ مَنْ تَعَبَّدَ مِنْهُمْ أَوْ لَبِسَ الصُّوفَ أَوْ تَوَحَّدَ فِي الْجِبَالِ وَالْمَوَاضِعِ الْمُعْتَزِلَةِ عَنِ الْأَمْصَارِ شَيْئًا مِنَ الْجِزْيَةِ أَوِ الْخَرَاجِ،

وَأَنْ يَقْتَصِرَ عَلَى غَيْرِهِمْ مِنَ النَّصَارَى مِمَّنْ لَيْسَ بِمُتَعَبِّدٍ وَلاَ رَاهِبٍ وَلاَ سَائِحٍ عَلَى أَرْبَعَةِ دَرَاهِمَ فِي كُلِّ سَنَةٍ أَوْ ثَوْبِ حِيرَةٍ أَوْ عَصَبِ الْيَمَنِ إِعَانَةً لِلْمُسْلِمِينَ وَقُوَّةً لِبَيْتِ الْمَالِ،

وَإِنْ لَمْ يَسْهُلِ الثَّوْبُ عَلَيْهِمْ طُلِبَ مِنْهُمْ ثَمَنُهُ وَلِيقُومَ ذَلِكَ عَلَيْهِمْ إِلاَّ بِمَا تَطِيبُ بِهِ أَنْفُسُهُمْ وَلاَ نَتَجَاوَزُ جِزْيَةَ أَصْحَابِ الْخَرَاجِ وَالْعَقَارَاتِ وَالتِّجَارَاتِ الْعَظِيمَةِ فِي الْبَحْرِ و الْأَرْضِ وَاسْتِخْرَاجِ مَعَادِنِ الْجَوْهَرِ وَالذَّهَبِ وَالْفِضَّةِ وَذَوِي الأَمْوَالِ الْفَاشِيَةِ وَالْقُوَّةِ مِمَّنْ يَنْتَحِلُ دِينَ النَّصْرَانِيَةِ أَكْثَرَ مِنْ اثْنَيْ عَشَرَ دِرْهَمًا مِنَ الْجَمْهُورِ فِي كُلِّ عَامٍ إِذَا كَانُوا لِلْمَوَاضِعِ قَاطِنِينَ وَفِيهَا مُقِيمِينَ،

وَلاَ يُطْلَبُ ذَلِكَ مِنْ عَابِرِ سَبِيلٍ لَيْسَ مِنْ قُطَّانِ الْبَلَدِ وَلاَ أَهْلِ الاجْتِيَازِ مِمَّنْ لاَ تُعْرَفُ مَوَاضِعُهُ.

وَلاَ خَرَاجَ وَلاَ جِزْيَةَ إِلاَّ عَلَى مَنْ يَكُونُ فِي يَدِهِ مِيرَاثٌ مِنْ مِيرَاثِ الْأَرْضِ مِمَّنْ يَجِبُ عَلَيْهِ فِيهِ لِلسُّلْطَانِ حَقٌّ فَيُؤَدِّي ذَلِكَ عَلَى مَا يُؤَدِّيهِ مِثْلُهُ وَلاَ يَجِبُ عَلَيْهِ وَلاَ يَحْمِلُ مِنْهُ إِلاَّ قَدْرَ طَاقَتِهِ وَقُوَّتِهِ عَلَى عَمَلِ الْأَرْضِ وَعِمَارَتِهَا وَقَبَالَةِ ثَمَرَتِهَا.

وَلاَ يُكَلَّفُ شَطَطَا وَلاَ يُتَجَاوَزُ بِهِ حَدُّ أَصْحَابِ الْخَرَاجِ مِنْ نُظَرَائِهِ وَلاَ يُكَلَّفُ أَحَدٌ مِنْ أَهْلِ الذِّمَّةِ مِنْهُمْ الْخُرُوجَ مَعَ الْمُسْلِمِينَ إِلَى عَدُوِّهِمْ لِمُلاَقَاةِ الْحُرُوبِ وَمُكْتَشِفَةِ الْأَقْرَانِ، فَإِنَّهُ لَيْسَ عَلَى أَهْلِ الذِّمَّةِ مُبَاشَرَةُ الْقِتَالِ وَإِنَّمَا أُعْطُوا الذِّمَّةَ عَلَى أَنْ لاَ يُكَلَّفُوا ذَلِكَ وَأَنْ يَكُونَ الْمُسْلِمُونَ ذُبَّابًا عَنْهُمْ وَجِوارًا مِنْ دُونِهِمْ، وَلاَ يُكْرَهُوا عَلَى تَجْهِيزِ أَحَدٍ مِنَ الْمُسْلِمِينَ إِلَى الْحَرْبِ الَّذِي يَلْقُونَ فِيهِ عَدُوَّهَمْ بِقُوَّةٍ وَسِلاَحٍ أَوْ خَيْلٍ إِلاَّ أَنْ يَتَبَرَّعُوا مِنْ تِلْقَاءِ أَنْفُسِهِمْ فِي كَوْنِ مَنْ فَعَلَ ذَلِكَ مِنْهُمْ وَتَبَرَّعَ بِهِ حُمِدَ عَلَيْهِ وَعُرِفَ لَهُ وَكُوفِئَ بِهِ.

وَلاَ يُجْبَرُ أَحَدٌ مِمَّنْ كَانَ عَلَى مِلَّةِ النَّصْرَانِيَةِ كَرْهًا عَلَى الإِسْلاَمِ وَلاَ تُجَادِلُوا أَهْلَ الْكِتَابِ إِلاَّ بِالَّتِي هِيَ أَحْسَنُ وَيُخْفَضُ لَهُمْ جَنَاحُ الرَّحْمَةِ وَيُكَفُّ عَنْهُمْ أَذَى الْمَكْرُوهِ حَيْثُ كَانُوا وَأَيْنَ كَانُوا مِنَ الْبِلاَدِ.

وَإِنْ أَجْرَمَ أَحَدٌ مِنَ النَّصَارَى أَوْ حَتَّى جَنَا جِنَايَةً فَعَلَى الْمُسْلِمِينَ نَصْرُهُ وَالْمَنْعُ وَالذَّبُّ عَنْهُ وَالْغُرْمُ عَنْ جَرِيرَتِهِ وَالدُّخُولُ فِي الصُّلْحِ بَيْنَهُ وَبَيْنَ مَنْ جَنَا عَلَيْهِ فَإِمَّا مَنَّ عَلَيْهِ أَوْ يُفَادَى بِهِ،

وَلاَ يُرْفَضُوا وَلاَ يُخْذَلُوا وَلاَ يُتْرَكُوا هَمَلاً لِأَنِّي أَعْطَيْتُهُمْ عَهْدَ اللهِ عَلَى أَنَّ لَهُمُ مَا لِلْمُسْلِمِينَ وَعَلَيْهِمْ مَا عَلَى الْمُسْلِمِينَ، وَعَلَى الْمُسْلِمِينَ مَا عَلَيْهِمْ بِالْعَهْدِ الَّذِي اِسْتَوْجَبُوا حَقَّ الذِّمَامِ وَالذَّبِّ عَنِ الْحُرْمَةِ واسْتَوْجَبُوا أَنْ يُذَبَّ عَنْهُمُ كُلُّ مَكْرُوهٍ حَتَّى يَكُونُوا لِلْمُسْلِمِينَ شُرَكَاءَ فِي مَالِهِمْ وَفِي مَا عَلَيْهِمْ.

وَلاَ يُحَمَّلُوا مِنَ النِّكَاحِ شَطَطًا لاَ يُرِيدُونَهُ وَلاَ يُكْرَهُ أَهْلُ الْبِنْتِ عَلَى تَزْوِيجِ الْمُسْلِمِينِ وَلاَ يُضَارُّوا فِي ذَلِكَ إِنْ مَنَعُوا خَاطِبًا وَأَبَوْا تَزْوِيجًا لِأَنَّ ذَلِكَ لاَ يَكُونُ إِلاَّ بِطِيبَةِ قُلُوبِهِمْ وَمُسَامَحَةِ أَهْوَائِهِمْ إِنْ أَحَبُّوهُ وَرَضُوا بِهِ.

وَإِذَا صَارَتِ النَّصْرَانِيَةُ عِنْدَ الْمُسْلِمِ فَعَلَيْهِ أَنْ يَرْضَى بِنَصْرَانِيَتِهَا وَيَتَّبِعَ هَوَاهَا فِي الاِقْتِدَاءِ بِرُؤَسَائِهَا وَالْأَخْذِ بِمَعَالِمِ دِينِهَا وَلاَ يَمْنَعُهَا ذَلِكَ، فَمَنْ خَالَفَ ذَلِكَ وَأُكْرِهَهَا عَلَى شَيْءٍ مِنْ أَمْرِ دِينِهَا فَقَدْ خَالَفَ عَهْدَ اللهِ وَعَصَى مِيثَاقَ رَسُولِهِ وَهُوَ عِنْدَ اللهِ مِنَ الْكَاذِبِينَ.

وَلَهُمْ إِنِ اِحْتَاجُوا فِي مَرَمَّةِ بِيَعِهِمْ وَصَوَامِعِهِمْ أَوْ شَيْءٍ مِنْ مَصَالِحِ أُمُورِهِمْ وَدِينِهِمْ إِلَى رِفْدِ الْمُسْلِمِينَ تَقْوِيَةً لَهُمْ عَلَى مَرَمَّتِهَا أَنْ يُرْفَدُوا عَلَى ذَلِكَ وَيُعَاوَنُوا، وَلاَ يَكُونُ ذَلِكَ دَيْنًا عَلَيْهِمْ بَلْ تَقْوِيَةً لَهُمْ عَلَى مَصَالِحِ دِينِهِمْ وَوَفَاءً بِعَهْدِ رَسُولِ اللهِ مَوْهِبَةً لَهُمْ وَمِنَّةً لِلَّهِ وَرَسُولِهِ عَلَيْهِمْ.

وَلَهُمْ أَنْ لاَ يُلْزَمَ أَحَدٌ مِنْهُمْ بِأَنْ يَكُونَ فِي الْحَرْبِ بَيْنَ الْمُسْلِمِينَ وَعَدُوِّهِمْ رَسُولاً أَوْ دَلِيلاً أَوْ عَوْنًا أَوْ مُخْبِرًا وَلاَ شَيْئًا مِمَّا يُسَاسُ بِهِ الْحَرْبُ. فَمَنْ فَعَلَ ذَلِكَ بِأَحَدٍ مِنْهُمْ

كَانَ ظَالِمًا لِلَّهِ وَلِرَسُولِهِ عَاصِيًا وَمِنْ ذِمَّتِهِ مُتَخَلِّيًا وَلاَ يَسَعُهُ فِي إِيمَانِهِ إِلاَّ الْوَفَاءُ بِهَذِهِ الشَّرَائِطِ الَّتِي شَرَطَهَا مُحَمَّدٌ بْنُ عَبْدِ اللهِ رَسُولُ اللهِ لِأَهْلِ مِلَّةِ النَّصْرَانِيَةِ،

وَاشْتَرَطَ عَلَيْهِمْ أُمُورًا يَجِبُ عَلَيْهِمْ فِي دِينِهِمْ التَّمَسُّكُ وَالْوَفَاءُ بِمَا عَاهَدَهُمْ عَلَيْهِ، مِنْهَا أَلاَّ يَكُونَ أَحَدٌ مِنْهُمْ عَيْنًا وَلاَ رَقِيبًا لِأَحَدٍ مِنْ أَهْلِ الْحَرْبِ عَلَى أَحَدٍ مِنَ الْمُسْلِمِينَ فِي سِرِّهِ وَعَلاَنِيَتِهِ، وَلاَ يَأْوِي مَنَازِلَهُمْ عَدُوٌّ لِلْمُسْلِمِينَ يُرِيدُونَ بِهِ أَخْذَ الْفُرْصَةِ وَانْتِهَازَ الْوَثْبَةِ وَلاَ يَنْزِلُوا أَوْطَانَهُمْ وَلاَ ضِيَاعَهُمْ وَلاَ فِي شَيْءٍ مِنْ مَسَاكِنِ عِبَادَاتِهِمْ وَلاَ غَيْرِهِمْ مِنْ أَهْلِ الْمِلَّةِ وَلاَ يَرْفُدُوا أَحَدًا مِنْ أَهْلِ الْحَرْبِ عَلَى الْمُسْلِمِينَ بِتَقْوِيَةٍ لَهُمْ بِسِلاَحٍ وَلاَ خَيْلٍ وَلاَ رِجَالٍ وَلاَ غَيْرِهِمْ وَلاَ يُصَانِعُوهُمْ، وَأَنْ يُقِرُّوا مَنْ نَزَلَ عَلَيْهِمْ مِنَ الْمُسْلِمِينَ ثَلاَثَةَ أَيَّامٍ بِلَيَالِيهَا فِي أَنْفُسِهِمْ وَدَوَابِّهِمْ حَيْثُ كَانُوا وَحَيْثُ مَالُوا يَبْذُلُونَ لَهُمُ الْقِرَى الَّذِي مِنْهُ يَأْكُلُونَ وَلاَ يُكَلَّفُوا سِوَى ذَلِكَ فَيَحْمِلُوا الْأَذَى عَلَيْهِمْ وَالْمَكْرُوهَ.

وَإِنْ احْتِيجَ إِلَى إِخْفَاءِ أَحَدٍ مِنَ الْمُسْلِمِينَ عِنْدَهُمْ وَعِنْدَ مَنَازِلِهِمْ وَمَوَاطِنِ عِبَادَتِهِمْ أَنْ يُؤْوُوهُمْ وَيَرْفُدُوهُمْ وَيُوَاسُوهُمْ فِيمَا يَعِيشُونَ بِهِ مَا كَانُوا مُجْتَمِعِينَ وَأَنْ يَكْتُمُوا عَلَيْهِمْ وَلاَ يُظْهِرُوا الْعَدُوَّ عَلَى عَوْرَاتِهِمْ وَلاَ يُخْلُوا شَيْئًا مِنَ الْوَاجِبِ عَلَيْهِمْ.

فَمَنْ نَكَثَ شَيْئًا مِنْ هَذِهِ الشَّرَائِطِ وَتَعَدَّاهَا إِلَى غَيْرِهَا فَقَدْ بَرِئَ مِنْ ذِمَّةِ اللهِ وَذِمَّةِ رَسُولِهِ، وَعَلَيْهِمُ الْعُهُودُ وَالْمَوَاثِيقُ الَّتِي أُخِذَتْ عَنِ الرُّهْبَانِ وَأَخْذُهَا وَمَا أَخَذَ كُلُّ نَبِيٍّ عَلَى أُمَّتِهِ مِنَ الأَمَانِ وَالْوَفَاءِ لَهُمْ وَحِفْظُهُمْ بِهِ،

وَلاَ يُنْقَضُ ذَلِكَ وَلاَ يُغَيَّرُ حَتَّى تَقُومَ السَّاعَةُ إِنْ شَاءَ اللهُ.

وَشَهِدَ هَذَا الْكِتَابَ الَّذِي كَتَبَهُ مُحَمَّدٌ بْنُ عَبْدِ اللهِ بَيْنَهُ وَبَيْنَ النَّصَارَى الَّذِينَ اشْتَرَطَ عَلَيْهِمْ وَكَتَبَ هَذَا الْعَهْدَ لَهُمْ.

عَتِيقُ بْنُ أَبِي قُحَافَةَ   عُمَرُ بْنُ الْخَطَّابِ   عُثْمَانُ بْنُ عَفَّانَ   عَلِيُّ إِبْنُ أَبِي طَالِبٍ

أَبُو ذَرٍ   أَبُو الدَّرْدَاءَ   أَبُو هُرَيْرَةَ   عَبْدُ اللهِ بْنُ مَسْعُودٍ   الْعَبَّاسُ بْنُ عَبْدِ الْمُطَّلِبِ

الْفَضْلُ بْنُ الْعَبَّاسِ   الزُّبَيْرُ بْنُ الْعَوَّامِ   طَلْحَةُ بْنُ عَبْدِ اللهِ   سَعْدُ بْنُ مُعَاذٍ
سَعْدُ بْنُ عُبَادَةَ   ثُمَامَةُ بْنُ قَيْسٍ   زَيْدُ بْنُ ثَابِتٍ وَوَلَدُهُ عَبْدُ اللهِ   حُرْقُوصُ بْنُ زُهَيْرٍ
زَيْدُ بْنُ الْأَرْقَمِ   أُسَامَةُ بْنُ زَيْدٍ   عَمَّارُ بْنُ مَظْعُونٍ   مُصْعَبُ ابْنُ جُبَيْرٍ
أَبُو الْغَالِيَةِ   عَبْدُ اللهِ بْنُ عَمْرٍو بْنُ الْعَاصِ   أَبُو حُذَيْفَةَ   كَعْبُ بْنُ مَالِكٍ
حَسَّانُ بْنُ ثَابِتٍ   جَعْفَرُ ابْنُ أَبِي طَالِبٍ
وَكَتَبَهُ مُعَاوِيَةُ بْنُ أَبِي سُفْيَانَ

And those who break the covenant of Allah after ratifying it, and sever that which Allah hath commanded should be joined, and make mischief in the earth: theirs is the curse and theirs the ill abode. (13:25)

Chapter 12

Text of the Covenant of the Prophet Muhammad with the Assyrian Christians

[*By the Prophet Muhammad*]
Translation Cited by Malech in 1910: 228–230

God has told me in a vision what to do, and I confirm His Command by giving my solemn promise to keep this agreement.

To the followers of the Islam I say: Carry out my command, protect and help the Nazarene nation in this country of ours in their own land.

Leave their places of worship in peace; help and assist their chief and their priests when in need of help, be it in the mountains, in the desert, on the sea, or at home.

Leave all their possessions alone, be it houses or other property, do not destroy anything of their belongings, the followers of Islam shall not harm or molest any of this nation, because the Nazarenes are my subjects, pay tribute to me, and will help the Moslems.

No tribute, but what is agreed upon, shall be collected from them, their church buildings shall be left as they are, they shall not be altered, their priests shall be permitted to teach and worship in their own way—the Christians have full liberty of worship in their churches and homes.

None of their churches shall be torn down, or altered into a mosque, except by the consent and free will of the Nazarenes. If anyone disobeys this command, the anger of Allah and His Prophet shall be upon him.

The tribute paid the Nazarenes shall be used to promote the teachings of Islam and shall be deposited at the treasury of *bayt al-mal*. A common man shall pay one dinar, but the merchants and people who own mines of gold and silver and are rich shall pay twelve dinars. Strangers and people who have no houses or other settled property shall not have taxes levied upon them. If a man inherits property he shall pay a settled sum to the *bayt al-mal* treasury.

The Christians are not obliged to make war on the enemies of Islam, but if an enemy attacks the Christians, the Mohammedans shall not deny their help, but give them horses and weapons, if they need them, and protect them from evils from outside and keep the peace with them. The Christians are not obliged to turn Moslems, until God's will makes them believers.

The Mohammedans shall not force Christian women to accept Islam, but if they themselves wish to embrace it, the Mohammedans shall be kind to them.

If a Christian woman is married to a Mohammedan and does not want to embrace Islam, she has liberty to worship at her own church according to her own religious belief, and her husband must not treat her unkindly on account of her religion.

If anyone disobeys this command, he disobeys God and his prophet and will be guilty of a great offense.

If the Nazarenes wish to build a church, their Mohammedan neighbors shall help them. This shall be done, because the Christians have obeyed us and have come to us and pleaded for peace and mercy.

If there be among the Christians a great and learned man the Mohammedans shall honor him and not be envious of his greatness.

If anyone is unjust and unkind to the Christians he will be guilty of disobeying the Prophet of God.

The Christians should not shelter an enemy of Islam or give him horse, weapon or any other help.

If a Mohammedan is in need the Christian shall for three days and nights be his host and shelter him from his enemies.

The Christians shall, furthermore, protect the Mohammedan women and children and not deliver them up to the enemy or expose them to view.

If the Nazarenes fail to fulfill these conditions, they have forfeited their right to protection, and the agreement is null and void.

This document shall be entrusted to the Christian chief and head of their church for safe keeping.

Signatures: *Abubakr Zadik, Omar Ben Chetab, Moavijah Ibn Abi Sofian, Abu Darda, Abuzar, Abubra, Abdula, Ibn Masud, Abdula Ibn Abas, Hamza Ibn Almulabb, Fazl Ibn Abas, Zaibar Ibn Aqam, Tilha Ibn Abdullah, Saad Ben Maaz, Saad Ibn Ebadah, Sabeh Ibn Kebis, Jazid Ibn Sabib, Abdullah Ben Jazid, Suhail Ibn Mifah, Othman Ibn Mazum, David Ibn Gijah, Abu Alalijah, Abdullah Ibn Omar Alqazi, Abu Harifah, Ibn Azir, Ibn Rabiah, Ebar Ibn Jaamir, Hashim Ibn Azijah, Hasan Ibn Zabid, Kab Ibn Kab, Ibn Malech, Jafar Ibn Abu Talib.*

[*Abu Bakr Siddiq, ʿUmar ibn Khattab, ʿUthman ibn ʿAffan, ʿAli ibn Abi Talib, peace be upon him, Muʿawiyyah ibn Abi Sufyan, Abu Dardaʾ, Abu Dharr, Abu Barah, ʿAbd Allah ibn Masʿud, ʿAbd Allah ibn ʿAbbas, Hamzah ibn al-Muttalib, Fadl ibn ʿAbbas, Zubayr ʿAwwam, Talhah ibn ʿAbd Allah, Saʿd ibn Muʿadh, Saʿd ibn ʿUbadah, Thabit ibn Qays, Yazid ibn Thabit, ʿAbd Allah ibn Yazid, Sahl ibn Sufya [or Sifa], ʿUthman ibn Matʿun, Dawud ibn Jibah, Abu al-ʿAliyyah, ʿAbd Allah ibn ʿAmr ibn al-Qadi, Abu Hudayfah, Ibn ʿAsir, Bin Rabiʿah, ʿAmmar ibn Yasir, Hashim ibn ʿAsiyyah, Hassan ibn Thabit, Kaʿb ibn Kaʿb, Kaʿb ibn Malik, Jaʿfar ibn Abi Talib*]

The peace of God be upon them all!

This agreement is written down by Moavijah Ben Sofian, according to the dictates of Mohammed, the messenger of God, in the 4th year of the Hegira in the city of Medina.

Reproduction of Original

The Covenant of the Prophet Muhammad with the Assyrian Christians

Reproduced from George David Malech's *History of the Syrian Nation and the Old Evangelical-Apostolic Church of the East* (1910)

عهدنامهٔ حضرت محمد

ترجمهٔ عهدنامهٔ حضرت رسول صلی الله علیه و آله که فیما بین امت خود و امت نصاری
منعقد فرموده است
این کتاب خطی است معروف و سجلی است مشهور و منشوری است مضبوط و عهدی است
که رعایت آن واجبست از برای جمیع ملت نصرانیه و غیره که در اطراف و اکناف
عالم از طرف مشرق عراق عرب و عجم یا از جانب مغرب بلاد عرب و عجم
ساکنند خواه دور باشند به بلاد مردم ایشان خواه نزدیک مردم یا ایشان
راه برند یا نبرند وصیت و عهدنامه ایست لازم الاطاعه و حفظ و یادداشتنی

بر همه اهل اسلام محتم است هر آنکه رعایت این امر و این وصیت را بر خود لازم شمارد به
اعتقاد او بمذهب اهل بیت راسخ خواهد بود و سزاوار ثواب خواهد بود و هر که او به تضییع
و شکست این عهد شود و مخالفت نماید و در گذرد و از آنچه امر کرده است ما و پس آنکس
سعی و جهد کرده باشد در نقض و شکست عهد و پیمان خدای عز و جل و بی ادبی کرده باشد
سزاوار لعنت گردد خواه از اولاد سلاطین باشند و خواه رعیت باشند از مومنان و مسلمانان
پس شروع کردیم در این عهدنامه بذکر و پیمان و میثاق که از جانب الله باز مأمور شدیم
و بستیم این عهد و پیمان خود را به سستی محکم که این چنین عهدی و پیمانی هیچ پیغمبری از
پیغمبران نه بسته و هیچ ملکی از ملائکه مقرب را میسر نشد که در باب طاعت و ادای
فرایض نموده باشد پس آنجائیکه امت من باشد باید که وفا بعهد معهود نماید
و نگاه داری ایشان کنند و اعانت ایشان را مومنان لازم دانند و نگاه داری ایشان
کنند در این ناحیه که باشند خواه دور خواه نزدیک در جماعت ایشان و جاهائیکه آنها
عبادت پروردگار میکنند و جاهائیکه رهبانان و کشیشان می باشند و در هر جائیکه
از امثال کوهستانها و بیابانها و عمارتها و سنگستانها و همواریها و بناهائیکه بوده باشد
نگاه داشت ایشان نماید و دین ایشان و ملک ایشان را محفوظ نمایند اگر در طرف شرق
و اگر در طرف مغرب و اگر در دریا و اگر در خشکی آنهائیکه رعایت خاطر ایشان نمایند
باید این گروه را داخل در امن و امان دانند و هر آزاری و گردهی که ایشان را
سانح باشد محافظت و سعادت ایشان را بر خود لازم شناسند چرا که ایشان

رعیت منند و اهل ذمهٔ منند و اتباع و اعوان امت منند و بدین سبب واجب است بمن رعایت
و حفظ و حراست ایشان را از هر مکروهی و آزاری و دفع کسانیکه سبب آزار ایشان باشند و باید
در مطالبات و خراج زیاده از قدر طاقت ایشان طلب ننمایند و از آنچه ایشان بآن راضی
باشند درنگذرند و ظلم و ستم با ایشان نکنند و تغییر در بناهای ایشان ننمایند و کشیشان را از عمل
خود باز ندارند و نصرانی را از دین و مذهب که دارند نگردانند و در صومعه و معبد خود بهر طریق که خواهند
عبادت کنند و در تخریب و انهدام کلیسای ایشان سعی جایز ندارند و از خانه و عمارات ایشان
داخل مساجد و بیوت اهل اسلام بعنف و تعدی و غصب ننمایند مگر برضای ایشان کسیکه
از فرموده درگذرد و خلاف معمول بجای آورد و پس عهد و میثاق را باطل کرده خود را بغضب خدا
و رسول خدا آورده باشد و از ایشان زیاده از چهار دینار جزیه طلب ننمایند یا یک جامه حریری
و آنچه خراج از ایشان حاصل میشود برای اعانت مسلمانان خواهد بود که داخل بیت المال نموده و در
مصرف معین صرف نمایند و زیاده ازین طلب ننمایند هرچه از اهل تجارت و صاحب جمعیت
خواه در بحر غواصی کنند و خواه معدن طلا و نقره یا مال بسیار بدست داشته باشد از ایشان در
زیاده از دوازده درهم طلب ننمایند بشرطیکه متوطن و قایم مقام باشند و از اهل ذمه جمعی که
راه گذر باشند و از سکنه بلاد نباشند و جای و مقام نداشته باشند خراجی و جزیه طلب ندارند
مگر آنکه در دست ایشان از میراث و غیره چیزی باشد که مال و حق امام در آن باشد پس
همان حق را از و طلب نمایند و جور و ستم را روا ندارند مگر بقدر طاقت او و طلب در عمارت دیرها
و بیوت آنها ننمایند و اهل ذمه را تکلیف نکنند که با مسلمانان اتفاق نمایند و در رفع
اعدای دین در محاربه و مقاتله که مسلمانان را با غیر ملت واقع شود و اهل ذمه را تکلیف نمایند

که با ایشان بر سر اعدا خروج نمایند و اگر ایشان را دشمنی به پیش آید مسلمانان اسب و سلاح
محاربه را از ایشان تقصیر نکنند پس بدین سبب پسندیده افعال خواهد بود و احدی از اهل ذمه را
به تعدی و جبر با سلاح یا در زند و جدل نه نمایند به هیچ وجهی و بال مرحمت و عاطفت خود را
بر ایشان گسترده و دفع ضرر اهل شر را از ایشان نمایند در هر مکانی و در هر جاییکه باشند از اهل
ذمه جنایتی نه نمایند در قتل و خطاء و غیره همه اهل در باب او لازم دانند که زیادت از
از ما فرض نشد و از طلب ندارند و طریق اصلاح را فیما بین ایشان جاری دارند و از فرموده آیه وا
به آیه فاما شاء و ابنه خیرا) در نگذرند بعد از این عهد و میثاق و اعطای جزیه و خراج احدی از ایشان را
با ایشان دست نه بست و مجلی ندارند و ایشان را نیز با اهل اسلام هیچ وجه نسبت و
نخواهد بود تا آن زمانیکه خدا بخواهد و همچنین مسلمانان به تعدی از ازواج و ابکار ایشان را بر جهت
ایشان تصرف نمی توانند کرد مگر آنکه برضا و رغبت تمام خود در حباله مسلمانان را می کردند
و به نکاح مسلمانان به عقد دوام یا غیر دوام تبیه و موقوف برضای ایشان دارند که هر که را دوست
دارند و راضی شوند مختارند و بعد از آنکه در نکاح ایشان درآیند آن زن را به نصرانیت خود واگذارند
و منع از عبادتخانه نصرانی نکنند و در دین و آیین خود بدان طریقیکه خواهد سلوک نماید و از
اقتدا به جماعت رهبانان آن زن را مانع نشوند و جبر و اکراه ننمایند در ترک و رفض آیین
و دینی که دارند پس اگر از فرموده (الکتاب) به عهدنامه تخلف نمایند مخالفت خدا کرده باشند
و از پیغمبر عاصی باشند عیاذا بالله بسبب نقض میثاق رسول خدا نزد حق سبحانه و تعالی از کلام بان
نوشته شود بر اهل ذمه را است و تعمیر مساجد و عبادتخانه ها و صومعه ها که داشته باشند
در مصلحت دین خود کرده ناحیه مسلمانان معاونت و امداد خود را در باره ایشان دریغ ندارند

و این اعانت را از قبیل ترحم و مرحمت نشمارند پس ایشان اطاعت کرده اند و امان خواسته اند
و در پناه ما آمده اند اعانت و امداد ایشان در این باب لازم است و اگر کسی از ایشان
رسول باشد و مصلح باشد سایر مسلمانان منع رسالت او ننمایند و اگر اعانت و امداد
است نمایند قبول دارند پس اگر او را منع نمایند از سلک ظالمان باشند و نزد رسول
عاصی بوده باشند و خلاف وصیت آن حضرت نموده باشند این است شرط حضرت محمد
رسول الله صلی الله علیه و آله با امت نصرانی شرطهائی که بعد از وصیت مذکور نموده و
مقرر نموده آن حضرت با ایشان در دین و آیین آن جماعت امری چند را که اهل ذمه بر ذمه
خود واجب داشته اند از آنها جایز نداشته اند و وفا بعهد بهمان نمایند یکی آنکه معاونت
مشرکین اهل حرب را آشکار و پنهان نکنند و دشمنان مسلمانان را در خانه خود راه که در
که در هیچ وقت با اهل اسلام دست یابند و اهل حرب را در خانه خود و صومعه خود
فرود نیاورند و ایشان را یاری و امداد ننمایند و سلاح تیر و شمشیر و اسب وغیره در این را
طریق نگیرند یا ندهند مال خود را امانت با ایشان نسپارند و حاجت خود را از اهل
حرب نبرند و بزبان و بدست امداد اهل حرب نکنند مگر در جایی که تقیه لازم باشد و اگر مسلمانی در
حوالی ایشان واقع شود تا سه روز و شب رعایت او را بر خود لازم دانسته زیاده لازم نیست
و آزار و اذیت اهل شر را از مسلمانان دور گردانند و اگر احتیاج افتد پنهان کردن یکی از مسلمانان
در منازل و اطاق عمارات خود او را جای دهند و مادامیکه پنهان باشند در حفظ تغافل
جایز ندارند و فرزندان و زنان مسلمانان را بدشمنان نه نمایند و نشان ندهند و از خود
نکنند پس اگر کسی از اهل ذمه در امری از این امور تهاون و تقصیر نماید و شرط و عهدها
نبوده باشد پس بیزار است از خدا و رسول خدا اما وجهی خواهم نمود باید وفا بعهد

و شرطها را بر خود لازم و واجب شمرند تا در روزی که خدای تعالی خواسته باشد و شاهد است
با این عهدنامه این خط در میان رهبانان و رؤسای ایشان از حضرت محمد المصطفی صلی الله
علیه و آله خواهد بود و شرطنامه در میان نیست والله اعلم حکم صورت امضای خلفاء و صحابهٔ کبار
که در روزنامهای خارجه نقل می شود و شهادت می دهند بر این مکتوب که محمد رسول الله برای
نصاری نوشته و با نها شرطها قرار داده و عهد بسته است

ابوبکر صدیق عمر بن خطاب عثمان ابن عفان علی ابن ابی طالب علیه السلام

معاویة ابن ابی سفیان ابو دردا ابو ذر ابو براه عبدالله ابن مسعود

عبدالله ابن عباس حمزه ابن المطلب فضل ابن عباس زبیر ابن عوام

طلحه ابن عبدالله سعد بن معاذ سعد ابن عباده ثابت ابن قیس

زید ابن ثابت عبدالله بن یزید سهل ابن سیفا عثمان

ابن مظعون داود ابن جبه ابو العالیه عبدالله ابن العمر القاضی

ابو حذیفه ابن عسیر ن ربیعه عمار ابن یاسر هاشم ابن

عصیه حسن ابن ثابت کعب ابن کعب کعب ابن مالک

جعفر ابن ابیطالب رضوان الله علیهم اجمعین نوشت این

عهدنامه را معاویه ابن ابوسفیان باملاء رسول خدا روز دوشنبه اخر ماه
چهارم از سال چهارم از هجرت نبویه علی صاحبها افضل السلام وکفی بالله شهیدا علی ما فی
هذا الکتاب

Part III

CHALLENGES

And dispute ye not with the People of the Book, except with a means better (than mere disputation), unless it be with those of them who inflict wrong (and injury); but say, "We believe in the Revelation which has come down to us and in that which came down to you; and our God and your God is One, and it is to Him we bow (in Islam)." (29:46)

Chapter 13

Examining the Authorities

The covenants of the Prophet Muhammad with numerous Christian communities provide many opportunities for research, the foremost of which is content analysis. The lists of authorities attached to them may also be of interest to scholars specializing in the history and development of *hadith* literature. These lists of witnesses can be treated in several ways. They can be treated as independent chains of authority. If this is the case, each and every covenant represents a separate line tracing back to the Prophet. They can be viewed as offshoots from a single source stem whether authentic or not. Subsequent scribes would have taken the liberty of adding or removing witnesses due to scholarly, political or religious motivations. Finally, they can be rejected outright as late additions which in no way compromise or undermine the content of the covenants. It should be recalled, however, that the covenants were largely accepted as valid by Muslim leaders and authorities for over a millennium after the Prophet's death and it was only in the 17th century that Western writers started to call them into question.

Although the content of *Covenant of the Prophet Muhammad with the Monks of Mount Sinai* is the same from scroll to scroll, the lists of witnesses vary from the standard twenty-two authorities to copies which cite thirty-seven to thirty-eight and others that quote sixteen. With rare exception, these witnesses are listed in more or less the same order. The first of these is ʻAli ibn Abi Talib (d. 661 CE), a man of impeccable integrity. The second is Abu Bakr (c. 573–634 CE) who is held in the highest esteem by Sunnis but who is criticized by Shiʻites for actions after the passing of the Prophet. The third is ʻUmar ibn al-Khattab (579–644 CE), who, for Sunnis, ranks second only to Abu Bakr in honesty but who, for Shiʻites, falls short like the former. The fourth is ʻUthman ibn ʻAffan (577–656 CE) who is criticized by both Sunni and Shiʻite authorities for his administrative shortcomings. Abu al-Darda' (d. 652 CE), who is admired by both Sunnis and Shiʻis, appears on three of the covenants but is conspicuously absent from two of them. He is followed by Abu Hurayrah (603–681 CE) who, likewise, appears only on three of the covenants. As mentioned earlier, the presence of Abu Hurayrah is problematic as he only moved to Medina during the last few years of the Prophet's life. He may, however, have been in Medina on a voyage at an earlier date. It is quite possible that the name Abu Hurayrah is a misreading of Abu Hudayfah ibn al-Yaman (d. 656 CE). It might also be Khuways ibn Hudayfah who died at Uhud. Otherwise, it could be Salim Mawla Abu Hudayfah who died fighting Musaylimah the Liar during the rule of Abu Bakr.

ʻAbd Allah ibn Masʻud (d. c. 650 CE) comes next. Respected by the Sunnis, he is held in the highest regard by Shiʻites due to his loyalty to Imam ʻAli. As for ʻAbbas ibn ʻAbd al-Muttalib (d. 652/653 CE), he was a paternal uncle to the Prophet and the forefather of the ʻAbbasid dynasty. His name, however, is missing from two covenants. Was he included at some later point to please the ʻAbbasids? Harith ibn Thabit is the next witness; however, this is probably a misreading of Hassan ibn Thabit (d. 674 CE), the Prophet's personal poet. He is followed by ʻAbd al-ʻAzim ibn Hasan, a figure I have not identified. Fadl ibn ʻAbbas, who also appears with the diminutive Fudayl, is the witness who follows. Trusted by Sunnis, he is revered by Shiʻites for refusing to pledge allegiance to Abu Bakr. He fought the Europeans and the Persians and died in Syria. As for Zubayr ibn al-ʻAwwam (594–656 CE) and Talhah ibn ʻUbaydullah (d. 656 CE), who appears as Talhah ibn ʻAbd Allah in all but one covenant, they are trusted by Sunnis but loathed by Shiʻites for joining ʻA'ishah's insurrection against Caliph ʻAli in the Battle of the Camel (656 CE).

Sa'd ibn Mu'adh (d. 627 CE) and Sa'd ibn 'Ubadah, a close Companion of Imam 'Ali who died during the rule of Abu Bakr, follow in succession. They are admired by both Sunnis and Shi'is. Thabit ibn Nafis appears on four of the covenants while Thabit ibn Qays appears on one. This latter is excoriated by Shi'ites for his role in the Saqifah, the secret meeting of tribal leaders that took place after the Prophet's death and that precipitously appointed Abu Bakr as Caliph without consulting with the community in any form or fashion. As for Thabit ibn Nafis, one wonders whether this is not really Nafi ibn al-Harith (d. 670), the name of the Prophet Muhammad's physician. The Prophet's personal scribe, Zayd ibn Thabit (c. 610–c. 660 CE) is next, found on four covenants, but absent on a fifth. The following witness caused great confusion among the scribes. His name was transcribed as Bu Hanifah ibn 'Ubayyah, Abu Hanifah ibn 'Attaba, Mou Khayetmeth, and Azur ibn Yasin. Khayetmeth could even be Khuzaymah, namely, Khuzaymah ibn Thabit (d. 657 CE), a Companion of the Prophet who sided with 'Ali, refused to pay allegiance to Abu Bakr, and died defending the Imam in the Battle of Siffin (657 CE). Perhaps this is really Khuwaylid ibn Asad who migrated to Abyssinia. It may also be Dhu Khuwaysirah al-Tamimi, the surname of Dhu al-Thudayyah Hurqus ibn Zuhayr al-Tamimi, the leader of the Kharijites. Still, considering this linguistic chaos, a positive identification is not possible at this point.

The next name is also confusing and appears as Hashim ibn 'Ubayyah, Hashim ibn 'Ubayd, Hashim ibn 'Abid, Hashim ibn Umayyah, and so forth. This could be Hashim ibn Utbah ibn Abi Waqqas, a Muslim army commander. Once again, any precise determination would be improper. The next witness is clearer: it is Mu'azzam ibn Qurayshi. The title Mu'azzam is an honorific for Companions of the Prophet and al-Qurayshi simply indicates that he belonged to the tribe of Quraysh. These are too few leads to identify this personality. The penultimate witness is 'Abd Allah ibn 'Amr ibn al-'As (d. 684 CE) who is respected by Sunnis but despised by Shi'ites for the crimes he committed in the name of the Umayyads. The final witness is 'Ammar ibn Yasir (c. 570–c. 657 CE) who appears on all but one covenant. An early Muslim convert and a deeply devoted follower of Imam 'Ali, he is respected by Sunnis and revered by Shi'ites. His name, however, also appears as 'Amir ibn Yasin on one covenant. Hence, this witness may possibly be Yasir ibn Amir al-Ansi, an early Companion of the Prophet who converted to Islam between 610 and 613 CE.

As for any scholar who may suspect that the *Covenant of the Prophet Muhammad with the Monks of Mount Sinai* is a Shi'ite forgery, its chain of authorities is inconsistent with Shi'ite standards of testamentary trustworthiness. Were a misguided Shi'ite to forge a list of witnesses, it would not feature Companions considered less than sincere. The *Covenant* would have been witnessed by Companions of the Prophet who stood staunchly on the side of the *ahl al-bayt*, the Household of the Messenger of Allah. This is, to all appearances, a Sunni chain of authority and, surprisingly, it seems to be relatively sound. If one removes Sa'd ibn Mu'adh, who died during the conflict with the Medinan Jews, and who may have been identified as Sa'd in an earlier version, thus leaving the scribe uncertain as to which one was the signatory, and treats Abu Hanifah as a corruption of Abu Hudayfah, the list of authorities would be acceptable to all Muslims. If Sa'd ibn Mu'adh was an actual witness, then this would date the *Covenant* to the first couple of years after the *hijrah*, the traditional date affixed to existing copies. If Sa'd ibn Mu'adh is excluded, and Abu Hurayrah is re-included, then the *Covenant* could only date to the last few years of the Prophet's life. While the list of witnesses on the *Covenant of the Prophet Muhammad with the Monks of Mount Sinai* is not without problems, it remains within the realm of possibility.

As for the covenants of the Prophet with the Christians of the World (1630 and 1538), Najran, and Assyria, the lists of authorities are also intriguing. The covenants in question commence with Abu Bakr. He is followed by 'Umar ibn al-Khattab on every covenant but that of 1630. 'Uthman ibn 'Affan appears next on all but the covenant with the Assyrian Christians. 'Ali ibn Abi

Talib is found on two of the covenants, with the exclusion of the covenant with the Christians of the World from 1630. Mu'awiyyah follows on every manuscript but the covenant with the Christians of the world from 1538. The presence of Mu'aw-iyyah on these covenants is always a problem as he was a latecomer to Islam who turned the Caliphate into a monarchy. He may, however, have been included as a respected dignitary among the Quraysh, even before he accepted Islam. It would have been just like him to express his admiration for the Prophet without taking the final step of pronouncing the *shahadah*, while speaking out of the other side of his mouth to certain of the Quraysh, promising them that if he ever became powerful among the Muslims he would return them to their former status. However, if the covenants were issued, or perhaps re-issued, during the last years of the Prophet's life, and the earlier signatories, some of whom had been martyred, were retained, the presence of Mu'awiyyah as both scribe and witness is perfectly sensible. However, since his name does not appear on the covenant of 1538, and suddenly appears on the covenant of 1630, where Imam 'Ali is not featured, anti-Shi'ite Sunni tampering may be at play. This does not mean that Mu'awiyyah did not appear as a scribe or witness on an earlier copy. Since he single-handedly destroyed the Caliphate of the Rightly-Guided many Muslims, both Sunni, Shi'i, and Sufi, viewed him with contempt and had plenty of reasons to suppress his name. There is no question that post-prophetic historical events have colored accounts from the life of the Prophet.

Abu Darda'(d. 652 CE) is found on all but one covenant while Abu Dharr (d. 652 CE) is found on all. A person by the name of Abu Barr is mentioned on two. This individual is most probably al-Bara' ibn Malik al-Ansari (d. 640 CE) who died at the Battle of Tustar while fighting the Persians. The brother of Anas ibn Malik (c. 612–709 or 712 CE), al-Bara' distinguished himself in the conquest of Persia. 'Abd Allah ibn Mas'ud appears on all of the covenants. Hamzah ibn al-Muttalib (568–625 CE) is found one two while Hisham ibn al-Muttalib is found on another. Considering how famous a figure the uncle of the Prophet is among Muslims, it seems odd that his name would be misrepresented. The problem with Hamzah is that he was martyred at the Battle of Uhud (625 CE). As such, the covenant would need to predate this event. The presence of persons who only embraced Islam at a later point poses evident problems. Again, if the Prophet was re-issuing these charters of protection or capitulations on a yearly basis, the earlier witnesses may have been retained out of respect.

Fadl ibn 'Abbas is found on all covenants but one. Talhah appears as the son of 'Ubaydullah on one and as the son of 'Abd Allah on the four others. Sa'd ibn Mu'adh and Sa'd ibn 'Ubadah appear in uniform fashion on all manuscripts. Sa'd ibn Mu'adh, as already mentioned, died during the early years of the *hijrah*. Thabit ibn Qays appears as such on three but as Thumamah ibn Qays on a fourth. Zayd ibn Thabit (c. 610–c. 660 CE) appears on two covenants but as Yazid ibn Thabit on others. 'Abd Allah ibn Yazid, an unidentified individual, is found on all but one. A person by the name of Sahl ibn Sufya or Sifa, Sahl ibn Bayda' or Sahl ibn Tamim is found on three covenants while absent from two others. This could be Sahl ibn Sa'd (709 CE) or perhaps Sahl ibn Bayda', a *muhajir* who died in the Battle of Badr. Sahl ibn Bayda', known as Shuhayl ibn Wahb ibn Rabi'ah, had also sought refuge in Abyssinia. The presence of this last Companion would push the date of the covenants back to a time before Islam emerged from obscurity. The name could also be Sahl ibn Hunayf (d. c. 658 CE), a partisan of 'Ali who refused to pay allegiance to Abu Bakr. Most interestingly, it might actually be Sahlah bint Suhayl ibn 'Amr. She was a female Companion of the Prophet who participated in the first *hijrah* to Abyssinia along with her husband, Abu Hudayfah ibn Utbah (d. 633 CE). She and her husband were the adopted parents of Salim Mawla Abu Hudayfah. The scribes may have masculinized her to conform to cultural norms. The name might also refer to Tamim ibn Aws al-Dari (d. 661 CE) or even to Mundhir ibn Sawa al-Tamimi, the ruler of

Bahrayn, to whom the Prophet had written. Again, it is difficult to be absolutely certain.

'Uthman ibn Ma'tun is found on three covenants and appears as 'Umar ibn Mazh'un on another. The correct identification is 'Uthman ibn Maz'un, a foster-brother of the Prophet who died during the lifetime of the Prophet. An unidentified person, by the name of Dawud ibn Jibah or David ibn Gijah is found on two covenants. Was this a Jewish or Christian witness? Or is this a corruption of Da'd bint Jahdam ibn Umayyah ibn Zarib, the mother of Suhayl ibn Bayda', who was another female Companion of the Prophet who migrated to Abyssinia. Only further research will tell. Abu al-'Aliyyah is found on three covenants along with the variant Abu al-Ghaliyyah on another. It the person is actually Abu al-'Aliyyah, he only embraced Islam during the rule of Abu Bakr. He was a follower of the Companions as opposed to a Companion of the Prophet himself. This certainly raises some questions. However, it may be that the covenant passed through the hands of the second generation of Muslims who, following tradition, included their names. This would be a primitive *isnad* from the Prophet to the Companions and then from the *ashab* to their followers, the *tabi'in*.

'Abd Allah appears as the son of 'Amr ibn al-Qadi on two covenants and as the son of 'Amr ibn al-'As (c. 592–664 CE) on three others. This could even be 'Abd Allah ibn 'Umar (c. 614–693 CE), the son of the Second Caliph, who related a large number of traditions. The identity of the next witness was difficult to discern, with some scribes providing Abu Hudayfah, others Abu Hanifah, and others Abu Ahrifah. If this is actually Abu Hanifah, the jurist, who lived from 699 to 767 CE, the entire list of authorities might be a late forgery. However, it would take a total incompetent to make such a mistake. In all likelihood, the name is Abu Hudayfah. The witness that follows is identified alternatively as Ibn 'Asir, Ibn 'Usayr, Abu al-'Azir, and Ibn 'Azir. This could be 'Asim ibn Thabit who died at the Battle of Badr (624 CE). Ibn Rabi'ah is found on only two covenants. If this is Sa'd ibn al-Rabi', he died at the Battle of Uhud (625 CE), which poses problems. It may also be al-Harith ibn Rabi' al-Ansari, a partisan of 'Ali who died during the Battle of the Camel. It could also refer to Abu al-'As ibn al-Rabi' who converted to Islam after the Conquest of Mecca. Abu Hudayfah ibn 'Utbah ibn Rabi'ah cannot be excluded nor can 'Amir ibn Rabi'ah, the Companion of the Prophet who participated in the first *hijrah* to the Kingdom of Axum and was one of the leaders of the group that returned to Medina in 615 CE. And Rabi ibn 'Amir, the ambassador of the Prophet who was sent to deliver his letter to the Persian emperor, is also a distinct possibility, not to mention 'Uthman ibn Rabi'ah ibn Uhban ibn Wahb ibn Hudhafa, who made the first migration to Abyssinia.

'Ammar ibn Yasir (c. 570–c. 657 CE) is found on two and misidentified as 'Umar ibn Yamin on a third. A person by the name of Hashim ibn 'Asiyyah is found on three but identified as Hashim ibn 'Abd Allah on a third. The individual in question appears to point to Hisham ibn al-'As who died in 635 CE at the Battle of Yarmuk. Alternatively, it could refer to Harith ibn 'Abd al-Muttalib, the uncle of the Prophet, one of his Companions, and a loyal partisan of 'Ali. Hassan ibn Thabit if found on two covenants; however, the name is rendered Hassan ibn Nabit on one and Hasan ibn Zabid on another. Ka'b ibn Ka'b is found on three while Ka'b ibn Malik is found on four. The former was a poet who died during the time of the Prophet while the latter died during the reign of Imam 'Ali.

Ja'far ibn Abi Talib (d. 629 CE) is found on four covenants. This is also an issue since he died during the early years of the *hijrah*. A person identified as Harfus ibn Zayd is found on one; as Farsus ibn Amir ibn Yazid on a second, and as Hurqus ibn Zuhayr on a third. The correct name is Hurqus ibn Zuhayr, a Companion of the Prophet who played an important role in the conquest of Persia during the rule of 'Umar ibn al-Khattab. A religious extremist and fanatic who had been reproached by the Prophet himself, Hurqus eventually became the leader of the Kharijites who waged war against the partisans of 'A'ishah and Mu'awiyyah and the partisans of 'Ali. Usamah ibn Zayd (615–673 CE) is found on two covenants as is Zayd ibn Arqam (d. 685 CE). The former was a famous commander in the Army of Muhammad. The latter was one of the earliest converts to Islam, the son of the first martyrs of Islam, who refused to acknowledge the appointment of Abu Bakr as Caliph. Abu Hurayrah is found on two and appears as Abu Harifah on a third. A person listed as ibn Zubayr or Ibn Jubayr is found on another but listed as Ibn Jamir on another. This could be Nafi ibn Jubayr. It could also be Jubayr ibn Mut'im who adopted Islam after the Treaty of Hudaybiyyah (628 CE). Suhayl ibn Mifah appears on but one covenant as does Mus'ah ibn al-Zubayr, 'Ubayd ibn Mansur, 'Abd al-'Azim, 'Abd al-'Azim ibn Husayn, Mu'azzam ibn Moshe. As for Mus'ab ibn al-Zubayr, this refers to Mus'ab ibn 'Umayr, a Companion of the Prophet killed on the day of Uhud. He had actually served as the first ambassador to Islam, representing Muhammad in Yathrib prior to the *hijrah*. As for the others, their identities are, as of yet, unclear.

As *hadith* scholars will recognize, the list of witnesses attached to the *Covenant of the Prophet Muhammad with the Monks of Mount Sinai* is more solid than the lists which follow the covenants of the Prophet with the Christians of the World (1630 and 1538), Najran, and Assyria. One unusual feature is that the names of the common witnesses on all of these covenants seem to follow the same order. This may suggest that all of the chains were produced *post factum* to meet the exigencies of Muslim scholarship. If this is the case, there may have been one source chain, which was adopted, expanded upon, and modified by other parties or each chain was put together independently. Otherwise, the similarities may point to a common origin, the Prophet Muhammad, who, for one reason or another, listed his Companions in a certain order. There also exists the possibility that all of these covenants were written during the same period of time, perhaps during the Year of Delegations (630–631 CE). He may have sat down and dictated all of these documents—to the Sinai, Egypt, the Levant, Assyria, and Armenia, among others that are no longer extant—during the same period, which would explain the presence of more or less the same witnesses. Again, since none of these covenants can be dated with certainty—we have seen, for example, that the covenant of 1630 included a date when its earlier incarnation was devoid of any such indicator—it is difficult to determine if we are dealing with documents produced during the early days of the *hijrah* or the last few years of the Prophet's life. The issue of dating is really a modern Western preoccupation. The *hadith* literature is generally undated. If the Prophet said: "I am the City of Knowledge and 'Ali is its Gate," the actual day, month, and year these words were uttered are of no import to Muslims.

The covenants of the Prophet with the Christians of the World (1630 and 1538), Najran, and Assyria contain some puzzling features. If one were to forge a list of authorities, one would expect the perpetrator to include the list of Companions most commonly known to most Muslims and to anyone familiar with Islam: Abu Bakr, 'Umar, 'Uthman, 'Ali, Salman al-Farsi, Abu Dharr, Abu Hurayrah, Bilal, Jabir ibn 'Abd Allah al-Ansari, and so forth. While those who wrote down these lists of authorities included some of the most prominent Companions of the Prophet, they also included the names of some very obscure Companions who are unknown to the Muslim masses and even unfamiliar to many scholars of Islam. Even some *'ulama'* would have to look up their names in specialized books on *'ilm al-rijal* [the science of men] or in works on Islamic history [*tarikh*] and biography [*sirah*]. In other words, this is not the type of information that is readily available to anyone. Furthermore, a significant number of these witnesses participated in the first *hijrah* to the Kingdom of Axum, including Abu Hudayfah ibn al-'Utbah, Sahlah bint Suhayl ibn 'Amr, 'Amir ibn Rabi'ah, 'Uthman ibn Ma'zun, Zubayr ibn al-'Awwam, Suhayl ibn Bayda', Ja'far ibn Abi Talib, 'Abd Allah ibn Mas'ud, and Mus'ab ibn al-'Umayr (Ibn Ishaq 146–150). The names Ibn Zubayr, Ibn Jubayr, and 'Abd al-'Azim, may point to al-Nadr ibn al-Harith ibn Khaladah who was known as Abu 'Aziz ibn 'Umayr, an early Companion of the Prophet from the Ansar.

The individual known as Ibn 'Ubayyah or Ibn Umayyah could be another early Companion and Ansar: Umayyah ibn Khalaf. It could also be 'Amr ibn Umayyah ibn al-Harith or Abu 'Ubayd ibn al-Jarrah, both of whom joined the first *hijrah*. The first, however, died in Abyssinia. It may even be 'Amr ibn Umayyah al-Damri, whom the Prophet sent to the Negus asking for the return of those who had migrated. Umaynah bint Khalaf ibn As'ad, the wife of Khalid ibn Sa'id ibn al-'As ibn Umayyah cannot be excluded. Most curious of all is the last name of 'Abd al-'Azim: al-Najashi, namely, the Abyssinian. Could this have been one of the Abyssinian converts to Islam that joined the refugees from the first *hijrah* on their return to Medina? Could this have been Arha, the son of Negus who was sent to the Prophet? The presence of early and obscure Companions of the Prophet associated with the first Emigrants and the Ansar who took them when they returned to Medina suggest that the covenants were composed at an early date. The presence of later, more prominent, Companions, point to a later date of creation. The only way that this could be reconciled is if these covenants were re-issued regularly and new witnesses were added to the old. The latter Companions simply ratified the covenants.

If the list of authorities on the *Covenant of the Prophet Muhammad with the Monks of Mount Sinai* might well survive the scholarly scrutiny of Muslim *hadith* scholars, resulting in an acceptable rating, the lists found on the other covenants would raise many red flags if examined independently. However, when viewed from comparative perspective, other possibilities present themselves and the covenants appear to be self-correcting. The scribes, it is evident, must have been dealing with a very defective script which may, in some cases, have been Kufic. For example, if one listed Abu Hanifah, which is impossible, and others wrote Abu Hudayfah, which is possible, the correct form cancels the incorrect one. We can also apply the maxim, "when in doubt, leave it out." For example, when there are two *hadith* of the same strength which contradict each other, one says that something is *halal* and the other says that it is *haram*, the permissible prevails over the prohibitive. Sometimes an identical saying has been passed down from the Prophet through various channels. Some of these are trustworthy and others are not. Simply because one of the authorities is untrustworthy or was not present at the time does not mean that the tradition is false if it was confirmed by trustworthy authorities who heard it in person. If we apply the principle of consensus, remove the witnesses upon which the scribes differed, and rely exclusively on the ones they agreed upon, we then have covenants with reasonably good references. If we assume that the covenants were renewed regularly, then we can divide the witnesses into early and late authorities. The early authorities might have witnessed the initial charter of protection and the later authorities witnessed later versions.

The study of the covenants of the Prophet Muhammad with the Christians of the World is in its infancy. The suggestions made here with regard to their lists of authorities are hypothetical, not definitive. With further study, these lists of authorities could potentially help substantiate the covenants. They could also, as others have already done, be used as a pretext to reject the covenants as a whole. However, since the list of witnesses found on the *Covenant of the Prophet Muhammad with the Monks of Mount Sinai* reportedly did not exist on the original, the same might well have been true of the remaining covenants. While these chains are of some scholarly interest, they should not deflect our attention from the content of the covenants which is by far the most important consideration. With primitive chains of authority or without them, the covenants should be judged primarily on the basis of their content. The acceptance of the covenants by early Muslim authorities, their compatibility with the *shari'ah*, and the arguments presented in this book against their being Christian forgeries—the Christians being the only likely candidates for such a role—should in themselves be sufficient evidence for their legitimacy. And if the inclusion of certain witnesses can cast doubt on the covenants, the historical record, which we have examined exhaustively, seems to fully support their antiquity and authenticity. The Qur'an itself is transmitted without chains of authority. Many books of prophetic traditions are passed down without lists of narrators and are accepted as authentic.

The absence of a fully developed *isnads* is not a sign of forgery; on the contrary, it is a sign of antiquity. Regarding the early decades after the death of the Prophet, Ibn Sirin said that "[t]hey did not ask about the *isnad*, but when civil war—*fitnah*—arose, they said 'Name to us your men'" (qtd. Azami 33). According to Azami, it was only by the end of the first century of the Islamic calendar that the science of *isnad* was fully developed (33). Still, many standards of hadith methodology can be retroactively applied to the covenants. Since they cite but a single generation of witnesses, as opposed to half a dozen to a dozen narrators as found in *isnads*, the covenants are not *mutawatir* [mass transmitted] by chain. They are, however, *mutawatir* by words and *mutawatir* according to meaning. As opposed to the overwhelming majority of *ahadith*, which are *ahad*, namely, related on the authority of a single witness, the covenants of the Prophet are *mashhur* or well-known; *marfu'*, tracing back to the Prophet; *musnad*, uninterrupted; and *muttasil*, unbroken.

Besides the question of chains, *hadith* scholars also evaluate traditions on the basis of their content. The general rules regulating the rejection of hadith have been summarized by Ibn Qayyim. Prophetic sayings containing any of the following elements are rejected:

> If the hadith contains an exaggerated statement that the Prophet could not have made...
>
> Experiment rejects it.
>
> Ridiculous kind of attribution.
>
> Contradicts a well-known *sunnah*.
>
> Attributes a statement to the Prophet which was supposed to have been made in the presence of a thousand Companions but all of them supposedly concealed it.
>
> The statement has no resemblance to other statements of the Prophet.
>
> Sounds like the saying of mystics or medical practitioners.
>
> Contradicts the clear and obvious meanings of the Qur'an.
>
> Inadequate in its style. (Azami 72)

The covenants of the Prophet contain nothing that is excessive in nature. Logic does not contradict them. They do not contain any ridiculous attributions. They do not contradict any well-known tradition. On the contrary, the content of the covenants is confirmed by the Qur'an, Sunnah, and practice of the pious successors of the Prophet. The covenants were witnessed by a large number of Companions and related by an equally large number which explains why parts of them have been found in various historical works. The content of the covenants is perfectly consistent with both the Qur'an and Sunnah. In fact, they cite, word for the word, the Qur'an, along with authentic sayings of the Prophet. The covenants do not contain any alarming mystical aspects that may suggest that they were falsified by some misguided Sufis. On the contrary, their socio-political and economic focus dismisses any such claims. The covenants of the Prophet confirm the content of the Qur'an. While some may claim that some of the covenants are inadequate in style, this study has shown that these shortcomings were due to problems of transcription and scribal error. All evidence indicates that the original copies of the covenants were in correct Classical Arabic. This content-based method of *hadith* evaluation was used by some scholars along with *isnad* criticism and by others in place of *isnad* criticism. It is therefore perfectly permissible to assess the authenticity of a text without regard to chain of narration. Furthermore, as Azami explains, the Prophet transmitted his teachings by different means: teaching, learning, and diffusion. The methods used in teaching included: 1) verbal teaching; 2) Written medium (dictation to scribes); and 3) practical demonstration (Azami 9). It goes without saying that the teaching of the Sunnah by the Prophet by means of the written method, namely, in his letters to kings, rulers, chieftains, and Muslim governors is not subject to the rules of *isnad*. In fact, since the covenants were revealed to Muhammad directly by Allah or by means of angelic intermediaries, the covenants of the Prophet Muhammad can thus be considered in a category of their own, similar, in a certain sense, to the sacred sayings or *al-ahadith al-qudsiyyah* but dealing with earthly and political as opposed to celestial and ethical matters.

As for subtle differences and variants of different kinds, they can be easily explained when one understands the methodology of quotations employed in hadith literature. These are: 1) word-for-word quotation; 2) word-for-word quotation with the addition of external material; 3) word-for word-quotation with the dropping of irrelevant material; and, finally, 4) paraphrasing (Azami 75–78). All of these modes of citation are applicable to the covenants. Some scribes may have attempted to quote the covenants integrally but made mistakes due to the difficult nature of early Arabic script. Some may have expanded upon the meaning for clarity; for example, adding more synonyms to elucidate the sense. Others, however, may have dropped material they viewed as pointless, redundant, irrelevant, obscure or incomprehensible. Finally, some may have attempted to convey the meaning through a free adaptation as opposed to a simple duplication.

Chapter 14

Tracking the Transmissions

From the point of view of *hadith* studies, this study has merely scratched the surface. Still, it provides important leads for subsequent scholars. In view of the fact that a detailed study of all the witnesses associated with the various covenants has not been completed due to issues of time and space, a few words concerning the possible modes of transmission of the covenants are in order. The possibilities, at this point, appear to be four: 1) multiple individual prophetic transmissions; 2) single source transmission with subsequent segmentation; 3) single source transmission with bifurcation; and 4) single source transmission from a Q source covenant.

The first, and most probable, mode of transmission consists of the Prophet Muhammad providing covenants of protection to all the major Christian denominations in the Middle East. The half a dozen covenants I have studied would all be unique; they would all have been dictated by the Prophet Muhammad and destined to specific communities. The similarities between these various covenants would be the result of their common origin: the Messenger of Allah. Early Islamic accounts unanimously agree that the Prophet sent and received emissaries from across the ancient world.

The second possible mode of transmission would consist of a single prophetic covenant which was appropriated by other Christian communities who claimed it as their own. Since the oldest such charter of protection is that of Najran, which dates to the 9th century CE, this may actually be the source covenant which was copied or adapted by the Christians of Egypt, the Sinai, the Levant, Persia, and Assyria. If the source covenant is in fact authentic, then the fact that it was appropriated by other communities, due to its universal directives, would not diminish the intrinsic merit of these various covenants.

The third possible mode of transmission involves a single source transmission with subsequent bifurcation. In this scenario, the Najran covenant represents the source covenant which was copied by the Christians of Egypt and the Levant. The Egyptian covenant, which traces back to Cairo, would have been copied by the monks of Mount Sinai; this *achtiname* would have been copied by the Armenian Christians of Persia which, in turn, was copied by the Assyrian Christians. Since they date from more or less the same period, it remains unclear as to whether the Sinai covenant is the precursor of the Egyptian covenant or the other way around. This approach, which establishes a chronology based on the dates of surviving copies, is full of flaws. Simply because the covenant of Najran dates to the 9th century CE and the *Covenant of the Prophet Muhammad with the Christians of the World* dates to 1630 does not necessarily mean that the former is older. There may exist or there may have existed earlier copies, perhaps all the way back to the 7th century CE.

A final source of transmission, which is influenced by Bible studies, presents the possibility of a Q source covenant. Since the *Covenant of the Prophet Muhammad with the Christians of Najran* is so elaborate in content and form, it would be unusual for it to sprout a primitive, almost bullet-point, covenant like that of the Sinai. The Najran covenant would stand on its own as a charter of protection received directly from the Prophet. The covenants from Egypt, the Levant, the Sinai, Persia, and Assyria, are all so similar in style and content that they may be variants of a single Q source covenant which has been lost.

Based on the available evidence, I remain in favor of the first hypothesis, namely, that most of the covenants are unique and not merely offgrowths from a single charter of protection. Were new discoveries to be made, I would be willing to modify this working hypothesis. However, for now, the argument that most of the covenants were prepared by the Prophet for different Christian communities and denominations is the one that agrees the most with the historical record. As for the connection between the *Covenant of the Prophet Muhammad with the Christians of the World* from 1538 and 1630, the case has yet to be closed. The covenant of 1630, which was supposedly found at Mount Carmel, may have been provided to the Christians of the Levant while the covenant of 1538 could have been intended for the Christians of Egypt. The rediscovery of further copies of the Prophet's covenants will certainly shed more light on the subject.

Chapter 15

The Covenants in Context

"Islam is a violent religion;" "There is no such thing as moderate Islam;" "Traditional Islam is radical Islam;" "Islam is a threat;" "Practicing Muslims cannot be loyal citizens;" "Mosques are Trojan horses;" "Muhammad was a terrorist;" "Islam and democracy are incompatible;" "Islam oppresses women;" and "Muslims are savages." Such are the slurs that law-abiding, family-loving, hard-working, and God-fearing Muslims have to endure regularly. Were this propaganda reversed to say: "Judaism is a violent religion;" "There is no such thing as moderate Judaism;" "Traditional Judaism is radical Zionism;" "Judaism is a threat;" "Practicing Jews cannot be loyal citizens;" "Synagogues are Trojan horses;" "Moses was a terrorist;" "Judaism and democracy are incompatible;" and "Jews are savages," the entire Western world would be up in arms. It is a sad testament that Westerners feel perfectly free to say that "Muslims are savages" but would never tolerate anyone saying that "Blacks are savages." Both the Bible and the Qu'ran condemn those who harass, abuse, slander, and defame others. So when the self-proclaimed and self-appointed guardians of "freedom" spend their time slandering that which is sacred to Muslims—and very often to Christians as well—the believers of the world turn away in disgust.

For Muslims, that Muhammad, the Messenger of Allah, was the very embodiment of goodness, is obvious; evil actions by those who claim to follow him cannot be laid to his account, but are the sole burden of those who have disobeyed him. According to a saying of the Prophet recounted in the *Sahih Bukhari*, "Whoever oppresses a Jew or a Christian I will testify against him on the Day of Judgment."

To anyone who accepts the premise that the Deity has sent sacred laws and established social orders based upon them, the Prophet Muhammad must appear as a mercy to humankind. Unlike Christianity, though similar in some ways to original prophetic Judaism, Islam was a Divinely-inspired union of the socio-political, religious, and economic orders. But there can be no doubt that many misguided Muslims have gone astray. That they have dishonored Islam and brought shame upon the Prophet is a sorrowful truth. However, despite all of their defects, and human shortcomings, Muslims have done much more good than harm. As Juan Vernet (b. 1923) readily recognizes, "Muslim tolerance undoubtedly contributed to the absorption of Arab culture, if not its religion, by the Christian faithful" (1992: 176). Whenever possible, Islam has attempted to solve problems pacifically, by means of discussion and dialogue, and not through forcible imposition of "solutions," though it was obviously necessary to establish the forms of government required to administer newly-acquired territories. Islam is the *sirat al-mustaqim*, the straight path. It is not a pacifist, non-violent movement nor is it a strictly warlike movement addicted to violence. The Islamic approach is to do the most good and avoid the most harm. Peace is sometimes the solution. In other instances, war may be the only option available. Any military option, however, must abide by the Islamic doctrine of Just War. During the early days of Islam, the Prophet Muhammad launched 68 military campaigns, in which it is estimated that there were no more than 1,000 casualties on all sides.

While it is true that the line that separates a just war and an unjust war is thin and delicate, the Prophet Muhammad never erred in this matter, and all of his battles were just. He fought solely in the defense of Truth, and never to conquer nations. His sole motivation was to secure and strengthen the Islamic State. Consequently, Islam was spread both by the word and the sword. It was spread by example and implementation, and, except in the case of those who violated the Prophet's directives, the sword was simply used to overthrow oppressors and provide all believers, Jews, Christians, and Muslims, the conditions in which they could prosper, physically, socially, and spiritually. As the Messenger of Allah is reported to have said, "I am the prophet of mercy, I am the prophet of battle" (Ibn Taymiyyah; Dhahabi; Tabari; Mawardi qtd. Hamidullah, *Muslim Conduct* 157). Facts are facts and there is no shame or contradiction in using both diplomacy and military action to further a just end (Siddiqui 25). As Nafziger (b. 1949 CE) and Walton recognize, "Muhammad proved a remarkably capable leader, tactician, and strategist" (14). In fact, as John Eric Adair's (b. 1934 CE) *Leadership of Muhammad* demonstrates, the Prophet is the very image of an ideal leader. Such a diplomatic and activist approach was also used by the First Four Caliphs who waged war when necessary but who always preferred peace when possible. 'Umar (579–644 CE), for example, prohibited his soldiers from plundering: "the conquered lands were not to be divided among the generals, but left to the existing cultivators, who paid rent to the Muslim state" (Armstrong, 2000: 31). The Second Caliph even forbade Muslims from settling in the cities: "[i]nstead, new 'garrison towns' (*ansar*) were built for them at strategic locations: Kufah in Iraq, Basrah in Iraq, Qum in Iran, and Fustat at the head of the Nile" (31). Mosques were also built in each of these Arab enclaves (31). The Qur'anic message was clear: "To you your religion and to me mine" (109:6). While they would soon come to rule an empire stretching from Western Europe to South-East Asia, the Muslims were very much a minority for centuries. As Richard Fletcher explains,

> There was an overriding practical reason for the Islamic leadership to remain on friendly terms with the Christian populations of the lands they conquered. Not only did the conquered peoples vastly outnumber their conquerors; in addition, only Christians commanded the necessary administrative expertise to make government possible. (21)

While scholars have written about the "Arab" conquests for centuries, the demographic reality on the ground was quite different. As Sir John Bagot Glubb (1897–1986 CE), known as Glubb Pasha, honestly admits,

> [F]rom 700 onwards in Syria, and later under the Abbasids in Baghdad, the 'Arab' armies consisted of regular troops, organized and trained on the lines of the professional Byzantine military forces. The personnel of these armies were not the descendants of the original Arabian conquerors, but of the indigenous peoples of these countries. (376)

Some might argue that these Muslims were like the lackeys of India without whom the English could never have remained as rulers for such a long time. However, this was not the case. These armies were composed of sincere Muslims who defended their countries since, as the Prophet is reported to have taught, the defense of one's homeland is a part of *din* or religion.

Despite the popularity of the myth of violent Islamic conquest, the archeological evidence shows an absence of destruction (Donner 248). As Donner (b. 1945) explains,

> Evidence of widespread destruction of towns, churches, and so on, is largely lacking in the archeological evidence of relatively well-explored areas, such as Syria-Palestine. Presumably, it is because most communities, which already consisted of monotheists, were not destroyed or even seriously disrupted but merely underwent a change of masters (and tax collectors). As we have seen, churches could still be—and, the archeological record shows, were—built after the 'conquest.' (115)

As Jonathan E. Brockopp has expressed, the early Islamic conquests were not missions of wanton destruction: "Tax structures, bureaucracies, and property ownership were all maintained as they were found and the populace was not forcibly converted" (10). "The millions of Christian Copts in Egypt today attest to this fact," he continues, "and Lebanon is still almost half Christian" (10).

In Iraq, even after the Arab conquest, "Christian communities continued on trajectories of growth" (Berkey 97). As Berkey explains, "The Nestorian church in particular proved vital: new monasteries were constructed in the wake of the conquests"

(97). "It comes as no surprise," then, "to find a number of Nestorian sources from the period following the Arab conquest commenting favorably upon the new rulers, recognizing them as worshipers of the one true God and describing them as respectful of churches, monasteries, the clergy, and their prerogatives within the Christian community" (97). Commenting on the conquest of Persia, the Nestorian patriarch Yeshuyab III informed a fellow cleric that "They have not attacked the Christian religion, but rather they have commended our faith, honoured our priests . . . and conferred benefits on churches and monasteries" (qtd. Armour 28–29). The Bishop of Adiabene, writing just after the Muslim invasion (650–660 CE), commented that the new masters were not nearly as bad as expected, respected the Christian clergy, protected Christian churches, and were not far removed from Christianity themselves (Fortuescue 92).

As Brandie Ratliff has shown, the early centuries of Islamic rule were periods of active growth and development for the Christian community ("The Christian communities . . . " 34). The Mesopotamian monk, John bar Penkaye (7th century CE), went so far as to claim that "there was no distinction between pagan and Christian" and that "the believer was not known from a Jew" (qtd. Hoyland, 2000: 293). The behavior of Muslims during this age of expansion differs radically from that of the Christians during the Crusades. If the purpose of the Muslim conquests was liberation, taxation, and invitation to Islam, "the point of the Crusades was not to convert Muslims but to exterminate them" (Mamdani 25). The Muslims, of course, "had a more nuanced view of the Other: they were specifically enjoined by the Qur'an to respect Jews and Christians as people to whom valid, if woefully incomplete and partly corrupted, revelations had been given" (O'Shea 15).

As skilled diplomats, the Companions made every attempt to maintain the treaties concluded by the Prophet and follow his example in establishing new ones. For example Abu Bakr (c. 573–634 CE), who was the First Caliph, renewed the Prophet's covenant with the Christians of Najran in the following terms, which are found in the *Kitab al-kharaj* by Abu Yusuf (d. 798 CE),

> In the Name of Allah, the Most Compassionate, the Most Merciful.
>
> This is the written statement of Allah's slave, Abu Bakr, the successor of Muhammad, the Prophet and Messenger of Allah.
>
> He affirms your rights as a protected neighbor: yourselves, your lands, your religious community, you wealth, retainers, and servants, those of you who are present or abroad, your bishops and monks, monasteries, and all that you own, be it great or small. You shall not be deprived of it, and shall have full control over it. (qtd. Danios)

When the people of Jerusalem surrendered to the forces of 'Umar ibn al-Khattab (579–644 CE), the Second Caliph, issued the made the following decree:

> This is the guarantee that 'Umar ibn al-Khattab makes with the inhabitants of Jerusalem. It protects their lives, their belongings, their churches, their crucifixes, and everything that pertains to their beliefs. Their churches will not be inhabited by Muslims nor will they be destroyed. Their household goods will not be taken from them. And they will not be forced to abandon their religion. (qtd. Haya 5)

After Patriarch Solonio showed 'Umar the various holy sites in the city in 659 CE, he invited him to pray in the Church of the Holy Sepulcher. The Caliph declined, saying he preferred to pray outside, as he did not want to set a precedent that Muslims could follow. In short, he wanted to ensure the protection of a Christian holy site. In order to do so, 'Umar entrusted the custody of the site to 'Ubadah ibn al-Samit, a Companion of the Prophet. His descendants, known by the family name of Nuseibeh, continue to administer the holy site to this day. 'Uthman was equally kind to the People of the Book. He was even married to a Jacobite Christian (Betts 9). Even Mu'awiyyah (602–680 CE), a person of little tolerance towards many Muslims, prayed at Golgotha, Gethsemane, and the grave of the Virgin after becoming "king" in Jerusalem in 659 (Crone and Cook 11).

The Caliph 'Abd al-'Aziz ibn Marwan (d. 705 CE) was also known for his love of the Christians (11). If 'Umar ibn al-Khattab continues to be portrayed as a person of little compassion towards the People of the Book, it is due in part to the polemical *Pact of 'Umar*, a series of discriminatory regulations attributed to the Second Caliph. The document, which takes the form of a letter written by a Christian community to the Second Caliph, and which is found in Muhammad ibn al-Walid al-Turtushi's (1059–1127 CE) *Siraj al-muluk*, is as follows,

In the Name of Allah, the Most Compassionate, the Most Merciful.

This is written to 'Umar from the Christians of such and such a city. When You [Muslims] marched against us [Christians], we asked of you protection for ourselves, our posterity, our possessions, and our co-religionists; and we made this stipulation with you, that we will not erect in our city or the suburbs any new monastery, church, cell or hermitage; that we will not repair any of such buildings that may fall into ruins, or renew those that may be situated in the Muslim quarters of the town; that we will not refuse the Muslims entry into our churches either by night or by day; that we will open the gates wide to passengers and travelers; that we will receive any Muslim traveler into our houses and give him food and lodging for three nights; that we will not harbor any spy in our churches or houses, or conceal any enemy of the Muslims.

That we will not teach our children the Qur'an; that we will not make a show of the Christian religion nor invite any one to embrace it; that we will not prevent any of our kinsmen from embracing Islam, if they so desire. That we will honor the Muslims and rise up in our assemblies when they wish to take their seats; that we will not imitate them in our dress, either in the cap, turban, sandals, or parting of the hair; that we will not make use of their expressions of speech, nor adopt their surnames; that we will not ride on saddles, or gird on swords, or take to ourselves arms or wear them, or engrave Arabic inscriptions on our rings; that we will not sell wine; that we will shave the front of our heads; that we will keep to our own style of dress, wherever we may be; that we will wear girdles round our waists.

That we will not display the cross upon our churches or display our crosses or our sacred books in the streets of the Muslims, or in their market-places; that we will not strike the clappers in our churches; that we will not recite our services in a loud voice when a Muslim is present; that we will not carry palm branches or our images in procession in the streets; that at the burial of our dead we will not chant loudly or carry lighted candles in the streets of the Muslims or their market places; that we will not take any slaves that have already been in the possession of Muslims, nor spy into their houses; and that we will not strike any Muslim.

All this we promise to observe, on behalf of ourselves and our co-religionists, and receive protection from you in exchange; and if we violate any of the conditions of this agreement, then we forfeit your protection and you are at liberty to treat us as enemies and rebels. (qtd. Marcus 13–15)

Despite its impact and application in parts of the medieval Muslim world, the *Pact* or *Covenant of 'Umar*, known as *'Ahd 'Umar*, has been dismissed as a forgery by both Sunni and Shi'ite scholars, such as Zaid Shakir (b. 1956 CE), Yusuf al-Qaradawi (b. 1956 CE), Maher Abu Munshar, and 'Abdulaziz Sachedina (Danios). It is also disputed by Western scholars such as Rabbi Abraham P. Bloch, M.J. de Goeje (1836–1909 CE), Leone Caetani (1869–1935 CE), and A.S. Tritton (1881–1973 CE) (Danios, Jewish Virtual Library). For Humphreys, "the so-called *Covenant of 'Umar*" cannot conceivably be authentic as it was only "composed in its definitive form ca. 1100" (257). Even Robert Spencer (b. 1962 CE), the anti-Islamic activist, admits that it is not authentic (Danios). Still, he does not hesitate to exploit the document to demonstrate that Muslims are intolerant. As the *Jewish Virtual Library* points out, the authenticity of the covenant is unlikely as "'Umar was known for his tolerant and friendly attitude toward the protected subjects who subordinated themselves to him." The genuine *Pact of 'Umar*, known also as the *Treaty of 'Umar*, is totally different and presents the policies of the Second Caliph in their true light. The authentic treaty, which is found in Imam al-Tabari's (838–923 CE) *Tarikh*, in the section on the history of nations and kings, is as follows,

In the Name of Allah, the Most Compassionate, the Most Merciful.

This is an assurance of peace and protection given by the servant of Allah, 'Umar, the Commander of the Believers to the people of Ilia' (Jerusalem). He gave them an assurance of protection for their lives, property, church, and crosses, as well as the sick and healthy and all its religious community.

Their churches shall not be occupied, demolished nor taken away wholly or in part. None of their crosses nor property shall be seized. They shall not be coerced in their religion nor shall any of them be injured. None of the Jews shall reside with them in Ilia'.

The people of Ilia shall pay *jizyah* tax as inhabitants of cities do. They shall evict all Romans and thieves.

He whoever gets out shall be guaranteed safety for his life and property until he reaches his safe haven. He whoever stays shall be (also) safe, in which case he shall pay as much tax as the people of Ilia' do. Should any of the people of Ilia' wish to move together with his property along with the Romans and to clear out of their churches and crosses, they shall be safe for their lives, churches and crosses, until they have reached their safe haven. He whoever chooses to stay he may do so and he shall pay as much tax as the people of Ilia' do. He whoever wishes to move along with the Roman, may do so, and whoever wishes to return back home to his kinsfolk, may do so. Nothing shall be taken from them after their crops have been harvested. To the contents of this convent here are given the Covenant of Allah, the guarantees of His Messenger, the Caliphs and the Believers, provided they (the people of Ilia') pay their due *jizyah* tax.

Witnesses hereto are:
Khalid ibn al-Walid, 'Amr ibn al-'As, 'Abd al-Rahman ibn 'Awf, Mu'awiyyah ibn Abi Sufyan
Made and executed in the year 15 AH.
(qtd. Isseroff)

As enlightened as this edict was for the epoch, it still has not escaped the criticism of scholars. However harsh it may seem to a modern mind-set, Ami Isseroff (d. 2011 CE) considers the true *Covenant of 'Umar* "to be very liberal" . . . "considering the fate of conquered populations in general at that time." After all, stresses the Jewish writer, "the intention was to protect and reassure the Christian population of Jerusalem."

Although he had defects and serious shortcomings, particularly in regard to the succession of the Prophet, namely, his denial of the claims of 'Ali, 'Umar (579–644 CE) had absorbed many good qualities thanks to his association with the religion of Islam. For example, one of the first actions he took after the conquest of Jerusalem was to remove the Christian ban which prevented Jewish people from entering the city for the purpose of worship (Akbar 77). 'Umar actually brought Jews back to the sacred city. There is thus a clear discrepancy between the historical 'Umar, who was gentle towards his subjects, and the 'Umar from the *Pact of 'Umar*, which appears to date from a later, less tolerant period, perhaps that of the Caliph 'Umar 'Abd al-'Aziz (r. 717–720), known as 'Umar II, who, according to Arab sources, was the first Muslim ruler to pass discriminatory legislation (Jewish Virtual Library). The *Pact of 'Umar*, then, would not be the *Pact of 'Umar I*, but rather, *the Pact of 'Umar II*. It may even have been attributed to 'Umar I to give it greater apparent authority.

In any event, not only is the *Pact of 'Umar* cited in Turtushi (1059–1127 CE) in clear contradiction with the *Treaty of 'Umar* cited in al-Tabari (838–923 CE), it is also the diametric opposite of the covenant that 'Umar concluded with the Christians in the year 638 CE (17 AH). This particular covenant, which came to light upon the publication of the *Chronicle of Séert*, an ancient history compiled by Nestorian Christians, reaffirms and reiterates the promises made by the Prophet to the Christians of Najran. It reads,

This edict is granted by the servant and slave of Allah, 'Umar ibn al-Khattab, the Commander of the Faithful, to the inhabitants of Selenia and Nahr Bir, to their Catholicos, their priests, and their deacons, as an inviolable commitment, a public document, and signed covenant, granting permanent protection. Whoever observes it will belong to the Muslim religion and will be worthy of that which it contains. On the contrary, any Muslim and believer, whether he be a sultan or a subject, who will betray it by breaking the covenant which it contains, who alters or transgresses its terms, he breaks the alliance of Allah and shows contempt for His Rights.

Now then, I make an alliance and a covenant with you on the behalf of Allah, and I place your lives, your wealth, your families and your people under the protection of His Prophets, His Messengers, and His Righteous Servants and Saints among the Muslims, and personally guarantee your safety and security. I have committed myself to protect you by myself and by means of my assistants, my representatives, and my companions who defend the heartland of Islam against all enemies who wish to harm me or any of you. I forbid the soldiers of faith from taking charge of you during their invasions. In all such matters, you will neither be bothered nor compelled.

None of your bishops or any of your leaders will be deposed. Your oratories and your churches will not be destroyed. No parts of your buildings will be used to construct mosques or the home of any Muslim. None of you who are traveling will be bothered in any way regardless of the country in which he finds himself. You are not obliged to go off to war with the Muslims in order to fight their enemies. No Christian will be forced to become a Muslim in accordance with what Allah revealed in His Book, which

says: 'Let there be no compulsion in religion: Truth stands out clear from Error: whoever rejects evil and believes in Allah hath grasped the most trustworthy hand-hold, that never breaks' [2:256] and 'And dispute ye not with the People of the Book, except with means better' [29:46].

My hands will protect you from any harm regardless of where you may be. Whoever acts contrary to this, will have violated the pact of Allah, his alliance, the pact of Muhammad (peace and blessings be upon him), and Allah's covenant of protection.

They deserved for us to make this pact which prevents us from spilling their blood and which obliges us to protect them from any and all injustice since they have been sincere with the Muslims, were good towards them, and granted them support. I have some conditions to impose upon them, namely, that no one act as a spy against a Muslim, be it secretly or openly, on behalf of an enemy during times of war; that no one harbor an enemy of the Muslims in his home, where he could wait for the moment to launch an attack; that no one support the enemies who are at war with the Muslims by providing them with weapons, horses, or men; that no one serve as a guide for the enemy or provide him with intelligence.

If it happens that a Muslim needs to take refuge in one of their homes, they must hide him, ensure that the enemy cannot reach him by helping him and treating him well so long as he remains with them.

They will not neglect any of these conditions which are imposed upon them. Whoever violates or alters any of these clauses will place himself outside of the protection of Allah and His Messenger, may the peace and blessings of Allah be upon him.

They must also fulfill all of the pacts and alliances they have made with the pontiffs, the monks, and the Christians who have a sacred code of law.

I affirm, once again, the alliance of Allah, and conclude, along with His Prophets in faith, the fulfillment of these promises in any place in which they are found. I myself will fulfill my obligations. It is up to the Muslims to observe this pact as well due to its prominence, and to respect it until the Day of Resurrection and until the end of the world.

Witnesses: *'Uthman ibn 'Affan, al-Mughirah ibn Shu'bah* on the 17th year of the *hijrah* (qtd. Scher 201–203 / 621–623)

As Scher (1867–1915 CE) observes, "This edict appears to be a summary of the covenant attributed to Muhammad" (303/623). Consequently, he concludes that "it is therefore probably apocryphal" (303/623). Once again, Scher's prejudices prevent him from conceiving of Muslims as tolerant, benevolent, and just rulers. He admits, however, that "with regards to the obligations imposed upon the Christians, these two false documents contain clauses from the act of capitulation of Jerusalem, which were renewed in the status of Syrian Christians redacted by the Caliph 'Umar" (303/623). In other words, he gives precedent to the apocryphal and ahistorical over the authentic and historical. It is clear to any critical mind that the notorious *Pact of 'Umar* and the *Treaty of 'Umar* were not written by the same person. If historians approve of the *Treaty of 'Umar* cited in al-Tabari's (838–923 CE) *Tarikh*, and reject the *Pact of 'Umar* cited in al-Turtushi's (1059–1127 CE) *Siraj al-Muluk* as a forgery, how can Scher give precedence to the latter over the former?

In accordance with the examples set by the Prophet (570–642 CE) and his other Companions, Khalid ibn al-Walid (592–642 CE), a Commander in the Islamic Army, promised the Christians that "they can ring their church-bells at any time, day or night, with the exception of the times when Muslims perform their daily prayers. They can also take out their crosses on their holy days" (qtd. Haya 5). The only thing that Muslims asked of Christians was respect for Muslim sensibilities, something that is sorely lacking in the Western world today where non-Muslims show the most callous of contempt towards Islamic sentiments. Not only did Christians play important roles in the administration of the Islamic State, many of them joined forced with the Muslims in times of war (Donner 176, 177, 181–183). They would even march in battle with the cross and banner of Saint Sergius (252).

While governor of Syria under the Caliph ʿUmar, Muʿawiyyah (602–680 CE) organized a navy manned, not only by Muslims, but by Monophysite Christians, Copts, and Jacobite Syrian Christian sailors, which resulted in the defeat of the Byzantine navy at the Battle of the Masts in 655 CE. Although he was ruthless and intransigent towards the Household of the Prophet, Muʿawiyyah promoted positive relations with the People of the Book. According to Betts, "Indigenous Syrian Christians, chiefly Jacobites, predominated among the literary, artistic, and scientific circles that revolved around the Damascus court of Muʿawiyyah, and some even rose to ranks of personal advisors and provincial administrators" (9). In fact, one of his closest advisors was Sarjun or Sergius, the father of John of Damascus (c. 645 or 676–749 CE). Muʿawiyyah was also surrounded by Christians in his personal life: his favorite wife was a Jacobite Christian and his son and successor, the infamous Yazid (r. 680–683 CE), "was raised in the Christian atmosphere of his mother's Christian Bedouin tribe, the Banu-Kalb" (Betts 9). As a result of all the factors, Muʿawiyyah's rule was a period of "peace and prosperity for Christians and Arabs alike" (Rhodes 105). It seems that he reserved his intolerance and oppression for the Family of the Prophet and those who supported their sublime status. Other Muslims leaders, like al-ʿAziz (r. 975–996 CE), the Fatimid Caliph, had Christian wives (Fortescue 234). According to Habib Levy, "Safavids mostly married Christian women" (265).

The tolerance that the early Muslim rulers exhibited towards the Christian majority was exemplary. As a study of Arab-Byzantine coins shows, Christian symbols were employed by Muslim rulers down to the time of ʿAbd al-Malik ibn Marwan (r. 685–705) (Foss 137). Far from proving that Islam was really a Christian heresy, the use of Christian images in coinage, including that of crosses, reflected the taste of the great majority of the population (137). As Clive Foss comments, "It seems that the new conquerors were far more tolerant of Christian symbols than often believed" (136). Consequently, "[t]hey produced coins that answered the desire and maintained the traditions of the Christian population" (136). This policy is perfectly in line with the Prophet's covenants which provided protection for Christian symbols.

While these are only a few examples of the benevolence of Islam towards the People of the Book, Islamic history provides hundreds of similar case studies. If this is how Muslims treated non-Muslims, it may be worthwhile to briefly explore how non-Muslims treated non-Muslims and how Christians sometimes treated Christians and non-Christians alike. Only then can a fair contrast be established. There have certainly been instances throughout history of Muslim persecution of Christians, for which all faithful Muslims will be moved to express their sincere regret; some of these happenings are detailed below. But the undeniable fact is that these actions took place in direct violation of the Holy Qur'an and the Sunnah of the Prophet. Likewise the excesses of the Spanish Inquisition cannot be laid at the doorstep of Jesus Christ, who said: "Love your enemies; do good to those who harm you."

Since time immemorial, it was considered the right of the conqueror to kill and enslave the conquered. In some extreme examples, such as the Aztecs, the conquered were ritually sacrificed to the gods. Those who were not slaughtered were subjected to heavy taxes, including payment in the form of slaves. Surrender was not considered an act of submission and a desire for peace; it was viewed as the culmination of cowardice. The conquered were enslaved and would forever bear the stigma of having surrendered. Those they did not slaughter, the ancient Romans enslaved in staggering numbers:

> In 177 BCE, during his campaign in Sardinia, Tiberius Sempronius Gracchus killed or enslaved 80,000 of the island's inhabitants. In 167 BCE the Roman senate granted the victorious Roman general in Greece the right to sack seventy cities on the west coast of Greece: 150,000 persons were enslaved. Although the nearly continuous wars of expansion of the last two [centuries] BCE came to an end under imperial Rome, the empire still waged wars and enslaved many of the conquered. To name a few, Augustus' wars against the Alpine tribes and in Spain, Tiberius' wars along the Rhine, Claudius' conquest of Britain, campaigns against the Parthians, Trajan's wars in Dacia, and Marcus Aurelius' campaign across the Danube all brought captives to Rome as slaves. Revolts in the provinces, though rarer, too, resulted in enslavements. In the Jewish War in 66–70 CE, to take a dramatic example, 97,000 people were enslaved. (Joshel)

Not only would the conquered lose their freedom, they would lose their identity. As Joshel explains, "men and women brought into the empire in the long-distance slave trade not only lost their natal cultures, they became outsiders, and their lack of power as bodies sold in the market likened them to the condition of defeated enemies who, like their goods, became plunder." The Huns were no better than the Romans, sacking and razing city after city, leaving nothing living in their wake. The Huns would pillage churches and monasteries, slaying monks and sexually assaulting virgins (Ferrill). Like the Chinese and the Mongols, the Huns adopted a scorched earth policy which aimed at preventing their enemies from ever rising again. Like the Romans, they would create deserts of destruction and death and call it peace. Romans and Mongols alike used to sow with salt the territory of defeated populations so that nothing could grow there again.

During the days of the Prophet, regional and world powers included Byzantium, the Sassanid Empire of the Persians, and the Visigoths in Spain, as well as the Franks in France, and the Sui Dynasty in China. As we have seen, the Byzantine Romans, who considered themselves civilized, were as savage as the so-called Barbarians hordes. In 614, during the final phase of the Sassanid-Byzantine War, the city of Jerusalem was laid siege. While the subject is contentious and continues to be the object of scholarly debate and research, the Persians are alleged to have slaughtered Christians and desecrated holy sites. While Islam preached an eye for an eye, such relatively moderate notions were unheard of in Europe where, in the year 782, Charlemagne slaughtered 4,500 Saxons in response to the death of two envoys, four counts, and approximately twenty nobles. The Sui people were equally ruthless. When their troops entered Nanjing, and the last emperor of the southern Chen surrendered, they razed the city to the ground. If the Prophet Muhammad embraced Jews and Christians as part of the Muslim Community, the Arian Visigoths in Spain were notoriously intolerant towards Jewish people, adopting an official church-state policy of systematic anti-Semitism. Circumcision, the observance of the Sabbath, and other Jewish rituals were outlawed. Jews were converted and baptized by force. They were subjected to exorbitant taxes. Their properties were confiscated. They were publicly flogged and even executed simply for being Jewish.

Under Islamic rule, the Jews and Christians of al-Andalus generally experienced a golden age of peace and prosperity over the course of nearly eight centuries. Although the Muslim rulers of Islamic Spain were intolerant towards those who were not Maliki Sunnis, they were extremely tolerant and benevolent towards Jews and Christians. They followed the Qur'anic commandment which proclaimed that:

> those who believe, those who follow Jewish scriptures, the Christians, the Sabians, and any who believe in God and the Last Day, and do good, all shall have their reward with their Lord and they will not come to fear or grief. (5:72)

Despite having defeated the Jews and Christians, ʿAbd al-Rahman III (r. 912–961 CE) allowed them to preserve their religion, language, and culture. In fact, it was under Muslim rule that the Hebrew language experienced a revival. In the rest of Europe, however, Jewish people were persecuted and deprived of some of the most elementary of rights. The Christians of al-Andalus also flourished under Muslim rule. Jews, Christians, and Muslims all worked closely together to translate books of all sorts, from Greco-Roman classics to scientific tracts, thus giving a powerful impetus to the European Renaissance. Seeing that Muslim rule in al-Andalus was far superior to the Christian rule in the rest of Europe, many Christian communities sided with the Muslims, and fought side to side with their believing brothers against the less civilized Christians from the north. This "Golden Age" has been studied in many works such as *The Ornament of the World: How Muslims, Jews, and Christians Created a Culture of Tolerance in Medieval Spain by* María Rosa Menoscal and *Convivencia: Jews, Muslims, and Christians in Medieval Spain* by Vivian B. Mann, Thomas F. Glick, and Jerrilynn Dodds, among many other notable works on the subject.

The fall of the Emirate of Granada to Catholic forces in 1492 marks two notable points which should serve as lessons. First, we need to understand why the Emirate came to an end after more than seven hundred years of real and effective rule under which the followers of the three revealed religions, namely, Jews, Christians, and Muslims, co-existed harmoniously. Secondly, we must compare the manner in which Muslims treated non-Muslims under Islamic rule to the treatment that Muslims received at the hands of Christians after they were overthrown. Why did the Emirate of Granada fall? Essentially, this occurred for the same reasons that the Ottoman Empire collapsed, for the same reasons that the Huns razed Baghdad, and for the same reasons that the civilization that brought light to the entire world entered a period of darkness that has lasted practically until the present day. And what were these reasons? They were essentially two-fold: 1) the failure to fulfill God's commands; and 2) ignoring, consciously or not, the orders of the Prophet Muhammad regarding his succession, the retribution for which worked itself out historically in the following way: the Umayyad Caliphate, built on the blood of ʿAli and the Family of the Prophet, ultimately became so hated as an institution that it was overthrown by the ʿAbbasids. The last Caliph of the Umayyads, ʿAbd al-Rahman I, escaped to found the Emirate of Córdoba in 756 CE, which was declared a Caliphate in 929 CE, under his successor, ʿAbd al-Rahman III, in response to a threat from the Fatimids, thus fracturing *dar al-islam*. And while the Caliphs of al-Andalus, as we have seen, administered a great spiritual civilization, their separation from the ʿAbbasid and Fatimid Caliphates of North Africa and the Middle East left them isolated, and consequently at the mercy of the Catholic *reconquista*.

In light of these two terrible transgressions, the power or virtue of the forces that defeated the Muslims should not be regarded as the primary causes of this defeat. Whether the non-Muslims were good, bad, or better than the Muslims, the central reason for the collapse of Islamic civilization is that the Muslims of al-Andalus, and elsewhere, prepared the path to their own destruction, humiliation, and disaster, by failing to fulfill the commands of the Qur'an and the Prophet Muhammad. How, then, were Muslims treated after the fall of the Emirate of Granada, the last stronghold of Muslim Spain? The treatment they received was truly shameful, independent of the fact that they were led to subjugation and slaughter as a direct result of the misguided policies of Muslim leaders at home and abroad. Rather than defend the besieged Muslims from al-Andalus, Sultan Bayazid II (r. 1481–1512 CE) committed his forces to Cyprus. Had he not heard the words of the Prophet in which he described the Muslim *ummah* as one body and that if one part hurt then the entire body suffered? While Bayazid II can be commended for sending his navy to al-Andalus in 1492 CE to evacuate the Jews from Spain and bring them to the Ottoman Empire, could he not have combated the Christians in defense of both Jews and Muslims? Consider, then, what happened to the abandoned Muslims in al-Andalus, abandoned like the Muslims of Palestine, Bosnia, Chechnya, Bangsamoro, Burma and beyond. . . .

Over seven hundred years of solidarity between the followers of Abraham—Jews, Christians, and Muslims—came to an abrupt end when the Emirate of Granada finally fell to Christian forces in 1492 CE. Of the 500,000 original inhabitants of Granada, 100,000 died fighting the Christian Crusaders or were enslaved, 200,000 fled (mostly to North Africa), and 200,000 stayed behind. Although the *Treaty of Granada*, signed and ratified between the king of Granada, Abu 'Abd Allah Muhammad Boabdil (1459–1533 CE) and the Catholic monarchs, Fernando (1452–1516 CE) and Isabela (1451–1504 CE), granted the Muslim population religious, cultural, and linguistic freedom, the treaty was soon broken by the Christian rulers on the pretext that covenants with "infidels" were not binding.

The terms of surrender negotiated by the Muslims in the Capitulation of 1492 CE contained sixty-seven articles, including the following:

> That their laws should be preserved as they were before, and that no-one should judge them except by those same laws; that their mosques, and the religious endowments appertaining to them, should remain as they were in the times of Islam; that no Christian should enter the house of a Muslim, or insult him in any way; that all Muslim captives taken during the siege of Granada, from whatever part of the country they might have come, but especially the nobles and chiefs mentioned in the agreement, should be liberated; that such Muslim captives as might have escaped from their Christians masters, and taken refuge in Granada, should not be surrendered; but that the Sultan should be bound to pay the price of such captives to their owners; that all those who might choose to cross over to Africa should be allowed to take their departure within a certain time, and be conveyed thither in the king's ships, and without any pecuniary tax being imposed on them, beyond the mere charge for passage; that after the expiration of that time no Muslim should be hindered from departing, provided he paid, in addition to the price of his passage, the tithe of whatever property he might carry along with him; that the Christians who had embraced Islam should not be compelled to relinquish it and adopt their former creed; that no Christian should be allowed to peep over the wall, or into the house of a Muslim or enter a mosque; that no badge or distinctive mark be put upon them, as was done with the Jews and *Mudéjares* [Spanish Muslims who refused to convert to Christianity]; that no muezzin should be interrupted in the act of calling the people to prayer, and no Muslim molested either in the performance of his daily devotions or in the observance of his fast, or in any other religious ceremony; but that if a Christian should be found laughing at them he should be punished for it. (al-Maqqari 389)

As Wiegers explains:

> According to the capitulations drawn up by Ferdinand and Isabella when the Christian troops entered Granada, the new subjects of the Crown were promised that they would be allowed to preserve their mosques and religious institutions, to retain the use of their language and to continue to abide by their own laws and customs. But within the space of seven years these generous terms had been broken. (10)

After the Catholic clergy was unsuccessful in converting the Muslim population, Cardinal Francisco Jiménez de Cisneros (1436–1517 CE) started to forcibly convert Muslims, burn Islamic books, and persecute the Muslims of Granada. As a result, the Muslims of Albaicín, Granada revolted in 1499 CE. The Christians took advantage of this revolt to claim that the Muslims broke the treaty, and that the Christians no longer had to honor it. Following the example of the Crusaders, they believed that while violating a pledge was a sin, honoring the pledge given to an infidel was a greater sin (Hamidullah, *Muslim Conduct* 71). In 1500 CE, many Muslims were compelled to convert to Christianity. In the Capitulations of 1500–1501, Muslims were prohibited from ritually slaughtering animals and were banned from bathing. On October 12th, 1501, all Arabic and Islamic books in Granada were burned. In 1501, the Spanish authorities gave the Muslims an ultimatum: convert to Christianity or be expelled. Although most

Muslims were compelled to convert, becoming known as Moriscos, a term they never accepted, always describing themselves as Muslims or believers, their conversions were superficial, and many continued to practice Islam secretly, reverting to the use of *taqiyyah* or pious dissimulation. As historian Ahmad ibn Muhammad al-Maqqari (1578–1632 CE) declares,

> Such of the Muslims as still remained in Andalus, although Christians in appearance, were not so in their hearts; for they worshipped Allah in secret, and performed their prayers and ablutions at the proper hours. The Christians watched over them with the greatest vigilance, and many were discovered and burnt. (391–392)

In 1502, the ultimatums were extended to the *mudéjares* of Castile and Leon. In 1508, Arabic and Islamic dress was prohibited by law. Between 1511 and 1513 a series of decrees were passed prohibiting the production, sale, and consumption of *halal* meat. The *mudéjares* of Navarre and Aragon were forced to convert or leave Spain by 1515 and 1525 respectively. In 1525, forced conversions were declared to be legally and religiously valid, and Charles V (1500–1558 CE) extended the decree of expulsion or conversion to Muslims in all of his kingdoms. In 1526 and 1527, he introduced even more restrictive legislation. Anything and everything associated with Islam or Arab culture was outlawed: Islamic clothing, amulets, jewelry, circumcision. . . . (Chejne, *The Moriscos* 9). The Moriscos were prohibited from possessing weapons of any sort and Islamic marriages were outlawed.

In 1565, Felipe II (1527–1598 CE) outlawed speaking, reading, and writing in Arabic; nullified all contracts written in Arabic; obliged the Moriscos to dress like Christians; prohibited Morisco women from wearing the headscarf or the veil, despite the fact that they were normative even for the Christian women of the time; banned Morisco music and dances; outlawed all celebrations on Friday; forbade the use of Muslim names; prohibited Morisco women from wearing henna; and banned and destroyed public baths (Bernabé Pons 34–35). The ritual of *'aqiqah*, namely, the shaving of a child's head and the sacrifice of a lamb, seven days after the baby's birth, was outlawed. Morisco children were forcibly baptized and Moriscos were obliged to attend mass. As Wiegers mentions, the new legislation "was directed not only against religion, but against all manifestations of traditional culture, such as all oral and written use of Arabic" (10). Besides prohibiting Islamic books, all customs connected with Islam, such as bathing, were outlawed (10). In fact, the simple possession of a book written in the Arabic alphabet was viewed by the Inquisition as a possible *corpus delicti* (11). Muslims were also expected to keep their doors open, particularly on Fridays, so that Christians could come and go as they pleased in their neighborly attempts to ensure that no ritual prayers were being conducted. Christians found it comical to randomly offer pork or bacon to Moriscos to "confirm" their Christianity. Any failure to consume the flesh of swine would result in a complaint to the Inquisition, an investigation, torture, and sometimes death. Since bathing and basic hygiene were viewed as evidence that one was a Crypto-Muslim, a failure to smell foul could also send one to the torture-chambers of the "Holy" Inquisition.

To add insult to injury, Philip II (1527–1598 CE) decreed that all Morisco children were to be turned over to Christian priests to be educated, leading to the Alpujarras uprising which lasted from 1568 to 1571. The uprising was brutally suppressed by Don Juan de Austria (1547–1578 CE). The town of Galera "was raised to the ground and sprinkled with salt, and all its 2,500 inhabitants, including women and children, were slaughtered" (11). After the revolt was crushed, the Spanish Crown forcibly deported and resettled 84,000 Moriscos from Granada and Castile, seeking to separate them from their brethren, thus ensuring their eventual assimilation into Christian culture.

In 1609, the final decision to expel the Moriscos was taken on the grounds of national security. The Moriscos were accused of conspiring with the Muslims of North Africa and the Ottomans to invade Spain. Unlike the expulsion of the Jews in 1492, which was completed in one step, the expulsion of the Moriscos was undertaken in stages. The Moriscos of Valencia were the first expelled in 1609, followed by the Moriscos of Castile in 1614. Under threat of death, the Moriscos were forced to leave Spain without their money or goods. They were even forced to leave their children behind. Morisco children under the age of seven were to serve the religious establishment, while Morisco children over the age of seven were to be sold as slaves to *cristianos viejos* or Old Christians, namely, families which had been Christians for over a thousand years (Boase 13).

Between October 1609 and July 1611, it is calculated that "over 50,000 Moriscos died resisting forcible expulsion, while over 60,000 died during their passage abroad by land or sea, or at the hands of their co-religionists after disembarking on the North Africa coast" (Boase 12). A total of 300,000 Moriscos, most of whom were from modern-day Aragon, Catalonia, and Valencia, were expelled from Spain during this second wave, eventually reaching the Ottoman Empire and Morocco. Of the 500,000 Muslims from Granada, only 10,000 to 15,000 remained after the expulsion of 1609. According to the lowest estimate, one fifth of the Morisco population perished in the space of a few years. According to other writers, two-thirds to three-quarters of the Morisco population perished (Boase 12). By other calculations, "110,000 Moriscos left Andalusia, Murcia, and Hornachos; some 50,000, Cataluña; 120,000, Aragon; 250,000, Castile, Mancha, and Estremadura" for a total of about half a million (Chejne, *The Moriscos* 13). But there is no doubt that nearly all of the afflictions suffered by Muslims from the passing of the Prophet to the present were the cumulative effect of a single cause: the refusal to recognize the rights of *ahl al-bayt*, the Holy Household of the Prophet. As the Messenger of Allah advised, "O people, I am leaving among you that which if you hold on to you shall never go astray: the Book of Allah and my kindred, my household" (Ahlul Bayt Digital Islamic Library Project).

When confronted with the exposure of such atrocities, some Christian apologists may simply protest that "those were dark days," or that they were "the norms of the time." And certainly the persecutions of Shi'ites and Sufis in parts of the Muslim world should not be swept under the rug. But while persecution of Muslims may have been the norm among European Christians, persecution of Christians was certainly not the norm among European Muslims. While the Moriscos were being persecuted and purged by the Christians in Spain, the Christians were treated with respect and tolerance by the Muslims of the Ottoman Empire. In contrast to the Catholics, the Turkish Muslims recognized the autonomy of the Athonite community after they took Thessalonica (Sherrard 28). After receiving a delegation of Athonites, Sultan Mehmet II (r. 1444–1446 CE and 1451–1481 CE) "agreed to protect their rights and safeguard their independence" (Speake 119–120). After the conquest of Bosnia in 1463, Sultan Mehmet II issued an edict to protect the basic rights of the Bosnians. Written 326 years before the French Revolution of 1789 and 485 years before the 1948 Universal Declaration of Human Rights, this *ahidname*, the original of which is housed in the Franciscan Catholic Church in Foznica, in Bosnia-Herzegovina, reads:

> Mehmet, the son of Murat Khan, always victorious!
>
> The command of the honorable, sublime Sultan's sign and shining seal of the conqueror of the world is as follows:
>
> I, the Sultan Mehmet Khan, inform the entire world that the ones who possess this imperial edict, the Bosnian Franciscans, have got into my good graces, so I command:
>
> Let nobody bother or disturb those who are mentioned or their churches. Let them dwell in peace in my empire and let those who have become refugees be safe. Let them return and let them settle in their monasteries without fear in all of the countries of my empire.
>
> Neither my royal highness, nor my viziers or employees, nor my servants, nor any of the citizens of my empire shall insult or disturb them. Let nobody attack or insult or endanger their lives, their property or the property of their church. Even if they bring somebody from abroad into my country, they are allowed to do so.

As, thus, I have graciously issued this imperial edict, hereby take my great oath.

In the name of the Creator of the Earth and Heaven, the One who feeds all creatures, and in the name of the seven mustaphas, and our great Messenger, and in the name of the sword that I wear, nobody shall do contrary to what has been written as long as they are obedient and faithful to my command. (Ottoman Souvenir)

As Speake explains, "The Ottomans had come to terms with the fact that the vast majority of their newly conquered subjects were adherents of another religion" (114). Since the goal of the Ottomans was smooth administration, they realized that inter-religious feuds were not in the best interest of the Empire. Unlike the Umayyads (r. 661–750 CE), the Almoravids (r. 1040–1147 CE), and the Almohads (r. 1121–1269 CE) in al-Andalus, these last two being Berber dynasties from Morocco that introduced a narrow and intolerant form of Islam, the Ottomans (r. 1299–1923 CE) were tolerant to both Muslims and non-Muslims alike. They generally accepted the presence of both "orthodox" and "heterodox" forms of Islam in their midst. They followed the Qur'anic doctrine in defense of diversity:

O humankind! We have created you male and female, and made you into communities and tribes, so that you may know one another. Surely the noblest amongst you in the sight of Allah is the most God-fearing of you. Allah is All-knowing and All-aware. (49:13)

Despite being a superpower, the Ottomans, never promoted cultural or religious uniformity as a general rule. On the contrary, they valued the fact that their empire was composed of Byzantine, Christian, Jewish, Arab, and Balkan elements. By making all religions subservient to the state, and appointing judges from all religious denominations, the Ottomans united the various ethnic, cultural, religious, and ethnic groups under the same "secular banner." Following the Prophet, who set up a system of central-local rule, the Ottomans maintained social boundaries between religious communities. As Karen Armstrong (b. 1944) explains,

The sultan did not impose uniformity on his subjects nor did he try to force the disparate elements of his empire into one huge party. The government merely provided a framework that enabled different groups—Christians, Jews, Arabs, Turks, Berbers, merchants, ulama, tariqahs and trade guilds—to live together peacefully, each making its own contribution, and following its own beliefs and customs. The empire was thus a collection of communities. (2000: 132)

Rather than undermine religious communities, the Ottomans granted them a significant degree of legal authority and autonomy. In so doing, the Ottomans not only strengthened the Greek Orthodox, Armenian, and Jewish communities, they maintained the internal religious and cultural composition of the Empire while earning the loyalty of their subjects. The Ottoman approach was, of course, inspired in the example of the Prophet, the Caliphs, and subsequent rulers. As Speake explains,

it had long been the practice of Muslim rulers to treat Christian minorities within their realms as *milets*, or nations, allowing them to govern themselves and maintain their own customs and religious practices under the supervision of their own religious hierarchy, which in turn ensure allegiance to the supreme power of the Caliph. (114)

The attitude of the Ottomans towards the monastery at Mount Athos can be seen in one document which states that "Athos is a place where the name of God is invoked continuously. It is a place of refuge for the poor and homeless" (qtd. Speake 121). The first sentence is actually drawn from the Holy Qur'an, which reads,

Did not Allah check one set of people by means of another, there would surely have been pulled down monasteries, churches, synagogues, and mosques, in which the name of Allah is commemorated in abundant measure. Allah will certainly aid those who aid his (cause); for verily Allah is full of Strength, Exalted in Might, (able to enforce His Will). (22:40)

The Turks, like all other true Islamic rulers, acted according to the spirit of the Qur'an, which teaches that it is the obligation of all Muslims to protect places of worship. The Mamluks (r. 1250–1517 CE), for example, signed a treaty with the French, under Louis XII (1462–1515 CE), in Cairo in 1500 CE, which subjected non-Muslim foreigners to the laws of their own land as opposed to Islamic Law. There were, evidently, excesses that took place at times, such as the confiscation of monastic estates by Sultan Selim II (r. 1566–1574 CE). He was also a drunken degenerate known by the title of "Selim the Drunkard." Such reviled rulers were very much the exception to the rule and are not representative of the values embodied by Islam and espoused by all true believers. Soldiers, of course, are sometimes difficult to control. The Convent of the Holy Transfiguration of God in Bulgaria was plundered and burned during the Ottoman conquest. However, in an effort to redress this wrong, the Sultan issued a *firman* in 1832 calling for its reconstruction. As R. Stephen Humphreys explains, incidents of excesses are rare in the totality of Islamic history and, when they occur, "one detects underlying emotions and attitudes on both sides which could easily explode into violence" (260). As history has shown us, most atrocities are motivated by money and issues of religion, race, and ethnicity are merely used as pretexts to usurp the rights of others. For Wigram, "a Church under Arab rule was an eternity of dullness, enlivened only by occasional risk of massacre, when anything occurred to irritate authority" (*The Assyrians* 34). As Abraham Rihbany has written, the history of Muslims "shows that they have been invariably well disposed toward non-militant Christians in their midst" (qtd. Emhardt and Lamsa 82).

The Christians, it is claimed, came close to being forcibly converted on two occasions. As Sir Charles Eliot (1801–1875 CE) alleges in *Turkey in Europe*, "Selim I and Ibrahim both formed projects of exterminating all the Christians in the Empire and were with difficulty dissuaded by their Muftis, who refused to declare that such a massacre was sanctioned by Moslim law" (247–248). "The same Selim, and, later, Murad III," writes Eliot, "threatened to convert all the churches of the capital into mosques, and were only prevented by deputations, headed by the Patriarch, who enforced their appeals to the privileges granted by the conqueror" (248). As Albert Howe Lybyer (1876–1949 CE) alleges,

> Selim the Grim disposed of the heretics in his dominions by wholesale execution, and punished, though he failed to crush, the Persians. . . . After he had got rid of Mohammedan heresy in his dominions, he was impressed with the absence of unity occasioned by the presence of the Christian subjects. Accordingly, he decided to order all these Christians to accept Islam on pain of death. To say that he desired to execute the Christians of his dominions would be to put the emphasis in the wrong place. He seems rather to have had in mind such a process as was carried through in Spain in the course of the sixteenth century, as a result of which none were left in that land who professed another than the dominant creed.
>
> But the Mufti Jemali intervened decisively. He had readily given a *fetva* authorizing the extermination of the heretics as in accordance with the Sacred Law, and he was later to sanction the Persian and Egyptian wars. In this case, Selim, it is said, deceived him by a hypothetical question into giving a response which might be interpreted to authorize the forcible conversion of the Christians. After the order was issued, however, Jemali, awakened to the situation, put the Greek Patriarch in possession of a sufficient defense by showing him that the Sacred Law provided that Christians who had accepted Mohammedan rule and agreed to pay *kharaj* and *jizyeh* (land tribute and poll-tax) were, aside from certain regulations, to be left unmolested in the exercise of their religion. This provision, the Patriarch, as instructed by the Mufti, claimed to be an irrevocable and eternal compact; therefore, he urged, since Selim's intention was contrary to it, his purpose was unlawful and must be abandoned. The argument prevailed, and the Christians were not disturbed as to their faith. (211)

For Lybyer, "Selim's idea was an excellent one from the point of view of statesmanship, and would, in the end, have resulted in a great advantage to the Moslem Institution" (211). As this Western academic explains, Christian churches were parallel and rival institutions and their removal would have provided the Ottoman Empire with a free field (211). "But the Mufti, as guardian of the Sacred Law, was right," admits Lybyer, as "[t]he position of the Christian subjects rested on a firm constitutional foundation" (212). "The Prophet Mohammed himself," admits the author, "had made the religious and social unity of the Ottoman Empire forever impossible" (212). So, while an occasional zealot or two conceived of the idea of uniting the Ottoman Empire through religious homogeneity, they were never able to enact their plans. They were prevented by the *shari'ah*, the sacred law of Islam, and, even more precisely by the covenants that the Prophet had concluded with various Christian communities. Most Ottoman rulers realized that the practice of granting relative autonomy to individual religious communities strengthened the empire as a whole. If the rights of distinct linguistic, religious, and cultural communities were recognized, what reasons would they have to seek separation from the Ottoman Empire?

In the estimation of Selim I (r. 1512–1520 CE), only Christian communities who had a *firman* could be considered *ahl al-dhimmah* or "protected people." Communities without such capitulations could be converted by force. Thanks to the documents, evidence, and arguments provided to him by the Chief Mufti, Patriarch Theoleptus (served from 1513–1522 CE) and a lawyer by the name of Xenakis, were able to persuade the Sultan that the churches of Istanbul had indeed surrendered during the 1453 fall of Constantinople and had been granted a *firman*. Since the *Capitulations* had been destroyed in a fire at the Patriarchate, no document could be exhibited. However, three elderly Janissaries, who had witnessed the events of 1453, swore on the Qur'an that the Christians had surrendered and received a patent of protection (Runciman 189). As Lybyer explains, a Sultan might, by act of violence, transgress its provisions. In so doing, however, he did it no damage and it remained what it always had been (26). In fact, "[t]he Sacred Law . . . even protected his Christian subjects from all efforts of his to bring them forcibly under its sway" (Lybyer 26). It should be stressed, however, that this is simply one of two views of Selim I. As Rossitsa Gradeva recognizes,

> Contemporary Orthodox men of letters are divided in their assessment of Sultan Selim I's (1512–1520) relations with his Christian subjects. Some of them describe him as an oppressor who ordered the seizure of all churches in Istanbul and their transformation into mosques as well as the enforced conversions of all Christians, which was neutralized by the Grand Vizier . . . others speak of him as a generous donor . . . and protector of monasteries on Mount Athos and elsewhere. (191, note 11)

Considering that he attempted to exterminate all the partisans of the Household of the Prophet in the entire Ottoman Empire, it is difficult to come to the defense of Selim I (r. 1512–1520 CE). It is quite possible that he commenced his rule as a protector and benefactor of the Christian community. Having met with success in eradicating Muslims who did not agree with his views, Selim I may have decided to bring even greater uniformity and unity by pressuring all non-Muslims to embrace Islam. If this was the case, then Selim I was the exception to the rule. Overall, however, "[t]he Ottomans proved good guardians of the holy places . . . providing a stable environment, arbitrating dispassionately between the conflicting Christian sects, and accommodating the growing Jewish presence in Palestine" (Wheatcroft: photo 34).

By empowering religious communities, and strengthening their ecclesiastical hierarchy, the Ottomans empowered themselves. If people are protected and included; if people have a voice and play an active role in governing themselves, they are far less likely to revolt due to dissatisfaction. Tolerance and inclusion were means of preserving social solidarity. Not only did Islam grant Muslims rights, it granted rights to non-Muslims from other states and nations. A case in point is *The Capitulations of the Ottoman Empire* which decreed that non-Muslim foreigners residing in Turkey would not be subjected to *shari'ah* law. Not only did it subject foreigners to the laws of their respective countries, it granted them semi-autonomy in matters regarding their personal status.

When French ambassador Antonio Rincón visited an Ottoman camp in Belgrade in 1532, he was noticeably impressed at the order which reined therein:

> Astonishing order, no violence. Merchants, women even, coming and going in perfect safety, as in a European town. Life as safe, as large and easy as in Venice. Justice so fairly administered that one is tempted to believe that the Turks are turned Christians now, and that the Christians are turned Turks. (qtd. Robinson 158)

As a result of its religious tolerance, the Ottoman Empire became a refuge for Huguenots, Anglicans, Quakers, Anabaptists, Jesuits, and Jews. As with the Moriscos who fled religious persecution in Spain, Jews, and Christians of numerous denominations were granted the right of residence and worship in the Ottoman Empire (Goffman 111). As evidence of their commitment to religious rights, the Ottomans even supported the Calvinists in Transylvania and Hungary as well as in France (111). This, however, might have been done as much as a way of exploiting dissention and conflict within Christian Europe as in service of religious freedom. If the Europeans remained divided, they represented a lesser threat to the *ummah*. Ironically, this is the same approach that has been employed by the West in its dealings with the Muslim world. In any event, Jean Bodin (1530–1596 CE), the French political philosopher, described the Sultan in the following terms:

> The great emperor of the Turks does with as great devotion as any prince in the world honor and observe the religion by him received from his ancestors, and yet detests he not the strange religions of others; but on the contrary permits every man to live according to his conscience: yes, and that more is, near unto his palace at Pera, suffers four diverse religions viz. that of the Jews, that of the Christians, that of the Grecians, and that of the Mahometans. (qtd. Goffman 111)

Sultan Mehmet II (r. 1444–1446 CE and 1451–1481 CE) granted even greater autonomy to the Jews, Greek Orthodox, and Armenians, without triggering any challenges to his standing as a devout believer (Karabell 179). The *Capitulations*, which granted Christians vast commercial rights and custody of certain holy places, remained current from 1517 to their abolishment by the *Treaty of Lausanne* in 1923. As Muhammad Hamidullah (1908–2002 CE) has shown, "There was no international law in Europe before 1856. What passed as such was admittedly a mere public law of Christian nations" (*Muslim Conduct* ix). In their relations with the Other, the Ottoman Muslims were more than one thousand years ahead of the West. It was only with the establishment of a secular Turkish state under Kemal Atatürk (1881–1938 CE) in 1923 that the rights of non-Muslims began to be encroached upon. As Karabell explains, it was when "the empire began to fray, and when it finally collapsed in the early years of the twentieth century" that "relations between Muslims, Christians, and Jews took a turn for the worse" (179). The fall of the Ottoman Empire broke the back of the Islamic *ummah* and Muslims have not recovered since. While it was certainly not perfect, the new society created by the Islamic revelation "was unlike anything the world had ever seen before: multiethnic, multicultural, multireligious, optimistic, open, curious, tolerant, literate, and cosmopolitan, united by a single language, brimming with cutting-edge science and technology, assured that the light of civilization burned brightest within its borders" (Barnard 9). Now, many Muslims shake their heads in shame, saying: "How far have we fallen!"

Since this is neither the time nor the place to provide a critical comparison of Islamic law and the legal systems which predominated in the Western world at the time of the Prophet, suffice it to say that the practice in Europe during the barbarian invasions was cruel and savage compared to the *shar'iah*. The Huns, for example, would kill anyone who committed a serious crime. Theft would result in the expropriation of the thief's property. Even minor crimes resulted in cruel punishment involving the crushing of bones. In fact, the *shar'iah*—the true *shari'ah* as understood by traditional Muslim scholars, of course, not the Wahhabi version—was the inspiration for the Napoleonic Code (though some scholars attempt to trace this Code back to the Laws of Justinian and other sources), and thus the forerunner of modern Western law in France and Québec. There is no doubt that Islam helped civilize the West and that the Prophet Muhammad lit the lamp that contributed to the end of Europe's Dark Ages. We must not forget, however, that the Roman Catholic Church also helped civilize the barbarian/Germanic West after the fall of the Roman Empire, almost single-handedly preserving much of the intellectual heritage of late antiquity; not for nothing was Ireland, for example, known as "The Isle of Saints and Scholars." And the Greco-Roman lore Islam helped re-introduce into the West was, of course, largely that preserved by the Christian scholars of the Byzantine Empire. Furthermore, a clear distinction must be made between "the Dark Ages" and the High Middle Ages, where Christianity, the heritage of Greek Philosophy preserved by it, the surviving lore and literature of the Germans and the Celts, and the many-faceted influence of Islam, united to produce a true spiritual civilization. In the past half-century, history has been re-written by people who have partly or mostly lost the knowledge that there was ever such a thing as a Christian Middle Ages and who act as if they believe that Europe was largely pagan up until the Renaissance. What we call the Dark Ages were not as dark as the secularist mind-set paints them. They were a time when great monasteries were both preserving and developing what was to become Western culture. After the fall of the Roman Empire, European populations were in decline and seemingly in despair; it was the emerging Christian civilization which brought them back to life, a process that was well under way before Islam existed. It was during the reign of the Merovingian Dynasty in the so-called Dark Ages that this Christian civilization began to emerge; the lies told about the Merovingians in books of spurious "scholarship" such as *Holy Blood, Holy Grail* and *The Da Vinci Code* have tended to suppress this knowledge. But there certainly would not have been the sort of Middle Ages or Renaissance we had in the West without the significant Islamic contribution, which greatly expanded Europe's knowledge of the literature of antiquity.

Evidently, when I speak of the *shari'ah* as a civilizational force, I speak not of the system denounced by secularists and non-Muslim religious extremists, as well as some people of good will, both Christian and non-Christian, who are not sufficiently informed to distinguish between the traditional *shari'ah* and the Wahhabi/Salafi perversion of it that is in force in many places today. For many misinformed Westerners, *shari'ah* law stands for cruel corporal punishments such as lashing, cutting off the hand of a thief, and stoning adulteresses—though atrocious punishments such as hanging, drawing and quartering were practiced in Europe up until modern times—as well as for refusing to grant the same legal status to testimony of women as that of men in court. The "honor-killing" of raped women by their relatives is also falsely identified as "*shari''ah* law" in many people's minds. Hence, it is important to make a distinction between the *shari''ah*, which encompasses all aspects of Islamic life, such as prayer, fasting, and charity, and certain cultural traditions that hark back to the pre-Islamic "time of ignorance." Likewise, it is imperative to distinguish between the spirit of the living *shari'ah*—which has been kept alive by traditional schools of jurisprudence through a continuation of the process of *ijtihad* or interpretation and application of immutable principles to changing times and circumstances—and the literalist, essentialist, and fundamentalist reading it receives by the Wahhabis/Salafis. While the *shari'ah* does contain rigorous punishments for what Islam considers as serious offenses, it also requires equally rigorous proof unlike the contemporary Salafi application of it where a person can sometimes be arrested or even executed with no more evidence than somebody's "denouncement."

Thanks to the Saudis, who have spread their Wahhabi cult throughout the world, to the point that much of Sunnism has morphed into Salafism, Islam is now something to be feared in the popular imagination of the West. When writing on the emergence of Islam, the Nestorian monks who authored the *Chronicle of Séert* asked God to strengthen it and help it to triumph (280 / 600). They stressed that of all sectarians the Muslims had treated the Christians the best: "They honored the Christians more than the followers of any other religion" (308 / 628). For them, Islamic rule was a God-send, and particularly in the case of the Caliphate of Imam 'Ali ibn Abi Talib (r. 656–661 CE) which brought great prosperity to Kufah (308 /628). Sadly, though, no credit is given where credit is due and the magnificent man who spread peace and justice around the world is mercilessly disparaged by those who benefited the most from his ideologically advanced ideas. Truly, in the Modern World, black is white, up is down, evil is good and good is evil. As the Prophet Muhammad prophesied in the 7th century: "Islam began as something strange, and it shall return to being something strange, so give glad tidings to the strangers" (Muslim).

And if they break their oaths after their treaty and defame your religion, then fight the leaders of disbelief, for indeed, there are no oaths (sacred) to them; (fight them that) they might cease. (9:12)

Chapter 16

General Conclusions

As a result of this study of the covenants between the Prophet Muhammad and the various Christian communities in the Middle East, a number of conclusions can be drawn. Whether it is the covenant of the Prophet Muhammad with the Christians of the Sinai, Egypt or Mount Carmel, or the covenant with the Christians of Najran, Assyria or Persia, these charters of protection have been passed down from the earliest days of Islam to the present. Ignored by most Muslims and Christians, these covenants have languished in the archives of libraries for centuries. It is time to bring out their light in this period of darkness in which the People of Scripture, Jews, Muslims, and Christians, have strayed from their sacred traditions of tolerance and co-existence. It is no coincidence, however, that the covenants of the Prophet Muhammad have been obfuscated for so long. It was certainly not in the interests of the imperialists, who devoted themselves to division instead of unification, to disseminate such ethically elevated instructions from the part of the Messenger of Allah. Muslim scholars are equally to blame for this complicity of ignorance and silence. From a monotheistic movement which embraced Jews, Christians, and Muslims, and which stressed esoteric similarity as opposed to exoteric conformity, Islam developed in a direction that was very different from that of its earliest expression.

The question of "authenticity" is unavoidable in scholarly circles, as it should be. Yet such an emphasis is sometimes no more than a manifestation of the power-motive by which intellectuals at the service of the secular world order seek to exert influence over Islam and Muslims, as if these scholars had the authority to determine truth for the followers of Allah's revelations. While they contain certain variations due to scribal shortcomings, the content of the covenants of the *Prophet Muhammad with the Christians of the World* is in complete agreement with the true teachings of Islam. From a content analysis approach, the covenants all seem to be sound. While they do not have chains of narration, this is not a requirement for authenticity as we are dealing with what purport to be primary sources. As for the lists of witnesses, it is quite possible that some of these figures were present during the signing of these covenants, however, many of them were not Muslims at the time, some were dead, and others cannot be identified in any of the works of *'ilm al-rijal* or the "study of men" which provides information about *hadith* transmitters. To all appearances, these lists of witnesses were appended to the covenants centuries after the fact in order to meet the demands of *hadith* scholars and to give them a greater air of authority. After all, the *Covenant of the Prophet Muhammad with the Christians of Persia* contains no signatories—suggesting, perhaps, that it predates all of the others.

Besides authority, the issue of applicability must also be addressed. Some scholars, such as Sir Paul Rycaut, recognize the *Covenant of the Prophet Muhammad with the Christians of the World* as authentic; they insist, however, that it was a ploy from the early days of Islam when Muslims were weak and feared that they would be attacked by both the polytheists and the Christians. In order to avoid fighting on two fronts, the Prophet, it is alleged, made a false peace with the Christians, only to violate it as soon as his forces grew sufficiently strong (Rycaut 102). Others have argued that the covenants of the Prophet are null and void as the Christians violated their terms over and over again throughout the course of history by siding with enemies of Islam, both ancient and modern. These arguments are ill-founded and can easily be dismissed based on basic historical facts. The *Covenant of the Prophet Muhammad with the Christians of the World* was supposedly concluded on the fourth year of the *hijrah*. History bears witness that the Messenger of Allah was actively engaged in signing treaties with people of all professions of faith during his final year in this earthly realm. Merely because some Jews from Medina had broken their treaties, the Prophet was not prevented from issuing charters of protection for other Jewish communities, such as those from Maqnah/Aylah. The precedent from the Prophet was not opportunistic treachery and hypocrisy, as Rycaut alleges, but turning towards people with the wing of mercy.

Whether one considers them authentic, weak or spurious, the covenants between the Prophet and the Christians from the Sinai, Egypt, the Levant, Assyria, Najran, and Persia, present Islam in an entirely new light. As any objective observer will admit, the standards set by such treaties are simply sublime, morally, ethically, socially, politically, and economically. Not only were they imminently just and merciful in the context of their time, but they were also superior to many of the forms of social organization of our own age. If General Juan Perón (1895–1974 CE) demonstrated a more enlightened attitude than the leaders of many other countries and even organizations like the United Nations when it came to the rights he proposed in the Argentine Constitution of 1949 with regards to workers, families, the elderly, women, children, education, property and health care, the Prophet Muhammad (570–632 CE) was virtually unique in his or any age for his establishment of social justice not on the revolutionary or "progressive" principles often invoked in our own time, but on transcendental spiritual values.

There are those that will argue that the *Treaty of Saint Catherine* and the *Treaty of Najran*, which are cited in Ibn Sa'd (784–845 CE), are authentic, while the longer covenants with the various communities which we have studied in this work have been tampered with; these scholars tend to believe that the short versions found in Ibn Sa'd later grew into the covenants we possess today as a result of varying degrees of interpolation at the hands of Christians. The question, again, must be: why would the Christians tamper with the texts, given that the treaties cited in Ibn Sa'd contain virtually the same clauses as those which are found in the covenants? The additional material is little more than literary adornment. If the treaties are authentic, then the monks of Mount Sinai and the Christians of Najran were already duly protected by the Prophet. It could well be argued, as I have done, that the treaties found in Ibn Sa'd are simply summaries of the complete covenants. If the covenants were interpolated, what kind of Christian would describe the Prophet as the rightful ruler of the entire world? And what sort of Christian would insist that the Law of Moses remains valid? And why is there no defense of Christian doctrine to be found? Besides these points, there is also the issue of dating.

The *Covenant of the Prophet Muhammad with the Christians of Najran* was said to have been found in a library in 878/879 CE. Hence, it was only rediscovered a couple of decades after the death of Ibn Sa'd (784–845 CE). Ibn Sa'd may only have had access to fragments of the covenant. While it is possible that some Christians seized upon the *Treaty of Najran* and then expanded upon it to suit their own interests, thus creating the *Covenant of the Prophet Muhammad with the Christians of Najran*, the time frame seems too short. Knowledge of the *Treaty of Najran*, which had only recently been published, must have been fresh in the minds of Muslim scholars. The sudden appearance of an overly inflated version would not have gone unnoticed. Some scholars will argue that the story of Habib the monk, and his discovery of the covenant of the Prophet, was simply a story fabricated to provide a frame of reference. They will insist that the *Chronicle of Séert*, in which the covenant is found, dates to the 11th century. However, most scholars believe that the work dates from the 9th century, which would support my contentions. Since the closer a text is to its source, the greater its likelihood of authenticity, it is pertinent to point out that the *Covenant of the Prophet Muhammad with the Christians of Najran* dates from the same period as the traditions of Bukhari, Muslim, and Nisa'i, which appeared in the 9th century; and predates the collections of *hadith* compiled by Ibn Khuzaymah, Sharif al-Razi, Saduq, and Kulayni, which date from the 10th century, as well as the works of Mufid and Tusi, which trace back to the 11th century. In terms of historicity, the *Covenant of the Prophet Muhammad with the Christians of Najran* has far more weight than even the encyclopedic *hadith* works of Hurr al-'Amili and Majlisi which were compiled in the 17th century.

Not only would some Muslim scholars reject any traditions transmitted on Christian authority, there are others who would reject any narration, regardless of its authenticity, if it seems to contain anything that might support Shi'ite claims concerning the succession of the Prophet. Such is the case with the *Treaty of Maqnah* in which the Prophet wrote that "Nobody will rule over you but a person from among yourselves or a member of the Household of the Prophet" (Qureishi 182). This treaty is accepted as authentic by Ibn Sa'd (784–845 CE) and Baladhuri (d. c. 892 CE), along with a large number of Orientalists such as Hershfield, Yashnki, and Rashprier (Qureishi 350). As we read in Gibbon (1737–1794 CE), "[t]he *Diploma securitatis aïlensibus* is attested by Ahmed Ben Joseph, and the author *Libri Splendorum* . . . but Abufeda himself, as well as Elmacin . . . though he owns Mahomet's regard to the Christians . . . only mention peace and tribute" (259, note 148). The treaty is also mentioned by Gregory Bar Hebraeus Abu al-Faraj (1226–1286 CE), the last great Syriac writer who is known in Latin as Abulpharagius. A note in Gibbon, however, points out that he was primate of the Jacobites, implying that this makes him untrustworthy (259, note 148). If Abu al-Faraj's works can be dismissed on the basis of the fact that he was a Christian, then the works of Gibbon, his editors, and all of their colleagues can equally be rejected on the ground that they were all Christians and Jews. More objective Christians, like Hieromonk Justin of Sinai, treat the *Treaty of Maqnah* as historical fact (50). In spite of all this evidence, however, the treaty is rejected by Ibn Qayyim al-Jawziyyah (1292/93–1286 CE), Muhammad Hamidullah (1908–2002 CE), and Muhammad Siddique Qureshi due to the presence of supposed "Shi'ite elements" (Qureishi 348–351) demonstrating that prejudice is also prevalent among some Sunni Muslim scholars.

The argument provided by Qureishi is completely contradictory. He claims that the *Treaty of Maqnah* was prepared by 'Abbassid Jews (349) during the reign of al-Mutawakkil, and then argues that it was prepared by Fatimid Jews (349, 351). However, al-Mutawakkil only ruled from 847 to 861 CE while Ibn Sa'd died in 845 CE. Since Ibn Sa'd died before the oppressive rule of Mutawakkil, it would have been impossible for him to record any treaty supposedly conjured up to protect Jews from Mutawakkil's tyranny. Qureishi claims that "Baladhuri has added many a things in the text of Ibn Sa'd" (349). However, as Qureishi himself relates, Baladhuri claimed to have received a copy of the treaty from a person who had seen it in Maqnah. It should be recalled that Baladhuri himself had traveled throughout greater Syria and Iraq in search of historical information. Furthermore, Baladhuri is recognized as a reliable source on early Islamic history. While it is true that the "Letter of Protection from the Prophet" found in the Cairo Geniza is a fake, probably inspired by the *Treaty of Maqnah*, this does not make the *Treaty of Maqnah* false as well. If this is the manner in which some scholars operate, they will surely reject the *Covenant of the Prophet Muhammad with the Christians of the World* on grounds that the Messenger of Allah speaks of himself, his family [*ahli*], and his successors [*khatimi*], thus leading them to suspect a Shi'ite bias. Objective academics, religious scholars, and laypeople, however, will not allow themselves to be swayed by such specious arguments.

As much as "liberal," "secular," and "civil" Muslims may insist that the Islamic State is imaginary (Tibi 145), that the system of divine governance has never existed in Islamic history (1), that Islamic law is a modern invention (4), and that the *shari'ah*-based Islamic State reflects a totalitarian order (215), the Qur'an as well as the covenants and treaties of the Prophet Muhammad make them out to be seriously misinformed. The word *hukm*, from the root *h-k-m*, from which the word *hukumah* or "government" is derived, is mentioned 192 times in the Qur'an (Shahin 198). The Qur'an commands believers to "obey Allah and obey the Messenger and those in authority from among you" (4:59). The theory of government in Islam is drawn directly from the Qur'an, the Sunnah, and the practices and consensus of the early Muslims (199). Muslim political theorists always insisted that the government, Caliphate or Imamate was "a necessary institution for fulfilling certain religious and temporal functions" (201). In fact, "Muslim political theorists believe that Islam ... was born to develop a state and a government" (201).

It is an undeniable fact that the Prophet Muhammad created an Islamic State in Medina. It had a constitution and it had an army. During the Messenger of Allah's decade-long rule, the Islamic State grew and spread until it incorporated all of Arabia. The powers that surrounded Arabia viewed the Prophet as a lord, king, and ruler. He was not a mere tribal elder or war-lord. The Prophet did not simply view himself as the leader of Arabia. He had eyes on the Byzantine and Persian empires. In fact, as he, himself, said: "I have been entrusted with the keys of the world" (qtd. Qureshi 30). And again, "Allah has given me the control over the whole earth. I have seen the eastern and western hemispheres where the government of my *ummah* will be established" (qtd. Qureshi 30). The Prophet did not simply raid, he conquered, and where he conquered he appointed governors, imposed a legal system, provided military protection from his army, introduced taxation, and offered government-based social services which were funded from the Treasury. These are all fundamental features of a State.

Bassam Tibi (b. 1944 CE) is correct to claim that "Islamism is not Islam" (1). Islam, after all, is a religion, a culture, and a civilization. Tibi, and many other Muslims, be they traditionalists or secularists, are wrong, however, to diminish or deny the role of politics. While Islam is not simply politics, it is a complete system in which politics plays a crucial part. Islam is not, and cannot be, complete without politics just like Islam is not, and cannot be, complete without all of its other branches. In order for Islam to fully and totally manifest itself, and for Muslims to develop in all their dimensions, an Islamic State and Society must be constructed. Otherwise, to what avail are all the laws that the Prophet brought down from Mount Hira? The rules and regulations contained in the Qur'an and Sunnah do not apply solely to personal morality and religious duties. They involve criminal law, civil law, business law, environmental law, and international law, along with every other branch of law imaginable. These are laws which can only be implemented by an Islamic State. The Prophet Muhammad was not simply a spiritual figure. Unlike Jesus, who said that his kingdom was not of this world, the kingdom of the Messenger of Allah spanned this life and the afterlife. He was a complete and total prophet: a spiritual guide, legislator, commander, and ruler.

If the Prophet did indeed create an Islamic State, as the *Constitution of Medina*, and his large number of treaties and covenants confirm, what shape did it take? If Muhammad's contemporaries viewed him as a king or a war-lord with imperial ambitions, it was because this was the only conceivable political system at the time. Modern scholars apply the same misguided approach to the Messenger of Allah by projecting upon him political ideologies as disparate as Monarchism, Marxism, Communism, National Socialism, Phalangism, Capitalism, Free-Marketism, and Parliamentary Democracy! Islam is none of the above. Islam is its own unique system. Instead of saying that Islam has Marxist, Nationalist, Liberal or Capitalist elements, it would be more dignified to describe these European ideologies as having certain points in common with Islam. The Islamic system should not be made to fit into a left- or right-wing mould. Whatever fits into the Muslim mould, Muslims should accept. Whatever is superfluous they should feel free to reject.

If it was *à la mode* in the sixties, seventies, eighties, and part of the nineties, to envision a socialist Islam, the trend since that time has been to show that Islam is compatible with "democracy." It is thought to be incumbent on Islam to live up to the "superior" standards of the modern West when a good case for the opposite evaluation might be argued. The Western world, due to the weakening of its Christian roots, is now grounded in materialism, individualism, and hedonism, despite its earlier ability to disseminate certain humane values that were ultimately derived from the Christian revelation. Consequently, by means of materialism both as an ideology and as the basis for a monstrous over-development of technology, it has brought the entire planet to the brink of destruction—though the former colonies of the West, in imitation of their one-time masters, are certainly playing their part. This is not a model any rational human being would seek to emulate. This is not to say that the contemporary Muslim world has anything better to offer. But, then again, whether they are military dictatorships or secular democracies, the systems applied in the Muslim world are largely of Western origin. If I speak of "democracy," between quotation marks, it is not because it is inappropriate to have a popular government which is freely-elected by the people. If the people have every opportunity to make a free and informed electoral choice concerning a political platform, any government chosen on this basis has the right to describe itself as "popular" or "democratically-elected." Unfortunately, the governments which currently claim to be "democratic" do not fit this description; they were not elected in a truly democratic fashion. In the year this book was published, ex-U.S. president Jimmy Carter, perhaps the most openly Christian president of the 20th century, stated that the United States is no longer a democracy. As Noam Chomsky and many other intelligent minds have made clear, the systems that pretend to be democratic, but which in reality are not, are adept at hiding their true nature. As a result of wide-spread social engineering, largely through the mass media, the established system gives people the illusion of "free choice," when, in reality, they are directed to make a pre-determined choice, or to "choose" between "alternatives" with no substantial difference between them. And although the media appear to present varying points of view, these nonetheless remain within a very narrow range of opinion, largely due to the fact that control of the mass dissemination of information remains largely concentrated in the hands of the power elites and their agents. As an example of this sort of illusory choice, we may draw an example from U.S. presidential politics. Partly due to his involvement of the United States in seemingly endless foreign wars, in Iraq, Afghanistan and elsewhere—and the revelation that the "weapons of mass destruction" Bush and his team claimed were possessed by Saddam Hussein not only did not exist, but were conjured into illusory existence by spurious intelligence reports—the "conservative" George W. Bush left office as one of the most unpopular presidents on record. He was succeeded by the "liberal" Barack Obama, whose relatively meaningless campaign slogan was "change we can believe in;" Obama was elected largely because he presented himself as an ideological alternative to Bush. At this writing, however, he is doing all that is humanly possible to involve the United States in the Syrian civil war, against the wishes of the vast majority of the American people, and apparently has his eyes set on Iran as well. Furthermore, in the economic arena, both Bush and Obama supported the TARP program, which bailed out Wall Street while leaving large sectors of the American population impoverished, perhaps permanently. In light of these facts, what real *democratic* choice is there any more between "liberal" and "conservative"? (For one example of the quite extensive literature on the subject of corporate and government control of the media, see Noam Chomsky, *Manufacturing Consent.*)

The word "democracy," as we use it today, means a number of different things which are not always compatible. We consider it as synonymous with "equality," with "partial or universal suffrage" and with "majority rule." And *equality* itself can also mean several different things: equality under the law; the practice of treating people with vastly different talents, abilities and degrees of virtue as if their talents, abilities and virtues were actually equal, coupled with the attempt to enforce by law this non-existent equality; and equality of economic opportunity, an unattainable ideal which we may also try to enforce by law, with mixed results. As for *partial or universal suffrage*, we tend to see it as the major or the only form of enfranchisement, though there are certainly many other types of social inclusion, some of them just as important or even more important than the right to vote—the right to own property, for example, or the ability to provide shelter and subsistence for our families. And when it comes to *majority rule*, the more absolute this becomes, the less room there is for the legal equality or the access to economic opportunity or the social enfranchisement of minorities.

While Muhammad's Islamic State was not a democracy per se, it did contains certain democratic elements. It certainly provided for a great deal of social inclusion and equality under the law. But what voting rights did the Prophet establish? The first caliph, Abu Bakr, seems to have been "elected" by a sort of acclamation; however, this was limited to a small circle of individuals who shared the same vision of succession and which excluded the participation of other parties. The collegiality of the *'ulama'* can also be seen as a kind of democracy. And undoubtedly there were certain democratic elements in the tribal patterns of authority and the civic administrations. It cannot be denied, however, that Islam, in many ways, is a theocracy, not a *hierocracy*, namely, the rule of a priestly class, but a kind of democratic theocracy which is fundamentally different from both modern western democracies and the sort of archaic theocracy represented by Pharaonic Egypt, for example.

It is often forgotten that in post-prophetic Islam, it is not the Caliph, Sultan, Imam or Rahbar who rules: it is Allah who rules by means of His Law. Having neglected this principle, Muslims, for far too long, have placed power in the hands of a single person, a strong-man, when the most powerful and immutable authority must be the Law of Islam. In Islam, the leader is a servant of Islam. Ruling on behalf of the Prophet, the ruler's responsibility is to ensure that the Law of Allah is applied. He or she is of little consequence otherwise. This obligation need not be invested in a single person. In fact, a Supreme Court of Islamic Clerics could make sure that all checks and balances are in place. So long as they do not violate Islamic legal and ethical principles, elected leaders are free to rule in the manner they see fit. And these leaders should indeed be elected by the people, held accountable by the people, and removed, when needs be, by the people. As for the laws of the land, they should always make matters easy for the people within the framework of the permissible. It is the most tolerant and not the most severe interpretations of the law that should become normative. What is not clearly prohibited is therefore permitted.

Although divinely-appointed, even the Prophet requested yearly pledges of allegiance from his followers, as did many of the early Caliphs. This was not an imposition, an obligation, or something simply ceremonial in nature, as found in the Kingdom of Morocco, for example. It was an opportunity for the people to express their support, or lack thereof, of their current ruler. Early Islamic rulers did not conscript soldiers. They consulted with tribal leaders in search for support. The people, under the first four Caliphs, had a voice and a vote. And unlike Western democracy, which can be the tyranny of the majority over the minority, even in cases of 51% to 49% votes, Islamic scholars and leaders also sought consensus. While it may be more time-consuming, this approach—which, incidentally is substantially the same that was employed by many Amerindian Nations—requires all parties to discuss, debate, and come to common terms. And though the citizens of the Islamic State can elect leaders and representatives, they cannot, for example, vote to de-criminalize fornication, adultery, or the consumption of intoxicants or legalize abortion on demand, pornography, and gay marriage. So, while there are democratic elements in Islam, the Islamic state is not a "liberal democracy" in the Western sense of the term. Democracy, for Muslims, must operate within the framework of Islam. Some Muslims, who seek to please the West, describe this as

"Islamic Democracy." I simply call it Islam. As for the much maligned *shari'ah* law, this study has shown that it was reasonable, flexible, and ever-evolving. If Wahhabism is a fossilized aberration of Islam, and Sunnism finds it difficult to modify the *shari'ah* to meet contemporary challenges insofar as it holds to the principle that "the door of *ijtihad* is closed," Shi'ism has maintained a living tradition of such *ijtihad*—namely, the interpretation and application of Islamic principles to changing times and circumstances.

While Orientalists, professional polemicists, and anti-Islamite activists—as well as some honest scholars who may not yet have given these documents the attention they deserve—will surely denounce them as forgeries, the covenants in question accord perfectly well with the spirit of Islam. Since they cannot possibly conceive of Islam in any positive fashion, Orientalists like Jean-Michel Mouton view the manifestation of Islam presented in the *Covenant of the Prophet Muhammad with the Monks of Saint-Catherine* as "legendary" (177). For him, "it is an Islam created from scratch by the monks and shaped to suit their interests" (177). For any individual with even a rudimentary understanding of Islamic sources, the contention that the *Covenant of the Prophet Muhammad with the Monks of Mount Sinai* was invented by Christian monks is astonishingly ignorant. Since they are saturated with references and allusions to Qur'anic verses, prophetic sayings, and specific historic events, only an individual immersed in the Islamic tradition could have produced such covenants. It seems highly unlikely that any Christian of the time could have had the capacity to create such treaties. As early Greek Orthodox, Armenian, Assyrian, and Catholic sources demonstrate, the Christians of the Middle East were grossly ignorant of Islamic history and beliefs. How it is that Christian historical sources all present a confused picture of Islam while the covenants of the Prophet held by these communities are in perfect accord with the Qur'an, the Sunnah, and the *shari'ah*? And, considering the fact that these antagonistic denominations had virtually no contact with one another, how did it come to be that they all possess covenants of the Prophet which are similar, and in some cases, the very same? If they could not agree upon basic beliefs and practices, and did not hesitate to call each other heretics and infidels, it is implausible that these hostile Christian factions would have joined forces to forge a covenant and attribute it to the Prophet. One denomination could easily have denounced another in an attempt to seek the favor of the Muslim rulers of the epoch.

To my knowledge, the only prophetic letter of protection which was forged in the history of Islam was produced, not by Christians, but by Jews. I refer to the *Letter of Protection of the Prophet* which was found in the Geniza of Cairo. As much as its ancient author attempted to present a convincing covenant of the Prophet for the purpose of evading taxes, it was never admitted as authentic and was proven to be a fake by both Muslim and non-Muslim scholars (Gil 29–30, note 27; Goitein 185). The covenants of the Prophet Muhammad with various Christian communities, however, have long been recognized as authentic by scholars both Muslim and Christian.

If the covenants of the Prophet Muhammad with the Christians of the world reveal something about Islam, the reaction they have received by some Orientalists reveals something about certain intellectual currents in the Western world: the complete refusal on the part of some influential scholars, based on little more than prejudice, to accept any positive presentation of Islam and the Prophet Muhammad. To the believing Muslim, however, the opinions of secularist scholars, when matched against the foundational sources of the Islamic revelation, carry little weight. And as it happens, those scholars who believe the covenants of the Prophet to be forgeries are in many cases the same people who maintain that the *hadith* literature is entirely ficticious, and that the Qur'an itself was forged by Muhammad, or perhaps by a charlatan who convinced the credulous religious fanatic that it was a genuine Divine revelation, if not by a ghost writer hired by Muhammad himself to produce it for the purpose of gaining influence over the Arabs. Nor is the basic worldview of such scholars very far different from those who hold analogous opinions about Jesus Christ, such Hugh J. Schonfield, author of *The Passover Plot*, who believed (unlike Muslims) that the crucifixion actually did take place, but saw it as part of an imposture concocted by Jesus and some of his disciples in order to amaze and mystify the Jews by staging a counterfeit resurrection. But as far as believing Muslims are concerned, the criteria for authenticity and certainty are clear: the Qur'an and authenticated Sunnah. As Jonathan A.C. Brown (b. 1977 CE) recognizes, "Western criticism of the *hadith* tradition can be viewed as an act of domination in which one worldview asserts its power over another by dictating the terms by which 'knowledge' and 'truth' are established" (198). In reality, "[t]he Authenticity Question is part of a broader debate over the power dynamic between 'Religion' and 'Modernity,' and between 'Islam' and 'the West'" (198). If anything, "attitudes towards... authenticity are necessarily based more on our critical worldview than on empirical fact" (198). For unbelievers, their default setting is denial. For believers, their default setting is belief. In the end, those who have found the truth will give little weight to the views of those who have not, especially when they presume to speak on sacred matters, though believers may be unable to entirely avoid the ultimate cultural, social and military consequences of those views.

If true believing Muslims have an agenda, it is the agenda of truth; the same can be said for the sincere believers in other revelations sent by Allah. If the enemies of monotheistic religions have an agenda, it is the agenda of relentlessly working to invalidate the belief in the Deity and replace it with the worship of what Muslims call *al-dunya*, and Christians, "This World." They may sincerely believe this falsehood, or cynically promote it, but neither sincerity nor cunning can make falsehood anything other than it is. And while it is one thing to dislike Muslims and to go on with one's life, it is quite another thing to devote one's entire life to attacking Islam, the Prophet, the Qur'an, employing in many cases the sort of tactics analyzed throughout this book. Understandably, the enemies of Islam will oppose anything and everything that presents the Prophet and Islam in a positive light. Likewise those who criticize Jesus Christ and his teachings will sometimes claim that it is "objectivity" that justifies slandering the Virgin Mary or calling into question the moral integrity of Jesus, while others feel free to daily satirize and blaspheme them in the media in terms that a century ago would have resulted in mass outrage throughout what was then "the Christian world."

Christians in the West are familiar with attacks upon their religion by militant atheists; what they may not realize is that the discipline of "Orientalism" plays a similar role in terms of Islam. As Edward Said has shown, Orientalism is often synonymous with European domination of the Orient (Hobbs 244). And although he defends Orientalists in his *Dangerous Knowledge*, Robert Graham Irwin (b. 1946) does a fine job of portraying many of their leading figures as people who approach Islam with sweeping skepticism and engage in deliberately destructive scholarship in an attempt to demolish Muslim tradition. Some Orientalists even claim to know more about the origins of Islam than Muslims themselves, on the theory that doubt, not certainty, is the road to truth. Their "source-critical" approach to early Islam does indeed spread doubts, but it does nothing to bring them any closer to historical reality. Seyyed Hossein Nasr (b. 1933 CE), for one, has described the use of such techniques to test the authenticity of Islamic sources as "one of the most diabolical attacks made against the whole structure of Islam" (qtd. Irwin 316). As Nasr explains, the issues these scholars seek to address

> arise not from scholarship but from a certain theological and philosophical position that is usually hidden under the guise of rationality and objective scholarship. For Muslims, there has never been the need to address these 'problems' because Muslim accept the revealed nature of the Qur'an, in the light of which these problems simply cease to exist. (qtd. Irwin 316)

As much as so-called "secularists" like Ibn Warraq, and those who take it as axiomatic that Islam is the enemy, may seek the "historical Muhammad," more objective scholars, like Walid A. Saleh, admit that "[t]he shadow of the historical Muhammad is . . . not far from the picture presented by Ibn Ishaq" (30), the author of the standard biography. The works of Muhammad Kurd 'Ali (1876–1953 CE), Jalal Al-e Ahmad (1923–1969 CE), René Guénon (1886–1951 CE), Muhammad Asad (1900–1992 CE), Seyyed Hossein Nasr (b. 1933 CE), Sayyid Qutb (1906–1966 CE), Maryam Jameelah (1934–2012 CE), Hamid Algar (b. 1940 CE), Abdul Latif Tibawi (1910–1981 CE), Ziyad-ul Hasan Faruqi, Ziauddin Sardar (b. 1951 CE), Fazlur Rahman Malik (1919–1988 CE), and Muhsin Mahdi (1926–2007 CE) among others, all show Orientalists in their true colors (see Irwin 310–330 for an unsympathetic overview of their main arguments). However, such dishonest attempts to extinguish the light of Islam shall be met with failure. Even G.R. Hawting, a student of Bernard Lewis (b. 1916 CE) and John Edward Wansbrough (1928–2002 CE), and colleague of the infamous Ibn Warraq, admits that "one cannot disprove the tradition or show that the image it presents is misleading or false" (423). "[I]n many areas of science," explain Michael E. Cremo and Richard L. Thompson (1947–2008 CE), "evidence exists primarily in the form of reports" (592). In essence, "everything depends upon how much faith one places in the reports" (592). Ultimately, it comes down to a question of trust. Muslims start with faith in their own tradition, whereas it is axiomatic to their opponents that Islam is not to be believed.

When attacking the covenants, the opposition has two approaches: to accuse Muslims of inventing them or to accuse Christians of inventing them. If the Muslims invented them, this actually presents Islam in a more positive light than its detractors wish to acknowledge—not a positive light from a purely Muslim point of view, however, since if it were true that Muslims actually falsified the words of the Prophet, they could in no way be called believers. The ideas enshrined in the covenants are so advanced that they represent a radical departure from the conventions of the time. However, considering the teachings of the Qur'an, the sayings of the Prophet, and the precedents he set, there would be no need for Muslims to invent anything. So, if the Muslims did not fabricate the covenants, it is conjectured that the Christians did. According to this scenario, it is the Christians, specifically their clergy, who are accused of being liars, imposters, and impersonators. Such allegations are deeply offensive, not only to Christians, but to Muslims as well, who respect all religions, and have a particular veneration for the learned and the pious. Again, considering that the teachings of the Qur'an were well-known, the sayings of the Prophet in ample circulation, and the precedents of the Prophet duly recorded, the Christians had no need to forge any covenants. They could simply have cited their rights as laid out in the Qur'an, the *hadith*, and the *shari'ah*. As always, the scholarly opponents of Islam seem to be engaging in an unproductive intellectual exercise like a dog chasing its own tail. Consequently, it is completely comprehensible that they would call into question the covenants of the Prophet with the Christians of Sinai, Assyria, Najran, Persia, and the World, as these present an image of Islam and Christianity that they would never accept.

How is it possible, asks Arthur Pillsbury Dodge (1849–1915 CE), that Christian clergy ignore the famous *Oath of the Prophet Muhammad* "which he entrusted to his Caliphs, expressing his authoritative Command to all his followers to respect and protect the followers of Christ?" (37). After all, "[a]ll of Islam were required to subscribe to that oath" (37–38). (He refers, obviously, to the covenant issued to the Christian monks of Mount Sinai, a document he describes as "remarkable" and "most strange") (38). For Pillsbury Dodge, the reason is one of two:

> 1. That there have been none in the Christian church familiar with these matters which so conclusively refute their teachings [against Muhammad and Islam]—far worse and more false than can be

found in the teachings of Judaism, to prejudice its followers against Christianity, or else:

2. That, knowing the truth reflected in the foregoing excerpts from Mohammedanism, yet they have knowingly, willfully deceived and misled the masses of the Christian church into diabolically false beliefs and practices; have persistently and criminally traduced and influenced the people against a great Prophet of God and his magnificent work for the people of the entire world without distinction or qualification. Which horn of the dilemma will they sit on? (38)

As Anton F. Haddad has witnessed, the attitude of many Christians towards the Prophet Muhammad is both unjust and intolerant (2). If he published an English translation of the *Covenant of the Prophet Muhammad with the Monks of Mount Sinai* in 1902, under the title *The Oath of the Prophet Mohammed*, it was to prove how unfortunate it was to accuse the Messenger of Allah of hatred and cruelty in his dealings with Christians (2). As a Baha'i, Haddad was neither Christian nor Muslim. If he challenged the prevalent view of the Prophet at the dawn of the 20th century, it was "for the sake of truth and Christian enlightenment" (2). These were, after all, "Mohammed's words, his valid oath, and covenant, concerning them" (2). If "[t]he emphatic teaching of the Christian Church has been to the effect that Mohammed was a false usurper and Mohammedanism a false religion, not of God, but of man," the reality remains that "Mohammed clearly and fully ratified and confirmed the Teachings of Jesus Christ and, as the Divine agent, messenger and instrument of God, actually saved Christianity, then at its lowest ebb, to the world" (Pillsbury Dodge 30). If Christianity has survived as a world religion, part of the credit belongs to Muhammad.

If, after moving forward by means of monumental civilizational leaps for centuries, Muslims have entered a regressive phase characterized by the adoption of much of what is worst in the civilization of the West, the responsibility for such failure falls upon the Muslims masses, not the Most Noble Messenger they pretend to follow, as well as upon those in both East and West who have led those masses astray for their own purposes. Following in the footsteps of Europe and the Americas has brought nothing but decay to *dar al-islam* or the Abode of Islam. We need to confront the evils we face in a spirit of grim sobriety. Like worms infecting an apple crop, the toxic attitudes of the Occident have spread from bushel to bushel, from tree to tree, and from grove to grove, putting the entire world crop in peril. The sole solution for Muslims is not to move backwards to some idealized frame frozen in time as the Salafis would have us do. The aim must be to move forwards while remaining firmly rooted in the fundamental, moral, ethical, and legal principles which represent the very essence of Islam and all of the authentic monotheistic religions. Once we realize that the Islamic revelation belongs to this age because it is truly perennial, and that everything it proposes contributes to the harmonious development of human beings, we can perfect the present and forge a new future founded on the fundamentals of True Universal Islam as opposed to the convoluted and corrupted religion which many cultural Muslims seem to follow.

If the advocates of terror knew anything about Islam, they would heed the command of the Prophet: "Observe scrupulously the protection accorded by me to non-Muslim subjects" (Mawardi, qtd. Hamidullah, *Introduction* 150). As for those who have become disconnected from the true Islamic tradition and the universal monotheistic movement of Muhammad, and who shirk their obligations by attacking innocents on the grounds that they are infidels, they should turn back to the Qur'an, the Sunnah, the *ahl al-bayt*, the *awliyya' al-salihin*, and the covenants of the Prophet, seek forgiveness from Allah, repent, atone, and reform their ways. For as Muhammad, the Messenger of Allah, has warned: "Whoever oppresses non-Muslim subjects shall find me to be their advocate on the Day of Judgment [against the Muslim oppressors]" (Abu Dawud). In fact, the Prophet of Allah foretold the consequences of failing to follow the covenants he had concluded in the following words:

> O Muhajirs, there are five things which may befall you and I pray Allah that you may escape them: moral decay never openly shows itself among a people but they suffer from pestilence and disease such as their fathers have never known; they do not use light weights and measures but they are smitten by famine and the injustice of rulers; they do not hold back the poor-tax from their herds but rain is withheld, for but for the beasts there would be no rain sent; *they do not break the covenant with Allah and His Messenger but an enemy is given power over them and takes much of their possessions*; and their imams do not give judgment about Allah's Book and behave arrogantly in regard to that Allah has sent down but Allah brings upon them the calamity they have engendered. (Ibn Ishaq 672) [emphasis mine]

If Muslims who had ruled over much of the world until the decline of the Ottoman Empire lost their power and were conquered and colonized by Western Europeans, it was not without reason. They were dispossessed by the Divinity because they violated the Covenants of Allah and His Messenger. If Muslims ever wish to regain the role they once played on the world stage, they must first begin by following the letter and spirit of Islam. And for those who, by any mean or scheme, would find fault with such sayings as a pretext to violate them, I take the Word of Allah as my witness: "Fulfill the contracts which ye have made," commands the Creator in the Qur'an (2:177). As Almighty Allah admonishes: "Those who break Allah's Covenant after it is ratified, and who sunder what Allah has ordered to be joined, and do mischief on earth: these cause loss (only to themselves)" (2:27). As he warned believers past, "Is it not (the case) that every time they make a covenant, some party among them throw it aside? Nay, most of them are faithless" (2:100). And while the following words were revealed concerning Moses, they have relevance to the covenant concluded between Muhammad and the Christian monks of Saint Catherine's Monastery: "And remember: We took your covenant and We raised above you (the towering height) of Mount (Sinai): (Saying): Hold firmly to what We have given you and bring (ever) to remembrance what is therein: perchance ye may fear Allah" (2:63). And Allah knows best.

And there are, certainly, among the People of the Book, those who believe in Allah, and the revelation to you, and in the revelation to them, bowing in humility to Allah: they will not sell the Signs of Allah for a miserable gain! For them is a reward with their Lord, and Allah is swift in account. (3:199)

Chapter 17

Suggestions for Future Scholarship

None but the Creator can make claims to perfection. Consequently, scholars and critics are reminded that any academic work is a thesis, namely, "something put forth" as an intellectual proposition. This work is very much an essay, from the French *essai*, which means an "attempt;" in other words, an attempt to advance an argument. The word *essai* derives from the Latin *exagium* which means a weight or an instrument of measure. I can only hope that the evidence I have presented has sufficient weight to convince my colleagues, and educated readers in general, of my thesis. It must be emphasized, however, that my conclusion, namely, that the covenants of the Prophet Muhammad are genuine, was arrived at only on the basis of meticulous and thorough examination of the evidence.

If I have come to a series of conclusions concerning the covenants, it was through a process of due diligence and deliberation. This does not, however, suggest that the documents themselves are without problems. However, the problems a researcher encounters are similar to those found in other ancient sources. As a general rule, the older the document, the more problems it poses. This is due to many factors, including, changes in language, style, and mode of thought, all of them the result of our distance from the text and its context. The difficulties presented by the covenants are similar to those one encounters with the *hadith* literature as a whole. However, considering that the *Covenant of the Prophet Muhammad with the Monks of Mount Sinai* has been deemed trustworthy for over one thousand years by scholars from all major schools of jurisprudence, Muslim scholars should maintain this consensus [*ijma'*]. Breaking scholarly consensus is not taken lightly by God-fearing jurists. As for the *Covenant of the Prophet Muhammad with the Christians of Najran* and the *Covenant of the Prophet Muhammad with the Christians of the World*, *ihtiyat* or scholarly precaution is in order. Considering the dire consequences of deliberately disobeying the command of Allah and His Messenger, compliance also certainly seems in order, especially since these covenants contain nothing which is contrary to the Qur'an and Sunnah, and much that is confirmed by them.

As for this study of the *Covenants of the Prophet Muhammad with the Christians of the World* its similitude is that of a brick, the solidity of which will be determined by time and the continuous process of peer review. Whether scholars or laypeople wish to accept it, ignore it, or discard it, is entirely up to them. I can only hope, and pray, that open and sympathetic minds will appreciate the solidity of its matter, and use it as the first building block of an entirely new edifice. And for those who are led to accept this work as foundational, many avenues of exploration are available. To begin with, the various notes found on the copies of the *Covenant of the Prophet Muhammad with the Monks of Mount Sinai* should be subjected to study as they are sure to provide us with a better understanding of this work and its transmission. The Monastery of Saint Catherine contains a large body of edicts, passed by jurists from the Hanbali, Hanafi, Shafi'i, Maliki, and Fatimid schools of jurisprudence, supporting the contents of the *Covenant of the Prophet Muhammad with the Monks of Mount Sinai*. The *fatwas*, and the arguments they advance, deserve serious scholarly study. Since there are some curious differences between some of the English and French versions of the *Covenant of the Prophet Muhammad with the Monks of Mount Sinai*, a study should be completed on the history of such translations. Scholars should determine, for example, whether the translators were all working from the same copy of the *Covenant* and whether they were working from the Arabic original or a Turkish translation. The Monastery of Saint Catherine should also make its early chronicles, which make mention of Muhammad, available to the scholarly community.

The Arabic editions and Latin translations of the *Testamentum et pactiones* or *Covenant of the Prophet Muhammad with the Christians of the World* produced by Gabriel Sionita (1577–1648 CE) and Johann Georg Nissel (1621–1662 CE) should be subjected to a critical comparative study. The origin of this document is also a mystery that has yet to be fully unraveled. According to currently available evidence, it appears to derive from the covenant brought to France by Father Scaliger and which dates from 1538. If so, where does this covenant come from? From which Christian monastery or community was it taken? Did it truly come from the monks of Mount Carmel?

Since it contains most of the same conditions as found in the *Covenant of the Prophet Muhammad with the Christians of Najran*, which are simply reiterated in different language, is the *Covenant of the Prophet Muhammad with the Christians of the World* a separate treaty or simply a variant? In fact, all of these covenants should be subjected to further linguistic and stylistic scrutiny. The *Covenant which was Written by Muhammad ibn 'Abd Allah ibn 'Abd al-Muttalib for all the Christians* (1538), and the entire manuscript in which it is found, MS Arabe 214 from the *Bibliothèque nationale de France*, merit much more attention. Who was Yuhanna ibn Ishaq al-Batanuni, the owner of the library for which the manuscript was copied? Who was Girgis al-Ifrangi, the scribe who completed the copy? Who were Girgis ibn Yuhanna al-Tamawi, Butrus ibn Diyab al-Halabi, Mansur ibn Sulayman Sahyun al-Ramadi, and Sim'an ibn Fadl Allah al-Barallusi? What was their connection to the *Covenant*? Who was this missionary who arrived in Old Cairo in 1592? And when exactly did Gabriel Sionita make notes on the copy of the *Covenant*? If the *Covenant* from 1538 was the one used by Gabriel Sionita and Johann Georg Nissel, why are their versions inferior to the original, full of errors, including omissions and additions? Why are the final two pages in a different handwriting? The expanded list of witnesses is clearly not in the hand of Girgis al-Ifrangi, the scribe. Did this ghost scribe simply complete the copy or is this evidence of interpolation? Were the final pages damaged or lost and then "recreated" at a later point? And who is the mysterious Michel who is apparently addressed at the end of the *Covenant* and who is asked to spread its message to Christian congregations far and wide? Imagine: Christian clergymen reading the *Covenant of the Prophet Muhammad with the Christians of the World* to the faithful as part of their liturgy with promises of ample rewards from the Messiah. This is simply startling. The complete details of this story need to be told. The ties between Gabriel Sionita and Cyril Lucaris also need to be examined. Not only were they both contemporaries, they were both connected to Protestants. Cyril Lucaris, the Patriarch of Constantinople, is known to have sent famous manuscripts to royalty, including a copy of the *Codex Alexandrinus* to King Charles I of England (Hadjiantoniou 93). Perhaps Cyril Lucaris was involved in dispatching a copy of the *Covenant of the Prophet Muhammad with the Christians of the World* to the King of France by means of Father Scaliger.

Besides European archives, scholars should focus their attention on Turkey where, I am confident, copies of various covenants of the Prophet must certainly remain. After all, the sacred relics of the Ottomans "had been stored for centuries in locked cases and stacks of bundles" (Aydin 11). While it sounds like work for the intrepid Indiana Jones, attempts to uncover older versions of these covenants, and even the actual originals produced by the Prophet, should most certainly be contemplated. Only God knows what revealing documents remain hidden in ancient monasteries, archives, mosques, and tombs. As Wendell Phillips acknowledged, the purpose of the 1950 expedition to the Monastery of Saint Catherine "was not so much to discover new material as to make accessible to scholars the unworked resources of this remarkable library" (Atiya xii). God knows what treasures remain to be found in the monasteries of Saint Catherine, Saint Anthony, and Saint Paul in

Egypt, not to mention hundreds of other such centers in the Old World. There are, after all, reports regarding the existence of other copies of the covenant of the Prophet. In 1850, Adrien Guibert's *Dictionaire géographique et statistique* included the following exciting entry:

> Deir-Saferan (Deïr-Saferan), city in Asian Turkey, located 15 kilometers north-west of Mardïn. — Residence of a Jacobite patriarch. It is said that the charter of Muhammad, which permits Christians the free exercise of their religion, is conserved in a convent. (579)

This report, it is hoped, will send an adventurous scholar scurrying to pack his or her bags and book a plane ticket to Turkey. There are also reports that other monasteries contain copies of prophetic covenants. Besides archival research in national libraries and monasteries, investigations of an archeological nature are in order. Paper graves should not be found by accident: they should be the result of conscious, deliberate, and determined efforts. Such efforts are only feared by those who are weak of faith. Why, only in 1822, the *Journal Asiatique* reported that they had received a "*Copy of the Pact of Muhammad in Favor of the Armenians, which an interlinear translation in Greek* . . . by M. J. Zohrab, an Armenian doctor" (Société Asiatique 116). In the same year, the *Bulletin des sciences mathématiques et astronomiques* made a passing mention of a *Traité de Mahomet*, found in Baghdad, which had appeared in an edition by Gregory (Darboux et al. 145). It is unclear whether this was the same as the *Pact of Muhammad in Favor of the Armenians* or a different covenant. Nor is it clear what the first name of Mr. Gregory was. Over five decades later, in 1899, the *Actes du Douzième congrès international des orientalistes* [*Acts of the Twelfth International Congress of Orientalists*] mention that M. Nallino presented the Arabic text of a *Charte de Mahomet en faveur des Chrétiens* along with its French translation (clxxxviii). While the acts note that it was "certainly apocryphal," they also report that "it does not differ much from the one which is conserved by Tabari and by other Arab authors." Scholars should also set off on a scholarly quest to uncover the source of Leon Arpee's *Covenant of the Prophet Muhammad with the Christians of Persia* which, so far, has eluded them.

Copies of all of these covenants, if they could be found again, should certainly be subjected to further comparative study. As for the existing copy of the *Covenant of the Prophet Muhammad with the Monks of Mount Sinai*, not to mention the letters of the Messenger of Allah, I see no reason why samples of these could not be subjected to modern, scientific, dating methods. In fact, I would have no objection to submitting the sacred strands of hair of the Prophet, and even the blood of Imam Husayn, to DNA sequencing. This would silence, once and for all, the claims of those who deny the historicity of Muhammad ibn 'Abd Allah.

So far, the majority of the surviving covenants of the Prophet come from communities that maintained the Christian faith after the Muslim conquests. However, most communities that came in contact with the Prophet not only surrendered to the power of Islam, they literally submitted to God by embracing Islam. Communications with such communities existed in the past and could conceivably be uncovered. Take, for example, the case of the Seven Saints of the Regraga, a sub-tribe of the Masmuda, from the region of Essaouira in Morocco. These seven saints are said to descend from three disciples of Jesus, Hamij, Harid, and Hirt, who brought the message of Christ to the Maghreb. They were members of a Berber Christian tribe that was awaiting the arrival of a final prophet. When they heard news that a man named Muhammad had declared his prophethood in Mecca, the seven saints set off on a long journey to Arabia in order to meet him. While they only spoke Tamazight, they were readily understood by the Messenger of Allah when they addressed him, asking: "Who is the one that was sent by God?" to which Muhammad replied, in the Berber language, "I am. Come!" His daughter, Fatimah, however, could not comprehend them, and asked her father *Ma hadhihi rajrajah* or "What is this mumbling?" at which the Prophet responded: "You have just given them their name." Not only did he give them a new name, he gave them his *barakah* or blessing, and instructed them to return to Morocco to spread the message of Islam. It is reported that they were the first to introduce the Qur'an to the Maghreb. Since they only spoke Tamazight, this was most probably a copy of the Qur'an in Tifinagh, the Berber script.

The seven saints, Sidi Ouasmine, Sidi Boubker ben Ashemas, Sidi Salah Ben Boubker, Sidi 'Abdallah Ben Salah, Sidi 'Isa Bou Khabia, Sidi Yala Ben Ouatil, Sidi Sa'id Sabek, who were now Muslim converts and Companions of the Prophet, succeeded in converting the Berber tribes *en masse*. Islam, according to the Berbers, was widespread in the Maghreb for decades prior to the Arab conquests. The seven holy warriors commenced the practice of visiting all of the tribes of the region to ensure that disbelief or apostasy did not raise its ugly head. This tradition, known as the Daour, continues to this day and includes visits to the tombs of forty-four saints over the course of thirty-nine days. And while they were responsible for spreading Islam in and around Essaouira, the Regraga Berbers always lived in peace and harmony with the large population of Jews who also inhabited the region. This founding tradition, believed by cynics to be a myth, confirms that the Qur'an, in complete form, was present with the Prophet in Mecca prior to the migration to Medina; that the Prophet had knowledge of all languages; that he had sent missionaries to the Berbers of the Maghreb; and that the Islam they spread is that which came to be known as Sufism. Since many Muslims are buried with copies of the Qur'an, a copy of this Berber translation of the Qur'an, provided by the Prophet himself, might, if it ever existed, be recovered some day as a result of archeological digs. Its historical value would be immeasurable.

The covenants of the Prophet also need to be studied in light of Ottoman *achtiname, ahidname* or *ahdname* tradition. These charters or capitulations played an important part in Turkish diplomacy. Some may suggest that the covenants of the Prophet are simply Ottoman capitulations which were attributed to Muhammad to give them greater weight. In reality, it seems that the Ottomans were actively imitating the structure of the covenants of the Prophet in the capitulations that they issued to various European powers. The introduction of the Ottoman *ahdname* consisted of the invocation of God, the *intitulatio*, which identified the person to whom it was directed, and the *salutatio*, or formal greeting. The main text featured the *expositio-narratio*, which explained why the document was issued, the *dispositio*, the decision that had been made in detail, the *sanctio*, which was both a confirmation of the decision, a warning, and an oath, the *corroboratio*, or authentication, the *datatio*, which was the date the document was issued, and the *legitimatio*, which was another form of authentication, typically the Sultan, the Grand Vizier or simply a seal. All of these features appear to imitate the structure of the covenants of the Prophet. The Ottomans appear to have been emulating the Messenger of Allah's method of dealing with Christian communities and countries.

While it will not be pleasing to many Muslims who believe that all of the *hadith* literature reflects the exact words of the Messenger of Allah, this study has shown that even documentary sources were in a minor state of flux from the time of the Prophet to more than half a millennium later. This finding, which was an unintended by-product of this study, will not come as a surprise to most Muslim and non-Muslim scholars who specialize in the study of Islamic literature. The issue of grammatical and orthographic variants in Qur'an manuscripts has long been studied and adequately explained by scholars such as Muhammad Hamidullah (1908–2002 CE) (*Le Saint Coran* xvi-xxx). The same goes for the *hadith* literature. My findings, I must emphasize, do not support the conclusions drawn by Patricia Crone (b. 1945 CE), Gerd R. Puin (b. 1940 CE), and company, who believe that the Qur'an, and the Sunnah, by extension, only reached its final form centuries after the fact. What I have found, however, is a lack of total textual stability which results from the phonetic shortcomings of early Arabic script. If modern written Arabic generally lacks short vowels, ancient Arabic also lacked *raqsh* or consonantal dots, meaning that a single symbol could represent the letters *ba*, *ta*, *tha*, *ya* or *nun*; *ra* and *zay* were the same; and even long vowels like *a* and *i*, the *ya* and the *alif maqsurah*, were indistinguishable as were numerous other letters.

This textual instability does not mean that the Qur'an has been corrupted. On the contrary, it was protected, not by the early Arabic writing system, but by the hearts of men, who merely used the vague and inaccurate Semitic script as a memory aid. For a person who knew the Qur'an by heart, the written text was easy to understand. Early Qur'ans, for people who did not know the Qur'an by memory, regardless of whether they were Arabs or not, were a serious cause for confusion. This explains the campaign of 'Uthman to standardize the Qur'anic script and Imam 'Ali's demand that the Qur'an be fully consonantalized and vocalized. If the Qur'an has reached us in an intact form, it was precisely because it was a *Qur'an*, a Recital, and not a *Maktub*, a Written Document. Were it not for the wise decision of al-Hajjaj ibn Yusuf, the notorious despot, to fully vocalize the Qur'an at the end of the first century of the *hijrah*, confusion and chaos would surely have ensued. Thanks to these reforms, namely, the use of consonant and vowel marks, "the Arabic alphabet became so perfect that a well vocalized text, like that of Qur'an, is more precise in Arabic characters than in any other writing system in the world." Unfortunately, this precision did not extend to other manuscripts. In fact, until modern times, no periods, commas, or punctuation marks of any kind were used in Arabic. Documents were all a single interminable run-on sentence. As a result, it is often difficult, even for Arabs, to determine when a sentence ends and another one begins leading to possible variants in meaning.

Comparing the various copies of the covenants of the Prophet provides a clear picture of how the *hadith* literature was passed down and the problems that scribes and scholars faced. They were not only transcribing defective early texts, they were also interpreting them, commenting upon them, updating them linguistically, and, quite often, improving upon them for the sake of clarity. Scribes and scholars may have been sincere in their struggle to decipher unvocalized consonants which were open to numerous interpretations; however, at times, their ideological inclinations, be they Sunni, Shi'i, or Sufi, surfaced in their final selection. Some were even inclined to expound or elaborate upon the text. While this may have been commentary which was confused with the text, it may also have been intentional interpolation. If the French say that *traduire est trahir*, or "to translate is to betray," we may rightfully say that to transcribe is textual treachery.

In the case of the covenants, the hand of the scribes is light. The scribes who worked on each respective covenant all appear to have been working from the same original sources. Some had superior knowledge of Arabic and produced a more eloquent transcription. Others struggled to comprehend the archaic original and made great numbers of mistakes. When faced with faded out words, sentences or entire sections, some scribes skipped them. Others evidently attempted to fill in the blanks. Some scribes improved the originals; others actually failed to do them justice by producing gibberish. While some might be taken aback by the spelling "mistakes" found in the covenants, such features would never startle genuine scholars who know full well that spelling was not stable, in any language, during medieval times, and that spelling is subject to linguistic evolution. For much of history, people spelled words as they wished. To denounce the covenants, or other documents for that matter, on grounds that the Prophet, Imam 'Ali, or the Caliph 'Umar could never have made a grammatical or spelling "mistake" is pathetically ignorant as Arabic grammar and orthography were not yet formalized at the time. The word *sirat* was spelled with both *sin* and *sad*. The word *Allah* was at times written with a single *lam* as *Alah*. There are entire works on this subject.

While textual variants may be disquieting and disheartening to many Muslims, this is not a new issue. Wathila ibn al-Aqsa' said that it was the meaning, and not the precise words, that mattered when relating traditions (Guillaume xxxix). Muhammad ibn Sirin (653–728 CE), for example, "used to hear traditions from ten different people in ten different words with the same meaning" (Guillaume xxxix). *Nahj al-balaghah* may be the work of Imam 'Ali ibn Abi Talib (d. 661 CE), however, this does not mean that every single word is the word of the Fourth Caliph. The *Sahifah al-sajjadiyyah* may, in large part, be the work of Imam 'Ali Zayn al-'Abidin (d. 712 CE); however, parts of it have been polished by subsequent scribes and scholars (Chittick xx). And some parts may not be authentic at all. In the case of the covenants, which were passed down in written form for over half a millennium, what should strike us is not the minor differences in wording; but rather, the general semantic stability of the text over the centuries. While the choice of words may vary, their meanings mostly remain the same. Instead of casting doubt on the integrity of the covenants, this fact actually helps to establish their trustworthiness. Unlike most traditions of the Prophet, which are based on hearsay passed down through oral tradition for one and a half centuries to over a millennium, the covenants are transcriptions of documents dictated by the Messenger of Allah. While an oral saying might require a chain of narrators, no such requirement can be demanded from a document derived directly from the Prophet Muhammad. The only problem revolves around problems of transcription. Since this study focused on the meaning of the covenants, a comparative linguistic analysis of the manuscripts was outside of its scope. Both the Arabic and Persian language covenants should be studied to see whether their language use is consistent with the 7th-century usage and whether there are signs of later linguistic developments. A scholar specializing in Arabic, Persian, and Turkish linguistics should examine the covenants seeking any of the subtle, but conclusive, signs of translation. The confusion of the letters *sin* and *sad* suggest that the scribes or translators of some of the covenants were not native speakers of the Arabic language. Mistakes in translation often provide clues as to the mother tongue of the translator. In other words, this is an open invitation to other Arabic linguists eager to expand our knowledge of these precious documents.

As for the variation in the lists of witnesses, Muslims should not be overly worried on their account since they may merely be late additions. Some copies of the *Covenant of the Prophet Muhammad with the Monks of Mount Sinai* feature lists of sixteen signatories while others include twenty-two. But even when the number is the same, the names of the witnesses are different. The number of Companions cited in the two versions of the *Covenant of the Prophet Muhammad with the Christians of the World* is the same at thirty-seven or thirty-eight. This is also the same number of witnesses found in the *Covenant of the Prophet Muhammad with the Christians of Najran*. One of the longest lists of signatories, however, is found on the *Covenant of the Prophet Muhammad with the Assyrian Christians* which stands at thirty-two. Why sixteen? Why twenty-two? And why thirty-seven or thirty-eight witnesses? Is there a symbolism behind these numbers? Were the scribes trying to meet a pre-established standard set by tradition? Did they simply list Companions at random? Or were the covenants passed down by different Companions? Once again, what appears as direct, first-generation, chains of narration may simply have been forged at a later point. If this were so, it would show that early Muslim scholars did not treat the *hadith* sciences very seriously. Chains of narration were simply padding used to fortify the sayings being cited.

The research upon which this book is based could also serve as a basis for a detailed study on the evolution of terms such as *mu'min* [believer], *muslim* [submitter], *mushrik* [associator / polytheist], *kafir* [infidel / unbeliever] and *munafiq* [hypocrite]. In modern Islamic usage, a *muslim* is a Muslim, a person who professes the religion of Islam, a *mu'min* is a Muslim who is a true believer, a *mushrik* is anyone who commits *shirk* or associates partners with God, including polytheists, Trinitarian Christians, and those who believe in the divinity of Christ, while *kafir* applies to all non-Muslims, be they Jews, Christians, Zoroastrians, Buddhists, Taoists, Hindus, animists, atheists or otherwise. The *Constitution of Medina* and the various covenants of the Prophet do not support these prevailing definitions. In these early sources, the followers of all Abrahamic religions—Jews, Christians, and Muslims—were viewed as *mu'minin* or believers. The term *muslimin* applied solely to Muslims: those who accepted Muhammad as the final Messenger of Allah, embraced Islam, and submitted to the Creator. The term *mushrikin* was reserved for polytheists and not to Christians who fell short of Islam's strict monotheism. As for the word *kuffar*, it described pagans, heathens, polytheists or atheists. It was not applied, as has been done in modern times, to the *ahl al-kitab* or People of the Book who were at peace with Islam although it could be used to describe those Jews and Christians who waged war against Muslims. The Prophet made a clear distinction between the Christians who were friends, like the Greek Orthodox, Armenians, and Assyrians, and the Christians who were foes, like the Byzantines. As the Qur'an says: "O you who believe! Do not take the Jews and the Christians for friends; they are friends of each other; and whoever amongst you takes them for a friend, then surely he is one of them; surely Allah does not guide the unjust people" (5:51). This verse applies to non-Muslims who are hostile to Islam. Furthermore, according to David Dakake in "The Myth of Militant Islam," from *Islam, Fundamentalism and the Betrayal of Tradition*, "friends" or *awliyya'* in this context probably does not denote "companions" but something more like "patrons" or "legal guardians." "If unbelievers have no dishonest intentions of plotting and aggression against Muslims and are inclined to coexist with them in peace," writes Ibrahim Amini, "an Islamic State, according to its diagnosis of the interests of Islam, can sign pacts of mutual coexistence with them. In the legitimate matters (permitted by the *shari'ah*) that are beneficial for both the sides, they are permitted even to cooperate" (Part 8). As the Qur'an stipulates:

> Allah does not forbid you respecting those who have not made war against you on account of (your) religion, and have not driven you forth from your homes, that you show them kindness and deal with them justly; surely Allah loves the doers of justice. Allah only forbids you respecting those who made war upon you on account of (your) religion, and drove you out from your homes and backed up (others) in your expulsion, that you make friends with them; and whoever makes friends with them, these are the unjust. (60:8–9)

As a religion of peace which seeks to spread socio-political, environmental, and spiritual peace, Islam is always open to dialogue: "If they incline to peace," advises the Qur'an, "then incline to it and trust in Allah; Surely He is the Hearing, the Knowing" (8:61). As Ibrahim Amini explains,

> It is evident from the Prophet's treaties with the unbelievers that the Islamic State, taking into consideration the interests of Islam and Muslims, can conclude treaties and pacts of friendship and cooperation with the unbelievers, polytheists and the People of the Book (*ahl al-kitab*) in matters of common welfare, such as exchange in spheres of science, agriculture, industry, commerce, economy and defence. Of course, such pacts should not pave way for the influence and interference of the unbelievers in the internal affairs of a Muslim State and should not hamper its independence and security, which is to be considered of the foremost importance at the time of concluding such pacts. In no way such pacts may be allowed to strengthen the position of the unbelievers and to endanger independence of Muslims.

Unlike today, when some scholars stress that all Christians are *ahl al-kitab*, even secular liberals and conservative fundamentalists, early Muslims distinguished between the followers of Christ who were friends and the so-called followers of Christ who were foes. A person like St. John of Damascus (Mansur ibn Sarjun) (d. 749/764 CE), who defined Islam as a Christian "heresy" could scarcely be considered *ahl al-kitab*. Patriarch Timothy I of Baghdad (727/8–823 CE), however, who defined Islam as a God-given faith that had led many to monotheism could be considered a friend (Becker, "Islam," 342). As Timothy L. Becker has written, "In times when the church was subject to Islamic control, there were more attempts to have a sympathetic understanding, and some degree of accommodation could be witnessed (along the lines that Muhammad had brought monotheism to his people, together with a sense of reverence for Scripture, and a moral code—all of which spoke of elements of divine inspiration" (644). If the Eastern Christians who submitted to Islam and showed respect for Muslim beliefs were *ahl al-kitab*, such a label could certainly never apply to the Byzantine Christians who viewed Muhammad as a false prophet, the Qur'an as a false scripture, and Islam as a false religion. Although it took 1,400 years, the Roman Catholic Church has very much come to terms with Islam. As the *Catechism of the Catholic Church* now teaches, "The plan of salvation also includes those who acknowledge the Creator, in the first place amongst whom are the Muslims; these profess to hold the faith of Abraham, and together with us they adore the one, merciful God, mankind's judge on the last day" (185: edict 841). Hence, simply because the Prophet preferred the Church of the East for political and perhaps theological reasons does not mean that his covenant does not extend to Catholics who are friendly towards Islam and Muslims. Finally, the *munafiqin* were unbelievers who pretended to be Muslims and who sided with their enemies. The term did not apply to Muslims who were weak in faith. Eventually, however, as Islamic unity disintegrated and Muslims splintered into schools and sects, terms such as *kafir* and *mushrik* were cast liberally from one group to another. As for Jews and Christians, there seems to have been some confusion among them as to the term *muslim* or submitter. Some communities appeared to have the impression that Islam or submission was simply political submission to the Prophet Muhammad and not necessarily submission to the religion he preached.

It appears that these terms suffered a semantic narrowing over the centuries as a result of confessional conflict. From brother and sister believers who belonged to the broader religion of Abraham, Jews and Christians eventually became infidels. Consequently, some jurists ruled that the People of the Book were ritually impure, that the meat of their slaughtered animals could not be consumed, and that their women could not be taken in as permanent or even fixed-term marriage by Muslim men. As Rula Jurdi Abisaab has shown, some of these rulings were the product of social and political forces (64–66). Not only were the People of the Book infidels and unbelievers, so were certain Muslims. Muhammad ibn 'Abd al-Wahhab (1703–1792 CE), the neo-Kharijite, is infamous for taking Qur'anic verses concerning polytheists and unbelievers and applying them to Sunni, Shi'ite, and Sufi Muslims. For the Wahhabis, only they are the true *muwahhidun* or monotheists while the rest of traditional Muslims are innovators and polytheists. Even "moderate" and "Modernist" jurists like Yusuf al-Qaradawi (b. 1926 CE) have echoed these ideas, ruling that Shi'ites are infidels who are worse than Jews and Christians. This speaks volumes of this demagogue's view of anyone who is not a Salafi. How, then, can one convince such people that peaceful People of the Book, at least those of them who are believing and observant Jews and Christians, are believers, when they believe that the followers of the four Sunni schools, along with Shi'ites, Sufis, and 'Ibadis, are all infidels? The situation is certainly tragic for there cannot be unity between Jews, Christians, and Muslims without there first being unity among Muslims themselves. The powers that be evidently understand this, which is why they are dedicated to inciting sectarian conflicts throughout the Muslim world. "Divide and conquer" remains the rule of the day. When the U.S. occupation in Iraq outlawed the Sunni Baath Party and installed a predominantly Shi'ite regime, even at the risk of inviting incursions from Iran, this acted to profoundly destabilize Iraq by inciting sectarian violence. And according to Noam Chomsky, in an email to the author of the Foreword to this book, the U.S., like Britain before it, has often supported Islamicist extremist groups so as to prevent the development of strong Islamic nation-states, who are seen as the "real enemy."

"[T]he legal protection of the People of the Book," writes Reza Shah-Kazemi, "is enshrined in the Islamic revelation, and it is based on the unity of the Abrahamic message." "This unity of essence," he continues, "transcends the differences between the faith-communities making up the Abrahamic family." While some superficial scholars have viewed the position of the People of the Book as secondary to that of Muslims, Shah-Kazemi rightly argues that "the legal principle of protection is in itself the expression of the fundamental unity of the Abrahamic faiths, an inward unity of spirit which is directly connected to 'that which is finest,' that which is *ahsan*, and which takes precedence over the differences between the faiths on the level of external forms." In other words, "just as the divine reality transcends all dogma, likewise, sincere devotion to that reality transcends the dogmatic framework within which it is accomplished" (Kazemi). As the covenants of the Prophet clearly demonstrate, the *ahl al-dhimmah* or People of Protection represent a fundamental component of the Muslim community or *ummah*. This shows the utter ignorance of individuals such as Richard L. Rubenstein who claim that "Islamic tradition envisages no such thing as genuine peace between faithful Muslims and infidels" (124).

If the Prophet perceived himself as the head of *Ale Ibrahim* or the Family of Abraham, a Patriarch who acted as the leader of Jews, Christians, and Muslims, this idealized alliance of the broader People of the Book broke down and he was eventually identified only as the leaders of the Muslims. According to Shi'ite eschatology, this lost balance will be restituted by Imam Muhammad al-Mahdi who will bring about the Universal Manifestation of the Great Kingdom of *Ale Muhammad* or the *Wilayah Muhammadiyyah* which was bestowed upon the Family of Abraham in the person of the Twelfth Imam from the Household of the Prophet. For Ayatullah Mirza Mahdi Pooya Yazdi, "This Twelfth Imam, and nobody else, can claim to combine in him all the spiritual and blood heritage from Adam to the Last Prophet, Muhammad. He represents both the branches of the House of Ibrahim, the Ishmaelite branch through his father and Israelite branch through his mother, Narjis, who was a direct descendant of Simon Peter, the true successor of the Holy Prophet Jesus" (Sa'eed 42). It may very well be that Imam Muhammad al-Mahdi will finally bring together Jews, Christians, and Muslims, into the Family of Abraham.

My commentary, as limited in scope as it may be, could easily be expanded upon, and the covenants analyzed from the perspective of Islamic jurisprudence, political science, and economics, as well as sociology, ethics, and leadership studies. Reza Shah-Kazemi, for example, has published a short, but insightful, commentary on the *Covenant of the Prophet Muhammad with the Monks of Mount Sinai* written from a Traditionalist perspective which is well-rooted in the Qur'an and Sunnah. Considering the large body of travel literature that was produced in Arabic, Persian, and other languages from Islamic lands in past centuries, these works should all be surveyed for references to Mount Sinai, the Monastery of Saint Catherine, and the *Covenant* or *Pact of the Prophet*. A meticulous survey of *diyarat* or monastery literature, namely, books written by Muslims on Christian holy places, should also be conducted, as well as an examination of geographical literature produced in Arabic and Persian. There also remains much to be found in European accounts of voyages to the Holy Land. There are literally hundreds of itineraries, journals, and travel logs, written in a large number of European languages, which have been published over the past millennium and a half (see Robinson and Smith 534–553). This does not even include the hundreds of books on the history, culture, geography, and religions of the Holy Land which were published by authors who had not themselves visited the region. While it would be a monumental endeavor, all of these sources should be surveyed to produce a complete history of the covenants of the Prophet. Finally, Arabists and Islamicists are invited to improve upon my translations and to produce new ones in other languages. Clearly, I have only touched upon a few of the aspects of the covenants that might be researched. Each of these, however, could be explored in greater depth—a possibility that I hope will spark the intellectual curiosity of my colleagues. So, I invite them to join the caravan, for the world continues to be a most interesting place filled with inexhaustible wonders.

Those who believe (in the Qur'an), and those who follow the Jewish scriptures, and the Christians and the Sabians—any who believe in Allah and the Last Day, and work righteousness, shall have their reward with their Lord; on them shall be no fear, nor shall they grieve. (2:62)

Part IV

BACKMATTER

But yes, whoever fulfills his commitment and fears Allah—then indeed, Allah loves those who fear Him. Indeed, those who exchange the covenant of Allah and their (own) oaths for a small price will have no share in the Hereafter, and Allah will not speak to them or look at them on the Day of Resurrection, nor will He purify them; and they will have a painful punishment. (3:77–78)

Appendix 1

Witnesses to the Covenants

MORROW	HADDAD	SKROBUCHA	RELIABILITY
ʻAli ibn Abi Talib	Ali Ibn Abi Talib	Ali the son of Abu Thaleb	Yes (S) / No (SH)
Abu Bakr ibn Abi Quhafah	Abou Bekr Ibn Kahafat	Abombake ibn Ambi Kaphe	Yes (S) / Yes (SH)
ʻUmar ibn al-Khattab	Omar Ibn El-Khattab	Homar, the son of Hat-tavi	Yes (S) / No (SH)
ʻUthman ibn ʻAffan	Ottman Ibn Affan	Ottoman, the son of Gafas	Yes (S) / No (SH)
Abu al-Darda'	Aboul Darda	*Missing*	Yes (S) / Yes (SH)
Abi Hurayrah	Abou Harirat	*Missing*	Yes (S) / No (SH)
ʻAbd Allah ibn Maʻsud	Abdullah Ibn Masood	Ambtelack, the son of Messutt	Yes (S) / Yes (SH)
ʻAbbas ibn ʻAbd al-Muttalib	Abbas Ibn Abdoul Mottaleb	*Missing*	Yes (S) / Yes (SH)
Harith ibn Thabit	El-Harith Ibn Thabit	*Missing*	Yes (S) / Yes (SH)
ʻAbd al-ʻAzim ibn Hasan	Abdoul Azim Ibn Haasan	Amphachin, the son of Hassan	Unknown
Fudayl ibn ʻAbbas	El-Fadhl Ibn Abbas	Phazer, the son of Abbas	Yes (S) / Yes (SH)
al-Zubayr ibn al-ʻAwwam	Ezzobier Ibn El-Awam	*Missing*	Yes (S) / No (SH)
Talhah ibn ʻAbd Allah	Talhat Ibn Abdullah	Talat, the son of Ampto-lack	Yes (S) / No (SH)
Saʻd ibn Muʻadh	Said Ibn Maath	Saith, the son of Maat	Yes (S) / Yes (SH)
Saʻd ibn ʻUbadah	Said Ibn Abada	Ziphir, the son of Abuan	Yes (S) / Yes (SH)
Thabit ibn Nafis	Thabit Ibn Nafees	Thavitt, the son of Nesis	Yes (S) / No (SH)
Zayd ibn Thabit	Zied Ibn Thabit	Saat the son of Abbatt	Yes (S) / Yes (SH)
Bu Hanifah ibn ʻUbayyah	Abou Hanifa Ibn Attaba	*Missing*	Unknown
Hashim ibn ʻUbayyah	Hashim Ibn Obied	Kasmer the son of Abid	Unknown
Muʻazzam ibn al-Qurayshi	Maazam Ibn Kariesh	Muathem, the son of Kasvi	Unknown
ʻAbd Allah ibn ʻAmr al-ʻAs	Abdullah Ibn Omar Ibn El-Aas	Ambtullack the son of Omar	Yes (S) / No (SH)
ʻAmmar ibn Yasir	Aamir Ibn Yasir	Azur, the son of Jassin	Yes (S) / Yes (SH)

MAUCHIN / GÉRAMB	POCOCKE	RELIABILITY
Aly ebn Taleb	Ali the son of Abu Thaleb	Yes (S) / No (SH)
Aboubekr Aly Kohafey	Abombaker ibnAmbi Kaphe	Yes (S) / No (SH)
Omar ebn el-Khattab	Homar, the son of Hattavi	Yes (S) / No (SH)
Otman ebn Hassan	Ottoman, the son of Gafas	Yes (S) / No (SH)
About el Darda	*Missing*	Yes (S) / Yes (SH)
Abou Horeyrah	*Missing*	Yes (S) / No (SH)
Abdallah Abou Massaoud	Ambtelack, the son of Messutt	Yes (S) / Yes (SH)
Abbas ebn Abdel Motteb	*Missing*	Yes (S) / Yes (SH)
Hareth ebn Thabet	*Missing*	Yes (S) / Yes (SH)
Adel Azim eben Hassan	*Missing*	Unknown
Fodeyl ebn Abbas	Phazer, the son of Abbas	Yes (S) / Yes (SH)
Zobeir ebn Aouan	Ziphir, the son of Abuan	Yes (S) / No (SH)
Talhat ebn Obeydallah	Talat, the son of Amptolack	Yes (S) / No (SH)
Saad ebn Maoz	Saat the son of Abbatt	Yes (S) / Yes (SH)
Saad ebn Obadey	Saith, the son of Maat	Yes (S) / Yes (SH)
Thabet ebn Kays	Thavitt, the son of Nesis	Yes (S) / No (SH)
Missing	Amprachin, the son of Hassan	Yes (S) / Yes (SH)
Mou Khayetmeth [?]	*Missing*	Unknown
Hachem ebn Omyeh	Kazmer, the son of Abid	Unknown
Meazzam ebn Kerachy	Muathem, the son of Kasvi	Unknown
Abdallah ebn Amrou Ebn el As	Ambtelack, the son of Omar	Yes (S) / No (SH)
Amer ebn Yassin	Azur, the son of Jassin	Yes (S) / Yes (SH)

WORLD (1655)	WORLD (1630)	WORLD (1538)	RELIABILITY
Abu Bakr al-Siddiq	Abu Bakr al-Siddiq	Abu Bakr al-Siddiq	Yes (S) / No (SH)
Missing	ʻUmar ibn al-Khattab	ʻUmar ibn al-Khattab	Yes (S) / No (SH)
ʻUthman ibn ʻAffan	ʻUthman ibn ʻAffan	ʻUthman ibn ʻAffan	Yes (S) / No (SH)
Missing	ʻAli ibn Abi Talib	ʻAli ibn Abi Talib	Yes (S) / Yes (SH)
Muʻawiyyah ibn Abi Sufyan	Muʻawiyyah ibn Abi Sufyan	*Missing*	Yes (S) / No (SH)
Missing	Abu al-Darda'	Abu al-Darda'	Yes (S) / Yes (SH)

Abu al-Darr	Abu Dharr	Abu Dharr	Yes (S) / Yes (SH)
Missing	*Missing*	*Missing*	Yes (S) / Yes (SH)
ʻAbd Allah ibn Masʻud	Abd Allah ibn Masʻud	ʻAbd Allah ibn Masʻud	Yes (S) / Yes (SH)
Ibn al-ʻAbbas	ʻAbd Allah ibn ʻAbbas	al-ʻAbbas ibn ʻAbd al-Malik	Yes (S) / Yes (SH)
Hamzah ibn ʻAbd al-Muttalib	Hamzah ibn ʻAbd al-Muttalib	Hisham ibn ʻAbd al-Muttalib	Yes (S) / Yes (SH)
Missing	Fadl	Fadl ibn al-ʻAbbas al-Zahri	Yes (S) / Yes (SH)
Missing	al-Zubayr ibn al-ʻAwwam	*Missing*	Yes (S) / No (SH)
Talhah ibn ʻAbd Allah	Talhah ibn ʻAbd Allah	Talhah ibn ʻAbd Allah	Yes (S) / No (SH)
Saʻd ibn Muʻadh	Saʻd ibn Muʻadh (twice)	Saʻid ibn Muʻazz	Yes (S) / No (SH)
Saʻd ibn ʻAbadah	Saʻd ibn ʻUbadah	Saʻid ibn ʻUbadah	Yes (S) / Yes (SH)
Thabit ibn Qays	Thabit ibn Qays	Thabit ibn Qays	Yes (S) / No (SH)
Zayd ibn Thabit	Zayd ibn Thabit	Yazid ibn Talit	Yes (S) / Yes (SH)
Missing	ʻAbd Allah ibn Zayd	ʻAbd Allah ibn Yazid	Yes (S) / No (SH)
Sahl ibn Bayda	Sahl ibn Bayda	Sahl ibn Tamim	Yes (S) / No (SH)
ʻUthman ibn Matʻun	ʻUthman ibn Matʻun	*Missing*	Yes (S) / Yes (SH)
Missing	Da'ud ibn Jubayr	*Missing*	Yes (S) / Yes (SH)
Abu al-ʻAliyyah	Abu al-ʻAliyyah	*Missing*	Unknown
ʻAbd Allah ibn ʻAmr ibn al-ʻAs	ʻAbd Allah ibn ʻAmr ibn al-ʻAs	ʻAbd Allah ibn ʻAmr ibn al-ʻAs	Yes (S) / No (SH)
Abu Ahrifah	Abu Ahrifah	Abu Hanifah	Yes (S) / Yes (SH)
Ibn ʻUsayr	Ibn ʻUsayr	Abu al-ʻAzir	Yes (S) / Yes (SH)
Ibn Rabiʻah	Ibn Rabiʻah	*Missing*	Yes (S) / Yes (SH)
ʻUmar ibnYamin	ʻUmar ibn Yamin	ʻAmr ibn Yasir	Yes (S) / Yes (SH)
Hashim ibn ʻAsiyyah	Hashim ibn ʻAsiyyah	Hashim ibn ʻAbd Allah	Unknown
Hassan ibn Thabit	Hassan ibn Thabit	Hassan ibn Nabit	Yes (S) / Yes (SH)
Kaʻb ibn Kaʻb	Kaʻb ibn Kaʻb	*Missing*	Yes (S) / Yes (SH)
Kaʻb ibn Malik	Kaʻb ibn Malik	*Missing*	Yes (S) / Yes (SH)
Jaʻfar ibn Abi Talib	Jaʻfar ibn Abi Talib	*Missing*	Yes (S) / Yes (SH)
Harfus ibn Zayd	Harfus ibn Zayd	Farsus ibn Amir ibn Yazid	No (S) / No (SH)
Usamah ibn Zayd	Usamah ibn Zayd	*Missing*	Yes (S) / Yes (SH)
Zayd ibn Arqam	Zayd ibn Arqam	*Missing*	Yes (S) / Yes (SH)
Missing	*Missing*	Abu Hurayrah	Yes (S) / No (SH)
Missing	*Missing*	*Missing*	Yes (S) / No (SH)

Missing	*Missing*	*Missing*	Yes (S) / Yes (SH)
Missing	*Missing*	ʻUbayd ibn Mansur	Unknown
Missing	*Missing*	ʻAbd al-ʻAzim	Unknown
Missing	*Missing*	ʻAbd al-ʻAzim ibn Husayn	Unknown
Missing	*Missing*	Muʻazzam ibn Moshe	Yes (S) / Yes (SH)

ASSYRIA (Morrow)	**ASSYRIA (Malech)**	**NAJRAN**	**RELIABILITY**
Abu Bakr Siddiq	Abubakr Zadik	ʻAtiq ibn Abi Quhafah	Yes (S) / No (SH)
ʻUmar bin Khattab	Omar Ben Chetab	ʻUmar ibn al-Khattab	Yes (S) / No (SH)
ʻUthman ibn ʻAffan	*Missing*	ʻUthman ibn ʻAffan	Yes (S) / No (SH)
ʻAli ibn Abi Talib	*Missing*	ʻAli ibn Abi Talib	Yes (S) / Yes (SH)
Muʻawiyyah ibn Abi Sufyan	Moavijah Ibn Abi Sofijan	Muʻawiyyah ibn Abi Sufyan	Yes (S) / No (SH)
Abu Darda'	Abu Darda	Abu al-Darda'	Yes (S) / Yes (SH)
Abu Dharr	Abuzar	Abu Dharr	Yes (S) / Yes (SH)
Abu Barah	Abubra	*Missing*	Yes (S) / Yes (SH)
ʻAbd Allah ibn Masʻud	Abdula Ibn Masud	ʻAbd Allah ibn Masʻud	Yes (S) / Yes (SH)
ʻAbd Allah ibn ʻAbbas	Abdula Ibn Abas	al-ʻAbbas ibn ʻAbd al-Muttalib	Yes (S) / Yes (SH)
Hamzah ibn al-Muttalib	Hamzah Ibn Almulabb	*Missing*	Yes (S) / Yes (SH)
Fadl ibn ʻAbbas	Fazl Ibn Abas	al-Fadl ibn al-ʻAbbas	Yes (S) / Yes (SH)
Zubayr ʻAwwam	Zaibar Ibn Aqam	al-Zubayr ibn al-ʻAwwam	Yes (S) / No (SH)
Talhah ibn ʻAbd Allah	Tilha Ibn Abdullah	Talha ibn ʻUbayd Allah	Yes (S) / No (SH)
Saʻd ibn Muʻadh	Saad Ben Maaz	Saʻd ibn Muʻadh	Yes (S) / No (SH)
Saʻd ibn ʻUbadah	Saad Ibn Ebadah	Saʻd ibn ʻUbada	Yes (S) / Yes (SH)
Thabit ibn Qays	Sabeh Ibn Kebis	Thumamah ibn Qays	Yes (S) / No (SH)
Yazid ibn Thabit	Jazid Ibn Sabib	Zayd ibn Thabit	Yes (S) / Yes (SH)
ʻAbd Allah ibn Yazid	Abdullah Ben Jazid	ʻAbd Allah ibn Thabit	Yes (S) / No (SH)
Sahl ibn Sufya [or Sifa]	*Missing*	*Missing*	Yes (S) / No (SH)
ʻUthman ibn Matʻun	Othman Ibn Mazum	ʻUmar ibn Mazh'un ʻAmmar	Yes (S) / Yes (SH)
Dawud ibn Jibah	David Ibn Gijah	*Missing*	Yes (S) / Yes (SH)
Abu al-ʻAliyyah	Abu Alalijah	Abu al-Ghaliyyah	Unknown

'Abd Allah ibn 'Amr ibn al-Qadi	Abdullah Ibn Omar Alqazi	'Abd Allah ibn 'Amr ibn al-'As	Yes (S) / No (SH)
Abu Hudayfah	*Missing*	Abu Hudayfah	Yes (S) / Yes (SH)
Ibn 'Asir	Ibn Azir	*Missing*	Yes (S) / Yes (SH)
Bin Rabi'ah	Ibn Rabiah	*Missing*	Yes (S) / Yes (SH)
'Ammar ibn Yasir	*Missing*	*Missing*	Yes (S) / Yes (SH)
Hashim ibn 'Asiyyah	Hashim Ibn Azijah	*Missing*	UNKNOWN
Hassan ibn Thabit	Hasan Ibn Zabid	Hassan ibn Thabit	Yes (S) / Yes (SH)
Ka'b ibn Ka'b	Kab Ibn Kab	*Missing*	Yes (S) / Yes (SH)
Ka'b ibn Malik	Ibn Malech	Ka'b ibn Malik	Yes (S) / Yes (SH)
Ja 'far ibn Abi Talib	Jafar Ibn Abu Talib	Ja'far ibn Abi Talib	Yes (S) / Yes (SH)
Missing	*Missing*	Hurqus ibn Zuhayr	Yes (S) / Yes (SH)
Missing	*Missing*	Usamah ibn Zayd	Yes (S) / Yes (SH)
Missing	*Missing*	Zayd ibn Arqam	Yes (S) / Yes (SH)
Missing	Abu Harifah	Abu Hurayrah	Yes (S) / No (SH)
Missing	Ebar Ibn Jaamir	Ibn Jubayr	Yes (S) / No (SH)
Missing	Suhail Ibn Mifah	*Missing*	Yes (S) / Yes (SH)
Missing	*Missing*	*Missing*	Unknown
Missing	*Missing*	*Missing*	Unknown
Missing	*Missing*	*Missing*	Unknown
Missing	Mus'ah ibn al-Zubayr	*Missing*	Yes (S) / Yes (SH)

Appendix 2
Possible Modes of Transmission of the Covenants

Prophet Muhammad

↓	↓	↓	↓	↓	↓	↓
Najran	Sinai	Assyria	Egypt	Levant	Persia	Other Christian Communities
↓	↓ ↓ ↓ ↓ ↓ ↓	↓ ↓ ↓ ↓ ↓ ↓ ↓ ↓ ↓ ↓ ↓ ↓	↓ ↓ ↓ ↓ ↓	↓ ↓ ↓ ↓ ↓ ↓ ↓ ↓	↓ ↓ ↓ ↓ ↓ ↓ ↓ ↓ ↓	
(9th c. CE)	(1561 CE)	(1822 or 1845 CE)	(1538 CE)	(Paris 1630)	(17th c. CE)	

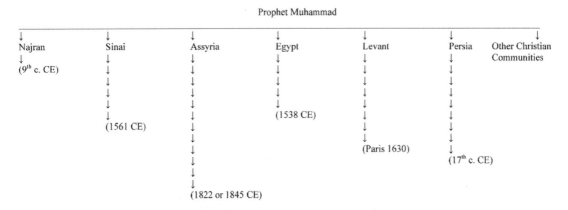

Table 1: Multiple Individual Prophetic Transmissions (above)

Prophet Muhammad
↓
Najran (9th c. CE)
↓
Egypt (1538)
↓
Sinai (1561)
↓
Levant (1630)
↓
Persia (17th c. CE)
↓
Assyria (1822 or 1845 CE)

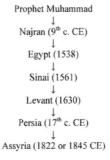

Table 2: Single Source Transmission with Subsequent Segmentation (above)

Prophet Muhammad

↓ Najran (9th c. CE) | ↓ Other Christian Communities

↓
Egypt (1538) → Sinai (1561) → Persia (17th c. CE) → Assyria (1882 or 1845) [or possibly] Sinai (1561) → Precursor of Egypt (1538)
↓
Levant (1630)

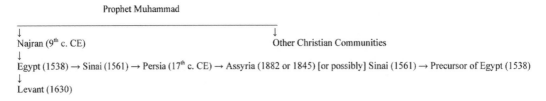

Table 3: Single Source Transmission with Bifurcation (above)

Prophet Muhammad

↓ Najran (9th c. CE) | ↓ Q Source Covenant | ↓ Other Christian Communities

Q Source Covenant:

↓ Egypt (1538) | ↓ Levant (1630) | ↓ Sinai (1561) | ↓ Persia (17th c. CE) | ↓ Assyrian (1822 or 1845)

Table 4: Single Transmission from Q Source Covenant Key:

Najran	=	*The Covenant of the Prophet Muhammnad with the Christians of Najran* (9th century CE)
Egypt	=	*The Covenant of the Prophet Muhammnad with the Christians of the World* (1538 CE)
Sinai	=	*The Covenant of the Prophet Muhammnad with the Monks of Mount Sinai* (1561 CE)
Levant	=	*The Covenant of the Prophet Muhammnad with the Christians of the World* (1630 CE)
Persia	=	*The Covenant of the Prophet Muhammnad with the Christians of Persia* (17th century CE)
Assyria	=	*The Covenant of the Prophet Muhammnad with the Assyrian Christians* (1822 or 1845–1847 CE)
Armenia	=	*The Covenant of the Prophet Muhammnad with the Armenian Christians of Jerusalem* (1538 CE)

3: The Sinai Peninsula from Space

List of Illustrations

4: Mount Sinai by Francis Frith (1822–1898)

5: Mount Sinai

6: Mount Sinai

7: Mount Sinai

8: Merchants at the top of Mount Sinai

9: View from the top of Mount Sinai

10: View from the top of Mount Sinai

11: Mount Sinai

12: Mount Sinai

13: View from the top of Mount Sinai

14: The Stairway of Repentance

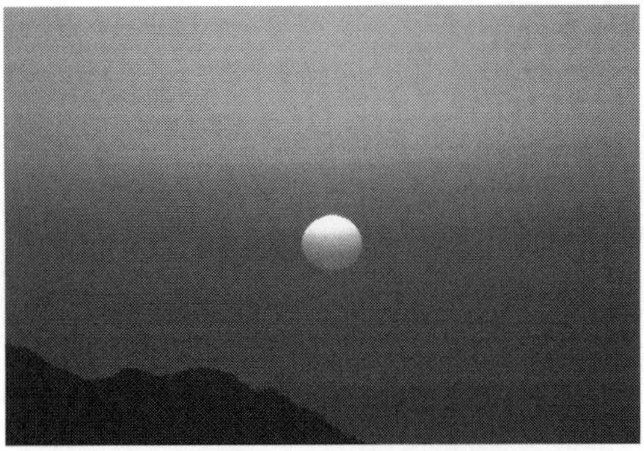

15: Sunset over Mount Sinai

16: St. Catherine's Monastery (Iacovos Moskos)

17: The Monastery of St. Catherine (Pierre Nicolas Ransonette, 1745–1810)

18: Monastery of St. Catherine c. 1891 by Helen Harris, with view of church tower & minaret

19: The Monastery of St. Catherine (Francis Frith, 1822–1898)

20: Monastery of St. Catherine in 1852
with view of minaret

21: Monastery of St. Catherine with
Mount Sinai in background

22: Monastery of St. Catherine with Mount Sinai in background

23: Monastery of St. Catherine viewed from the mountains above

24: Monastery of St. Catherine

25: Monastery of St. Catherine at Mount Sinai

26: Monastery of St. Catherine at Mount Sinai

27: Monastery of St. Catherine

28: Monastery of St. Catherine at Mount Sinai

29: Monastery of St. Catherine at Mount Sinai

30: Monastery of St. Catherine at Mount Sinai

31a: Church tower & minaret of mosque of Monastery of St. Catherine at Mount Sinai

33: The Burning Bush

31b: Inside the mosque in the Monastery of St. Catherine at Mount Sinai, with the 12th-century Fatimid mimbar

32: St. Catherine (Cosimo Rosselli, 17th c. CE)

34: Ottoman *Achtiname* (by permission of St. Catherine's Monastery, Sinai, Egypt)

35: Painting of Infant Jesus and Virgin Mary surrounded by angels, from Monastery of St. Catherine, a likeness of which was painted inside the Ka'bah

36: Top of Mount Sinai, by Adrien Egron (1837)

37: Chapel of the Holy Trinity on the top of Mount Sinai:
on the spot where God spoke to Moses

38: Chapel of the Holy Trinity on the top of Mount Sinai:
on the spot where God spoke to Moses

39: Cave where Moses received Ten Commandments and where Muhammad meditated

40: Secondary Entrance to Cave of Moses and Muhammad

41: Footprint of the Prophet Harun (Aaron) with his shrine in upper right

42: Print of Prophet Salih's she-camel or print of Buraq, the mystical beast that Muhammad rode during his Night Journey

43: *Jami' Fatimah* [Mosque of Fatimah], built on top of Mount Sinai by the Fatimids

44: *Jami' Fatimah* [Mosque of Fatimah], built on top of Mount Sinai by the Fatimids

45: Ilyas' [Elijah's] Hollow: where he heard the Voice of God when fleeing evil King Ahab and Queen Jezebel, 1 Kings 19: 8–9

46. Ilyas' [Elijah's] Hollow: where he heard the Voice of God when fleeing evil King Ahab and Queen Jezebel, 1 Kings 19: 8–9

47, 48, 49: The Gate of Repentance of the Prophet Ilyas [Elijah]

50: The Chapel of Repentance

51: Image of Golden Calf in mouth of Wadi Shu'ayb near Mount Sinai

52: Persian painting of meeting between Muhammad & Bahira the Monk

53: Inside the residence of Bahira, the Monk

54: Residence of Bahira, the Monk

55: Inside view of Cathedral of Bahira, the Monk

56: Outside view of Cathedral of Bahira, the Monk

57: Outside view of Cathedral of Bahira, the Monk

58: Prints of the Prophet Muhammad's camel in Busrah, Syria

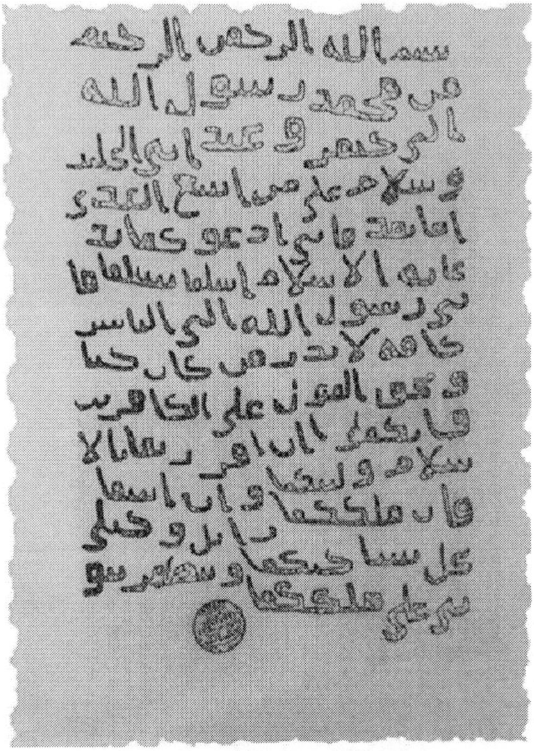

59: Letter of the Prophet to the Rulers of Oman (see page 51)

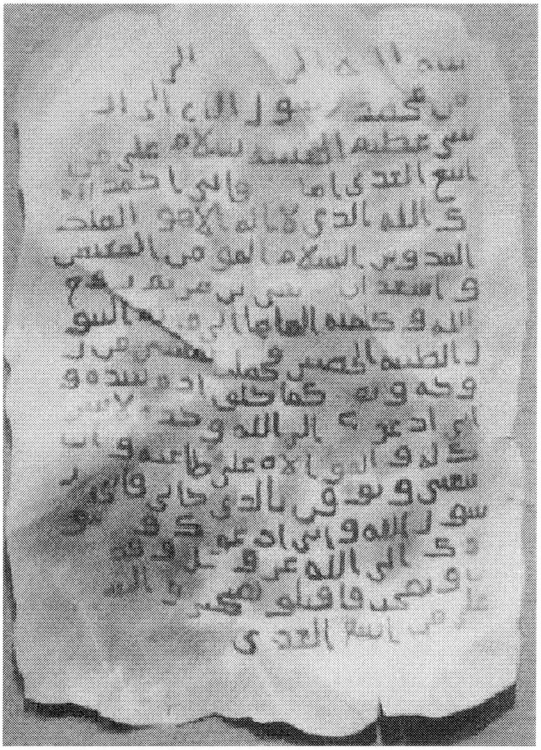

60: Letter of the Prophet to the Emperor of Abyssinia (See page 46)

61: Letter of the Prophet to the Rulers of Bahrayn (see page 50)

62: Letter of the Prophet to Muqawqis, Ruler of Egypt (see page 48)

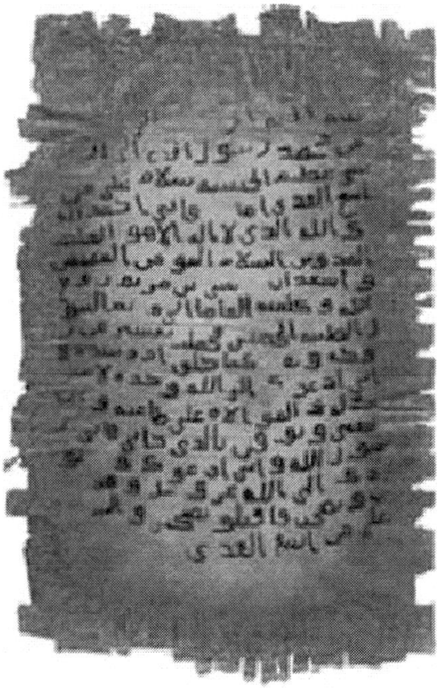

63: Letter of the Prophet to Emperor of Abyssinia

64: Letter of the Prophet to Ruler of the Ghassanids (see page 52)

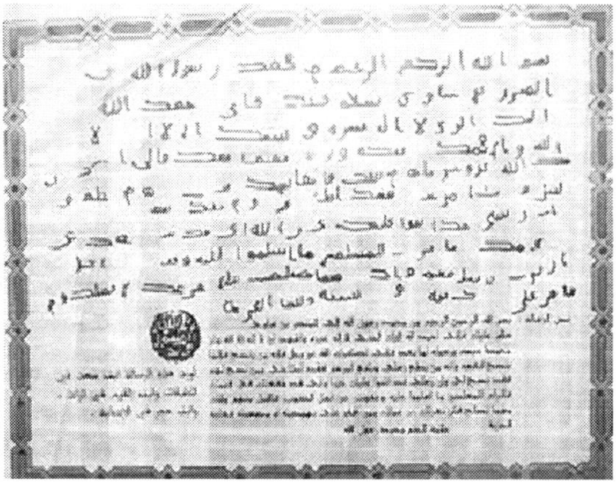

65: Letter of the Prophet to Mundhir ibn Sawa al-Tamimi (see page 49)

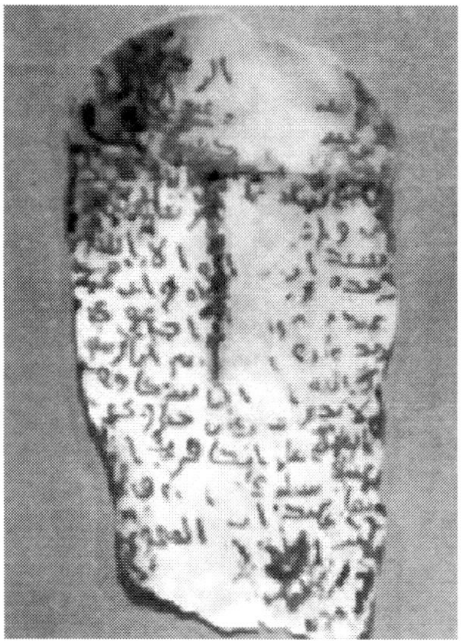

66: Letter of the Prophet to the Persian Emperor

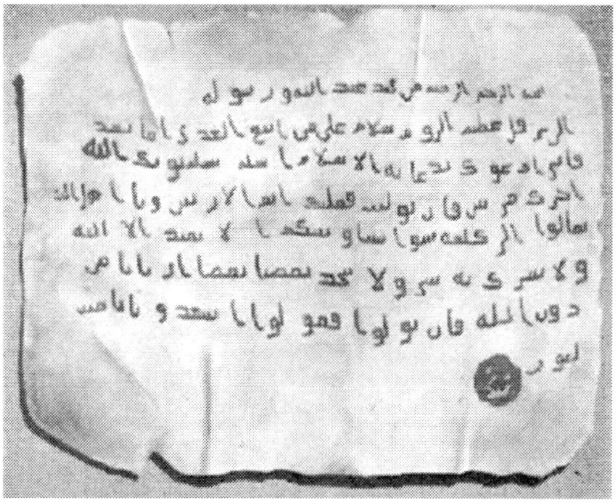

67: Letter of the Prophet to Heraclius (see page 47)

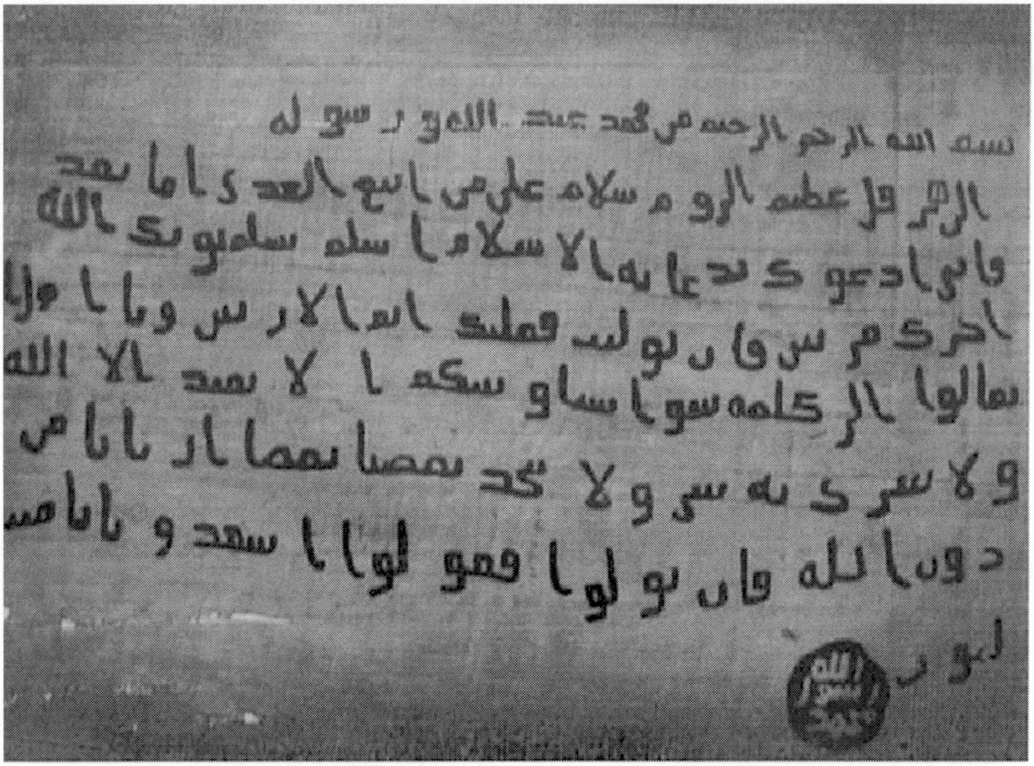

68: Letter of the Prophet to Heraclius

69: Letter of the Prophet to al-Najashi, Ruler of Abyssinia (see page 46)

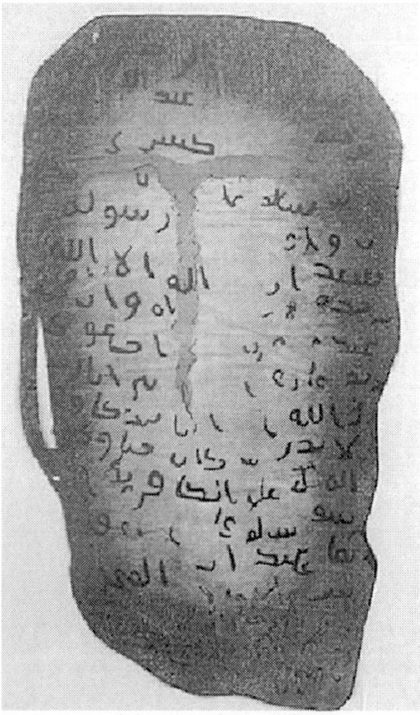

70: Letter of the Prophet to the Persians of Kisra, inviting them to Islam (see page 49)

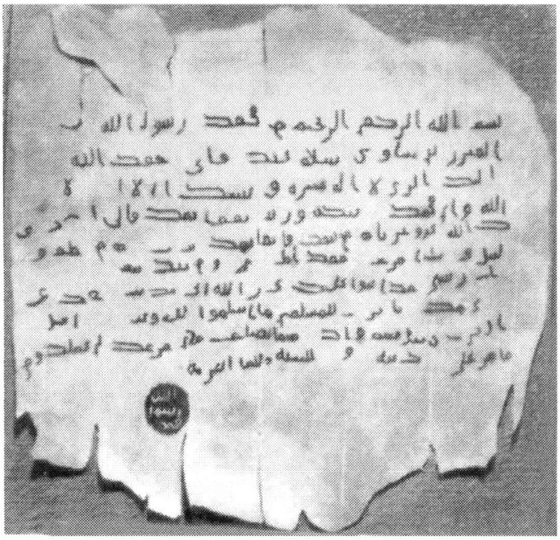

71: Letter of the Prophet to Mundhir ibn Sawa, Governor of Bahrayn

72: The Seal of the Prophet Muhammad

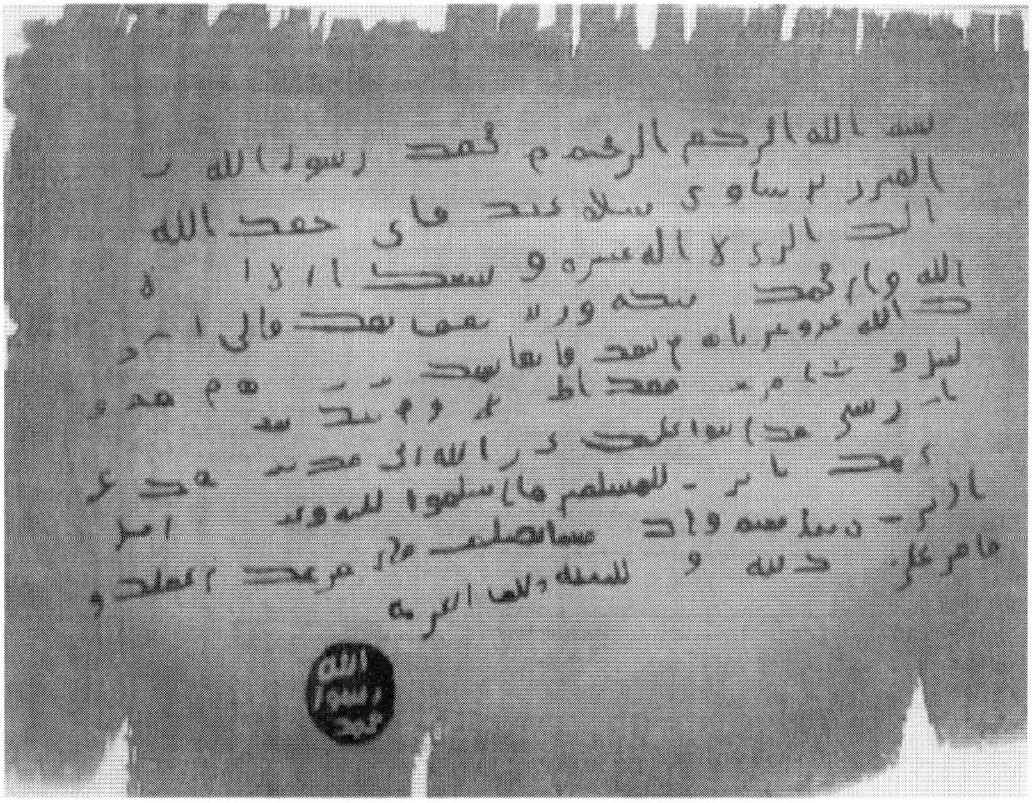

73: Letter of the Prophet to Mundhir ibn Sawa, Governor of Bahrayn

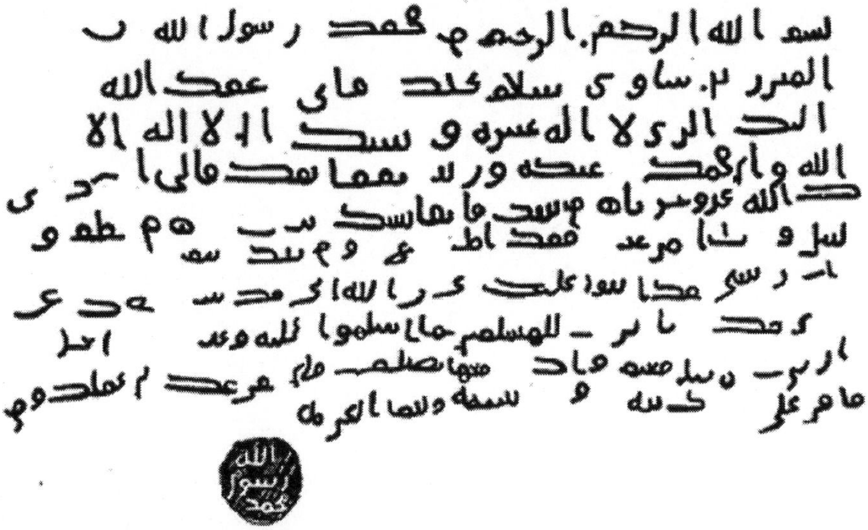

74: Letter of the Prophet to Mundhir ibn Sawa, Governor of Bahrayn

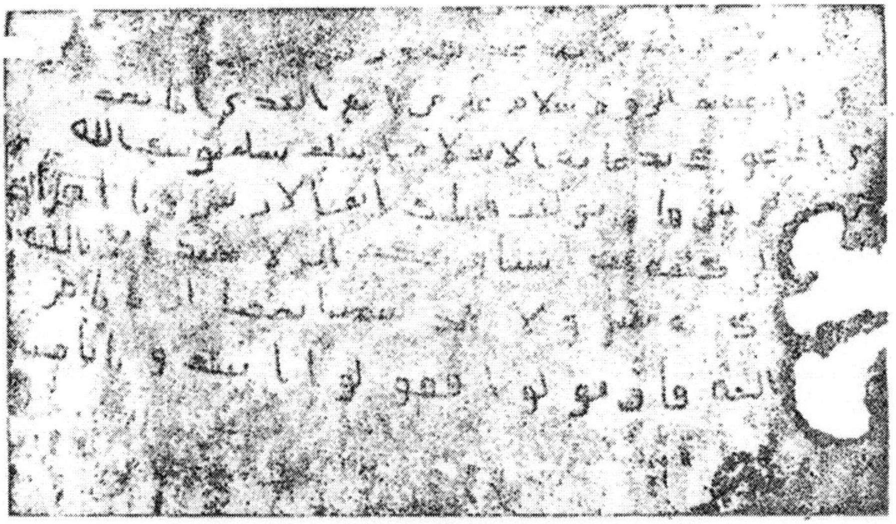

75: Letter of the Prophet to Heraclius

76. Letter of the Prophet to Musaylimah al-Kadhdhab

Bibliography

'Abd al-Malik, Sami Salah. "Les mosquées du Sinaï au Moyen Âge." *Le Sinaï durant l'antiquité et le moyen âge, 4000 ans d'histoire pour un desert*. Ed. Dominique Valbelle and Charles Bonnet. Paris: Éditions Érrance, 1998. 171–176.

Abu Dawud, Sulayman ibn al-Ash'ath al-Sijistani. *Sahih Sunan Abu Dawud*. Riyyad: Maktabah al-Tarbiyyah al-'Arabi li Duwwal al-Khalij, 1989.

Abu Riyya, Mahmud. *Light on the Muhammadan Sunnah or Defence of Hadith*. Trans. Hassan M. Najafi. Qum: Ansariyan Publications, 1999. Internet: http://www.maaref-foundation.com/english/library/islamic_history/light_on_the_muhammad an_sunnah/.

Adair, John. *The Leadership of Muhammad*. London: Koganpage, 2010.

Affagart, Greffin. *Relation de Terre Sainte (1533–1534)*. Ed. J. Chavanon. Paris: Librairie Victor Lecoffre, 1902. Internet: http://archive.org/details/relationdeterre sooaffauoft.

Ágoston, Gábor. "Information, Ideology, and Limits of Imperial Policy: Ottoman Grand Strategy in the Context of Ottoman-Habsburg Rivalry." *The Early Modern Ottomans: Remapping the Empire*. Ed. Virginia H. Aksan and Daniel Goffman. Cambridge: Cambridge University Press, 2007. 75–103.

Ahlul Bayt Digital Islamic Library Project. *Hadith al-thaqalayn*. Internet: http://www.al-islam.org/thaqa layn/nontl/index.htm.

Ahmad, Barakat. *Muhammad and the Jews: A Re-Examination*. New Delhi: Vikas, 1979.

Akbar, M.J. *The Shade of Swords: Jihad and the Conflict between Islam and Christianity*. London: Routledge, 2003.

Aksan, Virginia H. and Daniel Goffman. *The Early Modern Ottomans: Remapping the Empire*. Cambridge: Cambridge University Press, 2007.

'Ali, 'Abdullah Yusuf, trans. *The Holy Qur'an*. Brentwood, MA: Amana Corporation, 1983.

'Ali ibn Abi Talib. *Nahj al-balaghah*. Qum: Hawzah Publications, 1998.

'Ali Zayn al-'Abidin. *The Treatise on Rights / Risalat al-huquq*. Trans. Wm C. Chittick. Qum: Foundation of Islamic Cultural Propagation in the World, 1990.

Allen, Charles. *God's Terrorists: The Wahhabi Cult and the Hidden Roots of Modern Jihad*. Cambridge, MA: Da Capo Press, 2006.

'Amarah, Muhammad. *al-Islam wa al-akhar*. Maktabah al-Sharq al-Dawliyyah, 2002.

Amini, Ibrahim. *Foreign Policy of an Islamic State*. Qum: al-Tawhid, nd. Internet: http://www.al-islam.org/al-tawhid/foreign_policy/title.htm.

Armour, Sr., Rollin. *Islam, Christianity, and the West: A Troubled History*. Maryknoll, NY: Orbis Books, 2003.

Armstrong, Karen. *Muhammad: A Biography of the Prophet*. New York: HarperCollins, 1993.

———. *Islam: A Short History*. New York: Modern Library, 2000.

Arnold, John Muehleisen. Ishmael: *A Natural History of Islamism and its Relation to Christianity*. London: Rivingtons, 1859.

Arpee, Leon. *A History of Armenian Christianity from the Beginning to Our Own Time*. New York: The Armenian Missionary Association of America, Inc., 1946.

Arundale, Francis. *Illustrations of Jerusalem and Mount Sinai*. London: Henry Colburn, 1837.

Asia News. "Grand Mufti: All Churches on the Arabian Peninsula Should be Destroyed." *Asia News* (March 21, 2012). Internet: http://www.asianews.it/news-en/Grand-Mufti:-all-churches-on-the-Arabian-Peninsula-should-be-destroy ed-24294.html.

Atiya, Aziz Suryal. *The Arabic Manuscripts of Mount Sinai*. Baltimore: The John Hopkins Press, 1955.

Avdall, Johannes. "A Covenant of 'Ali, Fourth Caliph of Baghdad, Granting Certain Immunities and Privileges to the Armenian Nation." *Journal of the Asiatic Society of Bengal* 1–4 (1870): 60–64. Internet: http://www.globalarmenianheritage-adic.fr/oab/b_ali_ firman.htm.

Aydin, Hilmi. *The Sacred Trusts*. Somerset, NJ: Tughra Books, 2009.

Azami, M.M. *Studies in Hadith Methodology and Literature*. Indianapolis: American Trust Publication, 1977.

Azadian, Edmond Y. "Jerusalem in Limbo." *The Armenian Mirror Spectator* (May 29, 2011). Internet: http://www.mirrorspectator.com/2011/05/29/jerusalem-in-limbo.

Azraqi, al-. *Akhbar Makkah / Chroniken der Stadt Mekka*. Ed. Ferdinand Wuestenfeld. Np: Leipzig, 1858; reprint Beyrouth, 1964.

Badawi, Jamal. *Muhammad in the Bible*. Cairo: al-Falah Foundation, 2005. Internet: http://d1.islamhouse.com/data/en/ih_books/single/en_muhammad_in_the_bible.pdf.

Bahnasawy, Salim al-. *Non-Muslims in the Shari'ah*. Trans. Aisha Adel and Said Traore. Dar al-Nashr Li Jami'at, 2004.

Balagna, Josée. *L'imprimerie arabe en Occident: XVIe, XVIIe et XVIIIe siècles.* Paris: Éditions Maisonneuve & Larose, 1984.

Bangash, Zafar. *Power Manifestations of the* Sirah. Ed. Afeef Khan. Richmond Hill: Institute of Contemporary Islamic Thought, 2011.

Barnard, Bryn. *The Genius of Islam: How Muslims Made the Modern World.* New York: Alfred A. Knopf, 2011.

Basnage de Beauval, Henri. *Histoire des ouvrages des savans.* Rotterdam: Reinier Leers, 1698.

Bayhaqi, Ahmad ibn al-Husayn al-. *al-Sunan al-kubra.* Bayrut: Dar Sadr, 1968

Bayle, Pierre, John Peter Bernard, Thomas Birch, John Lockman, and George Sale. *A General Dictionary, Historical and Critical.* Vol. 1. London: J. Bettenham, 1735.

Becker, Timothy J. "Islam, Orthodoxy and." *The Encyclopedia of Eastern Orthodox Christianity.* Vol. 1. Ed. John Anthony McGuckin. Malden, MA: Wiley-Blackwell, 2011. 341–343.

———. "World Religions, Orthodoxy and." *The Encyclopedia of Eastern Orthodoxy Christianity.* Vol. 2. Ed. John Anthony McGuckin. Malden, MA: Wiley-Blackwell, 2011. 641–645.

Bell, Richard. *Introduction to the Qur'an.* Edinburgh: Edinburgh University Press, 1958.

Belleville Armenian Church. "Patriarchate of Jerusalem." *Belleville Armenian Church.* Internet: http://bellevillearmenianchurch.org/armtoday 11.htm.

Belon du Mans, Pierre. *Observations de plusieurs singularitéz et choses mémorables trouvées en Grèce, Asie, Judée, Égypte, Arabie, etc.* Paris: Hierosime de Marnef, 1538.

Berkey, Jonathan P. *The Formation of Islam: Religion and Society in the Near East, 600–1800.* Cambridge: Cambridge University Press, 2003.

Bernabé Pons, Luis F. *El cántico islámico del morisco hispano-tunecino Taybili.* Zaragoza: Institucion Fernando del Catolico, 1988.

Bernstein, Burton. *Sinai: The Great and Terrible Wilderness.* New York: The Viking Press, 1979.

Betts, Robert Brenton. *Christians in the Arab East: A Political Study.* Atlanta: John Knox Press, 1978.

Binns, John. *An Introduction to the Christian Orthodox Churches.* Cambridge: Cambridge University Press, 2002.

Boase, Roger. "The Morisco Expulsion and Diaspora: An Example of Racial and Religious Intolerance." *Cultures in Contact in Medieval Spain: Historical and Literary Essays Presented to L. P. Harvey.* Ed. David Hook and Barry Taylor. Exeter: King's College London Medieval Studies, 1990.

Bolman, Elizabeth S. "The White Monastery Federation and the Angelic Life." *Byzantium and Islam: Age of Transition, 7th–9th Century.* Ed. Helen C. Evans and Brandie Ratliff. New York: The Metropolitan Museum of Art, 2012. 75–77.

Boullata, Issa J. "*Fa-stabiqu'l-khayrat*: A Qur'anic Principle of Interfaith Relations." *Christian-Muslim Encounters.* Ed. Yvonne Yazbeck Haddad and Wadi Zaidan Haddad. Gainesville, FL: University Press of Florida, 1994. 43–53.

Bournoutian, George A. *A Concise History of the Armenian People: From Ancient Times to the Present.* 2nd ed. Costa Mesa, CA: Mazda Publishers, 2003.

Bowering, Gerhard, ed. *The Princeton Encyclopedia of Islamic Political Thought.* Princeton & Oxford: Princeton University Press, 2013.

Brevick, Harald. *Books were Opened.* Minneapolis: Thule Pub. Co, 1947.

Brockopp, Jonathan E., ed. *The Cambridge Companion to Muhammad.* Cambridge: Cambridge University Press, 2010.

Brown, Jonathan A.C. *Hadith: Muhammad's Legacy in the Medieval and Modern World.* Oxford: OneWorld, 2009.

Browne, J.G. "1937: The Assyrians: A Debt of Honor." *The Geographical Magazine* 4.6 (November 1936 to April 1937). Internet: http://www.atour.com/history/1900/20030922a.html.

Bucaille, Maurice. *The Bible, the Qur'an, and Science: The Holy Scriptures Examined in the Light of Modern Knowledge.* Trans. Alastair D. Pannell and the Author. Indianapolis: American Trust Publications, 1979.

Burckhardt, John Lewis. *Travels in Syria and in the Holy Land.* London: John Murray, 1822.

———. *Travels in Syria and in the Holy Land.* Adelaide: University of Adelaide, 2012. Internet: http://ebooks.adelaide.edu.au/b/burckhardt/john_lewis/syria/.

Busse, Heribert. *Islam, Judaism, and Christianity: Theological and Historical Affiliations.* Trans. Allison Brown. Princeton: Markus Wiener Publishers, 1988.

Cahen, Claude. "Note sur l'acceuil des chrétiens d'Orient à l'Islam." *Revue de l'histoire des religions* 166.1 (1964): 51–58.

Cansinos Assens, Rafael. *Mahoma y el Koran.* Editorial Bell: Buenos Aires, 1954.

Cantemir, Demetrius. *The History of the Growth and Decay of the Othman Empire.* Part 1. Trans. N. Tindal. London: James, John, and Paul Knapton, 1734.

———. *Histoire de l'empire othoman.* Paris: Despilly, 1743.

Catechism of the Catholic Church. Ottawa: CCCB, 1994.

Catholic Encyclopedia. "Gabriel Sionita." *Catholic Encyclopedia.* New York: Robert Appleton Company, 1913.

Internet: http://www.newadvent.org/cathen/06331a.htm.

Champdor, Albert. *Le Mont Sinaï et le Monastère de Sainte-Catherine*. Paris: Albert Guillot, 1963.

Chejne, Anwar G. *Islam and the West: The Moriscos, a Cultural and Social History*. Albany: SUNY Press, 1983.

———. *The Arabic Language: Its Role in History*. Minneapolis: University of Minnesota Press, 1969.

Chittick, William C., trans. *The Psalms of Islam:* al-Sahifat al-kamilat al-sajjadiyya. Qum: Ansariyan, 1987.

Christys, Ann. *Christians in al-Andalus: 711–1000*. New York: Routledge, 2007.

Clark, Kenneth Willis. *Checklist of Manuscripts in St. Catherine's Monastery, Mount Sinai, Microfilmed for the Library of Congress*, 1950. Washington: Library of Congress, 1952.

Clayton, Robert. *A Journal from Grand Cairo to Mount Sinai and Back Again*. London: William Boyle, 1753.

Congrès international des orientalistes. *Actes du Douzième congrès international des orientalistes*. Florence: Societe Typographique Florentine, 1901.

Constable, Olivia Remie. *Medieval Iberia: Readings from Christian, Muslim, and Jewish Sources*. Philadelphia: University of Pennsylvania Press, 1997.

Cremo, Michael A. and Richard L. Thompson. *Forbidden Archeology: The Hidden History of the Human Race*. Los Angeles: Bhaktivedanta Book Publishing, Inc., 1996.

Crone, Patricia and Michael Cook. *Hagarism: The Making of the Islamic World*. Cambridge: Cambridge UniversityPress, 1977.

———. *Slaves on Horses: The Evolution of Islamic Polity*. Cambridge: Cambridge University Press, 1980.

Cutillas Ferrer, José. "Political Plots, Espionage, and a Shi'a Text among the Moriscos." *Journal of Shi'a Islamic Studies* 5.1 (2012): 49–64.

Dadoyan, Seta B. *The Armenians in the Medieval Islamic World*. New Brunswick, NJ: Transaction Publishers, 2011.

Dadrian, Vahakn N. *German Responsibility in the Armenian Genocide: A Review of the Historical Evidence of German Complicity*. Watertown: Blue Crane Books, 1996.

Dahari, Uzi. "Les constructions de Justinien au Gebel Mousa." *Le Sinaï durant l'antiquité et le moyen âge, 4000 ans d'histoire pour un desert*. Ed. Dominique Valbelle and Charles Bonnet. Paris: Éditions Érrance, 1998. 151–156.

Dakake, David. "The Myth of a Militant Islam." *Islam, Fundamentalism and the Betrayal of Tradition*. Ed. Joseph E.B. Lumbard. Bloomington, IN: World Wisdom Books, 2004. 3–38.

Dalrymple, William. *From the Holy Mountain: A Journey among the Christians of the Middle East*. New York: Henry Holt and Company, 1997.

Daniel, Norman. *Islam and the West: The Making of an Image*. Oxford: OneWorld, 1993.

Danios. "The Protocols of the Elders of Mecca: The Final Word on the Pact of 'Umar." *Loonwatch* (March 1, 2010). Internet: http://www.loonwatch.com/tag/non-muslims/#refF18.

Dar Rah Haqq's Board of Writers. *A Glance at the Life of the Holy Prophet of Islam*. Trans. N. Tawheedi. Ed. Laleh Bakhtiar. Tehran: Islamic Propagation Organization, 1991.

Darboux, MM. G, J. Houël, and J. Tannery, et al. *Bulletin des sciences mathématiques et astronomiques*. Paris: Gauthier-Villars, 1882.

Davenport, John. *An Apology for Mohammed and the Koran*. London: J. Davy and Sons, 1869. Internet: http://archive.org/details/apologyformohammoodave.

Dawud, Abdul Ahad. *Muhammad in the Bible*. Internet: http://www.islamicsearchcenter.com/library/comparative/Muhammad%20in%20the%20Bible.pdf.

Deedat, Ahmed. *What the Bible Says about Muhammad*. Internet: http://www.kalamullah.com/Books/Deedat/What%20The%20Bible%20Says%20About%20Muhammad%20%7Bdeedat%7D.pdf.

Digbassanis, Hieromonk Demetrios. "The Library and the Archive: The Archive." *Sinai: Treasures of the Monastery of Saint Catherine*. Ed. Konstantinos Manafis. Athens: Ekdotike Athenon, 1990. 360–362.

Dobson, Richard Barrie et al. *Encyclopedia of the Middle Ages: A-J*. Paris: Editions du Cerf, 2000.

Dodge, Arthur Pillsbury. *Whence? Why? Whither?* Westwood, MA: Ariel Press, 1907.

Dodds, Jerrilynn, ed. *Al-Andalus: The Arts of Islamic Spain*. New York: The Metropolitan Museum of Art, 1992. 173–187.

Dollinger, Johann Joseph Ignaz von. *Origines du Christianisme*. Trans. M. Léon Boré. Paris: Hachette, 1842.

Donner, Fred M. *Muhammad and the Believers at the Origins of Islam*. Cambridge, MA: The Belknap Press of Harvard University Press, 2010.

Dumas, Alexandre. *Travelling Sketches in Egypt and Sinai*. Trans. A Biblical Student. London: John W. Parker, 1839.

École Pratique d'Études Bibliques, L'. "Bulletin: Golubovich, R.P. *I Frati Minori nel possesso de'luoghi santi di Gerusalemme*." *Revue Biblique* 30 (1921): 636–638.

Eliot, Sir Charles. *Turkey in Europe*. New York: Barnes & Noble, 1965.

Emhardt, William Chauncey, and George M. Lamsa. *The Oldest Christian People: A Brief Account of the History and Traditions of the Assyrian People and the Fateful History of the Nestorian Church*. New York: AMS Press, 1970.

Esposito, John L. *What Everyone Needs to Know about Islam: Answers to Frequently Asked Questions from One of America's Leading Experts*. Oxford: Oxford University Press, 2002.

Evans, Helen C. "Byzantium and Islam: Age of Transition (7th-9th Century)." *Byzantium and Islam: Age of Transition, 7th-9th Century*. Ed. Helen C. Evans with Brandie Ratliff. New York: The Metropolitan Museum of Art, 2012. 4–11.

———, with Brandie Ratliff. *Byzantium and Islam: Age of Transition, 7th-9th Century*. New York: The Metropolitan Museum of Art, 2012.

Evans, Helen C., Brandie Ratliff, eds. *Byzantium and Islam: Age of Transition, 7th–9th Century*. New York: The Metropolitan Museum of Art, 2012. 32–39.

Eversley, Lord. *The Turkish Empire: From 1288 to 1914*. New York: Howard Fertig, 1969.

Faizer, Rizwi, ed. and trans. *The Life of Muhammad: Al-Waqidi's* Kitab al-maghazi. Muhammad ibn 'Umar al- Waqidi. London and New York: Routledge, 2011.

Faroqhi, Suraiya. *The Ottoman Empire and the World around It*. London: Tauris, 2004.

Fattal, Antoine. *Le status légal des non-musulmans en pays d'Islam*. Beyrouth: Impr. Catholique, 1958.

Fazakerley, J. N. "Journey from Cairo to Mount Sinai, and Return to Cairo." *Travels in Various Countries of the East*. Ed. Rev. Robert Walpole. London: Longman, Hurst, Rees, Orme, and Brown, 1820.

Féraud-Giraud, Louis-Joseph-Delphin. *De la jurisdiction française dans les échelles du Levant et de Barbarie*. Paris: Durant & Pedone Lauriel, 1871.

Ferrill, Arther. "Attila the Hun and the Battle of Chalons." *MHQ: The Quarterly Journal of Military History*. Internet: http://history.eserver and.org/attila-at-chalons.txt.

Fine, Steven. "Jews and Judaism between Byzantium and Islam." *Byzantium and Islam: Age of Transition, 7th-9th Century*. Ed. Helen C. Evans with Brandie Ratliff. New York: The Metropolitan Museum of Art, 2012. 102–106.

Finkel, Caroline. *Osman's Dream: The History of the Ottoman Empire, 1300–1923*. New York: Basic Books, 2005.

Fletcher, Richard. *The Cross and the Crescent: Christianity and Islam from Muhammad to the Reformation*. New York: Viking, 2003.

Flood, Finbarr. "Faith, Religion, and the Material Culture of Early Islam." *Byzantium and Islam: Age of Transition, 7th-9th Century*. Ed. Helen C. Evans with Brandie Ratliff. New York: The Metropolitan Museum of Art, 2012: 244–258.

Fordham University. "Pact of 'Umar." *Fordham University* (1997). Internet: http://www.fordham.edu/halsall/source/pact-umar.asp

———. "Islam and the Jews: The Pact of 'Umar." *Fordham University* (1998). Internet: http://www.fordham.edu/halsall/jewish/jews-umar.asp.

Forsyth, George, and Kurt Weitzmann. *The Monastery of Saint Catherine: The Church and Fortress of Justinian*. Ann Arbor, University of Michigan Press, 1973.

Foss, Clive. "Arab-Byzantine Coins: Money as Cultural Continuity." *Byzantium and Islam: Age of Transition, 7th-9th Century*. Ed. Helen C. Evans and Brandie Ratliff. New York: The Metropolitan Museum of Art, 2012. 136–137.

Franck, Irene M, and David M. Brownstone. *The Silk Road: A History*. New York: Fact On File Publications, 1986.

Freeman-Grenville, G. S. P. *The Holy Land: A Pilgrim's Guide to Israel, Jordan, and the Sinai*. New York: Continuum, 1996.

Frescobaldi, Lionardo di Nicolo. *Viaggio di Lionardo di Nicolo Frescobaldi in Egitto ed in Terra Santa*. Roma: Stamperia Carlo Mordacchini, 1818.

Gabriel, Richard A. *Muhammad: Islam's First Great General*. Norman: University of Oklahoma Press, 2007.

Galey, John. *Sinai and the Monastery of St. Catherine*. Garden City, NY: Doubleday & Company, 1980.

Géhin, Paul. "La bibliotèque de Sainte-Catherine du Sinaï: Fonds anciens et nouvelles découvertes." *Le Sinaï durant l'antiquité et le moyen âge, 4000 ans d'histoire pour un desert*. Ed. Dominique Valbelle and Charles Bonnet. Paris: Éditions Érrance, 1998. 157–164.

Géramb, Baron Marie-Joseph de. *Pélerinage à Jerusalem et au Mont-Sinaï*. Tournay: J. Casterman, 1837.

————. *Pilgrimage to Jerusalem and Mount Sinai*. Vol. II. Philadelphia: Carey and Hart, 1840.

Gervers, Michael and R. J. Bizhazi. *Conversion and Continuity: Indigenous Christian Communities in Islamic Lands: Eighth to Eighteenth Centuries*. Toronto: Pontifical Institute of Mediaeval Studies, 1990.

Gibbon, Edward. *The History of the Decline and Fall of the Roman Empire*. Vol. VI. London: John Murray, 1887.

Gieseler, Johann Karl Ludwig. *A Text-Book of Church History*. Vol. 1. Trans. Samuel Davidson. Ed. Henry B. Smith. New York: Harper & Brothers, 1857.

Gil, Moshe. *A History of Palestine: 634–1099*. Cambridge: Cambridge University Press, 1997.

Glubb, Sir John. *The Life and Times of Muhammad*. New York: Madison Books, 1998.

Göçek, Fatma Müge. *East Encounters West: France and the Ottoman Empire in the Eighteenth Century*. Oxford: Oxford University Press, 1987.

Goddard, Hugh. *A History of Christian-Muslim Relations*. Chicago: New Amsterdam Books, 2000.

Goffman, Daniel. *The Ottoman Empire and Early Modern Europe*. Cambridge: Cambridge University Press, 2002.

Goitein, S. D. F. *Mediterranean Society: An Abridgement in One Volume*. Ed. Jacob Lassner. Berkeley: University of California Press, 1999.

Goujet, M. l'Abbé Claude-Pierre. *Mémoire historique et littéraire sur le Collège Royal de France*. Paris: Augustin-Martin Lottin, 1758.

Grabar, Oleg; Brown, Peter Robert Lamont; Bowersock, Glen Warren. eds. *Late Antiquity: A Guide to the Postclassical World*. Cambridge: Harvard University Press, 1999.

Gradeva, Rossitsa. "Conversion to Islam in Bulgarian Historiography: An Overview." *Religion, Ethnicity, and Contested Nationhood in the Former Ottoman Space*. Ed. Jorgen Nielson. Leiden: Brill, 2012.

Grassi (Alfio), M. *Charte Turque ou Organisation religieuse, civile et militaire de l'empire ottoman*. Paris: Librairie d'Ambroise Dupont, 1826.

Griffith, Sidney H. "Arab Christians." *Byzantium and Islam: Age of Transition, 7th-9th Century*. Ed. Helen C. Evans and Brandie Ratliff. New York: The Metropolitan Museum of Art, 2012. 60–62

Guibert, Adrien. *Dictionaire géographique et statistique*. Paris: Jules Renouard, 1850.

Guillaume, Alfred, trans. *The Life of Muhammad*. Ibn Ishaq. Oxford: Oxford University Press, 1987.

Guillaume, M. J., ed. *Procès-verbaux du Comité d'instruction publique de la convention nationale*. Tome sixième. Paris: Imprimerie Nationale, 1907.

Haddad, Anton F., trans. *The Oath of the Prophet Mohammed to the Followers of the Nazarene*. New York: Board of Counsel, 1902; H-Bahai: Lansing, MI: 2004.

Haddad, Yvonne Yazbeck and Wadi Zaidan Haddad, eds. *Christian-Muslim Encounters*. Gainesville, FL: University Press of Florida, 1994. 43–53.

Hadjiantoniou, George A. *Protestant Patriarch: The Life of Cyril Lucaris (1572–1638), Patriarch of Constantinople*. Richmond, VA: John Knox Press, 1961.

Hagopian, Arthur. "Jerusalem Armenian Story Finally Being Told." *The Armenian Reporter* (May 14, 2011). Internet: http://www.reporter.am/go/article/2011–05–14–jerusalem-armenian-story-finally-being-told.

Hamidullah, Muhammad, trans. *Le Saint Coran*. Brentwood, Maryland: Amana Corporation, 1989.

———. *Introduction to Islam*. Paris: Centre Culturel Islamique, 1969.

———. *Muslim Conduct of State*. Lahore: Sh. Muhammad Ashraf, 1961.

———. *Majmu'ah al-watha'iq al-siyasiyyah li al-'ahad al-nabawi wa al-khilafah al-rashidah*. al-Qahirah: n.p., 1956.

Harant, Christophe. *Voyage en Égypte*, 1598. Le Caire: L'Institut francais d'archeologie orientale du Caire, 1972

Hawting, G. R. "John Wansbrough, Islam, and Monotheism." *The Quest for the Historical Muhammad*. Ed. and Trans. Ibn Warraq. Amherst, NY: Prometheus Books, 2000. 510–526.

Haya, Vicente. "El cristianismo que conoció Muhammad." *Conferencia Huesca* (27 de octubre de 2007). Internet: http://www.vicentehaya.com/conferencias/

Hazleton, Lesley. *Where Mountains Roar: A Personal Report from the Sinai and Negev Desert*. New York: Holt, Rinehart and Winston, 1980.

Helke Sander/Barbara Johr: *Befreier und Befreite*. Frankfurth: Fischer, 2005.

Henniker, Sir Frederick. *Notes during a Visit to Egypt, Nubia, the Oasis, Mount Sinai, and Jerusalem*. London: John Murray, 1823.

Herf, Jeffrey. *Nazi Propaganda for the Arab World*. New Haven, CT: Yale University Press, 2009.

Hitti, Philip K. *Makers of Arab History*. London: MacMillan, 1969.

Hobbs, Joseph J. *Mount Sinai*. Austin: University of Austin Press, 1995.

Hook, David, and Barry Taylor, eds. *Cultures in Contact in Medieval Spain: Historical and Literary Essays Presented to L.P. Harvey*. Exeter: King's College London Medieval Studies, 1990.

Hoyland, Robert G. *Arabia and the Arabs: From the Bronze Age to the Coming of Islam*. London and New York: Routledge, 2001.

———. "The Earliest Christian Writings on Muhammad: An Appraisal." *The Biography of Muhammad: The Issue of Sources*. Ed. Harald Motzki. Leiden: Brill, 2000. 276–297.

Humphreys, R. Stephen. *Islamic History: A Framework for Inquiry*. Princeton: Princeton University Press, 1991.

Husayn, Sayyed Safdar. *Histoire des premiers temps de l'Islam*. Trans. Abbas Ahmad al-Bostani. Paris: Seminaire Islamique, 1991.

Husayn ibn 'Ali. *Le firman du Chérif de la Mecque et Gardien des Lieux Saints*. Global Armenian Heritage. Internet: http://www.globalarmenianheritage-adic.fr/oab/x9/husseinibnali...

Ibn Ishaq, Muhammad. *The Life of Muhammad*. Trans. A. Guillaume. Oxford: Oxford University Press, 1987.

Ibn Warraq, ed. and trans. *The Quest for the Historical Muhammad*. Amherst, NY: Prometheus Books, 2000.

Inter-Islam. "Hazrat Salman Farsi." *Inter-Islam*. Internet:

http://www.inter-islam.org/Bibliographies/SalmanfarsiR.htm.

Irwin, Robert. *Dangerous Knowledge: Orientalism and its Discontents.* Woodstock and New York: Overlook Press, 2006.

Islamic Supreme Council of Canada. "The Promise of Prophet Muhammad (Peace be upon Him) to the Christians of St. Catherine." *Islamic Supreme Council of Canada* (2001). Internet: http://www.islamicsupremecouncil.com/theeternalpromise.htm.

Islamic Web. "Abdullah Ibn Sallam." *Islamic Web.* Internet: http://www.islamicweb.com/history/sahaba/bio ABDULLAH_IBN_SAILM.htm.

Isseroff, Ami. "The Covenant of Omar." *MidEastWeb* (2004). Internet: http://www.mideastweb.org/covenantofomar.htm.

Jacobs, Steven Leonard, ed. *Confronting Genocide: Judaism, Christianity, Islam.* New York: Lexington Books, 2009. 119–137.

Jacques, Edwin E. *The Albanians: An Ethnic History from Pre-Historic Times to the Present.* Jefferson: McFarland, 1995.

Jafri, S.H.M. *The Origins and Early Development of Shi'a Islam.* Qum: Ansariyan Publications, 1989.

Jeffery, Arthur. "The Quest of the Historical Muhammad." *The Quest for the Historical Muhammad.* Ed. and Trans. Ibn Warraq. Amherst, NY: Prometheus Books, 2000. 339–357.

Jenkins, Philip. *The Lost History of Christianity: The Thousand-Year Golden Age of the Church in the Middle East, Africa, and Asia—and How it Died.* New York: HarperOne, 2008.

Jerusalem Patriarchate. *The Ahtiname (Treaty) of Caliph Omar Ibn al-Khattab.* Internet: http://www.jerusalem-patriarchate.info/en/axtinames/htm.

Jordac, George. *The Voice of Human Justice.* Trans. M. Fazal Haq. Qum: Ansariyan, 1990.

Joshel, Sandra. "Roman Slavery and the Question of Race." *Black Past: Remembered and Reclaimed.* Internet: http://www.blackpast.org/?q= perspective s/roman-slavery-and-question-race.

Jurdi Abisaab, Rula. *Converting Persia: Religion and Power in the Safavid Empire.* London: I.B. Tauris, 2004.

Karabell, Zachary. *Peace Be upon You: The Story of Muslim, Christian, and Jewish Coexistence.* New York: Alfred A. Knopf, 2007.

Kashif al-Ghita', Muhammad Husayn. *The Origin of Shi'ite Islam and its Principles.* Qum: Ansariyan, 1993.

Katsh, Abraham I. *Judaism in Islam: Biblical and Talmudic Backgrounds of the Koran and its Commentaries.* New York: New York University Press, 1954.

Khan, Ali. "The Medina Constitution." *Social Science Research Network* (2006). Internet: http://papers.ssrn.com/sol3/papers.cfm?abstract_id=945458.

Khan, Muhammad Zafrulla. *Muhammad: Seal of the Prophets.* London: Routledge & Kegan Paul, 1980.

Khan, Muqtedar. "Muhammad's Promise to Christians." *The Washington Post* (December 30, 2009). Internet: http://newsweek.washingtonpost.com/onfaith/guest voices/2009/ 12/prophet_ muhammads _promise_ to _christians.html.

Khitrowo, B. de. *Itinéraires russes en Orient.* Genève: J.-G. Fick, 1889.

Khomeini, Ruhullah. *The Imam Versus Zionism.* Tehran: Ministry of Islamic Guidance, 1984. Internet: http://www.hajij.com/library/component/k2/item/814–the-imam-versus-zionism.

King, G.R.D. "The Paintings of the Pre-Islamic Ka'ba." *Muqarnas: An Annual on the Visual Culture of the Islamic World* 21 (2004): 219–230.

Kingsley, Patrick, and Marwa Awad. "Mount Sinai Monastery Latest Victim of Egypt's Upheavals." *The Guardian* (September 5, 2013). Internet: http://www.theguardian.com/world/2013/sep/05/mount-sinai-monastery-egypt-closure.

Labevière, Richard. *Dollars for Terror: The United States and Islam.* New York: Algora Publishing, 2000.

Laborde, Simon Joseph Léon Emmanuel Marquis de. *Journey through Arabia Petrae, to Mount Sinai, and the Excavated City of Petra.* London: John Murray, 1838.

Lamartine, Alphonse de. *Oeuvres completes de Lamartine. Histoire de la Turquie.* IV. Tome vingt-sixième. Paris: Chez L'Auteur, 1862.

Lammens, Henri. "The Age of Muhammad and the Chronology of the Sira." *The Quest for the Historical Muhammad.* Amherst, NY: Prometheus Books, 2000. 188–217.

Lance, Peter. 1000 *Years of Revenge: International Terrorism and the FBI: The Untold Story.* New York: Reganbooks, 2003.

Layard, Sir Austen Henry. *Nineveh and its Remains: With an Account of the Chaldean Christians of Kurdistan...* New York: G.P. Putnam, 1849.

Lecker, Michael. "Glimpses of Muhammad's Medinan Decade." *The Cambridge Companion to Muhammad.* Ed. Jonathan E. Brockopp. Cambridge: Cambridge University Press, 2010. 61–79.

———. "Did the Quraysh Conclude a Treaty with the Ansar prior to the Hijra?" *The Biography of Muhammad: The Issue of the Sources.* Ed. Harald Motzki. Leiden: Brill, 2000. 157–169.

Levy, Habib. *Comprehensive History of the Jews of Iran.* Trans. George W. Maschke. Costa Mesa, CA: Mazda Publishers, 1999.

Lewontin, Richard. "The Demon-Haunted World." *The*

New York Review of Books (September 1, 1997): 28. Internet: http://www.drjbloom.com/Public%20files /Lewontin_Review.htm.

Lewy, Guenter. *The Armenian Massacres in Ottoman Turkey: A Disputed Genocide.* Salt Lake City: The University of Utah Press, 2005.

Limor, Ora. "Sharing Sacred Space: Holy Places in Jerusalem between Christianity, Judaism, and Islam." *In Laudem Hierosolymitani: Studies in Crusades and Medieval Culture in Honour of Benjamin Z. Kedar.* Ed. Iris Shagrir, Ronnie Ellenblum, and Jonathan Riley-Smith. Aldershot, UK: Ashgate, 2007. 219–231. Internet: http://www.openu.ac.il/Personal_sites/ora-limo r.html#a16–4.

Lindsay, Alexander William Branford Crawford. *Letters from Egypt, Edom, and the Holy Land.* Vol. 1. 3rd ed. London: Henry Colburn Publisher, 1843.

Lowney, Chris. *A Vanished World: Medieval Spain's Golden Age of Enlightenment.* New York: Free Press, 2009.

Luke, Sir Harry. *Mosul and its Minorities.* Piscataway, NJ: Gorgias Press, 2004.

Lumbard, Joseph E.B., ed. *Islam, Fundamentalism and the Betrayal of Tradition.* Bloomington, IN: World Wisdom Books, 2004.

Lunde, Paul. *Islam: Faith, Culture, History.* New York: DK, 2002.

Lybyer, Albert Howe. *The Government of the Ottoman Empire in the Time of Suleiman the Magnificent.* Cambridge: Harvard University Press, 1913.

M. "Remarks on the Defence of Gabriel Sionita." *The Classical Journal* XIII (September to December 1815): 254– 255.

Madrazo, Pedro de. *Córdoba.* Madrid: Parcerisa, 1855.

Mahmoud, Joseph. "Shiite Ayatollah Launches Fatwa: Iraqi Christians, Conversion to Islam or Death." *Asia News* (December 15, 2012). Internet: http://www. asianews.it/index.php?l=en&ar=26636&sendtofrie nd=9319.

Majlisi, Muhammad Baqir. *Hayat al-qulub: A Detailed Biography of Prophet Muhammad.* Vol. 2. Trans. Syed Athar Husain S.H. Rizvi. Qum: Ansariyan, 2010. Internet: http://www.al-islam.org/hayat-al-q ulub-v ol2–allamah-muhammad-baqir-al-majlisi/.

———. *Bihar al-anwar.* 104 volumes on CD Rom.

Malech, George David. *History of the Syrian Nation and the Old Evangelical-Apostolic Church of the East.* Minneapolis: n.p., 1910.

Malik ibn Anas, Imam. *al-Muwatta'.* Bayrut: Dar al-Gharb al-Islami, 1999.

Mamdani, Mahmood. *Good Muslim, Bad Muslim: America, the Cold War, and the Roots of Terror.* New York: Pantheon Books, 2004.

Manafis, Konstantinos A., ed. *Sinai: Treasures of the Monastery of Saint Catherine.* Athens: Ekdotike Athenon, 1990.

Manley, Deborah and Sahar 'Abdel-Hakim, eds. *Traveling through Sinai: From the Fourth to the Twenty-First Century.* Cairo: The American University in Cairo Press, 2006.

Mann, Vivian B., Thomas F. Glick, and Jerrilynn D. Dodds. *Convivencia: Jews, Muslims, and Christians in Medieval Spain.* New York: George Braziller Inc., 1992.

Maqqari, Ahmad ibn Muhammad al- and Ibn al-Khatib. *A History of the Mohammedan Dynasties in Spain.* Vol. 2. Ed. and Trans. Pascual de Gayangos. London: Oriental Translation Fund, 1843.

Mar Shimun, Theodore D. *The History of the Patriarchal Succession of the D'Mar Shimun Family.* Np: Mar Shimun Memorial Foundation, 2008.

Mar Shimun, Surma D'Bait. *Assyrian Church Customs and the Murder of Mar Shimun.* Ed. W.A. Wigram. Np: Assyrian International News Agency, 1920.

Marana, Giovani Paolo. *Suite de L'Espion dans les cours des princes chrétiens.* Tome quatrième. Cologne: Erasme Kenkus, 1697.

Marcus, Jacob. *The Jew in the Medieval World: A Sourcebook,* 315–1791. New York: JPS, 1938. Internet: http:// www.fordham.edu/halsall/jewish/jews-umar .asp.

Mattson, Ingrid. *The Story of the Qur'an: Its History and Place in Muslim Life.* Malden, MA: Blackwell Publishing, 2008.

McGuckin, John Anthony, ed. *The Encyclopedia of Eastern Orthodox Christianity.* Malden, MA: Wiley-Blackwell, 2011.

McMeekin, Sean. *Berlin-Baghdad Express: The Ottoman Empire and Germany's Bid for World Power.* Cambridge, MA: The Belknap Press of Harvard University Press, 2010.

Meimaris, Yiannis E. "The Library and Archive: The Arabic Manuscripts." *Sinai: Treasures of the Monastery of Saint Catherine.* Ed. Konstantinos Manafis. Athens: Ekdotike Athenon, 1990. 357–358.

Menoscal, María Rosa. *The Ornament of the World: How Muslims, Jews, and Christians Created a Culture of Tolerance in Medieval Spain.* Boston: Little, Brown, and Company, 2002.

Miltitz, Alexandre de. *Manuel des consuls.* Vol. 2. London and Berlin: A. Asher, 1838.

Mingana, A, ed. *A Charter of Protection Granted to the Nestorian Church in AD 1138 by Muktafi II, Caliph of Baghdad.* Manchester: The University Press, 1925; Birmingham: Antioch Gate, 2008.

M.L.M.D.C. *Jeux d'esprit et de mémoire.* Cologne: Fréderic Le Jeune, 1697.

Monconys, Balthasar de. *Journal des voyages de monsieur*

de Monconys. Première partie. Lyon: Horace Boissat & Georges Remeus, 1665.

———. *Le voyage en Égypte*, 1646–1647. Le Caire: Institut français d'archéologie orientale du Caire, 1973.

Morison Chanoine de Bar le Duc, Sieur Antoine. *Relation historique d'un voyage nouvellement fait au mont de Sinaï et à Jérusalem*. Toul: A. Laurent, 1704.

Moritz, Bernhard. "Sur les antiquités arabes du Sinai." *BIE*, 5e serie, tome iv.

———. *Beiträge zur Geschichte des Sinai-Klosters Im Mittelalter Nach Arabischen Quellen*. Berlin: Verlag Der Konigl; Akakemie Der Wissenschaften, 1918. Internet: http://www.archive.org/stream/beitrgezurgescoomoriuoft#page/no/mode/1up.

Morrow, John Andrew. *Religion and Revolution: Spiritual and Political Islam in Ernesto Cardenal*. Newcastle upon Tyne: Cambridge Scholars Publishing, 2012.

———. "Pre and Early Islamic Period." *A Cultural History of Reading*. Ed. Gabrielle Watling. Westport, CT: Greenwood Press, 2009. 521–540.

Mosheim, Johann Lorenz. *Mosheim's Institutes of Ecclesiastical History, Ancient and Modern*. London: W. Tegg and Co, 1878.

Motzki, Harald. *The Biography of Muhammad: The Issue of the Sources*. Leiden: Brill, 2000.

Moussaoui-Lari, Sayed Mujdtaba. *La dernière mission divine*. Trans. F. Khodaparasti. Qum: Seyed M. Moussaoui-Lari, nd.

Mouton, Jean-Michel. "Les musulmans à Sainte-Catherine au Moyen Âge." *Le Sinaï durant l'antiquité et le moyen âge, 4000 ans d'histoire pour un desert*. Ed. Dominique Valbelle and Charles Bonnet. Paris: Éditions Érrance, 1998: 177–182.

Mufid, Shaykh al-. *Kitab al-irshad: The Book of Guidance into the Lives of the Twelve Imams*. Trans. I.K.A. Howard. London: Muhammadi Trust, 1981.

Muhammad, Prophet. *al-'Ahd wa al-shurut allati sharataha Muhammad rasul Allah li-ahl al-millah al-nasraniyyah* [*Testamentum et pactiones initae inter Mohamedem Apostolum Dei, et Christianae fidei cultores*]. Trans. Gabriel Sionita. Paris: Antoine Vitré, 1630.

———. *al-'Ahd wa al-shurut allati sharataha Muhammad rasul Allah li-ahl al-millah al-nasraniyyah* [*Testamentum inter Muhammedem legatum dei et christianae religionis populous olim initum*]. Trans. Johann Georg Nissel. Lugduni Vatavorum: Elsevier, 1655.

Nagy de Harsany, Jacobo. *Colloquia familiar turco-latina*. Berlin: Typis Georgij Schultzij, 1672.

Nafziger, George F. and Mark W. Walton. *Islam at War: A History*. Westport, CT: Praeger, 2003.

Napoleoni, Loretta. *Terror Incorporated: Tracing the Dollars Behind the Terror Networks*. New York: Seven Stories, 2007.

Narkiss, Bezalel, ed. *Armenian Art Treasures of Jerusalem*. New Rochelle, NY: Caratzas Brothers Publishers, 1979.

Nersessian, Vrej Nerses. *Treasures from the Ark: 1700 Years of Armenian Christian Art*. Los Angeles: J. Paul Getty Museum, 2001.

Nisa'i, Ahmad ibn Shu'ayb. *Sunan al-Nisa'i*. al-Qahirah: Mustafa al-Babi al-Halabi, 1964–65.

Nissel, Johann Georg, trans. *al-'Ahd wa al-shurut allati sharataha Muhammad rasul Allah li-ahl al-millah al-nasraniyyah* [*Testamentum inter Muhammedem legatum dei et christianae religionis populous olim initum*]. Prophet Muhammad. Lugduni Vatavorum: Elsevier, 1655.

Ordoni, Abu Muhammad. *Fatima the Gracious*. Qum: Ansariyan, 1992.

Ormanian, Malachia. *The Church of Armenia: Her History, Doctrine, Rule, Discipline, Liturgy, Literature, and Existing Condition*. Trans. G. Marcar Gregory. London: A.R. Mowbray & Co., Ltd, 1912.

O'Shea, Stephen. *Sea of Faith: Islam and Christianity in the Medieval Mediterranean World*. New York: Walter & Company, 2006.

Ottoman Souvenir. "Ahdnama of the Fatih Sultan Mehmet." *Ottoman Souvenir*. Internet: http://www.ottomansouvenir.com/General/the_ahname_of_sultan.

Palter, Nurit. "2006: More Jews Converting to Islam." *Y Net News* (July 13, 2006). Internet: http://www.ynetnews.com/articles/0,7340,L-3274735,00.html.

Percy, Earl. "On Turkish Kurdistan." *Notices on the Proceedings at the Meetings of the Members of the Royal Institution of Great Britain with Abstracts of the Discourses Delivered at the Evening Meetings*. Vol. XVI (1899–1901). London: William Clowes and Sons, Limited, 1902.

Peters, Francis E. *Muhammad and the Origins of Islam*. Albany: State University of New York Press, 1994.

———. *The Hajj: The Muslim Pilgrimage to Mecca and the Holy Places*. Princeton, NJ: Princeton University Press, 1994.

Provins, [René de l'Escale] Pacifique de. *Relation du voyage de Perse*. Paris: Nicolas et Jean de la Coste, 1631.

Pococke, Richard. "A Description of the East and Some other Countries." *A General Collection of the Best and Most Interesting Voyages and Travels in All Parts of the World: Many of which are Now First Translated Into English*. Ed. John Pinkerton. London: Longman, 1809.

Porter, Venetia, ed. *Hajj: Journey to the Heart of Islam*. Cambridge: Havard University Press, 2012.

Pouillon, François. *Dictionnaire des orientalistes de langue française*. Paris: Karthala, 2008.

Qaturi, al-Safsafi Ahmad al-. "The Ottomans and Sacred Places in Jerusalem." *Fountain Magazine* 57 (January-March 2007). Internet: http://www.fountainmagazine.com/Issue/detail/The-Ottomans-and-Sacred-Places-in-Jerusalem

Qureshi, Muhammad Siddique. *Foreign Policy of Hadrat Muhammad*. New Delhi: Kitab Bhavan, 1991.

Qushayri, Muslim ibn al-Hajjaj al-. *Sahih Muslim*. Trans. Abdul-Hameed Siddiqui. Lahore: Sh. Muhammad Ashraf, 1990.

Rabino, Hyacinth Louis. *Le monastère de Sainte-Catherine du Mont Sinaï*. Le Caire: Impr. E. Spada, 1938.

Ramadan, Tariq. *In the Footsteps of the Prophet: Lessons from the Life of Muhammad*. Oxford: Oxford University Press, 2007.

Ratliff, Brandie. "Christian Communities during the Early Islamic Centuries." *Byzantium and Islam: Age of Transition, 7th-9th Century*. Ed. Helen C. Evans and Brandie Ratliff. New York: The Metropolitan Museum of Art, 2012. 32–39.

———. "To Travel to the Holy." *Byzantium and Islam: Age of Transition, 7th-9th Century*. Ed. Helen C. Evans and Brandie Ratliff. New York: The Metropolitan Museum of Art, 2012. 86–88.

———. "The Monastery of Saint Catherine at Mount Sinai and the Christian Communities of the Caliphate." *Sinaiticus: The Bulletin of the Saint Catherine Foundation* (2008): 14–17. Internet: http://www.saintcatherinefoundation.org/files/8013/2983/0724/Sinaiticus_2008–email.pdf.

Rehatsek, Edward. "Christianity in the Persian Dominions, from its Beginning till the Fall of the Sasanian Dynasty." *The Journal of the Bombay Branch of the Royal Asiatic Society*. Vol. XIII (1877): 18–108.

Rhodes, D. Bryan. "John Damascene in Context: An Examination of 'The Heresy of the Ishmaelites' with Special Consideration Given to the Religious, Political, and Social Contexts during the Seventh and Eighth Century Arab Conquests." *St Francis Magazine* 7.2 (April 2010). Internet: http://www.stf rancismagazine.info/ja/images/stories 7.%20Bryan %20Rhodes%20SFM%20April%202011.pdf.

Ricaut, Sir Paul. *Histoire de l'état présent de l'empire ottoman*. Trans. Monsieur Briot. Paris: Sebastien Mabre-Cramoisy, 1670.

Rikabi, Jaffar al-. "Baqir al-Sadr and the Islamic State: A Theory for 'Islamic Democracy.'" *Journal of Shi'a Islamic Studies* 5.3 (Summer 2012): 249–275.

Rizvi, Sayyid Muhammad. *Marriage and Morals in Islam*. Vancouver: Vancouver Islamic Educational Foundation, 1990.

Robinson, A. Mary F. *Margaret of Angouleme—Queen of Navarre*. Boston: Roberts Brothers, 1890. Internet: http://books.google.com.

Robinson, Edward, and E. Smith. *Biblical Researches in Palestine, and in the Adjacent Regions: A Journal of Travels in the Year* 1838. Vol. 2. Boston: Crocker and Brewster, 1874.

Rochetta, Don Aquilante. *Peregrinatione di Terra Santa*. Palermo: Giuseppe Roma, 1630.

Rodinson, Maxime. *Mohammed*. Trans. Anne Carter. New York: Pantheon Books, 1971.

Rogerson, Barnaby. *The Prophet Muhammad: A Biography*. Mahwah, NJ: HiddenSpring, 2003.

Roggema, Barbara. *The Legend of Sergius Bahira: Eastern Christian Apologetics and Apocalyptic in Response to Islam*. Leiden: Brill, 2009.

Rubenstein, Richard L. "Jihad and Genocide: The Case of the Armenians." *Confronting Genocide: Judaism, Christianity, Islam*. Ed. Steven Leonard Jacobs. New York: Lexington Books, 2009. 119–137.

Runciman, Steven. *The Great Church in Captivity*. Cambridge: Cambridge University Press, 1985.

Rycaut, Sir Paul. *The Present State of the Ottoman Empire*. New York: Arno Press & The New York Times, 1971.

Sa'eed, Shaykh Hasan, ed. *Fundamentals of Islam*. Tehran: The Chehel Sutoon School and Library, 1984.

Safi, Omar. *Memories of Muhammad: Why the Prophet Matters*. New York: HarperOne, 2009.

Salahi, M.A. *Muhammad: Man and Prophet. A Complete Study of the Life of the Prophet of Islam*. Rockport, MA: Element, 1995.

Saleh, Wadi A. "The Arabian Context of Muhammad's Life." *The Cambridge Companion to Muhammad*. Ed. Jonathan E. Brockopp. Cambridge: Cambridge University Press, 2010. 21–38.

Sanjian, Avedis K. "The Armenian Communities of Jerusalem." *Armenian Art Treasures of Jerusalem*. Ed. Bezalel Narkiss. New Rochelle, NY: Caratzas Brothers, Publishers, 1979. 11–20.

Santiago-Otero, Horacio. *Diálogo filosófico-religioso entre cristianismo, judaísmo e islamismo durante la edad media en la península ibérica*. Brépols: International Society for the Study of Medieval Philosophy, 1994.

Scaliger, Pacificus. See, Provins, [René de l'Escale] Pacifique de.

Scher, Addai and Robert Griveau, Trans. & Ed. "Histoire nestorienne inédite: Chronique de Séert. Seconde partie." *Patrologia Orientalis* 13.4 (1919). Internet:http://archive.org/details/patrologiaorient 13pariuoft.

Schoeps, Hans-Joachim. *Jewish Christianity: Factional Disputes in the Early Church*. Trans. Douglas R.A. Hare. Philadelphia: Fortress Press, 1964.

Schöller, Marco. "*Sira* and *Tafsir*: Muhammad al-Kalbi on the Jews of Medina." *The Biography of Muhammad: The Issue of the Sources*. Ed. Harald Motzki. Leiden: Brill, 2000. 18–48.

Schulz, Matthias. "Fortress in the Sky: Buried Christian Empire Casts New Light on Early Islam." *Spiegel* (2013). Internet: http:www.spiegel.edu/international /world/buried-christian-empire...

Schwartz, Stephen. *The Two Faces of Islam: Saudi Fundamentalism and its Role in Terrorism*. New York: Anchor Books, 2003.

Seidler/Zayas. *Kriegsverbrechen in Europa und im Nahen Osten im 20. Jahrhundert*. Hamburg, Berlin, Bonn: Mittler, 2002.

Shafi'i, Muhammad ibn Idris al-. *Risala: Treatise on the Foundations of Islamic Jurisprudence*. Cambridge: Islamic Texts Society, 1987.

Shah-Kazemi, Reza. "Illumination and Non-Delimitation: Lessons from Inter and Intra Faith Dialogue from the Wisdom of the Prophet of Islam. *Allama Iqbal*. Internet: http://www.allamaiqbal.com/publications/journals/review/oct05

Shahin, Emad El-Din. "Government." *The Princeton Encyclopedia of Islamic Political Thought*. Ed. Gerhard Bowering. Princeton & Oxford: Princeton University Press, 2013. 198–207.

Shboul, Ahmad. "Arab Islamic Perspective of Byzantine Religion and Culture." *Muslim Perceptions of Other Religions: A Historical Survey*. Ed. Jacques Waardenburg. Oxford: Oxford University Press, 1999.

Shedinger, Robert. *Was Jesus a Muslim? Questioning Categories in the Study of Religion*. Minneapolis: Fortress Press, 2009.

Sherrard, Philip. *Athos: The Holy Mountain*. New York: The Overlook Press, 1985.

Shoup, John A. *Culture and Customs of Jordan*. Westport, CT: Greenwood Press, 2007.

Shuqayr, Na'um. Tarikh *Sina al-qadim wa al-hadith wa jughrafiyatuha, ma'a khulasat tarikh Misr wa al-Sham wa al-'Iraq wa Jazirat al-'Arab wa ma kana baynaha min al-'ala'iq al-tijariyyah wa al-harbiyyah wa ghayriha 'an tariq Sina' min awwal 'ahd al-tarikh il al-yawm*. [al-Qahirah]: n.p., 1916.

Siddiqui, Kalim. *Political Dimensions of the Seerah*. London: The Institute for Contemporary Islamic Thought, 1998.

Siemon-Netto, Uwe. "Iraq's Church Bombers vs. Muhammad." *Christianity Today* (August 1, 2004). Internet: http://www.christianitytoday.com/ct/2004/aug ustweb-only/8-2-5...

Sinai, Hieromonk Justin of. "Sinai in the Seventh to the Ninth Century: Continuity in the Midst of Change." *Byzantium and Islam: Age of Transition, 7th-9th Century*. Ed. Helen C. Evans and Brandie Ratliff. New York: The Metropolitan Museum of Art, 2012. 50–51.

Sinai Monastery. "Mohammed and the Holy Monastery of Sinai." *Sinai Monastery*. Internet: http://www.sinaimonastery.com/en/index.php?lid=68.

Singleton, Esther. *Egypt as Described by Great Writers*. New York: Dodd, Mead, and Co., 1911.

Sionita, Gabriel, trans. *al-'Ahd wa-al-shurut allati sharataha Muhammad rasul Allah li-ahl al-millah al-nasraniyyah* [*Testamentum et pactiones initae inter Mohamedem Apostolum Dei, et Christianae fidei cultores*]. Prophet Muhammad. Paris: Antoine Vitré, 1630.

Skrobucha, Heinz. *Sinai*. London: Oxford University Press, 1966.

Slane, Le Baron de. *Catalogue des manuscrits arabes*. Paris: Imprimerie Nationale, 1883–1895.

Société Asiatique. "Ouvrages offerts à la Société." *Journal Asiatique* 1 (1822): 116.

Societé d'Amis de la Religion et de la Patrie. *Annales de la religion*. Tome cinquième. Paris: L'imprimerie Librairie Chrétienne, 1797.

Society for the Diffusion of Useful Knowledge, The. *The Penny Cyclopaedia*. Vol. XIX. London: Charles Knight, 1841.

Somel, Selcuk Aksin. *Historical Dictionary of the Ottoman Empire*. Lanham, MD: Sacrecrow Press, 2003.

Soskice, Janet. *The Sisters of Sinai: How Two Lady Adventurers Discovered the Hidden Gospels*. New York: Alfred A. Knopf, 2009.

Speake, Graham. *Mount Athos: Renewal in Paradise*. New Haven and London: Yale University Press, 2002.

Sprenger, Aloys. *Das Leben und die Lehre*. Vol. 1. Berlin: Nicolai'sche Verlagsbuchandlung, 1861–1865. 178–190.

———. "Mohammed's Zusammenkunft mit dem Eisiedler Bahyra." *ZDMG* 12 (1858): 238–249.

———. "Aus Briefen an Prof. Fleischer." *ZDMG* 7 (1853): 412–415.

———. "Mohammad's Journey to Syria." *Journal of the Royal Asiatic Society of Bengal* 21 (1852): 576–592.

———. "Gegenbemerkung." *ZDMG* 6 (1852): 457–458.

———. "Ueber eine Handschrift." *ZDMG* 3 (1849): 450–456.

Stafford, R.S. *The Tragedy of the Assyrians*. Piscataway, NJ: Gorgias Press, 2006.

Stanley, Dean Arthur Penrhyn, ed. *Sinai and Palestine in Connection with their History*. New York: A.C. Armstrong & Son, 1894.

———. "The Convent of St. Catherine." *Egypt as Described by Great Writers*. Esther Singleton. New York: Dodd, Mead, and Co., 1911. 339–346.

Stephens, J.L. *Incidents of Travel in Egypt, Arabia Petrae and the Holy Land.* Vol 1. 11th ed. New York : Harper & Brothers, 1853.

Tabataba'i, Sayyid Muhammad Husayn. *Shi'ite Islam.* Trans. Seyyed Hossein Nasr. Albany: State University of New York Press, 1977.

Tibi, Bassam. *Islamism and Islam.* New Haven & London: Yale University Press, 2012.

Thenaud, Jean. *Le voyage d'outremer (Égypte, Mont Sinay, Palestine).* Ed. Ch. Schefer. Paris: Ernest Leroux, 1874.

Thévenot, Jean de. *Relation d'un voyage fait au Levant.* Paris: Louis Billaine, 1665. Internet: https://play.google.com/store/books/details?id=HSqefSc9V9 QC&rdid=book-HSqefSc9V9QC&rdot=1.

———. *Voyages de Mr. de Thévenot au Levant.* 3ième édition. Tome second. Amsterdam: Michel Charles Le Cène, 1776.

Thomas, Thelma K. "'Ornaments of Excellence' from 'the Miserable Gains of Commerce:' Luxury Art and Byzantine Culture." *Byzantium and Islam: Age of Transition, 7th-9th Century.* Ed. Helen C. Evans and Brandie Ratliff. New York: The Metropolitan Museum of Art, 2012. 124–133.

Thomson, Ahmad, and Muhammad 'Ata'ur-Rahim. *Jesus: Prophet of Islam.* London: Ta-Ha Publishers, 1996.

———. *Blood on the Cross: Islam in Spain in the Light of Christian Persecution through the Ages.* London: Ta-Ha Publishers, 1989.

Thomson, Robert W. "Muhammad and the Origin of Islam in Armenian Literary Tradition." *Studies in Armenian Christianity.* Aldershot: Variorum, 1994. 829–858.

Tolan, John, Henry Laurens, and Gilles Veinstein. *Europe and the Islamic World: A History.* Princeton: University of Princeton Press, 2013.

Tomadakis, Nikolaos. "Historical Outline." *Sinai: Treasures of the Monastery of Saint Catherine.* Ed. Konstantinos Manafis. Athens: Ekdotike Athenon, 1990. 12–17.

Toomer, G.J. *Eastern Wisdom and Learning: The Study of Arabic in Seventeenth Century England.* Oxford: Oxford University Press, 1996.

Tschanz, David W. "Journeys of Faith: Roads of Civilization." *Saudi Aramco World* 55.1 (January/February 2004). Internet: http:www.saudiaramcoworld.com/issue/200401.

Twiss, Sir Travers. *Le droit des gens ou des nations.* Paris: A. Durand et Pedone-Lauriel, 1887.

Un religieux du même ordre. *Vie du très révérend père Ange de Joyeuse de l'ordre des ff. mineurs capucins.* Paris: Poussielgue, 1863.

Upton, Charles. "The Shepherds, the Baptist and the Essenes: A Response to *The Life of Christ and Biblical Revelations* by Anne Catherine Emmerich." *Findings in Metaphysics, Path and Lore: A Response to the Traditionalist/Perennialist School.* San Rafael: Sophia Perennis, 2010.

Valbelle, Dominique and Charles Bonnet. *Le Sinaï durant l'antiquité et le moyen âge, 4000 ans d'histoire pour un desert.* Ed. Dominique Valbelle and Charles Bonnet. Paris: Éditions Érrance, 1998.

Van Dyck, Edward A. *Capitulations of the Ottoman Empire: Report of Edward A. Van Dyck, Consular Clerk of the United States at Cairo, upon the Capitulations of the Ottoman Empire since the Year* 1150. Washington: Department of State, Government Printing Office, 1881.

Van Egmont van der Nyenburg, J.E. and John Heyman. *Travels through Parts of Europe, Asia Minor, the Islands of the Archipelago, Syria, Palestine, Egypt, Mount Sinai, etc.* London: L. Davis & C. Reymers, 1759.

Van Gorder, A. Christian. *Christianity in Persia and the Status of Non-Muslims in Modern Iran.* Lanham, MD: Rowman & Littlefield, 2010.

Vernet, Juan. "The Legacy of Islamic Spain." *Al-Andalus: The Arts of Islamic Spain.* Ed. Jerrilynn Dodds. New York: The Metropolitan Museum of Art, 1992. 173–187.

———. trans. *El Corán.* Barcelona: Editorial Planeta, 1991.

Volkoff, Oleg V. *Voyageurs russes en Égypte.* Le Caire: Institut francais d'archeologie orientale, 1972.

Volney, Constantin-François de Chasseboeuf. *Voyages en Égypte et en Syrie pendant les années* 1783, 1784 *et* 1785. Tome deuxième. Paris: Parmentier, 1825.

Waardenburg, Jacques, ed. *Muslim Perceptions of Other Religions: A Historical Survey.* Oxford: Oxford University Press, 1999.

———. "The Early Period: 610–650." *Muslim Perceptions of Other Religions: A Historical Survey.* Ed. Jacques Waardenburg. Oxford: Oxford University Press, 1999. 3–17.

Walpole, Robert, Ed. *Travels in Various Countries of the East.* London: Longman, Hurst, Rees, Orme, and Brown, 1820.

Watling, Gabrielle, ed. *A Cultural History of Reading.* Westport, CT: Greenwood Press, 2009.

Waqidi, Muhammad ibn 'Umar al-. *The Life of Muhammad: Al-Waqidi's* Kitab al-maghazi. Ed. Rizwi Faizer. Trans. Rizwi Faizer, Amal Ismail, and AbdulKader Tayob. London and New York: Routledge, 2011.

Wheatcroft, Andrew. *The Ottomans.* London: Viking, 1993.

Wiegers, Gerard A. *Islamic Literature in Spanish and*

Aljamiado. Leiden: Brill, 1994.

Wigram, William Ainser. *An Introduction to the History of the Assyrian Church: 100–640 AD*. London: Society for Promoting Christian Knowledge, 1910.

———. *The Assyrians and their Neighbours*. London: G. Bell & Sons, 1929.

Wolfe, Michael, ed. *One Thousand Roads to Mecca: Ten Centuries of Travelers Writing about the Muslim Pilgrimage*. New York: Grove Press, 1997.

Yohannan, Abraham. *The Death of a Nation, Or the Ever Persecuted Nestorians or Assyrian Christians*. New York and London: G.P. Putnam's Sons, 1916.

Zahoor, A and Z. Haq. "Prophet Muhammad's Charter of Privileges to Christians: Letter of the Monks of St. Catherine Monastery." *Cyberistan* (1990). Internet: http://www.cyberistan.org/ islamic/charter1.html.

Zeitlin, Irving M. *The Historical Muhammad*. Cambridge: Polity Press, 2007.

Index

F

G

About the Author

Dr. John Andrew Morrow was born in Montreal, Canada, in 1971. He completed his Honors B.A., M.A., and Ph.D. at the University of Toronto, as well as post-doctoral studies in Arabic in Morocco and at the University of Utah's Middle East Center. During the course of his studies, he specialized in Hispanic, Native, and Islamic Studies. Besides his academic training, he has also completed the full cycle of traditional Islamic seminary studies.

Dr. Morrow is currently Associate Professor of Spanish and French at Ivy Tech in Fort Wayne, Indiana, where he was recognized as a Master Teacher and Distinguished Faculty Member. He was formerly an Associate Research Scholar and Consultant on Middle Eastern Studies for the Area of Arabic and Islamic Studies at the National University of Rosario's Center for Oriental Studies in Argentina. He has worked for many universities, including the University of Toronto, Park University, Northern State University, and Eastern New Mexico University, as well as the University of Virginia's prestigious Semester at Sea Program. He has received fellowships to conduct research at Purdue, the University of Chicago, and Harvard University. He is a member of the Advisory Board for the *Journal of Shia Islamic Studies*, and peer-reviews academic articles and books for a number of scholarly journals and publishers.

Professor Morrow has published a multitude of scholarly articles in English, French, and Spanish, in academic, cultural, and literary journals in over a dozen countries. He has contributed book and encyclopedia chapters to *Identidades americanas: más allá de las fronteras nacionales: ensayos en homenaje a Keith Ellis* (2012), *Juan Felipe Toruño en dos mundos* (2006), *A Cultural History of Reading* (2008), *Latino America: State by State* (2008), *The Literary Encyclopedia*, and *Global English and Arabic: Issues of Language, Culture, and Identity* (2011). He has also authored, edited, and translated over a dozen books including: *Arabic, Islam, and the Allah Lexicon: How Language Shapes our Conception of God* (2006), *Amerindian Elements in the Poetry of Rubén Darío: The Alter Ego as the Indigenous Other* (2008), *Shi'ite Islam: Orthodoxy or Heterodoxy?* (2006, 2010), *El Islam chiita: ¿ortodoxia o heterodoxia?* (2010), *Humanos casi humanos* (2008), *Amerindian Elements in the Poetry of Ernesto Cardenal: Mythic Foundations of the Colloquial Narrative* (2010), *Kitab al-Tawhid / The Book of Divine Unity* (2010), *The Encyclopedia of Islamic Herbal Medicine* (2011), *Islamic Insights: Writings and Reviews* (2012), *Religion and Revolution: Spiritual and Political Islam in Ernesto Cardenal* (2012), and *Islamic Images and Ideas: Essays on Sacred Symbolism* (2013).

Say: "O People of the Book! Come to common terms as between us and you: that we worship none but Allah; that we associate no partners with Him; that we erect not, from among ourselves, lords and patrons other than Allah. If then they turn back, say ye: 'Bear witness that we (at least) are Muslims (bowing to Allah's Will).'" (3:64)